CA

What if Things Were Made in America Again

How consumers can rebuild the middle class by buying things made in American communities

James A. Stuber, J.D.

CA

Current Affairs Press

Philadelphia

CA Current Affairs Press, Inc.
1515 Market Street, Suite 1200
Philadelphia, PA 19102

First Current Affairs Press hardcover edition April 2017.

Current Affairs Press and colophon are trademarks of Current Affairs Press, Inc.

For information about special discounts for bulk purchases, please contact Current Affairs Press Sales at business@currentaffairspress.com. The Current Affairs Press Speakers Bureau can bring the author to your live event. For more information or to book an event contact the Current Affairs Press Speakers Bureau at speakers@currentaffairspress.com.

Book design by Current Affairs Press. Typeset in 12 point Cambria.

Manufactured in the United States of America.

10 9 8 7 6 5 4 3 2 1

Library of Congress Cataloging-in-Publication Data is available.

ISBN 978-0-9987818-0-8
ISBN 978-0-9987818-1-5 (eBook)

To Susan

and to

Daniel, Annie, Janie, and Molly

and their generation

Contents

Part II - Isn't that causing a problem?

Introduction

Why this Book Now?

You never know when an idea is going to sneak up on you, and not let go - when you are going to have that "light bulb" moment. Mine literally involved a light bulb.

One evening, at home, I took a light bulb out of its package, and noticed that on the top, besides a display of the wattage and voltage, were two things: The GE logo, and, in all caps, the word CHINA. It struck me that, if General Electric, founded by Thomas Edison and embodying all that has been great in American ingenuity and industry, is making its light bulbs in China, we might have a problem on our hands.

This "light bulb moment" came as I had recently been to the Boy Scouts store, and noticed that everything I bought for my son was made in China, Vietnam, and Bangladesh. And I had just heard a talk at my church's men's group by the chaplain of the prison in Coatesville, Pennsylvania. I had worked in a prison ministry for eight years and I knew there was never an excuse for committing a crime, but I thought, "Wouldn't it be easier to keep those young men in Coatesville straight if they still made things there?"

Shortly after, I bought a "Homeless Times" newspaper from a man in Philadelphia. He was a very regular looking guy, not mentally ill, not an alcoholic, just someone who had fallen through the ice. The newspaper contained a review of a new book by the economist Joseph Stiglitz about how many Americans are falling further behind while a few are getting ahead.[1] I suspected that the GE light bulb, and all the other products we are buying from "out there" instead of making here, might have a role in all of this.

So, I set out to answer three questions:

Why does it seem like everything is made somewhere else, especially China?

Isn't that causing a problem?

If it is, what can be done about it?

It has proven more difficult to find the answers to those questions than you might think.

Journalists often tend to skim the surface. For example, newspaper articles will quote the "top line" unemployment number, with a buried mention of stubborn long-term unemployment, when in fact, counting the underemployed and the discouraged, in 2016 we had unemployment that is worse than it was *during* the recession of 1990-91.

Economists engage in deep statistical analyses with the objective of proving a hypothesis that may be patently at odds with reality -- for example, that international trade is always a win-win proposition for all participants, or that the answer to globalization is to get Americans' wages down to the level of the rest of the world, so we can "compete" out there.

Perhaps most dangerous of all, think tanks and even government agencies pour out commentary and reports in which they cherry-pick facts in support of an ideological point of view, such as the benefits of "free trade."

All of this left me wanting to find out, with respect to my first two questions, "what's *really* going on?"

I have spent the better part of the last three years searching out answers, and I invite you to come on that journey as I retrace my steps in this book. I have tried to be open-minded and even-handed, initially playing the role of the finder of fact, and not of an advocate. My goal has been to pursue the evidence wherever it may lead.

I must say that in the beginning I had the mistaken impression that I was somewhat informed on these matters. To the contrary, I have made some surprising and disturbing discoveries. At risk of "spoiling the movie," here is some of what I have found:

Your smart phone was made in a labor camp, your clothes were made in a sweatshop, and your fish were caught on a slave ship. Not content to create sweat-shops abroad, we have created a whole new kind of sweatshop here at home, the "distribution centers" where workers receive, store, pick, pack, and ship all those cheap foreign products for below-subsistence pay in dangerous heat during the summer and cold during the winter.

These jobs could never replace the six million manufacturing jobs we have sent overseas, mostly to China. They are part of the "low-price, low-wage" economy applying the "big squeeze" up and down the ladder, hollowing out the middle class, and creating dependency and social ills as we have been caught in a vicious circle of economic stagnation and decline: eight years into the "recovery" from the Great Recession, most Americans are not back to their pre-recession economic status.

Without change, the future holds more of the same, or worse. We are caught in a holding pattern of anemic economic growth, and what growth we are experiencing is being captured disproportionately by those at the top. And there will be another recession, as the business cycle dictates. We will be ill-prepared for it, because in many ways, far too many of us are living in precarious, "permanent recession" conditions.

However, we seem hell-bent on perpetuating or worsening the situation, as many of us continue to beat the drum of "free" trade and seek to expand its reach, for example through the proposed Trans-Pacific Partnership and Transatlantic Trade and Investment Partnership.

In fact, I have become convinced that the future of the United States, and therefore in large measure, of the world, hangs in the balance. At a more personal level, the future of our children and grandchildren, hangs in the balance. I recently received a letter addressed to the parents of my daughter's high school Class of 2020, and saw a welcoming banner to the Class of 2020 at my college bookstore. What do we say to the Classes of 2020?

Do we say, here's a list of jobs you shouldn't train for, because there is someone in India who is ready to do it at one-fourth the pay, and can do so because of the Internet, and there are "American" consulting firms champing at the bit to teach companies how to offshore their jobs there? Do we say, don't bother studying to become a manufacturing process engineer, because those jobs can be filled in a town just over the Texas border for $20,000 per year? And that there are firms that are ready to help companies move operations there?

Do we try to figure out what jobs are "tradable," and guide our children only to prepare for those that are not? And if we give away all the tradable jobs, are there enough non-tradable jobs left, or do we end up with a fierce competition for them?

Could we in good conscience leave them on our current path? I believe the answer must be a resounding "No." I therefore took off my fact-finder hat, and have taken on the role of advocate for change.

The Way Forward

Fortunately, I have discovered that there is a way out. It begins by taking a fresh, clear-eyed look at what we want for ourselves, our families, and our communities – what is our view of the American Dream in 2017? What would we like the American future to look like for our children and grandchildren, based on our core values as a people and a nation?

It is not all about money. But surely it includes self-sufficiency and dignity for American families, so that if you go to work in a job that needs doing, you and your family can make a go of it without needing subsidies or charity. I take a hard look at how much that costs - how much is a living wage and a family wage in today's America? And then, we get to the answer:

> Bring the jobs home, and pay people
> a decent wage for performing them.

There is the answer, so elegant in its simplicity, that has been eluding most of the economists, policy-makers, and pundits all these years. While much has been written identifying the problem of the hollowing out of the American economy, almost always the associated prescriptions are inadequate, involving things like building infrastructure (creating one-time, rather than sustainable jobs, and going further into debt to pay for it), or having everyone go to college (most jobs don't require a college degree, and we're not all cut out for college). Meanwhile, we have been letting the air out of the very balloon we are trying to inflate, as we send trillions of dollars to other countries' economies through our offshore purchases. So, let me repeat the answer, in a little more detail:

> Bring home $500 billion in spending, enough to balance trade, create six million jobs, take the slack out of the labor market, and start a "virtuous circle" of growth.

But how to do that? Happily, the power to do so lies in your hands, as you hold this book, and the millions of other American consumers. *We* account for nearly 70 percent of the economy in our private purchases. *We* can solve this problem just by redirecting some of the money we already are spending, to products made in communities across America.

Not only can we do this, but *only* we, as consumers, have the capability to do this. A company facing lower-priced products from a competitor sourcing its goods in China will have trouble not following suit. But if consumers are *demanding* products made in American communities, then companies must respond. They will build new manufacturing capacity to make more of those products, employing working Americans, in the building, and in the making.

But, Jim, you say, that could be hard to do; there are whole stores where I have trouble finding anything made in America. I devote the last chapter to how we can do this, starting now. I refer to some helpful resources, including one I am working on which will use the Internet to connect us with the companies still making consumer products in communities all across America.

So, despite its gloomy diagnosis of the past and present, and its gloomy prognosis if nothing is done, this book has the happy distinction of having a last chapter with a blueprint for how we can solve these problems, beginning today, without having to ask the government or anyone else for permission or support.

How to Use this Book

This book looks longer than it is. There are a lot of footnotes! And there is a lot of white space, because I have included many figures in an effort to visually capture trends. I don't know about you, but I have trouble looking at a table of numbers and spotting trends. So, in order that you, as I, can "get the picture," I have used figures, usually very simple, with just a couple of lines, that can tell a big story. An example is the following, showing the goods we have bought from Vietnam compared to the goods we have sold to them since we began trade relations in 1992 and entered into a trade agreement in 2001:

Any questions? Other than, "Can that possibly be true?" "Why would we enter into such a lopsided trade relationship?" "How many jobs have we sent to Vietnam and what happened when we did?" and "What does the future hold; that imports curve is going out of sight!" These are exactly the questions I address in this book.

This book also includes some discussions that may go deeper into economics than you are accustomed to. I suggest that you go as deep as works for you, but feel free to skim and to fast forward to where I have set out my key findings in boxes at the end of a topic. However, I urge and encourage you to go deep. I believe this book contains material every American must know. I believe the situation is so urgent, and that our children's future is so endangered, that we each have a responsibility to know these facts and then to take some action in response to them.

A Call to Duty

Our situation is not unlike that at the end of the nineteenth and beginning of the twentieth century, when the slaughterhouses were turning out unsafe food products, when "medicines" were sold that didn't do anything, when advertising was full of other false and misleading claims and other shoddy business practices were rampant, when monopolists were grabbing market share by driving out competitors by selling below cost, and when "Lady Astor's 400" built fortunes from the resulting "trusts" on the backs of workers. We responded, during the presidencies of Theodore Roosevelt and William Howard Taft, by reigning in these forces through the food and drug safety, fair advertising, anti-trust, and labor protection laws that we take for granted today. But it is important to note that these responses only occurred because people demanded them, and they demanded them because they were informed.

They were informed because a group of investigative journalists, for whom Teddy Roosevelt coined the term "muckrakers," dug deep, and published the facts in magazines like McClure's. S.S. McClure said, "The vitality of democracy" depends on "popular knowledge of complex questions." "There is no one left," McClure said, "none but all of us." [2] Today, each of us has a duty, to each other and to our children and their children, to become similarly informed. I hope this book is a useful tool toward that end.

I have worried long and hard that I may have included too much information. But I have kept the full facts and discussions, for two reasons. First, I am hoping to do what is referred to in the law as "building a record" of facts entered into evidence, on which a decision can be based, a decision that is "supported by the record."

Second, as I said at the outset, there is a great deal of bad information out there. Information that is superficial, or so biased and misleading as to amount to "dis-information" -- information that is just incomplete or misleading enough to leave us wondering, *"What is really going on?"* I went digging for information sufficient for you and for me to answer that question.

It has been nearly three years in the digging, and I express my sincerest gratitude to my wife Susan, who has never doubted that I could complete this project even when I was not sure I could, and who "held down the fort" as I spent much more time than I would have liked away from her and our children, Daniel, Annie, Janie, and Molly. Thanks also to them, and it is to them and their generation, that this book is dedicated. Special thanks to Jean-Luc Ganivet, whose support made possible the first printing of this book. Thanks also to Alfred Glossbrenner at Firecrystal Communications for his insightful consultations, and to Terry Cunningham and Tom Petro for their helpful comments on the manuscript. Thanks also to Scott Andrews, Linda Duvall, Daniel Wideman, Mike McCairn, Lorraine Hays, and the rest of the staff at the University of Pennsylvania library, where I spent most of that time away from the family, and who make possible a place where one can go digging for answers.

So, I invite you to come with me now on a journey to discover why that GE lightbulb was made in China, if that is causing a problem, and what we can do about it. To do that, it turns out that we must go back and have a look at what was going on in 1945.

---

[1] Joseph E. Stiglitz, *The Price of Inequality: How Today's Divided Society Endangers Our Future* (New York: W.W. Norton & Co., 2012).

[2] Doris Kearns Goodwin, *The Bully Pulpit: Theodore Roosevelt, William Howard Taft, and the Golden Age of Journalism* (New York: Simon & Schuster, 2013).

Part One

Why does it seem like everything is made somewhere else, especially China?

Chapter 1

Getting to 1945

1945

As 1945 opened, thousands of ordinary Americans were in foxholes engaged in the Battle of the Bulge, Germany's last, desperate, and almost successful attempt to drive the Allies back out of Europe. Some of them had arrived in Normandy, France, on June 6, 1944, "D-Day." They had made it off the beach that day only because the Allies, in an effort unmatched in history, had put more men on the beach than the Germans could kill. Men who, through thousands of individual acts of courage, managed somehow to move forward into the hail of fire, exhorted by their noncommissioned officers to go forward or die on the beach. But many the Germans did kill, before being overwhelmed by courage and numbers.

In the following days and weeks, these "Citizen Soldiers," as Stephen Ambrose has called them, fought through fields bounded by "hedgerows," high, overgrown embankments of earth and stone, through which the Germans had punched holes for their tanks and machine guns. They spent the winter of the Battle of the Bulge, the coldest in Europe in a hundred years, in summer uniforms because General Omar Bradley thought the battle would be won months earlier. Again, as at Normandy, at Bastogne and dozens of other locations, through thousands of acts of individual courage, the tide was turned. As 1945 unfolded, they fought their way across France, the Rhine, and Germany. There, they encountered and liberated the concentration camps, and swore to each other that they must tell the world what they had witnessed, else no one would believe it had occurred.[1]

How could they manage to do all of this, and survive? The answer is that most of them who were on the front lines didn't. Richard Davis "Dick" Winters, the courageous leader whose story is recounted in Ambrose's book "Band of Brothers" and the television mini-series of the same name, was one of the "lucky ones," as they referred to themselves, who made it home. Ambrose noted a typical company that had arrived in Normandy on September 8, 1944 with 196 men: by V-E (Victory in Europe) Day on May 8, 1945, the unit had suffered 250 percent casualties; units involved longer fared worse. Most of the officers, the ordinary Americans who had developed into courageous and competent unit leaders like Winters, were dead.[2]

Similar sacrifices were being made by the Citizen Soldiers in the Pacific. In that theater, every few months ordinary Americans would run onto beaches on which Japanese forces had placed deadly crossfires, and fight their way to a conclusion against an enemy whose culture, unlike the Germans', called upon them to fight to the death. After V-E Day, the American soldiers in Europe were warned not to get too excited, because most of them would be transferring to the Pacific for the assault on Japan.[3] However, with the atomic bombing of Hiroshima and

Nagasaki, the war came to an end on "V-J Day," August 15, 1945.

The "lucky ones" came home. Some of them never recovered their faculties. But most of them came home, had nightmares for a while, and got on with their lives, marrying and having the children of the "baby boom," and going to work. One of the central themes of this book is, for what did those who died, and their families, and the lucky ones who came home, make this sacrifice, and have we squandered it?

Andy was one of the lucky ones. He had enlisted in the Army Air Force before the United States entered the war following the Japanese attack on Pearl Harbor on December 6, 1941. In Europe, the Allies' plan called for capturing North Africa from the Germans and then Italy; Andy's B-26 bomber unit, based in Tunisia, was to support the Italian campaign.

In the 1990 motion picture *Memphis Belle*, the crew's worst mission is their last before reaching the requisite number to go home. Andy's was his first: after flying his first mission as a gunner in a bomber crew, he wrote to his sister to tell his mother that we would not be coming home. However, he was one of the "lucky ones," and after surviving forty missions he earned the right to return to the U.S., where he finished the war serving as a gunnery instructor, and married. According to his wife, Betty, he lived out additional missions in his sleep until the nightmares subsided.[1]

Andy and Betty had met as teenagers in their hometown of Mingo Junction, Ohio, just south of Steubenville on

[1] Andy and Betty were my parents, now deceased, Andrew Stuber and Betty Long.

the Ohio River, and home to the steel mill featured in the 1978 motion picture *The Deer Hunter*. Andy's mother and father had emigrated, separately, from Czechoslovakia and married in the U.S., and his father worked in the mill. As did almost everyone, including Andy's and Betty's extended families. Betty's family had moved to the Pittsburgh area in search of work during a downturn at the mill. So, one thing Andy was familiar with was steel making.

Andy had heard they were making steel in Southern California, and thought that sounded like a better location than Mingo Junction or Pittsburgh. In fact, they were indeed making steel there, at Kaiser Steel in San Bernardino County, a place that will figure in this story later on. But it was farther from family than Betty would tolerate, and Andy entered an apprenticeship as a "roll turner" at Copperweld Steel in Warren, Ohio. He joined the 15 million American men and women who came home from the war, went to work, and began the thirty years of the "Golden Era" of unprecedented growth and widely shared prosperity.

America had won the war in no small part because it made steel. Steel that went into the construction of thousands of "Liberty Ships" carrying personnel and materiel, tanks that would defeat Rommel in Africa and Europe, aircraft that would destroy Germany's capacity to produce fuel, weapons and ammunition, and ships and aircraft that would defeat the Japanese in crucial naval battles in the Pacific. Now America began making the steel that would go into automobiles, bridges, skyscrapers, electrical transmission towers, and appliances during the "Golden Era." Andy would be one of those doing the making.

But even now, as the "Golden Era" was commencing, the seeds of its destruction had been sown.

Getting to 1945

America Steps onto the Road to Free Trade

Those seeds were sown before the war, in 1934. In that year, Congress enacted the Reciprocal Trade Agreement Act ("RTAA"), abrogating its tariff-making authority in favor of the Executive Branch.[4] The RTAA permitted the President to conclude bilateral, reciprocal trade agreements with other countries with a view toward reducing tariffs of mutual interest, without obtaining further Congressional approval. By June of 1940, agreements had been signed under the RTAA with 21 countries representing approximately 60 percent of U.S. trade. Through 1945, 32 agreements were negotiated.[5]

Enactment of the RTAA was the result of the election in 1932 of President Franklin D. Roosevelt, who had run on a platform of free trade. He appointed Cordell Hull as his Secretary of State to lead the charge for obtaining legislative authority and negotiating the tariff reductions.

In the campaign, and in the Congressional elections of 1932, Roosevelt and the Democrats framed the debate as free trade versus protectionism they said was embodied in the Smoot-Hawley Tariff Act of 1930, discussed below.

By pursuing a policy directed toward unrestricted trade with other countries, the Roosevelt administration and the Congress chose a different answer to a question that had faced the first administrations under the new American Constitution beginning in 1789: would the country pursue the open trade policies advocated by Adam Smith and David Ricardo, or the protected industrial development policies theretofore pursued by Great Britain?

English Mercantilism and the Tudor Plan

In his 2010 book, *The Betrayal of American Prosperity*, Clyde Prestowitz describes those policies and how they led Britain to become "the workshop of the world." [6] According to Prestowitz, the English monarch Henry VII, while spending his childhood in Burgundy, France, noticed that the French were getting rich making woolen textiles from wool provided in large part by England. On the throne, he instituted the first "catch-up" industrial growth program, designed to have Britain become the leading textile producer. The plan involved limits on exports of wool, tax relief and temporary monopolies for "infant" woolen textile manufacturers, incentives for importation of technological know-how in the form of craftsmen and entrepreneurs from Holland and Italy, and suppression of competition from other countries or colonies.

Queen Elizabeth went further, imposing a complete ban on wool exports, and the plan, which came to be known as the "Tudor Plan," was replicated in other industries. By means of the Navigation Acts, Britain also restricted shipping to British ships. In sum, the program subsidized domestic manufactures, imposed tariffs on imported manufactures, limited manufacturing in the British colonies, and subsidized colonial production of raw materials. The goal was to create a global economic structure in which raw materials flowed to Britain while Britain dominated the manufacture of high value-added goods.

This structure enabled an explosion in British exports, which may not only have enabled, but have been a prerequisite to, the Industrial Revolution. The final ingredient in the mix was British military and naval might. The result was that by 1815, at the end of the Napoleonic

Wars and conclusion of the Congress of Vienna, Britain stood at the pinnacle of economic and military power, with "a virtual monopoly on overseas colonies, worldwide naval power, and industrial production." [7]

Meanwhile, another approach was being formulated.

Adam Smith, David Ricardo and Free Trade

In 1776, Adam Smith published *The Wealth of Nations*.[8] In his treatise, he makes two assumptions: that the prime drive of mankind is self-interest, and the existence of a natural order which, operating like an "invisible hand," makes all the individual strivings for self-interest add up to the social good. Based on these assumptions, he concludes that the best policy is to leave the economic process alone - what has come to be known as *laissez-faire*, economic liberalism, or non-interventionism.

As a corollary to the third point, Smith generally concludes that trade, too, is best left alone, that is, open and unencumbered. However, it should be noted that this conclusion is subject to some substantial limitations, for example that free trade should not result in reliance on foreign sources for food or other items necessary in time of war.

Smith's thinking on trade was pursued further by David Ricardo, in his treatise, *The Principles of Political Economy and Taxation*, first published in 1817.[9] Ricardo made the case for free trade, and more specifically, for each nation producing the mix of goods in which it has a "comparative advantage." Importantly, under Ricardo's analysis, a nation could do better economically even if it removed barriers to others' goods and it did not, practicing what might be called "unilateral free trade." [10]

The ideas of Smith and Ricardo gained favor in Britain, and it is perhaps understandable why: according to Ricardo, "It is this principle that determines that wine will be made in France and Portugal, that corn shall be grown in America and Poland, and that hardware and other goods shall be manufactured in England." [11] That sounds like a pretty good arrangement for the British, doesn't it?

England was sitting at the pinnacle of economic and military power and was "the world's workshop," and it seemed like an immutable truth that it would remain so: if free trade and comparative advantage could improve its position even more, why not go for it?

And they did, adopting a policy of "*laissez-faire*, nonreciprocal free trade:" in the 1840s, they repealed the Corn Laws limiting corn imports into Britain, and the Navigation Acts limiting shipping to British ships, and in the 1850s and 1860s, they unilaterally removed virtually all tariffs.[12]

Thus, Britain became the world's first, and only, unilateral free trader. No other countries, including the United States, followed suit. And the British economy began a long decline.

So, the British made their choice, abandoning the system of mercantilism[13] and protected industrial development that had made them the world's number one economic and military power, and adopting a policy of unilateral free trade based on the idea of specialization in areas of comparative advantage.[14]

The American System

Now, the Americans were confronted with that choice as they embarked on their experiment in nationhood in

1789.[15] Opinions fell into two camps, reminiscent of the hit Broadway musical *Hamilton*:

Leading one camp was Thomas Jefferson, joined by James Madison, Thomas Paine, and Benjamin Franklin. They were generally in agreement with Smith's framework of free trade and specialization, as later more fully developed by Ricardo. In their view, the future lay in American specialization in agriculture, where it had the advantage of limitless fertile land and know-how, while importing manufactured goods.[16]

Alexander Hamilton led the other camp, which supported pursuing a program of protected industrial development along the lines that Britain had followed. He was joined by George Washington, who, it has been observed, likely supported a strong U.S. manufacturing base after experiencing difficulty clothing and arming his army during the Revolutionary War. He famously wore an American-made suit to his inauguration and promised a manufacturing association to do his best to buy American-made in carrying out the duties of his office.[17] Hamilton's "Report on Manufactures" in 1791 called for high tariffs to protect fledgling American industries.

When Jefferson took office, he took steps in the other direction. However, the War of 1812, during which the United States once again found itself inadequately prepared to produce the necessities of war, made him a believer; he switched positions and became an advocate of buy-American policies. Madison, Monroe, Adams, and Jackson all followed suit.[18]

Prestowitz notes that the politicians' views gained support among journalists and economists, notably Daniel Raymond, the "first systemic American economist."

Raymond questioned Smith's emphasis on the individual, believing that the focus should be on the general welfare. Of particular relevance in today's context, he took issue with Smith's proposition that consumers should buy less expensive foreign goods, and posited that consumers should not be patronizing foreigners "when their own fellow citizens were in want." Raymond did not assume that winners in trade would compensate losers, and did not believe that net gains meant a better society if the gains were concentrated in a few.[19]

And so, a consensus formed around what became known as the "American System." Espoused by Congressman Henry Clay of Kentucky, it included protection and subsidization of "infant" manufacturing industries; government-supported development of infrastructure including roads, railroads and waterways; expansion of the country's borders; and free trade only in cases of reciprocity.[20] It followed closely the British Tudor Plan, except that in my view it cannot be said to have been an "export-led" strategy; rather, it was designed to promote development of a broad range of American industry serving primarily the rapidly expanding American market.

The American System at Work

The backing for infrastructure included things you will remember from school: construction of the Cumberland (National) Road, the Erie Canal, and the transcontinental railroad and thousands of miles of additional track, supported with Federal land grants. The Federal government also gave land for the "land grant colleges" that are today's state universities, and supported developments such as the telegraph, sewing machine, and reaper. Earlier it had granted a contract to Eli Whitney, who had invented the cotton gin, to manufacture muskets. In the process, he applied the system of interchangeable parts that became known as the "American System of Manufacturing." All these inventions could be protected under the strong patent laws enacted in 1794.[21]

It worked. From 1820 to 1870, U.S. GDP increased tenfold. Between 1870 and 1900, the United States surged ahead of Britain in production and invention. The electric light bulb, typewriter, a variety of farm machinery, improved seeds and cures for animal diseases, railroad construction, machines for mechanization and automation, and a dramatic increase in the U.S. population and acreages under cultivation, with their attendant economies of scale, all added up to America's displacing Britain as the leader in per capita GDP. Germany and America each displaced Britain in percentage of world output and manufacturing output: Germany dominated in chemicals and America dominated in electrical and automotive technologies.

By 1900, Europe was complaining about the influx of American goods of superior quality and lower price, often newly invented by the Americans. By 1914, American GDP per capital exceeded Britain's and substantially exceeded Germany's - America had become the world's richest nation.

Britain hung on, partly by adding to its empire and exploiting its relationship with its colonies, and partly with income from the "invisible exports" of shipping, insurance, brokerage, and financing (referred to today as "trade in services"). It also benefited from increased exports of coal; taking a position heard in some quarters in America today, the *Economist* magazine opined that coal was as good as machine tools when it comes to exports.[22] However, World War I had a crippling effect on the British economy, creating an enormous debt, and permitting the U.S., Japan, and others to move into Britain's export markets in steel and other commodities. The British government nationalized many industries and reintroduced protective tariffs.[23]

Between the World Wars

The United States emerged from World War I in many ways as the "last man standing."

The United States had entered the war late, and was protected by two oceans. The toll exacted in death and injuries and economic costs was nothing like that experienced by the major combatants. U.S. GDP rose 204 percent from 1914 to 1918 and another 63 percent by 1921; a major shift was occurring. [24]

In 1914, the U.S. was world's largest debtor; in 1919, it was the world's largest creditor. By 1920, U.S. had displaced Britain as "the world's leading maritime country." The war also shifted leadership to America in aircraft and aviation. In 1915 the National Advisory Committee for Aeronautics (now NASA) had been formed, and America produced 14,000 airplanes in 1918. Enacting the Air Mail Act of 1925 and the Air Commerce Act of 1927, the U.S. also took the lead in aviation.[25]

With active involvement of the Federal government, the lead in radio telegraphy was seized from the British Marconi Radio Corp., with the formation of the Radio Corporation of America, a consortium of AT&T, Westinghouse, and others, with the U.S. Navy a 20% shareholder. RCA promptly captured a large percentage of Atlantic and Pacific cable communications traffic.[26]

The U.S. was emerging as an economic power. However, diplomatically and militarily, Great Britain remained the world's leading power. And Britain reverted to unilateral free trade.

The Roaring Twenties and Smoot-Hawley

The United States, to the contrary, reverted to high tariffs. The Fordney-McCumber Tariff Act of 1922 raised the effective tariff rate to 40 percent. The high tariffs had no discernible adverse effect on the performance of the economy, as the Roaring Twenties ensued.

In 1928, Herbert Hoover campaigned in part on a promise to struggling farmers to raise tariffs. Immediately before and following the stock market crash in the fall of 1929, Congress considered legislation that would raise tariffs not only on farm produce, but also manufactured products, the Smoot-Hawley Tariff Act of 1930.

If you are not engaged in economic policy-making, you may be having trouble recalling what may be ringing a faint bell from your high school or college days. Or from the film *Ferris Bueller's Day Off*, in which Ben Stein, playing a high school teacher, ad libs a monologue inquiring what his students know of the topic. Or the 1992 appearance of Al Gore and Ross Perot on the Larry King Live television show, in which Gore belittled Perot's opposition to the North American Free Trade Agreement by presenting him with a framed photograph of former Utah Senator Reed Smoot and former Congressman Willis Hawley. As chairmen of the committees with jurisdiction, they authored the Tariff Act of 1930, signed by President Herbert Hoover on June 17, 1930. The Act, which came to be referred to simply as "Smoot-Hawley," substantially increased tariffs on a large variety of agricultural and manufactured goods.

The run-up to the bill's passage was well-publicized and rancorous, and after its enactment Canada and a number of other countries imposed retaliatory tariffs. Prices were falling during the Depression, so the tariffs, many of which were posted in terms of dollars per unit of goods, increased as a percentage of the price of the imported goods, to as high a rate as had ever previously been in effect.

Imports declined, and exports declined even more. In a recent analysis, Dartmouth College economics professor Douglas A. Irwin reports that between 1929 and 1932, imports fell 40 percent, and exports 49 percent. However, most of this decline was due to the Depression - he estimates that five percentage points of the import decline was from the Act itself.[27]

That's pretty much where the facts end. From there, proponents of free trade and of electing Democrats jumped to the conclusion that Smoot-Hawley had caused the Depression, or tipped what would have been a recession into a Depression.

Stein, who is the son of the now-deceased prominent economist Herbert Stein and an attorney and economist himself in addition to doing some acting, has noted that at the time of Smoot-Hawley, exports accounted for only about five percent of U.S. economic output; to suggest that the bill, which raised tariffs on a minority of imports, caused the Depression "is almost comical." He called the popularization of the idea a "form of intellectual entrepreneurship, in which people carve out an appealing idea and then try to make capital of it." [28]

Alfred E. Eckes, Jr. spends a chapter of his 1995 book, *Opening America's Market*, refuting commonly-held misconceptions about Smoot-Hawley: that it imposed the highest tariffs ever; that it caused the stock market collapse; that is worsened the Depression; and that it invoked substantial retaliation. He concludes that it did none of these, which he refers to as "the Smoot-Hawley myth."[29]

In his 2011 study of the subject, *supra*, Douglas Irwin concludes that monetary and financial factors were the causes of the Great Depression; Smoot-Hawley made things worse, but played only a secondary role.[30] UC Berkeley economics professor Barry Eichengreen went further in a 1986 study, concluding that enactment of the Smoot-Hawley tariffs actually had a mildly positive effect on the U.S. economy, and a mildly negative effect on the world economy; however, their enactment did have a destabilizing effect on international financial markets.[31] He stood by this assessment in a column written in July of 2016, warning nevertheless of the potential pitfalls of protectionist measures.[32]

When the dust settles, I believe it is important to understand that the religious zeal with which free trade advocates invoke Smoot-Hawley against any steps to manage trade is unwarranted, and in fact misleading. As I already have noted, the Fordney-McCumber Tariff Act of 1922 raised the effective tariff rate to 40 percent, but the high tariffs had no discernible effect on the performance of the economy, which then entered the Roaring Twenties. And Irwin found that a small portion of the economic decline of the 1930s was attributable to the Smoot-Hawley tariffs. It appears, rather, that in any severe economic downturn, both imports and exports fall, in real terms and as a percentage of GDP. We will see later that this happened during the 2008-2009 recession, as well as the preceding recessions.

For our present purposes, the importance of Smoot-Hawley lies in the fact that in 1932, Congressional candidates and presidential candidate Franklin D.

Roosevelt did successfully invoke Smoot-Hawley in support of their election and of their subsequently setting the nation on a course toward free trade.

It is also important to note that Smoot-Hawley was not a departure from the previous 150 years of American trade policy; rather, it was the Reciprocal Trade Agreements Act of 1934 that deserved that honor. So, in 1945, as America began the voyage of the post-war era, American trade policy set off on a new tack.

Seven Snapshots

Seventy years have passed since then. I will try to capture them in a series of seven snapshots, with a discussion of events in the decade leading up to each. As we take that journey, watch out for the four actors playing out this saga:

- The U.S. public sector;
- The U.S. private sector;
- Foreign countries' public sector; and
- Foreign countries' private sector.

We also should note that there is another set of actors taking part in the situation: American consumers. In fact, there are three categories of consumers: individual consumers, companies acting as consumers, and governments acting as consumers. Without the participation of these consumers, nothing described in this book could be happening.[33] But now we leave 1945 and head toward our first snapshot, in 1955.

Notes to Chapter 1

---

[1] Stephen E. Ambrose, *Citizen Soldiers: The U S Army from the Normandy Beaches to the Bulge to the Surrender of Germany* (New York: Simon & Schuster, 1998), 463.

[2] Ambrose, *Citizen Soldiers*, 468.

[3] Ambrose, *Citizen Soldiers*, 466.

[4] Reciprocal Trade Agreements Act, Pub. L. No. 73-316, June 12, 1934. The Reciprocal Trade Agreements Act of 1934 is sometimes referred to as the Reciprocal Trade Act, or RTA. When being renewed, it was sometimes named the Trade Agreements Act and sometimes the Trade Agreements Extension Act. The initial law was valid for a three-year period. It was renewed repeatedly and has existed in some form since 1934 with a few major lapses: 1967–74, 1994–2002, and from 2007-2015. In June of 2015, Congress granted the President "fast track" trade promotion authority to negotiate the proposed Trans Pacific Partnership, as discussed below.

[5] Alfred E. Eckes, Jr., *Opening America's Market: U.S. Foreign Trade Policy Since 1776* (Chapel Hill: The University of North Carolina Press, 1995), 135, 141.

[6] Clyde Prestowitz, *The Betrayal of American Prosperity: Free Market Delusions, America's Decline, and How We Must Compete in the Post-Dollar Era* (New York: Free Press, 2010), 46 *ff.*

[7] Prestowitz, *Betrayal*, 46-48.

[8] Adam Smith, *An Inquiry into the Nature and Causes of the Wealth of Nations* (London: W. Strand and T. Cadell, 1776). Smith made some changes through five editions; the fifth and final edition was published in 1789, reprinted in Adam Smith, *An Inquiry into the Nature and Causes of the Wealth of Nations,* Edwin Cannan, Ed. (New York: The Modern Library, Random House, Inc., 1937.)

[9] David Ricardo, *The Principles of Political Economy and Taxation (London: J.M. Dent & Sons Ltd., 1911).*

[10] Prestowitz, *Betrayal*, 57, 162.

[11] Ricardo, *Principles*, 70-71.

[12] Prestowitz, *Betrayal*, 57.

[13] The practice of a nation intentionally selling to other nations more than it buys from them.

[14] Prestowitz points out that, despite British urging, none of the other European powers took the free trade path. In particular, the

German, Georg Friedrich List, wrote critiques arguing that a country should first industrialize by developing infant industries, and then trade freely with equally industrialized countries. Prestowitz, *Betrayal*, 58.

[15] It should be remembered that this was their second try: under the Articles of Confederation, the colonies-turned-states each had their own customs territories, levying tariffs against each other as well as other nations, and unable to negotiate with other nations as a group. The newly adopted Constitution gave Congress the power to regulate commerce with foreign nations and among the states, and gave Congress the power to impose duties (but not between the states), while generally prohibiting the states from doing so. *Constitution of the United States*.
http://www.archives.gov/exhibits/charters/constitution_transcript.html.

[16] Eckes, *Opening*, 9 *ff*. Prestowitz, *Betrayal*, 50.

[17] Eckes, *Opening*, 14. Prestowitz, *Betrayal*, 51.

[18] Prestowitz, *Betrayal*, 53.

[19] Prestowitz, *Betrayal*, 54.

[20] *Id*.

[21] *See* Vaclav Smil, *Made in the USA: The Rise and Retreat of American Manufacturing* (Cambridge, Massachusetts: The MIT Press, 2013), 21-60. Prestowitz, *Betrayal*, 53, 54, 55, 56, 59 *ff*. *See also* Robert J. *Gordon, The Rise and Fall of American Growth: The U.S. Standard of Living Since the Civil War (Princeton: Princeton University Press, 2016)*, 310, and generally, Part I. All of this is especially worthy of note in comparison to our current times, when we are sending the results of our research and development offshore for production, or even doing the R&D offshore, and giving away or failing to enforce patent rights. *Id*.

[22] Prestowitz, *Betrayal*, 63.

[23] Prestowitz, *Betrayal*, 66.

[24] Prestowitz, *Betrayal*, 67.

[25] Smil, *Made in the USA*, 64. Prestowitz, *Betrayal*, 68.

[26] *Id*.

[27] Douglas Irwin, *Peddling Protectionism: Smoot-Hawley and the Great Depression* (Princeton: Princeton University Press, 2011), 220-221.

[28] Ben Stein, "The Smoot Hawley Act Is More Than a Laugh Line," New York Times, May 9, 2009.
http://www.nytimes.com/2009/05/10/business/10every.html

[29] Eckes, *Opening*, 100 *ff*.

---

[30] Irwin, *Protectionism*, 220-221. *See also*, "The Great Depression - Was legislation sponsored by two Republicans to blame?" Book review in *The Economist*, March 24, 2011: ". . . Mr. Irwin's accessible analysis makes quite clear that the act cannot be said to have caused the Great Depression."

[31] Barry Eichengreen, "The Political Economy of the Smoot-Hawley Tariff," NBER Working Paper No. 2001, issued in August 1986. http://www.nber.org/papers/w2001,doi:10.3386/w2001.

[32] Barry Eichengreen, "What's the Problem with Protectionism?" *ProjectSyndicate.org*, July 13, 2016 https://www.project-syndicate.org/commentary/protectionism-geopolitical-problems-by-barry-eichengreen-2016-07

[33] There also is another group, who, though not actors, are influencers: individuals on university faculties, in private "think tanks," and in the press who conduct research and express opinions that influence the actors. In Chapter 4, I quote John Maynard Keynes as saying, "[T]he ideas of economists and political philosophers . . . are more powerful than is commonly understood. Indeed, the world is ruled by little else." [*See* Chapter 4, fn1.] However, as I discuss in Chapter 10, these members of our "elites," along with our government and business leaders, for the most part have failed us.

Chapter 2

1946-1995: Japan and the Era of Free Trade

1946 - 1955

American Leadership and the Postwar Framework

An understanding of the decade leading up to our first snapshot in 1955 is crucial to appreciating how we got to our current state of global economic and political affairs.

As after World War I, in 1946 America again was the "last man standing," but this time it was different: due to the extensive use of bombing during World War II, the industrial capacities of Japan, Germany, England, and numerous other countries lay in ruins. America, on the other hand, had built a dynamic and efficient industrial machine that had been protected by two oceans and was ready to be converted to civilian purposes.

Britain had emerged from World War I still the leading military and political power, even though the U.S. had taken the lead economically. However, following World War II,

America was far and away number one in all dimensions, and assumed the mantle of leadership in building a new world order — as it had almost done at the end of World War I before retreating behind its oceans.

The post-war order created structures for organizing world affairs in three dimensions: financial, political, and trade. Financial and monetary affairs were governed under a structure created at a conference at Bretton Woods, New Hampshire in July of 1944, establishing the International Monetary Fund and the World Bank.

The International Monetary Fund would manage a system anchored by a joint dollar/gold standard under which the U.S. dollar would be convertible to gold at $35 per ounce. (The United States held two-thirds of the world's gold at the end of the war.) Other currencies would be convertible to dollars (and, therefore, gold) at rates managed by the IMF. Individual countries' central banks would manage the business cycle through monetary policy applying the theories of John Maynard Keynes.

Reconstruction of Europe, and, later, economic development worldwide, would be financed via loans issued by the institution now known as the World Bank, under standard and concessionary terms. In addition, postwar recovery would be supported with funding from the United States, in Europe under the Marshall Plan, and in developing countries under President Harry Truman's Four Points Program. The United States, Canada, Australia, the western European countries, and Japan signed onto the Bretton Woods agreement; the Soviet Union declined.

International political affairs would be managed under the framework of the United Nations, established in the charter negotiated during the summer of 1945 and becoming effective that October. The United States would be the largest contributor to the United Nations budget.

The General Agreement on Tariffs and Trade

International trade was to be managed under a new international agreement, as part of a new International Trade Organization (ITO). The agreement, the General Agreement on Tariffs and Trade (GATT), became effective on January 1, 1948. However, the ITO did not gain Congressional support, and without U.S. participation, it was not implemented. Instead, an informal staff was established to administer the GATT.

The basic idea of the GATT was to eliminate tariffs and other barriers to trade in exchange for the member states' agreement to abide by certain rules to govern that trade. First and foremost was the principle of nondiscrimination, as implemented through two sub-principles. The first of those is "Most Favored Nation" treatment (also known as "Normal Trade Relations" in U.S. law since 1998). Under this principle, a country must extend to all countries the best terms it negotiates with any single country. The second principle is "National Treatment" -- that within a member country's borders, natural persons and companies from other countries will be treated the same as are citizens of the host country. Another foundational principle is that of "Reciprocity" - that relationships will be negotiated to be reciprocal, and not unilateral, in their effect.

In addition to these affirmative principles, the GATT established rules against bad behavior, such as "dumping" products on the world market at prices lower than the cost of production or domestic sales, and the provision of subsidies to domestic producers that would lower their costs vis-a-vis international competitors. Disputes over these and the GATT's other rules would be referred to "panels" for consultation, but the GATT had no power to impose or enforce a decision.[1]

Within this framework, in 1947 the countries participating in the GATT entered the "Geneva Round" of trade negotiations, and lowered the average duty from 27 percent to 15 percent.[2] In addition, the United States entered into a number of bilateral agreements under the authority of the Reciprocal Trade Agreements Act.

In all of this, the officials governing the United States were motivated by several beliefs: that free trade would foster peace and cooperation among nations; that the United States would be more secure with a prosperous, rebuilt Europe and Japan; and that more trade, regardless of the circumstances, would in the long run benefit the U.S. economy. Like the British before them in the 1840s, from the pinnacle of economic power the American policy makers assumed America would always win. They were wrong.

Early Signs of Problems

There were early signs that the new, open trade regime would not work, given the wide disparities in wages between the U.S. and new trading partners like Japan. As early as 1947 and continuing into the early 1950s, some U.S. apparel producers went to Japan and contracted with manufacturers there for production of blouses that would sell in U.S. stores for one dollar - the "dollar blouse." Comparable U.S.-made products were selling for three to four dollars per blouse.[3] Adjusting 1950 dollars for inflation, in 2016 dollars the dollar blouse was a "$10 blouse," competing against blouses selling for $30 to $40.

By 1949, it was clear that the new regime would benefit some industries at the expense of others. Makers of hats, bicycles, woolen gloves, and other products, coal producers, and fisheries operators, all found themselves facing competition from low-cost imported products.[4] Desperate post-war Japan was operating a low-price, low wage economy and sending to the U.S. imports that could be sold at a price below U.S. costs of production.

But even if these concerns might have been enough for American leaders to rethink their position, there arose a new motivation that would re-balance the scales - the onset of the Cold War.

The Cold War Begins

The United States had maintained an uneasy alliance with the Soviet Union during the Second World War, as a necessary expedient to defeat Nazi Germany. However, the war only deferred a brewing conflict.

Between World Wars I and II, the communists in Moscow had been busy spreading Marxist ideology around the world, in pursuit of Karl Marx and Vladimir Lenin's belief that the only way the socialist revolution could be successful was by its spreading throughout the world. Now, at the end of World War II, their successors in Moscow had two ways to accomplish that goal. First, they could, and did, install Moscow-controlled communist governments in all the territory controlled by Soviet troops at the end of the war, including countries they only half-controlled, such as Germany and Korea.[5] By March of 1946, Soviet plans to effectively annex the countries under its control by making them "satellites" had become clear, and former British Prime Minister Winston Churchill declared in a speech that an "iron curtain" had fallen across Europe. The later construction of the Berlin Wall confirmed that this was not an exaggeration.

Second, they could support the movements they had been planting since the Bolshevik revolution in 1917 and the end of the Russian civil war in 1922, acting through the Communist International (the "Comintern").[6] They nearly succeeded in France, where the communists had played a major role in the Resistance and fully expected to come into power at war's end. As described with considerable drama by Larry Collins and Dominique Lapierre in the 1965 book *Is Paris Burning*, it was only through a deft and audacious maneuver by Charles De Gaulle that they were thwarted and France installed a democratic government.[7]

In Japan, communists initially controlled a number of unions, but fought an ultimately losing battle for control.[8] The Soviets also were active in since the early 1930s in Southeast Asia, acting through the Vietnamese party leader Ho Chi Minh, the agent for the Comintern for Southeast Asia, to support communist parties in Malaysia and other Southeast Asian countries.

In China, the Moscow-connected, urban-oriented communists lost out to the rural peasantry-oriented Mao Zedong, who proved more adept at fighting the Nationalist armies, and who emerged as the leading force at war's end after leading his followers on the "Long March." In 1949, Mao's Chinese Communist Party and its People's Liberation Army defeated the Nationalist forces led by Chiang Kai-Shek, and established the People's Republic of China. Chiang Kai-Shek and his followers retreated to the island of Taiwan where they established a separate government. Thousands fled to Taiwan and to Hong Kong, taking with them the money, skill, and acumen to establish new textile, apparel, and other industries. After coming to power, Mao considered it China's place to lead the spread of communism in Asia, and he competed with the Soviets to do so.

The Korean War and its Aftermath

The Soviet post-war sphere of influence included Korea north of the 38th Parallel. Soviet troops had liberated that area from the Japanese, and a communist government led by Kim Il-sung was in control. U.S. troops had moved into the South, and neither government recognized the other. On June 25, 1950, after receiving approval from Soviet leader Joseph Stalin on his second try, Kim Il-sung ordered North Korean forces to invade the South. The United Nations responded by sending armed forces, primarily from the United States, to the defense of the South, which was on the verge of defeat. In September, the U.S./U.N. forces launched a daring amphibious landing at Inchon and forced the North Korean forces almost to China. In October, China entered the war on the North Korean side, pouring thousands of Chinese troops into the conflict.

At the end of World War II, many of the "lucky ones" who had made it home to America had joined the armed forces reserves, thinking that showing up once a month for a drill was a good way to make some extra money. Now those units were called up as the U.S. hastily responded to the Korean emergency. They found themselves mired in a protracted, deadly war, through a couple of winters worse than the one in the Battle of the Bulge, and, tragically, many of them didn't make it home. The war was fought to a stalemate and an uneasy truce on July 27, 1953 around a "demilitarized zone" at the 38th Parallel, where it had begun. As time went on, the differences between the North under Kim and his progeny and the South under a democratic, capitalist regime, would become stark indeed.

But the Korean War had other, momentous effects for the post-World War II economic and political order. When China invaded Korea, the United Nations responded by imposing a trade embargo on China. Additionally, the United States included in the U.S.-Japan peace treaty in 1951 an embargo on Japanese trade with mainland China, to prevent China from again becoming a market for Japan's textile and other industrial production. The goal was to contain communism and link Japan to the Western democracies.[9]

Korea, Taiwan, Hong Kong, and Singapore, as well as other Southeast Asian countries, also historically had sold many of their goods into China. Like Japan, if they were to survive economically, that market must be replaced.

Furthermore, the Korean War demonstrated the seriousness of the new power struggle between the western democracies and the two poles of the communist world, the sometimes allied, sometimes competing, Soviet Union and China. In Asia, these concerns were amplified by the defeat of the French colonial forces by Ho Chi Minh's Vietnamese communist forces at Dien Bien Phu in 1954.

In this new context, rights to build and operate military bases and the creation of political and military alliances became major concerns. American trade and economic policies came to be driven by geopolitical considerations.

Geopolitics Prevails

Bolstered by these national security concerns, the United States doubled down on its efforts to promote the economic development of Japan and of South Korea, Taiwan, Hong Kong, and Singapore, the "Asian Tigers." The U.S. did so by supporting the creation of new industries, such as textiles, and opening the American market to the low-priced products of those industries. Japan was to be re-industrialized by making it "America's workshop in Asia," followed by its former colonies.[10]

There also was a need for an adjustment to be made from Japanese colonialism. For fifty years prior to 1945, Korea and Taiwan were colonies of Japan, which transformed them into plantation economies exporting rice, tea, and sugar to Japan, and importing Japanese manufactured goods. Taiwan and Korea were recovering from the effects of colonization and war, and the U.S. sent them millions of dollars to support the process.

The U.S. also provided aid to other former colonial and newly independent nations, including Hong Kong, Malaysia, Thailand, the Philippines, Indonesia, and Singapore. In these countries, the U.S. promoted export-led industrialization designed to link them to the Japanese "workshop," and thus to the West.[11] In 1954 and 1955, the United States conducted trade negotiations with Japan that resulted in tariff cuts on 56 percent of total U.S. imports from Japan versus 1.6 percent of U.S. exports to Japan.[12]

There were two reasons the U.S. was willing to support these new industries and import their production from these Asian countries. One was that the U.S. was willing to pay the price of harm to its own industries in return for strengthening countries threatened by communism and maintaining basing rights there, particularly in Japan.[13]

The other was simply American hubris. As I have mentioned, like the British in the 1840s, the United States was "king of the mountain" and thought its position was unassailable. For example, Clyde Prestowitz reports that the U.S. Secretary of State said Japan should focus on exports to Asia because they weren't capable of making anything Americans would want to buy, and that the chief U.S. negotiator in the 1954-1955 negotiations said the Japanese would be foolish to make cars, which they should import from the United States.[14]

However, the Japanese did not see it that way at all.

The Japanese Response

In Japan, industry was in ruins, and many of its cities, residential and industrial sectors alike, had been leveled by American bombing, not to mention Hiroshima and Nagasaki. The country was occupied and administered by the Americans, under the leadership of General Douglas MacArthur. There were food shortages and the country was in a desperate situation.

To recover from these difficult conditions, the Japanese did not follow the prescription of the American model of free trade and pursuit of "comparative advantage." As one Japanese official told Clyde Prestowitz, if they had done so, then the Japanese would specialize in the production of tuna while the United States specialized in the production of automobiles.[15]

Neither did the Japanese subscribe to the Adam Smith theory of a "hands off," *laissez-faire* approach in which the government would leave industrial development to the "invisible hand" of the market. To the contrary, Japan intentionally followed a carefully planned industrial development program, led by the Ministry of International Trade and Industry (MITI). MITI "helped decide in which industries Japan would concentrate its limited resources, which companies would receive vital government subsidies, and which potential imports Japan would discourage." [16]

Japan had a great deal of low-cost labor, and relatively little capital and technology. According to theory, the Japanese should have focused on low-technology, labor-intensive sectors. They did the opposite, targeting industries such as steel and shipbuilding that would be the foundation for a diversified industrial economy.

And, contrary to the United States, which was pursuing a virulent anti-trust policy that resulted in the breakup of AT&T and the export of much of its hard-won technology to foreign companies in Japan and elsewhere, Japan required that companies like Sony deal only with other companies in the "family" of Japan's AT&T equivalent, Nippon Telephone & Telegraph. The Japanese sealed the country's market against exports, and prohibited direct investment by foreigners except on the condition that it be accompanied by technology transfer.[17]

The very name of MITI, emphasizing international trade even before industry, demonstrates the Japanese emphasis on exports as a means of driving the growth of their economy. It can be said that the Japanese followed the very "American System" that had built America and which America had abandoned, except with the addition of an emphasis on exports to the exclusion of imports - a "mercantilist" strategy for national economic growth.

In addition, Japan succeeded in undervaluing the exchange rate of the Yen to the dollar at the IMF, making Japanese goods cheaper in America, and American goods more expensive in Japan. And to boost savings, they instituted a cash-payment economy.

Despite all this activity in clear contravention of the principles of mutuality and reciprocity integral to the General Agreement on Tariffs and Trade, Japan was admitted to the GATT in 1955.

Snapshot in 1955

In 1955, America was engaged in an effort to rebuild the world's economies and establish a stable world order in the face of the attempts of the Soviet Union and China to export communism and bring more countries into their orbit.

To do so, the U.S. was prepared to assist other countries in the development of their industries and to open its market to low-priced foreign goods, in the hope that this would work out in the long run under the new mutual trade rules of the GATT. Particular industries such as apparel and textiles already were being damaged by these policies. However, in general the U.S. economy was growing fast in the new "Golden Era," masking these ill effects.

Japan, on its knees, was determined to create a "catch-up economy" like the ones operated by the British in the early 1800s and the Americans from 1870 to 1920. The Asian "tigers" of Korea, Taiwan, Hong Kong, and Singapore were following suit.

The seeds of "free trade" that had been sown in 1934 were beginning to sprout, and would soon bear fruit.

1956 - 1965

Low- and High-Wage Worlds Colliding

In the decade after 1955, the Cold War intensified, with the coming to power of a communist regime in Cuba in 1959 followed by the Cuban Missile Crisis in October of 1962. International tensions also included a brief war between India and China over disputed territory along those countries' mutual border, in October-November 1962.

With respect to trade, the collision between the U.S. economy and the low-wage economies of Asia became evident. As a result of the low-wage foreign competition, U.S. textile wages dropped, from being 16 percent lower than other manufacturing industries in 1947 to 30 percent lower in 1957. Even after these wage reductions, in 1960, textile workers in Japan and Hong Kong earned $1.22 per hour (in 2016 dollars), nine percent of the average U.S. wage of $13.40 (in 2016 dollars).[18]

But the difference lay not just in wages. Harkening back to the "mill girls" that made the textile industry of Lowell and Lawrence, Massachusetts so profitable during the 1800s, the Asian companies operated what I call "Factory Labor Camps." South Carolina textile manufacturer Walter T. Forbes reported on conditions in the Hong Kong textile industry in 1960:

> Dormitories housed 500 men and 1,000 girls each. The average age was about 21, with the "best workers" between 18 and 23 years old; after age 25, they were sent off to other jobs. 85 percent of the workers were women, and 85 percent of all employees were housed in mill dormitories. The girls were paid [$227] per month [in 2016 dollars;

> $1.05 per hour assuming a 50-hour work week], plus room and board. In the off hours they were given training. After four or five years, they could return home with a "dowry" of about $5,000, a sewing machine, and a hand held knitting machine, in a good position to find a husband.[19]

By 1961, the apparel industry could see what was coming. The President of the American Trouser Institute wrote that one could at any moment arrange for the offshore production of identical products at a 20 to 30 percent discount. And in 1961 Lawrence Phillips, then vice-president of the American shirt maker Philipps-Van Heusen, testified that the industry feared that the Hong Kong experience could be replicated in any of a number of countries, even someday communist China. Philipps-Van Heusen soon began producing offshore.[20]

American Attempts at Managed Trade

As these disparities hit home, the United States embarked on an effort to manage the problem.

Voluntary Restraints

One method of "management" was to obtain agreements for voluntary restraints on the rate at which foreign imports were penetrating the U.S. market. On Nov. 1, 1955 Japan began to place voluntary export restraints on cotton textiles, plywood, and other goods to the United States to avoid possible restrictive import measures to protect U.S. domestic markets.[21]

In 1957, Japan agreed to further voluntary export restraints on textile and apparel exports to the U.S. However, no such agreements existed with Taiwan or Hong Kong, which established a thriving business producing for

U.S. businesses whose representatives came there regularly to place orders. (In 1959, under the "Lancashire Agreement." Britain began to limit imports of textiles, so Hong Kong turned more toward the American market.)[22]

The Japanese voluntary restraints on textiles were broadened into a multi-party agreement under the GATT, first, on July 21, 1961, in the "Short-Term Arrangement on Cotton Textiles," and then, on Oct. 1, 1962, in the "Long-Term Arrangement on Cotton Textiles." However, these agreements only slowed the rate of increase of imports of the low-priced foreign products into America, and the U.S. continued to promote export-led development in low-wage Asian countries by expansion of apparel industries there.

It is important to note that this policy of a "slow death" for American industries was no longer limited to a desire to build up the Asian economies to fight communism; now the "competition" argument began to emerge. As one high-ranking State Department official put it: "The problem is to find a way to shift American manpower as swiftly and painlessly as possible, out of the industries that cannot stand up to foreign competition into those which have stood the test." [23] We will see this argument emerge in forcc in the 1980s, as discussed below. However, we should stop for a moment right now and ask, just what does it mean to "stand up to foreign competition" when that competition is paying its workers one-tenth of the U.S. wage?

Trade Adjustment Assistance

The other means of "managing" trade was the establishment of programs of assistance to workers and companies being harmed by trade. This injury is euphemistically referred to in trade policy circles as "adjustment," so the program to alleviate it is referred to as the "Trade Adjustment Assistance" program, or "TAA."

The TAA program was established in the Trade Expansion Act of 1962,[24] which also established the Office of the Special Trade Representative (USTR). For workers, the TAA offered income assistance, relocation assistance, and job training. For companies, it offered assistance including accelerated depreciation for new equipment to assist in becoming more efficient to meet the foreign competition. The law also equalized the price of American cotton, which, amazingly, was being sold to foreigners at a lower price so as to promote the foreign industries.

More Free Trade

As astonishing as it may seem, even as the United States was dealing with the problem of the low-priced textile, apparel and other imports, it embarked on further actions toward even freer trade: the Trade Expansion Act of 1962 authorized the White House to conduct negotiations for further mutual tariff reductions.

By the time of the 1964 United Nations Conference on Trade and Development (UNCTAD), developing nations were demanding that the United States open its market to promote their economic development and make up for their colonial past.[25] In the "Kennedy Round" of negotiations held in 1964-67, U.S. tariffs on manufactures were lowered by a third.[26]

So, during this period, we saw the U.S. pursuing a schizophrenic trade policy under which, on the one hand, it was making half-hearted and ineffectual efforts to mitigate and compensate for the damage being done by cheap foreign imports, and on the other, negotiating further tariff reductions making it easier for them to be brought into the U.S.

The U.S.-Canadian Automobile Pact

1965 also saw a preview of what would later become a trend - the negotiation of "free trade" agreements, in this case, the U.S.-Canada Agreement Concerning Automotive Products, commonly referred to as the U.S.-Canadian Automobile Pact. The agreement, signed on January 16, 1965, established tariff-free treatment of automobiles traded between Canada and the United States. Canada was fearful that all the production would end up in the United States, which had a strong "comparative advantage" in its economies of scale. So, the pact required that 60 percent of the cars sold in Canada must be made in Canada, with at least 60 percent Canadian content. Since a factory in Canada would be required, the auto makers might as well make it a large one that could serve both markets (the U.S. had no similar requirement), so the upshot of the pact was the establishment of multiple large automobile assembly plants on the Canadian side of the border, with much of their output destined for the U.S.[27]

Mexican Maquiladora Plants

The other significant development of 1965 was Mexico's establishment of the "*Maquiladora*" program. This program provided for the establishment, in towns on the Mexican side of the U.S.-Mexican border, of export processing zones where foreign companies could set up a manufacturing operation, import parts and materials duty-free, manufacture products, and then export them (but not sell them in the Mexican market). Various tax holidays and other incentives were offered for companies to locate operations there. Of course, the major market for the output of the *Maquiladoras* was the U.S. market. It was an example of a country, in this case Mexico, trying to grow its economy through an "export-led" strategy.

Licensing to Japan

With respect to Japan, here is an example of shooting oneself squarely in both feet: In the 1960s, American television manufacturers were effectively blocked out of the Japanese market through Japan's various formal and informal protections. The U.S. companies responded by licensing their technology to the Japanese companies in exchange for royalty payments.[28] Of course, the Japanese companies would soon be exporting that technology back to the U.S. in the form of television sets destined for the U.S. market.

Two Industries of Note

This period also saw textile and apparel companies moving out of New York, where the apparel industry had won relatively high wages through their unions, to states in the Southern U.S., where wages were low and workers were not organized. The furniture industry already had made its way south, and during this period it was running full-tilt, not yet facing foreign competition.[29] As we will see, eventually, even these lower Southern wages could not stand up to the extremely low-wage Asian producers.

Snapshot in 1965

By 1965, we saw numerous U.S. industries, especially textiles and apparel, suffering under the influx of foreign products produced in Asia by extremely low-paid labor working under adverse conditions.

The U.S. had made its first attempts at a response, by entering into voluntary restraint agreements and the short- and long-term textile agreements, and by instituting the Trade Adjustment Assistance Program to assist workers and companies being harmed by imports. However, as we will see, the restraint agreements only slowed down the rate of import penetration and decline of the affected industries, and the trade adjustment assistance was not even implemented for some ten years, and then was woefully inadequate.

The year 1965 also saw the implementation of the first free trade agreement, dealing with U.S.-Canadian trade in automobiles, which resulted in auto assembly plants being built on the Canadian side of the U.S.-Canadian border, and the establishment of the "*maquiladora*" program encouraging the construction of manufacturing plants on the Mexican side of the U.S.-Mexican border. – all to the detriment of U.S. manufacturers and trade.

Finally, the Kennedy Round of GATT negotiations for further tariff reductions had begun. None of this augured well for the coming decade, when things really started coming off the rails.

1966 - 1975

Tumultuous Times

The decade after 1965 was a tumultuous time in many respects. Rioting was occurring in American cities in 1967 and 1968. In 1968, Martin Luther King and Robert Kennedy were assassinated, and the nominating convention of the Democratic Party saw violent confrontations between anti-Vietnam War protesters and police. In 1970, when President Nixon authorized bombing of North Vietnamese forces in Cambodia, protests broke out on American college campuses, and several students tragically were killed by national guardsmen at Kent State University. In 1973 the cover-up of the burglary of the Democratic Party headquarters at the Watergate apartment complex led to President Nixon's resignation from office on August 9, 1974.

On the economic front, as the U.S. imported more foreign goods, the U.S. trade in goods surplus was disappearing. However, the U.S. was still spending a great deal of money abroad, on military bases, diplomatic posts, and the like. So, contrary to the problem of the 1950s, when the war-ravaged countries hadn't enough dollars, dollars now were piling up offshore. Eventually there were three times more dollars abroad than the United States had gold to redeem, leading foreign countries to want to exchange their dollars for gold while they still could.

To prevent a run on Fort Knox, on August 16, 1971, President Nixon "temporarily suspended" the convertibility of dollars to gold. The dollar/gold standard was no more, and the value of the dollar depended entirely on other countries' assessment of its security. The Bretton Woods system of managing the international monetary system had collapsed; however, the resulting devaluation of the dollar provided some temporary relief from the underpricing of imports and overpricing of U.S. exports.

At the same time, President Nixon imposed temporary U.S. wage and price controls, as well as import surcharges. The U.S. economy was experiencing strong inflation, in part due to spending on the Vietnam War, which had begun in earnest with the U.S. troop buildup in 1965.

Then, on October 16, 1973, the first of two OPEC[30] oil price shocks occurred, beginning with the Arab oil embargo, eventually quadrupling the price of crude oil. In addition to causing serious inflationary shocks throughout the economic system, the oil price increase had several specific effects with respect to trade. First, the U.S. trade deficit was worsened, because the imported oil now was being paid for with so many more dollars. Second, the American automobile industry was caught flatfooted as consumer preferences quickly moved from the large, "gas guzzling" cars the American car companies were producing to the smaller, fuel efficient cars being produced in countries where energy costs were much higher. The Japanese share of the U.S. market, in particular, began a dramatic increase.

More Voluntary Restraints

From the standpoint of trade, the onslaught of inexpensive foreign products expanded beyond textiles and apparel. The U.S. continued its efforts to abate the influx through voluntary restraint agreements. On January 1, 1969, Japan and the members of the European Coal and Steel Community agreed to place voluntary export restraints on steel products destined for the United States.

On October 1, 1971, The United States reached voluntary export restraint agreements with Hong Kong, Japan, South Korea, and Taiwan for textiles made with wool and man-made fibers, in addition to the existing agreements regarding cotton textiles. On Jan. 1, 1974, The GATT Multifiber Arrangement governing trade in textiles and apparel entered into effect, succeeding the 1962 GATT Long-Term Arrangement on Cotton Textiles. The stated purpose was to balance the needs of developing countries for export markets with the needs of industrialized countries to regulate the rate at which imports of textiles and apparel expanded.[31]

Continued Trade Losses

However, these voluntary restraint agreements were only slowing the shift of the balance of trade against the U.S., and by December 31, 1971, the United States recorded its first merchandise trade deficit in the twentieth century–a deficit of approximately $2.5 billion in 1971.

A number of factors were at work. First and foremost, foreign costs of production were "shockingly lower" than in the U.S., chiefly due to lower labor costs. America had opened its market wider than other countries and was still promoting imports into the U.S. The U.S. also was putting up with other countries' restrictions on U.S. imports and requirements for transfer of U.S. technology in connection with U.S. foreign direct investment.[32]

There also was a problem with the overvaluation of the dollar. Despite all the progress made by Japan, the Yen was still valued at the rate set by the IMF in 1947, so the dollar was seriously overvalued - U.S. products were made more expensive, pricing them out of foreign markets. Many manufacturers therefore built facilities overseas to serve the overseas markets, instead of exporting from the U.S. On the other hand, Japanese and other foreign imports into the U.S. were made even more inexpensive.[33]

As a result of all of these factors, Japan and the "Asian Tigers" were capturing the U.S. market. In 1965, every color television sold in the U.S. was produced in a U.S. manufacturing facility, by a host of American companies.[34] By 1972, Sony and other Japanese companies had captured 62 percent of sales of black-and-white television sets and 45 percent of color sets, and totally dominated radio, stereo, and recorder sales.[35] The Japanese companies were achieving this market penetration by "dumping" their television sets in the American market at lower prices than they sold for in Japan; for example, Zenith noted sets selling for $500 in Japan and $300 in the United States. The U.S. International Trade Commission imposed anti-dumping fines and tariffs on the Japanese makers; however, appeals and maneuvering followed and only nominal amounts were paid. By the time the dust settled on this and other litigation, the U.S. television industry was nearly gone - only Zenith remained. [36]

Meanwhile, despite the harm being caused to domestic industries, the Trade Adjustment Assistance program enacted in 1962 hadn't gotten off the ground. For the first seven years of its existence, Congress appropriated no funds for the implementation of the program. In 1970, a small office was established. By 1973, a half dozen firms had been funded.[37]

Trade Act of 1974

In response to these conditions, Congress enacted the Trade Act of 1974.[38] Having attempted to "manage" trade through voluntary restraint agreements and the provision of assistance to workers and companies being harmed by trade, Congress now tried to implement "trade remedies" to halt unfair trade practices. Responding to some foreign countries' continued practices of excluding U.S. products, subsidizing exports, and dumping exports at prices below domestic prices or cost of production, and frustrated with the GATT mechanisms for combating these practices, Congress enacted Section 301 of the Trade Act of 1974, providing tariff and other remedies to companies that could prove harm from such practices.

Demonstrating the continued schizophrenic nature of American trade policy, the Act also included provisions that would increase imports of low-priced products, in the case of developing countries, through a new Generalized System of Preferences providing lower tariffs to those countries, and, in the case of the non-market economies of the Soviet bloc countries of Eastern Europe, providing the lower tariffs of most favored nation status so long as they permitted emigration (the "Jackson-Vanik amendment"). And, ominously, the GATT "Tokyo Round" of multilateral trade negotiations had begun.

Ultimately more important than any of this, in my view, was this fact: on February 21 through 28, 1971, President Richard Nixon visited China, meeting with Chairman Mao Zedong and engaging in substantive discussions that led to the creation of economic and diplomatic relations between the U.S. and China for the first time since 1949.

Product Sectors under Attack

During this period, a number of specific U.S. industries came under attack.

Microwave Ovens

An example of the pattern adopted by the Japanese government and companies was the microwave oven industry. Raytheon had developed the technology as a defense contractor in the 1940s, and microwave ovens started appearing in homes in the 1950s. In 1967, Amana brought out a countertop model, and sales took off, from 60,000 units sold in 1970 to 1.1 million in 1975. Several U.S. companies followed Amana's lead.

It wasn't long, however, before a number of Japanese companies jumped in, following the classic formula of selling in volume at prices below what they charged in Japan. In 1972, Amana filed a complaint with the Commerce Department, and was rebuffed on the basis that there was no showing of harm to the U.S. industry.

Furniture

In the 1960s, as Asian radios, televisions and auto parts were pouring into the U.S. market, many thought furniture would be immune, due to its weight and bulk. Even in 1967, one former worker told Beth Macy, you could plan on having a job the same day as you went looking.[39] However, the foreign suppliers learned that they could ship chairs and occasional tables in pieces and assemble them in the U.S. By the mid-1970s, a lot of furniture for the U.S. market was being made offshore.

Textiles

In textiles, the "Kennedy comprise" of 1962 had some effect. Through 1970, U.S. textile production expanded.[40] By the mid-1970s, a modernized, more concentrated textile industry was operating in the U.S. South, dominated by companies like Burlington and J.P. Stevens. However, as we will see, this respite would be brief.

Snapshot in 1975

In 1975, the United States concluded a tumultuous decade with the last American helicopter leaving the roof of the U.S. embassy, abandoning Vietnam after ten years of war. The U.S. was only beginning to recover from the shock of the quadrupling of oil prices in 1973 and was experiencing "stagflation" - stagnant growth coupled with strong inflation. The American social fabric had been torn by urban riots and anti-war protests. And major shares of entire industries were being captured by imports from Japan and other countries due to low wages and subsidies, while American exports were hampered by foreign barriers and lopsided exchange rates. The U.S. was trying to stem the tide of foreign imports with voluntary restraint agreements, and, in the Trade Act of 1974, with new remedies against unfair trade practices. Most importantly, the U.S. had stepped onto the road to trade and other economic relations with China.

1976 - 1985

Japanese Mercantilism plus Tigers

The decade running up to 1985 witnessed the "second oil shock." 1979 saw the Iranian Revolution and beginning of the hostage crisis at the U.S. Embassy in Iran. By year's end, the price of oil had doubled, with further increases to follow upon the commencement of the Iran-Iraq war in September of 1980. A severe, "double-dip" recession followed.

The decade also witnessed a step-up in Japan's export-led, catch-up growth strategy; the Japanese were resisting efforts by the U.S. to get Japan to open its market, and were moving aggressively to keep exports growing. Acting through the Ministry of International Trade and Industry, they instructed businesses to buy Japanese, provided capital on preferential terms to targeted companies, provided tax rebates and other incentives for exports, imposed myriad regulations and unique Japanese standards; operated programs to promote the electronics industries, and required IBM, Texas Instruments, and other such companies to transfer proprietary technology and/or enter into joint ventures in order to enter the Japanese market.

Furthermore, Japanese private companies operated cartels that engaged in the targeted dumping of products into the U.S. market. Televisions were one such market, and, as a result, between 1960 and 1980, 27 American TV makers were reduced to three. Other industries had similar experiences, including automobiles, steel, machine tools, batteries, optics, semiconductors, printed circuit boards, flat panel displays, videotape recorders and other consumer electronics, and many others, as the Japanese claimed one market after another.[41]

At the conclusion in 1979 of the Tokyo Round of the GATT trade negotiations, Japan agreed to remove most quotas and cut tariffs. However, it employed the other tools of mercantilism to keep exports out: regulations, standards, distribution arrangements, subsidies, buy-Japanese incentives, and management of the value of the Yen relative to the dollar to keep Japanese goods relatively low-priced. Clyde Prestowitz has noted that after the negotiations, the Japanese press would proclaim that the concessions would not increase imports. So, in point of fact, the Japanese market remained closed.[42]

Meanwhile, the "Asian Tigers," Singapore, South Korea, and Taiwan, emulated the Japanese model. They adopted strategic export-led strategies including industrial policies, suppression of domestic demand (to promote saving), maintenance of undervalued currencies, subsidization of exports, and subsidization of inbound foreign direct investment. That is, they practiced "State Capitalism," with an export-led, catch-up strategy. [43]

In this, they were greatly aided by the large U.S. retailers and their suppliers. Sears, K-Mart, and U.S. apparel makers began pro-actively taking advantage of contract manufacturers in the Asian Tigers. In a move that ultimately would dwarf all the other players in significance, Wal-Mart opened its first Asian direct buying office, in Hong Kong, in 1981. Offices in Taipei and other Taiwanese cities followed; by 1989, Wal-Mart would have a staff of 90 in these offices.[44]

The U.S. Response

The U.S. response was confused and ineffectual. On the one hand, the U.S. tried to tighten enforcement against dumping. On February 15, 1978, the U.S. Treasury Department introduced a trigger-price mechanism to monitor dumping of steel imports in the United States. And Congress enacted the Trade Agreements Act of 1979, easing the requirements for obtaining relief from dumping and other unfair practices,[45] and the Trade and Tariff Act of 1984, expanding the reach of section 301 to cover foreign investment regulations.[46] The U.S. also pursued more "voluntary restraint" arrangements.[47]

But there also were refusals to act. For example, Congress wanted to move against the continued and growing influx of textiles and apparel from the low-wage Asian countries, and both houses passed the Jenkins-Hollings bill that would have imposed new limits. However, President Reagan vetoed the bill.[48]

U.S. trade officials wanted to utilize the tools of the GATT and/or U.S. law to counter the dumping, subsidy, and unfair trade practices of the Japanese. However, security officials in the Departments of State and Defense gave top priority to maintenance of U.S. bases in Japan. The U.S. computer chip industry was decimated.[49] So, too, in 1985, a presidential strike force headed by Clyde Prestowitz wanted to take on the Europeans for the subsidies to the Airbus. Secretary of State George Schultz stopped the move because it would "shatter NATO." [50] Again, geopolitics won.

Rather than pursuit of an industrial policy or of remedies for the trade mercantilism being practiced by other countries, the response of the U.S. government mostly was benign neglect.[51] The U.S. trade deficit and current account deficit worsened to the point that they were unsustainable. The situation came to a head in 1985, as the "twin deficits" of the federal government and international trade soared. On September 22, 1985, the United States, West Germany, France, the United Kingdom, and Japan agreed to the "Plaza Accords," providing for a gradual devaluation of the dollar with reference to the Japanese yen and the German mark.[52]

More Free Trade

Meanwhile, in 1979 the "Tokyo Round" of GATT negotiations concluded, with the U.S. agreeing to another cut in U.S. tariff rates.

The Caribbean and Central America

While all of this was transpiring, there was occurring a surprising resurgence of Marxism across the globe. Beginning in 1975, Communist or Marxist regimes came to power in North Vietnam, Laos, Cambodia, Angola, Mozambique, Ethiopia, South Yemen, Grenada, Nicaragua, Afghanistan, and Suriname. Other insurgencies were active in areas including Latin America. The Reagan administration responded by providing material support to counterinsurgencies in countries where Marxist regimes had taken hold, and to governments that were combating Marxist insurgencies.[53]

The administration and the Congress determined that an effective way to combat the insurgencies was to support the economic development of the countries where they were active. Toward this end, Congress enacted the U.S. Caribbean Basin Economic Recovery Act,[54] also known as the Caribbean Basin Initiative, providing preferential duty treatment for eligible products imported into the U.S. from twenty-two countries in Central America and the Caribbean.

Puerto Rico

The Congress also engaged in some more foreign-aid-through-trade, on behalf of the U.S. territorial possession of Puerto Rico. In 1976, Congress enacted "Section 936" of the tax code, providing that companies that set up operations in Puerto Rico would not pay federal income tax on the profits from those operations. The provision was utilized primarily by U.S. pharmaceutical companies, to the extent that Puerto Rico developed the world's largest concentration of pharmaceutical operations. To benefit from the law, the pharma companies closed mainland manufacturing facilities and re-opened them in Puerto Rico, destroying tens of thousands of well-paying U.S. jobs to create the same jobs, at much lower pay, in Puerto Rico.

The effects on individuals, families, and communities in the U.S. were predictably devastating. The effects on the U.S. treasury were dramatic, with many billions of dollars of lost tax revenues. The effects on the economy in Puerto Rico were miniscule, to the point that the General Accounting Office panned the program and Congress repealed it in 1996. However, as of September, 2016, with the Puerto Rico economy still on the skids and the government nearly bankrupt, proposals were being floated to bring it back.[55]

China takes a new tack

Meanwhile, in 1978, a world-changing event occurred: At after an historic five-day meeting December 18 to 22, 1978, The Third Plenary Session of the Eleventh Central Committee of the Communist Party of China issued a communique committing the Chinese Communist Party to reform the economic structure and open the economy to more foreign trade.[56] The "reform and opening" strategy fostered by reformists led by Deng Xiaoping, dubbed "Socialism with Chinese Characteristics," included permission for entrepreneurs to start and own businesses, privatization of many state-owned businesses, and lifting of price controls and other regulations. The "opening" included permission for foreign investment under certain conditions and a fostering of foreign trade, especially exports.

As part of the reform and opening initiative, in 1978 the Chinese government named four "special export zones" (later renamed "special economic zones" or "SEZs") in four cities on the southeast coast of China: Zhuhai, Shantou and Shenzhen in Guangdong province across from Hong Kong, and Xiamen in Fujian province. The zones offered foreign investors incentives in the form of duty-free importation of materials and components and exportation of products and low corporate taxes. Taiwanese companies and investors were the first in, bringing with them investment funds and manufacturing know-how they had acquired during Taiwan's run as one of the "Asian Tigers."

Thereafter, in 1980 and 1983, China signed trade agreements with the U.S. During this period, China developed a modern textile manufacturing capability, and a large percentage of the new trade was in textiles and apparel. In a portent of things to come, the Chinese government unofficially encouraged exporters to use false documentation to make shipments to the U.S., exceeding agreed-upon quotas. Eventually, the U.S. cut China's quotas due to its continued violations of the GATT.[57]

Product Segments under Attack

U.S. product sectors continued to suffer under attack from abroad. As we will see, these attacks often succeeded with the complicity of the U.S. government.

Microwave Ovens, Continued

In 1979, when microwave oven imports had seized more than one-third of the U.S. market, the U.S. industry filed an anti-dumping complaint with the U.S. International Trade Commission, requesting the imposition of tariffs. The Commission made a preliminary finding in favor of the complainants, but the Treasury Department overruled it and declined to impose tariffs, on the ground that there was substantial doubt that the industry was, or was likely to be, injured by the imports. (Fast forward to 1995: most of the U.S. producers were out of business, and imports accounted for 85 percent of microwave oven sales in the U.S.)[58] And so it goes with U.S. trade policy.

Footwear

In 1976, in response to requests for relief from the U.S. shoe industry, the U.S. International Trade Commission ruled that Brazil was causing harm to the industry through trade policies that violated international trade law, and that the U.S. industry should be provided the tariff relief available under the anti-dumping and anti-subsidy laws. However, President Ford refused to provide the relief. In 1978, President Carter also refused to impose tariffs on the Brazilian imports. When the first petition was filed in 1976, the industry employed 172,000 workers. By 2012, employment was fewer than 15,000.[59] The industry had been wiped out.

Mobile Phones

From 1882 through 1985, Western Electric Co. made all the telephones for AT&T, employing as many as 43,000 workers at its Hawthorne works outside of Chicago. By the mid-1980s, U.S. trade policy favored manufacture of the newly-invented cellular phones outside the United States. By 1986, the Hawthorne works were closed, and those 43,000 jobs were gone.

Flatware

In the early 1980s, Japan, Korea and Taiwan started flooding the U.S. market with stainless steel knives, forks and spoons. The domestic industry petitioned the U.S. International Trade Commission to impose higher tariffs. On May 1, 1984, the Commission issued a decision refusing the requested relief. Applying the applicable law, the Commission determined that the flatware was not being imported "in such increased quantities as to be a substantial cause of serious injury, or the threat thereof, to the domestic industry." The Commission found that the economic data regarding the industry "fail to demonstrate the required degree of serious injury mandated by the statute. Rather, the industry is doing reasonably well." [60] In 2016, there were no domestic producers of flatware save one: Sherrill Manufacturing, doing business as Liberty Tabletop, which operates the former Oneida factory in Sherrill, New York. All the rest were forced out of business, and Sherrill only recently has re-started operations. Once again, the "trade remedies" of U.S. trade law and the GATT failed to save a U.S. industry from the predatory practices of America's trade "partners."

Machine Tools

One of the more interesting, and alarming, stories is that of the U.S. machine tool industry. These are the machines that make the machines - machine tools are used to make the parts that comprise the finished products, be they automobiles, appliances, or medical devices. They historically have been small businesses, often family owned, but nevertheless highly innovative - a sector where "American ingenuity" has been deployed with great success, making the U.S. the world leader through most of the 20th century. Employment and sales in the industry grew throughout the 1950s, 60s, and 70s; employment reached a peak of 108,000 in 1980.

However, as recounted by investigative reporters Donald L. Barlett and James B. Steele, [61] in the 1950s, the Japanese Ministry of International Trade and Industry decided to promote a large, export-oriented machine tool industry. Toward this end, MITI deployed low-cost loans and loan guarantees, subsidies, and export assistance, and sealed off the Japanese market from imports. Amazingly, during the 1960s, the American companies that were shut out of the Japanese market licensed their technology to the Japanese in return for royalty payments. Japan used this licensed technology to produce American-designed machine tools for export to the U.S. market. The Japanese targeted the U.S. market because it was the largest, but also because it was the most open. A trickle of Japanese machine tool imports became a flood, increasing from $300,000 in 1961 to $854 million in 1985.[62]

In response, in 1982, the U.S. machine tool industry filed petitions for tariff relief from the Japanese subsidies, market protection, and below-market pricing. There was an ensuing debate between those who believe the U.S.

needed a vital machine tool industry and unmitigated free traders. President Reagan landed on the side of the latter, declining to grant the requested relief, on the ground that "free trade was the best way to bring the benefits of competition to American consumers and businesses." [63]

When the industry went into a further slide, the Defense Department weighed in with concerns over the national security implications of the loss of this vital industry. The Reagan administration responded with half a loaf, negotiating a Voluntary Restraint Agreement limiting the growth of the imports through 1993.[64] Nevertheless, from 1986 through 1995, the United States ran deficits in machine tools trade with ten industrialized countries, especially Japan. Employment in the industry plunged from 108,000 in 1980 to 58,000 in 1995, and wages for those still employed were lower in real dollars than they had been in 1975.[65]

Furniture's Turn

As I mentioned in the previous snapshot, by the mid-1970s the furniture industry, previously thought to be immune from the Asian threat, was beginning to feel the impact of Asian imports. Now it was furniture's turn to feel the full brunt of the Asian onslaught.

In her 2014 book, *Factory Man*,[66] Beth Macy reports that in 1979, Robert Spillman, the head of Bassett Furniture, made his first tour of Chinese furniture factories. They were crowded, often had dirt floors, and lacked safety precautions. The workers lived in adjacent dormitories, alternating shifts, sending money back to their families in the country. In the early 1980s, the average U.S. furniture worker's wage, measured in 2016 dollars, was $12.65; his or her counterpart in Taiwan averaged $3.37, and in China

$0.84. What the Chinese lacked in technology, they made up for in diligence and low cost. [67]

But that would change. Macy describes how a Chinese-born, Wharton-trained Taiwanese businessman, Larry Moh, expanded out of traditional Asian rattan furniture, starting with hotel furniture for booming Hong Kong, and then turned to the American market, starting with end tables and dining room furniture, which they assembled at several American locations; other companies soon followed.[68]

In the early 1980s, as the Asian occasional tables and chairs began flooding into the U.S. market, the initial response of many American furniture manufacturing executives was to resist sourcing from Asian countries. According to Macy, Spillman told an investment banker he couldn't source offshore, because of concern for what would happen to the people who worked in the plants. The investment banker responded that it would only be a matter of time.[69] He was right.

Major U.S. brands began importing at prices permitting a retail price 20 to 30 percent below market. Those prices were below U.S. costs, and bankruptcies ensued; Macy reports that in 1986 seventeen American furniture factories closed. Once this process got started, the American companies started teaching their Asian suppliers their production techniques for finishes, veneers, and details, in order to get more salable products from them. Personnel from Taiwan and Hong Kong would visit the American factories to be taught how to perform their various functions, and American personnel were dispatched to Asia.[70] The new Asian furniture factories begat other companies supplying veneer, glue, fixtures, cartons, tooling and machines - the entire furniture supply chain was being replicated offshore.[71]

Snapshot in 1985

1985 capped a decade of a rapidly deteriorating American position in trade, as Japan, and to a lesser extent other Asian countries, captured entire sectors of the U.S. economy and major parts of others, through the practice of export promotion and home market protection. The U.S. response was tepid, including further voluntary restraint agreements, which did nothing but slow down the Japanese onslaught. U.S. commercial officers who wanted to fight back using the tools of the GATT were overruled by national security officials focused on maintaining American military bases in Japan. A similar story played out with European dumping of steel and subsidies for the development of the Airbus commercial aircraft business, where concerns about the trans-Atlantic alliance trumped U.S. economic interests.

In addition, to counter growing Marxist movements in the Americas, the U.S. implemented the Caribbean Basin Initiative, providing duty preferences for imports from twenty-two Central American and Caribbean countries. Meanwhile, by the 1980s, the latest technologies in textile production had become globally dispersed, leveling the technological playing field among the U.S., Europe, and the Far East.

All of this resulted in the U.S. buying a lot more from overseas than it sold: during the decade 1976-1985, the U.S. balance of payments in goods and services totaled a negative $1.1 trillion in 2016 dollars. Finally, in 1985, the U.S. obtained an agreement for a significant devaluation of the dollar, in an attempt to stem the flow of dollars abroad.

1986 - 1995

As bad as the previous decade had been for U.S. trade and business, the decade leading up to 1995 would be worse, as it ushered in truly world-changing developments on the international economic scene.

More of the Same in Japan and the U.S.

Japan's deficits continue, worsen

In response to the Plaza Accords, the dollar fell, especially against the yen.[72] With U.S. goods less expensive, the trade balance should have improved, and, indeed, the U.S. trade deficit with Europe fell. However, the deficit with Japan increased.[73]

The deficit was not only due to Japanese exports to the U.S. In a 1994 report, the U.S. Trade Representative noted that, despite the reduction of tariffs, Japan imported relatively fewer manufactured goods than any other developed country, that Japanese imports had not increased to any substantial extent, and that, despite years of market-opening efforts, the Japanese market remained significantly less open to imports and investment.[74]

So, the Japanese continued to capture U.S. industries while their market remained relatively closed. Numerous U.S. firms went out of business or contracted for production in Japan. These conditions persisted even when the Japanese real estate bubble burst in 1992. During each year of this decade, Japan accounted for between 40 and 60 percent of the total U.S. trade in goods deficit.

More Enforcement and Export Promotion

In the face of this onslaught from Japan and other mercantilist countries, the U.S. continued to pursue voluntary restraints and better enforcement of trade rules. On September 2, 1986, the second U.S.-Japan semi-conductor agreement was reached. In 1988, Congress enacted the Omnibus Trade and Competitiveness Act of 1988,[75] introducing "super" and "special" section 301 trade remedies and requiring annual reports on foreign trade barriers.

The U.S. also pursued promotion of exports. On January 9, 1992, a U.S.-Japan agreement on auto and auto parts was reached to voluntarily increase Japanese imports of U.S.-made automobile parts. In October of 1992, the U.S. Export Enhancement Act of 1992 was enacted,[76] calling for a government-wide strategy for U.S. export promotion. This strategy was announced in September of 1993 as the "National Export Strategy." As we will see, none of these efforts would prove sufficient to address the trade imbalance.

More South American Aid through Trade

In Latin America, in 1990 the U.S. launched the Enterprise for the Americas Initiative (EAI), designed to expand investment in and provide some debt relief to countries in Latin America and the Caribbean. Except for the negotiation of free trade agreements, the EAI basically is a foreign aid program.[77]

There was another angle, too: the Andean Trade Preference Act (ATPA)[78] was enacted to combat drug production and trafficking in the Andean countries: Bolivia, Colombia, Ecuador and Peru.[79]

"If the U.S. can't compete . . ."

So, during this period, we see the U.S. government pursuing a schizophrenic policy agenda of at least going through the motions of promoting trade and protecting against unfair trade while at the same time giving away the U.S. market to fight drugs and poverty in Latin America.

However, During the 1980s and early 1990s, there also arose a mantra in Washington government and policy circles that if American companies "can't compete," then they deserve to lose out to imports. Of course, by adopting unilateral free trade, these policy makers established a scenario in which American companies must compete with foreign companies where pay was one-tenth that in the U.S.

Big Changes in the Organization of Trade

The World Trade Organization is formed

On September 20, 1986, the GATT "Uruguay Round" of multilateral trade negotiation began, with the general aim of removing non-tariff trade barriers and opening markets.[80] On December 15, 1993 the negotiations concluded, with 125 countries signing the Uruguay Round Agreements, including significant further reductions in tariffs.

However, the real big story coming out of the Uruguay Round was the folding of the GATT into the new World Trade Organization (WTO), effective on January 1, 1995. The WTO wrought two major changes from the GATT: First, it included compulsory dispute resolution, binding upon the member nations. Second, it expanded the concept of trade, to include intellectual property law, economic development financing, health regulations, and government procurement. It also included the Agreement on Textiles and

Clothing, providing for the phasing out of tariffs and quotas on textile and apparel imports by 2005.[81]

The International Trade Organization that was envisioned as part of the new post-war economic order had now arrived. In the eyes of many observers, the WTO represented a revolution in the operation not only of international trade, but of the world economy.[82]

The European Union is formed

A related development involved a regional trading bloc. In 1994, the European Economic Community further integrated into the European Union, with a common currency, the "Euro," replacing national currencies, and the elimination of immigration limitations within the union.

NAFTA enters into effect

Another major development during this period was the entry into effect on January 1, 1994 of the North American Free Trade Agreement (NAFTA) among the United States, Canada, and Mexico. The United States and Canada previously had entered into the U.S.-Canada Free Trade Agreement, effective January 1, 1989.[83] The new NAFTA agreement followed the same framework, but now integrated the three countries into a common set of rules. It is notable that this was the first attempt to implement a free trade-type agreement between high-wage countries (the U.S. and Canada) and a low-wage country (Mexico).[84]

The *Maquiladora* Run-up to NAFTA

The likely effects of NAFTA should have been evident from the *Maquiladora* program, which had been in operation since 1965. Barlett and Steele reported that from 1965 through 1990, more than 1,800 manufacturing plants, employing some 530,000 workers, were constructed and began operating under the *Maquiladora* program.

Barlett and Steele reported on one of them, a fluorescent light components factory that opened in 1989 in Matamoros, Mexico, across the Rio Grande from Brownsville, Texas. The plant had its origins in Paterson, New Jersey, as a plant operated by Universal Manufacturing Company, founded in 1947, making ballasts for fluorescent lights. Universal's owners knew the employees, and there was a family atmosphere typical of many American manufacturing businesses.

Universal was acquired in 1986 by MagneTek, Inc., an entity created by a Los Angeles investment company funded with junk bond debt. Facing steep payments of debt and management fees, the company opened a 150,000 square-foot manufacturing facility in Matamoros, and closed the Paterson manufacturing operation, converting the facility to a distribution center.

Barlett and Steele shined a light on the differences between a woman who lost her job in Paterson, and one who gained her job in the Matamoros plant: the former made $7.91 an hour and lived in a house with electricity, running water, and sewer services in a working class neighborhood with paved roads; the latter made $1.45 an hour and lived with her husband and two children in a one-room, ten foot by twelve-foot dwelling with a tin roof, along a dirt footpath. She worked an additional full-time job in addition to her husband, so they could send their children to school. However, the biggest difference between the two women was that the one in Matamoros had a job while the one in Paterson did not.[85]

NAFTA – Maquiladoras on Steroids

Immediately following the entry into effect of NAFTA on January 1, 1995, the number of Mexican *Maquiladora* manufacturing plants increased dramatically.[86]

NAFTA was sold to the American public by the President and Congress, industry, and the press as being to American advantage: that the larger reductions being made to Mexican tariffs than to already-low U.S. tariffs would result in net gains from sales of U.S. products to Mexico's eighty-five million consumers. U.S. Rep. Bill Archer, R., Texas, said during the floor debate on the NAFTA implementation bill:

> NAFTA really is the ultimate win-win situation. Mexico will modernize its economy, buying machinery, products, and equipment from the USA, creating better jobs for its own workers. Its consumers will then spend their new-found wealth on everything from autos, refrigerators, and diapers made in the USA, creating better paying jobs for Americans.[87]

With the benefit of twenty years of hindsight, one doesn't know whether to laugh or cry in response to these arguments – the automobiles and refrigerators would not be going from the United States to Mexico. As in the case of the MagneTek worker in Matamoros, the jobs created in the *Maquiladora* plants didn't pay enough to support that. The cars and refrigerators would be going in the other direction.

And in fact, the wrongheadedness of these arguments was immediately evident: upon NAFTA's entry into effect, the U.S. trade in goods with Mexico jumped from a small surplus in 1993 and 1994 to a $16 billion deficit in 1995.[88]

The Age of Oversupply begins

China confirms reform and opening

As we have seen, under the leadership of Deng Xiaoping, beginning in 1978 China engaged in the "reform and opening" of its economy. After the brutal suppression of the Tiananmen Square-related demonstrations across the country in 1989 by the Communist Party and People's Liberation Army, Deng Xiaoping made a trip to the south of the country in 1992 known as the "Southern Tour," and confirmed the movement toward an export-oriented, quasi-capitalist system. (By then, the United States already accounted for one-third of China's exports.)[89]

Like the Asian Tigers, China was following the Japanese model. It planned for development of key industries for the domestic and export markets; engaged in state-aided development of those industries through low- or no-cost financing and land, subsidized energy and other factors of production, and tax incentives; provided significant incentives to promote exports, managed the currency to be undervalued against the dollar,[90] and maintained incentives for savings by the populace.

More so than the Japanese, China welcomed and encouraged foreign investment. Like the Japanese, China made that investment contingent upon transfer of technology and/or operation through joint ventures with domestic firms.[91] China pursued the goal of making the country an "export platform" for multinational companies as a way of jump-starting its development.[92]

Motorola typified the American-based companies that were suffering from Japanese import penetration and were both looking for a way to cut costs and also wanting to sell to the incipient enormous Chinese consumer market. In 1992, Motorola built a plant in Tianjin, and it was soon followed by many other companies.[93] Meanwhile, Taiwanese businessmen were establishing companies that would use cheap labor and enormous economies of scale to become the world's largest manufacturers of such products as brassieres and shoes.[94] China was off and running.

Russia and India enter the fray

In 1985, the leader of the Soviet Union, Mikhail Gorbachev, initiated political and economic reforms known as "glasnost" and "perestroika" that eventually would bring the 400 million people living in the Soviet Union and Eastern Europe into the global economy. Following the collapse of the Soviet Union in 1992, Russia came out from behind the "economic iron curtain" and joined the world economy. Although the Russian economy was fraught with obsolescence, inefficiency, corruption, and cronyism, it was now connected to the world as it had not been since 1917.

With the demise of the Soviet Union, in 1991 India began moving from socialism toward market-based capitalism, removing barriers to trade and investment and joining the world economy more fully than ever before, joining the World Trade Organization in 1995.

India did not adopt the export-oriented manufacturing model of Japan and the Asian Tigers. Rather, it capitalized on its large reservoir of a well-educated, English speaking populace to create a different kind of export platform - one for the provision of services. These included a wide range of activities, from customer service call centers to the provision of information technology, engineering and design, and other professional services. A cottage industry grew up among U.S. consulting firms, offering "outsourcing" and "offshoring" services to manage the transfer of back office, research and development, financial, and all sorts of work from the U.S. to India.

The Age of Oversupply

It would be difficult to overstate the magnitude of the effect of this move of China, Russia, and India out from behind their socialist walls, bringing three billion people into the world economy, around 1992. This development ushered in what has been called the "Age of Oversupply," with dramatic effects on the world economy.

Oversupply of People

Two of these, China and India, had a population of over one billion each. Others, taken as a group, added another billion: the Russian Federation and Eastern Europe with 400 million, and the formerly socialist/statist countries of Indonesia, Brazil, Bangladesh, Pakistan, Mexico, and Vietnam, accounting for another 450 million, joined the world economy.

These nations previously had been cut off from the world economy because they were operating socialist economic systems that precluded investment and profit, both internally, and through rules against foreign investment. Now, they were connected to the world economy in communication, shipping, capital access, and financial services.

So, in a span of a very few years, three billion people joined the world economy, nearly two billion of them potentially in the workforce. And yes, many of these are unskilled workers just in from the family farm. However, many have received technical- and university-level training. In his 2013 book, *The Age of Oversupply*, Daniel Alpert reports that the number of Chinese college graduates increased from 830,000 in 1998 to 6.8 million in 2012, and the Indian university system expanded from 390,000 seats in 2000 to 1.5 million in 2011.[95]

This dynamic applies not only in the market for goods, but also for services. The Internet, which accounted for so much of the growth of the American economy during the 1990s, also was undermining the services economy, by creating the ability for skilled and unskilled workers alike in remote locations such as India to perform work nearly as efficiently as if sitting in the next cubicle. As I discuss elsewhere, much research and development is being offshored, often in connection with new offshore manufacturing capacity.

As documented by Brown, Lauder and Ashton in their 2011 book, we are caught up in a "Global Auction" with an oversupply of qualified workers, from the least to the most skilled.[96] Writing in 2011, Gallup Organization Chairman Jim Clifton summed it up this way: of the seven billion people on earth, five billion want a full-time job; however, the world's economies only produce 1.2 formal, full-time jobs, leaving a 1.8 billion shortfall.[97]

Oversupply of Capacity

Importantly, these countries did not fully adopt capitalism. Rather, they practiced a hybrid form of "state capitalism" that included a lot of planning and devotion of state resources to the development of favored industries. China, of course, still has its five-year plans, but I was surprised to learn that India, too, still utilizes five year plans.[98] The problem is that these countries, with the state so heavily involved in industrial development, have a strong tendency toward the creation of overcapacity, for example, in steelmaking and photovoltaics (just as Japan did in its day with respect to automobile manufacturing capacity). So, not only is there a built-in overcapacity of labor, but also there is a built-in tendency to overbuild production capacity.

Oversupply of Money

The third part of this trifecta is this: as these countries have pursued an export-led strategy of economic development, their exports have greatly exceeded their imports, and, therefore, the payments they received for their exports greatly exceeded the payments they made for their imports. And so there has been a tremendous accumulation of financial capital in the fast-growing, low-wage, export-oriented countries, especially China.[99]

We are left with the oversupply of workers, physical capital, and financial capital described by in *The Age of Oversupply*, Brown, et al., in *The Global Auction*, and Clifton in *The Coming Jobs War*.

Globalization

Each of the developments I have reviewed so far were momentous enough in their own right. However, they pale in comparison to an overarching development that reached maturity toward the end of this decade, when international trade morphed into globalization. Although it can be hard to pin down just what is meant by "globalization," the key components include flows of capital, information, and technology across national borders, and a convergence of the rules for regulating those flows. That is a pretty dry, academic-sounding definition, but we will see that the thing called "globalization" has had profound effects on individuals' lives worldwide.

The stage was set for this new phenomenon by the creation of the World Trade Organization, plus several other changes in the worldwide business environment.

Shipping and Communications Revolutions

First was a revolution in shipping, on two fronts. One was rapid shipping: In the early 1990s, FedEx, followed by UPS, expanded service to Asia, and then to Europe and the rest of the world. The other front was the internationalization and containerization of shipping: giant container ships flying flags of convenience staffed by personnel paid low wages could carry as many as 15,000 containers and on-load or offload them in 24 hours in modern, mechanized ports around the world.[100]

This revolution in the speed and scale of the movement of goods was accompanied by an analogous revolution in the communication of information. Speed and scale in communication were an important enabler of both revolutions in shipping.

However, there was another dimension to the communication revolution: with the advent of the Internet, suddenly anything that could be communicated digitally could be done anywhere in the world. As we have seen, in the new "age of oversupply," call center operators, computer coders, accountants, and engineers in America and Western Europe were competing with their counterparts in India and Eastern Europe, who could now perform their functions as if they were sitting down the hall.

The Revolution in Retailing: The Wal-Mart/ China Joint Venture

Second, this period saw a transformation of the relationship between manufacturers and retailers, with retailers now dictating what they wanted made in response to real-time information on customer preferences. This transformation was led by Wal-Mart.

The revolution had three components. First, retailers began deciding what would be sold and when, based upon sophisticated computer analysis of their customers' buying habits. Wal-Mart led the way on this component, developing its own "super computer" for collecting and analyzing big data and managing worldwide inventory on a day-to-day basis. There was a move from "push production" of manufacturers bringing products to retailers, to "pull production" of retailers calling the shots.

The second component was a move by retailers, again led by Wal-Mart, toward expanding, improving, and aggressively marketing their own private-label product offerings. The retailers were competing on their own shelves with their name-brand suppliers. But consumers were caring less about brands, and low price was outselling brand loyalty. For the private-label products, retailers would deal directly with contract manufacturers of their choosing.

The third component was a move toward foreign sourcing in low-wage countries, primarily in Asia, and especially in China. As mentioned earlier, Wal-Mart had opened an Asian buying office in 1981.[101]

Not only was Wal-Mart sourcing its private-label products in Asia; it effectively was forcing its branded product suppliers to do the same. Wal-Mart was telling suppliers, including branded manufacturers, what price it was willing to pay for a product. And that price typically was the price for which it could be gotten in China – what Alexandra Harney has called "The China Price."[102]

Brands became price takers, providing Wal-Mart and the chains and big box stores the products they specified, at the prices they specified. Since that price was "the China Price," many American manufacturers had little choice but to redefine themselves as "branded distributors" for overseas goods. Instead of making their own products, they would use their own brand names to market Chinese-made goods to retailers.

Remaining U.S. producers effectively became contract manufacturers responding to Wal-Mart's and other retailers' needs, and saw their profits squeezed. Wal-Mart's profits took off. Reau Berry, owner of Johnston/ Tombigbee furniture, told Beth Macy that if people understood what was going on, they'd never go to Walmart again.[103]

Development of Global Supply Chains

A third, and related, development contributing to globalization was the movement by manufacturers and brands toward global production via global supply chains. This trend was enabled by countries' elimination or reduction of bars to foreign investment, permitting companies to make capital expenditures to create new plants on their soil and transfer their technologies to those plants. (In some cases, most notably China, a local share in ownership is required.)

It also was enabled by a trend in manufacturing toward dividing the manufacturing process into smaller, discreet steps, each capable of being distributed over a widely-dispersed supply chain.

As already had occurred with apparel, textiles, and footwear, production of all manufactured goods became "footloose," unmoored from the country where the company was headquartered or the products were sold.

Case Studies during 1986-1995

How did these enormous changes in the international business landscape play out on the ground in America during this decade?

Automobiles

In 1986, the Korean conglomerate Hyundai began selling cars into the U.S. market. Justin Lin tells of sitting at a conference next to the president of the North American division of the Hyundai automobile company. Lin commented that other countries must be envious of South Korea's success selling automobiles in the United States. The executive replied that Hyundai had been running losses in the U.S. market for many years. From this, Lin inferred that Hyundai must have been receiving a great deal of South Korean government support in the form of subsidies and protective trade barriers, and that the Hyundai success in the U.S. must have come at a great cost, at least initially. Perhaps you, as I, were wondering how they were selling sedans in the U.S. for $15,000 that were the equivalent of cars other companies sold for $30,000. Now you know.[104]

Commercial Aircraft

In January of 1990, Boeing employed 155,900 people, at its home facility in Seattle and in Wichita and Philadelphia. In February 1996, the company had cut its workforce by one-third, to 103,600. A big reason the job losses was that Boeing struck deals with other countries for placing component manufacturing there in exchange for their purchase of aircraft. In China, the setup was the same as we have seen in other industries: The Xianjin factory where 737 components were being made employed 20,000 workers living in barracks adjacent to the factory.[105]

Color Television Sets

In 1991, twenty-one million color television sets were sold in the U.S., most of them imported -- only one American company was making them, Zenith, at its plant in Springfield, Missouri, employing some 1,350 workers. In 1992, Zenith closed the plant and moved its production to a Zenith plant in Reynosa, Mexico. The company explained that it was doing so to cut costs, from the $5 to $11 an hour it paid workers in Springfield, to an average of $1.60 an hour in Reynosa.[106]

Glassware

Venerable American brands like Anchor Hocking glassware came under relentless pressure. That company was sold to Newell and in November, 1987, Newell closed the Anchor Hocking plant in Clarksburg, West Virginia.[107]

Furniture

The Chinese furniture factories were enormous, and didn't have to worry about workplace safety. In 1994 an American furniture executive visited a factory three times as large as any he'd seen, but where he had trouble breathing due to the fumes in the finishing room - the workers lasted two years and died, he said, and there would be plenty more workers lined up to take their place.[108]

Textiles

By the 1980s, the latest technologies in textile production had become globally dispersed, leveling the technological playing field among the U.S., Europe, and the

Far East.[109] Now it was a contest over wages, a contest the U.S. and Europe would lose.

Imports of textiles and apparel from the low-wage Asian countries continued to rise dramatically from 1986 through 1990. The Customs Service did not have sufficient resources to track the movement of goods between countries to circumvent quotas, and existing executive authority to curb imports was not fully utilized. In 1986, Congress passed a bill that would have limited the growth of imports of textiles and apparel from the low-wage Asian countries to the rate of growth of the U.S. Market. However, President Reagan vetoed it. And in 1990, Congress passed another bill to place new limits on these imports; this one was vetoed by President George H.W. Bush.[110]

Cut Flowers

The U.S. Agency for International Development was supporting and promoting exports of roses and other cut flowers from Colombia into the U.S. market. While Europe and Japan remained essentially closed to cut flowers, U.S. imports of roses, mostly from Colombia, from one million stems in 1971 to 752 million stems in 1995 (66% of the market).[111]

Trade Legislation and Results through 1995

These events on the ground were the results of actors including foreign companies and governments, U.S. companies and the U.S. government (and, of course, U.S. consumers). But they were the result in large part of the U.S. policy response, as embodied in the U.S. trade laws.

As Barlett and Steele have pointed out, from the time Congress debated the 1973 trade bill, when the U.S. had a $900 million merchandise trade surplus, through 1995, after enacting five major pieces of legislation, the U.S. United States recorded twenty consecutive years of deficit, accumulating a massive $1.7 trillion in total merchandise trade deficits. How could this happen? In their view, "Congress had no intention of putting real teeth in any trade legislation, and the executive branch had no intention of using the teeth it had." But the real story, they said, was the results, in terms of millions of lost jobs and a declining standard of living.[112] In later chapters, I will confirm that that was the case.

In their third book, Barlett and Steele capture quotes from the members of Congress in support of each trade bill. It is indeed dismaying to read them. With each bill, members of the House and Senate stand in the chamber and pronounce the dawn of a new era of tough enforcement of fair trade rules and the opening of other markets to American products, knowing that in the years following the enactment of each of these laws, the U.S. trade deficit continued to increase.[113]

It is useful, but indeed dismaying, to take a moment to stop and take stock of the major trade policy legislation that was enacted over the decades through 1995 (Amounts are expressed in 2016 dollars): [114]

The Trade Act of 1974 was touted by its sponsors as providing the U.S. government with authority to "take action" in response to unfair trade practices. In 1973, when the law passed the Congress, *U.S. trade in merchandise had a surplus of $5 billion. By 1979, it had a deficit of $91 billion.*

So, Congress enacted the Trade Agreements Act of 1979. It was touted by President Carter as opening "vast new opportunities" for American exports and revising the rules of international trade toward a more equitable and open system. *The trade in goods deficit rose from $91 billion in 1979 to $260 billion in 1984.*

So, Congress enacted the Trade Remedies Reform Act of 1984. It was touted by President Reagan as putting real teeth in U.S. trade remedies and expanding exports. *The trade in goods deficit remained constant, from $260 billion in 1984 to $258 billion in 1988.*

So, Congress enacted the Omnibus Trade and Competitiveness Act of 1988. Its sponsors said America would insist on opening markets and would no longer "roll over" on trade. *The trade in goods deficit rose from $258 billion in 1988 to $269 billion in 1994.*

So, Congress enacted the 1994 legislation ratifying the General Agreement on Tariffs and Trade and the new World Trade Organization.

With each trade law and subsequent increase in the trade in goods deficit, I am reminded of the late Charles Schultz's comic strips, in which Lucy pulls the football away as Charlie Brown tries to kick it, choosing to believe, every year, that this time it will be different.

Snapshot in 1995

- In U.S. trade relations –
  - The Japanese continued to capture U.S. industries while their market remained relatively closed.
  - In 1992, China confirmed its "reform and opening" movement toward an export-oriented, quasi-capitalist economy welcoming foreign investment to become an "export platform" for multinational companies.
  - The enactment of the North American Trade Agreement began an accelerated move of U.S. companies' operations into Mexico.
  - The World Trade Organization was created, implementing new, lower tariffs and establishing new rules with compulsory dispute resolution.
- We entered the "Age of Oversupply:"
  - Russia and India came out from behind their socialist protections, with India becoming an "export platform" for services. U.S. consulting business sprang up to assist U.S. companies in "offshore outsourcing" of company functions.
  - Three billion people were added to the world economy. We entered the "age of oversupply," of everything but consumer demand. The countries joining the world economy did not have sufficient internal consumer demand, so they turned to the U.S. and other developed nations' markets for growth.

- Several trends ushered in the era of "globalization:"
  - A revolution in shipping, via courier companies and containerized vessels, and a revolution in communication, bringing people into close virtual proximity via the Internet.
  - A revolution in retailing, with a move to retailers telling manufacturers what would be produced and at what cost, expansion of retailers' private-label programs, and foreign sourcing in low-wage countries. Brands were forced to follow retailers in sourcing offshore, and remaining U.S. manufacturers were squeezed by the "China Price." Wal-Mart led the way, in what was dubbed the "Wal-Mart-China joint venture."
  - A revolution in production, in which retailers and brands moved into production via global supply chains. As already had occurred with apparel, textiles, and footwear, production of all manufactured goods became "footloose," unmoored from the country where the company was headquartered or the products were sold.
- By 1995, these trends were having devastating effects on U.S. industries from automobiles to cut flowers. The U.S. went through the motions of enacting laws that were supposed to foster fair and beneficial trade. However, in the sixteen years from 1980 to 1995, the U.S. had a perfect record of sixteen years of merchandise trade deficits, while Japan and Germany had sixteen years of consecutive trade surpluses.
- By 1995, when it came to trade, the United States had become, to paraphrase the recent television show, "the biggest loser."

Notes to Chapter 2

---

[1] For a review of the principles of the GATT and its early implementation, see Richard Baldwin, "The World Trade Organization and the Future of Multilateralism," Journal of Economic Perspectives, Volume 30, Number 1—Winter 2016—Pages 95–116. http://dx.doi.org/10.1257/jep.30.1.95.

[2] Robert E. Baldwin, "U.S. Trade Policy Since 1934," in *The Oxford Handbook of International Commercial Policy*, eds. Mordechai E. Kreinin and Michael G. Plummer (New York: Oxford University Press, 2012), 36.

[3] Alexandra Harney, *The China Price: The True Cost of Chinese Competitive Advantage* (New York: Penguin Press 2007), 19.

[4] Ellen Israel Rosen, *Making Sweatshops: The Globalization of the U.S. Apparel Industry* (Berkeley: University of California Press, 2002), 59.

[5] They wanted Denmark, which had been occupied by the Germans in 1940, for its warm-water ports. However, the Allies learned of their plans and sent the Allied armies there ahead of the Soviets, so the Danes were liberated instead of occupied. Ambrose, *Citizen Soldiers.*

[6] Joseph Stalin moved away from these international movements, focusing on building up the Soviet Union under a policy of "National Socialism." However, the respite was brief, as after his death the Soviet Union continued to support communist movements worldwide well into the 1980s.

[7] Larry Collins and Dominique Lapierre, *Is Paris Burning?* (New York: Simon and Shuster, 1965).

[8] David Halberstam, *The Reckoning* (New York: William Morrow and Company, Inc., 1986), 120-123.

[9] Rosen, *Sweatshops,* 37.

[10] Rosen, *Sweatshops,* 15.

[11] *Id.*

[12] Prestowitz, *Betrayal,* 91. Earlier, the Trade Agreements Extension Act of 1951 (Pub. L. No. 82-50, June 16, 1951) had been enacted, authorizing negotiations and establishing a statutory "escape clause" procedure to deal with harmful imports.

[13] The Truman and Eisenhower administrations and the businessmen favoring imports argued that the damage would be limited, because imports were only a small fraction of consumption, imports competed with only a small segment of American industries,

and imports' poor quality would prevent them from injuring U.S. producers.

[14] Prestowitz, *Betrayal*, 92.

[15] Prestowitz, *Betrayal*, 89.

[16] Halberstam, *Reckoning*, 27.

[17] Prestowitz, *Betrayal*, 78, 88.

[18] Rosen, *Sweatshops,* 48, 49.

[19] Congressional testimony of Walter T. Forbes, quoted in Rosen, *Sweatshops,* 82.

[20] Rosen, *Sweatshops,* 105, 106.

[21] Rosen, *Sweatshops*, 50.

[22] *Id.*

[23] Quotation attributed to George Ball, Under Secretary of State for Economic and Agricultural Affairs from 1964 to 1966, in testimony of R. Dave Hall, president of the American Cotton Manufacturers' Association, U.S. House of Representatives, Committee on Education and Labor, Impact of Imports and Exports on Employment (Textiles).

[24] Enacted on Oct. 11, 1962 (Pub. L. No. 87-794).

[25] Rosen, *Sweatshops,* 75.

[26] Baldwin, Robert, "Trade Policy," 36. It is worth noting that earlier, in 1958, Congress had enacted the Trade Agreements Extension Act of 1958 (Pub. L. No. 85-686, August 20, 1958), establishing procedures that limited the president's authority to reduce tariff rates when negotiating a foreign trade agreement.

[27] It is also worth noting here that another, multilateral "free trade" agreement had entered into effect on January 1, 1958 - the Treaty Establishing the European Economic Community ("Treaty of Rome").

[28] Donald L. Barlett and James B. Steele, *America: What Went Wrong* (Kansas City: Andrews and McMeel, 1992), 52.

[29] Beth Macy noted that in 1963, her newspaper, the Roanoke Times, ran a series about Martinsville and surrounding Henry County as the industrial powerhouse of Virginia. Bassett, Stanley, and American in furniture, and DuPont in textiles, were all expanding their operations, and unemployment was below one percent. Beth Macy, *Factory Man: How One Furniture Maker Battled Offshoring, Stayed Local - and Helped Save an American Town* (New York: Little, Brown & Company, 2014), 324.

---

[30] Certain oil producing countries had organized a cartel named the Organization of Petroleum Exporting Countries, led by Saudi Arabia and the other Arab oil producing nations. (*See* http://www.opec.org.)

[31] Rosen, *Sweatshops,* 111.

[32] Prestowitz, *Betrayal*, 92, 93.

[33] *Id.*

[34] Barlett and Steele, *What Went Wrong*, 35.

[35] Prestowitz, *Betrayal*, 92.

[36] Barlett and Steele, *What Went Wrong*, 36.

[37] Rosen, *Sweatshops,* 90.

[38] Pub. L. No. 93-618, January 3, 1975.

[39] Beth Macy, *Factory Man: How One Furniture Maker Battled Offshoring, Stayed Local - and Helped Save an American Town* (New York: Little, Brown & Company, 2014), 147, 343.

[40] Rosen, *Sweatshops,* 91.

[41] Prestowitz, *Betrayal* 97, 103

[42] *Id.*

[43] Prestowitz, *Betrayal*, Prestowitz, *Betrayal*, 97, 123.

[44] Nelson Lichtenstein, "Walmart's Long March to China," in *Walmart in China,* ed. Anita Chan (Ithaca: ILR Press, an imprint of Cornell University Press 2011), 23-24.

[45] Pub. L. No. 96-39, July 26, 1979. The Act also implemented the market opening agreements reached during the "Tokyo Round."

[46] Pub. L. No. 98-573, October 30, 1984. The law also provided bilateral trade negotiating authority for the U.S.-Israel and U.S.-Canada Free Trade Agreements.

[47] On May 2, 1981 Japan announced voluntary export restraint measures on its automobile exports to the United States. On November 9, 1983, the first U.S.-Japan semiconductor agreement was reached. On January 28, 1985, the U.S.-Japan Market-Oriented Sector-Specific talks opened, concerning electronics, forest products, medical equipment, pharmaceuticals, and telecommunication products.

[48] Rosen, *Sweatshops,* 127.

[49] Prestowitz, *Betrayal*, 99, 101.

[50] Prestowitz, *Betrayal*, 105.

[51] There were exceptions, such as the Chrysler bailout in 1979-80, and the creation in the mid-1980s of Sematech, a 50-50 private/public semiconductor R&D partnership. Also, the National Science Foundation

took over from DARPA the development and commercialization of the Internet. (Ironically, the Internet became a tool for offshoring service, design, and manufacturing jobs, as discussed below.)

[52] Prestowitz, *Betrayal* 108.

[53] In the case of Grenada, where Cuba was building an air base and had stockpiled arms sufficient for a 10,000-man army, U.S. action included the use of military force. "The Invasion of Grenada," http://pbc.org.

[54] Pub. L. No. 98-67, Aug. 5, 1983.

[55] Barlett and Steele, *What Went Wrong*, 95. Jose Aponte-Hernandez, "No to the return of 936," *The Hill,* September 2, 2016. http://thehill.com/blogs/congress-blog/economy-budget/294141-no-to-the-return-of-section-936.

[56] Justin Yifu Lin, *Demystifying the Chinese Economy,* (Cambridge: Cambridge University Press 2012), 3.

[57] Rosen, *Sweatshops,* 122, 123.

[58] Donald L. Barlett and James B. Steele, *America: Who Stole the Dream?* (Kansas City: Andrews and McMeel, 1996), 127.

[59] Donald L. Barlett and James B. Steele, *The Betrayal of the American Dream,* (New York: Public Affairs, 2012), 57.

[60] Barlett and Steele, *Who Stole the Dream,* 57.

[61] Barlett and Steele, *Who Stole the Dream*, 114 *ff.*

[62] *Id.*, 117.

[63] *Id.*, 119.

[64] *Id.*

[65] *Id.*, 212.

[66] I strongly recommend this readable and compelling account of an American industry mostly capitulating to the forces of globalization, the destructive effects of that capitulation on hundreds of communities, and the successful resistance of one man and a band of like-minded company owners who thought they had a duty to their communities.

[67] Macy, *Factory Man,*147, 148.

[68] Macy, *Factory Man,* 161, 162, 196, 197.

[69] *Id.*

[70] Macy, *Factory Man*, 163, 170, 246.

[71] *Id.*, 246.

[72] On February 22, 1987, the United States, Japan, West Germany, France, the United Kingdom, and Canada signed the Louvre Accord to

stabilize the value of the U.S. dollar on foreign-exchange markets, whose decline began after the Plaza Accord 18 months earlier.

[73] From 1985 to 1986, the U.S. trade in goods deficit with Japan increased from $103 billion to $121 billion, measured in 2016 dollars. In the next several years the deficit declined as there was some improvement in U.S. exports to Japan. However, this trend was short-lived, and by 1995 the deficit was back up to $93 billion.

[74] Barlett and Steele, *Who Stole the Dream,* 56.

[75] Pub. L. No. 100-418, August 23, 1988. The Act also established the negotiating principles for further trade talks, including a focus on services, intellectual property rights, and investments.

[76] Pub. L. No. 102-429, October 21, 1992.

[77] The three components of the EAI are: the development of free-trade agreements, including the North American Free Trade Agreement (NAFTA); a US$1.5 billion grant fund to support the implementation of investment reform programs; and a program of official debt relief. Except for the negotiation of free trade agreements, the EAI is administered by the Agency for International Development (AID). The EAI was authorized by Sec. 602(a) of the Jobs Through Exports Act of 1992 (Public Law 102-549; 106 Stat. 3664), which amended the Foreign Assistance Act by adding Part IV--Enterprise for the Americas Initiative, secs. 701-710. https://www.usaid.gov/biodiversity/TFCA/enterprise-for-the-americas-initiative.

[78] Pub. L. No.102-182, December 4, 1991.

[79] The program offered preferential duty treatment for eligible products from these countries to help them develop and strengthen legitimate industries to replace trafficking in coca. The ATPA was expanded under the Trade Act of 2002, and called the Andean Trade Promotion and Drug Eradication Act (ATPDEA). Due to Colombia's and Peru's implementation of Free Trade Agreements with the U.S. (see below), and Bolivia and Ecuador becoming ineligible, the ATPDEA expired on July 31, 2013.

[80] It also is worth noting that in 1986 Mexico joined the GATT.

[81] *See* Baldwin, Richard, "Future."

[82] See, *e.g.* Prestowitz, *Betrayal,* 114.

[83] That agreement was in effect an extension of the U.S.-Canadian Automobile Pact of 1965.

[84] NAFTA had been negotiated by the administration of President George W. Bush. It was controversial, and Bush's successor, Bill Clinton, pushed for its implementation after negotiating two supplemental agreements, the North American Agreement on Environmental

Cooperation (NAAEC) and the North American Agreement on Labor Cooperation (NAALC).

[85] Barlett and Steele, *What Went Wrong*, 32.

[86] Joshua Cohen, "The Rise of the Maquiladoras," Business Mexico 1994, excerpted at: http://www.mruniversity.com/courses/international-trade/maquiladoras]

[87] U.S. House of Representative video archives, captured in *American Jobs*, documentary film directed by Greg Spotts, at 0.16:17.

[88] Barlett and Steele, *Betrayal*, 53 *ff.*

[89] Harney, *China Price*, 31.

[90] In 1994, China dramatically devalued its currency, from roughly five to eight yuan to the dollar, fueling its export promotion program by effectively slashing the prices of its products to the rest of the world. During the Asian currency crisis of 1997, China took measures to keep the yuan steady.

[91] Justin Lin has expressed the belief that "The completely different economic performances before and after reform in China also demonstrated how critical borrowing technology is to the economy. . . . The main reason for China's rapid growth after its reform and opening is borrowing technology at low costs to achieve rapid technological change." Lin, *Demystifying*, 15, 16.

[92] Prestowitz, *Betrayal*, 136.

[93] *Id.*

[94] Prestowitz, *Betrayal*, 30, 31.

[95] Daniel Alpert, *The Age of Oversupply* (New York: Portfolio/Penguin, 2013), 12.

[96] Phillip Brown, Hugh Lauder and David Ashton, *The Global Auction* (New York, 2011).

[97] Jim Clifton, *The Coming Jobs War* (New York: Gallup Press, 2011), 2.

[98] Brown, *et al.*, *Global* Auction, 33.

[99] There also has been an accumulation of capital outside these countries, as western companies have "parked" profits in various tax havens, and as western central banks have created trillions of dollars out of thin air ("quantitative easing") in a desperate attempt to jump-start their economies.

[100] Rose George, *Ninety Percent of Everything* (New York: Picador, 2013), 3, 9.

---

[101] Following the suppression of the Tiananmen Square demonstrations, in 1991 Wal-Mart had set up an exclusive buying agent, Pacific Resources Export Limited (PREL), to serve as a cover for Wal-Mart's buying in Asia. PREL also permitted Wal-Mart to continue promoting the "Buy American" campaign it had begun in 1985, even while emphasizing its Asian sourcing to meet its low-price requirements. (The company quietly ended the campaign in 1992, after *Dateline NBC* exposed that "Buy American" signs had been placed on imported goods from Asia.) Sam Hornblower, "Wal-Mart & China: A Joint Venture," *PBS Frontline*. http://www.pbs.org/wgbh/pages/frontline/shows/walmart/secrets/wmchina.html. Lichtenstein, "Walmart's Long March."

[102] Harney, *The China Price*. In many cases, they were told outright by Wal-Mart that they had to source the product in China. Nelson Lichtenstein, "Walmart's Long March to China," in *Walmart in China,* ed. Anita Chan (Ithaca: ILR Press, an imprint of Cornell University Press 2011).

[103] Macy, *Factory Man*, 394.

[104] Lin, *Demystifying*, 134.

[105] Barlett and Steele, *Who Stole the Dream*, 49 *ff.*

[106] Barlett and Steel, *What Went Wrong*, 37.

[107] Barlett and Steele, *Betrayal*, 79.

[108] Macy, *Factory Man*, 298.

[109] Rosen, *Sweatshops,* 94.

[110] Rosen, *Sweatshops*, 124, 127.

[111] Barlett and Steele, *Who Stole the Dream*, 59 *ff.*

[112] Barlett and Steele, *Who Stole the Dream*, 131, 132.

[113] Barlett and Steele, *Betrayal*, 50 *ff.*

[114] Source: U.S. Census Bureau, International Trade Data.

Chapter 3

1996-2015: China and the Era of Globalization

1996 – 2005

The decade 1996 to 2005 was the first experience with the new phenomenon of globalization in the age of over-supply, and would include what was arguably an even larger upheaval: the full arrival of China on the scene.

Problems at the WTO

In the first several years of its operation, the scope of the World Trade Organization was expanded, with the entry into effect of new agreements.[1] But it was about to run into heavy head winds: a rift between the "have" and "have not" nations, and a growing anti-globalization movement.

In December of 1999, when the WTO Ministerial Conference convened in Seattle, Washington, it was met with large anti-globalization demonstrations. Protesters focused on issues including workers' rights, sustainable economies, and environmental and social issues. When downtown streets and intersections could not be cleared, and after downtown businesses were vandalized, the Mayor and Governor declared a state of emergency.[2]

The conference itself was faring no better. A week before the meeting, delegates admitted failure to agree on the agenda and acknowledged deep disagreements between developed and developing countries. Developing country representatives resented being excluded from talks between the United States and the European Union toward a mutual deal on agriculture.[3] The conference was intended as the launch of a new round of multilateral trade negotiations that would have been called "The Millennium Round", however, the negotiations broke down and the conference was terminated early.

The negotiations that collapsed in Seattle were reconvened in November 2001 at Doha, Qatar, for negotiation of the "Doha Development Round;" however, due to an impasse over agricultural subsidies and other issues between developed and developing nations, the round has been suspended and reconvened in fits and starts, with no agreement in sight.[4]

We will see in Chapter 9 that, by 2016, it had become evident that the Seattle demonstrators were the "canary in the coal mine," as globalization was shown to be failing, for developing and developed nations alike.

U.S. Trade with Developing Countries

In the U.S., Congress continued to pursue trade as a means of supporting economic development in developing countries: The Trade and Development Act of 2000, enacted in May of that year,[5] provided duty-free treatment for eligible products from designated developing countries and territories. One part of the Act provided duty- and quota-free treatment for certain products from eligible sub-Sahara African countries. [6] The Act also amended the 1984 Caribbean Basin Initiative to re-authorize duty- and quota-free treatment for apparel from qualifying Caribbean-area countries, a status they had lost with the coming of NAFTA.[7]

Enforcement, Voluntary Restraints & TAA

The U.S. also continued efforts to "manage" trade through enforcement and voluntary restraints. On March 20, 2002, the United States imposed increased tariffs and tariff-rate quotas on fourteen steel products under the "safeguard" or "escape clause" provisions of Section 201 of the U.S. Trade Act of 1974. And on November 8, 2005, the U.S.-China Memorandum of Understanding was signed, limiting exports of Chinese textiles and clothing to the United States during 2006-08. Congress also enacted the Trade Act of 2002, including the reauthorization of trade adjustment assistance. [8]

First Decade under NAFTA

This period also ushered in the first decade of experience under NAFTA. As we saw in Chapter 2, during the floor debate on the NAFTA implementation bill, U.S. Rep. Bill Archer had promised the American people that Mexican consumers would "spend their new-found wealth on everything from autos, refrigerators, and diapers made in the USA, creating better paying jobs for Americans." [9]

It didn't work out that way. Instead, this period was marked by a dramatic increase in U.S. companies moving production there. As for autos, during these years, automobile industry investment in Mexico accelerated, especially among American manufacturers and parts suppliers seeking lower labor costs than at their U.S. factories.[10]

As for appliances, the rush to move production to Mexico was exemplified by Maytag's move from Galesburg, Illinois, to Reynosa, Mexico, chronicled by Chad Broughton in his 2015 book, *Boom, Bust, Exodus: The Rust Belt, the Maquilas, and a Tale of Two Cities*.[11]

From the 1970s through 2002, Maytag produced appliances at a unionized manufacturing plant known as "Appliance City" in Galesburg, "described in a 1974 Chicago Tribune article as an 'industrial Eden' peopled by 'mid-Americans straight out of a Norman Rockwell Saturday Evening Post cover,' the very epitome of 'stability in [the] heartlands.'" [12] However, all that changed after Maytag's announcement in October of 2002 that it would shut down its Galesburg operations and move them to Reynosa.

The Mexican workers couldn't afford to buy appliances made in the USA or even the ones they were making for Maytag, because they weren't making even the $2.60 an hour claimed by the McAllen Economic Development Corporation – Broughton verified that their base wage rate was 78 cents an hour. One of the workers told Broughton he not only couldn't afford to buy one of the refrigerators, the job didn't pay "nearly enough to raise a family." Broughton also determined that many of the workers had been forced to move to Reynosa seeking work after their *ejido* common farm land had been privatized under the rules of NAFTA, the IMF, and the World Bank.

In Reynosa, poverty reigned, living conditions were grim, and crime was rampant. Broughton found that companies like Maytag could avoid U.S.-level wages, pensions, taxes, and regulations, as well as any responsibility to the place where they operated; they could operate nearly anonymously among the proliferation of factories doing likewise.

Meanwhile, back in Galesburg, workers went on public assistance and took menial jobs where they could find them. Footnote: Broughton reports that Maytag CEO Ralph Hake, who had come to Maytag from Whirlpool and presided over its sale to that company, left Maytag after three years with $10 million in severance pay to take up residence in a Las Vegas country club.[13]

Other Free Trade Agreements

During this period, the U.S. entered into a number of other free trade agreements: In the middle East, The U.S.-Jordan Free Trade Agreement (effective December 17, 2001) and the U.S.-Morocco Free Trade Agreement (effective January 1, 2006); in Asia, the U.S.-Vietnam Bilateral Trade Agreement (effective December 10, 2001), the U.S.-Singapore Free Trade Agreement (effective January 1, 2004), and the U.S.-Australia Free Trade Agreement effective January 1, 2005); in Latin America, the U.S.-Chile Free Trade Agreement (effective January 1, 2004) and the U.S.-Central America-Dominican Republic Free Trade Agreement (effective January 1, 2006).[14]

Asian Currency Crisis

In 1997, a real estate and investment bubble in Thailand that had been built with foreign capital burst. The foreign investors pulled their capital out of the country, and the Thai currency collapsed. Other nations followed, and the "Asian currency crisis" drove down Asian currencies by 40 percent.[15] The cheaper currencies meant that products were suddenly 40 percent cheaper, and Asian textile imports into the U.S. soon were up 80 percent. Hundreds of textile mills closed. Ninety percent of these mills were in small southern towns, where the closings hit people and the local economies extremely hard.[16]

China joins the WTO

The signal event of this decade was the conclusion of an agreement to bring China into the World Trade Organization, and the related enactment of U.S. legislation to grant China permanent most favored nation treatment under the U.S. tariff laws. As Clyde Prestowitz has pointed out, this amounted to providing the treatment intended for market-based countries practicing free trade to a country that is authoritarian and highly state-directed, pursuing a mercantilist, export-oriented economic strategy and program.[17]

Full access to the U.S. market now was granted to Chinese companies and to U.S. companies that moved their factories there. Prestowitz has well noted that this would be the equivalent of Britain moving its textile mills to Portugal.[18] U.S. companies were willing to do the equivalent, both to gain access to the Chinese market and to set up low-cost production to serve the U.S. market. However, they would pay a high price, because they must operate through a joint venture business structure, to which they must transfer their hard-won, proprietary technology.

There also was a view among President Clinton and other U.S. officials that the new arrangements would set China on the road to democracy, as they believed this is what inevitably happens when nations become rich. Some Chinese indeed would become rich, but at the expense of Chinese and U.S. workers, and as we will see in Chapter 8, democracy and even basic human rights appear farther away than ever.

The Peterson Institute, among others, predicted that U.S. exports to China would rise faster than Chinese imports into the U.S., rejecting predictions to the contrary by the Economic Policy Institute.[19] They should have known better. The trade in goods deficit with China already was large and growing at an increasing pace, as shown in the following figure:

And this had happened even under the uncertainty of year-to-year renewal of China's normal trade relations status. What would happen if this dampening effect were removed through the grant of permanent NTR status should have been predictable: even more rapid growth in the trade deficit. And that is exactly what happened, as shown in the following figure:

There had been much talk about how the legislation granting China permanent normal trade relations status would open the huge Chinese market to exports from U.S. companies. In fact, however, there was a great deal of pent-up demand among companies who wanted to do the opposite - to move from the U.S. to China the production of their products for sale into the U.S.[20]

And so, although U.S. exports to China increased substantially, they were far outweighed by the dramatic increase in imports from China, which increased from $140 billion to $373 billion from 2000 to 2007, an increase of 166%. The result was a blowout in the U.S. trade in goods deficit with China, which increased from $117 billion in 2000 to $300 billion in 2007. (All amounts are in 2016 dollars.)[21]

Wal-Mart in China

With China's acquisition of permanent normal trade relations with the U.S. and admission to the World Trade Organization under President Clinton's leadership, and with a politically entrenched free trade movement, Wal-Mart's leadership no longer saw any need to hide its ties to China. The company established a new global sourcing group based in Shenzhen, China, to succeed PREL in 2002.[22]

Industry Sectors – The "Tipping Point"

Developing countries drawn into export-led development compete against each other for concessions they can offer to investors locating manufacturing operations. As more manufacturers move overseas, the pressure intensifies on U.S. manufacturers to follow suit.[23] The industry then reaches a "tipping point," where the major brands become importers.

Apparel

Such was the case in the apparel industry. In the case of Guess? jeans, the company had 97 percent of its production in the U.S., but was violating wage and hour laws. When the Labor Department enforced the laws and imposed fines, in 1997 the company moved most of its operations to Mexico. So, too, Levi Strauss tried to stay in the U.S., but, facing competition from competitors operating in Mexico, the company moved its production there in 1997 and 1999. [24]

Consumer Electronics

The case of Apple computers seems also to be an example of an industry "tipping point." Founded by Steve Jobs and Steve Wozniak, Apple built the first personal computer in 1976. It built its "Macintosh" computers at factories in San Francisco, then Fremont, CA. In 1992, the company opened factories in Elk Grove, California, near Sacramento, and in Fountain, Colorado, near Colorado

Springs. The Apple plants were the core of high tech clusters of industries in Sacramento and Colorado Springs.

Then, in 1996, Apple, following other companies in the electronics industry, began moving production to China. It sold the Fountain plant with a three-year production contract that ended in 1999; the Elk Grove plant closed in 2004.[25]

Case Study: Furniture

I believe many of us have had tended to regard the offshoring of the textile/apparel/footwear and electronics industries as something inevitable. However, another industry reached a "tipping point", one that may be a bit of a surprise. That industry is furniture.

We have seen that during the decade 1986-1995 the U.S. furniture industry, previously thought to be immune from foreign competition due to the products' bulk, came under intense pressure from Asian imports. How this story unfolded in the subsequent decade is a classic example of how globalization is not working, and serves as a cautionary tale for other industries. Fortunately, investigative reporter Beth Macy provided an up-close account in her 2014 book, *Factory Man*.[26]

At first, the U.S. furniture companies tried to adopt a "blended strategy" of including some imports in their product lines. By 1998, imports constituted nearly a third of U.S. sales of wooden furniture, up from one-fifth five years previous. In the late 1990s through the early 2000s, U.S. furniture companies were rushing to the south of China to find contract manufacturers who would make furniture to sell under the U.S. companies' brand names.

As we have previously noted, there was an additional trend: retailers could cut out the American-based manufacturers altogether and buy direct from the Asian suppliers. Remaining U.S. manufacturers tried to overcome the Chinese advantages, by installing the latest equipment, slashing delivery times, and highlighting customer service. Nevertheless, the tide was going out. China's entry into the World Trade Organization in 2001 accelerated the trend.

Knock-offs were the *modus operandi* of the foreign suppliers. Lax or non-existent safety and environmental laws, cheap labor, and subsidies and direct export rewards from the government meant the Chinese could offer an extremely low-priced product. However, the Chinese and other Asian suppliers did not stop at selling at prices enabled by their low wage structure, or even by government subsidies. They were prepared to sell below their own cost to capture a place in the U.S. market.

John Bassett's Vaughan-Bassett Furniture encountered this when they noticed that a knock-off of their Louis Phillipe bedroom suite was selling at wholesale for $399 - even cheaper than the prices in the Taiwanese-owned factories in southern China. They learned that it was being made in the Chinese port city of Dalian, which lies in the far north on a peninsula between Beijing and North Korea.

They also learned that the company was building an entire factory complex dedicated to the American furniture market, intended to employ over 20,000 workers. The owner's intention was to become the world's number one furniture manufacturer. Macy reports that the owner told John Bassett that he intended to put every American bedroom furniture factory out of business, including Bassett's, by selling products below their cost of production - taking the loss as the cost of entry into the U.S. market. The owner suggested that Bassett close all his factories and turn his manufacturing over to him.

However, John Bassett III was an outlier in the furniture industry; he wasn't going to close his factories and put all his people out of work. He led the formation of a coalition of bedroom furniture manufacturers to seek the imposition of tariffs in response to the "dumping" of the Chinese bedroom furniture that He YunFeng exemplified.

Bassett's coalition ultimately was successful. The initial duties were not high, but during the annual reviews, the U.S. manufacturers were able to calculate dumping margins that resulted in high enough tariffs to make the American products price competitive. Furthermore, in this case the tariffs were paid to the companies, who could use them to modernize their factories and take other steps to stay in business.

What transpired is a cautionary tale about how industries become captive to foreign sourcing, and of the limits of the "trade remedies" in the WTO and U.S. law. In fact, the bedroom furniture case is instructive as to *why we cannot rely on "trade remedies" to keep international trade fair:*

First and foremost, relief is not available until harm already has been done. The law provides that an industry must suffer substantial harm *before* it can file a petition.

Second, it is difficult to know where the harm is coming from: orders start declining, but no one knows why. Tremendous resources must be deployed to identify the source of the harm and to quantify it. John Bassett's pursuit of the "Dalian dresser" is illustrative.

Third, it is necessary to prove the foreign manufacturers' actual cost of production and the extent of sales below those costs, a daunting and expensive process.

Fourth, it is necessary to define the affected industry and to obtain the participation of fifty-one percent of it. This requires striking at the right moment, before too much of the industry has turned to offshoring. In the case of furniture, the "tipping point" already had been reached, and only companies "standing on principle" were still manufacturing in the United States.

Fifth, there will be much opposition from importers, retailers, academia, the press, and government, raising the costs of the matter. This was so in the furniture case.

Sixth, the entire process is extremely expensive and time-consuming. Many industries are not able to muster the necessary financial and management resources. As John Bassett III told Beth Macy, making furniture "should not be this laborious." [27]

Seventh, the remedy is never sufficient. Past harm is not compensated, except to the extent that a company or workers obtain benefits under the Trade Adjustment Assistance program, and prospectively, the tariffs may be insufficient to restrain the foreign imports. Importers and foreign suppliers can move their operations to another low-wage country not affected by the tariffs, and foreign suppliers can surreptitiously sell their products to non-affected suppliers in their own or other countries.

Nevertheless, these remedies can help to prevent the total loss of an industry, as is currently occurring with respect to Chinese dumping of steel and other products.

The Process at the Company Level

Many industries have not reached such a "tipping point" toward offshoring, and still have suffered severe losses from offshoring. Reading the company stories collected by Barlett and Steele in their three books and other reports, a pattern emerges:

A company is founded, often by the inventor of the product, and grows through the second generation of family ownership. Typically, the owners know and have contact with their employees, who feel valued and part of a family.[28]

Then the company is acquired, perhaps in a leveraged buyout, perhaps by a private equity firm, or perhaps by a conglomerate like Newell Corp. Often, these are perfectly profitable companies. But perhaps because the third generation of family owners are no longer interested or wanted to cash out, they are sold.[29] Often, they are financially troubled, due in part to cutthroat competition from foreign suppliers, either directly or through Wal-Mart requiring them to match the foreign prices.[30]

The new owners put on the "big squeeze," always asking for more output for less in wages.[31] They may be looking for more profit, to "squeeze more juice out of the orange." Or they may be responding to market pressures from competing low-cost imported products. Or they may be responding to pressure from Walmart or other customers.

Then the plant is closed, and the production is sent offshore.[32] The former workers and the community are left to try to pick up the pieces, but they never do. The communities, and, with few exceptions, the former workers, end up depressed, and never make it back.[33] So, there they are, scattered across America.

Snapshot in 2005

By 2005, the World Trade Organization had grown in scope, but the 1999 Seattle protests showed growing discontent with globalization, and a division was growing between the developed and developing nations.

The United States was pursuing its agenda of supporting developing nations through trade, with a new initiative to authorize duty-and-quota-free entry of products from sub-Saharan Africa, Central America and the Caribbean.

At the same time, the U.S. pursued voluntary restraints of the very products whose production it was promoting, and Congress reauthorized Trade Adjustment Assistance for dealing with economic injury caused by the imports.

The U.S. also placed new emphasis on free trade agreements, concluding agreements with Vietnam and with countries in the Middle East, Asia, and Latin America. The U.S. also launched an initiative to pursue further such agreements in Southeast Asia.

Meanwhile, the Asian financial crisis of 1997 caused a significant devaluation of Asian countries' currencies, effectively lowering the price of their goods by 40%. U.S. imports of textiles from Asia increased dramatically, as this industry reached a "tipping point" and offshore production became the norm.

The electronics and furniture industries also reached a "tipping point" where most of the production went offshore. Some producers fought back, but their efforts showed the limits of remedies for dumping and other unfair trade practices, and opposition from some surprising quarters including the U.S. government, academia, and the press.

Other industries hadn't reached such a "tipping point," but suffered nonetheless. They often followed a pattern where founder/inventors or their heirs sold companies to investors or conglomerates who squeezed the life out of them and then took them offshore.

The most far-reaching development leading up to 2005 was the United States' granting permanent normal trade relations status to China, and China's admission to the World Trade Organization in 2001. This event set the stage for a new era in world trade and international economics.

After enduring the recession that ran from March 2001 through November 2001, the U.S. economy rebounded, and it was not obvious what harm was being done or might lie in the future from the China events.

But when trade in goods and services was tallied up for the decade ending in 2005, *the U.S. had sent a net $4.8 trillion overseas, up from $1.7 trillion during the previous decade.* China was a game changer, as the next decade would show.

2006 – 2015

We now come to the decade leading up to our final snapshot in 2015.

U.S. Government Initiatives

During the decade 2006 - 2015, the U.S. government continued efforts to foster trade and exports.

Enterprise for ASEAN Initiative

On October 26, 2002, President George W. Bush announced a new trade initiative with the Association of Southeast Asian Nations (ASEAN), the "Enterprise for ASEAN Initiative." [34] The goal was to create a network of bilateral free trade agreements between the United States and ASEAN countries that are committed to economic reforms and openness in furtherance of free and open trade and investment in the Asia Pacific region.[35]

National Export Initiative

The Obama administration also sought to up its game in export promotion, as part of the recovery from the Great Recession of 2008 - 2009. On March 11, 2010, President Obama issued an Executive Order establishing the National Export Initiative (NEI).[36] Previously, under the Export Enhancement Act of 1992, the President had established the Trade Promotion Coordinating Committee (TPCC).[37]

Now, in pursuit of "my Administration's goal of "doubling exports over the next five years," the President established the cabinet-level "Export Promotion Cabinet" to work with the TPCC to remove trade barriers abroad and help U.S. firms overcome financial and other hurdles to entering new export markets.

So, how did we do towards the President's goal doubling exports, i.e., a *100% increase?* Measured in 2016 dollars, exports of goods and services were $2.039 trillion in 2010. In 2015, they were $2.284 trillion, *an increase of 12%, not 100%, over five years*. So much for government programs to increase exports.

Trade Adjustment Assistance

As part of the legislative response to the Great Recession, Congress enacted legislation reauthorizing and amending the Trade Adjustment Assistance programs for workers and firms. [38] The legislation was designed to improve the program, for example, by providing for a simplified and extended enrollment deadline for worker assistance.

However, the 2013 edition of the Department of Labor's annual report on Trade Adjustment Assistance reported that less than half of the 4.8 million workers declared eligible for TAA benefits since the program's inception had received them.[39]

Trade Agreements

Another Decade under NAFTA

This period marked the second decade of experience under NAFTA. How did it go? "Blame it on NAFTA," read the opening paragraph of Brendan Case's January 31, 2014 report that Mexico was projected to surpass Japan as the number two exporter of automobiles to the United States in 2015.[40] Case reported that from 1993 to 2013, Mexican automobile exports to the U.S. more than quadrupled.

Mexico's percentage of North American automobile production rose from 6.5 percent in 1990 to 11 percent in

2000, to 18 percent in 2013. Mexico's vehicle exports to the U.S. and Canada exploded from fewer than 250,000 in 1990 to some 1.9 million in 2015.[41]

Total Mexican exports added up to $397.5 billion in 2014, and the United States was the destination for 80 percent of them. 85 percent of Mexico's exports were from manufacturing; they included, in addition to oil and cars, flat-screen televisions, mobile phones, computers and airplane components.[42] How did these statistics play out on the ground in the U.S. in Mexico? Let's look at some examples.

Evansville, Indiana

In February of 2010, Whirlpool announced that it would transfer the manufacturing operations of its Evansville, Indiana refrigerator factory to Mexico, by June of that year, displacing 1,100 jobs. It was not the first time for Evansville; in the 1980s, Zenith Electronics laid off 1,000 workers.[43] But the effects were felt. Two years later, *PBS Newshour* reported on a typical husband and wife who had worked at the plant, and had seen his pay go down twenty percent, hers fifty percent.[44] A firm that made refrigerator shelves lost two hundred jobs, and more recently, a packaging manufacturer cut 100 jobs. The Indiana Economic Development Corp., had awarded Whirlpool $1.1 million in tax credits in 2004. The state clawed back $800,000 of that amount in 2012.[45]

Fort Smith, Arkansas

A similar story played out the following year: on October 28, 2011, Whirlpool announced that it would move the production of its Fort Smith, Arkansas plant, making mainly side-by-side refrigerators, to a plant in Ramos

Arizpe, Mexico. The plant was the largest in Fort Smith, population 86,200, and employed 4,600 people as recently as 2004. It had been down-sized steadily since then, and the closing would eliminate about a thousand jobs.

Once the state's manufacturing capital, Fort Smith still had other manufacturers, and had diversified into some other industries; nevertheless, it was reported to have lost 33 percent of its manufacturing jobs in the previous ten years.[46]

One study estimated an annual loss of $57 million in wages for the 974 Whirlpool workers and about 500 other local workers like plastic makers connected to the Whirlpool plant, according to Gregory Hamilton, an economist at the University of Arkansas at Little Rock.

A city official told Reuters that the company paid $1.1 million in local property taxes, which now would be lost to the public services it supported, especially the school district.

The closing came during the lingering downturn of the Great Recession, and a local food bank administrator said it likely foretold another year of double-digit growth of their business. A local plumbing business told of taking payment plans, post-dated checks, and even barter from those who couldn't afford to pay for services.[47]

Meanwhile in Reynosa

The adverse effects on the communities that lost their jobs to Mexico were predictable and severe. What about on the other side of the border, where the jobs went? We saw in Chad Broughton's account of the Maytag move in 2002 from Galesburg, Illinois to Reynosa, Mexico, that things were not going so well for the workers there. Were things going better for Mexican workers during the second decade of NAFTA? Charlie LeDuff marked the twentieth anniversary of the agreement by taking his documentary film crew to Reynosa to find out.[48] What he encountered there was not pretty.

LeDuff's driver, a former reporter and Reynosa city official, advises not to get out of his van. Driving on unpaved streets past ramshackle shanties, the guide says "life here for humans is little better than for an animal." There is no running water, and no electric power; a donkey-drawn cart serving as a sanitation truck goes by. They stop, and a woman shows them her pay stub from an American factory – she earns about $1.15 per hour, in a plant making automobile air conditioning units. Like the Magnetek worker in Matamoros, she cannot afford to buy what she makes.[49]

A Sad, Typical Case

Rosa Moreno was a typical *Maquiladora* worker during this period. She also worked in Reynosa. A 38-year-old mother of six, she had worked for eleven years in various plants making cell phone components, medical devices, and automobile air conditioners. Now she was working for a subcontractor that made metal backings for flat-screen televisions.

She operated a 200-ton hydraulic press, feeding it thin aluminum sheets that were stamped into shape for each model of television. The workers pursued high production goals without bathroom breaks or changing position. Modest workplace safety protections under NAFTA were being honored in the breach, especially since the 2008-2009 recession. One night in February of 2011, the machine malfunctioned and the press dropped while her hands were still placing the metal sheet. Her hands were forged to the sheet, and eventually amputated. The machine had a fail-safe requiring the pushing of two buttons, but it failed; a worker reported that the company had deferred maintenance on the machine.

Moreno's case provides an instructive window on the operations of the *Maquiladora* plants under NAFTA. She worked in a plant operated by HD Electronics, which had come from Korea to Reynosa to serve its only customer, the giant Korean firm LG Electronics. LG had acquired the formerly U.S.-owned Zenith plant in Reynosa in 2000. The world's second-largest supplier of liquid crystal and plasma televisions, LG announced in 2012 that its Reynosa factory made $2.5 billion in sales in the North American market, with plans for $3 billion the following year.

HD offered to pay Moreno $3,800 as a lifetime settlement for the loss of her hands. An employee at HD had been crushed to death in one of the larger presses two years earlier and his family had taken a settlement of approximately $11,500.

Moreno could not rely on Mexico's laws, which are woefully inadequate: Mexico's federal labor law mandates that the loss of each hand was worth 75 percent of two years' wages. Rosa made $4,800 a year. That meant under the law her settlement should be about $14,400, to replace a lifetime of lost wages.

NAFTA also is inadequate: The NAFTA side agreement intended to protect workers hasn't worked. Under the agreement, workers like Moreno with grievances can request a hearing at a government entity called the National Administrative Office. From there, the complaint is sent to the respective country's labor secretary for further consultation and eventual resolution.

But the system has never worked. The handful of cases submitted were never resolved. A decade after NAFTA took effect, UCLA researchers found that workers were already abandoning the process. "They are disillusioned and frustrated by the weak outcomes of ministerial consultations and the governments' refusal to pursue even the best-documented cases," the study concluded. Most *Maquiladora* workers aren't even aware that a grievance process through NAFTA exists.

The problem of workplace injuries is widespread. The companies under-report these incidents. In 2011, the year Moreno had her accident, the Mexican social security agency reported 17,302 workplace accidents. That same year, the United States, with three times the population of Mexico, reported 2.8 million workplace accidents.

Caught in the Global Big Squeeze

Mexico and its workers are caught in a bind. During the 2000s, some 200,000 Mexican jobs were lost to new, lower-wage competition from China. Now that Chinese wages have risen, those jobs are coming back. But the government and the companies are desperate not to let wages or other costs of employment rise, because they fear the multinationals will move somewhere else. The workers have no choice but to take the jobs under current conditions. It can be argued that LG can afford to treat its workers better. Profits at the multinationals have been piling up. But it is possible that the multinationals also are caught in the trap of the "race to the bottom." To the extent that a company's products are price sensitive, it may not be able to do any better by its workers than its competitors do.

So, at the end of the day, the problem may lie with American consumers' relentless pursuit of "the lowest price." In any event, Mexican workers are bearing the brunt of the system. As one of them told a reporter, "We are disposable." That can also be said of the American workers whose jobs were sent south.[50]

NAFTA's Perverse Feedback Loop

Which brings us to just how perverse this NAFTA relationship is. Charlie LeDuff ticked off the "American" companies operating in Reynosa: Caterpillar from Illinois, Kohler from Wisconsin, Corning from New York, textiles from the South, and Delphi Delco from Flint, Michigan.

LeDuff took his film crew to the abandoned Delphi factory in Flint, the birthplace of General Motors, Delphi's one-time parent company, and to the gate of the Delphi factory currently humming along in Reynosa, one of fifty Delphi operates in Mexico.[51] LeDuff points out that "Flint is now the murder capital of America. But Reynosa's worse, thanks to the drug and smuggling wars there."

So, there we have it – under NAFTA, we send Flint's jobs to Reynosa, creating demand for drugs in Flint, demand that is filled by gangs in Reynosa. We have "employed" workers living in shanty towns in Reynosa, and jobless workers living in slums in Flint, and drug wars going on among suppliers in Reynosa and distributors in Flint. And so things stood at the end of the second decade under NAFTA.

More Free Trade Agreements

Despite the experience under NAFTA, during the decade ending in 2015 the United States stepped up its trade agreement activities, concluding a number of new bilateral trade agreements.

On May 31, 2006, the U.S. and Vietnam signed an agreement updating the previous bilateral trade agreement, providing for the terms to govern trade between the two countries upon Vietnam's admission to the World Trade Organization. The agreement significantly reduced tariffs on nearly all goods. Textile and apparel quotas applied to Vietnam were to be removed upon accession by Vietnam to the WTO, and Vietnam agreed to terminate a major textile subsidy program. The agreement became effective upon Vietnam's admission to the World Trade Organization on January 11. 2007.[52]

The U.S. also entered into the U.S.-Korea Free Trade Agreement, effective March 15, 2012.[53] The White House fact sheet regarding the agreement claimed that the tariff cuts in the agreement would increase U.S. merchandise exports to Korea by $10 billion to $11 billion, creating 70,000 jobs, plus more jobs created by reduction of non-tariff barriers to goods and opening the Korean market to U.S. services.[54] As usual, the fact sheet made no mention of increased imports from Korea or how many U.S. jobs might be *lost* due to those imports. In Chapter 3, we will see how it turned out. Several other, less important free trade agreements also became effective during this period.[55] A list of current and proposed trade agreements is provided the Appendix.

Proposed Regional Trade Agreements

Also during this period, the U.S. pursued negotiations directed at two proposed major regional trade agreements.

The Trans-Atlantic Trade and Investment Partnership would establish special, regional rules of trade between the United States and the European Union. The White House and the European Commission have issued reports claiming that the agreement would create jobs and economic growth by increasing trade between the regions. Opponents have argued that the agreement would reduce the "regulatory barriers to trade for big business, things like food safety law, environmental legislation, banking regulations and the sovereign powers of individual nations."[56]

Such concerns, especially regarding corporations' rights to contest nations' environmental protection and safety laws, almost derailed the Canadian-European Trade Agreement. It was approved by both sides in 2016 only after amendments addressing these concerns. I would point out that Europe is by no means homogenous, and includes many nations that are middle, even low-wage, that could be problematic in a free trade relationship with the U.S.

The proposed Trans-Pacific Partnership is more problematic, in that it would establish free trade agreement-type rules among eleven countries rimming the Pacific Ocean, many of which are low-wage, developing countries. (See Appendix.) The NAFTA agreement with Canada and Mexico also would be rolled into the new agreement. Proponents saw it as opening opportunities for exports of U.S. services, opening data transfer, and protecting U.S. pharmaceutical and other patents. Opponents saw it as sending more U.S. jobs to Asia and undermining remaining jobs in the U.S., and transferring power from governments to corporations. The agreement became controversial during the 2016 presidential campaign, and upon taking office, President Trump announced the United States' withdrawal from the agreement.[57]

Worker and Environmental Protections

These new free trade agreements, and authority to negotiate the TPP and TTIP, gained congressional approval due to an agreement reached in May of 2007 between the George W. Bush White House and Democrats in the House of Representatives, to attach environmental and worker protections to the pending trade agreements with Colombia, Panama, Peru, and South Korea, and to serve as a template for future global, regional, and bilateral agreements. The agreed provisions would guarantee workers the right to organize, ban child labor and prohibit forced labor. They also would require trading partners to enforce environmental laws already on their books and comply with several international environmental agreements.[58]

Why it Can't Work

The Democratic members of the House and the labor unions fooled themselves into thinking that if labor rights and environmental protections were included, then trade agreements would not be harmful to the United States.

Let us first consider a hypothetical perfect world in which all the U.S. laws on these subjects were in effect in the foreign country and enforced to the same degree as in the U.S. There still would be the fundamental problem, never addressed, that the wages in the low-wage trading partner would be significantly lower than in the U.S. Given the freedom of investment and technology transfer, the foreign party to the trade agreement will always have an advantage that would not be overcome until the U.S. wages dropped enough, and the foreign country's wages rose enough, to equalize. This, of course, would be disastrous for U.S. workers, since the cost and standard of living in the U.S. are both higher than in the low-wage country. However, the harm would not stop there. Given the "footloose" character of the multinational companies, they would just move on to another low-wage country, as we have seen with companies leaving Mexico for China, and then returning to Mexico from China - all the while paying wages that are about one-tenth of the wages paid to equivalent U.S. workers.

But as bad as it would be, this hypothetical perfect world does not exist. Parties to our trade agreements do not adopt, and certainly do not enforce, labor and environmental laws that are equivalent to those of the U.S. A case in point is that of Rosa Moreno, the Mexican Maquiladora factory worker who lost her hands due to a malfunctioning machine. President Clinton and the Congress held off on approving NAFTA until side agreements on labor rights and environmental protection were agreed upon. The mechanism for workers to bring complaints of cases such as Moreno's is laughable. Most workers do not know it exists, and certainly do not have the resources to utilize it, and when they do the results are ineffectual. So, the situation is even worse than if they had done nothing, because now Washington has a fig leaf, and can say "we addressed the issue of labor protections," when in reality there are no protections. In China, similar or worse conditions prevail, as reported by Alexandra Harney in *The China Price* and by Beth Macy in *Factory Man*.

And yet the Obama administration, many members of Congress, and many academics and commentators have projected that the proposed Trans Pacific Partnership would result in the participating countries' adopting and enforcing labor, environmental, and other standards that are equivalent to those of the U.S.

In sum, labor and environmental protections in the less developed nations will never be equivalent to those in the

U.S., and if they were, wages in those countries will always be lower, dragging production to those countries, or dragging U.S. wages down, or both.

Product Sectors under Attack

During the decade leading up to 2015, American industries continued to suffer at the hands of foreign competitors and "American" corporations sending production offshore. The following examples give a flavor of what was going on.

Light Bulbs in Winchester, Virginia

I had the "light bulb moment" that led to this book in December of 2012. A couple of years earlier, I would have been able to find an incandescent light bulb that bore the GE logo and the legend "USA" instead of "CHINA." However, in September of 2010, GE closed its last incandescent light bulb factory, located in Winchester, Virginia. There was some irony involved. The Obama administration and members of Congress had been saying that new technology, especially in the green sector, would create many new American jobs. However, in this case, federal standards enacted in 2007 pushed the lighting industry toward compact fluorescent light (CFL) bulbs; because their production was more labor-intensive, their production grew up offshore, primarily in China. It was not clear why GE could not convert the Winchester plant to production of halogen lights, as Sylvania had done with its plant in St. Mary's, Pennsylvania. Or why no one was interested in working with a Chinese CFL producer who wanted to open a plant in the U.S. It was clear, however, that the terminated workers would have great difficulty finding other work in the Shenandoah Valley that would pay anywhere near the $30 an hour they had been earning at the GE plant, especially those in their late 40s and 50s. As one worker put it, "We gave GE the best years of our lives."[59] I drove through Winchester recently, and it had that all-too-familiar feel of a formerly lovely town that had seen better days and faced an uncertain future.

Bridge Steel from China

The eight-mile Bay Bridge linking San Francisco and Oakland was damaged in an earthquake in 1989, and the State of California needed to replace it. The project included a multi-billion-dollar contract to supply the steel components of the bridge. California governor Arnold Schwarzenegger encouraged the Chinese to submit a bid. [60]

Zhenhua Heavy Industries operated a Steel plant thirty minutes outside Shanghai. Compared to a typical American steel fabricating facility, which might have 300 to 1,000 people, the Chinese facility employed 32,000 people. One American steel executive remarked, “It is not even a contest.” American Bridge Company of Coraopolis, Pennsylvania, that had provided steel for the Golden Gate Bridge and the Brooklyn Bridge, but now was only an assembler, wanted to put together a consortium of American companies that could do the job. The project went to the Chinese firm. Schwarzenegger traveled to China to celebrate with the Chinese workers.[61]

The project was plagued with quality problems and cost overruns. However, the major point that jumps out is that it does not seem to have occurred to California’s politicians and bureaucrats that companies and individuals making the steel for the bridge would have income from which to pay taxes to the cash-strapped state. Or that the Inland Empire, which once made steel for liberty ships but now, as a distribution center for imported products, was economically depressed and a drain on state coffers, could be making steel again.

New York made the same miscalculations with respect to specialty steel plates for renovation of the Verrazano-Narrows Bridge, North America's longest suspension bridge. The agency that awarded the contract claimed that the U.S. steel industry has atrophied to the point where the contract winner had to reach out to a Chinese firm to produce the plates. However, the United Steel Workers asserted that it had located two firms who could do the work. And, as with the Bay Bridge, welding quality issues have arisen. And so it goes.[62]

IBM in Endicott, New York

IBM was founded in Endicott, Broome County, New York, and its first factories were located there. From 2001 to 2015, Broome County employment in computer and electronics manufacturing fell from about 9,000 to 3,000. Laid-off workers were reemployed in warehouses and at transportation companies at less than half their former pay.[63]

Circuit Boards in Chicago

From its origins in the first plant outside Chicago in 1952, the U.S. printed circuit board industry grew to some $10 billion in sales in 2000, accounting for 30 percent of world production. Chinese, Korean, and other producers, subsidized by their governments, began selling into the U.S. at prices that undercut the U.S. domestic producers. The U.S. industry turned to Congress for help, but received none. By 2012, the industry's sales were down from $10 billion to $3 billion.[64]

Solar Photovoltaics

Solar photovoltaics were invented at Bell Laboratories in 1954. In the 1980s, the United States was the leading producer of the panels that used the process to convert the sun's rays to electricity. However, the Chinese government decided to capture the market, and began a program to build a solar photovoltaic industry in China. Barlett and Steele report that the program included low-cost loans, land purchase subsidies, water and power at discounted prices, tax exemptions, and export grants. All these practices are illegal under the WTO rules, but China pursued them nevertheless, and produced an industry that, through low-cost pricing, has taken over the world market. The U.S. industry sought tariff relief from these practices, citing the closure of multiple U.S. plants and resulting job losses in states from California to Massachusetts. The resulting tariffs were too low to make a difference. Chinese imports surged from $21.3 million in 2005 to $2.65 billion in 2011. By 2011, Chinese imports accounted for more than 50 percent of the U.S. market.[65]

GM sells Isuzu trucks as "GM"

General Motors used to produce medium-duty trucks, under the Chevrolet Kodiak and GMC Topkick nameplates, at a plant in Flint, Michigan. GM shut down the line while it was in bankruptcy during the 2008-2009 recession and couldn't find a buyer for the plant. GM dealers with fleet customers had been asking for years that GM reintroduce the medium-duty trucks, because those customers typically needed such trucks for their fleets and wanted one-stop shopping, and they were missing out on these sales.

Rather than re-starting its line in Flint, and yes, that's the same economically depressed Flint that lost the Delco plant, with plenty of underutilized manpower available, in 2015 GM arranged to purchase a line of medium-duty trucks made in Japan by Isuzu and slap the GM logo on them (some models would have the option of a GM engine) – another lost opportunity to re-employ American workers.[66]

Job Deserts: Milwaukee, Wisconsin

Flint is an example of how we have been creating "job deserts" in American cities and communities. Milwaukee is another. From 1990 to 2014, more than half of Milwaukee's neighborhoods experienced declines of median household income of between 25 and 50 percent, some more than 50 percent. A major contributor was the closing of the Tower Automotive factory, putting thousands of workers out of a job.[67]

Information Technology

The offshoring was not limited to manufacturing jobs. On July 29, 2010, PriceWaterhouseCoopers announced that PwC's entire information technology division, comprising some eight hundred employees in Tampa, Florida, was being closed, and its functions would be performed in India by Tata Consultancy Services of India.[68]

Conditions Abroad – "I am a feminist"

This decade saw continued utilization abroad of the "Factory Labor Camp" model, with employees working ten- and twelve-hour shifts, often standing the entire time, and living in Spartan dormitories, often with inadequate toilet and laundry facilities.

We will see in Chapter 8 how the model has been applied with a vengeance in China. However, these practices have been widespread; in Chapter 2, we saw how as early as 1960 the Hong Kong textile industry was reported to be using them. During the decade 2006-2015, these conditions persisted, as evidenced by an ironic episode unearthed by the British newspaper the Daily Mail.

A British women's labor rights group, The Fawcett Society, backed by the fashion magazine Elle, launched a campaign in which the British retail chain Whistles was selling T-shirts bearing the message "I am a feminist," with profits to go to the Society. The T-shirts were donned by members of Parliament and other luminaries.

However, the Daily Mail discovered that the T-shirts had been produced by a company on the Indian Ocean island of Mauritius operating a classic factory labor camp. Migrant women from India, Bangladesh, Sri Lanka, and Vietnam signed four-year contracts to work at the facility, without contact with their families. 2,800 women workers were expected to produce 50 shirts a day and disciplined for failing to meet their quota.

They earned 77 cents an hour, far below prevailing wages on Mauritius, working shifts of up to twelve hours. They lived sixteen to a twenty-square-foot room furnished only with metal bunk beds with thin mattresses and some shelves for their belongings, and were confined to the facility during the work week. They told the Daily Mail that they didn't feel like feminists at all; to the contrary they felt "trapped." Meanwhile, Whistles was selling the T-shirts, which cost a reported eleven dollars to make, for $56 and change.[69]

Snapshot in 2015

Beginning with the demonstrations in Seattle in 1999, the World Trade Organization became unable to advance further multilateral agreements, due to disputes between the "have" and "have not" countries. The U.S. government tried to fight the Great Recession with a goal of doubling exports in five years. In fact, exports increased a mere twelve percent.

Under NAFTA, Mexican auto exports to the U.S. exploded, with Mexico surpassing Japan as the number two exporter to the U.S. Nevertheless, the U.S. pursued further trade agreements, signing an updated trade agreement with Vietnam and a new agreement with South Korea, plus several others, and negotiating regional agreements with Europe and in the Pacific Rim.

Whole industries were being wiped out by imports, including such high-tech products as circuit boards and solar photovoltaics. Governments awarded large infrastructure projects such as the Oakland Bay Bridge and the Verrazano-Narrows Bridge to Chinese steel companies. GM slapped its logo on trucks made by Isuzu rather than restart its closed medium-duty truck plant in Flint, Michigan.

When trade in goods and services was tallied up for the decade ending in 2015, the U.S. had sent a net $6.1 trillion overseas (in 2016 dollars). For the decade ending in 1985, that figure had been $1.1 trillion; in 1995, $1.7 trillion; and in 2005, $4.8 trillion. Now it was $6.1 trillion. Do we see a trend here? What will the number be in 2025? We will address that important question in Chapter 9. But first, we will consider, *why* did all of this happen?

Notes to Chapter 3

---

[1] The Information Technology Agreement, on July 1, 1997; the Basic Telecommunications Agreement, on Feb. 6, 1998, and the Financial Services Agreement, on Jan. 29, 1999.

[2] World Trade Organization Protests in Seattle," Seattle Municipal Archives. http://www.seattle.gov/cityarchives/exhibits-and-education/digital-document-libraries/world-trade-organization-protests-in-seattle.

[3] "World leaders resist joining Seattle talks," *Financial Times*, November 24, 1999.

[4] *See* Baldwin, Richard, "Future." Meanwhile, China has signed bilateral trade agreements with dozens of countries in Africa, Asia, and Latin America. In return for loans and technical or business support, Chinese companies receive rights to develop the country's oil and other commodities.

[5] Pub. L. No. 106-200, May 18, 2000.

[6] The African Growth and Opportunity Act (AGOA), amending the Generalized System of Preferences program.

[7] U.S. Caribbean Basin Trade Partnership Act, amending the Caribbean Basin Economic Recovery Act (CBERA).

[8] Pub. L. No. 107-210, August 6, 2002. The Act also included the authorization of trade promotion (formerly "fast track) authority for negotiation of further trade agreements.

[9] U.S. House of Representative video archives, captured in *American Jobs*, documentary film directed by Greg Spotts, at 0.16:17.

[10] Christina Rogers and Dudley Althaus, "It's Getting Harder and More Expensive to Make Cars in Mexico," Wall Street Journal, August 14, 2016. http://www.wsj.com/articles/mexicos-auto-production-boom-is-driving-up-labor-costs-1471201920

[11] Chad Broughton, *Boom, Bust, Exodus: The Rust Belt, the Maquilas, and a Tale of Two Cities* ((Oxford: Oxford University Press, 2015).

[12] Jose Skinner, Book Review: How NAFTA Transformed a Mexican Border Town," Texas Observer, April 22, 2015.
https://www.texasobserver.org/how-nafta-transformed-a-mexican-border-town/.

[13] *Id.*

---

[14] In December of 1994, at the Summit of the Americas, the participants pledged to complete negotiations for a free trade agreement of the Americas by 2005. However, this did not come to pass.

[15] In 1998, the crisis spread to Russia and Argentina.

[16]Rosen, *Sweatshops,* 248; Prestowitz, *Betrayal,* 124.

[17] Prestowitz, *Betrayal,* 140.

[18] Prestowitz, *Betrayal,* 141.

[19] Prestowitz, *Betrayal,* 142.

[20] Pierce and Schott captured some of this pent-up demand in the quotes assembled in the appendix to their paper, "The Surprisingly Swift Decline of US Manufacturing Employment." *See* discussion at Chapter 6.

[21] After a drop during the 2008-2009 recession, the deficit has continued to grow, as I describe in the next chapter, to some $370 billion during 2015.

[22] Hornblower, "Joint Venture."

[23] Rosen, *Sweatshops,* 230.

[24] *Id.*

[25] Barlett and Steele, *Betrayal,* 83 *ff.*

[26] Beth Macy, *Factory Man: How One Furniture Maker Battled Offshoring, Stayed Local - and Helped Save an American Town* (New York: Little, Brown & Company, 2014). I highly recommend this compelling, readable, and informative narrative of an industry's capitulation to the forces of globalization, except for one man and a band of like-minded manufacturers who thought they had a responsibility to their communities. The following discussion refers to facts reported by Macy in *Factory Man,* at 168-363.

[27] Macy, *Factory Man,* 362.

[28] Rubbermaid: "It was like a big family." Barlett and Steele, *Betrayal,* 41. Vise Grip: "You couldn't ask for a better place to work." Barlett and Steele, *Betrayal,* 75. Apple: "There was such a camaraderie. When we got off work, all we could talk about was Apple, Apple, Apple." Barlett and Steele, *Betrayal,* 87. Clyde Hooker, Jr., of Hooker Furniture in Martinsville, Virginia, knew every employee by name. Macy, *Factory Man,* 333.

[29] That was the case with Vise Grip, which was sold by the family in 1985 and ultimately purchased by Newell in 2002.

[30] That was the case with Rubbermaid, when Newell purchased it in 1999.

[31] See, for example, Vise-Grip under Newell, at Barlett and Steele, *Betrayal*, 77.

[32] The Rubbermaid plant in Wooster, Ohio was closed by Newell in 2004, the rubber division production sent to Mexico, and corporate staff to Atlanta. Barlett and Steele, *Betrayal*, 39 *ff*. In 2008, Newell closed the Vise-Grip plant in DeWitt, Nebraska, and moved its operations to China. Barlett and Steele, *Betrayal*, 78.

[33] We will pick up these stories in Chapters 6 and 7.

[34] The ASEAN countries are Indonesia, Malaysia, Philippines, Singapore and Thailand, Brunei Darussalam, Viet Nam, Lao PDR, Myanmar, and Cambodia.

[35] The only agreements reached were an agreement with Singapore, in 2004, and an amendment to the 2001 Vietnam agreement, in 2006. Brunei, Malaysia, and New Zealand would have been included in the Trans Pacific Partnership. However, in 2017, the U.S. withdrew from that agreement.

[36] Executive Order 13534. https://www.whitehouse.gov/the-press-office/executive-order-national-export-initiative.

[37] Public Law 102-429; The TPCC was established by Executive Order 12870 in September of 1993.

[38] Trade and Globalization Adjustment Assistance Act of 2009, part of the American Recovery and Reinvestment Act, Public Law 111-5.

[39] Alex Lawson, "DOL Gives Strong Review of TAA Program," Law360, June 14, 2016.

[40] Brendan Case, "Mexico Surpassing Japan as No. 2 Auto Exporter to U.S.," *Bloomberg*, January 31, 2014.
http://www.bloomberg.com/news/articles/2014-01-31/mexico-surpassing-japan-as-no-2-auto-exporter-to-u-s-.

[41] Some of the Mexican increase came at the expense of exports from Japan: several Japanese companies opened plants in Mexico to serve the U.S. market. However, it should be noted that these plants could have been built in the United States, as Japanese companies have done in the past.

[42] Ben Bain, "Mexico auto exports forecast to hit record in 2015," Automotive News/Bloomberg, February 6, 2015.
http://www.autonews.com/article/20150206/OEM01/302069972/mexico-auto-exports-forecast-to-hit-record-in-2015

[43] Dustin Ensinger, "Whirlpool Moving Jobs to Mexico," economyincrisis.org, February 22, 2010.
http://economyincrisis.org/content/whirlpool-moving-jobs-mexico

[44] PBS Newshour, "Revisiting Evansville, Two Years After Whirlpool's Move South," *Need to Know*, October 28, 2011. http://www.pbs.org/newshour/bb/business-july-dec11 needtoknow_10-28/

[45] Susan Orr, "Whirlpool Benefits Clawed Back." Indiana Business Journal, October 20, 2016. http://www.ibj.com/articles/60906-mayor-unsure-how-much-of-rexnord-incentives-city-could-claw-back

[46] Suzi Parker, "Arkansas town braces as Whirlpool shuts big plant," Reuters, October 31, 2011. http://www.reuters.com/article/us-whirlpool-arkansas-idUSTRE79U5QK20111031

[47] There has been occasional good news. In December of 2013, Whirlpool announced that it was moving some of its washing-machine production from Monterrey, Mexico to a plant in Clyde, Ohio, creating 80 to 100 jobs. James R. Hagerty, "Whirlpool Shifts Some Production to U.S. From Mexico," Wall Street Journal, December 19, 2013. http://www.wsj.com/articles/SB100014240527023047731045792 68560299331976.

[48] Charlie LeDuff, "Happy Twentieth Anniversary, NAFTA!" *The Americans with Charlie LeDuff.*

[49] While I was watching LeDuff's documentary, the YouTube algorithm presented me with the following advertisement: "This July fourth, let's think about what it means to be independent, to be free; that's what built manufacturing in America, and it's what will rebuild it." Caption: "Because work is a beautiful thing." Logo: "Walmart. Save money. Live better." I swear; you can't make this stuff up.

[50] Melissa del Bosque, "We are disposable," Texas Observer, December 11, 2013. https://www.texasobserver.org/disposable/.

[51] LeDuff reported that Delphi, whose U.S. employment dropped from 50,000 workers to 5,000, now employs 50,000 in Mexico. The company declared bankruptcy in 2005, effectively dumping its pension obligations onto the American taxpayer, and received billions in bailout money from General Motors, then created a tax shelter in England. Meanwhile, its profits are soaring, and the company declares in the Form 10-Q on its web site that it delivers "industry-leading shareholder value."

[52] Office of the U.S. Trade Representative. http://www.trade.gov/press/press_releases/2006/vietnam_053106.asp.

[53] The Korea-U.S. FTA was negotiated and signed on June 30, 2007, by President George W. Bush. However, President Bush did not submit the legislation because of differences with the Democratic leadership over treatment of autos and beef, among other issues. On December 3, 2010, after a series of negotiations, President Obama and South Korean President Lee announced that they had reached an agreement on addressing the outstanding issues. The final implementing legislation modified certain provisions of the 2007agreement, primarily focused on trade in agriculture and autos; the agreement retained some tariffs protecting the U.S. auto industry, which it scheduled to expire in 2021. Brock R. Williams, et al, "The U.S.-Korea Free Trade Agreement (KORUS FTA): Provisions and Implementation." *Congressional Research Service*, September 16, 2014.

[54] "The U.S.-South Korea Free Trade Agreement: More American Jobs, Faster Economic Recovery Through Exports."
https://www.whitehouse.gov/sites/default/files/fact_sheet_overview_us_korea_free_trade_agreement.pdf.
See also Chrissie Thompson, "Obama: South Korean free trade creates 70,000 U.S. jobs," USA Today and Detroit Free Press, October 14, 2011. http://content.usatoday.com/communities/driveon/post/2011/10/obama-south-korean-free-trade-will-create-70000-us-jobs/1#.WB3dIvorJPa.

[55] In the Middle East, the U.S.-Bahrain Free Trade Agreement (effective August 1, 2006) and the U.S.-Oman Free Trade Agreement (effective January 1, 2009); in Latin America, the U.S.-Peru Trade Promotion Agreement (effective February 1, 2009), the U.S.-Colombia Free Trade Agreement (effective May 15, 2012), and the U.S.-Panama Trade Promotion Agreement (effective October 31, 2012).

[56] Lee Williams What is TTIP? And six reasons why the answer should scare you, *The Independent*, October 6, 2015.

[57] Kevin Granville, "The Trans-Pacific Partnership Trade Deal Explained," New York Times, May 11, 2015.
http://www.nytimes.com/2015/05/12/business/unpacking-the-trans-pacific-partnership-trade-deal.html?_r=0
Jonathan Weisman, "Trade Authority Bill Wins Final Approval in Senate," New York Times, June 24, 2015.
http://www.nytimes.com/2015/06/25/business/trade-pact-senate-vote-obama.html
Kevin Granville, "This Was the Trans-Pacific Partnership," New York Times, November 11, 2016.
http://www.nytimes.com/interactive/2016/business/tpp-explained-what-is-trans-pacific-partnership.html.

"The United States Officially Withdraws from the Trans-Pacific Partnership," Office of the United States Trade Representative, January 30, 2017. http://www.ustr.gov.

[58] Other provisions would ease the sale of generic drugs in foreign countries; preserve the right of the U.S. to prevent foreign companies from running American ports; and prevent foreign investors from acquiring more rights than American investors in the U.S. There also was agreement to step up training for workers losing their jobs to imports. Steven R. Weisman, "Bush and Democrats in Accord on Trade Deals, New York Times, May 11, 2007.
http://www.nytimes.com/2007/05/11/business/11trade.html

[59] Peter Whoriskey, "Light bulb factory closes; End of era for U.S. means more jobs overseas," *Washington Post*, September 8, 2010.

[60] Barlett and Steele, Betrayal, 225.

[61] *Id.*

[62] Staten Island Advance Editorial, "What's the deal on Verrazano-Narrows Bridge steel? (editorial)," sillive.com, June 19,2014. Peter Navarro, "The Price of 'Made in China,'" *New York Times*, August 3, 2013.

[63] Jon Hilsenrath, "Tech Boom Creates Too Few Jobs," Wall Street Journal, October 13, 2016.

[64] Barlett and Steele, *Betrayal,* 223.

[65] Barlett and Steele, *Betrayal,* 234.

[66] Mike Colias, "GM returns to medium-duty truck market, partners with Isuzu," Automotive News, June 15, 2015.

http://www.autonews.com/article/20150615/OEM01/150619921/gm-returns-to-medium-duty-truck-market-partners-with-isuzu.

[67] Shibani Mahtani and Scott Calvert, "City Neighborhoods Declined as Factory Jobs Evaporated," *Wall Street Journal*, August 15, 2016.

[68] Barlett and Steele, *Betrayal*, 115.

[69] Ben Ellery, "62p an Hour: What women sleeping 16 to a room get paid to make Ed and Harriet's £45 'This Is What a Feminist Looks Like' T-shirts."
http://www.dailymail.co.uk/news/article-2817191/62p-HOUR-s-women-sleeping-16-room-paid-make-Ed-Harriet-s-45-Feminist-Looks-Like-T-shirts.html#ixzz3TlJCh72M.

Chapter 4

Why did this happen?

The Move to Unregulated Markets & Free Trade

We have seen in Chapters 1 through 3 *how* America's trade policy and participation in globalization have unfolded over seven decades, resulting in large trade imbalances. But *why* did this happen? We saw hints in the U.S. government's goals of combatting communism and supporting economic development in the third world, and in companies' goals of maximizing profits. However, it turns out that economic and political *ideas* have played an important role. As John Maynard Keynes wrote:

> . . . [T]he ideas of economists and political philosophers, both when they are right and when they are wrong, are more powerful than is commonly understood. Indeed, the world is ruled by little else.[1]

And indeed, there is a link between economic theory and politics, since it is the political process that often takes economic ideas and expresses them in the form of policy or regulation.

The Invisible Hand and Laissez-Faire

To understand why we arrived at our present juncture, we must return to Adam Smith and his economic treatise published in 1776, *The Wealth of Nations*.[2]

Smith's thinking has been passed down and adopted under the concept of the "Invisible Hand," the proposition that buyers and sellers, by pursuing their self-interest in an open market free of any government interference, will arrive at an "optimal" pricing and distribution of goods and services, as if guided by an unseen hand.[3]

Smith did not propose the principle in as pure a fashion as this; for example, he spent a good deal of his writing discussing when the government should and should not be involved in the guidance and regulation of markets.[4] However, what is important for our purposes is how his idea has been interpreted and promoted. In shorthand, it is this: because of the movement of the "invisible hand," markets, when left alone ("*laissez-faire*"), will provide socially desirable, or at least "efficient," results.[5]

The trouble with the invisible hand is that it doesn't comport with experience. Smith wrote just before the industrial revolution visited all sorts of privations and suffering in the factories, mines, and cities of England, Scotland, and Wales. These continued on the other side of the Atlantic in America, into the nineteenth and twentieth centuries. To these troubles we may add pricing distortions created by monopolists and cartels, and fake and unsafe products - quite literally "snake oil."

As these experiences and others indicate, no invisible hand was guiding the market to socially optimal results. Several modern studies discredit the idea of an invisible hand, going so far as to call it "tooth fairy economics."[6] And yet, the idea has guided much economic and political thought and policy in America and other parts of the world.[7]

The American Mixed Economy

Over time, the United States adopted a market economy largely based on Smith's principles, but tempered by a public sector owning and operating "public goods" such as roads and schools, and by rules designed to rein in abuse of the market.

For example, at the beginning of the twentieth century, when Standard Oil and others captured market share by throwing their weight around, we enacted antitrust laws to protect against the monopolies and anticompetitive practices that Adam Smith had railed against. And when hucksters were selling snake oil and adulterated products, we enacted truth in advertising and safe food and drug laws.

In the 1930s, when banks took too much risk with people's deposits and stocks were sold based on false or limited information, we enacted banking and securities laws. We also adopted policies, based on the work of John Maynard Keynes, to temper the business cycle through fiscal policy (expanding or contracting taxing and spending) and monetary policy (expanding or contracting the money supply). We also enacted wage and collective bargaining laws and national old age, survivors, and disability insurance ("Social Security").

In the 1960s and 70s, after Rachel Carson published *Silent Spring* and the Cuyahoga river caught fire in Cleveland, we took steps to clean up our air, land, and water, and protect against injuries in the workplace and from consumer products. And we enacted medical care for the elderly and protections for private pensions.

Operating a market economy within this framework of rules, referred to as a "mixed economy," [8] from 1947 through 1974, the U.S. experienced the thirty years of economic growth known here as the "Golden Age" and in France as the "Golden Thirty." [9]

The "Efficient Market"

Meanwhile, in the 1960s and 1970s, Smith's invisible hand was being resuscitated, in what came to be known as the "Efficient Market Hypothesis." The EMH holds that rational, intelligent profit-maximizers participating in the stock market where information is freely available leads to an "efficient market" in which the current price of a stock will reflect its intrinsic value. [10] The participants may not act rationally, over- or under-reacting to information, but the average of their decisions will be rational.[11]

The Efficient Market Hypothesis has been contested by critics such as Yale University economist Robert Shiller. Schiller has noted that people are influenced in their behavior in the market by the stories they tell themselves and each other about the economy.[12] And, indeed, we see markets driven by optimism, herd mentality, and greed, experiencing business cycles and bubbles that should not exist at all under the Efficient Market Hypothesis.[13]

Nevertheless, the Efficient Market Hypothesis has been widely held, and led to the proposal of a corollary principle: that regulation only causes distortions, so removing regulations increases efficiency and reduces risk. This line of thinking, sometimes referred to as "market fundamentalism,"[14] adopts market effectiveness as the foundational principle of action, with the accompanying goal of reduction of state involvement in the economy. Based on the work of Friedrich von Hayek and Milton Friedman, this line of thought proposes that a market freed of state controls can best deliver economic growth, and that economic growth will lead to well-being, freedom, democracy, and liberty. There is a tendency to believe, and insist, that whatever outcomes the unfettered (domestic and global) market produces are by definition "the good." Closely akin to this is the belief that the unfettered market will produce a predefined social good.[15]

Another formulation of this line of thought has been under the rubric of "competitiveness."[16] The idea is that if an efficient market creates the greatest social welfare, then welfare will be maximized when firms compete successfully in the market, through productivity and efficiency. At the national level, "national competitiveness" is proposed as essential to a country's ability to improve its citizens' quality of life. Higher productivity increases return on investment, which generates economic growth, which is an important factor in improved quality of life.[17]

The Washington Consensus

This line of reasoning gained force in the 1980s as it was adopted in the United States and the United Kingdom.[18] In the international realm, it has been adopted by international development agencies such as the International Monetary Fund. In this context, it is known as the "Washington Consensus," and has been spread to other countries as it was imposed as a condition of loans made to struggling counties by the IMF. In the international context, the Washington Consensus --

> . . . rests on two main planks. The first is increased competition—achieved through deregulation and the opening up of domestic markets, including financial markets, to foreign competition. The second is a smaller role for the state, achieved through privatization and limits on the ability of governments to run fiscal deficits and accumulate debt."[19]

General Theory of Free Trade

The Washington Consensus includes as one of its main planks the opening-up of markets to international competition. This has been done through the adoption by American and global policy makers of the principle of "free trade." As I discussed in Chapter 1, the policy has its roots in the writings of Adam Smith and David Ricardo, particularly in the application of the principle of "comparative advantage." [20]

The idea is that nations will realize the "best" economic results if they sell to other nations those goods in which they have a "comparative advantage." Doing so "distributes labor most effectively and economically" and "increas[es] the general mass of productions" to the general benefit, binding nations together: "It is this principle which determines that wine shall be made in France and Portugal, that corn shall be grown in America and Poland, and that hardware and other goods shall be manufactured in England." [21]

Ricardo uses the example of trade between England and Portugal in cloth and wine. If Portugal is more efficient at making wine than cloth, it will be better off selling England wine and purchasing cloth, even if Portugal can make both wine and cloth at lower cost than can England. Ricardo's work also is interpreted as meaning that even if one country excludes or taxes the goods of a second country, the second country may still be better off buying the products of the first country than in producing them at home at a higher price. That is, even "unilateral free trade" can benefit a country.[22]

In the twentieth century, Ricardo's theory was updated and expanded into the "Hecksher-Ohlin factor proportions" model, that added land, capital and technology to the factors of production and distinguished between skilled and unskilled labor. This model has been referred to as the "benchmark model."[23]

The benchmark model is applied under the following assumptions: markets are completely open and competitive and free of distortions such as subsidies; firms are small and there are no economies of scale; Each country's economy is operating at full capacity and full employment; there are no costs of entry into business; labor is perfectly mobile and fungible; all goods and services are tradable, exchange rates are fixed, and trade is always balanced.

As is immediately obvious, this is a list of quite unrealistic assumptions. Quite frankly, I was shocked as I researched this book to learn that the theory underpinning free trade policy was based on assumptions so patently inapplicable to the real world. In recent years, there has developed a widespread recognition among economists that the model is generally inapplicable to reality.[24]

And yet, free trade continues to dominate U.S. policy at all levels of government, business, and academia. I will now try to tease out the various ways we have seen it applied: I believe many of these will sound familiar to you.

Specific Theories of Free Trade

Have everything done by someone else

Let me begin with a hypothetical case; it has not been proposed, but it is not far off some of the policies that have been proposed and followed and it is a helpful point of departure. The case is this: let's just have everything made and done by someone else somewhere else, and sit back and relax. As in the Veggie Tales® episodes my kids used to watch, we can be "the pirates who don't do anything."

However, some work must be performed in person, and so is not "tradable." We could solve this problem through immigration - just bring in foreign workers to do all the non-tradable work. So, the tradable work could be done abroad, and the non-tradable work done by immigrants.

The obvious question posed by this approach is, how would we earn a living? Economic activity consists of producing goods or services and exchanging at least some of them for goods and services others have produced. Even fishermen and farmers must produce somewhat in excess of their needs to exchange for the things they cannot produce.

The only escape from this formula seems to be the case where one owns a resource such as land or mineral deposits, the rights to which one can sell or lease to another, and can just sit back and collect the income. This can be done at the national level, for example, in the case of North Sea Oil. Or, where the social system permits, one may save, or be the beneficiary of gifts or inheritance of, enough money or other assets that throw off income or can be sold.

At the end of the day, however, the general rule is that we each need to produce salable goods and services to earn a living. So, the question becomes, *how much of this productive activity can we have done outside our borders*?

Have everything tradable done offshore

One answer is everything possible - that is, everything that is "tradable," and we will do only the things that must be done in person. Due to the revolutionary improvements in shipping and communications, one hundred percent of manufacturing, and all services except those that must be done in person, are "tradable" - that is, we can have them made or done outside the U.S.

The first problem with this approach is that we must pay for the foreign work - how will we earn the money to pay for it, if we are only performing non-tradable services? One way is to sell the non-tradable, domestic services to foreign persons who are visiting the United States, for example, tourism, medical care, or education.

This actually is a fairly accurate picture of Grenada, a Caribbean island with hotels and a medical school - these were its source of income with which to pay for all of the tradable goods and services it purchased off-island. However, is it possible to operate a large economy of more than 300 million people in this manner? The answer certainly is no.

Another way to pay for foreign-produced goods and services is to sell assets. And, in fact, we have done a good deal of that, as in the case of the sale of the Rockefeller Center and the Pebble Beach golf resort to Japanese interests to cover the large trade deficit we were running with Japan. We also can sell companies, and a good bit of that is going on now, especially with China. However, this obviously is not a sufficient or sustainable strategy.

A closely related approach is the sale of natural resources. This is what the oil-rich Persian Gulf countries do. They buy nearly everything that is tradable, in exchange for their oil. This is not a sustainable strategy even for them, because they will run out of oil, and in the meantime, cannot control its price. (So, they are trying to diversify, to tourism and other activities.) It is certainly not a sustainable strategy for the United States due to our size and lack of excess capacity of such resources.

The final asset that may be sold is savings. The oil producing countries like Saudi Arabia are doing this now, but even with their extensive "sovereign wealth funds," they already have had to resort to the final way to pay for foreign-produced goods and services: through borrowing.

I have led you through this exercise partly to emphasize this conclusion: tourism and sales of real estate and oil will never be sufficient to pay for a sizable trade deficit: the only significant way to do so is to borrow the money, and that is what the United States has been doing these many years now.

But back to the question at hand. We can safely conclude that it is not feasible to have everything tradable made and done abroad, if only because we must earn enough money to pay for what we buy. So, if we do not send *all* the tradable work offshore, the question becomes:

> *What part of the tradeable work will we send abroad, and what part will we retain at home?*

This is where we pick up the half-baked and destructive policies that we have been pursuing for the past seventy years.

Have the low-skill tradable work done offshore

The next line of reasoning was, okay, then, we will offshore all the *low-skill* manufacturing and tradable service functions, and only engage in the high-skill ones -- both to serve our own market and to sell in the foreign markets in exchange for the low-skill functions we would buy from them. It is surprising how prevalent this line of thinking has been.

The first problem with it is that it assumes that all Americans are high-skilled, or capable of becoming high-skilled. I call it the "Lake Wobegon" view of America, after Garrison Keillor's fictional town "where all the women are strong, all the men are good looking, and all the children are above average."

The fact is, intelligence quotient ("IQ") is distributed across the population in a bell curve. Half of Americans have below-average intelligence, and just as many have very low intelligence as have very high. [25] *Sending all the tradable low-skill work overseas does not leave behind enough of such work for the low-skill population. Low-skill workers wind up competing against each other and driving down wages for the remaining, non-tradable low-skill jobs.*

The second problem with this approach is that *the foreign countries refuse to buy into it.* The high-skill functions, both in manufacturing and in services, are "high value added," and tend to be compensated at higher rates in proportion to that value. So, everyone is constantly trying to move up the value chain, and they are quite capable of doing so, often with the assistance of American education, capital and technology. They are not about to sign on to an arrangement where America keeps all the high-skill work.

The third problem with this approach is that *the "American" companies refuse to buy into it.* Because they don't think of themselves as "American" at all: Ford, Boeing, General Electric, all of them now refer to themselves as "global" companies. All of them are actively placing high-skill functions in research, development, and manufacturing facilities in China, Korea, and other locations abroad.[26]

For these reasons, this strategy hasn't worked. By 2005, this had become evident to U.S. Senator Pete Dominici, who said, "We thought we'd keep the high-end jobs, and others would take the low-end jobs. We're now on track to [be] a second-rate economy and a second-rate country." [27] So, if we are tempted to think that it is a good idea to locate that toy factory or call center abroad, we need to remind ourselves that, *no, we need those jobs.*

Stick with our "comparative advantage"

Another answer to the question has been that we should make those things and perform those services where we have a comparative advantage - because that is where we will be able to "out-compete" the rest of the world. This proposition is applied both at the company level, and at the national level.

Here is where we confront the limitations inherent in the theory of comparative advantage.

Perhaps the most important is this: *it is strategically unwise for a country to specialize.* First, specializing leaves a country dependent on others for entire segments of its economy. This leads to a loss of independence: the foreign producer, if it has market power, can raise the price. This is what the members of the Organization of Petroleum Exporting Countries (OPEC) did in 1973, quadrupling the price of oil in one fell swoop, and, I would submit, ending the thirty-year run of increasing prosperity in the western economies.

On the other side of the coin, specialization can leave a country subject to the vagaries of the world market. So, for example, Russia and Venezuela have specialized heavily in production of crude oil, and now are suffering as the price has dropped from $100 to $50 a barrel. South Africa is suffering as tastes are shifting toward synthetic diamonds and away from the real thing. Specialization tends to be worse for producers of commodities, but it also is dangerous in manufactured goods, and that leads us to the next shortcoming of the theory:

Comparative advantage is not static and immutable - it can be here today and gone tomorrow.[28] This is probably the major limitation to Ricardo's theory: it assumes that countries have inherent advantages that never change. But we have already seen that America was not content to produce corn and get its manufactured goods from England. So, too, Japan was not content to produce tuna, or even to produce low-price, labor-intensive products. Like the U.S. in earlier days, Japan intentionally embarked on a path of industrialization, until it had a comparative advantage in many sophisticated manufactured goods.

Reserving our production of goods and services to only those sectors where we have a comparative advantage ultimately will fail - especially in today's world, where "American" companies are busily sending our hard-won proprietary technologies to their joint venture partners and subsidiaries in China, Korea, and elsewhere.

And, as we have seen, even if we could hang onto comparative advantage, *a specialized economy is a vulnerable economy*. Perhaps Iceland and Luxembourg have no choice but to specialize. But for a large economy such as that of the United States, *a diversified economy must be the goal.*

Have everything made somewhere else

In addition to high-skill versus low-skill and comparative advantage, another answer has been offered to our question of what to import and what to export: going back as far as the 1980s, it was suggested that we would become a "post-industrial" society that would not make anything, but rather would only produce services. We would buy all our manufactured goods from foreign suppliers. In exchange, we would sell them services that we produced in excess of our domestic needs. I am amazed at how much traction this idea got, at the highest levels of academia and government.

There were numerous problems with this approach. First, the foreign countries did not want to buy our services, and they put up all kinds of barriers to them. Second, with the advent of the Internet, foreign countries wanted to *sell* services into the U.S. market, not buy them. So, we couldn't count on the domestic services sector replacing manufacturing, because so much of the U.S. service sector was being performed offshore, for example, in India. Third, as discussed, it is a bad idea to become dependent on foreign sources for manufactured goods, especially for products necessary for national security.

Finally, we should note that sending manufacturing offshore pulls a lot of things with it. For example, extraction also can be sent overseas. In many, probably most, cases, the foreign country doing the manufacturing would also like to be mining the iron or aluminum or silica used in the making. So, when a steel mill closes in Indiana, an iron mine closes in Minnesota. In any event, for the reasons I have discussed, it would be imprudent to focus on extraction to the exclusion of manufacturing, for example, producing lumber sent abroad to make furniture for the U.S. market. Perhaps more importantly, offshore manufacturing also can take with it a myriad of related services, including design, engineering, and financial services.

So, *having everything made somewhere else, and being "post-industrial," is not a sustainable strategy for the United States or any other major country.*

Have low-tech things made and done offshore

Another answer looks not to the nature of the work (high-skill versus low-skill), but the nature of the products and services: we should have all the low technology products and services made and performed somewhere else, and make and perform the high-technology products and services here. This answer has the same problems as the division based on the nature of the work.

Again, *the foreign countries won't settle for this bargain.* And they don't need to - they are perfectly capable of producing high-technology goods (especially China) and services (especially India). For one, the production of sophisticated, high technology products involves a great deal of low-skill assembly work. That work can be done abroad at very low wages, and so we have seen the production of computers, smart phones, and other electronics products and components offshored to Taiwan, then China, and now Vietnam.

And that is why *"American" companies haven't bought into this proposition either*, and are doing more and more foreign sourcing of high-technology products. As things stand now, we are importing more "high technology" products than we are exporting. This strategy hasn't worked, and will work even less so in the future.

Make and do where we can "out-compete"

Another answer to the question is that we should make and perform only the products and services in which we can successfully out-compete the rest of the world.[29]

This argument ignores the facts on the ground. *We cannot compete against low- or high-skill labor that is being supplied for a tenth to a third of the cost in the United States.* If we try to improve the quality of our labor, they can match it. If we try to compensate through technological advantage, they can adopt it, often with our assistance.[30] For the foreseeable future, we cannot look to technology to even the playing field and give us a sufficient competitive edge.

But *there will never be a level playing field*, for several reasons. The first is that *there are billions of people who are ready to work for a fraction of what it costs to live in America.* We have elites espousing the laughable proposition that Americans are paid too much, and that they need to be paid less so that American products can be competitive against the low-wage countries. That is, we just need to get our wages down to world market-clearing levels. But we will never succeed in that race to the bottom.

The second is that *other countries will always try to build in an advantage for themselves.* The list of methods by which they do this is long, indeed. Even when they agree not to do these things, as in the WTO rules or in trade agreements, they continue to do them. For example, they will ignore workplace health and safety standards. To level the playing field, the U.S. would have workplaces where the air is full of stuff that gives the workers brown lung disease, where it is so cold they get frostbite or so hot they get heat stroke, where they don't get a break to go to the bathroom, and where the workforce includes children, often as low- or non-paid "interns."

And they don't have, or don't enforce, environmental standards. To level the playing field, we would remove the scrubbers from our smokestacks and the waste water treatment and ground contamination protection systems. And they subsidize the industries we are "competing" with. To level the playing field, we would have land grants, no-interest loans, subsidized electricity, and cash bonuses for exports.

Finally, let me add this important point: *Even if the playing field were level, we have no duty to compete with other countries for the privilege of producing the goods and services for the American economy.* Under the "out-compete" theory, we are telling the American worker that they must compete with the hundreds of millions of workers in Indonesia and who knows where else for the privilege of producing the goods and services used in the U.S. economy. That is quite a different thing than competing with them to produce the goods and services that are used in the Indonesian market or the rest of the world. *Those* are the venues where it makes sense to talk about competing.

Yes, we want to make sure there is sufficient competition in the U.S. market to protect against price gouging and shoddy goods. But so long as that is present, we have no obligation to "compete" with foreign producers in our own marketplace. More importantly, as I have discussed, there will never be a "level playing field" - the foreign countries, all of whom are engaged in adversarial trade, will see to that. *The notion of "competitiveness," which has gained wide adoption over the years in guiding U.S. economic policy, is not a sufficient basis for deciding what we make and what we import.*

So, with the failure of these various attempts to apply some form of "comparative advantage" to achieve a workable application of free trade, we are left with two prevailing rationales for pursuing free trade as national policy.

First Rationale: Low price is worth the sacrifice

The first is this: the sacrifice of lost jobs, low pay, and social ills resulting from sending U.S. production offshore is outweighed by the widespread benefit of the lower prices paid for the imported products and services.

To consider this proposition, we must first consider, how much lower are the prices? One analysis concluded that the cost of baby and toddler clothes in the United States fell ten percent between 1999 and 2013.[31] In her book *Factory Man*, Beth Macy makes several references to competing foreign products being sold for thirty percent less. The savings likely depend on the industry and product mix.

Benefits Outweighed by Costs

The benefit of lower prices for foreign goods must be weighed against the costs. One cost is the reduction in pay caused by the offshoring of jobs. This reduction has two causes: one is the lower pay the remaining *production* workers experience due to (i) employers' threats to move production offshore, and/or (ii) employers' stated need to match the lower pay of other employers threatening offshoring, and/or (iii) employers' stated need to compete with the lower prices charged for foreign-sourced goods.[32]

The second cause is the slack in the larger labor market caused by the loss of production jobs to offshore producers. With workers chasing fewer jobs, employers can and do bid down the price paid for an hour of work, *not just in production jobs, but in all jobs*. Lower pay is experienced in the remaining production jobs and, also, throughout much of the rest of the economy.

A Hypothetical Case Study

How might this play out? Let's consider a ten percent reduction in overall pay due to these causes. A family making $50,000 a year with take-home pay of $40,000 may spend $10,000 on consumer products that potentially could be sourced overseas. A 30% reduction in the price of those consumer products would save that family $3,000, which it would be free to spend on other things, perhaps a family vacation. However, a ten percent reduction in gross pay would mean a $4,000 reduction in take-home pay: This loss in pay would exceed the benefit of the cheaper products by $1,000.[33]

This family is $1,000 worse off under the low-price, low pay economy.

We also should consider this question at a national level. Let's assume that U.S. consumers purchased $700 billion of goods overseas, at a thirty percent price savings. Free trade advocates would say of $700 billion spent overseas, "you saved $300 billion on those goods – you just got a pay raise." That is like the person who is lured into the department store by the holiday sale, purchases $1,000 worth of merchandise for $700, and goes home thinking "I saved $300 today," when her or she actually spent $700 today. The fact is, our economy lost $700 billion, and the other countries' economies gained $700 billion. *Was the $300 billion in savings worth the $700 billion lost?*

Finally, I would add that the job losses caused by trade occur most among the working class, pushing down working class wages as more workers compete for the remaining jobs. So, the theoretical benefits of free trade may skew the benefits of lower prices toward the better off, and the costs of lower wages toward the less well-off.

Trade can lower wages farther than prices

Paul Samuelson, who won the Nobel prize in economics and whose textbook was long the standard for undergraduates, predicted these outcomes in an article he published in 2004.[34] In the article, he rebutted the "popular polemical truth" that the American economy always benefits in the long run from any-and-all forms of international trade. To the contrary, Samuelson noted conditions when trade *can* cause American wage losses that are *not* necessarily offset by the lower prices paid for imports.

Samuelson wrote that when a low-wage nation like China or India is rapidly improving its technology in fields like call centers and computer programming, the "new labor-market-clearing real wage has been lowered," reducing per capita income in the U.S. In an interview regarding the article, Samuelson told Steve Lohr of the New York Times, "If you don't believe that changes the average wages in America, then you believe in the tooth fairy." [35]

Furthermore, the lower costs of sourcing the products offshore do not necessarily provide a net benefit to the U.S. economy: "being able to purchase groceries 20 percent cheaper at Wal-Mart does not necessarily make up for the wage losses," he told Lohr. Samuelson wrote that the proposition that "the gains of the American winners are big enough to more than compensate for the losers" is "only an innuendo." Samuelson told Lohr that he had written the article to "set the record straight" because "the mainstream defenses of globalization were much too simple a statement of the problem." [36]

A Race to the Top?

The response to Samuelson's article also is illuminating. Jagdish N. Bhagwati, a leading international economist and professor at Columbia University and author of *In Defense of Globalization* (Oxford University Press, 2004), and some colleagues published an article minimalizing the number of educated of workers produced by the Indian and Chinese educational systems, and noting that Samuelson's conclusions only apply when the other country is closing the gap on the U.S. technologically – Bhagwati told Lohr that the U.S. could solve the problem by "moving up the technology ladder." [37]

That would leave us engaged in what I call a "race to the top" – I can picture a Looney Tunes cartoon with the two characters frenetically racing up Bhagwati's "technology ladder," the rungs disappearing behind them as they go. However, like the "race to the bottom," *it is a race we cannot win* – because we are constantly training the Indians and Chinese in our universities, because both countries are building universities by the dozens,[38] and because American companies are avidly transferring the U.S. technological advantage to operations in China, India, Korea, and elsewhere – *we are making sure there is no technology gap.* Samuelson was writing in 2004, and events since then support his conclusions: *Trade need not be a win-win, and the gains of lower prices can be offset by larger losses of American wages.*

A Race to the Near-Bottom

Samuelson was applying what is referred to as the "factor-price equalization theorem," a fancy name for a commons-sense prediction: wages across nations will converge until they are equal, with wages in low-wage countries (*e.g.*, China) going up, and wages in high-wage countries (*e.g.*, the U.S.) going down.

Writing in 2008,[39] Josh Bivens suggested that the following conditions must be in effect for the theory to apply:

- Prices (of goods, labor, and capital) are set on a global level;
- Each country has access to the same production technologies;
- Each country produces some of each good (trade is not specialized by product); and
- All goods are tradable.

These conditions are currently in effect, and so, we see Chinese wages rising, and U.S. wages falling. The gap is still large, so U.S. wages still have a long way to fall, if we leave this dynamic in effect. So, you could say we are engaged, if not in a race to the bottom, then in a race to nearly the bottom, certainly far below the cost of living in the United States.

Failure to Calculate Other Costs

And this comparison of benefits and costs is inadequate, because the overall decline in wages is only the beginning of the story. The individual whose job was offshored has seen his or her lifetime earnings destroyed or severely limited. It is not unlike the case where someone suffers traumatic brain injury in an automobile accident; in those cases, the net loss in lifetime earnings is calculated and reduced to present value. In the case of someone losing a manufacturing job, that is a very large number.

Secondary effects are felt by the businesses that supplied goods and services to the manufacturer and to the laid-off workers. Third-level effects are felt by the local, state, and federal governments, who lose the taxes formerly paid by the manufacturer and the laid-off employees, and at the same time incur greater expenses in dealing with the dependency and social ills of the formerly self-supporting workers.

So, even in terms of a simple national cost-benefit analysis, the benefits of the low prices have been outweighed by the costs. But, as we will discuss, there are other ethical considerations as well: even if, on a national basis, the "benefits" outweighed the "costs," we will see in Chapter 10 that it would be unethical to impose those costs without the consent of the harmed.

Second Rationale: Sacrifice to Cure Poverty Abroad

The second prevailing rationale for the pursuit of free trade is this: the sacrifice of lost jobs, low pay, and social ills resulting from sending production offshore is outweighed by lifting millions of foreign workers and their families out of poverty.

This issue is usually posed as "lifting hundreds of millions out of poverty" and "building a global middle class." But what is the reality? I would sum it up as follows: Many people have moved from abject poverty to extreme or middling poverty, and there has been a small increase in the middle and upper class, mostly concentrated in China. However, these gains have been achieved at a high cost to workers in the developed and developing countries alike.

Trading away American jobs in pursuit of alleviating world poverty has practical limits, and raises ethical concerns about its impacts abroad; equally important are the ethical concerns raised by its impacts in the U.S. We will pick up these topics in Chapters 10 and 11.

But meanwhile, you may be wondering, how has seventy years of pursuing free trade and unregulated markets turned out? We address that question in the following chapters.

Notes to Chapter 4

---

[1] In the concluding words of his principal work, Keynes continued: "Practical men, who believe themselves to be quite exempt from any intellectual influences, are usually the slaves of some defunct economist. Madmen in authority, who hear voices in the air, are distilling the frenzy from some academic scribbler of a few years back... [S]oon or late, it is ideas, not vested interests, which are dangerous for good or evil." John Maynard Keynes, *The General Theory of Employment Interest and Money* (New York: Harcourt, Brace and Company, 1936), 383-384.

[2] Smith, *An Inquiry into the Nature and Causes of the Wealth of Nations* (London: W. Strand and T. Cadell, 1776).

[3] Smith wrote: "Every individual... neither intends to promote the public interest, nor knows how much he is promoting it... he intends only his own security; and by directing that industry in such a manner as its produce may be of the greatest value, he intends only his own gain, and he is in this, as in many other cases, led by an invisible hand to promote an end which was no part of his intention. Nor is it always the worse for the society that it was no part of it. By pursuing his own interest he frequently promotes that of the society more effectually than when he really intends to promote it." Adam Smith, *The Wealth of Nations*, Book IV, Chapter II, p. 456.

[4] Dogan Gocmen has suggested that Smith recognized the need for a legal system enforcing certain rights as the context within which market prices would be set. This framework would lead market prices toward Smith's ideal of "natural prices," which reflected the costs of rent, wages, and profit in bringing a product to market. Without such a framework, Smith thought, market prices are subject to manipulation and can obscure the forces of supply and demand that produced them. Dogan Gocmen, "The 'Adam Smith Problem' and Adam Smith's Utopia," in *New Essays on Adam Smith's Moral Philosophy*, eds. Wade L. Robinson and David B. Suits (Rochester: RIT Press, 2012), 45-70.

[5] It is also worth noting that what modern economists call "optimal," Smith referred to as the "public interest," the "public good" and the "interest . . . of society."

[6] For example, Joseph Stiglitz has cited his work with Bruce Greenwald as demonstrating that due to the imperfect information of the market, the invisible hand seems invisible because it isn't there. Stiglitz concludes that Smith was "dramatically wrong." D. Joseph Stiglitz, "Moving Beyond Market Fundamentalism to a More Balanced Economy," *Annals of Public and Cooperative Economics*, 80:3 (2009):

345-360. *See* also Jonathan Schlefer, "There is No Invisible Hand," *Harvard Business Review* (April 10, 2012), https://hbr.org/2012/04/there-is-no-invisible-hand.

Smith's fallibility regarding the existence of a welfare-optimizing mechanism that might be called an "invisible hand" is confirmed in the other place where he utilizes the concept. In his *Theory of Moral Sentiments*, he writes: "[The rich] consume little more than the poor, and in spite of their natural selfishness and rapacity...they divide with the poor the produce of all their improvements. They are led by an invisible hand to make nearly the same distribution of the necessaries of life, which would have been made, had the earth been divided into equal portions among all its inhabitants, and thus without intending it, without knowing it, advance the interest of the society, and afford means to the multiplication of the species." Adam Smith, *The Theory of Moral Sentiments*, Knud Haakonssen, Ed. (Cambridge: Cambridge University Press, 2002). Here, again, real-world observations negate the proposition that the rich act anything like Smith's description, in his time or especially now, when more and more income and wealth is being drained off at the top.

[7] For a treatment of how these theories came to gain popularity, see Fred Block and Margaret R. Somers, *The Power of Market Fundamentalism: Karl Polanyi's Critique* (Cambridge: Harvard University Press, 2014.).

[8] Arthur Okun described and proposed improvements to the mixed economy in Arthur M. Okun, *Equality and Efficiency: The Big Tradeoff* (Washington, D.C.: Brookings Institution Press, 1975). *See also* Hacker and Pierson, *Amnesia.*

[9] This is not to say that any and all regulation is good. Just as an unregulated market can lead to problems, so, too, an overregulated market can become "sclerotic," unable to produce to its full potential.

[10] Eugene F. Fama, "Random Walks in Stock-Market Prices," University of Chicago Graduate School of Business, Selected Papers No. 16 (1965), 3. https://www.chicagobooth.edu/~/media/34F68FFD9CC04EF1A7690 1F6C61C0A76.PDF.

[11] Fama postulated that "[i]n an efficient market ... the actions of the many competing participants should cause the actual price of a security to wander randomly about its intrinsic value" – the "Random Walk" theory. *Id.*, 4.

[12] The other failing of the Efficient Market Hypothesis is that market participants don't all have "all available" information at the same time, and "all available" information may not be enough for a

rational decision. Joseph Stiglitz has pointed out that the market's information is always imperfect. Joseph Stiglitz, "Moving Beyond Market Fundamentalism to a More Balanced Economy," *Annals of Public and Cooperative Economics*, 80:3 (2009): 345-360. http://www8.gsb.columbia.edu.

[13] For a history of the EMH, see Justin Fox, *The Myth of the Rational Market: A History of Risk, Reward, and Delusion on Wall Street* (New York: HarperCollins, 2009).

[14] See, e.g., Stiglitz, *Moving Beyond*; Block and Somers, *Beyond*. It also is referred to as Neoliberalism or the Neoliberal Agenda.

[15] In the first case, we are left to whatever result the market produces. In the second case, we will likely be disappointed as the market fails to deliver the defined good.

[16] See Davies, *Limits*, 109.

[17] See, for example, the Harvard Business School U.S. Competitiveness Project, discussed in Chapter 11. *See also* Reut Institute, http://reut-institute.org/en/Publication.aspx?PublicationId=1301.

[18] The United States pursued deregulation of the transportation industry in the 1970s and the financial industry in the 1908s. Despite a move toward deregulation, by some measures regulation in the United States has grown dramatically since 1974. The George Washington University Regulatory Studies Center reports that the number of pages in the Code of Federal Regulations increased from 71,224 in 1975 to 178,227 in 2016. https://regulatorystudies.columbian.gwu.edu/reg-stats.

[19] Jonathan D. Ostry, Prakash Loungani, and Davide Furceri, "Neoliberalism: Oversold?" *Finance & Development*, International Monetary Fund, Vol. 53, No. 2 (June 2016). http://www.imf.org/external/pubs/ft/fandd/2016/06/ostry.htm.

[20] David Ricardo, *The Principles of Political Economy and Taxation* (London: J.M. Dent & Sons Ltd., 1911, orig. pub. 1817), Chapter VII, On Foreign Trade, 77 *et seq*.

[21] *Id.*, 81.

[22] Paul Krugman laid out this view in a 1997 article: "If economists ruled the world, there would be no need for a World Trade Organization. The economist's case for free trade is essentially a unilateral case: a country serves its own interests by pursuing free trade regardless of what other countries may do." Paul Krugman, "What Should Trade Negotiators Negotiate About?" *Journal of Economic*

Literature, 35 (1), 1997, 113-120. Cited in Autor et al., *China Shock*, 2. Krugman subsequently modified this view.

[23] Sven W. Arndt, "Free Trade and Its Alternatives," in *The Oxford Handbook of International Commercial Policy*, eds. Mordechai E. Kreinin and Michael G. Plummer (New York: Oxford University Press, 2012), 3-31; Prestowitz, *Betrayal*, 163.

[24] See Ardnt, "Free Trade," 27; Prestowitz, *Betrayal*, 165.

[25] I spoke recently with two men who serve on the board of a non-profit that employs low-IQ workers in contract manufacturing. They employ several hundred people, and told me they could employ several hundred more, but for the competition they face from China and India. My daughter Jane has Down syndrome and autism. She is 14 and their facility could offer her an opportunity to be productive and support herself. Except that in pursuit of half-baked theories like sending all our low-skill work offshore, our leaders would relegate her to spending her days in front of a TV, instead of engaged in productive work.

[26] For example, General Motors designed its new electric car, the Bolt, at its research and development center in South Korea.

[27] "Losing the Edge," Times of India, November 17, 2005, quoted in Frank, *Falling Behind*, 113.

[28] A couple of important exceptions are natural resources, geography, climate and size. With respect to size, I especially note the comparative advantage enjoyed by China.

[29] See, *e.g.*, Harvard Business School's "U.S. Competitiveness Project," discussed in Chapter 11.

[30] There could be a case where manufacturing technology reduces the labor input to the point where the foreign producer no longer has a labor advantage, and even if the foreign producer adopts the same technology, the drawbacks of shipping time and distance and cultural differences and communications shortcomings give domestic production the competitive advantage. These situations are in the minority. If they become prevalent at some time in the future, we will need to address how to spread income through an increasingly "workerless" economy.

[31] Peter S. Goodman, "More Wealth, More Jobs, But Not for Everyone," New York Times, September 29, 2016, citing analysis by Pietra Rivoli, author of *Travels of a T-Shirt in the Global Economy*.

[32] This phenomenon is sometimes referred to as the "threat effect." *See* Josh Bivens, "Using standard models to benchmark the costs of globalization for American workers without a college degree," *Economic Policy Institute*, Briefing Paper #354 (March 22, 2013).

http://www.epi.org/publication/standard-models-benchmark-costs-globalization/.

[33] This hypothetical is consistent with work by Josh Bivens, in which he found that in 2011, international trade depressed wages for non-college educated workers by 5.5 percent, not including losses from the "threat effect." Bivens, "Standard models," *supra*.

[34] Paul A. Samuelson, "Where Ricardo and Mill Rebut and Confirm Arguments of Mainstream Economists Supporting Globalization." *Journal of Economic Perspectives*, 18(3) (2004): 135-146. DOI: 10.1257/0895330042162403.

[35] Steve Lohr, "An Elder Challenges Outsourcing's Orthodoxy," New York Times, September 9, 2004.

[36] Furthermore, Samuelson pointed out that he had touched on these matters as early as 1972, in a lecture he delivered shortly after he won his Nobel Prize, titled "International Trade for a Rich Country." Importantly, Samuelson said he was applying Ricardo's theory of competitive advantage, and this is where it takes us. At the global level, he still believed there is a net gain; however, the gain is not necessarily shared among trading nations. Lohr, "An Elder Challenges," *supra*. *See also*, Josh Bivens, *Everybody Wins, Except Most of Us* (Washington, D.C.: Economic Policy Institute, 2008).

[37] Lohr, "An Elder Challenges," *supra*.

[38] There is a global race to produce college graduates, especially in technical fields. In May of 2012, the OECD studied trends in higher education in the in the major economies of Europe and Asia. Looking at 25- to 34-year-olds with education beyond secondary school, they found that in 2000, the U.S. and China each had 17 percent of the total; in 2010, China had 18 percent and the U.S. had 14 percent; in 2020, they projected that China would have 29 percent and the U.S. 11 percent. The OECD projected that by 2020, China and India would account for 40 percent of this population, compared to just over 25 percent for the U.S. and Europe. The study noted that these projections are subject to change, because many of these countries, including the U.S., China, and Europe, have launched ambitious programs to increase their percentage of college graduates. If China reaches its goal of 20 percent in 2020, it will have 195 million people with college degrees - more than the entire projected population of 25-64 year-olds in the United States. OECD, "Education Indicators in Focus. - 2012/5 (May)," Organization for European Cooperation and Development (2012).

[39] Bivens, *Everybody Wins, supra.*

Chapter 5

So, how has that worked out?

On January 16, 2014, the U.S. Senate Finance Committee held a hearing to consider a bill sponsored by Senator Max Baucus, the Democratic Senator from Montana whom we met in Chapter 1, and Rep. Dave Camp, a Republican Congressman from Michigan. The bill would give the President "fast-track" authority to negotiate the proposed Trans Pacific Partnership regional trade agreement and propose it to the Congress for an up-or-down vote.

Larry Cohen, President of the Communication Workers of America, was testifying. Mary Bottari, of the Center for Media and Democracy, was present. She reported that Cohen "looked Baucus in the eye and demanded answers to a few pointed questions."

> After 20 years of NAFTA, Cohen demanded, when are we going to start to actually measure the results?
>
> When, asked Cohen, will we start to document the net effect of these trade deals on employment? "What has happened to our jobs, our communities,

> the North Philadelphia that I grew up in? The Cleveland that I can picture now? The devastation throughout those communities, no replacement for those jobs," said Cohen.
>
> When, asked Cohen, will we document the effect of trade on pay and standards of living?
>
> The Senators shifted uncomfortably in their seats, but had no answers for the CWA chief. . . . [1]

In this chapter and the next, I attempt to provide those answers. As I mentioned in the Introduction, they are surprisingly hard to come by. The U.S. Trade Representative, whose purpose purportedly is to look after U.S. trade interests, talks only about exports, never about the corresponding imports. So, too, the Department of Commerce. The information is available, from the Census Bureau and the Bureau of Labor Statistics, if one goes digging deep enough; I have done that. So, let's have a look, beginning in this chapter with trade, and, in answer to Larry Cohen's question, "actually measure the results."

Measuring the Trade in Goods Deficit

But how to measure this? We do so by adding up our imports and exports each year; if imports are higher than exports, we have a "trade deficit."

Just how large is that deficit? U.S. imports and exports of goods from 1960 through 2015 are presented in the following figure:[2]

As the figure indicates, during this period the United States has substantially increased its trade in goods with the world; however, as shown in the gap between the two curves, beginning in 1976 we have experienced a chronic trade in goods deficit, importing substantially more goods than we export. In 2015 the deficit was some $770 billion,[3] as presented in the following figure:

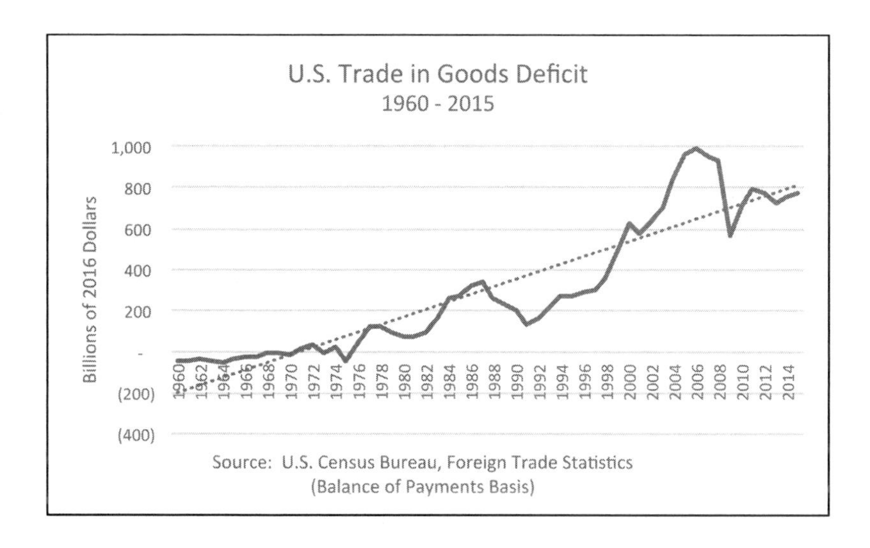

Considering Trade in Services

In addition to goods, we also import and export services. There, we have seen an opposite effect, beginning with a deficit, then turning into a recurring surplus of exports over imports. The following figure presents the balance of trade, either surplus or deficit, for goods and for services from 1960 through 2015 (goods are indicated by the dark bars and services by the light bars).

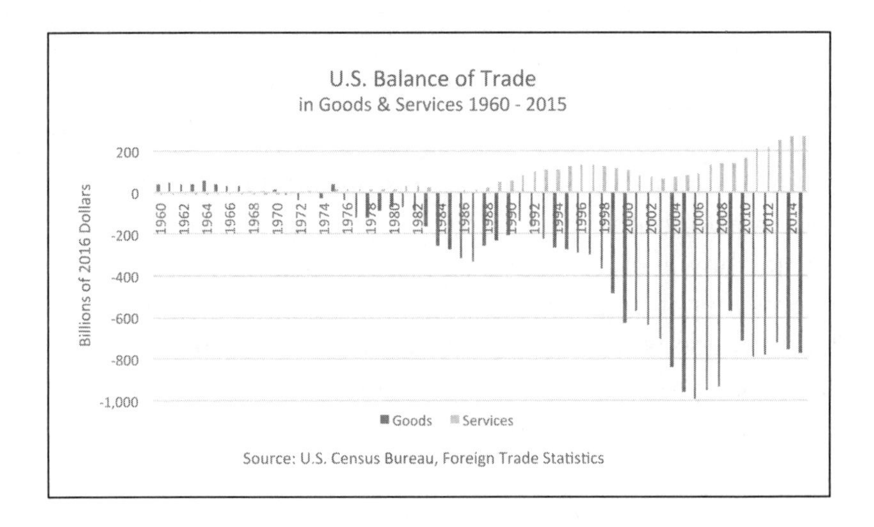

We see the annual balance for goods starting out in surplus, then shifting to permanent deficit by 1976. Trade in services, on the other hand, changes to a surplus, which becomes substantial in the late 1980s.[4] However, *the surplus in services always remains small in comparison to the deficit in goods*, so there remains a substantial deficit, some $505 billion in 2015. The size of that deficit is illustrated in the following figure:

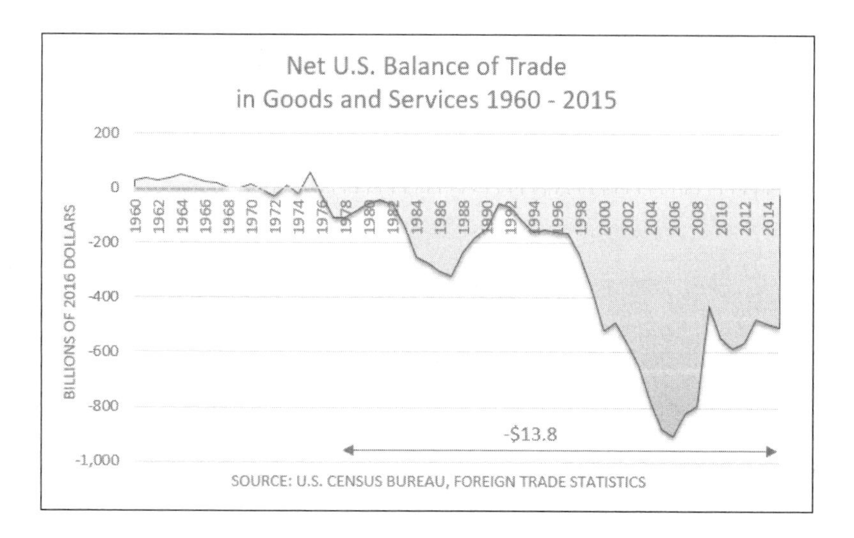

The entire area under the zero line, which shows where trade would be balanced, constitutes money sent to other countries' economies, some $13.8 trillion, expressed in 2016 dollars. So, even when the surplus in services is considered, the U.S. has been experiencing very large deficits in its trade with other nations.

The Trade in Goods Deficit and the Economy

Returning to the trade in goods deficit, we consider, is it really a lot in relation to the size of the U.S. economy? Since 2000, these trade-in-goods deficits have represented a substantial sum compared to total U.S. economic output -- over four percent of Gross Domestic Product except during the recession of 2008-2009, and ballooning as high as 6 percent in 2005-2006, as shown in the following figure:

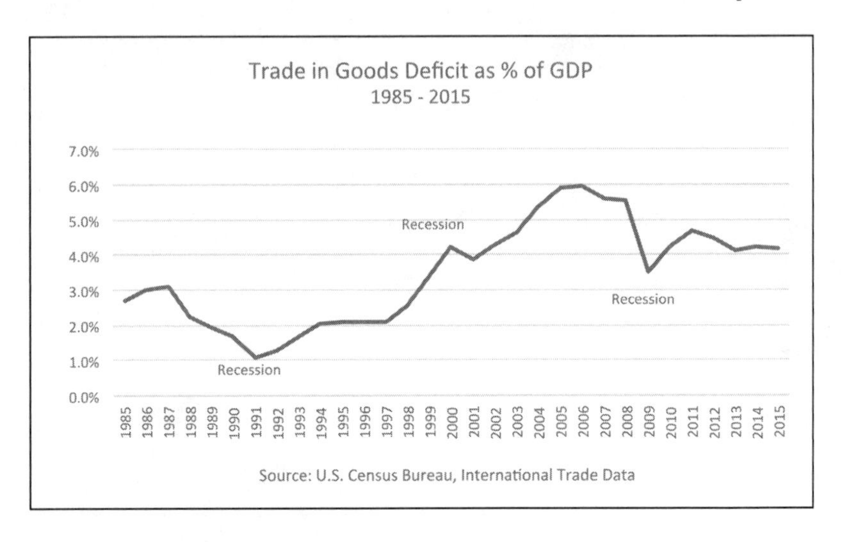

This means that, if we had spent that money on U.S.-made goods rather than foreign goods, GDP could have been at least four to six percent larger than it was during those years, when we were barely eking out annual increases in GDP. However, the loss was actually greater than that: each dollar spent on a manufactured product has ripple effects through the economy, generating more production of goods and services. So, the four to six percent of GDP spent on excess imports would have generated about one and a half times that much economic activity, an increase of about six to nine percent in GDP.

Another way to consider whether this is a lot of money is just to add it up: during the period 1985 through 2015, we sent just shy of $16 trillion dollars to other countries.

And the pace was accelerating: during the first 16 years, through 2000, we accumulated $4.4 trillion in trade in goods deficits, 28% of the total; during the 15 years 2001 through 2015, we accumulated $11.5 trillion in deficits, 72% of the total. As we will see later, that translates into a lot of lost jobs.

Snapshot of Trade in Goods

So, where are we today? As of 2015, our trade in goods situation looked like this:

Sources of the Trade in Goods Deficit

Where are all those imports in excess of exports coming from? It turns out that the lion's share, currently some 80%, of our excess imports, has come from a handful of countries, as presented in the following figure:[5]

We see that we have a lot of trade with Canada and Mexico, and deficits that, while proportionally small, are substantial. We see that with Japan and Germany, trade is seriously out of balance. We see that with China, trade is enormously out of balance, both in size and proportion.

Trade in Goods Deficit Over Time

It also is instructive to look at the trade in goods deficit we have been running with each of these trading "partners" over time, as presented in the following figure:

As my children, would say, "Wait, what . . .?" Can that be correct? The figure shows China breaking out of the pack with a dramatic, rapid increase beginning in 2001, reaching $370 billion in 2015, and dwarfing the other countries' deficits by comparison. The following figure shows each country's contribution to the total trade in goods deficit, plus the OPEC [6] countries and the rest of the world:

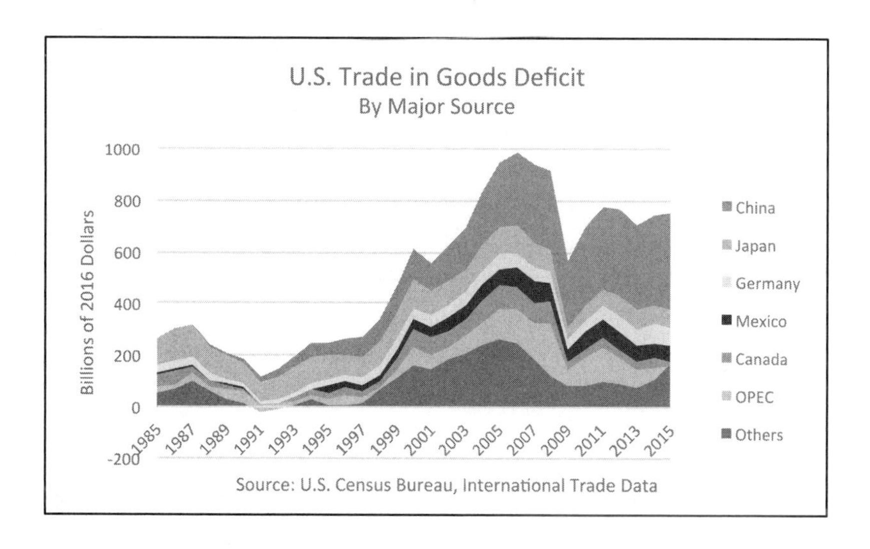

Several things stand out in these figures and the accompanying tables:

- OPEC's contribution to the trade in goods deficit swelled from 2001 through 2011 due to the run-up in oil prices to around $100 per barrel. With the collapse of prices to half that amount, OPEC's exports to the U.S. have shrunk to a level below their imports from the U.S.

- All other factors are dwarfed by the dramatic and continued (except for a pause during the 2008-9 recession) increase in the trade in goods deficit with China, both in real and percentage terms.

In fact, China's trade in goods deficit has grown to 49% of the U.S. trade in goods deficit, per the following figure:

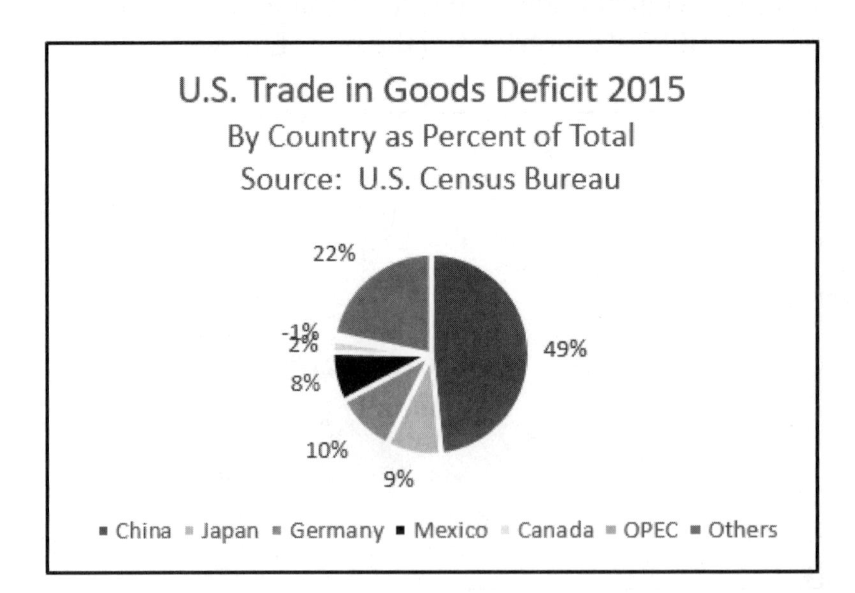

Sources Country by Country

So, that's a good start in beginning to understand what's going on. To get a more complete picture, including imports and exports as well as the deficit and the composition of trade, let's take a quick walk through each country's figures over time.

Germany

U.S. trade in goods with Germany is presented in the following figure:

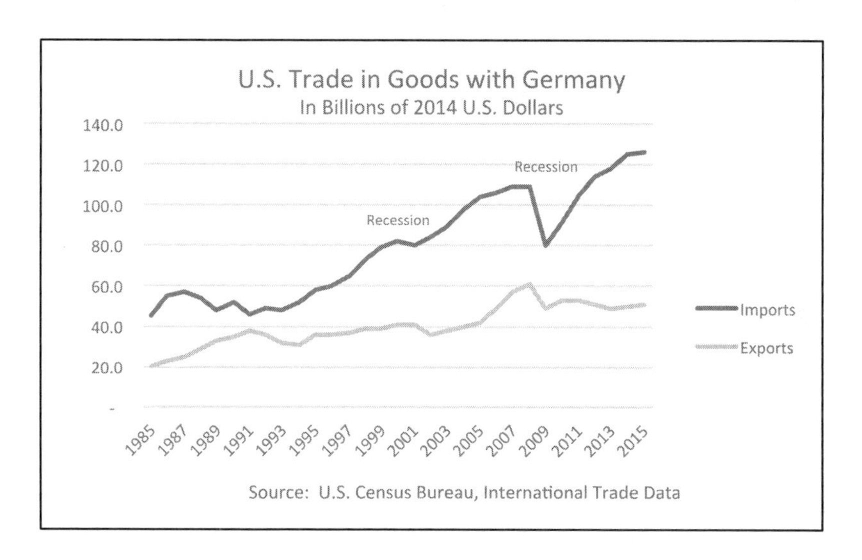

Over this entire period, Germany has been exporting to the U.S. roughly double what it imports. The size of the deficit has been increasing since 1991 (except for the 2008-9 recession), to a deficit of $75.6 billion in 2015. Where is this deficit coming from? U.S. trade with Germany by major groupings of goods during 2015 is presented in the following table and figure.

U.S. - Germany Trade Profile
Trade in Goods 2015
Billions of 2016 U.S. Dollars
15.0
5.0
(5.0)
(15.0)
(25.0)
(35.0)
(45.0)
Agricultural, Livestock &
Oil & Gas, Coal, Lumber &
Waste & Scrap and Used
Food & Beverage Products
Textiles, Apparel & Leather
Wood & Paper Products
Furniture & Fixtures
Petroleum, Chemicals, &
Primary Metals &
Machinery, Fabricated
Transportation Equipment
Computer & Electronic
Miscellaneous
Exports to Germany
Imports from Germany
Source: U.S. Census Bureau, International Trade Data
http://usatrade.census.gov

U.S. Trade in Goods with Germany 1985-2015 in Billions of 2016 Dollars							
Year	**Imports**	**Exports**	**Balance**	**Year**	**Imports**	**Exports**	**Balance**
1985	45.1	20.2	(25.0)	2001	80.3	40.8	(39.6)
1986	55.0	23.1	(31.9)	2002	83.8	35.7	(48.1)
1987	57.1	24.8	(32.3)	2003	89.2	37.8	(51.5)
1988	53.5	29.1	(24.4)	2004	98.1	39.9	(58.2)
1989	48.2	32.7	(15.5)	2005	104.2	42.0	(62.2)
1990	51.8	34.5	(17.3)	2006	106.0	49.0	(57.0)
1991	46.0	37.5	(8.5)	2007	109.2	57.3	(51.9)
1992	49.3	36.3	(12.9)	2008	109.2	61.0	(48.2)
1993	47.4	31.4	(16.0)	2009	80.1	48.5	(31.6)
1994	51.4	31.2	(20.3)	2010	90.7	53.0	(37.7)
1995	58.2	35.4	(22.8)	2011	105.6	52.7	(52.8)
1996	59.6	35.9	(23.6)	2012	114.7	51.2	(63.4)
1997	64.7	36.7	(28.0)	2013	117.8	48.8	(69.0)
1998	73.3	39.2	(34.1)	2014	125.4	49.9	(75.6)
1999	79.5	38.6	(40.9)	2015	126.1	50.5	(75.6)
2000	81.9	41.2	(40.7)	TOTAL	2,462.5	1,246.0	(1,216.5)
Source: U.S. Census Bureau, Foreign Trade Statistics							

What do we learn from this table and figure?

Key Findings: A snapshot of U.S. trade in goods with Germany in 2015 shows –

- Most of the U.S. trade in goods deficit with Germany comes from high-value manufactures, especially motor vehicles and other transportation equipment ($28.4 billion), machinery, fabricated metal and electrical products, and appliances ($20.6 billion) and chemical, petroleum, and plastic and rubber products ($17.3 billion).
- The only U.S. surpluses with Germany are in farm products, raw materials, and scrap.

Japan

U.S. trade in goods with Japan is presented in the following figure:

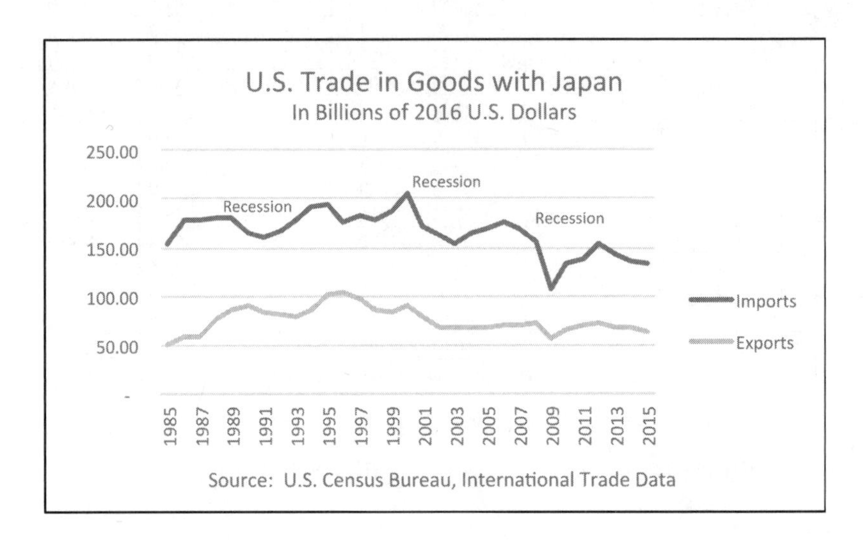

As we see, by 1985, Japan already was running a large trade deficit with the U.S., over $100 billion in 2016 dollars. Japanese imports have been drifting down and have not returned to their pre-recession levels, probably in part due to Japan's losing U.S. market share to China and perhaps Korea and Germany. However, Japan still accounts for a substantial deficit: in 2015, Japan exported $69.6 billion more to the U.S. than it imported from the U.S.

Where is this deficit coming from? U.S. trade with Japan by major groupings of goods during 2015 is presented in the following table and figure.

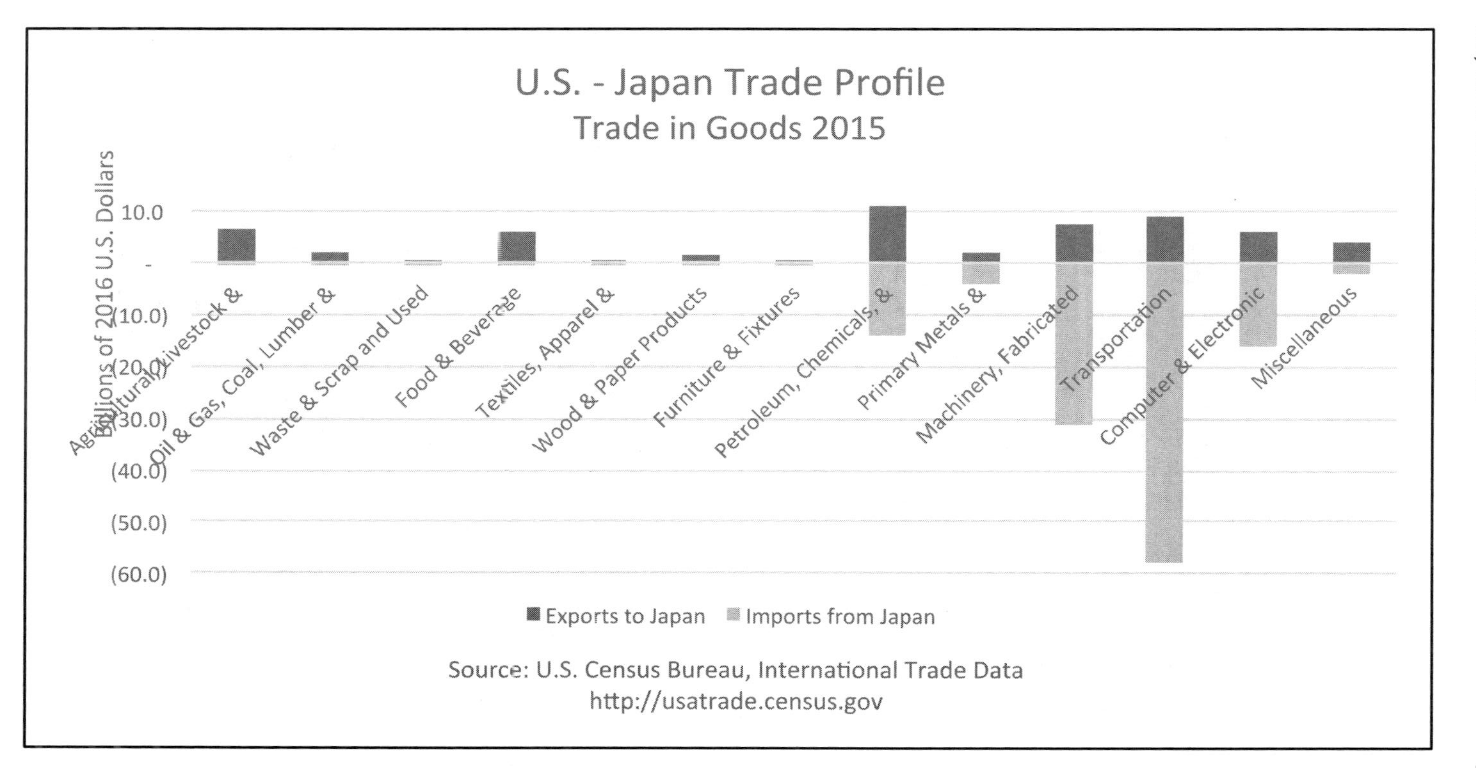
U.S. - Japan Trade Profile
Trade in Goods 2015
Billions of 2016 U.S. Dollars
10.0
-
(10.0)
(20.0)
(30.0)
(40.0)
(50.0)
(60.0)
Agricultural, Livestock &
Oil & Gas, Coal, Lumber &
Waste & Scrap and Used
Food & Beverage
Textiles, Apparel &
Wood & Paper Products
Furniture & Fixtures
Petroleum, Chemicals, &
Primary Metals &
Machinery, Fabricated
Transportation
Computer & Electronic
Miscellaneous
Exports to Japan
Imports from Japan
Source: U.S. Census Bureau, International Trade Data
http://usatrade.census.gov

U.S. Trade in Goods with Japan 1985-2015 in Billions of 2016 Dollars							
Year	Imports	Exports	Balance	Year	Imports	Exports	Balance
1985	153.4	50.5	(102.9)	2001	172.0	78.1	(93.9)
1986	179.4	58.9	(120.5)	2002	162.7	68.9	(93.8)
1987	178.5	59.6	(118.8)	2003	154.6	68.1	(86.5)
1988	181.7	76.6	(105.1)	2004	164.9	68.0	(96.8)
1989	181.5	86.3	(95.2)	2005	169.7	67.3	(102.5)
1990	165.0	89.4	(75.6)	2006	176.3	69.6	(106.8)
1991	161.1	84.7	(76.4)	2007	168.7	70.9	(97.8)
1992	166.6	81.8	(84.8)	2008	156.0	73.0	(83.0)
1993	178.0	79.5	(98.5)	2009	107.3	57.3	(50.0)
1994	193.0	86.6	(106.4)	2010	132.6	66.5	(66.1)
1995	195.1	101.7	(93.4)	2011	138.0	70.4	(67.5)
1996	176.2	103.4	(72.8)	2012	153.8	73.5	(80.3)
1997	182.5	98.3	(84.2)	2013	142.7	67.2	(75.5)
1998	179.1	85.0	(94.1)	2014	135.8	67.5	(68.3)
1999	188.4	82.8	(105.7)	2015	132.7	63.1	(69.6)
2000	205.1	90.9	(114.2)	TOTAL	5,132.5	2,214.7	(2,649.2)
Source: U.S. Census Bureau, Foreign Trade Statistics							

What do we learn from this table and figure?

Key Findings: A snapshot of U.S. trade in goods with Japan in 2015 shows that, much like Germany --

- Most of the U.S. trade in goods deficit with Japan comes from high-value manufactures, especially motor vehicles and other transportation equipment ($48.8 billion), machinery, fabricated metal and electrical products, and appliances ($23.6 billion), and electronics ($9.9 billion).

- The only substantial U.S. surpluses with Japan are in farm products ($6 billion) and lumber and other raw materials.

Mexico

U.S. trade in goods with Mexico is presented in the following figure.

The United States has a much more active trading relationship with Mexico than with Japan or Germany, including substantial exports. However, beginning in 1994, the year of entry into effect of the North American Free Trade Agreement (NAFTA), a widening gap appeared between U.S. exports to and imports from Mexico, with a 2015 trade in goods deficit of over $61 billion, approaching that of Japan.

Where is this deficit coming from? U.S. trade with Mexico by major groupings of goods during 2015 is presented in the following table and figure.

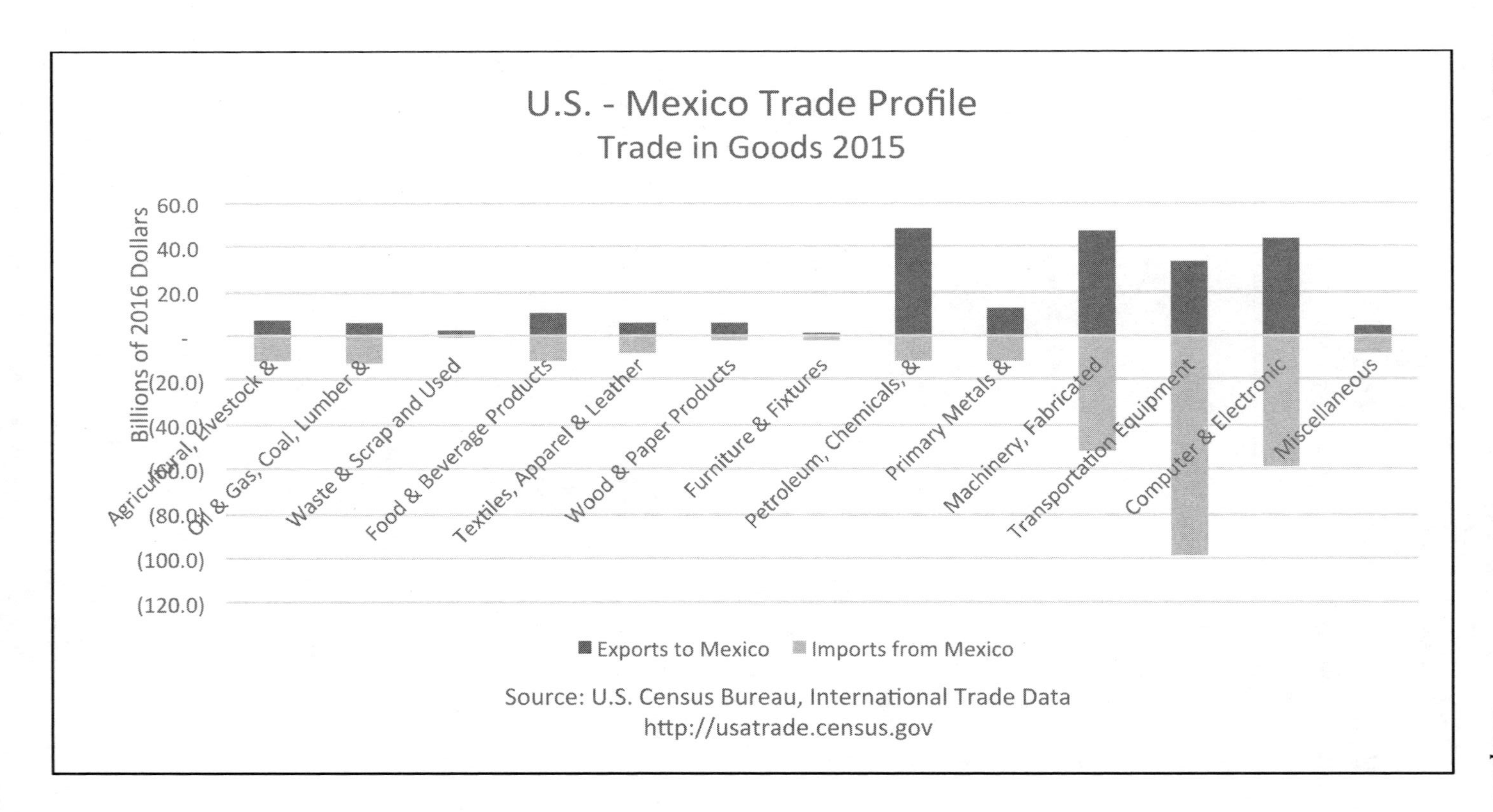
U.S. - Mexico Trade Profile
Trade in Goods 2015
Billions of 2016 Dollars
60.0
40.0
20.0
-
(20.0)
(40.0)
(60.0)
(80.0)
(100.0)
(120.0)
Agricultural, Livestock &
Oil & Gas, Coal, Lumber &
Waste & Scrap and Used
Food & Beverage Products
Textiles, Apparel & Leather
Wood & Paper Products
Furniture & Fixtures
Petroleum, Chemicals, &
Primary Metals &
Machinery, Fabricated
Transportation Equipment
Computer & Electronic
Miscellaneous
Exports to Mexico
Imports from Mexico
Source: U.S. Census Bureau, International Trade Data
http://usatrade.census.gov

U.S. Trade in Goods with Mexico 1985-2015 in billions of 2016 dollars							
Year	**Imports**	**Exports**	**Balance**	**Year**	**Imports**	**Exports**	**Balance**
1985	42.7	30.4	(12.3)	2001	178.6	137.8	(40.9)
1986	37.9	27.1	(10.8)	2002	180.4	130.6	(49.8)
1987	42.8	30.8	(12.0)	2003	180.9	127.6	(53.2)
1988	47.2	41.9	(5.3)	2004	198.0	140.6	(57.4)
1989	52.7	48.5	(4.2)	2005	209.2	147.9	(61.3)
1990	55.5	52.0	(3.5)	2006	235.9	159.1	(76.8)
1991	54.8	58.6	3.8	2007	244.4	157.7	(86.8)
1992	60.2	69.4	9.2	2008	241.9	169.4	(72.5)
1993	66.3	69.0	2.8	2009	197.9	144.4	(53.5)
1994	80.2	82.4	2.2	2010	253.0	180.0	(73.0)
1995	98.1	73.1	(25.0)	2011	281.3	212.2	(69.1)
1996	113.7	86.9	(26.8)	2012	291.5	226.7	(64.8)
1997	128.9	107.1	(21.8)	2013	289.0	232.7	(56.2)
1998	139.1	115.8	(23.3)	2014	298.7	242.7	(56.0)
1999	158.0	125.1	(32.8)	2015	299.4	238.1	(61.3)
2000	190.3	155.9	(34.4)	Total	4,948.2	3,821.5	(1,126.7)
Source: U.S. Census Bureau, International Trade Data							

What do we learn from this table and figure?

Key Findings: A snapshot of U.S. trade in goods with Mexico in 2015 shows that --

- We have a lot of trade with Mexico; however, we are running a large deficit, both in manufactured goods ($48.9 billion) and in farm products and raw materials ($10.5 billion).
- We enjoy a $36.9 billion surplus in petroleum, chemical, plastic and rubber products.
- However, this is more than offset by a huge deficit in motor vehicles and other transportation products ($65.2 billion – even larger than Japan).

Canada

U.S. trade in goods with Canada is presented in the following figure:

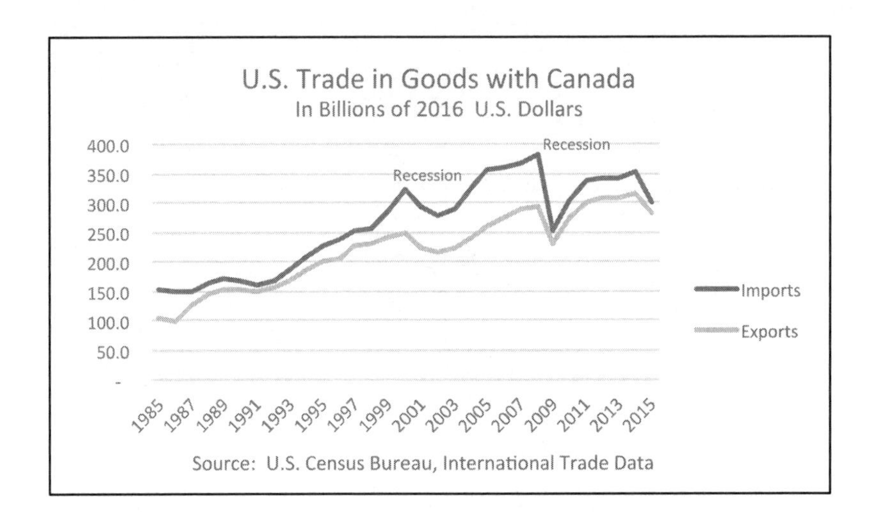

Canada historically has been the United States' largest trading partner, and this two-way trade has increased substantially during the period 1985 through 2015, on an order of magnitude similar to Mexico's. Like Mexico, Canada was running a persistent and widening trade in goods deficit until the recession of 2008-2009. However, neither overall trade nor the deficit has returned to its pre-recession level. In 2015, the U.S. trade in goods deficit with Canada stood at $15.7 billion.

U.S. trade with Canada by major groupings of goods during 2015 is presented in the following table and figure.

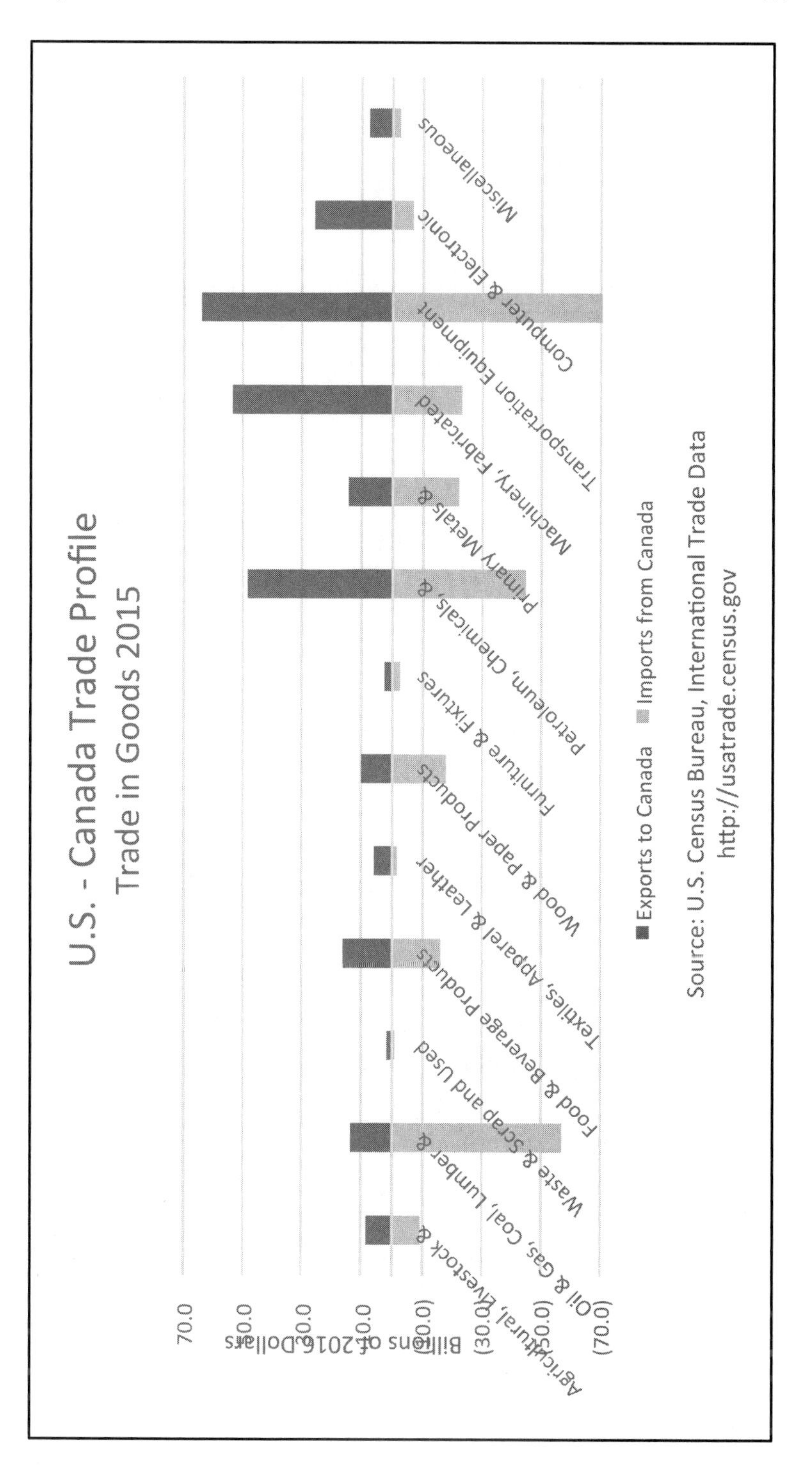
U.S. - Canada Trade Profile
Trade in Goods 2015
70.0
(70.0)
Billions of 2016 Dollars
Agricultural, Livestock &
Oil & Gas, Coal, Lumber &
Waste & Scrap and Used
Food & Beverage Products
Textiles, Apparel & Leather
Wood & Paper Products
Furniture & Fixtures
Petroleum, Chemicals, &
Primary Metals &
Machinery, Fabricated
Transportation Equipment
Computer & Electronic
Miscellaneous
Exports to Canada
Imports from Canada
Source: U.S. Census Bureau, International Trade Data
http://usatrade.census.gov

U.S. Trade in Goods with Canada 1985-2015 in billions of 2016 dollars							
Year	Imports	Exports	Balance	Year	Imports	Exports	Balance
1985	153.9	105.4	(48.5)	2001	294.1	222.3	(71.9)
1986	149.5	99.3	(50.2)	2002	280.2	215.6	(64.5)
1987	150.0	126.2	(23.8)	2003	290.3	222.6	(67.7)
1988	165.2	145.4	(19.8)	2004	325.6	241.1	(84.4)
1989	170.6	152.9	(17.7)	2005	357.2	260.6	(96.5)
1990	168.1	154.0	(14.2)	2006	359.9	274.5	(85.4)
1991	160.3	149.9	(10.4)	2007	367.8	288.7	(79.1)
1992	168.7	154.9	(13.7)	2008	380.2	292.5	(87.7)
1993	184.6	166.7	(17.9)	2009	253.4	229.2	(24.2)
1994	208.0	185.4	(22.6)	2010	305.4	274.2	(31.2)
1995	228.1	201.0	(27.1)	2011	337.4	301.0	(36.4)
1996	238.5	205.3	(33.2)	2012	340.5	307.3	(33.2)
1997	250.9	227.7	(23.2)	2013	342.5	309.8	(32.7)
1998	254.7	230.2	(24.5)	2014	352.8	315.9	(36.8)
1999	286.1	239.9	(46.2)	2015	299.1	283.4	(15.7)
2000	323.2	250.5	(72.7)	TOTAL	8,146.7	6,833.4	(1,260.8)
Source: U.S. Census Bureau, Foreign Trade Statistics							

What do we learn from this table and figure?

Key Findings: A snapshot of U.S. trade in goods with Canada in 2015 shows that --

- We are running a large deficit in crude oil and natural gas, some $44.7 billion dollars.
- We enjoy a large surplus in manufactured goods, just shy of $40 billion, mostly attributable to machinery, metal, electrical and appliances ($30.6 billion) and computer and electronic products ($18.8 billion).
- Unlike Mexico, our large trade with Canada in transportation equipment is nearly balanced, with a $7.4 billion deficit.

China

I've saved the most important of the five for last. U.S. trade in goods with China is presented in the following figure:

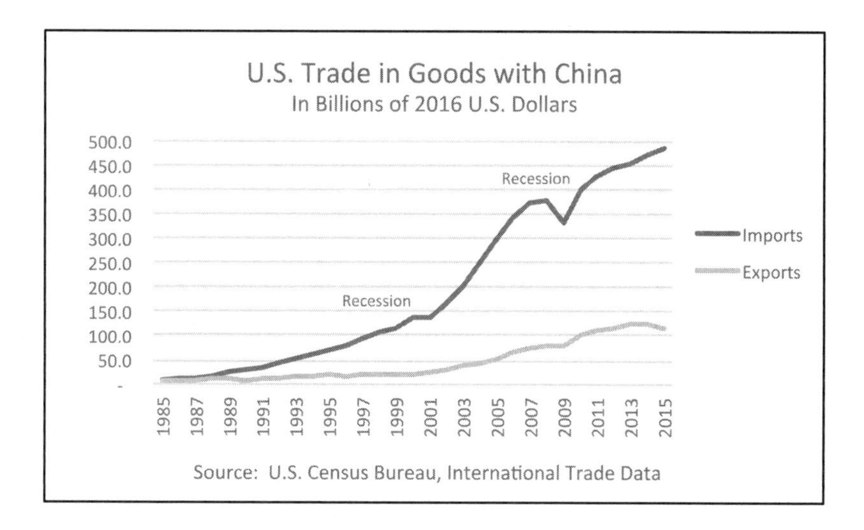

This is indeed an alarming graph. China's exports to the United States have grown exponentially, especially since 2001, blowing past Mexico's and Canada's levels. That would be no problem whatsoever if it were a reciprocal relationship and the United States' exports to China had kept pace. However, from the outset, U.S. exports to China have been a fraction of China's exports to the U.S., resulting in an enormous trade in goods deficit that reached $370 billion in 2015.

What accounts for this great disparity in imports and exports? U.S. trade with China by major groupings of goods during 2015 is presented in the following table and figure.

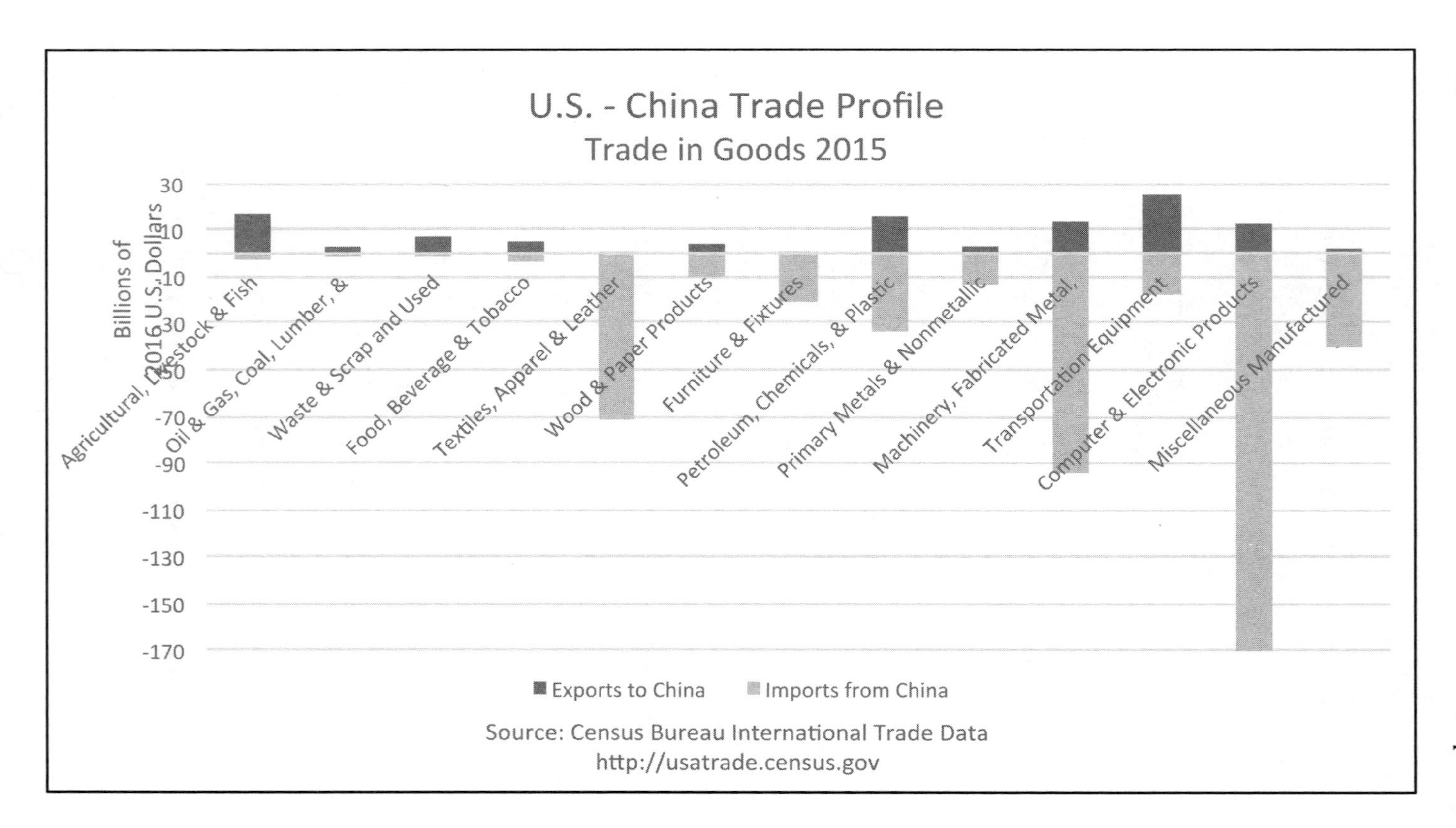
U.S. - China Trade Profile
Trade in Goods 2015
30
10
-10
-30
-50
-70
-90
-110
-130
-150
-170
Billions of 2016 U.S. Dollars
Agricultural, Livestock & Fish
Oil & Gas, Coal, Lumber, &
Waste & Scrap and Used
Food, Beverage & Tobacco
Textiles, Apparel & Leather
Wood & Paper Products
Furniture & Fixtures
Petroleum, Chemicals, & Plastic
Primary Metals & Nonmetallic
Machinery, Fabricated Metal,
Transportation Equipment
Computer & Electronic Products
Miscellaneous Manufactured
Exports to China
Imports from China
Source: Census Bureau International Trade Data
http://usatrade.census.gov

U.S. Trade in Goods with China 1985-2015 in billions of 2016 U.S. dollars							
Year	Imports	Exports	Balance	Year	Imports	Exports	Balance
1985	8.6	8.6	(0.0)	2001	139.1	26.1	(113.0)
1986	10.4	6.8	(3.6)	2002	167.8	29.7	(138.1)
1987	13.3	7.4	(5.9)	2003	199.7	37.2	(162.5)
1988	17.3	10.2	(7.1)	2004	249.8	43.7	(206.1)
1989	23.3	11.2	(12.1)	2005	299.5	50.7	(248.8)
1990	28.0	8.8	(19.2)	2006	342.5	63.9	(278.6)
1991	33.4	11.0	(22.3)	2007	372.9	73.0	(299.9)
1992	44.0	12.7	(31.3)	2008	378.3	78.1	(300.2)
1993	52.4	14.5	(37.8)	2009	331.9	77.8	(254.1)
1994	62.8	15.0	(47.8)	2010	401.4	101.1	(300.3)
1995	72.0	18.6	(53.4)	2011	427.3	111.4	(315.9)
1996	78.8	18.3	(60.5)	2012	446.9	116.0	(330.9)
1997	93.8	19.3	(74.5)	2013	453.6	125.4	(328.2)
1998	104.6	20.9	(83.7)	2014	473.2	124.9	(348.3)
1999	117.8	18.9	(98.9)	2015	488.1	117.2	(370.8)
2000	140.0	22.7	(117.4)	TOTAL	6,072.4	1,401.1	(4,671.3)
Source: U.S. Census Bureau, International Trade Data							

What do we learn from this table and figure?

Key Findings: A snapshot of U.S. trade in goods with China in 2015 shows that --

- We are running an enormous deficit in computers and electronics, over $158 billion dollars.

- We also have a huge deficit in high-value manufactured products, in machinery etc. ($80.2 billion), chemicals etc. ($18.5 billion), and steel etc. ($10.5 billion).

- We also have a large deficit in lower-value goods, in textiles and apparel ($70.7 billion), furniture ($20.4 billion), and miscellaneous manufactured goods ($38.2 billion).

Key Findings, China, continued:

- We have an $8 billion surplus in transportation products.
    - In 2015, we sold a net $14.4 billion worth of civilian aircraft.
    - We also sold China a net $8.1 billion worth of motor vehicles.
    - However, these vehicle sales were more than offset by net imports of $11.9 billion worth of motor vehicle parts.
- In 2015, we sold China a net $22.5 billion worth of farm products, raw materials, and scrap. With the exception of civilian aircraft, these were the only categories of goods in which we had a trade surplus with China.

The U.S. trade with China in transportation equipment is presented in more detail in the following table:

U.S. - China Trade in Transportation Equipment during 2015
In Millions of 2016 Dollars

	Exports 1/	Imports 2/	Balance
	Exports	Imports	Balance
Aircraft and Other Aerospace Equipment (3364)	15,245.1	845.3	14,399.9
Motor Vehicles (3361)	8,426.4	228.8	8,197.6
Motor Vehicle Parts, Bodies & Trailers (3362, 3)	1,973.0	13,859.5	(11,886.5)
Railroad, Water, & Other Trans. Equip. (3365, 6, 9)	102.9	2,767.4	(2,664.5)
	25,747.4	17,700.9	8,046.5

1/ Domestic Exports Value. 2/ Customs Import Value.
Source: Census Bureau International Trade Data, http://usatrade.census.gov
Data do not include certain adjustments made in NAICS 980 and 990.

The trade in motor vehicle parts is especially worthy of note. China is busily developing its domestic motor vehicle manufacturing capacity, often in joint ventures with U.S. vehicle manufacturers. Meanwhile, the U.S. has had little exports of vehicle parts to China, while China's exports of those goods to the U.S. have been growing exponentially. The following figure shows the trend:[7]

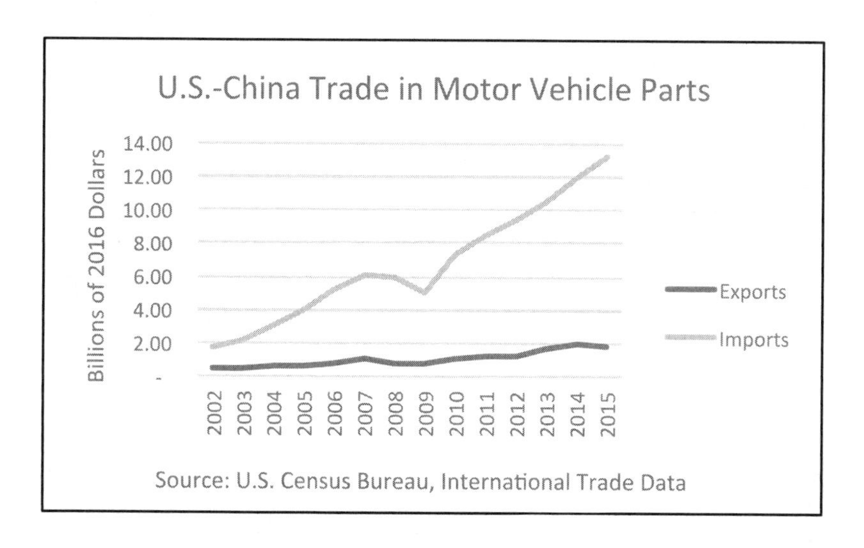

Another striking aspect of the U.S. – China trade is that China is achieving large trade surpluses in categories of goods both at the high-value-added and lower-value added ends of the spectrum. We have observed this phenomenon with respect to electronics, machinery and the like, and steel and other primary metals goods, on the one hand, and textiles and apparel and furniture on the other. The "Miscellaneous Manufactured Commodities" subsector (NAICS 339) brings this aspect of China trade into focus, as presented in the following table. Here we see China running substantial surpluses in surgical and ophthalmic products, while it also has a total predominance in sales of toys, sporting goods, and the like.

U.S. - China Trade in Miscellaneous Manufactured Commodities during 2015 In Billions of 2016 U.S. Dollars			
	Exports 1/	Imports 2/	Balance
3391 Medical Equipment & Supplies			
339112 Surgical & Medical Instruments	781	796	(15)
339113 Surgical Appliances & Supplies	505	2,118	(1,613)
339114 Dental Equipment & Supplies	99	94	5
339115 Ophthalmic Goods	142	1,788	(1,645)
339116 Dental Laboratories Products	14	49	(35)
Total Medical Equipment & Supplies	1,542	4,844	(3,303)
3399 Miscellaneous Manufactured Commodities			
33991 Jewelry & Silverware	280	3,908	(3,628)
33992 Sporting & Athletic Goods	68	5,253	(5,185)
33993 Dolls, Toys & Games	23	17,089	(17,066)
33994 Office Supplies (except Paper)	5	1,018	(1,014)
33995 Signs	6	150	(144)
33999 Other Manufactured Commodities	341	8,198	(7,857)
Total Miscellaneous Manufactured Commodities	723	35,616	(34,893)
Total	2,264	40,461	(38,196)
1/ Domestic Exports Value. 2/ Customs Import Value. Source: Census Bureau International Trade Data, http://usatrade.census.gov Data do not include certain adjustments made in NAICS 980 and 990.			

Key Findings:

- In sum, in its trade with the U.S., China is operating a sustained, dominant position of trade surplus in manufactured goods across the entire spectrum of value-added, in nearly every category of goods. The exceptions are civilian aircraft, and motor vehicles, which is more than offset by Chinese exports of motor vehicle parts.

- The other area where the U.S. runs a trade surplus with China is farm products, raw materials, and scrap. In this respect, the U.S. appears to be practicing a kind of reverse colonialism, in which it sells a few of these kinds of things to China in return for a deluge of manufactured merchandise.

Summary of the "Big Five"

While it is useful to consider the U.S. trade relationship each of these five countries individually, it is important also to gain an appreciation of those relationships in the context of each other. For example, the sheer magnitude of the U.S.-Chinese trade relationship is not evident from viewing the individual country charts, as the Chinese chart is on a whole different scale.

I therefore have prepared the following two figures.[8] The first figure displays the thirteen categories of merchandise we have been using, and, within each category, each of the five countries. For each country, U.S. exports of the category of products are displayed as a bar on the positive scale, and imports of the category as a bar on the negative scale.

So, for example, in the category of Machinery, Fabricated Metal, Electrical Equipment and Appliances, we see deficits of $21 billion and $24 billion, respectively, with Germany and Japan, a deficit of about $4 billion with Mexico, a surplus of some $30 billion with Canada, and an enormous deficit of over $80 billion with China.

The deficits (or surpluses) should not be considered in isolation, however. We also should be aware of the total volumes of our exports to, and imports from, these countries in these categories of goods. I therefore have prepared the second chart. It displays the same pairings, except that within a category, for each country, exports and imports are displayed as separate bars (exports on the positive scale, and imports on the negative scale).

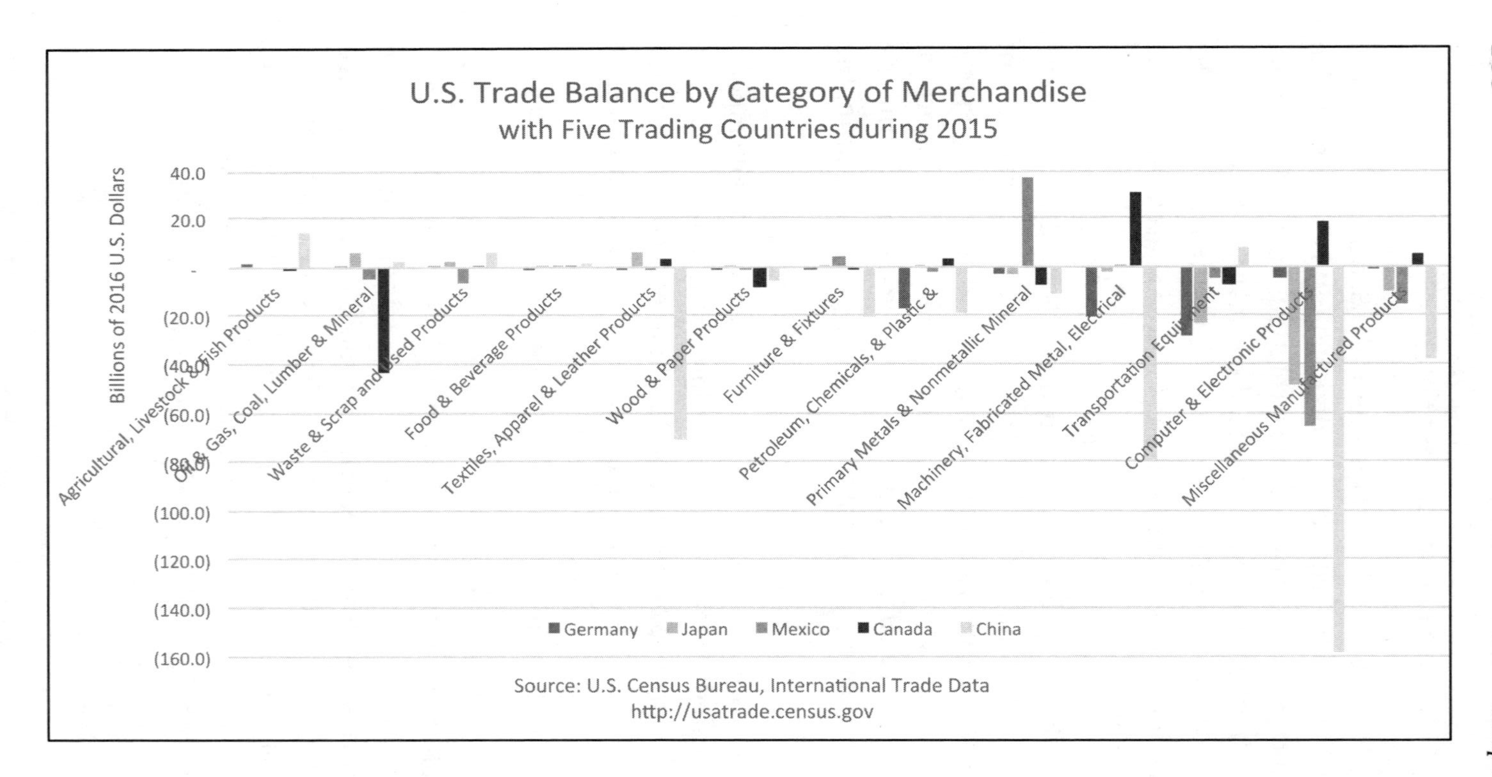
U.S. Trade Balance by Category of Merchandise
with Five Trading Countries during 2015
Billions of 2016 U.S. Dollars
40.0
20.0
-
(20.0)
(40.0)
(60.0)
(80.0)
(100.0)
(120.0)
(140.0)
(160.0)
Agricultural, Livestock & Fish Products
Oil & Gas, Coal, Lumber & Mineral
Waste & Scrap and Used Products
Food & Beverage Products
Textiles, Apparel & Leather Products
Wood & Paper Products
Furniture & Fixtures
Petroleum, Chemicals, & Plastic &
Primary Metals & Nonmetallic Mineral
Machinery, Fabricated Metal, Electrical
Transportation Equipment
Computer & Electronic Products
Miscellaneous Manufactured Products
Germany
Japan
Mexico
Canada
China
Source: U.S. Census Bureau, International Trade Data
http://usatrade.census.gov

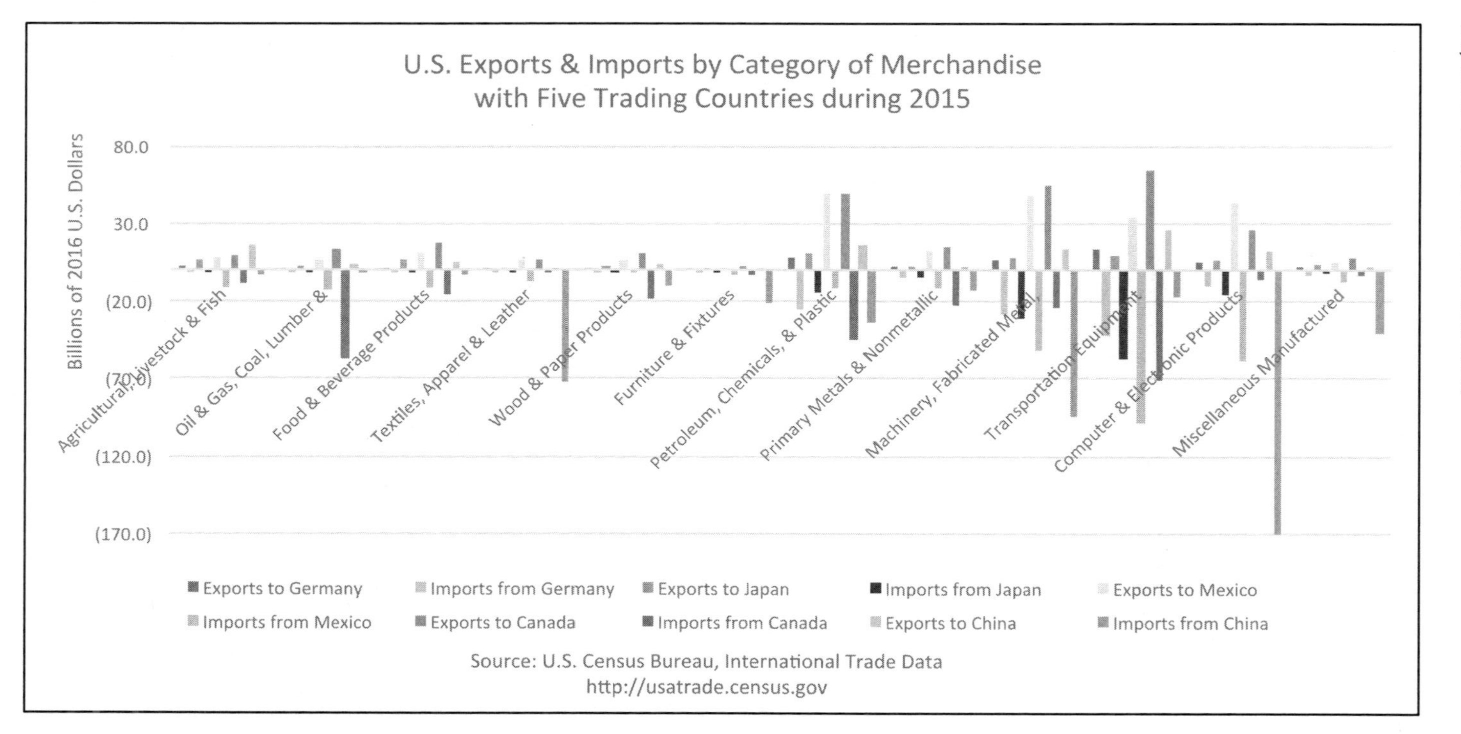
U.S. Exports & Imports by Category of Merchandise
with Five Trading Countries during 2015
Billions of 2016 U.S. Dollars
80.0
30.0
(20.0)
(70.0)
(120.0)
(170.0)
Agricultural, Livestock & Fish
Oil & Gas, Coal, Lumber &
Food & Beverage Products
Textiles, Apparel & Leather
Wood & Paper Products
Furniture & Fixtures
Petroleum, Chemicals, & Plastic
Primary Metals & Nonmetallic
Machinery, Fabricated Metal
Transportation Equipment
Computer & Electronic Products
Miscellaneous Manufactured
Exports to Germany
Imports from Germany
Exports to Japan
Imports from Japan
Exports to Mexico
Imports from Mexico
Exports to Canada
Imports from Canada
Exports to China
Imports from China
Source: U.S. Census Bureau, International Trade Data
http://usatrade.census.gov

In this case, again looking at the category of Machinery, Fabricated Metal, Electrical Equipment and Appliances, we see small exports to Germany and Japan outweighed by large imports, a fairly even balance between exports and imports with Mexico, and a large surplus of exports over imports with Canada. With respect to China, we see that we are importing an enormous sum of $94 billion, that is slightly offset by exports of some $23 billion, to result in the deficit of over $80 billion. What can we learn from these figures?

Key Findings: Taking a snapshot of the U.S. trade relationship with the five countries responsible for most of the U.S. trade in goods deficit during 2015 --

- The U.S. deficit in computer and electronics equipment from China of $158 billion is larger than the combined total deficit for Germany ($73 billion) and Japan ($71 billion).

- The U.S. has deficits with China in machinery, fabricated metal, electrical, and appliances ($80 billion) and textiles, apparel, and leather products ($70 billion) that, combined, are as large as the combined total deficit for Germany and Japan.

- The U.S. is running a very large deficit with Mexico in motor vehicles and parts and other transportation equipment, over $65 billion, nearly as much as Germany and Japan combined ($28 billion and $49 billion, respectively).

- The U.S. is running a substantial surplus only in aircraft sold to China, chemicals/plastics sold to Mexico, and machinery, etc. sold to Canada.

A Note about the "Other Countries"

In addition to the five major trade deficit countries of China, Japan, Germany, Mexico and Canada and OPEC, I have noted a catch-all "other" category that accounts for 22% of the trade in goods deficit, $167 billion in 2015.

Vietnam

Of these countries, Vietnam merits a special call out. The United States established diplomatic and economic relations with Vietnam in 1992, and entered into the U.S.-Vietnam Bilateral Trade Agreement in 2001. U.S. trade in goods with Vietnam since 1992 is presented in the following figure:

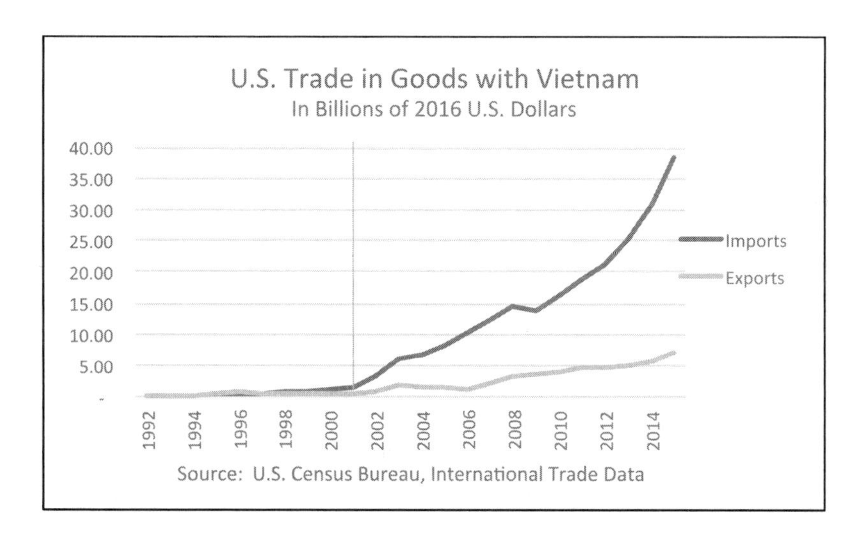

This figure is not dissimilar to the figure showing the Chinese trade in goods deficit exploding beginning in 2001: since 2001, U.S. imports from Vietnam are exploding at an ever-increasing rate, to nearly $40 billion in 2015, while exports to Vietnam are small and growing slowly, to $7 billion. Although Vietnam's population is not in China's league, it has over 93 million people, on a par with Japan's 127 million, Germany's 90 million, and Mexico's 120 million. Vietnam has the potential to surpass these other countries as a contributor to the U.S. trade in goods deficit.

South Korea

In the "Other Countries" category, South Korea also is worth noting. U.S. trade in goods with South Korea is presented in the following figure:

Since 1998, United States has run a persistent trade in goods deficit with Korea, except the 2008-9 recession. Since the entry into effect of the U.S.-Korea Free Trade Agreement in 2011, this deficit has widened to nearly $30 billion.

Countries with Free Trade Agreements

Overview of Trade Agreements

With respect to Canada, Mexico, Vietnam, and Korea I have mentioned the entry into trade agreements with the

United States. Our review of "what's really going on with trade" cannot be complete without considering the countries with which the U.S. has entered into bilateral or regional trade agreements. These agreements typically provide for elimination or reduction of tariffs on goods traded between the parties, for rules against "non-tariff barriers to trade" and against subsidies and/or sales below market or cost of production, and for mechanisms for enforcing the agreement. In Chapters 2 and 3 we considered when and why we entered into them. Now, we consider our historical and current trade in goods balances with these countries. Here is a list:

U.S. Free Trade Agreements in Effect as of 2016					
	Country	Entry		Country	Entry
	Israel	1985	CAFTA-DR 4/	El Salvadore	2006
NAFTA 1/	Canada 2/	1989	CAFTA-DR	Guatemala	2006
NAFTA 1/	Mexico	1994	CAFTA-DR	Honduras	2006
	Jordan	2001	CAFTA-DR	Nicaraugua	2006
	Vietnam 3/	2001	CAFTA-DR	Dom. Repub.	2007
	Chile	2004	CAFTA-DR	Costa Rica	2009
	Singapore	2004		Oman	2009
	Australia	2005		Peru	2009
	Bahrain	2006		South Korea	2012
	Morocco	2006		Colombia	2012
				Panama	2012

1/ North American Free Trade Agreement
2/ U.S.-Canada Free Trade Agreement, subsumed into NAFTA.
3/ This agreement is a "bilateral trade agreement."
4/ Central American Free Trade Agr. Incl. Dominican Republic.

These agreements are always touted as promising jobs and economic growth. So, now we ask, "how's that working out for you?" The answer, it seems, is sometimes pretty well, but more often than not, not so very well at all. The facts are summarized in the following figure.[9]

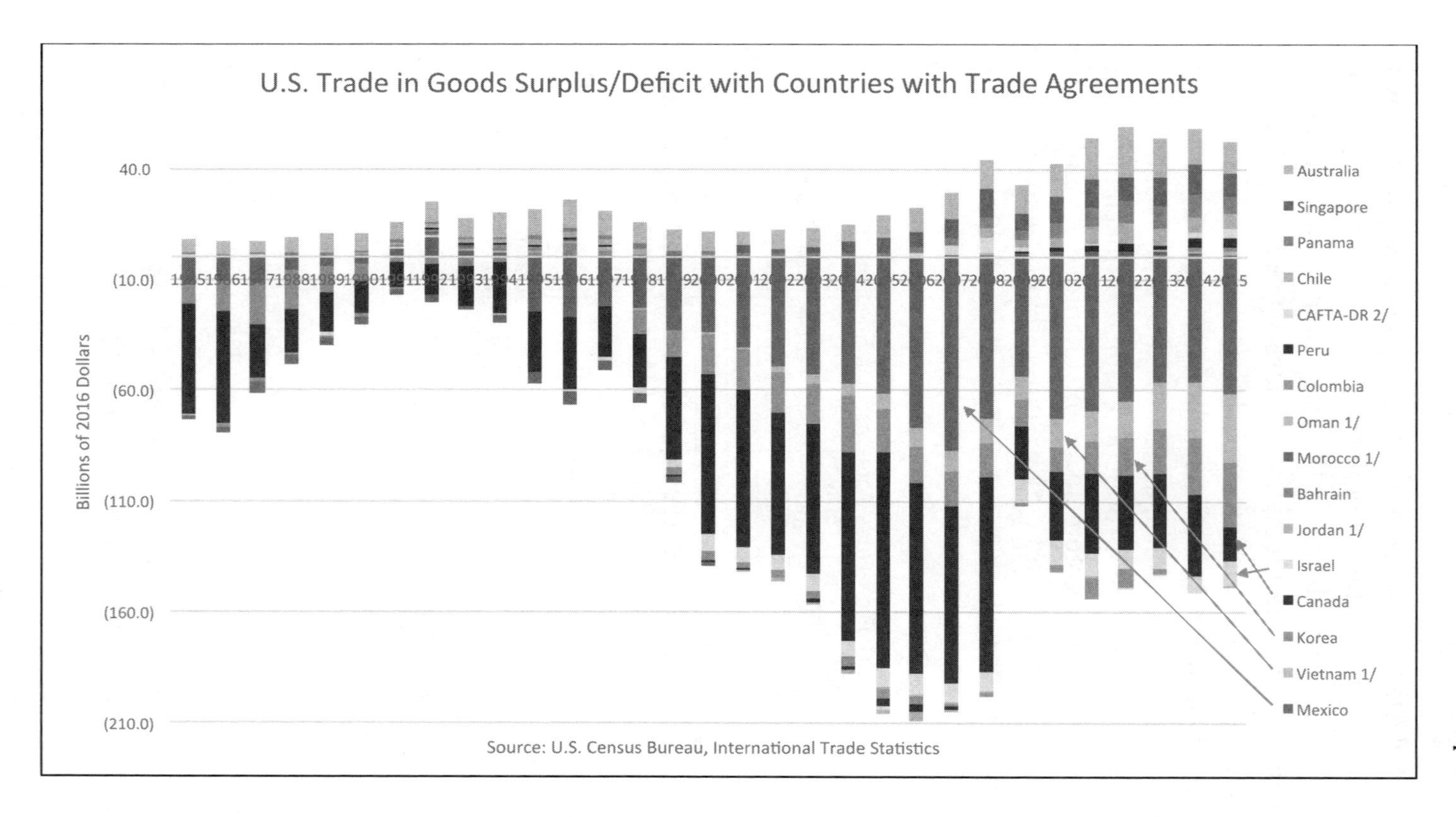
U.S. Trade in Goods Surplus/Deficit with Countries with Trade Agreements
40.0
(10.0)
(60.0)
(110.0)
(160.0)
(210.0)
Billions of 2016 Dollars
Australia
Singapore
Panama
Chile
CAFTA-DR 2/
Peru
Colombia
Oman 1/
Morocco 1/
Bahrain
Jordan 1/
Israel
Canada
Korea
Vietnam 1/
Mexico
Source: U.S. Census Bureau, International Trade Statistics

The figure displays graphically the U.S. balance of trade in goods with each of the party countries during the years 1985 through 2015. A surplus is shown on the positive scale, a deficit on the negative scale. What does the figure tell us?

Experience under Each Agreement

The experience under each of the major agreements can be summarized as follows:

Key Findings and Conclusions:

- A glance at the figure shows that there is a great deal more trade in negative territory than in positive: taken as a whole, the parties to these agreements have engaged in a lot more imports into the U.S. than exports from the U.S.
- A group of five countries, Mexico, Vietnam, South Korea, Canada, and Israel, are running substantial-to-large trade in goods deficits, totaling $148 billion in 2015.
- A group of seven parties, Australia, Singapore, Panama, Chile, CAFTA-DR, Peru, and Colombia, are running small-to-substantial trade in goods surpluses, totaling $50 billion in 2015.
- A group of four small Middle Eastern countries, Oman, Morocco, Bahrain, and Jordan, are running negligible surpluses (and one deficit), for a total surplus of $2.3 billion in 2015.

Mexico

As we have discussed, the experience with Mexico under NAFTA has been for greatly increased trade, but with a catch – significantly more trade was created on the Mexican side. A very large trade gap of some $65 billion has opened, which easily could grow larger.

Vietnam

The agreement with Vietnam has been an unmitigated disaster, as discussed above under "Other Countries." I was shocked to learn that this agreement provided that during the first several years, tariffs would be lowered by the U.S., but not by Vietnam, in order to protect against the U.S. taking over its markets. That is indeed a laughable concern given the experience under this agreement, with inconsequential exports by the U.S. accompanied by increasing exports by Vietnam, with no end in sight.

South Korea

The agreement with South Korea also has not been beneficial in its effect, as discussed above under "Other Countries." U.S. trade deficits with Korea only worsened after the entry into effect of the agreement in 2011.

Canada

As discussed above, the trade relationship with Canada has been mostly salutary. When the price of crude oil was high, the U.S. ran a substantial overall deficit with Canada. However, the deficit has become more manageable, and the U.S. runs a considerable surplus in manufactured goods.

Other Countries

The U.S. trade relationships with other parties to trade agreements are illustrated in the following figures:

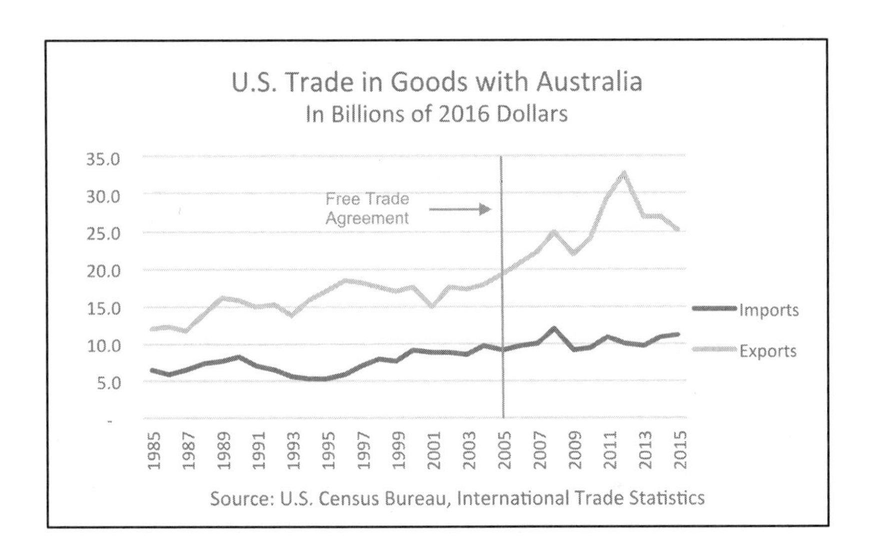

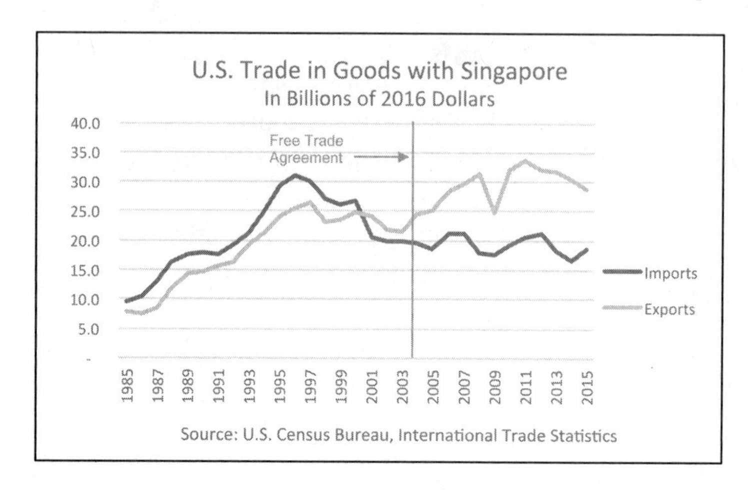
U.S. Trade in Goods with Singapore
In Billions of 2016 Dollars
40.0
35.0
30.0
25.0
20.0
15.0
10.0
5.0
-
Free Trade Agreement
1985
1987
1989
1991
1993
1995
1997
1999
2001
2003
2005
2007
2009
2011
2013
2015
Imports
Exports
Source: U.S. Census Bureau, International Trade Statistics

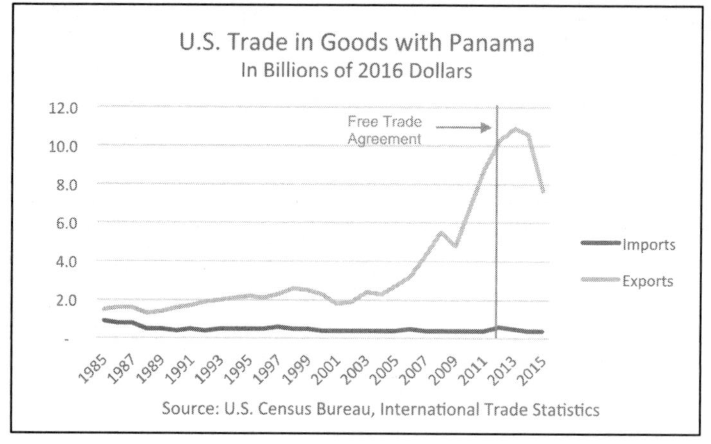
U.S. Trade in Goods with Panama
In Billions of 2016 Dollars
12.0
10.0
8.0
6.0
4.0
2.0
-
Free Trade Agreement
1985
1987
1989
1991
1993
1995
1997
1999
2001
2003
2005
2007
2009
2011
2013
2015
Imports
Exports
Source: U.S. Census Bureau, International Trade Statistics

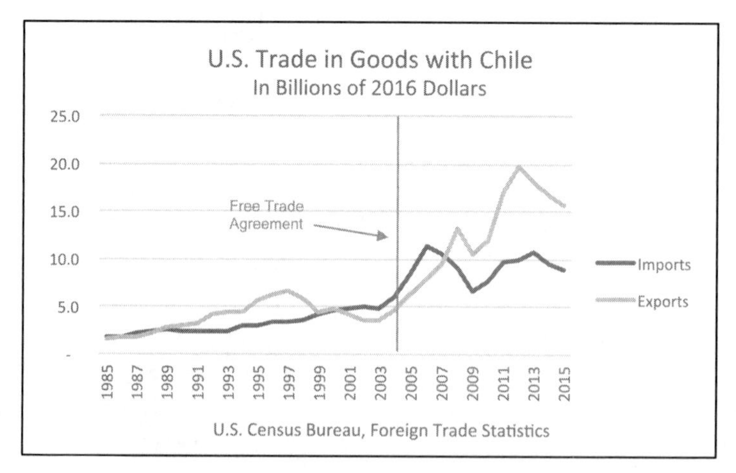
U.S. Trade in Goods with Chile
In Billions of 2016 Dollars
25.0
20.0
15.0
10.0
5.0
-
Free Trade Agreement
1985
1987
1989
1991
1993
1995
1997
1999
2001
2003
2005
2007
2009
2011
2013
2015
Imports
Exports
U.S. Census Bureau, Foreign Trade Statistics

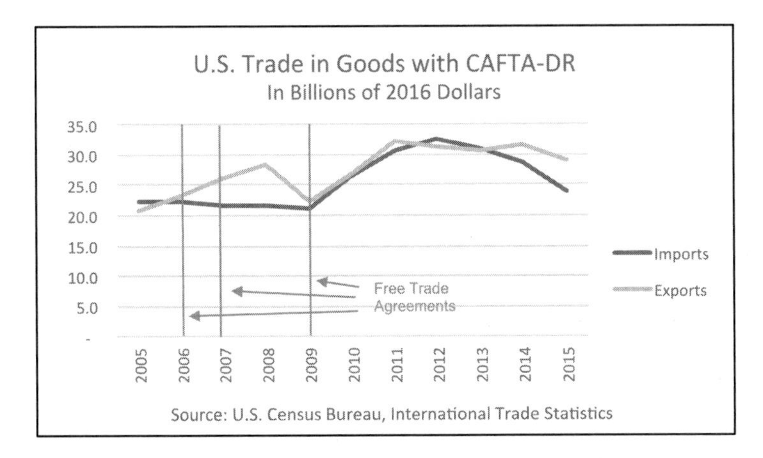
U.S. Trade in Goods with CAFTA-DR
In Billions of 2016 Dollars
35.0
30.0
25.0
20.0
15.0
10.0
5.0
-
Free Trade
Agreements
Imports
Exports
2005
2006
2007
2008
2009
2010
2011
2012
2013
2014
2015
Source: U.S. Census Bureau, International Trade Statistics

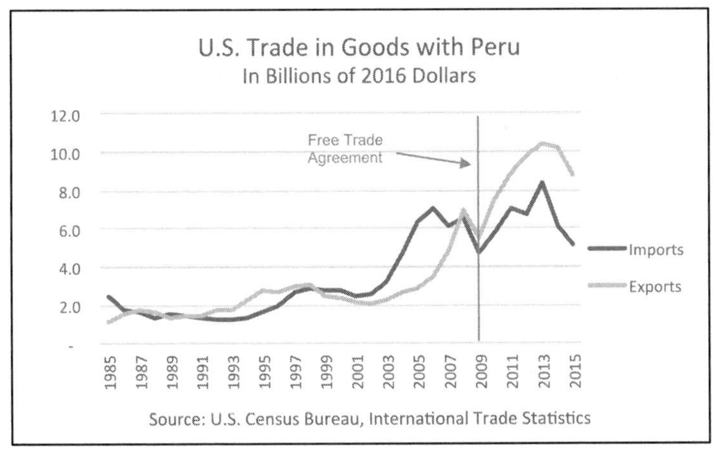
U.S. Trade in Goods with Peru
In Billions of 2016 Dollars
12.0
10.0
8.0
6.0
4.0
2.0
-
Free Trade
Agreement
Imports
Exports
1985
1987
1989
1991
1993
1995
1997
1999
2001
2003
2005
2007
2009
2011
2013
2015
Source: U.S. Census Bureau, International Trade Statistics

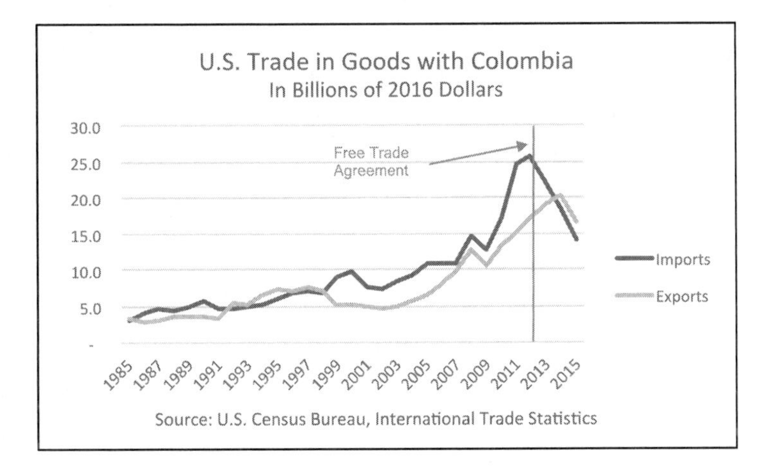
U.S. Trade in Goods with Colombia
In Billions of 2016 Dollars
30.0
25.0
20.0
15.0
10.0
5.0
-
Free Trade
Agreement
Imports
Exports
1985
1987
1989
1991
1993
1995
1997
1999
2001
2003
2005
2007
2009
2011
2013
2015
Source: U.S. Census Bureau, International Trade Statistics

The first thing to notice about these other countries is that the volume of trade is relatively small compared to "the big five;" however, they are significant. The other thing that jumps out is that with each of these countries except Israel and Columbia, the U.S. has been running a surplus, selling to them more goods than we purchase from them.

Conclusions

So, where do we come out in our quest to find out, "what's *really* going on with trade?" The picture that emerges is this:

Key Findings:

- Since 1993, the U.S. has experienced a chronic trade in goods deficit: In 2015, the annual trade in goods deficit stood at some $753 billion.

    - The trade in goods deficit is substantial: in 2015, it was the equivalent of 4.2% of U.S. Gross Domestic Product. In recent years, it been the equivalent of from four to six percent of GDP, which, considering multiplier effects, would have added six to nine percent to the economy, if the spending on excess imports had stayed home.

    - In dollar terms, the trade in goods deficit has meant draining trillions of dollars from the U.S. economy into the economies of other countries: $15.9 trillion (in 2016 dollars) from 1985 through 2015.

    (continued)

  - In the 16 years from 1985 through 2000, the U.S. spent $4.4 trillion on net imports of goods. But the pace accelerated dramatically:

  - In the 15 years from 2001 through 2015, the U.S. spent $11.5 trillion on net imports of foreign goods.

- China and four other countries, Japan, Germany, Mexico, and Canada, account for 80% of the U.S. trade in goods deficit.

  - For two of these countries, the deficit has been declining, but is still substantial: Japan ($70 billion in 2015) and Canada ($15.7 billion in 2015).

  - For two of these countries, the deficit has been increasing: Germany ($75.6 billion in 2015) and Mexico ($61.3 billion in 2015).

- Regarding the rest of the world --

  - Of the remaining countries, Vietnam is of special concern: since the 2001 U.S.-Vietnam trade agreement, Vietnam's trade in goods deficit has grown at an ever-increasing pace, from less than $1 billion in 2001to over $31 billion in 2015.

  - South Korea also is of concern; since the 2011 U.S.-Korea Free Trade Agreement, South Korea's deficit has grown steadily, from $14 billion in 2001 to nearly $30 billion in 2015.

- In all of this, one country stands out --
    - The U.S. trade in goods deficit with China grew steadily from essentially zero in 1985 to over $113 billion in 2001, and then exploded to over $370 billion in 2015, accounting for 49% of the total U.S. trade in goods deficit.

So, as to our first question, "why does it seem like everything is made somewhere else?", our initial answer is that we have been importing most of the things consumers buy from a handful of countries, especially China, and we are importing from them a great deal more than we've been exporting to them.

But, if we have sent a net $16 trillion in 2016 dollars to China and other countries since 1985, and uncounted trillions before that, we are left wondering, "Isn't that causing a problem? We take up that question in Part II.

Notes to Chapter 5

[1] Mary Bottari ,"Like Gravity" Fast Track Trade Sinks Jobs and Wages, *Center for Media and Democracy*, January 21, 2014 http://www.prwatch.org/news/2014/01/12367/%E2%80%9C-gravity%E2%80%9D-fast-track-trade-will-sink-jobs-and-drag-down-wages.

[2] For an apples-to-apples comparison, I express all values in 2016 dollars. The tables from which the figures in this Chapter are derived are published at http://currentaffairspress.com/titles/what-if-things-were-made-in-america-again/.

[3] The values are calculated by the Customs Bureau on a "Balance of Payments" basis, including certain adjustments in order to make the values comparable to the data for services. When calculated on a "Customs Basis," the trade in goods deficit for 2015 is $753.1 billion. Except as otherwise noted, all trade figures in this book are reported on a Customs Basis. The trade in goods deficit as reported on a Customs Basis is presented in the following table:

U.S. Trade in Goods Deficit 1985-2015
As Percentage of GDP
In Billions of 2016 U.S. Dollars

Year	GDP	Deficit	% of GDP	Year	GDP	Deficit	% of GDP
1985	9,693	262.5	2.7%	2001	14,450	560.2	3.9%
1986	10,052	302.8	3.0%	2002	14,713	627.5	4.3%
1987	10,276	321.0	3.1%	2003	15,081	697.4	4.6%
1988	10,663	240.6	2.3%	2004	15,592	831.6	5.3%
1989	10,976	212.2	1.9%	2005	16,107	950.0	5.9%
1990	11,002	187.2	1.7%	2006	16,491	985.3	6.0%
1991	10,866	117.4	1.1%	2007	16,797	938.2	5.6%
1992	11,182	144.5	1.3%	2008	16,487	914.1	5.5%
1993	11,419	191.8	1.7%	2009	16,148	564.0	3.5%
1994	11,840	244.0	2.1%	2010	16,454	699.0	4.2%
1995	12,109	250.9	2.1%	2011	16,621	776.2	4.7%
1996	12,393	260.4	2.1%	2012	17,057	767.1	4.5%
1997	12,913	270.8	2.1%	2013	17,304	709.5	4.1%
1998	13,361	337.7	2.5%	2014	17,522	742.5	4.2%
1999	13,919	473.5	3.4%	2015	18,126	753.1	4.2%
2000	14,406	610.5	4.2%	Total	432,021	15,943.7	3.7%

Source: U.S. Census Bureau, International Trade Data

---

[44] U.S. trade in services during the year 2015 is presented in the following table:

U.S. Exports and Imports of Services during 2015			
By Major Category in Billions of 2016 Dollars			
	Exports	Imports	Balance
Maintenance & Repair Servcies	24.3	9.1	15.2
Transport	88.1	98.0	(9.9)
Travel	206.6	114.0	92.6
Insurance Services	17.3	48.2	(30.9)
Financial Services	103.5	25.4	78.1
Intellectual Property Charges	125.9	39.9	86.0
Tel., Computer, & Info. Services	36.3	36.8	(0.6)
Other Business Services	136.0	100.3	35.6
Government Goods & Services	20.5	21.7	(1.3)
Total Services	758.4	493.5	264.8
Source: Bureau of Economic Analysis U.S. International Trade in Goods and Services, Annual Revision for 2015 http://www.bea.gov/newsreleases/international/trade/2016/trad1316.htm Details may not equal totals due to seasonal adjustment and rounding.			

[5] The figure is derived from the following table:

U.S. Imports & Exports 2015			
(Billions 2016 $)	Exports	Imports	Balance
China	117.2	488.1	(370.84)
Germany	50.5	126.1	(75.60)
Japan	63.1	132.7	(69.61)
Mexico	238.1	299.4	(61.27)
Canada	283.4	299.1	(15.70)
Rest of World	765.3	925.4	(160.09)
Total	1,517.6	2,270.7	(753.12)
Source: U.S. Census Bureau			

[6] The Organization of Petroleum Exporting Countries. See http://www.opec.org.

---

[7] The figure is derived from the following table:

U.S.-China Trade in Motor Vehicle Parts 2002 - 2015 In Billions of 2016 U.S. Dollars							
Year	**Exports**	**Imports**	**Balance**	**Year**	**Exports**	**Imports**	**Balance**
2002	0.4	1.7	(1.3)	2009	0.8	5.0	(4.2)
2003	0.5	2.2	(1.7)	2010	1.1	7.3	(6.2)
2004	0.7	3.0	(2.4)	2011	1.3	8.5	(7.3)
2005	0.6	4.0	(3.3)	2012	1.3	9.5	(8.2)
2006	0.8	5.1	(4.4)	2013	1.8	10.4	(8.7)
2007	1.0	6.1	(5.1)	2014	2.0	11.9	(9.9)
2008	0.8	5.9	(5.2)	2015	1.9	13.2	(11.3)
Source: U.S. Census Bureau, International Trade Data							

[8] The figures are derived from the following tables:

U.S. Imports & Exports by Category of Merchandise with Five Trading Countries during 2015					
	Germany	Japan	Mexico	Canada	China
Agricultural, Livestock & Fish Products	1.6	6.0	(4.6)	(0.5)	13.5
Oil & Gas, Coal, Lumber & Mineral Products	0.4	2.0	(6.8)	(43.3)	2.7
Waste & Scrap and Used Products	1.1	0.1	0.8	0.8	6.3
Food & Beverage Products	(0.8)	5.6	(0.4)	0.7	1.4
Textiles, Apparel & Leather Products	(0.3)	0.1	(1.3)	3.8	(70.7)
Wood & Paper Products	(0.5)	1.1	4.5	(7.9)	(5.8)
Furniture & Fixtures	(0.3)	0.0	(1.9)	(0.1)	(20.4)
Petroleum, Chemicals, & Plastic & Rubber Products	(17.3)	(3.1)	36.9	3.7	(18.5)
Primary Metals & Nonmetallic Mineral Products	(2.7)	(2.1)	0.9	(7.6)	(10.5)
Machinery, Fabricated Metal, Electrical & Appliances	(20.6)	(23.6)	(4.2)	30.6	(80.2)
Transportation Equipment	(28.4)	(48.8)	(65.2)	(7.4)	8.0
Computer & Electronic Products	(4.4)	(9.9)	(15.2)	18.8	(158.1)
Miscellaneous Manufactured Products	(0.4)	1.5	(2.9)	5.3	(38.2)
	(72.6)	(71.3)	(59.4)	(3.1)	(370.5)

Exports are Domestic Exports Value. Imports are Customs Import Value.
Source: Census Bureau International Trade Data, http://usatrade.census.gov/perspective60
Data do not include certain adjustments made in NAICS 980 and 990.

U.S. Imports & Exports by Category of Merchandise
with Five Trading Countries during 2015 (Part 1)

	Exports to Germany	Imports from Germany	Exports to Japan	Imports from Japan
Agricultural, Livestock & Fish Products	1.9	(0.3)	6.3	(0.3)
Oil & Gas, Coal, Lumber & Mineral Products	0.5	(0.0)	2.0	(0.0)
Food & Beverage Products	0.6	(1.5)	6.1	(0.5)
Textiles, Apparel & Leather Products	0.3	(0.6)	0.6	(0.6)
Wood & Paper Products	0.8	(1.3)	1.6	(0.6)
Furniture & Fixtures	0.1	(0.4)	0.1	(0.1)
Petroleum, Chemicals, & Plastic & Rubber Products	7.6	(24.8)	10.9	(14.0)
Primary Metals & Nonmetallic Mineral Products	2.0	(4.7)	2.0	(4.1)
Machinery, Fabricated Metal, Electrical & Appliances	7.0	(27.6)	7.5	(31.1)
Transportation Equipment	13.1	(41.4)	8.9	(57.7)
Computer & Electronic Products	5.1	(9.5)	6.0	(15.9)
Miscellaneous Manufactured Products	2.7	(3.1)	3.8	(2.3)
Total	41.7	(115.3)	55.8	(127.2)

Exports are Domestic Exports Value. Imports are Customs Import Value.
Source: Census Bureau International Trade Data, http://usatrade.census.gov/perspective60
Data do not include certain adjustments made in NAICS 980 and 990.

U.S. Imports & Exports by Category of Merchandise
with Five Trading Countries during 2015 (Part 2)

	Exports to Mexico	Imports from Mexico	Exports to Canada	Imports from Canada	Exports to China	Imports from China
Agricultural, Livestock & Fish Products	7.102815	-11.6729	8.858253	-9.36973	16.32387	-2.7834
Oil & Gas, Coal, Lumber & Mineral Products	6.1928	-12.9694	13.72807	-57.0114	3.085414	-0.42416
Food & Beverage Products	10.9864	-11.396	16.84433	-16.1086	5.034915	-3.62713
Textiles, Apparel & Leather Products	6.146646	-7.48062	5.808128	-2.03939	0.923776	-71.6036
Wood & Paper Products	6.438444	-1.97012	10.45237	-18.3224	3.84926	-9.69825
Furniture & Fixtures	0.80791	-2.69343	2.712043	-2.82521	0.189283	-20.6185
Petroleum, Chemicals, & Plastic & Rubber Products	48.69177	-11.7862	48.7039	-44.9889	15.54526	-34.0032
Primary Metals & Nonmetallic Mineral Products	12.411	-11.5249	14.86896	-22.4283	2.367954	-12.8451
Machinery, Fabricated Metal, Electrical & Appliances	47.54484	-51.7622	53.95273	-23.3979	13.64515	-93.8654
Transportation Equipment	33.85907	-99.0921	63.65882	-71.0717	25.74742	-17.7009
Computer & Electronic Products	43.63398	-58.8113	25.54189	-6.7399	12.08789	-170.201
Miscellaneous Manufactured Products	5.172512	-8.04574	8.238138	-2.94757	2.264298	-40.4605
Total	228.9882	-289.205	273.3676	-277.251	101.0645	-477.831

Exports are Domestic Exports Value. Imports are Customs Import Value.
Source: Census Bureau International Trade Data, http://usatrade.census.gov/perspective60
Data do not include certain adjustments made in NAICS 980 and 990.

[9] The table from which the figure is derived is presented in the Online Appendices.

Part Two

Isn't that causing a problem?

Chapter 6

Job Losses and their Effects

> When, asked Cohen, will we start to document the net effect of these trade deals on employment? "What has happened to our jobs, our communities, the North Philadelphia that I grew up in? The Cleveland that I can picture now? The devastation throughout those communities, no replacement for those jobs," said Cohen.[1]

Looking at the persistent excess of imported goods over exports, one must suspect, hasn't this caused a loss of manufacturing jobs? If so, where did those jobs go? And what happened when the jobs left? In this chapter, we will consider these questions.

Job Losses in Manufacturing

From the first post-war year of 1946 through 1979, the number of people employed in manufacturing in the United States rose by 44 percent, from 13.5 million to 19.4 million, as shown in the following figure.[2]

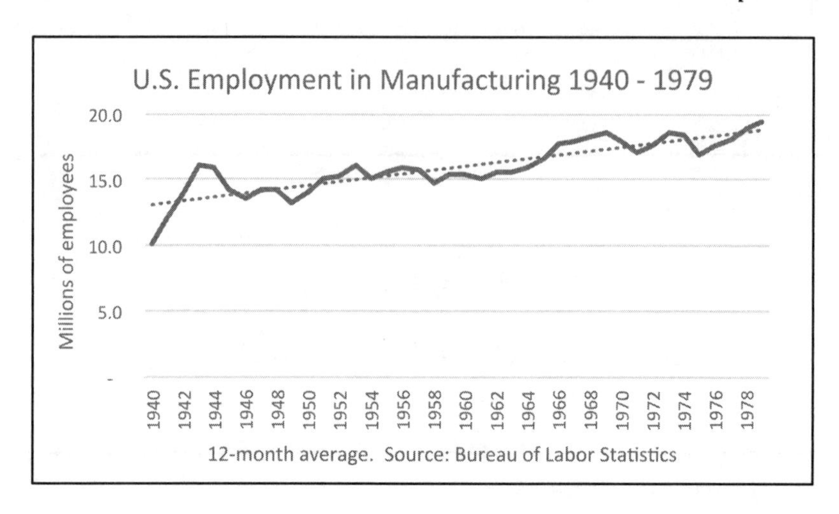

From then on, it has been all downhill: manufacturing employment in the United States dropped from a peak of 19.4 million in 1979, to 12.3 million in 2016. That is a decline of 7.1 million, some 37% -- nearly four of every ten manufacturing jobs, as shown in the following figure.[3]

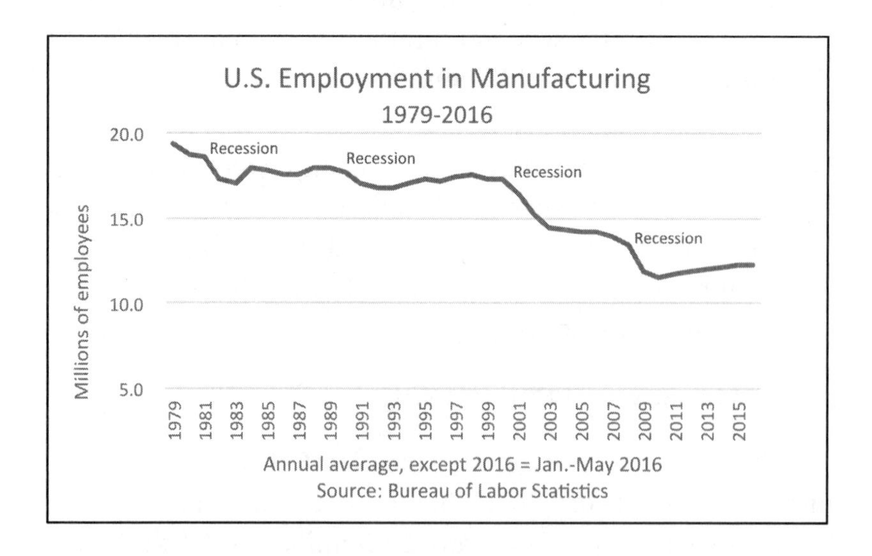

But what lies behind these totals?

The trouble with the use of the single word "manufacturing" is that it tends to evoke a picture in the mind's eye of something smaller than the whole. An assessment of employment in manufacturing requires that we consider the extraordinary breadth, depth, and richness of this sector of the economy.[4]

Consider the "built environment." Every edifice, from a row house in Baltimore to the World Trade Center, consists entirely of components from the manufacturing sector. As you read this book, I urge you to begin looking at the exterior and interior of buildings you visit, and to imagine the structural components in between (or observe them in buildings under construction). Then consider the "furnishings, fixtures and equipment" inside the building. Then do the same for your home. Then consider all the cranes, bulldozers, and other machinery used in constructing all of this.

Then begin to observe the roads, bridges and tunnels, railways, ports, and airports, and all the automobiles, trucks, and other transportation equipment that operate on them, and all the facilities that service that equipment. Then consider all the facilities and equipment used in converting petroleum, coal, wind, sunshine, and moving water into fuels and electricity. Then consider the clothing, packaged and processed food and beverages, medical equipment and medicines, and recreational equipment we use every day. Then, consider all the machinery used in creating all of the foregoing. Manufacturing produces the framework of our lives.

So, the U.S. manufacturing sector is very large and diverse, and we must take this into account if we are to grasp the scope and extent of these job losses. To structure this review, I use The North American Classification System

("NAICS"), which divides the manufacturing sector into subsectors, together with the Bureau of Labor Statistics reports on employment in each subsector.[5] I separated the 20 BLS subsectors into nine groupings having similar characteristics.

I consider employment during the period 1990-2016, partly because data before 1990 are not readily available. However, that period is useful in that it follows the manufacturing sector through the three recessions of 1990-91, 2000-2001, and 2008-2009 and their very different aftermaths. This period also corresponds well to changes in the global economy.

Each industry follows its own variant of the overall path of employment in the preceding figure. Some industries, such as apparel, textiles, and electronics, were already in decline when the 1990-91 recession hit in July of 1990. For these industries, peak employment registers at the beginning of 1990; they then were caught in three repetitions of the cycle of employment declines with inadequate recovery, each time hitting a new low, from which they have made only a modest, if any, recovery.

Other industries, such as furniture, recovered from the 1990-91 recession and rode the 1990s' economic expansion up to a new high of employment in 2000. This peak is followed by a disastrous fall-off beginning after 2000, coincident with the 2001 recession and the granting of permanent normal trade relations status and WTO membership to China. This drop is followed by a pause or shallower fall-off during 2003-2008, and another disastrous fall-off beginning with the start of the Great Recession in 2008.

After this "double dip" effect, we see a general bottoming out, followed by a true "flat line" (to borrow a medical term) for a number of industries, and a modest recovery for others. At the end of the day, all industries are far below their peak employment. And the effect is worse than the graphs suggest, because the population was growing during this time.

What is startling, is the breadth of these losses, across industries and geographies. Each of the twenty-one industry subsectors has within it a number of discreet, viable, and important industries. Each industry has its own sad tale to tell. And behind these numbers lie the real effects on individuals, families and communities.

I invite you to read each industry's story. The cumulative effect is powerful.

Group 1 – Apparel, Textiles, and Textile Products [6]

Apparel

We first consider job losses in apparel manufacturing (NAICS 315). Here we find establishments producing a vast array of clothing and accessories for men, women, boys, girls, and infants, including suits, coats, jackets and vests, shirts, blouses, slacks, dresses and skirts, hosiery, sweaters, shirts and blouses, dresses, outerwear, athletic wear, swimwear, underwear, nightwear and robes, hats and caps, mittens and gloves, neckwear, belts and other accessories.[7]

The extent of job losses in this sector is striking: American apparel factories, which employed 938,600 workers at the beginning of 1990, employed an average 133,600 during 2016, per the following figure: [8]

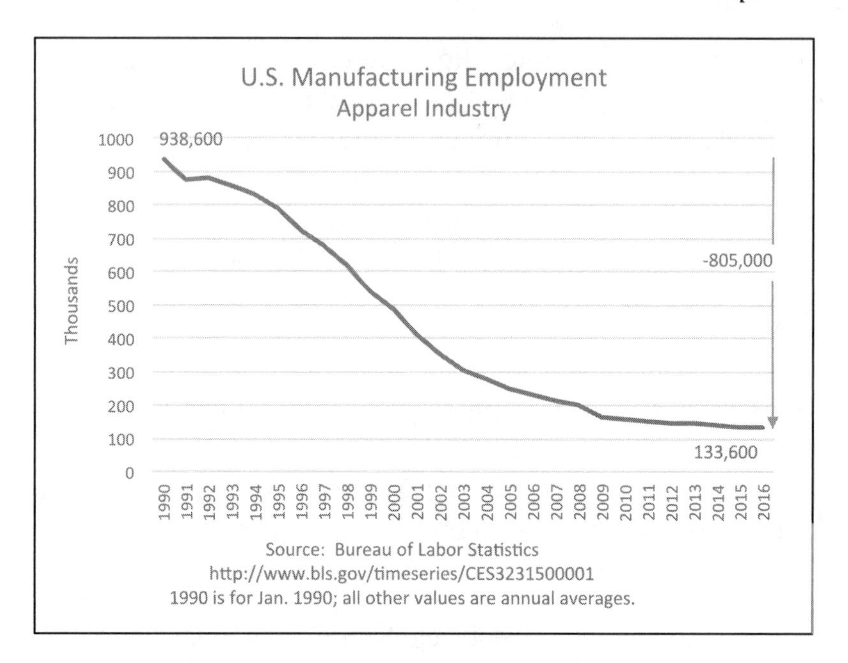

Key Finding: Between 1990 and 2016, employment in the apparel industry fell by some 805,000 jobs, an 86% decline, nearly nine in every ten jobs.

Textiles

We next consider job losses in textile mills (NAICS 313). Here we find establishments producing yarns, thread, broad-woven fabrics, knit fabrics, and vinyl and rubber-coated fabrics.

As with apparel, employment in textile mills has demonstrated an extraordinary decline: American textile mills, which employed 503,300 workers at the beginning of 1990, employed an average 114,217 during 2016, as illustrated in the following figure:

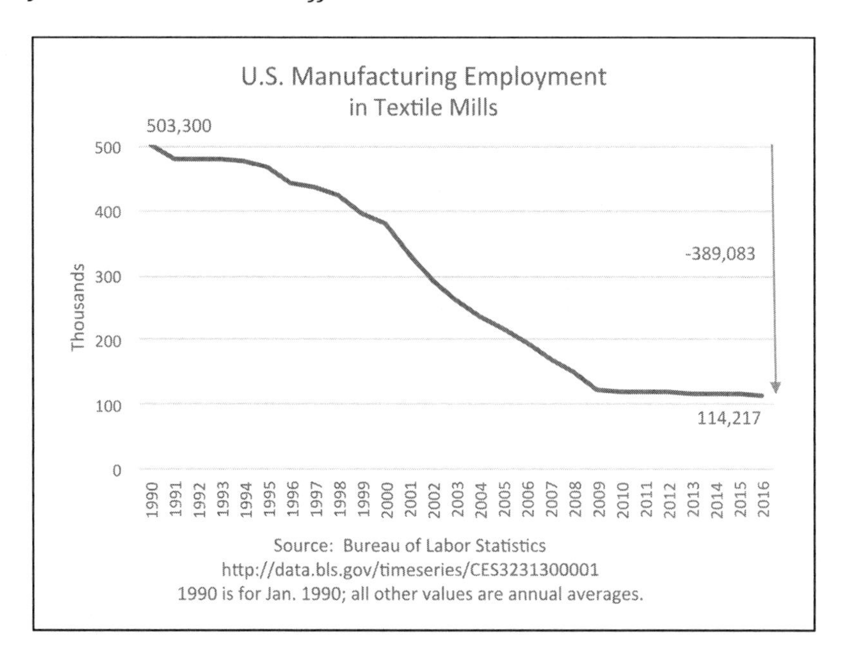

> **Key Finding:** Between 1990 and 2016, employment in textile mills fell by some 390,000 jobs, a 77% decline, nearly eight in every ten jobs.

Textile Products

We next consider job losses in textile product mills (NAICS 314). Here we find establishments producing carpet and rugs, curtains and draperies, upholstery components and other household furnishings, bedspreads, sheets and pillowcases, towels and washcloths, textile bag and canvas products, and rope, cordage and twine (including tire cord).

American textile product mills, which employed 243,500 workers at the beginning of 1990, employed an average 117,417 during 2016, as illustrated in the following figure:

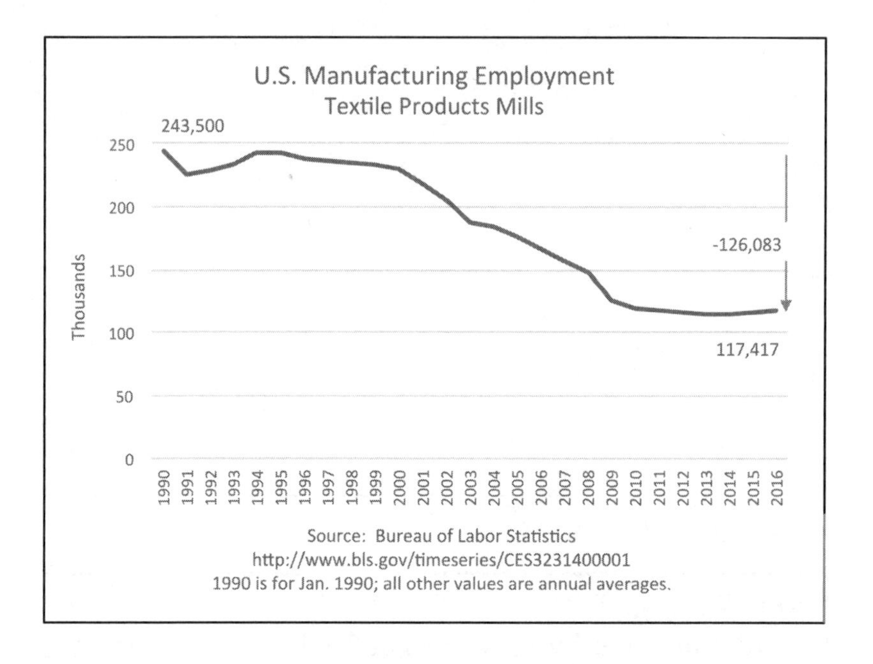

Source: Bureau of Labor Statistics
http://www.bls.gov/timeseries/CES3231400001
1990 is for Jan. 1990; all other values are annual averages.

Key Finding: Between 1990 and 2016, employment in the textile products industry fell by some 126,000 jobs, a 52% decline, five in every ten jobs.

Group 2 – Paper and Printing Products

Paper and Paper Products

We next consider job losses in paper and paper products (NAICS 322). Here we find a wide assortment of products from raw to finished, including pulp mill products, paper mill products, newsprint, paperboard, corrugated and solid boxes, paperboard containers, paper bags, wallpaper, wrapping paper, cut paper and stationery products, disposable diapers and other sanitary products.

This is another hard hit-industry: American paper mills and paper product plants, which employed 647,100 workers at the beginning of 1990, employed an average 372,433 during 2016, per the following figure:

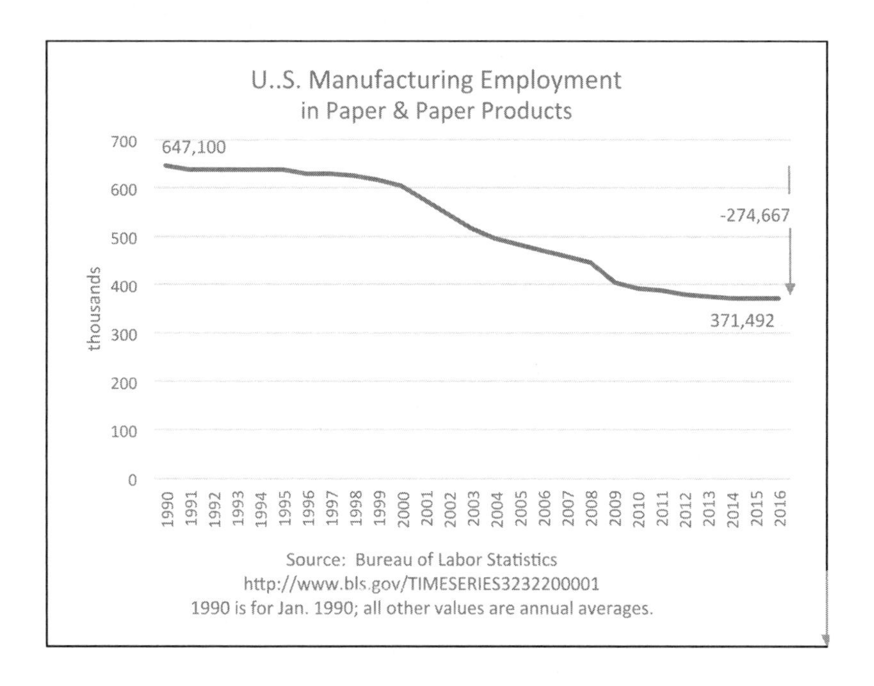

Key Finding: Between 1990 and 2016, employment in the paper and paper products industry fell by some 275,000 jobs, a 42% decline, four in every ten jobs.

Printing and Related Support Activities

We next consider job losses in printing and related support activities (NAICS 323). Activities in this subsector include the printing of magazines and periodicals, catalogs and directories, labels and wrappers, business forms and checkbooks, advertising materials, and loose leaf binders; screen printing on labels and garments; and printing and binding of books and pamphlets.

Not surprisingly, printing has followed the path of paper products: American printing establishments, which employed an average of 808,608 workers in 1990, employed an average 445,633 during 2016, as illustrated in the following figure:

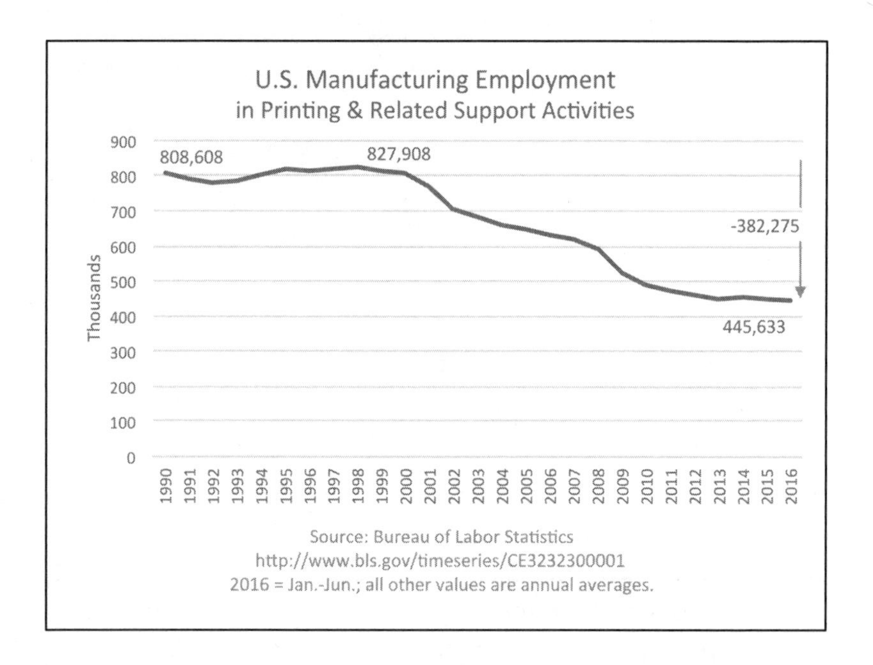

Key Finding: Between 1990 and 2016, employment in printing and related support activities fell by some 382,000 jobs, a 46% decline, nearly five in every ten jobs.

Group 3 – Computer and Electronics Equipment

Computer and Electronic Products

We next consider job losses in computer and electronic product manufacturing (NAICS 334). Here we find computers, servers, storage devices, terminals, and peripherals; telephones, televisions, audio equipment, and camcorders; circuit boards and components; electro-medical equipment; navigation equipment; process, laboratory, and test instruments; watches and clocks; and recording media. Factories in these industries, which employed 1,940,900 workers in January 1990, employed an average 1,042,950 in 2016, per the following figure:

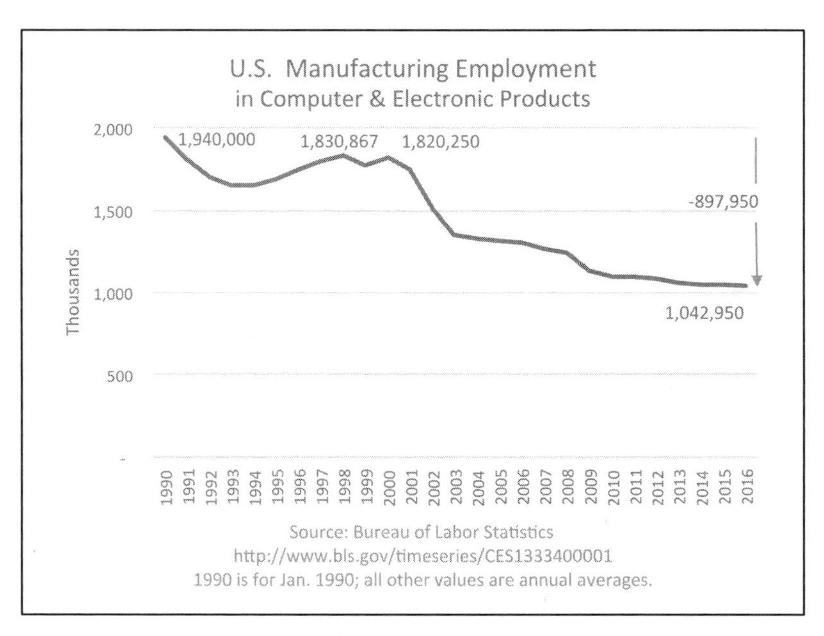

> **Key Finding:** Between 1990 and 2016, employment in the computer and electronic product industry fell by some 898,000 jobs, a 46% decline, nearly five in every ten jobs.

Group 4 –Primary Metals, Appliances & Electrical Products, and Chemicals Manufacturing

Steel and Other Primary Metals

We next consider job losses in primary metal manufacturing (NAICS 331). Here we find the steel and other primary metal products that are the fundamental building blocks of an industrial economy: ingots and shapes, sheet, bars and wire, pipes and tubes, and extruded shapes of steel, aluminum, copper, zinc, nickel, titanium, and other metals; and die-casting and other foundry products from primary metals. Manufacturing facilities in this subsector, which employed 692,700 workers in April of 1990, employed an average 378,071 during 2016, per the following figure:

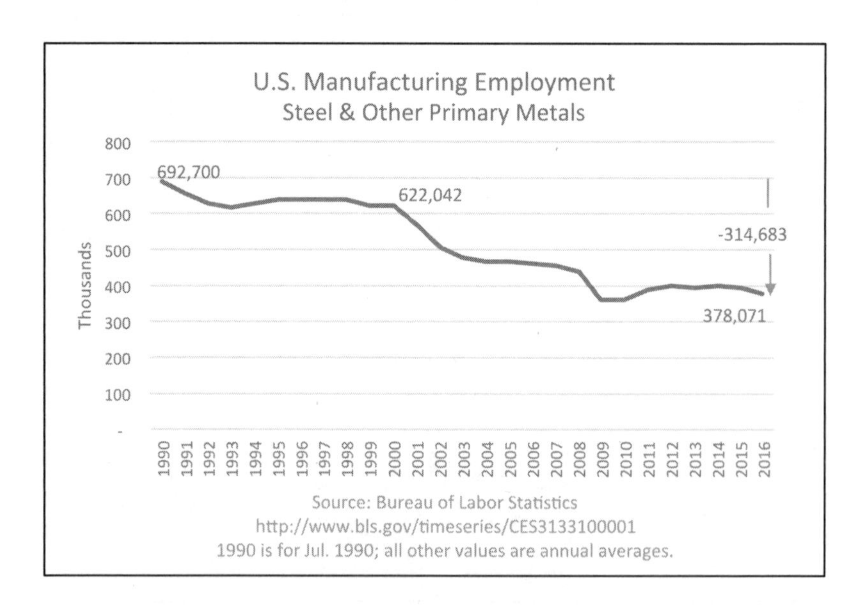

Key Finding: Between 1990 and 2016, employment in the primary metal industries fell by some 315,000 jobs, a 45% decline, nearly five in every ten jobs.

Appliances and Electrical Equipment

We next consider job losses in appliances and electrical equipment manufacturing (NAICS 335). Here we find household ranges, ovens, refrigerators, freezers, laundry equipment, water heaters, and other household appliances; electric lighting fixtures, bulbs and tubes; and a variety of equipment including transformers, motors and generators, circuit breakers, industrial controls, batteries, fiber optic cable, power transmission wire, carbon and graphite products, and miscellaneous other electrical equipment. Manufacturing facilities in this subsector, which employed 647,500 workers at the beginning of 1990, employed an average 385,267 during 2016:

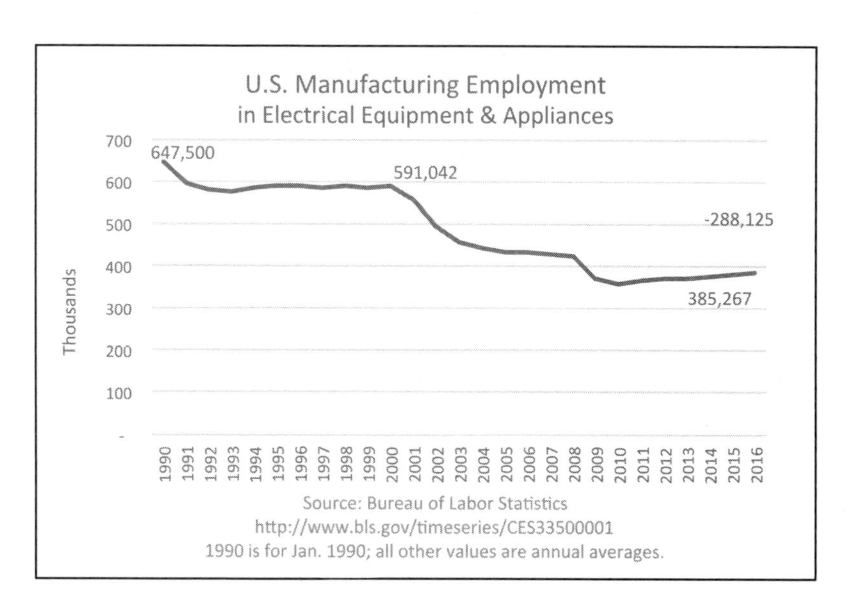

Key Finding: Between 1990 and 2016, employment in the appliance and electrical equipment manufacturing industries fell by some 262,000 jobs, a 40% decline, four in every ten jobs.

Chemical Manufacturing

We next consider job losses in chemical manufacturing (NAICS 325). Here we find a wide range of products including basic chemicals, intermediate products such as resins, synthetic rubber, fibers, and filaments, and finished products including paints, coatings and adhesives, soaps and cleaning compounds, agricultural chemicals, and pharmaceuticals and medicines.

American chemical manufacturing plants, which employed 1,035,600 workers at the beginning of 1990, employed an average 817,317 during 2016, as illustrated in the following figure:

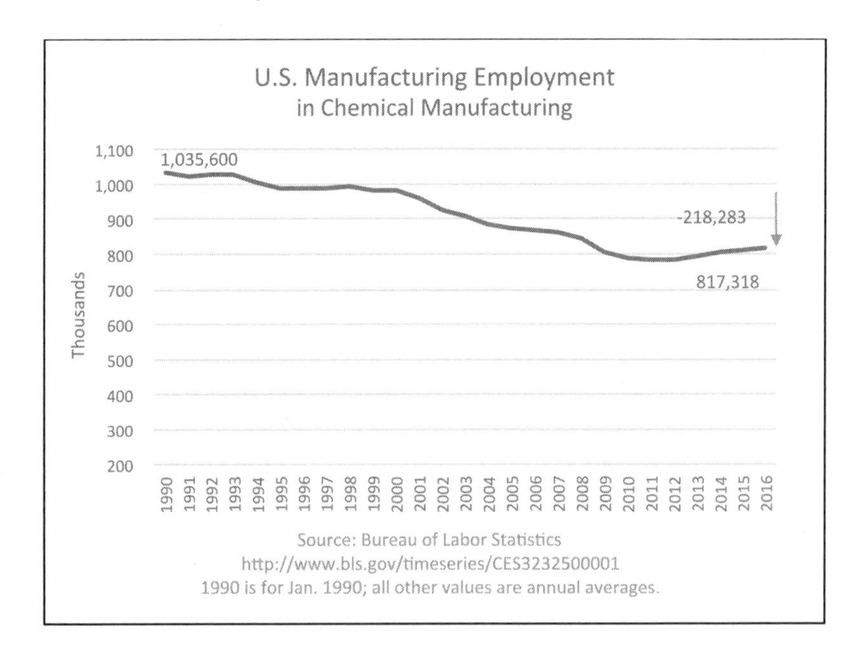

Key Finding: Between 1990 and 2016, employment in the chemical manufacturing industry fell by some 218,000 jobs, a 21% decline, two in every ten jobs.

Group 5 – Furniture, Wood Products and Non-Metallic Mineral Products

Furniture

Next, we consider job losses in furniture and related products manufacturing (NAICS 337). Here we find establishments producing upholstered and non-upholstered wood and metal household furniture; mattresses, blinds and shades; wood kitchen cabinets and countertops; office furniture; and school, public building, restaurant, and other institutional furniture. American furniture manufacturing plants, which employed 680,342 workers at the beginning of 1990, employed an average 389,300 in 2016, per the following figure:

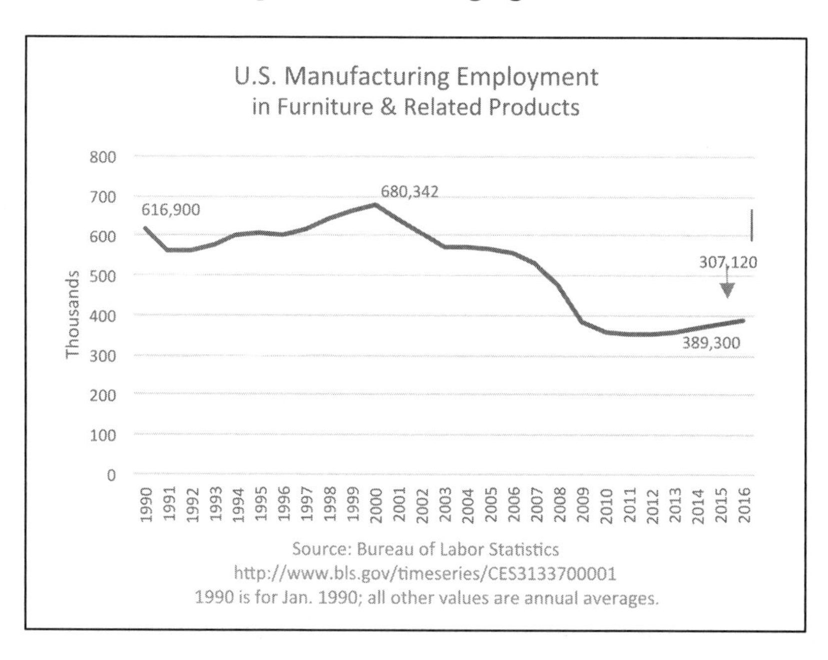

Key Finding: Between 2000 and 2016, employment in the furniture industry fell by some 291,000 jobs, a 43% decline, more than four of every ten jobs.

Wood Products

We next consider job losses in wood products manufacturing (NAICS 321). Here we find lumber, siding, shingles, and shakes from sawmills, treated wood, veneers and plywood, engineered wood members and trusses, particle board and other reconstituted wood products, window and door frames, cut stock, moldings, and flooring, wood containers and pallets, mobile homes, and prefabricated wood buildings. American saw mills and wood product plants, which employed 557,300 workers at the beginning of 1990, employed an average 383,133 during 2016, as illustrated in the following figure:

Key Finding: Between 1999 and 2016, employment in the wood products industry fell by some 240,000 jobs, a 38% decline, nearly four of every ten jobs.

Nonmetallic Mineral Products

We next consider job losses in Nonmetallic Mineral Product Manufacturing, including glass, clay and brick, cement and concrete, lime and gypsum products (NAICS 327). Here we find a wide variety of ceramic, porcelain, earthenware and glass products for household, commercial, and industrial uses, and building products derived from cement, clay, and stone.

Manufacturing facilities in this subsector, which employed 540,000 workers at the beginning of 1990, employed an average 400,183 during 2016, as illustrated in the following figure:

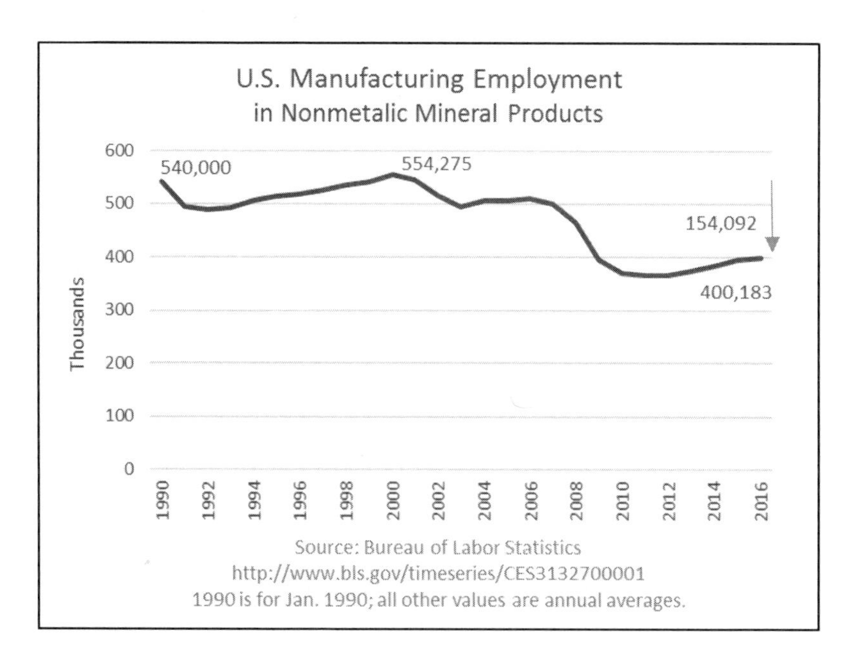

Key Finding: Between 2000 and 2016, employment in nonmetallic mineral products manufacturing fell by some 154,000 jobs, a 28% decline, nearly three of every ten jobs.

Group 6 – Plastics and Rubber Products and Miscellaneous Durable Goods

Plastics and Rubber Products

We next consider job losses in plastics and rubber products manufacturing (NAICS 326). Here we find a wide array of products including plastic packaging, shapes, plumbing fixtures, and table ware; plastic components of transportation, electrical, construction, machinery, furniture, and other products; and rubber products. American plastics products and rubber products plants, which employed 823,900 workers at the beginning of 1990, employed an average 691,117 during 2016:

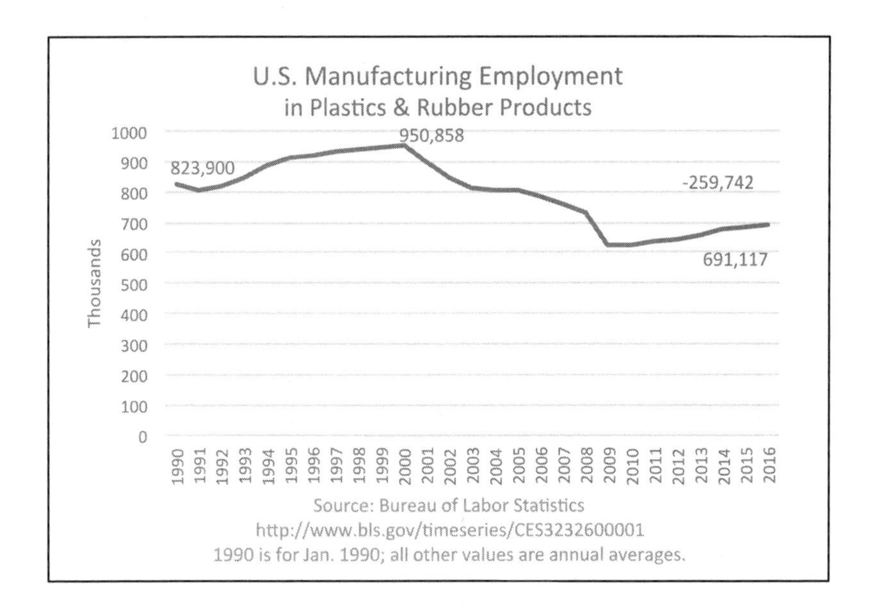

Key Finding: Between 2000 and 2016, employment in plastics and rubber products manufacturing fell by some 260,000 jobs, a 27% decline, nearly three of every ten jobs.

Miscellaneous Durable Goods

We next consider job losses in the miscellaneous durable goods subsector (NAICS 339). Here we find medical equipment and supplies and a potpourri of durable goods including sporting goods; dolls, toys and games; office supplies; eyeglass frames and lenses; jewelry and silverware; musical instruments; and picture frames and framed pictures. Manufacturing facilities in this subsector, which employed 688,000 workers in September of 1990, employed an average 598,417 during 2016:

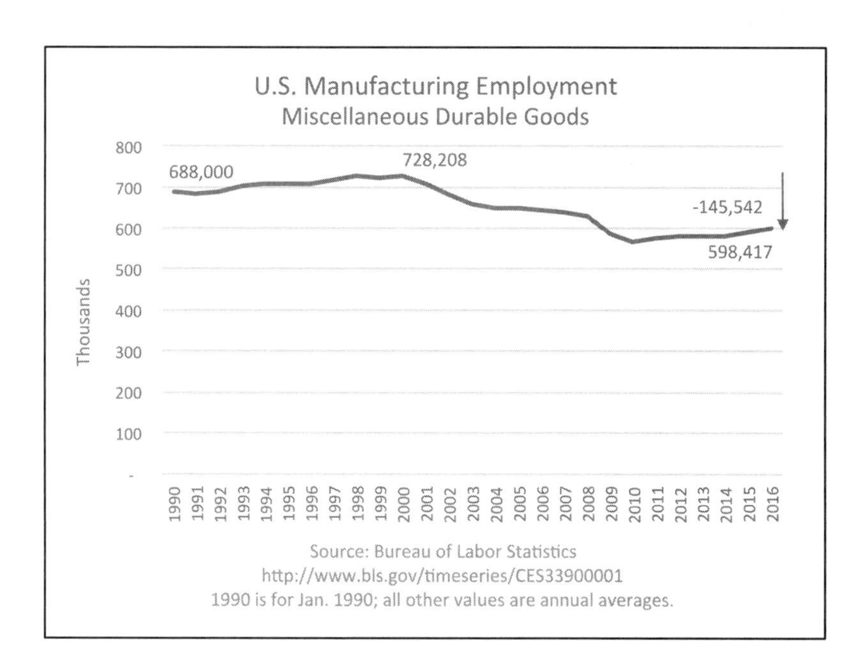

Key Finding: Between 2000 and 2016, employment in manufacturing in the miscellaneous durable goods subsector fell by some 130,000 jobs, an 18% decline, nearly two of every ten jobs.

Group 7 –Fabricated Metal Products, Machinery, and Transportation Equipment

Fabricated Metal Products

We next consider job losses in fabricated metal product manufacturing (NAICS 332). Products include iron, steel, and other metal forgings and stampings, prefabricated metal buildings, structural metal and reinforcing bars, metal windows and doors, sheet metal products for air conditioning, roofing, awnings, ornamental and architectural metal products, hand tools and saw blades, kitchen utensils, cutlery, and razor blades. Manufacturing facilities in this subsector, which employed 1,620,300 workers at the beginning of 1990, employed an average 1,435,317 in 2016, per the following figure:

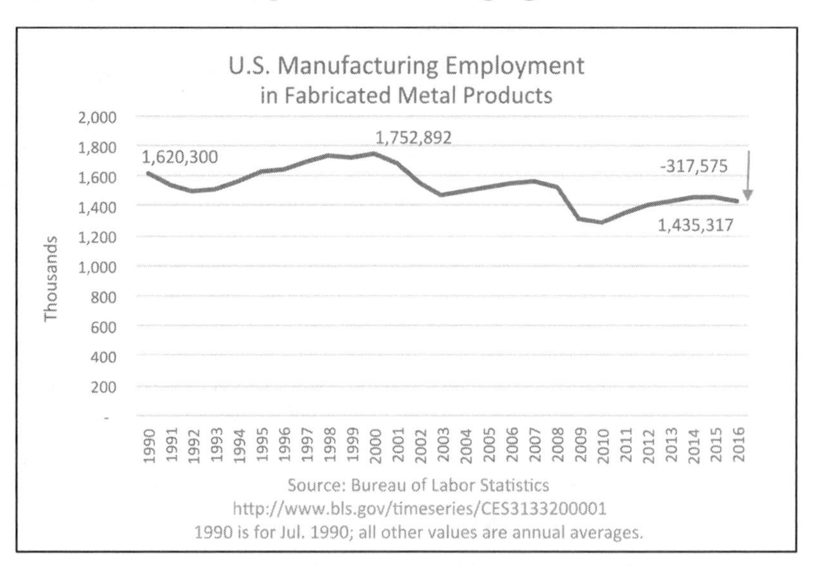

Key Finding: Between 2000 and 2016, employment in fabricated metal products manufacturing fell by 318,000 jobs, an 18% decline, nearly two of every ten jobs.

Machinery

We next consider job losses in machinery manufacturing (NAICS 333). If you are thinking that sounds like a big category, you are right.[9] Here we find:

- Machinery used in farming and extraction, including farm machinery and equipment including tractors and planting and harvesting equipment, mining machinery including drilling and processing equipment, and oil and gas drilling rigs and other equipment;
- Machinery used in construction including cranes, loaders, dozers, trucks, mixers, pavers, and backhoes;
- Machinery used in general manufacturing including Industrial process furnaces and ovens, boilers, furnaces, and other heating equipment, Industrial molds, dies, tools, jigs and fixtures, hydraulic and pneumatic power cylinders and pumps, industrial fans, blowers and purification equipment, rolling mill and other metalworking machinery, overhead cranes and hoists, Industrial trucks, tractors, trailers, and stacking machines, machine tools including lathes, milling, cutting, punching, and other metal forming tools, Conveyors and conveying equipment, and packaging machinery; machinery used in specific manufacturing including food and beverage processing equipment, semiconductor machinery, sawmill, woodworking, paper, and printing machinery, plastics and rubber working machinery, textile, chemical, and foundry machinery, and optical instruments and lens production machinery;
- Industrial and commercial intermediate and end-use machinery including mechanical power transmission equipment, pumps and pumping equipment, air and

gas compressors, turbines and turbine generator sets, internal combustion engines, elevators and escalators, welding and soldering equipment, power-driven hand tools, and air-conditioning and warm air heating equipment and commercial and industrial refrigeration equipment; and

- Commercial and service industry machinery including photographic and photocopying equipment, vending machines, laundry and dry cleaning machinery, mailing and other office machines, commercial cooking and food service equipment, commercial and industrial vacuum cleaners, automotive maintenance equipment, and teaching machines.

Manufacturing facilities in this large and diverse subsector, which employed 1,423,100 workers at the beginning of 1990, employed an average 1,088,900 during 2016, as illustrated in the following figure:

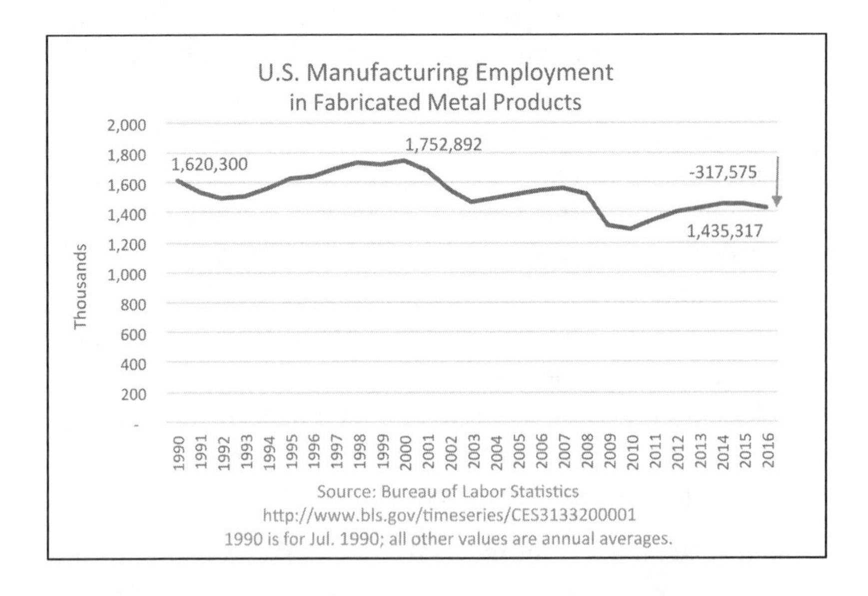

Key Finding: Between 2000 and 2016, employment in machinery manufacturing fell by some 426,000 jobs, an 18% decline, nearly two of every ten jobs.

Transportation Equipment

We next consider job losses in transportation equipment manufacturing (NAICS 336). Here we find products in the motor vehicle, aerospace, railroad, shipping, and other transportation categories. Product categories include:

- Motor vehicles, including automobiles, light duty trucks and utility vehicles, heavy duty trucks and trailers, buses, firefighting vehicles, motor homes, travel trailers, and campers, and motor vehicle components including bodies, gasoline engines and parts, electrical and electronic equipment, steering and suspension components, brake systems, transmissions and drive trains, seating and interior trim, metal stampings, air-conditioning systems, exhaust systems, filters, and wheels;

- Civilian and military aircraft, engines, and parts and guided missiles and space vehicles; railroad locomotives and freight and passenger cars and trolley, subway and rapid transit cars;

- Civilian and military ships, barges and platforms; motorboats and sailboats; motorcycles, bicycles, and parts; military armored vehicles and tanks; and all-terrain vehicles and golf carts.

Manufacturing facilities in this large and important subsector, which employed 2,171,400 workers at the beginning of 1990, employed an average 1,607,667 in 2016, as illustrated in the following figure:

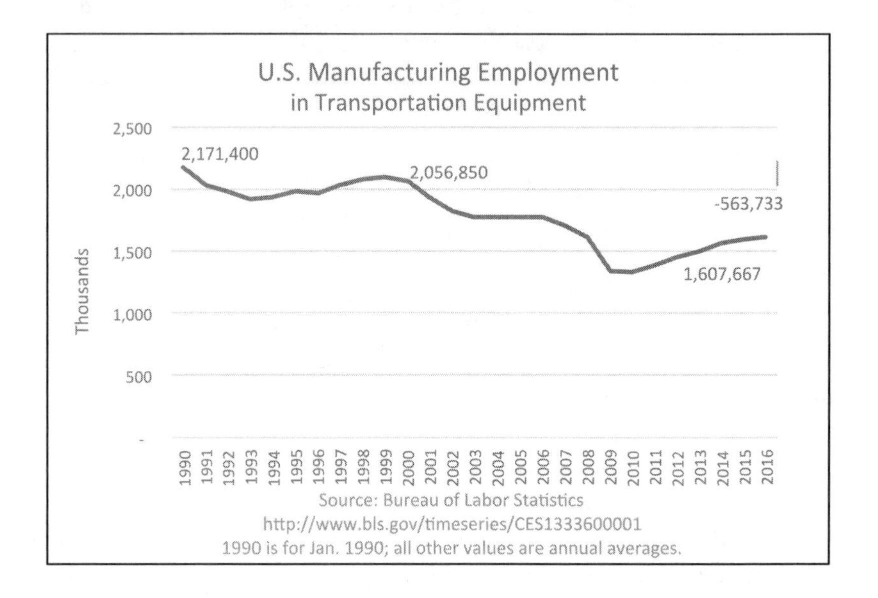

> **Key Finding:** Between 1990 and 2016, after experiencing a partial recovery since 2010, employment in transportation equipment fell by some 564,000 jobs, a 26% decline, one of every four jobs.

Group 8 – Petroleum and Coal Products and Miscellaneous Nondurable Goods

Petroleum and Coal Products

We next consider employment in petroleum and coal products manufacturing (NAICS 324). Here we find refined petroleum products such as heating oil, diesel fuel, and gasoline and further processed products such as asphalt coatings and motor oil.

American petroleum refineries and other petroleum and coal products manufacturing facilities, which employed 806,400 workers at the beginning of 1990, employed an average 115,650 during 2016, as illustrated in the following table and figure:

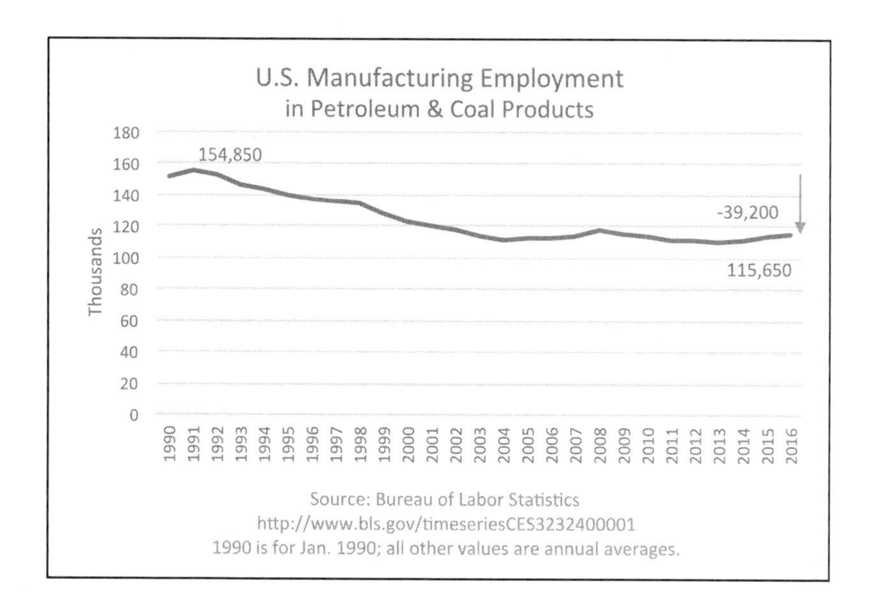

Key Finding: Between 1991 and 2016, employment in the petroleum refining and coal products industries fell by some 39,000 jobs, a 25% decline, one of every four jobs.

Beverage, Tobacco and Leather Goods

The Bureau of Labor Statistics has published employment statistics for "Miscellaneous Nondurable Goods" comprising the following three-digit NAICS codes: Beverage and Tobacco Manufacturing (NAICS 312): Non-alcoholic and alcoholic beverages and intermediate and finished tobacco products; Leather and Allied Products (NAICS 316): Tanned and finished leather and hides, and footwear, luggage and other products made from leather or leather substitutes. Facilities in this grouping, which employed an average of 353,900 workers during 1990, employed an average 265,517 during 2016, per the following figure:

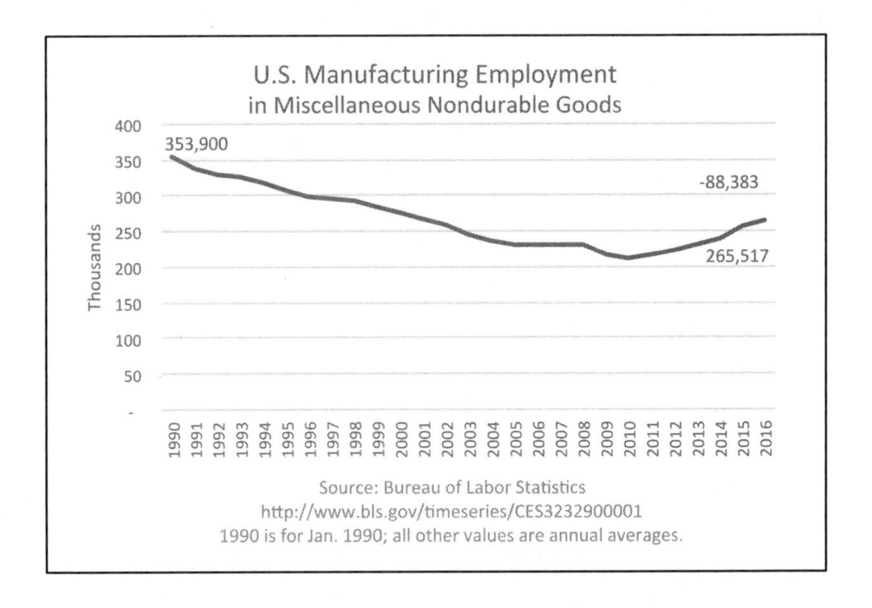

Key Finding: Between 1990 and 2016, employment in the beverage, tobacco and leather manufacturing industries declined by some 88,000 jobs, a 25% decline, one of every four jobs.

Group 9 – Food Manufacturing

Food Manufacturing

We next consider employment in food product manufacturing (NAICS 311). Here we find intermediate food products including animal feed, corn sweeteners and oil, soybean and cotton seed products, wheat, corn, rice, and other milling products, and raw beet and cane sugar, and the final food products one would find in a supermarket. Manufacturing facilities in this subsector, which employed an average of 1.507 million workers during 1990, employed an average 1.523 million during 2016:

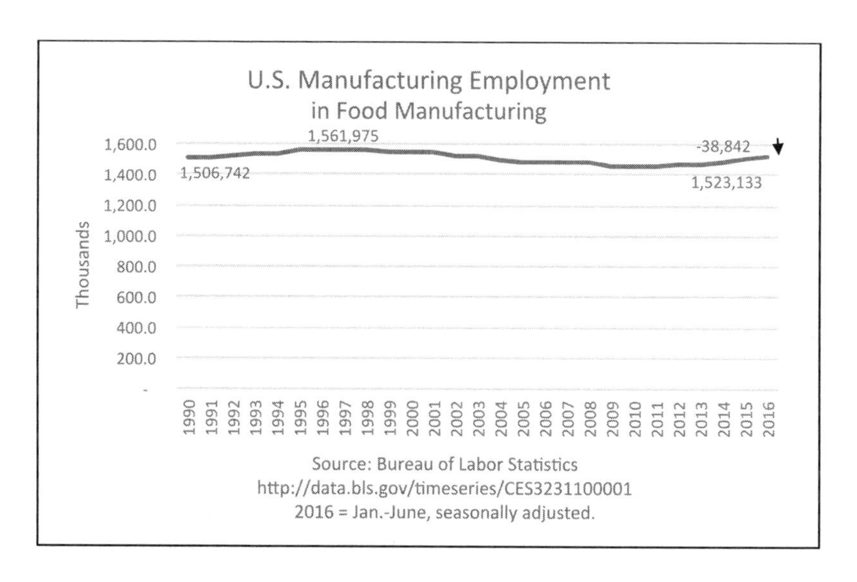

Key Finding: Between 1996 and 2016, after experiencing a partial recovery in 2010-2016, employment in the food product manufacturing fell by some 39,000 jobs, a loss of 2.5%.

What does this all add up to?

Let's try to synthesize this information, with reference to the table that follows:[10]

Key Findings:

- Taken together, peak employment in the industries in the nine groups totaled 18.5 million. (For some, the peak occurred in 1990, in others around 2000.)
- These industries shed 7.16 million jobs from peak to bottom, a loss of 39%, four of every ten jobs.
- For some industries, there was a partial recovery: 945,000 jobs were regained – 13% of the lost jobs.
- Despite these gains, by 2016, these industries were 6.2 million jobs below their peak, a loss of 34%, or one of every three manufacturing jobs.

U.S. Manufacturing Job Losses 1990 - 2016, with Reference to Peak Employment

In Thousands of Jobs, by Three-Digit NAICS Code, Sorted by Group

Industry NAICS Code	Industry	Year of Peak Employment	Employed at Peak	Year Reached Bottom	Employed at Bottom	Total Lost Peak to Bottom	Percent Lost Peak to Bottom	Employed in 2016	Number of Jobs Recovered	Percent of Lost Jobs Recovered	Net Jobs Lost Peak to 2016	Percent Lost Peak to 2016
Group 1	**Steady decline from 1990, then flatline.**											
315	Apparel	1990	939	2016	134	805	86%	134	-	0%	805	86%
313	Textile Mills	1990	503	2016	114	389	77%	114	-	0%	389	77%
314	Textile Product Mills	1990	244	2013	114	129	53%	117	3	2%	126	52%
	Total Group 1		1,685		362	1,323	79%	365	-	0.0%	1,320	78%
Group 2	**Slow decline from 90-91 (paper)/recovery & growth (printing), (then double-dip decline to flatline**											
322	Paper and Paper Products	1990	647	2016	372	275	42%	372	-	0%	275	42%
323	Printing and Related Activities	1993	828	2016	446	382	46%	446	-	0%	382	46%
	Total Group 2		1,475	2017	818	657	45%	818	-	0%	657	45%
Group 3	**Near recovery from 90-91, then "double dip" decline to flatline**											
334	Computer & Electronic Products	1990	1,941	2016	1,043	898	46%	1,043	-	0%	898	46%
	Total Group 3		1,941		1,043	898	46%	1,043	-	0%	898	46%
Group 4	**Decline, then flat through 2000, then "double dip" decline until modest recovery.**											
331	Primary Metals	1990	693	2009	362	331	48%	378	16	5%	315	45%
335	Electrical Equipment & Appliances	1990	648	2010	359	288	44%	385	26	9%	262	40%
325	Chemical Manufacturing	1990	1,036	2011	783	252	24%	817	34	13%	218	21%
	Total Group 4		2,376		1,505	871	37%	1,581	76	9%	795	33%
Group 5	**Decline, then increase to peak in approx. 2000, then "double dip" decline until modest recovery.**											
337	Furniture and Related Products	2000	680	2012	351	329	48%	389	38	12%	291	43%
321	Wood Products	1999	623	2011	337	286	46%	383	46	16%	240	38%
327	Non-Metallic Mineral Products	2000	554	2012	366	189	34%	400	35	18%	154	28%
	Total Group 5		1,857		1,054	804	43%	1,173	119	15%	685	37%

U.S. Manufacturing Job Losses 1990 - 2016, with Reference to Peak Employment

In Thousands of Jobs, by Three-Digit NAICS Code, Sorted by Group

Industry NAICS Code	Industry	Year of Peak Employment	Employed at Peak	Year Reached Bottom	Employed at Bottom	Total Lost Peak to Bottom	Percent Lost Peak to Bottom	Employed in 2016	Number of Jobs Recovered	Percent of Lost Jobs Recovered	Net Jobs Lost Peak to 2016	Percent Lost Peak to 2016
Group 6	**Decline, then increase to peak in approx. 2000, then "double dip" decline until modest recovery.**											
326	Plastics and Rubber Products	2000	951	2009	625	326	34%	691	67	20%	260	27%
339	Miscellaneous Durable Goods	2000	728	2010	567	161	22%	598	32	20%	130	18%
	Total Group 6		1,679	2017	1,191	488	29%	1,290	98	20%	390	23%
Group 7	**Decline, then increase to peak in 2000, then "double dip" decline with moderate recovery.**											
336	Transportation Equipment	1990	2,171	2010	1,333	838	39%	1,608	275	33%	564	26%
332	Fabricated Metal Products	2000	1,753	2010	1,282	471	27%	1,435	153	33%	318	18%
333	Machinery Manufacturing	1998	1,515	2010	996	518	34%	1,089	93	18%	426	28%
	Total Group 7		5,439		3,611	1,827	34%	4,132	520	28%	1,307	24%
Group 8	**Increase/decline through 2000, then "double dip" decline until moderate recovery.**											
324	Petroleum and Coal Products	1991	155	2013	110	45	29%	116	5	12%	39	25%
312, 6	Beverage, Tobacco & Leather	1990	354	2010	211	143	40%	266	54	38%	88	25%
	Total Group 8		509		322	187	37%	381	60	32%	128	25%
Group 9	**Increase through 2000, then "double dip" decline until robust recovery.**											
311	Food Manufacturing	1996	1,562	2010	1,451	111	7%	1,523	72	65%	39	2%
311-339	**All Manufacturing**		18,523		11,357	7,166	39%	12,305	945	13%	6,218	34%
Groups 1 through 7			**16,452**		**9,584**	**6,868**	**42%**	**10,401**	**814**	**12%**	**6,052**	**37%**

Source: Bureau of Labor Statistics, Employment, Hours, and Earnings from the Current Employment Statistics Survey (National)
http://www.bls.gov/webapps/legacy/cesbtab1.htm

Key Findings and Conclusions

Further insight can be gained by considering each group.

First, *reports of a recovery of employment in American manufacturing are greatly exaggerated.*

- The very best case can be made for Group 7, which includes transportation equipment, fabricated metal products, and machinery. After losing 1.8 million, or 34% of its jobs, this group recovered 520,000 jobs – that is 28% of the lost jobs. 1.3 million jobs have not been recovered, a loss of one in every four jobs in these industries.
- And that is the best case. The next best case, Group 6, plastics and miscellaneous durable goods, recovered 98,000 (20%) of 488,000 jobs.
- The next best case, Group 5, furniture, wood, and mineral products, recovered 119,000 (15%) of 804,000 lost jobs.
- The next best case, Group 4, primary metals, electrical and appliances, and chemicals, recovered 76,000 (9%) of 871,000 lost jobs.
- Group 3, computers and electronics, recovered none of 898,000 lost jobs.
- Group 2, paper and printing, recovered none of 657,000 lost jobs.
- Group 1, apparel and textiles, recovered none of 1.3 million lost jobs.

Second, *in several key industries, I have noted a disturbing trend: even the recovery experienced since the Great Recession has ended,* as employment has begun to decline once again. And this, even though the total economy has continued to grow, albeit at a slow pace.

- In Group 7, which has seen the best, though inadequate, recovery, employment has gone flat in transportation equipment (NAICS 336), and has begun to decline in fabricated metal products (NAICS 332) and machinery (NAICS 333).
- So, too, in Group 4, employment has begun to decline in manufacturing of steel and other primary metals (NAICS 331).

What is the cause of these declines? One may speculate that these employment losses are due to increased automation in manufacturing processes, and some no doubt are. However, a more obvious reason is the aggressive dumping of steel and other products into the American market by Chinese firms, as they have built overcapacity and the Chinese economy's growth has slowed. The "recovery" of employment in American manufacturing, as anemic and inadequate as it has been, is threatened by China's attempts to sustain domestic employment and growth by selling their excess capacity elsewhere, even at prices below their already low, subsidized cost of production. We will look more closely at this in the following chapters.

Third, *one cannot assume that even the modest increases in employment in some subsectors will continue.* As discussed in a later chapter, the Bureau of Labor Statistics is forecasting a decline in employment in all subsectors of manufacturing through 2024.

Fourth, *these employment statistics, though mere numbers, represent dire effects on individuals, families, and communities across America.*

We will look at the effects of these employment losses on individuals, families, and communities. But first, we must consider:

Where did the jobs go?

A hint lies in the curve on the graph showing manufacturing employment from 1979-2014, reproduced here:

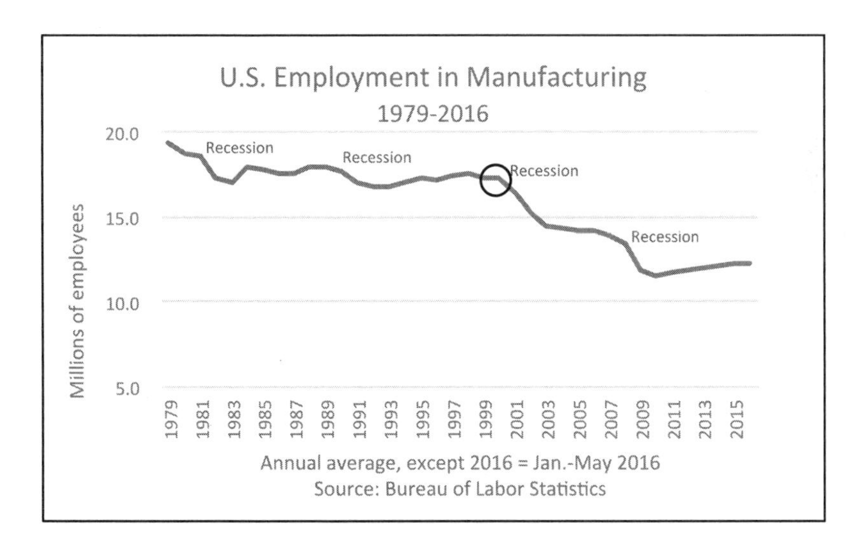

Even to the untrained eye, something jumps out: in 2001, there is a sharp break in the curve, with employment declining at a rapid rate. At the same time, in 2001, we see a similar, but upward break in the curve for net Chinese exports to the United States, in the figure reproduced here:

This relationship is made clearer when U.S. manufacturing job losses and net Chinese exports to the U.S. are displayed together. The following chart does so, with the trade in goods deficit (U.S. exports to China net of U.S. imports from China) expressed as a negative number:[11]

Again, to the untrained eye, there is a strong relationship between manufacturing job losses and the

Chinese trade in goods deficit. It is not much of a leap to connect the dots and conclude that *the jobs went to China*, with goods formerly produced in the U.S. being produced in China for export to the U.S. It turns out that there is some social science research that confirms this conclusion.

The Pierce & Schott Study

Two economists at the National Bureau of Research, Justin R. Pierce and Peter K. Schott, considered the question in a December 2012 paper, "The Surprisingly Swift Decline of U.S. Manufacturing Employment."[12] In particular, they considered whether the sharp decline in U.S. manufacturing employment beginning in 2001 was linked to the United States' granting permanent normal trade relations ("PNTR") status to China via an act of Congress in October 2000.

Prior to that action, the application to China of the lower tariffs flowing from normal trade relations ("NTR") status was uncertain, because they were granted on an annual basis and were politically contentious.[13] The authors investigated whether there was a link between the losses of U.S. manufacturing employment and the elimination of uncertainty with respect to PNTR status.[14] After an extensive data review and analysis, they concluded that, indeed, there was.

In particular, they looked at products for which there was a large difference between the NTR tariff and the tariff the product would face if NTR status were not renewed (the "NTR gap"). They hypothesized that the removal of uncertainty regarding these products' tariffs through the granting of PNTR status could result in market shifts.

Pierce and Schott's key findings included the following:

- PNTR status provided Chinese producers with incentives to invest in entering or expanding in the U.S. market, putting further price pressure on U.S. producers. The same incentives encouraged U.S. firms to invest time and resources in locating or establishing Chinese suppliers, encouraged U.S. producers to exit, and discouraged U.S. producers from entering markets.

- U.S. imports grew in exactly the same group of products where the U.S. manufacturing employment losses occurred, and the new imports came from China, the country that was the subject of the PNTR policy change.

- There was a strong association between products with higher NTR gaps and the value of imports from China, the number of U.S. firms importing from China, and the number of Chinese firms exporting to the U.S.

- Where PNTR status pushed upstream supply offshore to China, U.S. customers of those suppliers often followed them there to take advantage of lower transportation and other costs.

With respect to manufacturing job losses, the authors found:

- Much of the manufacturing job loss was caused not directly, but rather when a U.S. firm's downstream customers disappeared – either moved to China or went out of business. Other data suggested that companies competing directly with China may simply go out of business rather than move production there.

- There were employment losses in upstream and downstream industries stemming from simultaneous offshoring of several stages of a supply chain.

- There was a significant relationship between the reduction in tariff uncertainty flowing from PNTR for China, on the one hand, and losses in U.S. manufacturing employment on the other, for up to six years after the 2001 peak: employment losses were highest in the industries that experienced the largest reduction in the threat of tariff hikes.

- The negative impact of PNTR was greater for production workers (-17% from 1997-2007) than for non-production workers (-4.6% from 1997-2007).

- PNTR status for China was associated both with increased manufacturing job destruction and decreased manufacturing job creation, and helped to explain the widely recognized "jobless" aspect of the recovery from the 2001 recession in manufacturing.

- **Key Finding:** Without PNTR status for China, manufacturing employment in the U.S. *would have gone up 10 percent* between 2001 and 2007, instead of declining 15 percent – a 25 percent swing and a difference of some *4 million jobs.*

The authors also examined the data to consider whether the manufacturing employment declines could be caused by non-trade-related, technical changes replacing low-skilled labor with human or physical capital. They concluded not, for several reasons:

- The job losses were concentrated in industries with high NTR gaps, and persisted even when technology and capital factors were controlled for;
- The employment losses were concentrated in the period after 2000; and
- PNTR coincided with increases in U.S. imports from China compared with all other trade partners.

Pierce and Schott's statistical analysis was consistent with other "facts on the ground," which they have presented in an appendix of anecdotal evidence, including quotations capturing the pent-up demand and the headlong rush of U.S. firms into Chinese production. I was particularly struck by this quotation from the U.S. Trade Deficit Review Commission:

> In the months since the enactment of Permanent Normal Trade Relations (PNTR) legislation with China there has been an escalation of production shifts out of the U.S. and into China. According to our media-tracking data, between October 1, 2000 and April 30, 2001 more than eighty corporations announced their intentions to shift production to China, with the number of announced production shifts increasing each month from two per month in October to November to nineteen per month by April.[15]

Key Findings: In sum, the Pierce and Schott study concludes that --

- Much of the dramatic decline in U.S. manufacturing employment beginning in 2001 during the "jobless recoveries" from the 2001 and 2008 recessions resulted from the removal of uncertainty regarding U.S. tariffs on Chinese goods, and the resulting shift of U.S. manufacturing production to China for export to the United States.

- The destruction of jobs and inhibiting of new jobs was felt up and down the supply chain as suppliers lost U.S. customers and U.S. customers followed suppliers to China.

- Between 2001 and 2007 alone, there would have been four million more manufacturing jobs without the granting of PNTR status to China.

China and "The Great U.S. Employment Sag"

In a second recent study,[16] Daron Acemoglu, David Autor *et al.* considered the contribution of the rise in imports from China to the loss of manufacturing jobs and stagnation of overall employment during the 2000s. Noting that what they called "the Great U.S. Employment Sag of the 2000s" coincided with the rapid increase of net imports from China, they explored how much of this employment "sag" could be attributed to the increased imports from China.

They took two approaches to the question. First, they considered industry-level manufacturing employment from 1991 to 2011 in relation to each sector's exposure to import competition from China. They found that without the increase in Chinese penetration of the U.S. market that began after 1999, there would have been 560,000 fewer direct job losses in manufacturing. In addition to these direct effects, they considered effects on the upstream suppliers and downstream purchasers of an industry's manufactured products. These supply chain effects apply both within and outside the manufacturing sector; for example, import penetration of the steel manufacturing industry can have negative employment effects on upstream iron-ore producers. Including these "input-output" effects increased the number of manufacturing job losses to 985,000, and total job losses in manufacturing and its supply chain to 1.98 million.

Their second approach considered two other questions: (i) to what extent did the affected manufacturing industries reallocate their resources to non-affected sectors, and (ii) what ripple effects ("aggregate demand effects") did the Chinese import penetration have on economic sectors that were not directly exposed to the competition from imports. They studied these effects at a local level, within "commuting zones."

As to the first question, they found no statistically significant evidence of reallocation of employment to non-exposed industries:

Key Finding: At the local level, a hit to employment from imports was not compensated for by increases in employment in non-affected industries.

As to the second question, they estimated that the growth of imports from China from 1999 to 2011 resulted in a loss of *2.4 million jobs,* including losses both within and outside manufacturing. They found this estimate to be consistent with their earlier finding of 1.98 million job losses, since this second approach picked up job losses outside the manufacturing supply chain, which were not included in the first approach.

They noted that their study differed from that of Pierce and Schott, in that their industry-level analysis picked up supply chain job losses in the manufacturing supply chain that occurred in industries outside manufacturing, such as the extraction industries; also, their local-level analysis considered reallocation effects (they found none), and ripple effects ("changes in aggregate demand"), which were significant.

Even so, they noted that *their estimate likely understates the total job losses,* because it does not include supply chain and ripple effects that don't have a counterpart in the local market.

Although their focus was on the period 2000 through 2011, the authors studied effects beginning in 1991. During the 1990s there already was some penetration of the U.S. market by Chinese imports; this penetration was accelerated after the granting of U.S. permanent normal trade relations and China's accession to the World Trade Organization in 2000 and 2001. Considering the entire period from 1991 to 2011, the estimates of job losses are even larger: 2.6 million under the first approach, and 3.1 million under the second. The results are summarized in the following tables:

Implied Employment Changes from Exposure to Chinese Imports (First Methodology; In Millions)			
	Time Period		
	1991-1999	1999-2011	1991-2011
Manufacturing	(0.421)	(0.985)	(1.406)
Non-Manufacturing	(0.224)	(0.994)	(1.218)
Total	(0.645)	(1.979)	(2.624)

Source: Acemeglu, Autor et al 2015.

Includes direct and first- and second-order input-output effects.

Implied Employment Changes from Exposure to Chinese Imports (Second Methodology; In Millions)			
	Time Period		
	1991-1999	1999-2011	1991-2011
All Employment in Commuting Zone	(0.743)	(2.367)	(3.110)

Source: Acemeglu, Autor et al 2015.

As indicated in the following tables, most of these job losses occurred after 1999:

Implied Employment Changes from Exposure to Chinese Imports (Second Methodology; In Millions)			
	Time Period		
	1991-1999	1999-2011	1991-2011
Manufacturing	30%	70%	100%
Non-Manufacturing	18%	82%	100%

Source: Acemeglu, Autor et al 2015.

Includes direct and first- and second-order input-output effects.

Implied Employment Changes from Exposure to Chinese Imports (Second Methodology; In Millions)			
	Time Period		
	1991-1999	1999-2011	1991-2011
All Employment in Commuting Zone	24%	76%	100%

Source: Acemeglu, Autor et al 2015.

Key Findings: In sum, Acemoglu, Autor and their colleagues found that *the sharp increase in Chinese imports and the sharp decrease in manufacturing employment from 2000 to 2011 were not merely coincidental.* By their estimates:

- without the increased imports during this period, there would have been nearly a million more manufacturing jobs in the United States in 2011, and another million more jobs in the manufacturing supply chain.
- These losses came on top of millions lost during the 1990s: from 1999 through 2011, 1.4 million manufacturing jobs and 1.2 million manufacturing supply chain jobs went missing.
- Total job losses were as high as 2.4 million from 1999-2011, and 3.1 million from 1991-2011.

These studies are confirmed in the stories of the manufacturing job losses, which often are inextricably tied to the movement of the company's production offshore, or to the company's demise in the face of foreign production.

Import Penetration of the U.S. Market

These economic studies have used statistical methods to identify the connection between the increased Chinese imports and the decline in U.S. manufacturing employment and stagnation in other employment. There is another method for gaining insight into the question of whether the decline in manufacturing employment was caused by imports. Using information gathered by the U.S. Census Bureau, one can determine how much of the U.S. consumption of a manufacturing subsector is from imports – the "import penetration" of the subsector.

This is more difficult than it might sound, because the Commerce Department organizes the National Income and Product Accounts differently for domestic production and for imports and exports. Fortunately, in 2012 and again in 2014, the Department of Commerce prepared a comprehensive compilation of data permitting a comparison of domestic production, exports, and imports by detailed NAICS category.[17] I have organized this information for the year 2014 in the following table.

To see how to read the table, consider the first item, NAICS 315, Apparel. In 2014, U.S. apparel production was $12.5 billion in 2016 dollars. Of this, we exported $4.4 billion, leaving $8.1 billion consumed domestically. We also consumed $118.5 billion in imported apparel, for a total consumption of $126.6 billion. Of this total consumption, six percent was from domestic production, and 94 percent was from imported products. So, the import penetration rate of the U.S. apparel market is 94 percent; that is, *94 percent of our clothes come from abroad.*

When a subsector has a high import penetration rate coupled with job losses, it is likely that the jobs went overseas. However, that is not the complete picture. It is possible that a subsector may import a sizable percentage of total U.S. consumption, but also export a sizable amount of U.S. production. In that case, the employment in producing the exports would offset the employment lost to the imports. An example is primary metal manufacturing (steel, aluminum, and other primary metals, NAICS 331). The import penetration is relatively high, some 37 percent;

however, a significant amount is exported. At the end of the day, we are consuming 1.18 times as much steel and other metals as we are producing. This difference is a good measure of the jobs lost. In the case of apparel, we are exporting very little, so we are consuming 10 times as much as we are producing: it is clear that many jobs are being lost to apparel imports.

Looking at the last column in the table, we see that the worst offenders are apparel and leather goods, followed by computers and electronics. Each of these subsectors has a very high import penetration with little offsetting exports.

Groups 4, 5, 6, and 7, which perhaps comprise the subsectors one usually would think of as "manufacturing," all show a substantial import penetration and also consumption that is significantly higher than production. In each of these subsectors it is clear that a substantial number of jobs are being lost to imports.

Key Findings: Taking manufactured products as a whole, excluding food, beverage, tobacco and petroleum,

- Imports account for 39 percent of our total consumption of these products.
- Counting production for both domestic consumption and export, we are consuming 22% more than we are producing, with the difference coming from imports.

Analysis of Domestic Production, Exports, Imports, and Domestic Consumption for Manufacturing Sector in 2014
In Billions of 2016 Dollars

NAICS Code	Commodity	Domestic Production Shipped	Domestic Production Exported	Domestic Production Less Exports	Consumption Import Value of Goods	Total Domestic Consumption	Consumption from Domestic Production	Consumption from Imports	Consumption/ Production Ratio 1/
315	Apparel Manufacturing	12.5	4.4	8.1	118.5	126.6	0.06	0.94	10.1
316	Leather and allied product manufacturing	4.7	3.4	1.3	38.9	40.2	0.03	0.97	8.5
314	Textile product mills	23.6	2.9	20.7	19.8	40.5	0.51	0.49	1.7
313	Textile mills	25.9	9.5	16.4	8.5	24.9	0.66	0.34	0.96
	Total Group 1	**66.7**	**20.2**	**46.6**	**185.6**	**232.2**	**0.20**	**0.80**	**3.5**
322	Paper manufacturing	183.8	24.2	159.6	21.1	180.7	0.88	0.12	0.98
323	Printing and related support activities	72.7	5.5	67.1	5.3	72.5	0.93	0.07	1.00
	Total Group 2	**256.5**	**29.7**	**226.8**	**26.4**	**253.2**	**0.90**	**0.10**	**0.99**
334	Computer and electronic product manufacturing	288.8	126.2	162.6	368.1	530.7	0.31	0.69	1.84
	Total Group 3	**288.8**	**126.2**	**162.6**	**368.1**	**530.7**	**0.31**	**0.69**	**1.84**
331	Primary metal manufacturing	236.6	59.3	177.4	102.5	279.8	0.63	0.37	1.18
335a	Appliance manufacturing	19.9	8.5	11.4	25.5	36.9	0.31	0.69	1.85
335b	Electrical equipment & component mfg.	99.4	39.8	59.6	73.2	132.8	0.45	0.55	1.34
325a	Chemical manufacturing	542.9	141.0	401.9	122.9	524.8	0.77	0.23	0.97
325b	Medicines, diagnostics & biologics manufacturing	185.2	52.4	132.7	122.9	255.6	0.52	0.48	1.38
	Total Group 4	**1,084.0**	**301.0**	**783.0**	**447.0**	**1,230.0**	**0.64**	**0.36**	**1.13**

Author's calculations; data are from Manufacturing and International Trade Report 2014, U.S. Census Bureau, published January 29, 2016.
Excludes some production for which export and import data are not avaliable.

Analysis of Domestic Production, Exports, Imports, and Domestic Consumption for Manufacturing Sector in 2014
In Billions of 2016 Dollars

NAICS Code	Commodity	Domestic Production Shipped	Domestic Production Exported	Domestic Production Less Exports	Consumption Import Value of Goods	Total Domestic Consumption	Consumption from Domestic Production	Consumption from Imports	Consumption/ Production Ratio 1/
337	Furniture and related products manufacturing	73.4	6.8	66.6	39.4	106.0	0.63	0.37	1.44
321	Wood product manufacturing	80.8	7.3	73.5	16.8	90.3	0.81	0.19	1.12
327	Nonmetallic mineral product manufacturing	110.2	12.6	97.6	21.6	119.1	0.82	0.18	1.08
	Total Group 5	**264.3**	**26.7**	**237.7**	**77.7**	**315.4**	**0.75**	**0.25**	**1.19**
326	Plastics and rubber products manufacturing	193.3	31.4	161.9	49.6	211.5	0.77	0.23	1.09
339a	Medical, dental & opthalmic product manufacturing	86.7	26.6	60.1	31.2	91.3	0.66	0.34	1.05
339b	Miscellaneous durable product manufacturing	55.8	18.9	36.9	80.9	117.8	0.31	0.69	2.11
	Total Group 6	**335.8**	**76.9**	**258.8**	**161.8**	**420.6**	**0.62**	**0.38**	**1.25**
336a	Automobiles & light trucks	276.3	59.3	217.0	173.2	390.3	0.56	0.44	1.41
336b	Trucks, bodies, trailers, motor homes & campers	68.1	19.3	48.8	16.7	65.6	0.74	0.26	0.96
336c	Motor vehicle parts & components	238.2	44.8	193.3	103.7	297.1	0.65	0.35	1.25
336d	Aerospace products and parts	234.7	103.9	130.8	54.1	184.9	0.71	0.29	0.79
336e	Railroad, maritime, military & other trans. equipment	70.6	10.2	60.4	9.4	69.9	0.87	0.13	0.99
332	Fabricated metal product manufacturing	236.6	43.9	192.7	65.2	258.0	0.75	0.25	1.09
333	Machinery manufacturing	374.0	134.6	239.5	153.4	392.9	0.61	0.39	1.05
	Total Group 7	**1,498.5**	**416.0**	**1,082.6**	**575.9**	**1,658.5**	**0.65**	**0.35**	**1.11**
324	Petroleum and coal products manufacturing	729.8	116.9	612.8	114.2	727.0	0.84	0.16	1.00
312	Beverage and tobacco product manufacturing	144.2	8.3	136.0	20.3	156.2	0.87	0.13	1.08
311	Food manufacturing	704.8	70.1	634.7	57.6	692.3	0.92	0.08	0.98
	Total Group 8	**1,578.7**	**195.3**	**1,383.4**	**192.0**	**1,575.5**	**0.88**	**0.12**	**1.00**
	Total Groups 1 through 7	**3,794.7**	**996.7**	**2,798.0**	**1,842.5**	**4,640.5**	**0.60**	**0.40**	**1.22**
	Total Groups 1 through 8	**5,373.4**	**1,192.0**	**4,181.4**	**2,034.5**	**6,216.0**	**0.67**	**0.33**	**1.16**

Author's calculations; data are from Manufacturing and International Trade Report 2014, U.S. Census Bureau, published January 29, 2016.
Excludes some production for which export and import data are not avaliable.

Recent Trends in Import Penetration

Having taken this "snapshot" of import penetration and how much we consume compared to how much we produce, it is important also to consider, what is the trend – is the tide going in or out?

To get a feel for the recent trend, I compared the Commerce Department's 2014 report to the 2012 report.[18] Unfortunately, the news is not good. In general, the 2014 values for import penetration and consumption to production ratio were quite similar. However, some industries showed changes. In the following table, I have assembled the reported values for those industries that saw a two percent or greater change in import penetration from 2012 to 2014.

Only one industry, Machinery Manufacturing (NAICS 333), saw an improvement in the import penetration: it declined by 3.3 percentage points, from 42.4% to 39.0%. However, this subsector also saw a decline in exports, so the ratio of imports compared to domestic production worsened by two percentage points.

In six other industries, there was a worsening of import penetration of between 2.0 and 5.1 percentage points, with corresponding worsening of the imports to domestic production ratio. So, during the two-year period from 2012 to 2014, industries that saw a significant change were moving in the wrong direction: In nearly every case, imports accounted for a larger percentage of consumption, and in every case, the excess of consumption over domestic production worsened:

Key Findings: From 2012 to 2014 --

- Medicines and pharmaceuticals show a disturbing trend: 48.1 percent of our medicines came from abroad, an increase of 5.1 percentage points in just two years. Import penetration of medical and dental equipment also increased.

- Computer and electronics equipment also moved strongly in the wrong direction: we imported 69.4 percent of these goods, up 4.7 percentage points in just two years.

- Electrical equipment and appliances also deteriorated: imports accounted for 58.2 percent of these goods, an increase of 3.5 percentage points. Nearly 70 percent of our appliance purchases were from imports.

- We managed to send even more of our leather goods manufacturing offshore, with imports increasing from 94.5 to 96.7 percent of consumption.

- Overall, import penetration of manufactured products increased from 31.4 to 32.4 percent, and the ratio of consumption to domestic production increased from 1.14 to 1.15 percent.

Conclusion: For manufacturing as a whole, the tide is still going out: foreign goods are accounting for more of our domestic consumption, and we are continuing to consume more than we produce.

	Consumption from Imports by Manufacturing Subsector 2012 Compared to 2014						
		Consumption from Imports			Consumption/Prod'n Ratio		
	Subsector	2012	2014	Change	2012	2014	Change
316	Leather and allied product manufacturing	94.5%	96.7%	2.2%	7.66	8.51	0.85
325b	Medicines, diagnostics & biologics manufacturing	42.9%	48.1%	5.1%	1.24	1.38	0.14
333	Machinery manufacturing	42.4%	39.0%	-3.3%	1.03	1.05	0.02
334	Computer and electronic product manufacturing	64.7%	69.4%	4.7%	1.72	1.84	0.12
335	Electrical equipment, appliance, and component mfg.	54.7%	58.2%	3.5%	1.38	1.42	0.04
3352	Appliances	66.2%	69.1%	2.8%	1.83	1.85	0.05
339a	Medical, dental & opthalmic products manufacturing	32.2%	34.2%	2.0%	1.04	1.05	0.02
335	Electrical equipment, appliance, and component mfg.	54.7%	58.2%	3.5%	1.38	1.42	0.04
	All manufacturing subsectors	31.4%	32.4%	1.0%	114.2%	115.1%	0.9%

Source: Author's calculations; data are from Manufacturing and International Trade Report 2012 and Manufacturing and International Trade Report 2014, U.S. Census Bureau

Excludes some production for which export and import data are not avaliable.

Measuring Manufacturing by "Value Added"

Despite the studies connecting the manufacturing job losses to imports, especially from China, and despite the data showing high penetration of U.S. markets by foreign imports, there is a persistent assertion of the proposition that the U.S. job losses in manufacturing are not due to imports, but rather to some other cause, such as automation and increased productivity.[19] The argument is that, although employment has been declining, U.S. manufacturing production has been increasing when measured by "value added," that is, total output less intermediate inputs. The disparity with employment levels is explained by increased productivity, often with reference to productivity measures. I will refer to this proposition as the "value-added narrative."

Of course, this narrative is at odds with facts on the ground. If it were true, there would be highly automated furniture factories pumping out ever greater quantities of bedroom sets in the towns of North Carolina. But as Beth Macy has documented in her book *Factory Man*,[20] we know that the factories are closed, and the executives went off to China and Indonesia to teach their new suppliers how to make furniture.[21]

Nevertheless, the argument is so persistent, I needed to test it. To do so, I downloaded the Bureau of Economic Analysis' numbers for manufacturing value added by industry.[22] What I found is at odds with the value-added narrative.

Manufacturing is not doing very well.

First, overall, the manufacturing sector hasn't been doing very well, as shown in the following figure:

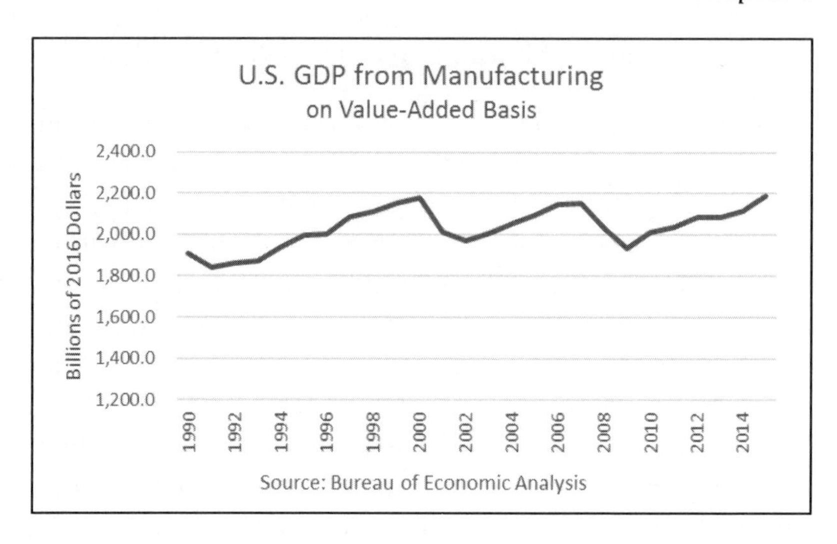

Looking at the figure, we see that by 2015, manufacturing measured by value added barely recovered to its 2000 level after the 2001 and 2008 recessions.[23] Like the "jobless recoveries" from an employment point of view, we have had two "insufficient recoveries" from a production point of view.

Manufacturing output is lower than it should be.

But if manufacturing output basically is flat since the 2000-1 recession, where should it be?

Two standards come to mind. The first is where manufacturing output would be if it had continued to increase at the average rate experienced from 1990 through 2000. (Including the 1990-91 recession, the average rate of increase is 1.35% per year.)

The second is this: where would manufacturing output be if we captured our net imports of manufactured goods, measured on a value-added basis – if, instead of purchasing these goods abroad, we had spent this amount on domestic goods?[24] The answers are displayed in the following figure:

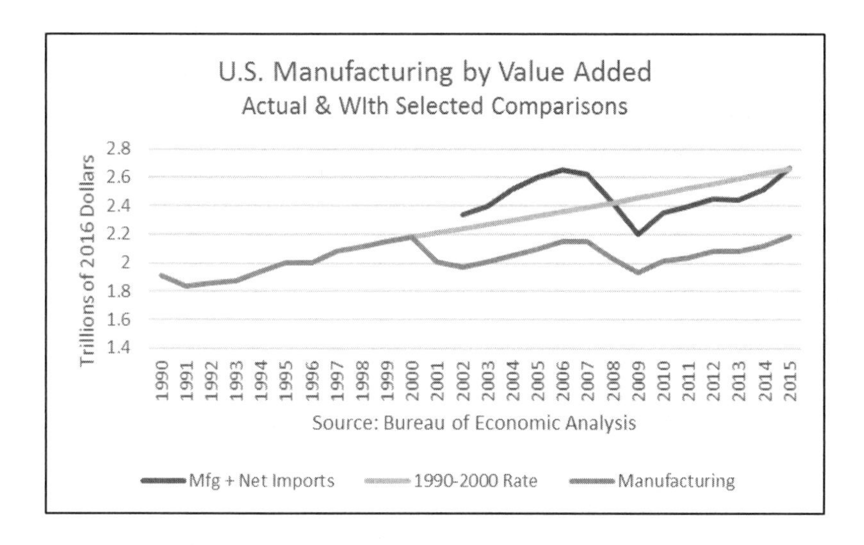

This is a striking figure in several respects. First, growing manufacturing value added at the pre-2001 rate, and adding in the excess imports, have exactly the same effect – we end up at the same point. The trade deficit in manufactured goods in 2015 was nearly exactly equal to the gap between actual manufacturing and where production would be at the pre-2001 growth rate. *The loss in production was equal to the excess imports.*

Second, the shortfall is substantial: actual production was $477.2 billion lower when compared to GDP plus the excess imports, and $472.1 billion lower when compared to GDP grown at the pre-2001 rate. And it should be noted that the estimate for capturing the excess imports likely is on the low side, because each dollar of spending retained would have a "multiplier effect", creating additional spending as it rippled through the U.S. economy.

Failure to Keep Pace with GDP & Population

Two other benchmarks can be considered as to where manufacturing value added should be: the growth of the overall economy, as measured by Gross Domestic Product, and the growth of the U.S. population: Has manufacturing output been keeping pace with GDP? With population growth?

In my view, neither of these standards is adequate: the actual overall GDP number is substantially lower than it should be, for the reasons I describe in this book. And we should not be satisfied with any sector of the economy growing only at the rate of population growth, because that means that, on a per capita basis, it is standing still. Nevertheless, I thought it would be useful to consider these reference points as a lower bound on what we have lost in manufacturing. The following figure shows reported manufacturing by value added in 2016 dollars from 1990 through 2015, and what it would have been had it grown at the same pace as the overall economy and the population:

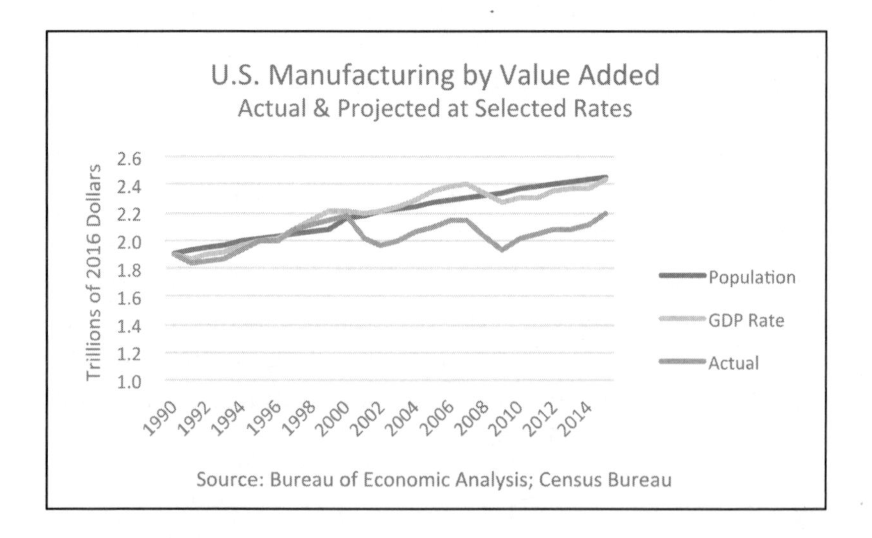

The figure illustrates that growth in manufacturing value added has *not* kept pace, either with growth of the economy or with growth of the population:

- In 2015, manufacturing value added was $251 billion lower than it would have been had it kept pace with growth of the economy.
- In 2015, Manufacturing value added was $270 billion lower than it would have been had it kept pace with population growth.
- As with the previous comparison with the pre-2001 growth rate, the figure also illustrates that U.S. manufacturing recovered from the 1990-91 recession, returning to the population trend line by 1995, but did not do so after the 2000-1 and 2008-9 recessions: the result is the $251-$270 billion gap.

Key Findings:

- Manufacturing measured by value added recovered after the 1990-91 recession, but did not do so after the 2000-1 and 2008-9 recessions:
- In 2015, MVA was $472 billion lower than it would have been at pre-2001 growth rates, and $477 billion lower than if excess imports were included. *The shortfall from the pre-2001 rate was exactly equal to the losses to imports.*
- Manufacturing output also did not keep pace with overall economic growth or population growth: in 2015, it was $251 billion lower than if it had grown with GDP, and $270 billion lower than if it had kept pace with the population.

Explaining the Value-Added and Employment Gap

That said, we still must address the question of why the manufacturing output curve is different than the manufacturing employment curve: while the former is lower than it should be, it recovers to pre-2001 levels, while the latter does not:

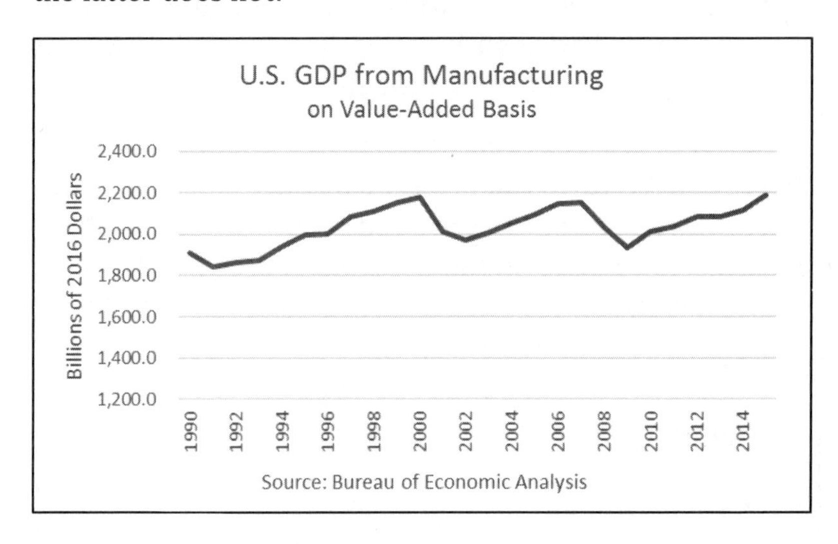

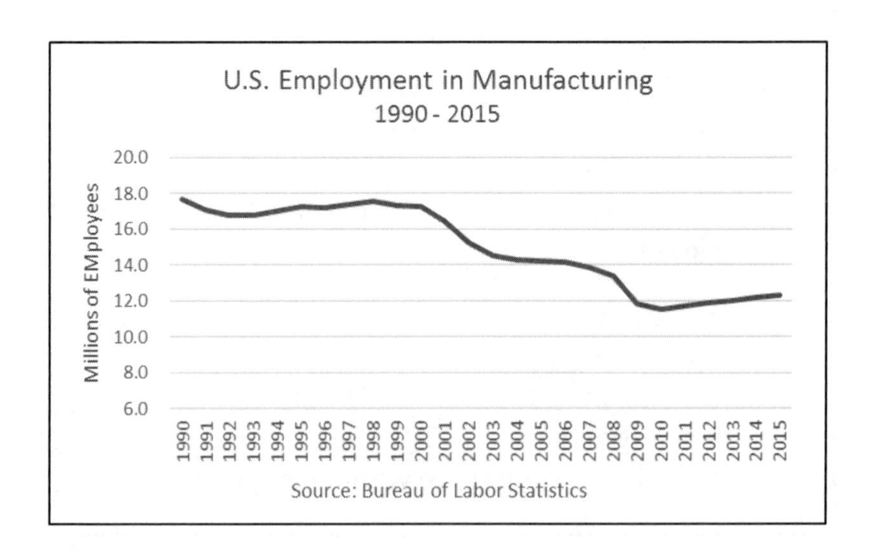

Combined figures are not representative.

One important possibility is that the BEA's figures overstate the U.S. manufacturing value added, as I discuss below. But the major answer for the disparity between the employment numbers and the value-added numbers is that *the combined value-added numbers for manufacturing are not representative of most subsectors.* When value-added output is considered by subsector, the results look a lot more like the employment numbers, as shown in the following figures.

For apparel, leather goods, and textile products, we see that the curves look much like the curves for employment: a steady and dramatic decline to "flat line," except that the value-added curves trend slightly upward towards the end, perhaps due to productivity increases. Electrical equipment and appliances also show a steady decline.

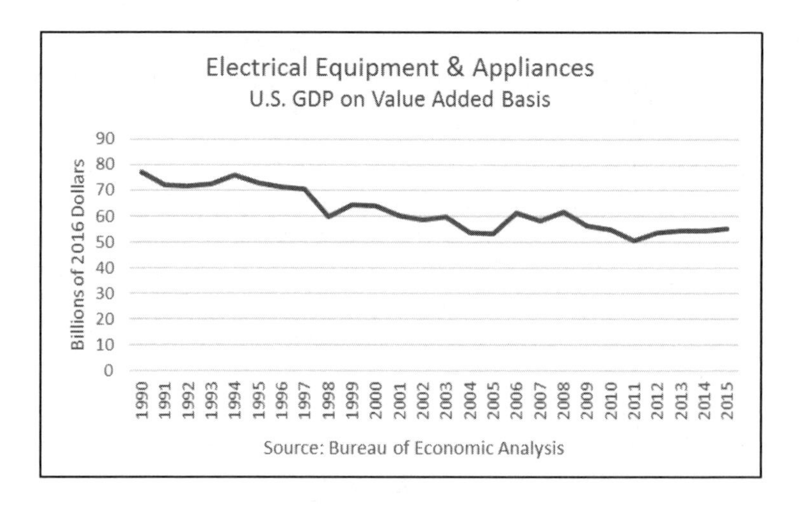

Furniture, wood products, and nonmetallic mineral products also track their employment curves closely, with substantial losses and only partial recovery. This group is particularly interesting because it largely comprises building materials. So, we see the production losses in these three industries beginning in the 2005 – 2007 timeframe, before declines spread to the rest of the economy during the Great Recession.

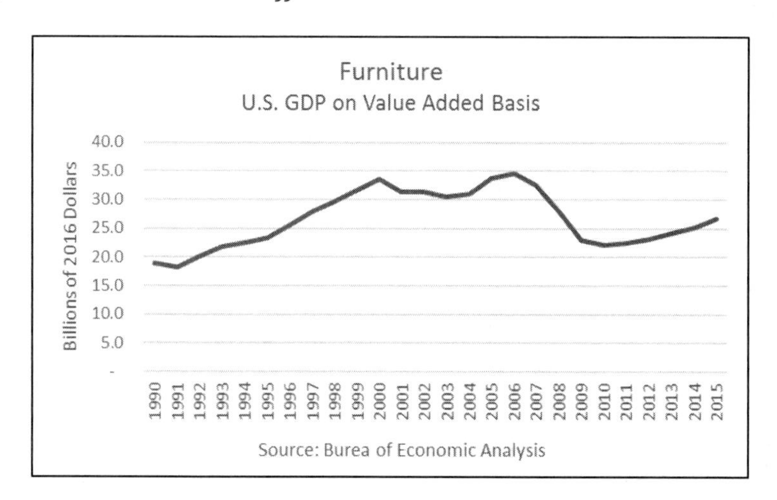
Furniture
U.S. GDP on Value Added Basis
Billions of 2016 Dollars
40.0
35.0
30.0
25.0
20.0
15.0
10.0
5.0
-
1990 1991 1992 1993 1994 1995 1996 1997 1998 1999 2000 2001 2002 2003 2004 2005 2006 2007 2008 2009 2010 2011 2012 2013 2014 2015
Source: Burea of Economic Analysis

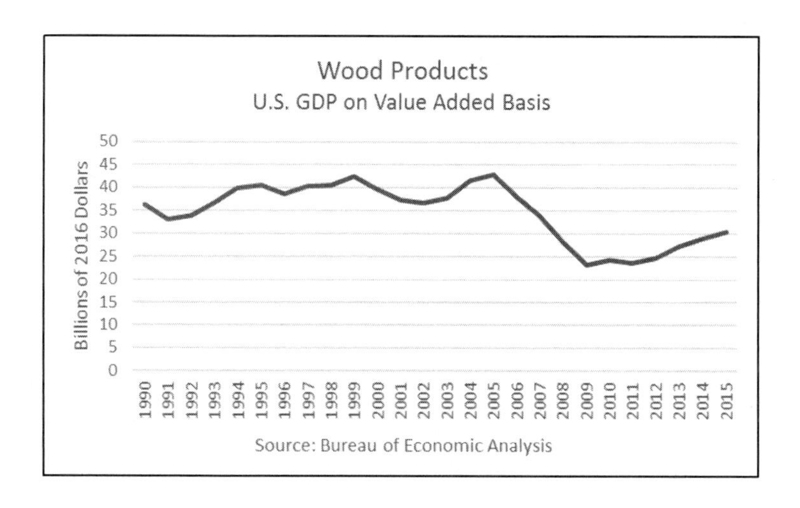
Wood Products
U.S. GDP on Value Added Basis
Billions of 2016 Dollars
50
45
40
35
30
25
20
15
10
5
0
1990 1991 1992 1993 1994 1995 1996 1997 1998 1999 2000 2001 2002 2003 2004 2005 2006 2007 2008 2009 2010 2011 2012 2013 2014 2015
Source: Bureau of Economic Analysis

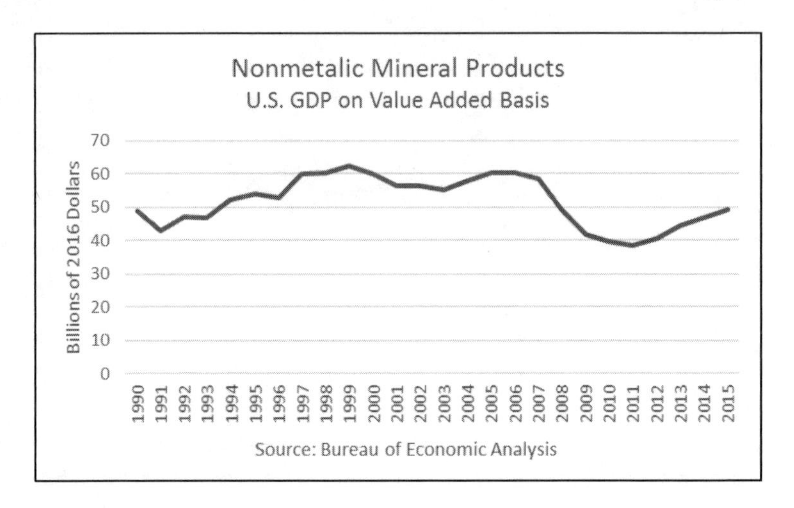

Paper, Printing Products, and Machinery are almost flat, with little increase or slight decline over the time period.

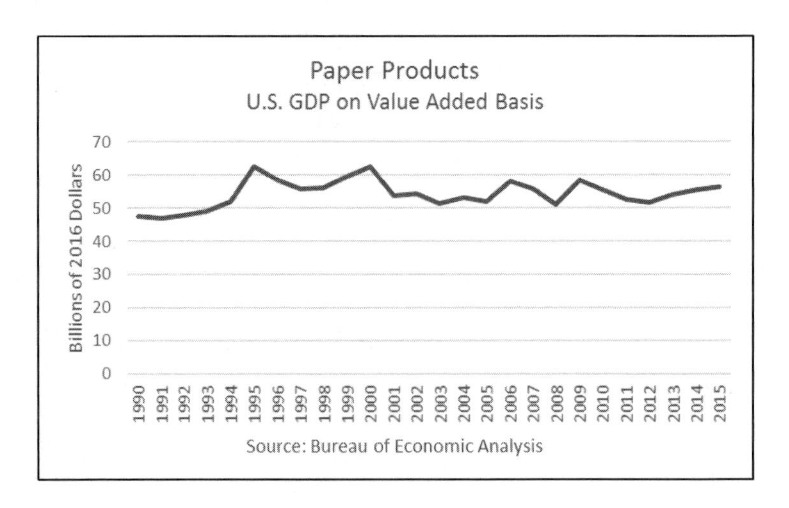

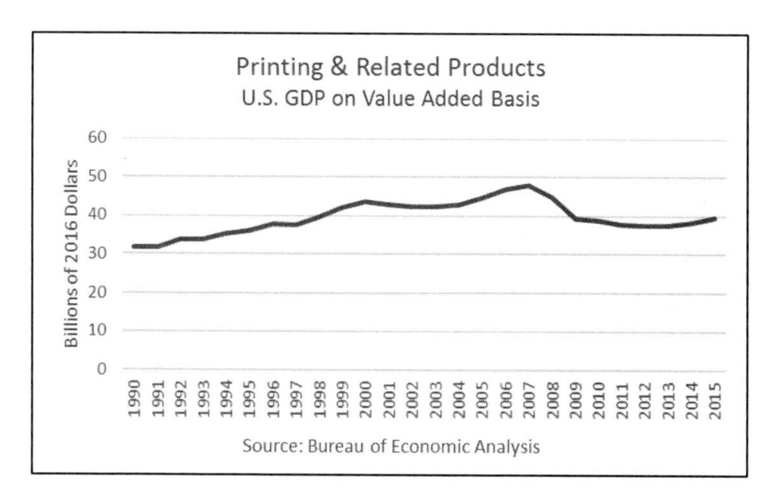

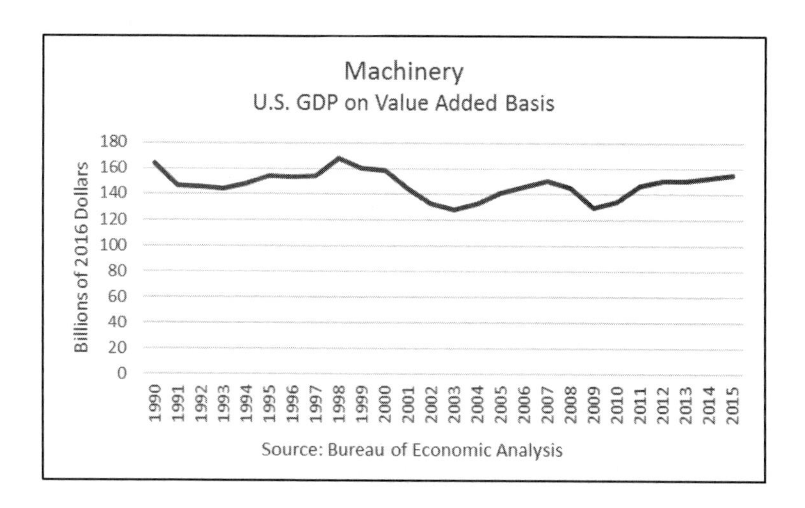

Primary Metal Products, Miscellaneous Durable Products, and Food and Beverage and Tobacco Products show small gains over the time frame.

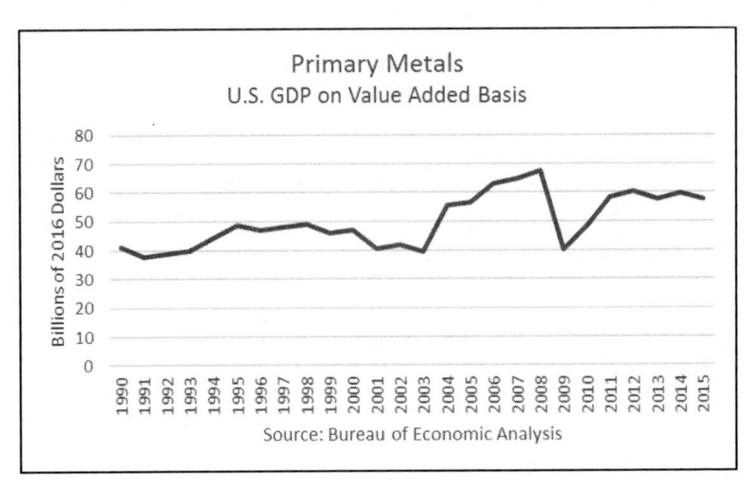
Primary Metals
U.S. GDP on Value Added Basis
Billions of 2016 Dollars
80
70
60
50
40
30
20
10
0
1990 1991 1992 1993 1994 1995 1996 1997 1998 1999 2000 2001 2002 2003 2004 2005 2006 2007 2008 2009 2010 2011 2012 2013 2014 2015
Source: Bureau of Economic Analysis

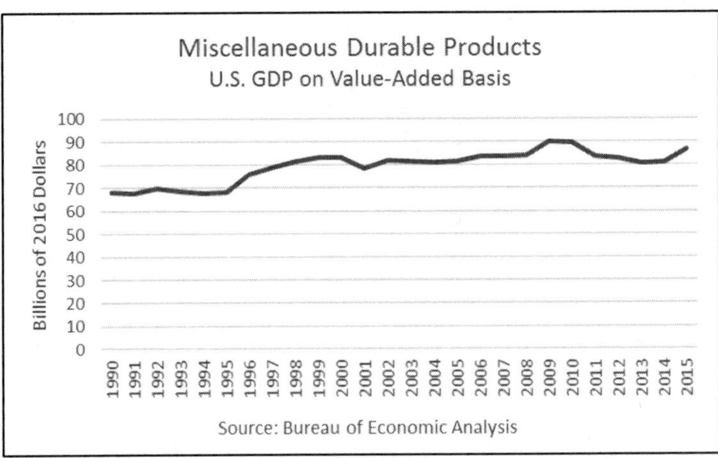
Miscellaneous Durable Products
U.S. GDP on Value-Added Basis
Billions of 2016 Dollars
100
90
80
70
60
50
40
30
20
10
0
1990 1991 1992 1993 1994 1995 1996 1997 1998 1999 2000 2001 2002 2003 2004 2005 2006 2007 2008 2009 2010 2011 2012 2013 2014 2015
Source: Bureau of Economic Analysis

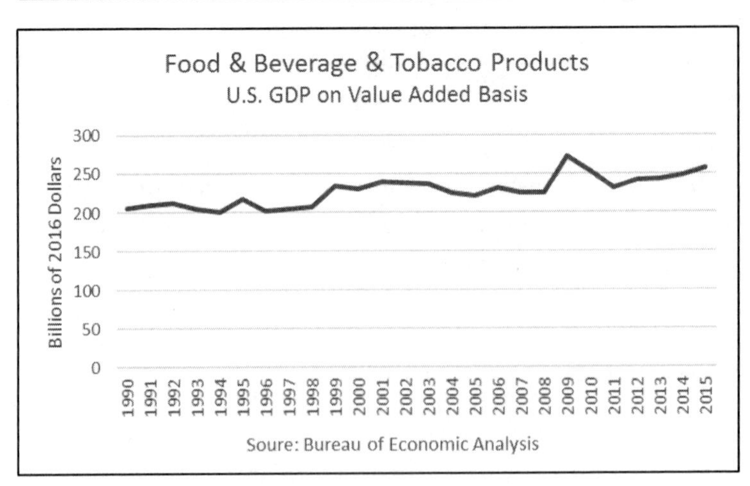
Food & Beverage & Tobacco Products
U.S. GDP on Value Added Basis
Billions of 2016 Dollars
300
250
200
150
100
50
0
1990 1991 1992 1993 1994 1995 1996 1997 1998 1999 2000 2001 2002 2003 2004 2005 2006 2007 2008 2009 2010 2011 2012 2013 2014 2015
Soure: Bureau of Economic Analysis

Chemical products, Motor Vehicles, and Other Transportation Equipment all show the kind of steady increase in output that is recited in the value-added narrative (excepting motor vehicles, which showed a severe dip during the 2008-9 recession). Fabricated Metal Products also show net increases after the recessions. These may constitute subsectors in which the value-added narrative might be operative.

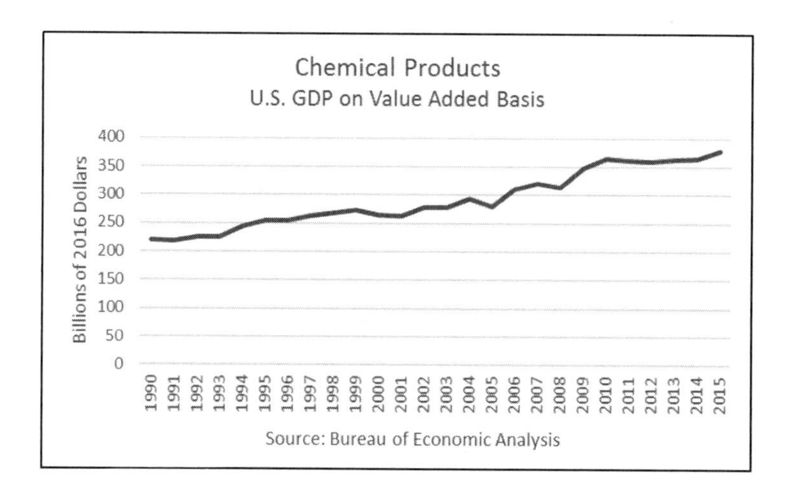

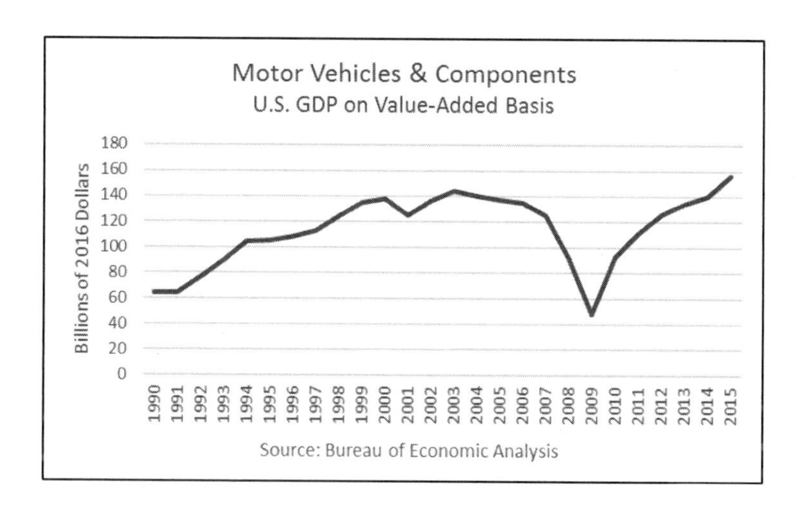

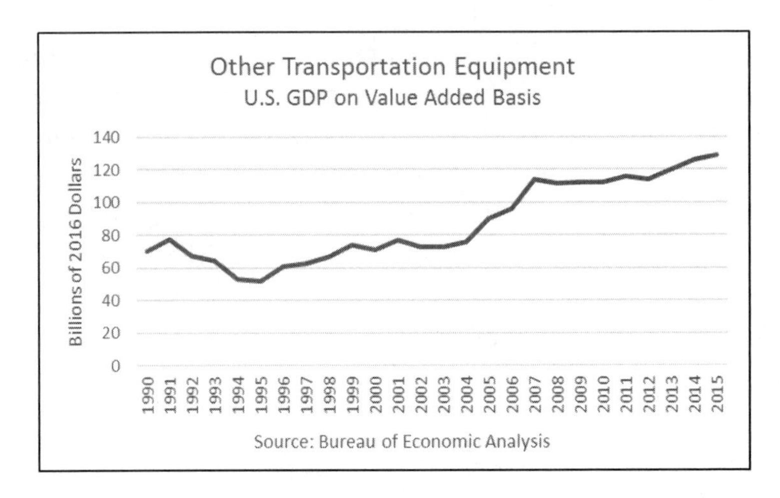

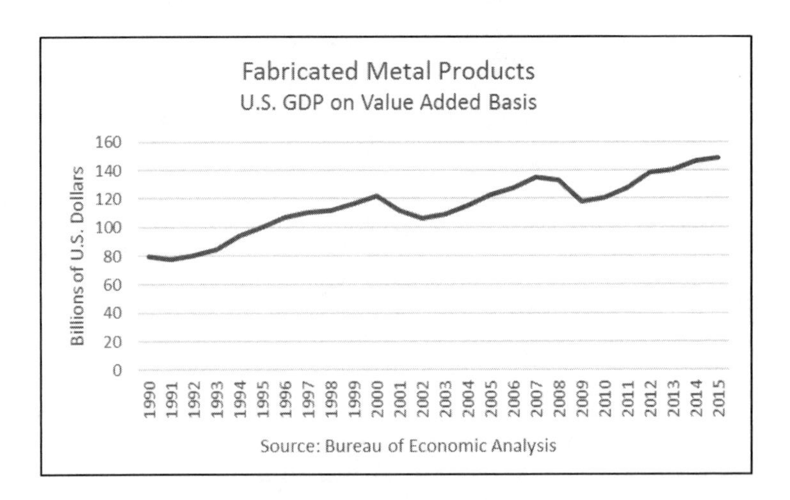

Petroleum and Coal Products show sharp increases in output; however, this is increase likely is attributable to idiosyncrasies in the statistical methods used by the Bureau of Economic Analysis. Reported output by volume of product does not correspond to the reported output by value added.[25]

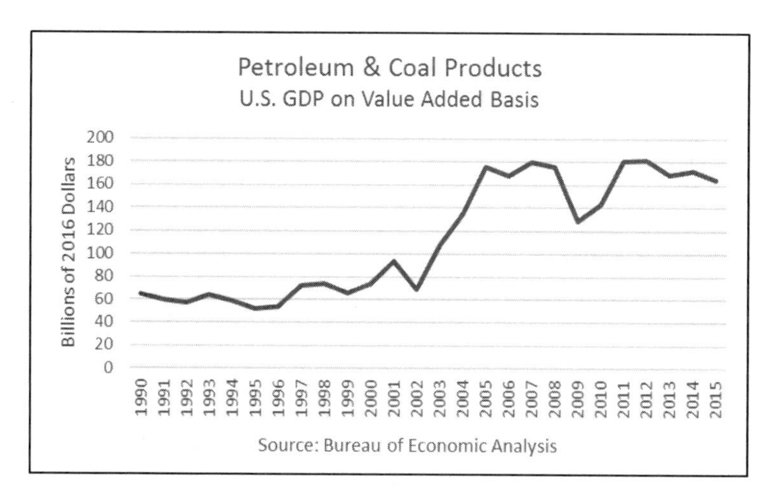

Computers are a different story. After a drop during the 2001 recession, output in this subsector has seen a steady increase. Meanwhile, employment declined in the 2001 and 2008 recessions, with little recovery. As I discuss below, computers likely are subject to overestimation of the U.S. value-added, due to an underestimation of the foreign inputs. However, value added output in computers likely is subject to an overstatement of output for another reason: the government calculates it using formulas intended to capture increases in computing power per dollar spent. [26]

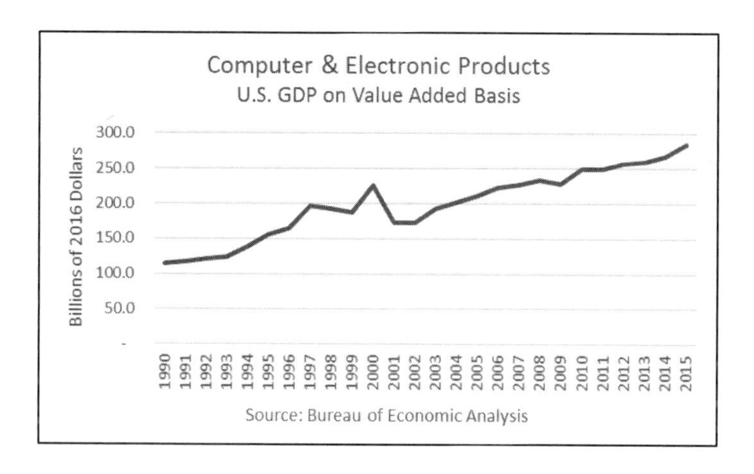

What, then, do we learn from this closer look at value added in manufacturing?

Key Findings:

A review of U.S. manufacturing output measured by value added during the period 1990 through 2015 for each of the 18 subsectors reported by the BEA shows:

- Six subsectors saw substantial declines in value added: Apparel and Leather Goods, Textiles and Textile Products, Electrical Equipment and Appliances, Furniture, Wood Products, and Nonmetallic Mineral Products.
- Six subsectors were flat or with small gains: Paper Products, Printing Products, Machinery, Primary Metal Products, Miscellaneous Durable Products, and Food and Beverage and Tobacco Products.
- Four subsectors saw substantial gains: Chemical Products, Fabricated Metal Products, Motor Vehicles, and Other Transportation Equipment.
- Petroleum and Coal Products saw gains likely peculiar to the subsector, and Computer and Electronic Equipment, saw gains likely due to accounting methods.

Overstatement of Value Added

What of the four subsectors that saw substantial gains? Might the value-added narrative be operative there, and to some extent in the six subsectors where output was flat, but higher than employment? Might the gap between output and employment in these subsectors be explained by increased productivity?

There is a growing body of thought among economists that the answer is no, and that *in these manufacturing subsectors, output, as measured by value added, is overstated.* As U.S. manufacturers have moved more of their intermediate production to low-cost foreign suppliers such as China, it is likely that the shift to foreign suppliers, and the lower costs of these intermediate products, are not being captured by government statistics: it looks like the U.S. company is buying less foreign input than it really is, so that the remaining U.S. value-added is overstated.[27] *If this bias were taken into account, the curves for manufacturing value added following the 2001 and 2008 recessions would become more like the flat curves for employment.*

Conclusion:

The value-added narrative is an exaggeration bordering on a myth. It is neither true that U.S. manufacturing is healthy, nor that U.S. manufacturing job losses can be accounted for by increases in productivity.

What Happened When the Jobs Left?

We have confirmed that the unbalanced overseas sourcing of products and services for the American market has led to significant direct job losses, due either to the movement of a company's production offshore, or to demise of the company in the face of foreign production. And we have confirmed that a large portion of the lost jobs went to China and other such places – U.S. manufacturing has not kept pace with previous growth rates, GDP growth, or population growth. Now we consider, what have been the effects of sending these jobs overseas?

Predictable Mirror Effects

Canadian economist Brian McCaig did a study of the impacts experienced in Vietnam in the years immediately following the entry into effect of the U.S.-Vietnam bilateral trade agreement in 2001. He found an exponential increase in net Vietnamese exports to the U.S., and that exports resulted in a substantial reduction in poverty in that country. In an article discussing the study, Nathaniel Popper reports:

> By [McCaig's] estimate, only about 250,000 jobs were created in export-based manufacturing in Vietnam during those two years. But those jobs, which were better-paying than almost anything else available before, had an enormous ripple effect: every new factory position led to several other new jobs nearby. In general, the more specialized a region was in producing exports, the faster poverty declined."[28]

Taking Popper's summary, we can easily predict the mirror effect that was experienced in American manufacturing towns at the same time:

> *The loss of* those jobs, which were better-paying than almost anything else available *after*, had an enormous ripple effect: every *lost* factory position led to several other *lost* jobs nearby. In general, the more specialized a region was in producing *products*, the faster poverty *increased*.

Studies of Effects on Communities

These seem to be the same effects as we saw in the examples reviewed in Chapters 1, 2, and 3. Is there evidence beyond those anecdotal reports? In recent years, the evidence has been growing, in a number of studies by economists.

Chinese Imports and the Local Economy

In a study first reported in 2012,[29] economist David Autor and colleagues at MIT sought to get a better handle on the local effects of the influx of products imported from China. To do so, they identified product sectors where a high percentage of U.S. consumption was from Chinese imports. They then looked at data on local economies with concentrations of industries making these products. They looked at the period 1990 through 2007; as we have seen in Chapter 2, this was the time of the great run-up of China's manufacturing exports, especially to the United States.

As would be expected, they found significant declines in employment in the import-competing manufacturing industries.[30] But what about the rest of the local economy? Here they found significant reductions in earnings: *a combination of reduced demand for local services and increased supply of available workers created downward pressure on non-manufacturing wages.* Overall, the researchers found that import competition caused an involuntary drop in labor force participation and had a negative effect on household incomes that was "statistically significant and economically large."

The researchers also found that Chinese import exposure was related to a significant increase in dependency, as evidenced by increased spending on government transfer programs.[31] The researchers acknowledged that "gains" from trade with China could include "gains to consumers from lower product prices or increased product variety," . . . "gains to firms from having inputs at lower cost and greater variety," and gains to productivity growth due to trade-induced innovation by U.S. firms. However, they concluded that there were costs, identified in their study, that must be weighed against these gains.

Chinese Imports at the Worker Level

Autor and his colleagues Dorn and Hanson followed with another study, this time seeking "hard evidence" of the effects of the Chinese onslaught on individual workers, during the period 1992 - 2007. [32]

They found that workers who were employed in 1991 in an industry that subsequently became subject to increased import competition from China experienced markedly lower cumulative earnings: the difference between a manufacturing worker with high industry trade exposure and one with low exposure amounted to *reduced earnings equal to 46 percent of initial yearly income.*[33]

These workers also experienced somewhat lower cumulative employment, lower earnings per year worked, and greater reliance on Social Security Disability Insurance. They found that these impacts were felt the most by those least able to bear them: they fell to a greater degree on workers who started out with lower wages and lower tenure and who were employed by large firms with low wages; higher-earning workers fared better, moving to new jobs, often outside manufacturing, without much effect on wages.[34]

Effects of Imports on Wages

In a study published in 2015,[35] Avraham Ebenstein and colleagues took a different approach, keying on *occupations*, rather than industries, that were subject to import competition from China. Using data that followed individual workers over time, their research indicates that *"occupational exposure to globalization puts significant downward pressure on wages" due to the movement of workers out of manufacturing and into lower-wage services.* Even larger losses are experienced when workers also change occupations in the process.[36] *For each ten percent increase in the share of a market that is captured by Chinese imports, they found a six percent decline in the wages of affected U.S. workers.*

More Research on Local Effects

In February of 2016, Autor, Dorn and Hanson updated their 2013 "China Syndrome" paper with a new study, "The China Shock." [37] The authors discuss how far the real-world experience of the U.S. with the China surge has departed from textbook theoretical predictions: employment in the import-facing industries has fallen as predicted, but offsetting gains in employment in export-oriented or non-tradable industries have not materialized. The new paper amplifies the earlier findings of the negative effects experienced in local labor markets facing import competition from China. Among their findings:

> Labor-market adjustment to trade shocks is stunningly slow, *with local labor-force participation rates remaining depressed and local unemployment rates remaining elevated for a full decade or more* after a shock commences.[38]

The work of Autor and his colleagues provides statistical corroboration of the reports we saw in Chapters 1, 2, and 3 of communities deeply harmed by the loss of manufacturing jobs to imports from China and other low-wage countries. But the "China Shock" paper serves perhaps an even more important purpose. In my research, I have been frustrated in my attempts to identify the widely-heralded benefits of "trade for the sake of trade." Autor, Dorn and Hanson identify the reason -- the economics profession hasn't done a very good job of identifying or quantifying them:

> Finally, we argue that having failed to anticipate how significant the dislocations from trade might be, it is incumbent on the [profession] to more convincingly estimate the gains from trade, *such that the case for free trade is not based on the sway of theory alone*, but on a foundation of evidence that illuminates who gains, who loses, by how much, and under what conditions.[39]

What is the evidence of the effects at the national level? We consider this question in the next chapter.

Notes to Chapter 6

---

[1] Testimony of Larry Cohen, President of the Communication Workers of America, before U.S. Senate Committee on Finance, January 16, 2014. Quoted in Mary Bottari ,"Like Gravity" Fast Track Trade Sinks Jobs and Wages, *Center for Media and Democracy*, January 21, 2014. http://www.prwatch.org/news/2014/01/12367/%E2%80%9C-gravity%E2%80%9D-fast-track-trade-will-sink-jobs-and-drag-down-wages.

[2] The figure is derived from the following data:

U.S. Employment in Manufacturing 1940 - 1979 (millions)							
Year	Employees	Year	Employees	Year	Employees	Year	Employees
1940	10.1	**1950**	14.0	**1960**	15.4	**1970**	17.8
1941	12.1	**1951**	15.1	**1961**	15.0	**1971**	17.2
1942	14.0	**1952**	15.3	**1962**	15.5	**1972**	17.7
1943	16.2	**1953**	16.1	**1963**	15.6	**1973**	18.6
1944	15.9	**1954**	15.0	**1964**	15.9	**1974**	18.5
1945	14.3	**1955**	15.5	**1965**	16.6	**1975**	16.9
1946	13.5	**1956**	15.9	**1966**	17.7	**1976**	17.5
1947	14.3	**1957**	15.8	**1967**	17.9	**1977**	18.2
1948	14.3	**1958**	14.7	**1968**	18.2	**1978**	18.9
1949	13.3	**1959**	15.3	**1969**	18.6	**1979**	19.4
Source: Bureau of Labor Statistics http://data.bls.gov/timeseries/CES3000000001 Values are annual averages.							

[3] The figure is derived from the following data:

U.S. Employment in Manufacturing 1979 - 2016 (millions)							
Year	Employees	Year	Employees	Year	Employees	Year	Employees
1979	19.4	**1989**	18.0	**1999**	17.3	**2009**	11.8
1980	18.7	**1990**	17.7	**2000**	17.3	**2010**	11.5
1981	18.6	**1991**	17.1	**2001**	16.4	**2011**	11.7
1982	17.4	**1992**	16.8	**2002**	15.3	**2012**	11.9
1983	17.0	**1993**	16.8	**2003**	14.5	**2013**	12.0
1984	17.9	**1994**	17.0	**2004**	14.3	**2014**	12.2
1985	17.8	**1995**	17.2	**2005**	14.2	**2015**	12.3
1986	17.6	**1996**	17.2	**2006**	14.2	**2016**	12.3
1987	17.6	**1997**	17.4	**2007**	13.9		
1988	17.9	**1998**	17.6	**2008**	13.4		
Source: Bureau of Labor Statistics http://data.bls.gov/timeseries/CES3000000001 Values are annual averages.							

[4] Manufacturing is preceded by the extraction industries, and succeeded by distribution, installation, maintenance and use. Can any large society survive and thrive without the manufacturing component? If we send this entire sector of the economy to other countries, because it can be done at lower cost there, can the resulting economy, with this hole punched in it, be sustainable? And even if it could, would we want to be dependent on other countries for all of this? And if we are not to send it all offshore, which ones of these industries are we to say are not important? Important from the point of view of the consumer? From the point of view of strategic economic or security concerns? Which products don't matter, and which jobs producing them don't matter? We will consider these questions in this and subsequent chapters.

[5] There are 21 NAICS subsectors, but the Bureau of Labor Statistics has combined NAICS 312 Beverage and Tobacco Products and NAICS 316 Leather and Allied Products into one reporting group, "Miscellaneous Nondurable Goods", in a table numbered 329. I report on the 20 BLS subsectors.

[6] I also would include in Group 1 NAICS 316, Leather and Allied Products Manufacturing, and I do so with respect to trade and GDP statistics. However, the Bureau of Labor Statistics does not report leather products separately, but rather with NAICS 312, Beverage and Tobacco Manufacturing in a grouping called Miscellaneous Nondurable Goods. I have included this miscellaneous BLS grouping in my Group 8, with NAICS 311, Food Manufacturing.

[7] In each case I seek to give a fulsome description of the products produced, because I believe it is important to appreciate the richness, breadth and depth of the economic activity involved in each subsector.

[8] The data from which the figures in this chapter are derived are published at http://currentaffairspress.com/titles/what-if-things-were-made-in-america-again/.

[9] It is important to note that many of these products are used in the manufacture of other products. So, if the manufacture of those products goes offshore, then these machinery industries die, except to the extent that we can sell this machinery to foreign manufacturers.

[10] A note regarding methodology: I have counted job losses during the period 1990-2016 from the highest level of employment experienced by a subsector during that period. Some industries have never regained the level of employment they enjoyed at the beginning of 1990. For them it is appropriate to count job losses since then. However, other industries, usually after a dip following the 1990-91 recession, saw job gains during the 1990s to a new high, typically in the

year 2000. For these industries, it would not be informative to refer to their 1990 employment level, and it is appropriate for our purposes to count job losses since their highest point. As noted previously, I have separated the 20 NAICS subgroups into eight groupings having similar characteristics. There are 21, but the Bureau of Labor Statistics has combined NAICS 312 Beverage and Tobacco Products and NAICS 316 Leather and Allied Products into one reporting group, "Miscellaneous Nondurable Goods", in a table numbered 329.

[11] Apologies for a chart with different scales on the y axis. However, if it is borne in mind that the curves are on different scales, I believe the resulting graphic provides a valid representation of the relationship.

[12] Justin R. Pierce and Peter K. Schott, "The Surprisingly Swift Decline of U.S. Manufacturing Employment." NBER Working Paper Series, Working Paper 18655. National Bureau of Economic Research. Cambridge, MA December 2012. http://www.nber.org/ papers/ w18655.

[13] The United States utilizes two tariff classification: "NTR" or "column 1" tariffs applicable to countries with which it has normal trade relations (including countries that are members of the World Trade Organization) and higher, "Non-NTR" or "column 2" tariffs that are applied to countries with which it does not (e.g., Iran, Cuba, and North Korea). The Trade Act of 1974 gives the President the power to temporarily grant NTR status to countries with non-market economies, subject to potential Congressional disapproval. China was granted temporary NTR status in 1980 (shortly after the "reform and opening" initiated by Deng Xiaoping in 1978). Following the Tiananmen Square events of 1989, the annual renewals became contentious and uncertain; if either the President failed to act or Congress overturned his action, large increases in tariff rates could result. The October 2000 legislation granting permanent NTR status to China removed the uncertainty and paved the way for China's entry into the World Trade Organization in December 2001. Pierce and Schott found that there was no significant change in tariffs applied to Chinese imports; only the uncertainty of renewal of NTR status was removed. *Id.*, 10.

[14] Another important, but not sufficient, condition was already in place: China's previous action permitting foreign investment and establishing special export production zones via the "reform and opening" begun in 1978 and confirmed with Deng Xiaoping's trip to the southern provinces in 1992.

[15] "Impact of U.S.-China Trade Relations on Workers, Wages and Employment," http://govinfo.library.unt.edu/tdrc/ research/33.

Quoted in Online Appendix for "The Surprisingly Swift Decline of U.S. Manufacturing Employment," Justin R. Pierce and Peter K. Schott, *infra*.

[16] Daron Acemoglu, David Autor, David Dorn, Gordon H. Hanson, and Brendan Price, "Import Competition and the Great US Employment Sag of the 2000s," Journal of Labor Economics, Vol. 34, No. S1 (Part 2, January 2016): S141-S198, doi:
http://www.jstor.org/stable/10.1086/682384.
The authors summarize their study in Daron Acemoglu, David Autor, David Dorn, Gordon Hanson, and Brendan Price, "The rise of China and the future of US manufacturing," *VOX*, September 28, 2014.
http://voxeu.org/article/rise-china-and-future-us-manufacturing.

[17] "2014 Manufacturing and International Trade Report," Census Bureau, U.S. Department of Commerce, January 29, 2016, http://www. census.gov/foreign-trade/PressRelease/MITR/2014/index. html

[18] "2012 Manufacturing and International Trade Report," Census Bureau, U.S. Department of Commerce, January 29, 2016, "2014 Manufacturing and International Trade Report,"
http://www.census.gov/foreign-trade/Press-Release/MITR/2012/index.html?eml=gd.

[19] Representative assertions of the narrative are collected at Susan N. Houseman, "The Debate over the State of U.S. Manufacturing: How the Computer Industry Affects the Numbers and Perceptions," *Employment Research*, 19(3) (2012): 1-4, footnote 1,
http://dx.doi.org/10.17848/1075-8445.19(3)-1.

[20] Beth Macy, *Factory Man, supra*.

[21] In Macy's narrative, John Bannister did install the latest machinery and techniques; in the factories that remain open, there likely has been some job loss attributable to productivity improvements.

[22] The data are available at http://www.bea.gov/industry/ gdpbyind_data.htm.

[23] In the discussion that follows, please note that the BEA statistics likely overstate value added from manufacturing, for the reasons discussed below.

[24] I have added the amount of the trade deficit in manufactured goods to the manufacturing value added. The Census Bureau does not record imports by value added, but rather by gross sales. I have approximated a value-added measure of imports by removing 25 percent of the gross import value. That is, I have assumed that 25 percent of imports are attributable to U.S. content, for example, a U.S.-made microchip inserted into a laptop computer that is imported into

the United States. The Census Bureau data are only available since 2002. The average proportion of imports to domestic production during the period 2002 through 2015 was 19.5%.

[25] *See* Robert D. Atkinson, Luke A. Stewart, Scott M. Andes, and Steven J. Ezell, "Worse Than the Great Depression: What Experts Are Missing About American Manufacturing Decline," Information and Technology Innovation Foundation (March 2012), 36.
http://www2.itif.org/2012-american-manufacturing-decline.pdf

[26] In a recent article, Susan Houseman concluded that looking behind these contrived numbers, job losses in the computer and electronics industry have been caused by the shift of production to Asia, and not by productivity improvements to domestic production. Susan N. Houseman, "The Debate over the State of U.S. Manufacturing: How the Computer Industry Affects the Numbers and Perceptions," *Employment Research*, 19(3) (2012): 1-4,
http://dx.doi.org/10.17848/1075-8445.19(3)-1
See also, Atkinson, et al., "Worse Than the Great Depression," 33.

[27] Susan Houseman, Christopher Kurz, Paul Lengermann, and Benjamin Mandel. "Offshoring Bias in U.S. Manufacturing." *Journal of Economic Perspectives* 25 (2) (2011): 111–32. *See also*, Atkinson, et al., "Worse Than the Great Depression," and summary and commentary by Robert D. Atkinson at:
http://www.huffingtonpost.com/robert-d-atkinson-phd/worse-than-the-great-depr_b_1368219.html

[28] Nathaniel Popper, "How Much Do We Really Know about Global Trade's Impacts?" *New York Times Magazine*, September 6, 2016.

[29] David Autor, David Dorn, and Gordon H. Hanson, "The China Syndrome: Local Labor Market Effects of Import Competition in the United States," Massachusetts Institute of Technology Department of Economics Working Paper Series, Working Paper 12-2. May 2, 2012. http://ssrn.com/abstract=2050144. *American Economic Review* 103:6 (2013): 2121-2168. http://doi.org/10.1257/aer103.6.2121.

[30] Interestingly, they did not find wage reductions, perhaps because those industries made internal production changes resulting in a higher-skilled workforce. See discussion of Ebenstein *et al.*, below.

[31]These transfer programs included Unemployment Insurance benefits, Social Security Disability Insurance (SSDI) benefits, federal income assistance benefits from SSI (Supplemental Security Income), TANF (Temporary Assistance for Needy Families), and SNAP (Supplemental Nutrition Assistance), education and training assistance, and in-kind medical transfer benefit programs, *i.e.*, Medicare and

Medicaid, (Of far lesser significance was increased temporary spending on Trade Adjustment Assistance.)

[32] David H. Autor, David Dorn, Gordon H. Hanson, and Jae Song, "Trade Adjustment: Worker Level Evidence," Massachusetts Institute of Technology Department of Economics Working Paper Series, Working Paper 13-21, June 30, 2013. http://ssrn.com/abstract=2323054, NBER Working Paper No. 19226, Released on July 23, 2013. http://www.nber.org/papers/w19226.
© 2013 by David H. Autor, David Dorn, Gordon H. Hanson, and Jae Song. Also published in Quarterly Journal of Economics, Oxford University Press, vol. 129(4): 1799-1860.

[33] Claire Brunel, "Employment Effects of International Trade," National Bureau of Economic Research.
http://www.nber.org/digest/nov13/w19226.html.

[34] In their study, they took pains to "control for," i.e., to exclude, impacts from technological changes such as increased automation.

[35] Avraham Ebenstein, Ann Harrison, and Margaret McMillan, "Why are American Workers getting Poorer? China, Trade and Offshoring," NBER Working Paper No. 21027 issued in March 2015, doi: 10.3386/w21027 http://www.nber.org/papers/w21027.

[36] These researchers did not find a relationship between globalization and reduction in labor force participation; other factors such as increased use of computers and capital equipment seemed to be at work.

[37] Autor, David H., David Dorn, and Gordon H. Hanson. "The China Shock: Learning from Labor Market Adjustment to Large Changes in Trade." NBER Working Paper No. 21906, Issued in January 2016. doi: 10.3386/w21906. http://www.nber.org/papers/w21906
Published: David H. Autor & David Dorn & Gordon H. Hanson, "The China Shock: Learning from Labor Market Adjustment to Large Changes in Trade," Annual Review of Economics, vol 8(1), 2016.

[38] Autor, *et al.*, "China Shock," 38. Emphasis added. Another study found that in Canadian families where the father suffered a job loss from a firm closure, the children had lower annual earnings and were more likely to receive unemployment insurance and social assistance. Philip Oreopolous, Marianne Page, and Ann Huff Stevens, "The Intergenerational Effect of Worker Displacement," *National Bureau of Economic Research*, Working Paper No. 11587 (2005)

[39] *Id.*, 4. Emphasis added.

Chapter 7

The Vicious Circle and the Hollow Economy

At the national level, the loss of six million manufacturing jobs has led to a cascading series of effects.

Slack Labor Market

We begin with the immediate effect of these job losses: reducing demand for workers, creating slack in the labor market:

- **Slack labor market**
    - Underemployment & low pay
        - Dependency and social ills
            - Slack consumer demand
                - Stagnant economy

Immediately, the question arises, has the slack been taken up? That is, *have the manufacturing job losses been made up through employment in other industries?* To answer that question, we must begin with an assessment of the general employment situation. It may seem like a tough slog, but I believe you will be surprised at where we come out.

Unemployment - Many lost jobs haven't been replaced

How to Measure Employment and Unemployment

Assessing employment and unemployment is easier said than done: the employment and unemployment reports from the Bureau of Labor Statistics (the "BLS") contain a bewildering and overlapping array of concepts, and media accounts don't make much sense of them.

As we will see, "employment" is defined too broadly, and "unemployment" too narrowly, to be useful. The "broader measure" of unemployment often referred to in news accounts is vague, leaving one wondering, "What is that?" So, I have set out to find out, "What's really going on with employment and unemployment?"

Toward that end, I have sought to lay out in a clear way the BLS concepts and how they fit together.[1] I have teased out eight categories of potential workers that are included in the BLS numbers. (I know this may seem tedious, but we really must get this to understand what's going on.) The categories are as follows:

1. Employed full-time
2. Employed part-time voluntarily

3. Employed part-time involuntarily ("for economic reasons"): Want a full-time job but have had to settle for part-time work.

4. "Unemployed": Do not have a job and are available for work, and actively looked for work in the last four weeks (or were waiting to be called back to a job from which they had been temporarily laid off).

5. "Discouraged workers": Do not have a job and are available and actively looked for work in the last twelve months (or since they last worked if they worked within the last 12 months), but did not actively look for work in the last four weeks because they were discouraged.[2]

6. Others "marginally attached to the labor force": Do not have a job and are available for work and actively looked for work in the last twelve months (or since they last worked if they worked within the last 12 months), but did not actively look for work in the last four weeks for reasons other than discouragement.[3]

7. Looked during the last year but not available for work: Do not have a job and actively looked for work in the last twelve months (or since they last worked if they worked within the last 12 months), but did not actively look for work in the last four weeks and are not currently available.

8. Want a job and are available for work, but did not actively look for work during the last year.

The categories are displayed in the following figure:

Categories of Workers as Reported by Bureau of Labor Statistics

"Civilian Non-Institutional Population 16 Years and Over"								
"Civilian Labor Force"				"Not in Labor Force"				
"Employed"			"Unemployed"	"Marginally Attached"				
Cat. 1	Cat. 2	Cat. 3	Cat. 4	Cat. 5	Cat. 6	Cat. 7	Cat. 8	Cat. 9
Employed Full-Time	Employed Part-Time Voluntary	Employed Part-Time Involuntary	Unemployed Looked Last 4 Weeks	Looked in Last Yr., Not Last 4 Wks. because Discouraged	Looked in Last Yr., Not Last 4 Wks., for Other Reasons	Looked in Last Yr., Not Last 4 Wks., Not Avail.	Want Job, Didn't Look in Last Year	Not Employed, Do Not Want Job

Source: Author's comiplation of Bureau of Labor Statistics data categories

"Employed" Defined Too Broadly

The BLS statistics include Categories 1, 2 and 3 in the definition of "Employed".[4] As I discuss below, that term is too broad to be useful: first, by definition it includes, in Category 3, those who are working part-time but want to be working full-time; second, the definition of "employed" includes individuals who did *any work at all* during the survey week, and thus includes individuals who are only sporadically employed, and many individuals who are underemployed in other ways.

"Unemployed" Defined Too Narrowly

On the other hand, the definition of "unemployed" in Category 4 (which is the "U-3" official unemployment rate), is too narrow: it includes only unemployed individuals available for work who actively sought work[5] during the four weeks preceding the survey interview (or are waiting to be recalled from a temporary layoff).

We will consider broader measures; but first, using the "U-3" narrow definition of unemployment, let us look at what we might call *the severity of unemployment*. The percentage unemployed, whatever the definition, does not capture the additional dimension of what we might think of as "how badly unemployed are you?"

One measure of this dimension is to ask the unemployed in the survey, "*how long* have you been unemployed?" The Census Bureau does ask this question in the monthly survey. The average response over time is shown in the following figure:

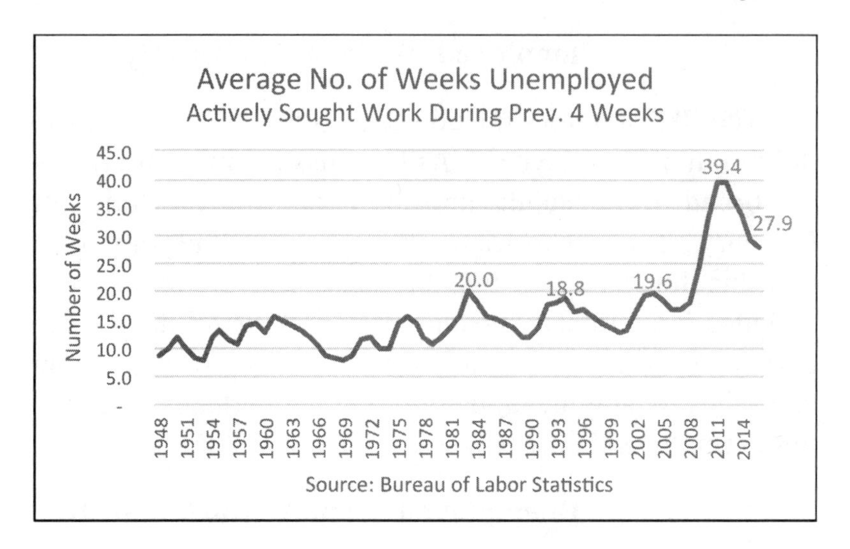

What does this figure tell us about what it is like to be unemployed in 2016? That on average, the unemployed have been out of work for 28 weeks. That is an astonishing figure, especially when we compare it to previous recessions.

Key Finding: Seven years into "recovery" from the Great Recession, the average duration of unemployment is 28 weeks, far more than the duration experienced at the *worst* points of the previous three recessions. The percentage unemployment rate is measuring a different phenomenon than before the Great Recession.

We now turn to consideration of more realistic definitions of unemployment.

Measuring Unemployment: Unemployed, Discouraged Workers

Alternative Measures: The "U-6" Unemployment Rate

The BLS has acknowledged the shortcoming of the narrow definition of the "U-3" official unemployment rate, and has published alternative measures of unemployment, as discussed in the online appendix, "Demystifying Unemployment.[6] The measure most commonly referred to is "U-6," which includes my Categories 3, 4, 5, and 6:

- Unemployed (Cat. 4)
- Employed part-time involuntarily (Cat. 3)
- Discouraged Workers (Cat. 5)
- Marginally attached to the labor force (Cat. 6)

The U-6 unemployment rate for 1994-2016 is presented in the following figure:[7]

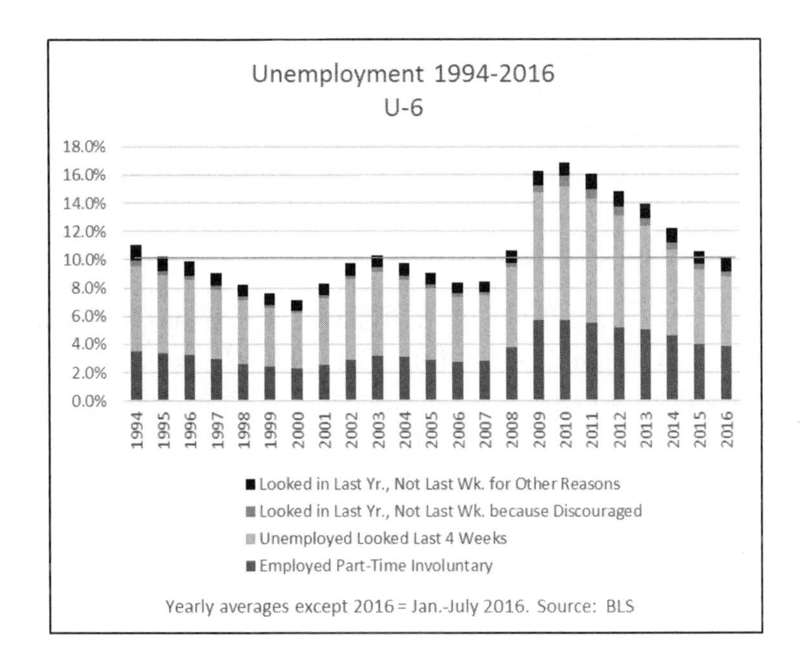

Yearly averages except 2016 = Jan.-July 2016. Source: BLS

So, where do we stand?

Key Finding: In July of 2016, the "U-6" unemployment rate stood at *10.2%*. Seven years after the official end of the Great Recession in June of 2009, the U-6 unemployment rate was still on a par with the *worst point* reached during the previous recession, 10.3% in 2003. That is, seven years into the "recovery," *we were still experiencing recession-level unemployment*; the U-6 rate was nowhere near the post-recession "recovery" lows of 7.1% in 2000 and 8.3% in 2006.

Next Step: U-6 plus Available but Not Looking

However, there is another category that should be paid attention to: my Category 8, those who want a job but are even more discouraged than the "discouraged workers" in Category 5 - they have become so discouraged that they didn't undertake any active job seeking activities in the twelve months preceding the survey interview. And yet, they are willing and available. We might think of them as the "super-discouraged" workers.

So, we can track the "potential workforce" as Categories 3 through 8 (but excluding Category 7, who are not available for work), as a full measure of those who (i) are unemployed, want a job, and are available for work, or (ii) are working part-time and want a full-time job. Those percentages, as annual averages from 1994 through 2014, are presented in the following figure:

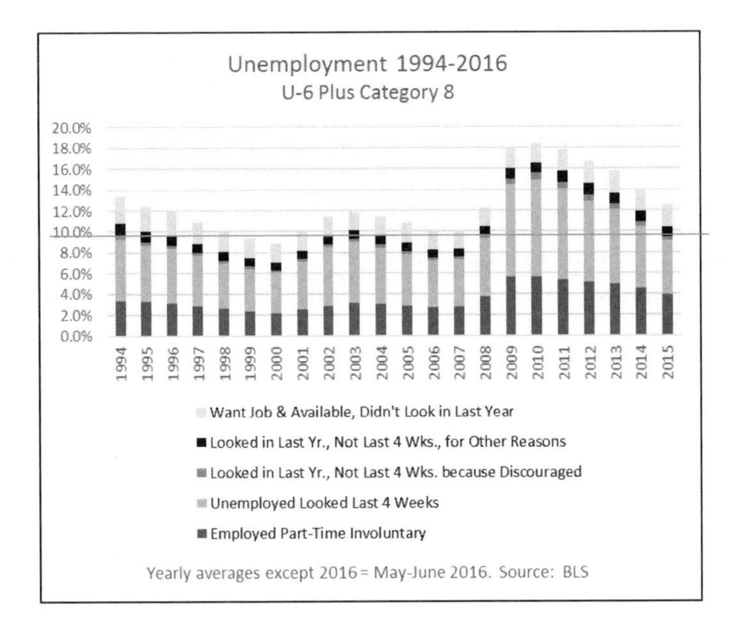

What does this chart tell us?

Key Finding: In July of 2016, this "U-6 plus Category 8" unemployment rate stood at *12.1%*. Seven years after the official end of the Great Recession, this "U-6 plus Category 8" unemployment rate was on a par with the *worst points* reached during the two previous recessions, 13.4% in 1994, and 11.9% in 2003. That is, seven years into the "recovery," *we were still experiencing recession-level unemployment*; it was substantially more than the post-recession "recovery" lows of 8.8% in 2000 and 10.0% in 2006.

Able Workers Who Dropped Out of the Workforce

Is there anyone else we should be considering to get a full picture? It turns out that there is.

Since the onset of the Great Recession, the population has been growing, but the labor force has not. BLS defines the "Labor Force" as those who are employed (my Categories 1, 2 and 3) and those who are unemployed and actively looking for work (my Category 4). I use the more expansive "potential workforce" concept I have described above, including Categories 1-6 and Category 8. Under both definitions, the labor force has remained flat since 2008 while the population has grown, as illustrated in the following figure:[8]

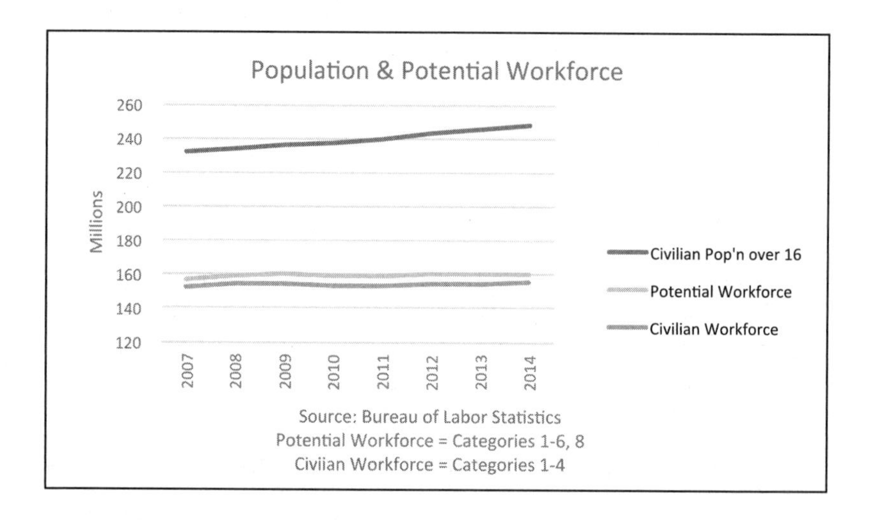

In fact, as a percentage of the population (The BLS refers to this concept as the "Labor Force Participation Rate"), labor force participation is declining. The following figure shows both the BLS definition of workforce and my broader concept of potential workforce as percentages of the civilian population over age 16:[9]

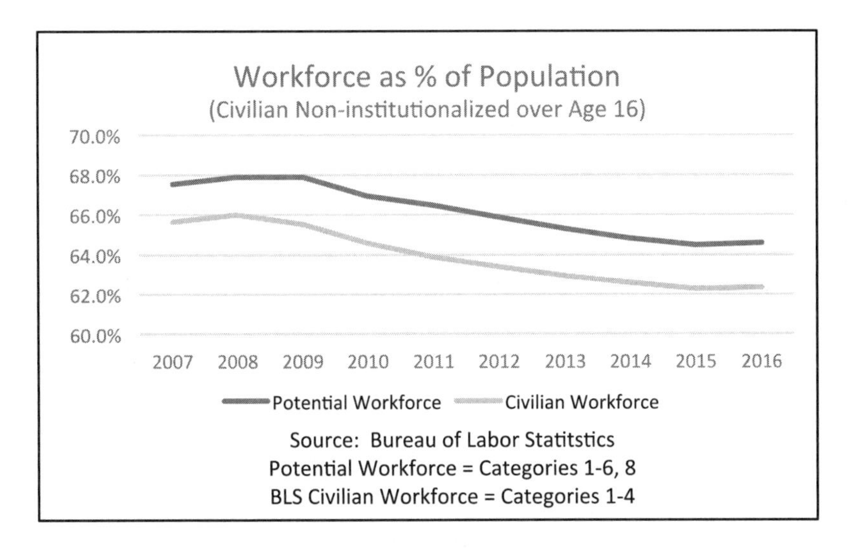

This chart illustrates a potential problem for the economy: both the narrower BLS measure of the Labor Force Participation Rate and our broader measure of potential workforce have declined steadily since the depths of the Great Recession in 2009.

Why is a smaller percentage of the working-age population participating in the workforce? Two members of the staff of the Boston Federal Reserve, Christopher Erceg and Andrew T. Levin, considered the causes of the post-2007 decline in the U.S. labor force participation rate in a paper published in April 2013.[10]

They concluded that the entire decline in the labor force participation rate since 2007 was attributable to workers' responses to the *persistent shortage of demand* for their services in the aftermath of the Great Recession. Some went back to school (nearly all the decline for youths aged 16-24 years and a substantial portion of prime age workers), some went on Social Security disability benefits (a substantial percentage of the older workers aged 55-64 years), and some retired (only a small net fraction, as retirements were largely offset by individuals staying in the workforce longer).

Focusing on the drop in the participation rate of prime-age adults (age 25-54), they concluded that only about half the decline could be explained by these factors. The other half, about a million individuals, simply dropped out of the workforce.

Key Finding: It therefore appears that there is indeed one more group, not included in Categories 1-8, who have left the workforce in response to the "persistent shortfall in labor demand" since the Great Recession, and who respond "no" when asked in the BLS survey whether they want a job and are available for work – true "workforce dropouts," the term I will use to refer to them.

Measuring Employment: The Employment Gap

The gap between the number of potential workers and the number of jobs created by the economy is even clearer when we shift our focus from unemployment to employment.

First, just as we considered the workforce as a percentage of the working age population, we can look at employment as a percentage of that population, as illustrated in the following figure:[11]

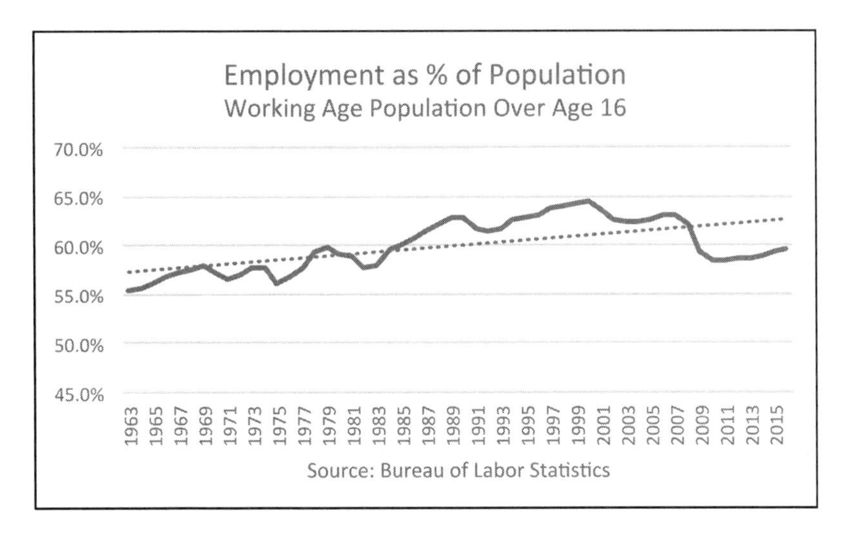

The result is similar:

Key Finding: Employment as a percentage of the working age population has shown a marked decline, beginning with the 2001 recession, and worsening with the 2008 recession, with only a minimal recovery.

If we really want to know how we are doing, however, we must compare our current employment levels to those preceding the Great Recession. The following figure[12] presents (i) projected employment if the percentage of the potential workforce[13] employed in 2006 (90%) had been maintained through 2016, and (ii) actual employment (defined as full-time and voluntarily part-time).

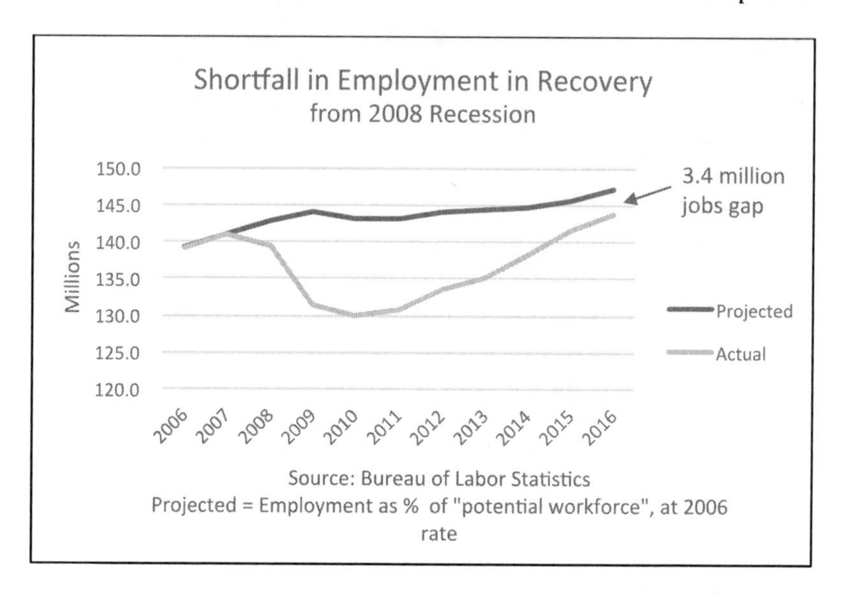

Key Finding: In July of 2016, the gap between the number of jobs at the 2006 employment rate and actual employment stood at 3.4 million jobs.

However, given our focus on what has happened in trade, jobs and employment since 2000, it is even more instructive to consider the jobs gap that has resulted from both the 2001 and 2008 recessions.

The following figure[14] presents (i) projected employment if the percentage of the potential workforce employed in 2000 (91.3%) had been maintained through 2016, and (ii) actual employment (defined as full-time and voluntarily part-time).

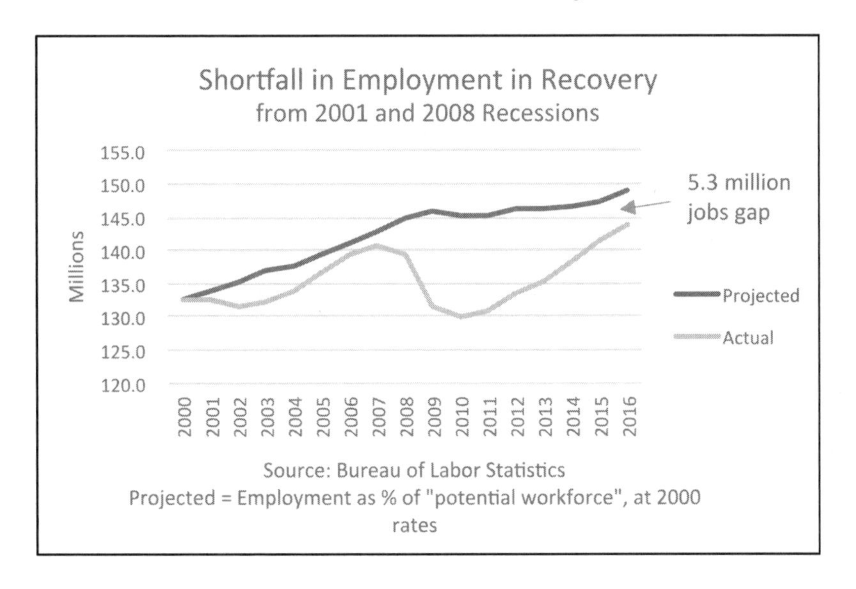

Key Finding: In July of 2016, the gap between the number of jobs at the 2000 employment rate and actual employment stood at 5.3 million jobs.

However, there is something striking about this figure. It is evident that during the period 2000 through 2009, even during the recession of 2001, the "potential labor force" (my Categories 1-6 and 8) was growing at a steady rate. Then, in 2009, there is a break in the curve, and it remains lower than its previous trajectory. These are the lost workers studied by Erceg and Levin, reflected in the decline in the labor participation rate discussed above, who have dropped out of the labor force.

A true measure of the "jobs gap" would be to compare actual employment with what employment would be if the same percentage of the *working-age population* were employed as was employed in 2000, before the 2001 and

2008 recessions. That comparison is made in the following figure:[15]

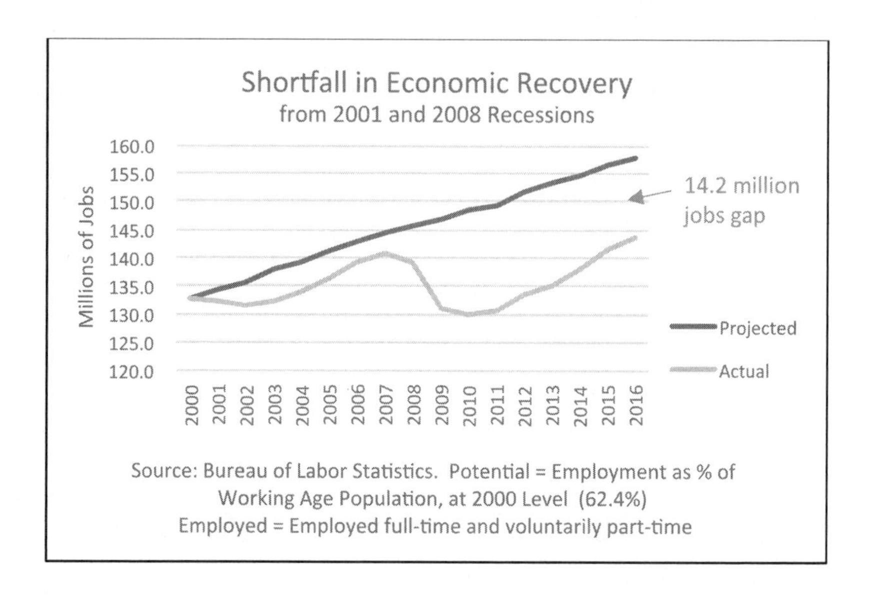

The figure shows that employment has barely recovered – it only matched the 2007 level of 132.7 million in 2012, standing at 143.7 million in 2016. However, at the 2000 rate of employment as a percentage of the working age population, we should be at 157.9 million jobs – we are short 14.2 million jobs.

Conclusion: So, our answer is, no, we have not replaced many of the offshored manufacturing jobs lost during the last two recessions with other jobs – we are still 14.2 million jobs short.

This "jobs gap" hits some groups harder than others. Unemployment has a perverse "trickle down" effect on teenagers, as unemployed adults are forced into jobs previously filled by teenagers. A Drexel University study noted that from the late 1940s through 2000, between forty and fifty percent of American teenagers were employed. However, around the year 2001,[16] something changed: teenage employment dropped from 46 percent employed in 2000 to 25.5 percent in 2011, in March of 2015, it remained at 28.7 percent. In 2015, only one in ten black male teenagers in Philadelphia had a job.[17] In the past, teenage jobs played an important role in preparing young people for participation in the adult work force. Now, their absence is an invitation for entry into behaviors such as pregnancy and crime.

Unemployment also hits older workers hard: a recent AARP study found that workers older than 45 who lost their jobs in the last five years have had trouble finding work[18]

Underemployment and Low Pay

We now turn to the second stage in the cascade of effects, underemployment and low pay.

- Slack labor market
  - **Underemployment & low pay**
    - Dependency and social ills
      - Slack consumer demand
        - Stagnant economy

Depressed Wages & Working Conditions

It's bad enough that those jobs are lost, but the losses also are depressing wages and working conditions at home.

Most of the replacement jobs are the wrong kind

As we have seen, many of the manufacturing jobs lost to offshoring have not been replaced. But what of those jobs that have been created? Unfortunately, the jobs that have been created during the recovery from the Great Recession have tended to be in lower-paying sectors of the economy. The National Employment Law Project (N.E.L.P.) reported this trend early in the recovery, but with the caveat that it may be temporary.[19] In a new report issued in April 2014,[20] the N.E.L.P. concluded that "low-wage job creation was not simply a characteristic of the early recovery, but rather a pattern that has persisted for more than four years now." [21]

The report found that during the recession, employment *losses* were concentrated in mid-wage and high-wage industries; however, during the recovery, employment *gains* were concentrated in lower wage industries. By the spring of 2014, the economy had re-generated a number of jobs exceeding the number that had been lost during the Great Recession. However, there were:

- 976,000 *fewer* jobs in higher-wage industries,
- 958,000 *fewer* jobs in mid-wage industries, and
- 1,850,000 *more* jobs in lower wage industries

than at the start of the recession.[22]

As the New York Times reported: "With joblessness high and job gains concentrated in low-wage industries, hundreds of thousands of Americans have accepted positions that pay less than they used to make, in some cases, sliding out of the middle class and into the ranks of the working poor." [23]

Just as troubling, the N.E.L.P. found a tendency toward an "hourglass" employment situation: "Service-providing industries such as food services and drinking places, administrative and support services, and retail trade have led private sector job growth during the recovery. These industries, which pay relatively low wages, accounted for 39 percent of the private sector employment increase over the past four years." [24]

On the other hand, the N.E.L.P. reported strong growth in some high-paying industries. As the Times reported: "Economists worry that even a stronger recovery might not bring back jobs in traditionally middle-class occupations eroded by mechanization and offshoring. The American work force might become yet more 'polarized,' with positions easier to find at the high and low ends than in the middle." [25]

Key Findings:

- During the Great Recession, employment *losses* were concentrated in mid-wage and high-wage industries; however, during the recovery, employment *gains* were concentrated in lower wage industries:
- In July of 2014, five years into the recovery, the number of jobs was back to pre-recession levels; however, there were approximately 1.9 million *fewer* jobs in mid-wage and higher-wage industries, and 1.9 million *more* jobs in lower-wage industries.

Fewer jobs leads to depressed wages and working conditions

As we have seen in our discussion of the "jobs gap" and the slack labor market, there are more American workers chasing fewer jobs.

Although one hears occasional talk of an "inherent" value of the work performed in a certain job, wages are set largely by supply and demand: when there is an excess of supply of workers hunting for work, employers can bid down the hourly pay and working conditions offered.

Offshoring low-skill-intensive tasks reduces the home-country demand for low-skill workers; the excess of supply over demand drives their wages down. The result is "sweated labor" in the United States, as well as abroad. A prime example of this effect is the warehousing, or "goods movement" industry, in which Amazon and Wal-Mart are principal players.

Case Study: The Warehousing Industry

One of the big reasons for the movement toward lower-paying replacement jobs is that many of the new jobs are low-pay jobs in the warehouses and distribution centers that receive the foreign goods and distribute them to U.S. retailers and online buyers.

Distribution centers often are operated by contracted logistics or warehouse management companies, who in turn outsource and subcontract their work, frequently to temporary worker agencies. The bid to move goods as quickly and cheaply as possible has led to a "time and profit squeeze" along the supply chain, with ill consequences for the wages and working conditions of logistics workers.

For example, an Allentown, Pennsylvania newspaper reported in September 2011 on working conditions in the Amazon fulfillment warehouse located there. In words strikingly paralleling the reports of conditions in the sweatshop factories in China, the newspaper reported:

- Workers endured temperatures soaring to 100 degrees, with Amazon responding not by lowering temperatures but by parking paramedics in ambulances outside;
- Workers were pushed to meet unsustainable work flows and were frequently reprimanded regarding their productivity and threatened with termination, with employees falling short being fired and publicly escorted from the facility;
- Workers were hired by a temporary help agency paying $11 to $12 per hour, with few moving to permanent employment by Amazon; instead, employees reported that they were pushed harder and harder to work faster and faster until they were terminated, they quit or they got injured." [26]

As one worker told the newspaper, "They can do that because there aren't any jobs in the area." The Morning Call reported:

> In a better economy, not as many people would line up for jobs that pay $11 or $12 an hour moving inventory through a hot warehouse. But with job openings scarce, Amazon and Integrity Staffing Solutions, the temporary employment firm that is hiring workers for Amazon, have found eager applicants in the swollen ranks of the unemployed. [27]

Walmart follows similar practices at its warehouses in the United States. For example, Workers at Wal-Mart's "Inland Empire" warehouse in Mira Loma, California filed a federal lawsuit complaining that Wal-Mart is pressuring the contractor and subcontractors who operate the warehouse to work more quickly and is complicit in working conditions that include lack of air conditioning in an area that routinely sees triple-digit heat, and lack of safe drinking water and breaks. The case is particularly notable because this is the "Inland Empire" warehouse that receives containers from the ports of Los Angeles and Long Beach that have traveled from China, and reships them to Wal-Mart distribution centers and stores across the U. S. (and used to produce steel -- see Chapter 1). [28]

Amazon and Wal-Mart may be the largest actors in the "goods moving" industry, but they are not outliers. Unfortunately, they are representative of general conditions in the industry, which may be extrapolated from a 2010 study of the warehousing industry that has sprung up in Wills County outside Chicago, one of the nation's largest goods-moving hubs.[29] The study reported the following findings:

- 63% of workers in warehouses were temps;
- The majority of warehouse workers made poverty-level wages, and temps had it worse than direct hires. The median hourly wage for a temp was $9.00 an hour–$3.48 an hour less than direct hires;
- One in four warehouse workers had to rely on government assistance to make ends meet for their families;
- 37% of current warehouse workers had to work a second job to provide for their families;

- Temps were far less likely to have basic benefits. For example, only 5% of temps had sick days and 4% had health insurance;
- 20% of warehouse workers had been hurt on the job. Of those, one in three were disciplined or fired when they reported their injury.[30]

Key Finding: we have moved our manufacturing to sweatshops offshore, and have created new, domestic sweatshops for receiving and distributing the products made in the offshore sweatshops – a "gulag archipelago" of sweatshops scattered around the world and around the United States.

Case Study: Long-Haul Trucking

The "time and profit squeeze" along the supply chain in the bid to move goods as quickly and cheaply as possible has led to ill consequences for the wages and working conditions of another group of workers -- the long-haul truck drivers picking up and delivering the goods at the warehouses and other points in the supply chain, in what have been described as "sweatshops on wheels."

With the regulation of the industry via the Interstate Commerce Commission in 1935, by the 1950s, truck drivers were as well paid as steel and auto workers, working 50 to 60 hours a week at most, and home for dinner with their families at night or at least every other night. However, with deregulation in 1979, truck driving became subject to the "time and profit squeeze" in the supply chain.

Current conditions were documented by University of Pennsylvania lecturer Steve Viscelli, who spent six months training and working as a long-haul trucker.[31] Today's truckers basically work two jobs for not much more than minimum wage. Viscelli found that he made $9.42 an hour, not including the other ten hours a day spent living out of the truck, waiting for work. He would be on the road 12 to 19 days at a time, arrive home and sleep for ten hours, then head back out a day and a half later.

Viscelli determined that a few companies pay their drivers well, but most, rather than pay the $70,000 the market would demand, follow a business model of using government-funded programs to train drivers for two months, and then pay them $35,000 to $40,000 for six months until they burn out, and hire another batch. They can accomplish this by treating the drivers as independent contractors who lease their rigs, but are completely subject to the company's direction. [32]

Stagnant Wages for Ordinary Workers

The problem of depressed wages is widespread across industries. To measure it, we can turn to what I believe to be the truest marker of compensation for ordinary American workers, a statistic the BLS gathers: average hourly earnings of production and nonsupervisory employees in the private sector. This is the average of the wages earned by the vast majority of working Americans. Since it is expressed as an hourly wage, it is a better marker than annual or household earnings, which can increase because people are working longer or more people are working.

As shown in the following figure, this wage, expressed in 2016 dollars, rose steadily, with a few pauses and dips, from $11.67 in 1946 to a high of $22.45 in 1978. Since then, it has not fared well; ordinary American households have held their own or increased their income only by one or both spouses working more hours.[33]

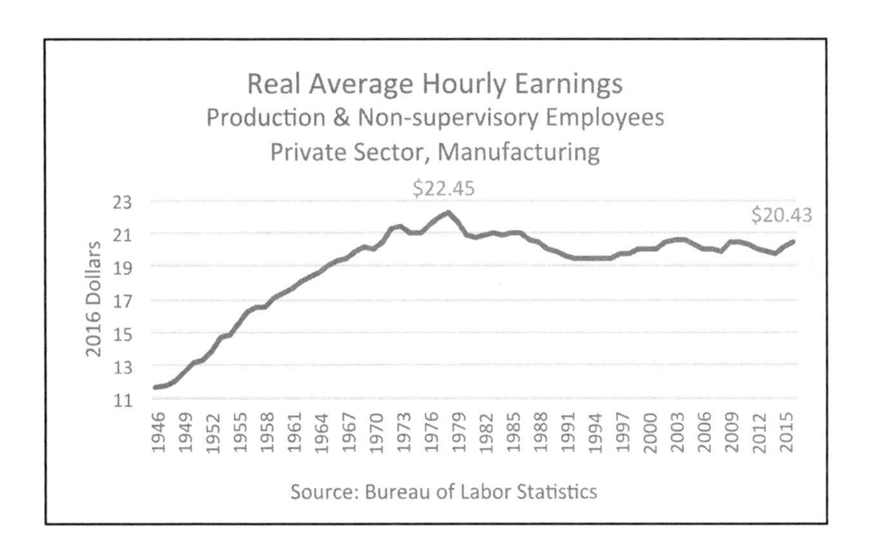

The Depressing Effect of the Threat of Offshoring

We have discussed two causes of this stagnation in wages -- the slack in the labor market and the growth of low-paying jobs. There is another reason, however -- the competition from abroad: domestic employers claim that they "must compete" with foreign wage scales, by paying lower wages in the U.S., under threat of sending the jobs overseas. This is especially true of traditionally better-paying jobs in manufacturing.

The Bureau of Labor Statistics has provided the following comparison of manufacturing wages among countries:

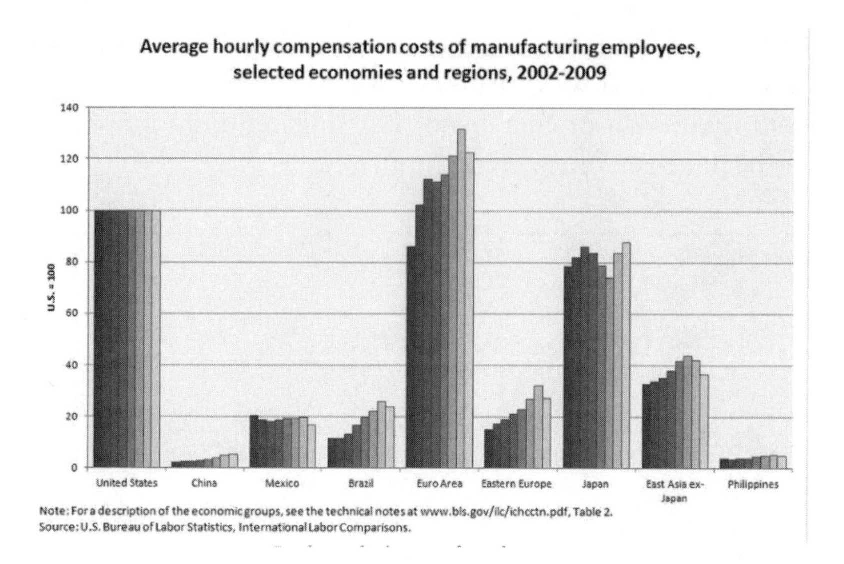

BLS stopped gathering these statistics in 2009, and China's average manufacturing wages have continued to rise, to the point where they are said to becoming comparable to Mexico's.[34]

Even with that, what is striking about this chart is the stark contrast between the wages being paid in the United States and the other developed industrialized nations, on the one hand, and the rest of the world on the other.

As we have seen, many manufacturing jobs have been sent overseas, especially to China, in pursuit of these low wages. However, U.S. employers have used these foreign wages in negotiating wage rates for domestic jobs as well. The effects also can be seen in the "two tier" wage scales being imposed in industries such as aerospace and automobile manufacturing.

For example, the 2011 contract approved by the United Auto Workers provided for a two-tier wages system under which the big three U.S. auto makers could hire new workers at $15.78 per hour (rising to $19.28 by 2015), compared with the existing factory workers' rate of about $28 per hour.[35] Automobile assembly formerly embodied the job that would support a family. As we will see, $19.28 won't support a family, even if two parents are holding down two full-time jobs earning that rate. With the downward pressure flowing from the threat of offshoring to low-wage sites, U.S. workers in what formerly were our flagship jobs are being offered wages and benefits that bear no relationship to the true cost of living of an American family today.

The Big Squeeze

We are living in the Big Squeeze: up and down the American economy we have imposed pressure on each other, to do more, with less, at a lower price. At the high end, a banker at a leading American bank recently returned from a ten-day training. I asked her how it went, and she replied that it was terrible – she is a "top producer," and yet she is facing constant pressure to produce more. She is expected to spend her evenings handling company emails, but during that time, her priority is her children.

In the middle of the spectrum, the Boeing case shows how the threat of offshoring plays into the larger trend of extracting more for less: Boeing threatened to move the 777 production to lower-wage locations in the U.S., and, ultimately, abroad, until the Seattle workers agreed to significant wage and benefit concessions.

At the low end of the spectrum, we have seen how low-wage workers in distribution centers are constantly pressured to meet increasing quotas until they eventually are let go. But the pressure is ubiquitous: a young woman working at an ice cream parlor is taught how to up-sell when dealing with customers; the store uses a computer program to track the employees' up-selling, and only the successful up-sellers (she bragged that she is one) will "get their hours" in the schedule. Even minimum wage workers are feeling the Big Squeeze.

The Big Squeeze extends to governments: state and local governments and their economic development agencies are reduced to trying to outbid each other in tax holidays, tax credits, and cash grants to lure manufacturing businesses into their economies. The tax base for building and maintaining schools, roads, and other infrastructure is undermined, and another community is often the loser as an existing facility relocates away. It is a negative sum game for the national economy, and, not infrequently, one that everyone loses as the company decides to locate offshore after all.

For workers, the Big Squeeze too often means being offered a wage that bears no relation to their families' cost of living. (See "When Life Doesn't Add Up," below.)

Underemployment and Job/Skills Mismatch

Another indirect result of the lost manufacturing jobs is underemployment and a mismatch of many workers' skills and jobs, causing a "productivity gap" of lost opportunity.

In December of 2016, Payscale reported that 46 percent of the American workers it surveyed said they were under-employed, that is, they were working part-time but wanted full-time work (24%), or they were holding a job that didn't require or utilize their education, experience or training (76%). [36]

Recent college graduates, especially, have experienced underemployment: The Wall Street Journal reported that in

2015, 34.4 percent of all college graduates, and 44.5 percent of recent college graduates, were employed in jobs that didn't require their degree.[37]

A 2015 Accenture study found that 49 percent of 2013 and 2014 graduates considered themselves "under-employed" in 2015, and 41 percent of the classes of 2013 and 2014 was earning $25,000 or less per year.[38]

Underemployment also hits older workers hard: a recent AARP study found that workers older than 45 who lost their jobs in the last five years and got new jobs often settled for less pay and fewer hours than they had in the previous positions.[39]

Job Insecurity

Across America, workers go to work each day not knowing if they will be informed that their plant is being moved to China or Mexico or their work moved to India. Workers stay in jobs that underutilize their skills and experience, because they lack confidence in the job market.

Dependency and Social Ills

We now turn to the third stage in the cascade of effects, dependency and social ills:

- ➢ Slack labor market
  - ➢ Underemployment & low pay
    - ➢ **Dependency and social ills**
      - ➢ Slack consumer demand
        - ➢ Stagnant economy

Working Americans experiencing the effects of the slack labor market often experience a profound disconnect between their pay and working conditions on the one hand, and the costs of providing for basic needs for themselves and their families on the other. When they compare the income and cost sides of the ledger, life just doesn't add up.

When Life Doesn't Add Up

You may ask, "But what about the federal poverty guidelines? Reading the reports, it seems like a relatively small proportion of Americans are actually living in poverty.

Measuring Poverty

There are two federal poverty measures: the "poverty thresholds" and the "poverty guidelines."

The *poverty thresholds* are issued annually by the U.S. Census Bureau, and are used in making statistical calculations of the number of Americans living in poverty. But how are they determined? I went digging, and you are not going to believe what I found:

The federal poverty thresholds are determined by taking a "low cost" food plan for "needy families and others who wished to keep food costs down" *from 1961* and *reducing it by another 20-25 percent* to arrive at an "economy" plan, for "temporary or emergency use when funds are low", then adjusting it for inflation, and then multiplying it *by three* to allow for non-food expenses based on 1955 statistics, with *no allowance for variation by geography.*[40] No, I mean, that's really it, no exaggeration on my part!

The *poverty guidelines* are issued annually by the U.S. Department of Health and Human Services (HHS).[41] They are a simplified version of the poverty thresholds, and are used in determining financial eligibility for certain federal programs.[42] The poverty guidelines for 2016 are as follows:

Federal Poverty Level Guidelines by Family Size Guidelines for 2016			
Family Size	Week	Month	Year
1	$ 228.46	$ 990	$ 11,880
2	$ 308.08	$ 1,335	$ 16,020
3	$ 387.69	$ 1,680	$ 20,160
4	$ 467.31	$ 2,025	$ 24,300
5	$ 546.92	$ 2,370	$ 28,440
6	$ 626.54	$ 2,715	$ 32,580
7	$ 626.54	$ 2,715	$ 32,580
8	$ 626.54	$ 2,715	$ 32,580
For families/households with more than 8 persons, add $4,160 per person.			
Source: Department of Health & Human Services https://aspe.hhs.gov/poverty-guidelines			

A cursory glance leads one to conclude that these amounts are not sufficient to provide for basic necessities.

Key Finding: It is fair to say that the federal poverty guidelines do not represent a socially acceptable minimum standard of living, below which one can be deemed to be living in poverty.

That standard surely lies somewhere north of these numbers, a fact implicitly acknowledged by Congress and federal agencies in setting eligibility for many means-tested federal programs at levels higher than 100% of the poverty guidelines.

Of what use are these standards, then? Even the Census Bureau, which publishes the poverty thresholds, points out: "Although the thresholds in some sense reflect families' needs they are intended for use as a statistical yardstick, not as a complete description of what people and families need to live." [43]

They can be useful in tracking trends over time. And we can be sure that individuals and families living at or below these levels are living in poverty, by anyone's definition. However, it is clear that *many people with incomes above these levels are "poor" by any reasonable definition*: we should never read statistics on poverty in America based on the poverty thresholds and assume that they accurately describe the number of Americans who are not able to provide for the basic necessities of life.

The Minimum Wage

Well, then, what of the federal minimum wage? Doesn't it establish a "floor" for wages at a place where people can make ends meet?

One way to answer this question is to look at the history of the minimum wage. If at some point it was sufficient to cover one's basic expenses, there has been no mechanism to keep it so, whether by indexing it to inflation or otherwise. Rather, it has been sporadically increased by Congress, and then had its purchasing power eroded by inflation until such time as Congress might enact another increase. Here is what the actual wage has been since 1967:[44]

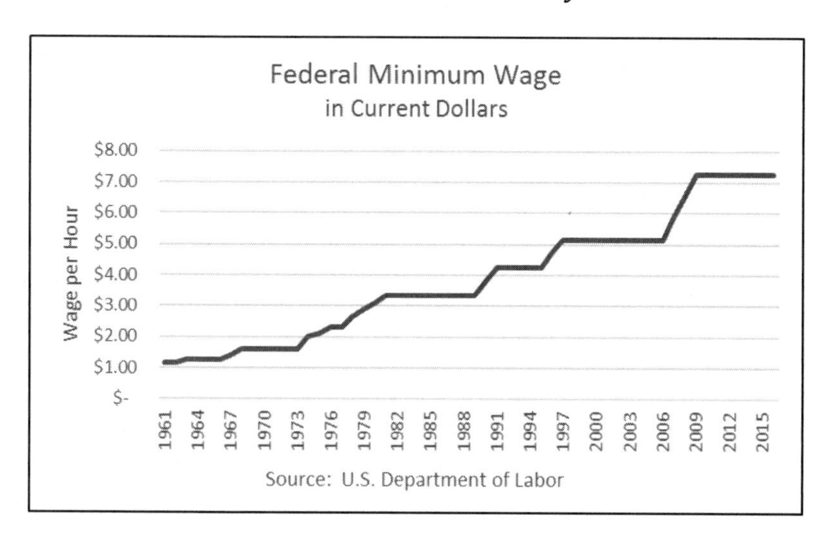

Of course, one cannot compare a 2016 dollar to a 1967 dollar, which could purchase a lot more, so in order to compare the minimum wage over time, it is necessary to express it in one year's currency, i.e., adjusted for inflation. Adjusting each year's amount to 2016 dollars, the minimum wage since 1967 looks like this:

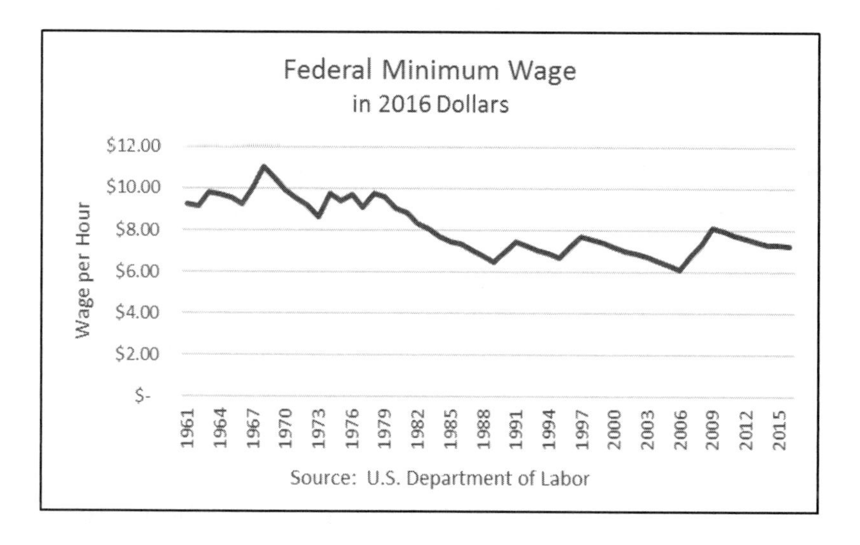

The chart shows the value of the wage eroding over time as inflation eats into it, until the next time Congress increases it. The dollar amounts, in 2016 dollars, are as follows:

Federal Minimum Wage in 2016 Dollars							
1961	1962	1963	1964	1965	1966	1967	1968
$ 9.23	$ 9.14	$ 9.81	$ 9.69	$ 9.54	$ 9.26	**$ 10.07**	**$ 11.04**
1969	1970	1971	1972	1973	1974	1975	1976
$ 10.48	$ 9.90	$ 9.49	$ 9.20	$ 8.66	**$ 9.74**	**$ 9.39**	**$ 9.71**
1977	1978	1979	1980	1981	1982	1983	1984
$ 9.11	**$ 9.75**	**$ 9.60**	**$ 9.05**	**$ 8.84**	$ 8.34	$ 8.07	$ 7.74
1985	1986	1987	1988	1989	1990	1991	1992
$ 7.47	$ 7.34	$ 7.07	$ 6.80	$ 6.50	**$ 6.99**	**$ 7.48**	$ 7.27
1993	1994	1995	1996	1997	1998	1999	2000
$ 7.06	$ 6.89	$ 6.72	$ 7.27	**$ 7.73**	$ 7.57	$ 7.42	$ 7.21
2001	2002	2003	2004	2005	2006	2007	2008
$ 7.00	$ 6.90	$ 6.75	$ 6.54	$ 6.33	$ 6.13	**$ 6.79**	**$ 7.34**
2009	2010	2011	2012	2013	2014	2015	2016
$ 8.12	$ 7.98	$ 7.76	$ 7.61	$ 7.47	$ 7.32	$ 7.32	$ 7.25

Source: Bureau of Labor Statistics
Years when increased are indicated in bold.

An interesting question to consider is, how has the minimum wage related to the economy's ability to pay? The ability to pay can be measured as the amount of Gross Domestic Product per employee. For example –

- in 1967 (in 2016 dollars) –
    - GDP was 6.2 trillion, and the population was 197.3 million.
    - GDP per capita was $31,390.
    - Assuming a labor force participation rate of 60%, the GDP per employed person was $52,317.

  - The annualized minimum wage was $20,937 ($10.07/hr. x 2,080 hrs.)

- In 2015 (in 2016 dollars) –

  - GDP was $17.9 trillion and the population was 321,418,820.

  - GDP per capita was $56,395

  - Assuming a labor force participation rate of 60%, GDP per employed person was $93,992.

  - The annualized minimum wage was $15,231 ($7.32/hr. x 2,080 hrs.).

These values, and the corresponding amounts for the intervening years, are expressed in the following Figure:

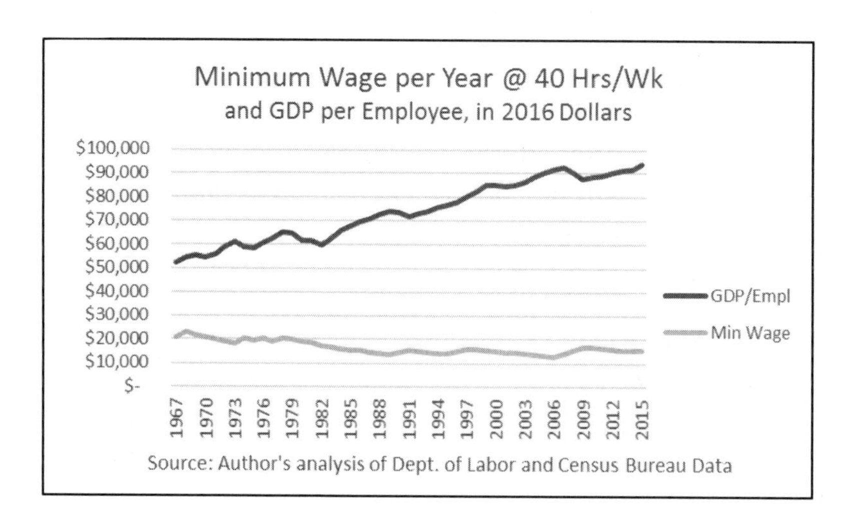

The chart shows an increasing disparity between the minimum wage and the ability to pay: from $20,937 on a per-employee GDP of $31,390, to $15,231 on a per-employee GDP of $93,992.

This disparity is expressed by the minimum wage as a percentage of per-employee GDP, in the following Figure:

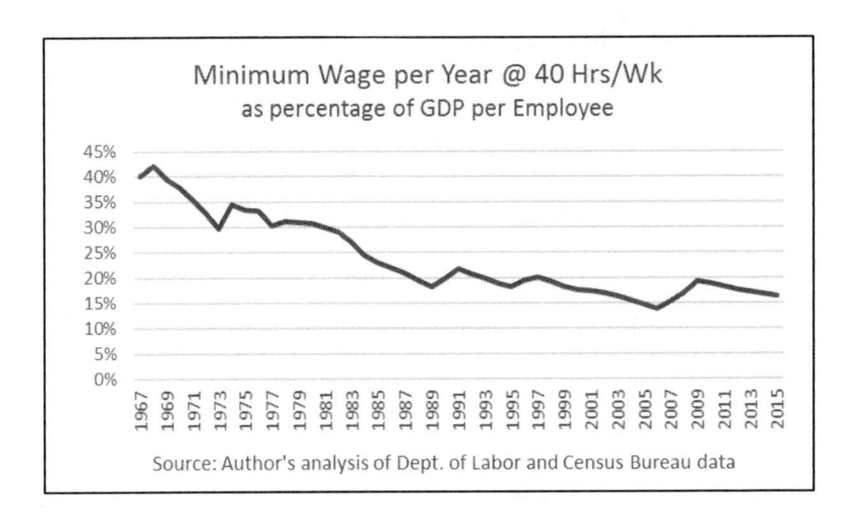

Key Findings:

- Measured in 2016 dollars, from 1961 through 1980, the federal minimum wage only once (in 1973) dipped below $9.00 an hour. Since then it has swung up and down within the $6.00-$8.00 range, now being at $7.25.
- Compared to per-employee GDP, the minimum wage declined from a high of 42% in 1968 to 18% in 1989, and since then has moved up and down within the 14%-21% range, now being at 17%.
- The federal minimum wage has not borne a consistent relationship either to inflation or to the economy's ability to pay.

But the real question is, what relationship does the minimum wage bear to the cost of living in America today? How far does $7.25 go in 2016?[45] To answer that question, we must make an honest inquiry into how much it costs to live in America.

The Real Cost of Living in America

In considering the consequences of the low price, low wage economy, it is necessary to establish a point of reference: how much does it really cost to live in America today? Much has been written on this subject. However, in the spirit of honest inquiry, I thought it worthwhile to pursue the question independently, wherever the facts may lead.

A Subsistence Budget

As an initial point of reference, we consider what it costs to pay for a minimal level of the necessities of life without having to resort to subsidies or charity, what I will refer to as a "Subsistence Budget." The Subsistence Budget is made up of minimum, "bare bones" amounts for necessary living expenses of food, clothing, shelter, transportation, medical care, and, where applicable, child care and school expenses.[46]

The Subsistence Budget does not include provision for many ordinary living expenses, such as modest Christmas and/or birthday gifts, children's participation in sports or other activities, or other recreation. It does not include any provision for saving for immediate extraordinary expenses, retirement, or post-secondary education. It does not include any provision for contributions to church or charities. Even for the included categories, these amounts are obviously very "bare bones."

I have prepared three versions of the Subsistence Budget, as follows. The first budget is for an individual, applicable, for example, to a 25-year-old who has not yet married, and to a 55-year-old who is single, divorced, or widowed. The second and third budgets are "family" budgets – one for a family of two adults and two children, and the other for a family of a single adult and two children.

Individual Budget - Can you make a living doing that?"

The Individual Budget is summarized in the following table:

Subsistence Budget - Individual - Summary				
	Week	Month	Year	Percent
Food, Clothing & Other Items	$ 135	$ 583	$ 6,996	15%
Health Care	$ 113	$ 489	$ 5,870	12%
Housing & Utilities	$ 303	$ 1,312	$ 15,744	33%
Transportation	$ 171	$ 743	$ 8,916	19%
Saving, Insurance, Recreation & Charitable Giving	$ -	$ -	$ -	0%
Total Expenses	$ 722	$ 3,127	$ 37,526	78%
Taxes	$ 199	$ 862	$ 10,339	22%
Pay Required for Expenses and Taxes	$ 920	$ 3,989	$ 47,865	100%
Required pay per hour @ 40 hrs./week	$ 23.01			
Source: Author's calculations using referenced sources.				

Family Budgets - Can you support a family doing that?

Two Parents, Two Children

The first "family" budget is for a family of two adults and two children.[47] There is a rather broad range of options when there are two parents in the home.

- One or both parents working more than one job (probably in low-paying jobs, trying to make ends meet).

- Both parents working full-time.
- One parent working full-time, one part time.
- One parent working full-time, the other not working.

For this Subsistence Budget, I have assumed both parents working full-time. Many American households are pursuing this option, perhaps for career fulfillment, perhaps for income to support a better lifestyle, and likely often for a mixture of both reasons. In any event, it maximizes the number of hours worked (excluding the extreme option of more than two full-time jobs), and thus minimizes the hourly wage required to meet the subsistence budget, providing the most conservative result. So, the budget assumes 80 hours worked per week, resulting in an average hourly wage between the two parents necessary to pay subsistence expenses and taxes. Having one parent work part-time increases the required hourly rate.

It should be noted that this assumption does require a second car and child care, the trade-off that every family must calculate in deciding whether and how much the second parent will work. There is tremendous variety in the arrangements families make for child care where both parents are working or only one parent is present (see below). For purposes of the Subsistence Budget, I use the average amount reported by the U.S. Census Bureau for a family with two children under age 15. In 2011, the amount was $169 per week. Adjusted per the increase in the Consumer Price Index, in 2014 dollars the amount is $177 per week, i.e., $769 per month.

With respect to housing costs, in the case of a two-parent family, I assume that the family is able to purchase a home. Therefore, in determining effective income tax rates, I assume deductions for $300 a month for property taxes and $600 per month for mortgage interest.

The Subsistence Family Budget for Two Parents and Two Children is summarized in the following table:[48]

Subsistence Budget - Two Parents, Two Children - Summary				
	Week	Month	Year	Percent
Food, Clothing & Other Items	$ 342	$ 1,482	$ 17,784	18%
Health Care	$ 194	$ 842	$ 10,099	11%
Housing & Utilities	$ 418	$ 1,811	$ 21,732	23%
Transportation	$ 343	$ 1,486	$ 17,832	19%
Child Care	$ 177	$ 769	$ 9,227	
Saving, Insurance, Recreation & Charitable Giving	$ -	$ -	$ -	0%
Total Expenses	$ 1,475	$ 6,390	$ 76,675	80%
Taxes	$ 374	$ 1,622	$ 19,469	20%
Pay Required for Expenses and Taxes	$ 1,849	$ 8,012	$ 96,144	100%
Required pay per hour @ 80 hrs./week	$ 23.11			
Source: Author's calculations using referenced sources.				

One Parent, Two Children

It is important to also consider the case of the single parent with children. The number of these households, both absolute and as a percentage of households, has been increasing.

As I have noted, there is tremendous variety in the arrangements families make for child care where both parents are working or only one parent is present.[49] The arrangements include care by grandparents and other family members, sharing child care duties with neighbors, and commercial day care, preschool, and after school providers, often in combination. As noted, for the Subsistence Budget, I have utilized the reported national average, adjusted to 2014 dollars, i.e., $769 per month.

In the case of single parents, the parent often will receive child support payments that may offset some of the costs of child care and other costs of supporting a child. This is not always the case, and most single parents do not receive all the child support payments that they are due. The Subsistence Family Budget for One Parent and Two Children is summarized in the following table:

Subsistence Budget - Single Parent with Two Children - Summary				
	Week	Month	Year	Percent
Food, Clothing & Other Items	$ 288	$ 1,249	$ 14,988	20%
Health Care	$ 194	$ 842	$ 10,099	13%
Housing & Utilities	$ 375	$ 1,624	$ 19,488	26%
Transportation	$ 171	$ 743	$ 8,916	12%
Child Care	$ 69	$ 300	$ 3,603	
Saving, Insurance, Recreation & Charitable Giving	$ -	$ -	$ -	0%
Total Expenses	$ 1,098	$ 4,758	$ 57,094	76%
Taxes	$ 356	$ 1,542	$ 18,506	24%
Pay Required for Expenses and Taxes	$ 1,454	$ 6,300	$ 75,600	100%
Required pay per hour @ 40 hrs./week	$ 36.35			
Source: Author's calculations using referenced sources.				

Subsistence Budget Conclusions

Let us recall that the Subsistence Budget is designed to measure only what it costs to pay for a minimal level of the necessities of life without having to resort to subsidies or charity. It is made up of minimum, "bare bones" amounts for necessary living expenses of food, clothing, shelter, transportation, medical care, and, where applicable, child care and school expenses; that is, those expenses that are necessary to provide for an individual's (and his or her family's) "health and welfare and/or production of income."

Not only are the amounts for these categories minimal, but many categories are entirely excluded. As I have noted, it does not include provision for many ordinary living expenses, such as modest Christmas and/or birthday gifts, children's participation in sports or other activities, or other recreation. It does not include any provision for saving for immediate extraordinary expenses, retirement, or post-secondary education. It does not include any provision for contributions to church or charities. Even for the included categories, these amounts are obviously very "bare bones."

One could say that on this budget, one is "surviving but not thriving." And what is the wage required for such an existence in an average American city?[50] In sum, it is:

Individual	$23.01 per hour
Two Parents, Two Children Both parents working 40 hrs./wk. Full child care	$23.11 per hour
Two Parents, Two Children One parent working 20 hrs./wk. No child care	$27.11 per hour
Two Parents, Two Children One parent working 20 hrs./wk. Half child care	28.96 per hour
One Parent, Two Children Full child care	$36.35 per hour

These numbers may be startling, but if anything, they are conservative. For example, I believe that this budget underestimates health care costs – but that is a subject beyond the scope of this book. Also, it is important to note that in much of America, living costs are much higher than these. The Census Bureau ranks for 329 cities run from a low of 82.8 in Harlingen, TX, to a high of 216.7 in Manhattan.) Meanwhile, The Bureau of Labor Statistics reported that during the first eleven months of 2016, hourly earnings of production and nonsupervisory employees in the private sector averaged $21.53 per hour.

Key Finding: When we compare these subsistence budgets with reported wage levels, we see a gap, sometimes a yawning gap, between even a minimal cost of living and average pay levels in ordinary jobs – it becomes clear that for ordinary Americans, life is not adding up.

A "Middle Class" Budget

As I have pointed out, the Subsistence Budget does not make adequate provision for many items, and no provision for others. What would be the cost of the things we would typically consider to make up the "American dream" for a family of four? This question was the subject of a special report published in USA Today on July 4, 2014.[51]

The USA Today analysis concluded that supporting the life most Americans aspire to would require a household income of $130,000 per year: $58,491 for essentials (housing (mortgage on a house costing $275,000), groceries, one car, medical, education, apparel, and utilities); $17,009 for extras (vacation, entertainment, restaurants, cable, etc. and miscellaneous); $32,357 for taxes (income, property, and sales taxes), and $22,500 for savings (retirement and college). The report noted that adding a second car and another child could easily take the total to $150,000, and that with regional variations in cost, the number is much higher in many areas of the country.

Noting that only one in eight U.S. households earned $130,000 in 2013, with the median at about $51,000, the report concluded that the American dream of owning a home, having time and money for a vacation and some modest recreation, paying their fair share of taxes, and saving for retirement and their kids' college education, has become out of reach for most Americans.

> **Key Finding:** For most Americans, the "American dream" of some discretionary income and savings for emergencies, children's college and retirement has become out of reach.

What We Get: Dependency

So, we see that a great number of Americans are working full-time, and often in an additional job, and receiving an income that bears no relation to their families' actual costs of food, clothing, shelter, medical care and education. Rather than creating an economy in which they can be self-sustaining, we have relegated them to dependency, and have created a plethora of state and federal programs designed to assist them in meeting those needs.

A 2006 study by the Congressional Research Service[52] inventoried 84 federal means-tested programs. The Department of Human Services has provided a short list of 39 of those programs[53]. These include: Community Services Block Grant, Head Start, Low-Income Home Energy Assistance Program, parts of Medicaid, Children's Health Insurance Program, subsidized prescription drugs under Medicare, the Supplemental Nutrition Assistance Program (formerly Food Stamp Program), Special Supplemental

Nutrition Program for Women, Infants, and Children (WIC), National School Lunch Program, School Breakfast Program, Child and Adult Care Food Program, Weatherization Assistance for Low-Income Persons, Job Corps and Workforce Investment Act Youth Activities, Supplemental Security Income (SSI), Earned Income Tax Credit (EITC), Section 8 low-income housing assistance, and low-rent public housing.

And researchers have established an increase in the use of these programs in areas impacted by competition from imports. In their 2012 study, David Autor and colleagues at MIT found that in labor markets exposed to rising imports from China between 1990 and 2007 transfer benefits payments for unemployment, disability, retirement, and healthcare rose sharply.[54]

However, even with these programs in place, we have millions of *working* Americans who are having their electricity and water cut off and cannot fill their fuel oil tanks, feed their children regularly, or fill their doctors' prescriptions, in short, who cannot make ends meet, and for whom life does not add up.

For example, in 2015, an estimated 12.7 percent of U.S. households were food insecure, meaning they had difficulty at some time during the year providing enough food for all their members due to a lack of resources. The 2015 prevalence of food insecurity was down from a high of 14.9 percent in 2011, but still above the 2007 pre-recessionary level of 11.1 percent. The prevalence of food insecurity varied considerably from State to State. Estimated prevalence of food insecurity in 2013-15 ranged from 8.5 percent in North Dakota to 20.8 percent in Mississippi.[55] 59 percent of those experiencing food insecurity received assistance from one of the federal food assistance programs.

A proposition: There will always be some individuals in need of assistance. But how much better would it be if working Americans could make their own way and lead a life of independence, rather than having to rely on these inefficient subsidies and income transfers?

What We Get - Social Ills

But it is not just dependency -- we also experience a broad array of social ills. At the individual level, we see increased alienation, depression, and substance abuse, and at the family level increased spouse and child abuse and divorce.

We have seen Barlett and Steele tell the story of the young man who committed suicide the day he was terminated from his computer programming job at the Bank of America, to be replaced by an Indian working on an H-1B visa.

We hear these stories, and we feel bad, and we dismiss them as isolated, one-off incidents. But if they are so rare, why did the suicide help-line signs go up at each of the regional rail stations around Philadelphia, and why are they still there? Are there dots to be connected between the ongoing offshoring of every "tradable" job in America, white-and blue-collar alike, and the ongoing wage and performance pressure being applied in the jobs remain, on the one hand, and on the other the national epidemics of suicides and overdoses from heroin and opioid painkillers?

Of course, there is a connection, and now there is statistical evidence. Angus Deaton, Princeton economist and winner of the 2015 Nobel Prize for economics, and his wife Anne Case, in research published in 2015 documented a measurable increase in deaths among non-college-educated middle-aged white men in America, largely due to suicides and drug overdoses. The researchers suggested that a likely explanation was in the job losses and economic insecurity experienced in the areas hit by globalization and automation.[56]

This speculation was confirmed by a subsequent study by Justin R. Pierce and Peter K. Schott.[57] Pierce and Schott determined that counties with high exposure to import competition from China saw a four percent increase in suicide rates, with the increase concentrated among white males, and a 28 percent increase of deaths from accidental poisonings including drug overdoses.[58]

At the community level, we see failures of commercial districts and residential neighborhoods and increased crime. And, as individuals fall into dependency, not only do they draw government subsidies, but they pay less income, property, and sales taxes, undermining the tax base. Local governments are less able to fund roads, schools, and parks, police and fire departments, and other essential infrastructure and services. The problem is worsened as communities try to outbid each other with tax abatements in attempts to lure employers from other locations.

Slack Consumer Demand

We now turn to the fourth stage in the cascade of effects, slack consumer demand:

- Slack labor market
  - Underemployment & low pay
    - Dependency and social ills
      - **Slack consumer demand**
        - Stagnant economy

The Engine of Consumer Demand

We have seen that offshoring jobs and the resulting slack labor market cause unemployment, under-employment and depressed wages, leading to dependency and social ills at the individual, family and community level. At the macroeconomic level of the entire economy, these trends result in the next cascading effect: slack consumer demand.

The secret of the American prosperity of the second half of the twentieth century was the economy's creation of a prosperity that was widely shared. Postwar consumers with savings and earnings in their pockets created demand for a wide array of goods from houses to toasters, and companies hired workers at good wages to produce those goods. Improvements in productivity were shared with employees in the form of increased pay, and consumer spending became a major engine of the national economy.

The necessity of consumer spending for a vital economy has not diminished. For example, observers of the Chinese economy, both within and outside China, have concluded that the country must shift toward a consumer-oriented economy, and the Chinese government is pursuing policies toward that end.

A recent Reuters article on Mexico brought the issue into clear focus.[59] The article considered the cause of Mexico's economic stagnation despite the robust growth of its manufacturing sector, and concluded that an oversupply of labor due to population growth was driving down wages, preventing consumers from spending enough to fuel the economy. Among the article's findings:

- Lower wages mean lower consumer spending, which accounts for more than two-thirds of the economy.
- Spending by the wealthy helps, but falling wages among the poorest half of the population is putting a drag on retail sales, which are basically flat.
- A government economist attributes the stagnation to the failure to create enough high quality jobs and over-reliance on abundant cheap labor. *Id.*

These findings apply equally to the United States. So, too, China has largely failed to engage its consumers in the economy, relying to date on investments in infra-structure and capital-intensive industries. At the end of the day, it is consumers who drive the economy, and they can't do so if they are struggling to make ends meet. However, in the United States, we have been killing the goose that laid the golden egg.[60]

The Hourglass Economy

In April 2014, a leading consulting firm to the retail industry gave a briefing in which it identified ten trends reshaping the U.S. retail landscape.[61] Number one was the emergence of an "hourglass economy,' in which there was more spending among high and low income levels as the middle class is being squeezed.

As evidence for the trend these experts noted, on the one hand --

- Growth of the American luxury market at an annual rate of 4 percent from 2008-2013;
- Growth of luxury brands and channels like Louis Vuitton, BMW and Neiman Marcus.

And on the other –

- Growth in sale of less-expensive store brand products;
- Growth of stores like Dollar General aimed at lower-tier customers;
- Continued post-recession growth of deals and discounts offered by major stores;
- Fast casual restaurants gaining at expense of casual and midscale restaurants.

The resulting advice, and prevailing wisdom for retailers, is to focus on either end of the spectrum and avoid the middle, where it is increasingly difficult to make a go of it: Embrace the hourglass economy and look for ways to exploit opportunities at the top or bottom, and don't get caught in the middle.

This advice may be helpful to individual retailers and brands; however, it does not solve the problem for the larger economy -- *consumers who are not able to make ends meet are not able to prime the pump of the economy with their spending.*

Stagnant/Declining Economy

We now turn to the fifth stage in the cascade of effects, the slack economy:

- Slack labor market
  - Underemployment & low pay
    - Dependency and social ills
      - Slack consumer demand
        - **Stagnant economy**

Without demand to drive it, the economy goes stagnant and declines. During the years 2010 through 2016, U.S. Gross Domestic Product has grown at annual rates of 2.5%, 1.6%, 2.2%, 1,7%, 2.4%, 2.6%, and 1.9%, respectively.[62]

However, even this relatively anemic growth was not being realized by typical American households. In September of 2016 the Census Bureau reported:

> Median household income in the United States was $56,516 in 2015, an increase in real terms of 5.2 percent from the 2014 median of $53,718. *This is the first annual increase in median household income since 2007*, the year before the most recent recession.

> *In 2015, real median household income was 1.6 percent lower than in 2007, the year before the most recent recession, and 2.4 percent lower than the median household income peak that occurred in 1999.*
>
> The real median earnings of men and women who worked full time, year-round between 2014 and 2015 increased by 1.5 percent and 2.7 percent, respectively. *This is the first significant annual increase in median earnings for men or women since 2009.* [Emphasis supplied.] [63]

The Slack economy causes a slack job market, and we repeat the cycle of cascading effects. It's a race to the bottom, except that the bottom is never reached – rather, it is a vicious circle that keeps repeating itself. As we have seen, each decade and each recession brings another round of job losses from which we do not fully recover, starting the cycle all over again. So, the pattern looks more like this:

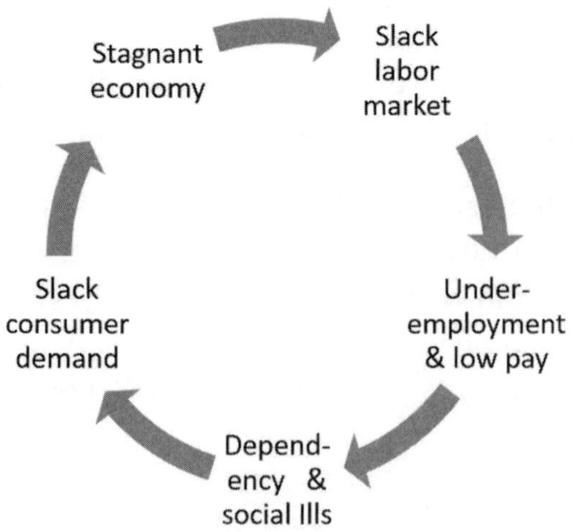

I have referred to a recent Reuters article that considered the cause of Mexico's economic stagnation despite the robust growth of its manufacturing sector. It concluded that an oversupply of labor due to population growth was driving down wages, preventing consumers from spending enough to fuel the economy. This article could just as well have been written about the United States, except that in the U.S. case, the oversupply of labor is due to offshoring jobs (many to Mexico), not population growth. I invite you to substitute U.S. facts for Mexico's:

[America's problem is the same as Mexico's – a lack of consumer demand:]

- Between ~~1992 and 2012~~ <u>2012 and 2013</u>, the economy grew by an annual average of only ~~2.8~~ <u>2.4</u> percent, although exports were up ~~8.6~~ <u>.54</u> percent annually.
- Worker pay is a large part of the problem, with pay per capita household income falling ~~six~~ <u>eight</u> percent from ~~2005 to 2012~~ <u>2007 to 2013</u>.
- Lower wages mean lower consumer spending, which accounts for more than two-thirds of the economy.
- Spending by the wealthy helps, but falling wages among the poorest half of the population is putting a drag on retail sales, which are basically flat.
- A government economist attributes the stagnation to the failure to create enough high quality jobs and over-reliance on abundant cheap labor.

Other trends have worsened these effects

These developments have occurred against a backdrop of other, interrelated economic and social trends, which have worsened their effects.

Automation of Work

One trend that has worsened the effects of sending jobs offshore is what I will refer to simply as the "automation of work." In Chapter 6, I discussed how automation and increased productivity could not account for all the shortfall in manufacturing employment. Nevertheless, these trends are significant. In recent years there has been an accelerating trend toward greater automation, both of manufacturing (including the use of ever-more-productive robots) and also of many non-manufacturing functions.[64] The resulting job losses have put more slack into the labor market, contributing to the vicious circle.

Failed Immigration Policies

Another trend that has worsened the effects of sending jobs offshore has been the immigration into the U.S. of foreign workers willing to work for less than prevailing U.S. wages, and creating excess supply in the labor market. Increased numbers of immigrants have resulted from more relaxed legal immigration since the Immigration Act of 1965, and increased illegal immigration not countered by effective enforcement.

The largest effects have been upon those least able to bear them: high-school dropouts who make up approximately the lowest one-tenth of the workforce. Timothy Noah has cited research concluding that from 1980 to 2000, immigration reduced the average annual income of this group by 7.4 percent, and another study finding that during that period, Mexican immigration reduced that group's income by 8.2 percent.[65] And the job losses and downward pressure on wages are not the only effects: the arrival of poor, unskilled immigrant families creates great stress on community education, health-care, and other social support systems, effectively requiring subsidies for the immigrants' low-paying jobs.

But it is not just the low-skill jobs that are being undermined through immigration - there is another piece of the immigration problem has to do with well-paying jobs in technical fields.

In Chapter 3, we saw how PriceWaterhouseCoopers outsourced their entire 800-person IT operation from their offices in Tampa to an Indian IT consulting firm, Tata Consulting. In addition to this "offshore outsourcing," there is another insidious practice, outsourcing to "onshored" foreign workers. Greg Spotts captured a vivid example in his documentary film, *American Jobs*.[66]

On Friday, March 21, 2003, the entire software testing department at the Watchmark company in Seattle was told they were being outsourced to an Indian consulting firm. They were informed that "you are expected to train your replacements" who would be flying in over the weekend and would arrive on Monday. They were employees of Tata Consulting, the same firm to whom Price Waterhouse Coopers would offshore their entire IT operation in 2010, as we saw in Chapter 3. The American workers felt "thrown away," after Watchmark had invested a great deal of training in them; now "my Indian replacement is sitting at my desk, answering my phone."

Tata and Watchmark were exploiting a provision of the U.S. immigration laws, the "L-1B" visa, which permits the temporary transfer to the U.S. of employees with "specialized knowledge" of a company's products or processes. Except that this was a total abuse of the provision, since the Indian workers had only basic IT knowledge, and had to be trained in Watchmark's intellectual property.

Another visa category, the "H-1B" visa also is used to bring in technology workers and other "members of the professions." [67]

As with the L-1B, there is no requirement for a showing of a shortage or inability to recruit U.S. workers - only that the foreign worker be paid the "prevailing wage" (a requirement more honored in the breach - it is for low pay that the H-1B workers are brought here.) H-1B visas are subject to an annual cap, and they are dispensed to U.S. employers via an annual "lottery."

Unlike the H-1B visa category, the L1-B is not subject to annual caps on visas issued, or to a requirement for the payment of "prevailing wage" rates. The Indian workers reportedly were paid $$3,000 per month, from which Tata deducted $2,000 for hotel and rental car expenses. Meanwhile, the U.S. workers were out of jobs, and as one worker pointed out, whatever computer programming jobs remained in the market, "the value of those jobs has declined . . . the threat of offshoring will suppress the salary you can pay to an American."[68]

And the trend continues -- in October of 2014, Walt Disney Parks and Resorts in Florida laid off 250 information technology workers who would train their Indian replacements; in May of 2015, Disney of California did the same thing to 35 IT workers there.[69]

Shareholder Value

Another trend that has worsened the effects of sending jobs offshore has been the widespread adoption of "shareholder value" as the guiding principle of American business.

Shareholder value has two forms. One is that shareholder value is all that matters, because that's what we are in business to do: to maximize shareholder value, i.e., return on investment. We (companies) are not in business to accomplish any social ends.

The second is that social ends do matter, but that they will necessarily follow if we maximize shareholder value. This is a variant of the "invisible hand" argument that markets will always deliver socially desirable conditions. In this case the particular market mechanism is the pursuit of shareholder value, as established via the stock market for publicly traded companies, and the merger and acquisition market for privately held companies.

That is just more tooth fairy economics. If that were true, then all the companies would be pursuing workers' and communities' interests. But they are not. If that were true, then Carrier would not be moving to Mexico to realize $46 million a year in operating savings. The single-minded pursuit of shareholder value sends Carrier to Mexico, the employees and the community be damned.

Cornell Law School professor Lynn Stout has pointed out that shareholder value only recently displaced managerial capitalism, under which companies could and did pursue more than one goal simultaneously, and that this shift was not required under American corporate law.[70]

Fortunately, some American business leaders still subscribe to a broader view of the purpose of a company. An NAACP leader told Beth Macy she was grateful that John Bassett III understood that as a business owner, ". . . you are responsible for your community, and you don't just turn around and walk away!" [71] And Bassett was not alone -- Reau Berry, owner of Johnston/Tombigbee who joined Bassett in the furniture anti-dumping case, told Beth Macy that in his view the real value of manufacturing is creating a community with a vibrant economy.[72] At the institutional level, the National Association of Corporate Directors has raised the importance of sustainability, which may include consideration of the economic and social health of communities. [73]

Nevertheless, shareholder value continues to hold sway, as a trend that contributes to the offshoring of American jobs. For example, Chad Broughton describes Maytag's transformation from "a family-run, customer-centered, paternalistic company to one obsessed with 'shareholder value,'" as exemplified by the move of the Maytag factory in Galesburg, Illinois to Reynosa, Mexico.[74]

Gains Unequally Shared

During the "Golden Thirty" years of American economic growth following World War II, the nation's new-found prosperity was broadly shared. The following figure from the Economic Policy Institute shows the average annual growth of income for families in each fifth of the distribution. From 1947 through 1979, there was a remarkably even distribution of income growth of about 2.4 percent, with the bottom fifth actually being the biggest gainer, and the top five percent gaining at the lowest rate (although gains were much larger in absolute dollar terms).

Then, during the period 1979 through 2007, there was a remarkable breach of this order, with almost no growth at all for the bottom fifth, and slowly ascending growth through subsequent fifths, up to the top five percent, which was the biggest gainer by far. During 1979-2007, there was less growth overall, and it was skewed strongly towards the top earners, with the lowest fifth basically left out.

Figure 2C Average family income growth, by income group, 1947–2007

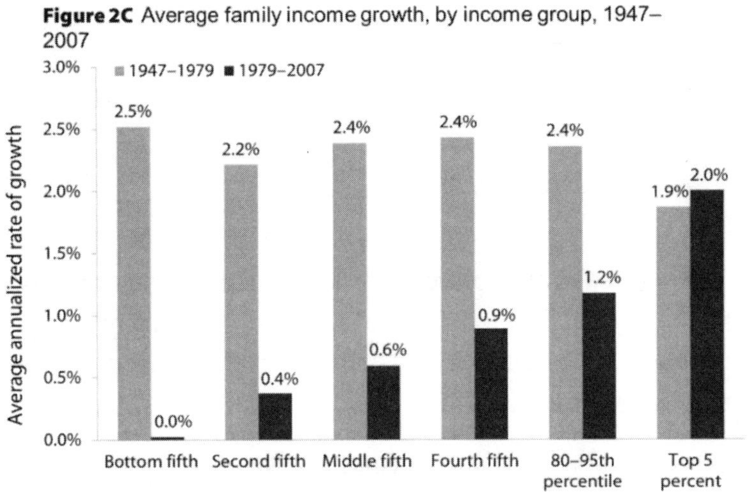

*Data are for market based income of tax units.
Source: Authors' analysis of Current Population Survey Annual Social and Economic Supplement *Historical Income Tables* (Table F-2, F-3, F-5), and Piketty and Saez (2012)

There is a simple explanation for this "before and after" disparity in sharing of income growth. Real economic growth (as opposed to inflation) occurs primarily as a result of increases in productivity. During the post-war period through the mid-1970s, productively grew steadily, and hourly compensation grew in lock step with it: that is, productivity-induced economic growth was shared proportionately with workers. However, as the following figure from EPI illustrates, in the mid-1970s, a sharp break occurred, after which productively continued to grow, but ordinary production workers' wages went flat.

Figure 4U Cumulative change in total economy productivity and real hourly compensation of production/nonsupervisory workers, 1948–2011

Note: Data are for production/nonsupervisory workers in the private sector and productivity of the total economy.
Source: Authors' analysis of unpublished total economy data from Bureau of Labor Statistics Labor Productivity and Costs program, wage data from BLS Current Employment Statistics program, and Bureau of Economic Analysis National Income and

The gains from productivity went elsewhere, as shown in the bar chart. The capture of income growth by a small percentage of households is further illustrated in the following figure from EPI:

Figure 2Y Share of total household income growth attributable to various income groups, 1979–2007

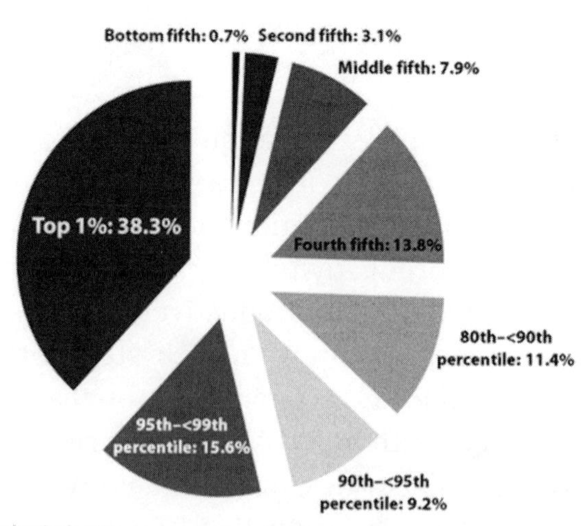

Note: Data are for comprehensive income.
Source: Authors' analysis of Congressional Budget Office (2010)

This extraordinary figure is worth a long look. It is immediately obvious that the largest portion of the pie of economic growth is captured by the tiniest percentage: the top one percent, with 38.3 percent. The top 20 percent of households captured three fourths of the income growth during this period; the remaining fifths received progressively smaller shares until the bottom fifth was nearly entirely left out.

The extent to which income is now being skewed to the small percentage of top earners has been captured in a series of studies published by the economist Emmanuel Saez, most recently in June of 2016.[75] Saez has found that from 1993 to 2015, average real family incomes of the bottom 99% grew by 14.3%, while top one percent incomes grew by 94.5%. That is, top one percent incomes captured 52% of the overall economic growth of real incomes per family over the period 1993-2015. *Id.*

During the period since the Great Recession, from 2009 to 2015, average real income per family of the bottom 99% incomes grew by 7.6% while top one percent incomes grew by 37.4%. That is, the top one percent captured 52% of the income gains in the first six years of the recovery. *Id.*

This skewing of income *growth* toward the top has skewed real *incomes* as well. The following figure and table show incomes of each fifth of American households from 1967 through 2015, expressed in 2016 dollars.[76]

Incomes of the bottom fifth went from $11,504 to $12,582, up nine percent; incomes of the top five percent went from $200,705 to $327,594, *up 75 percent.* As the figure indicates, all the increases in income and disparities occurred in the period beginning after 1981.

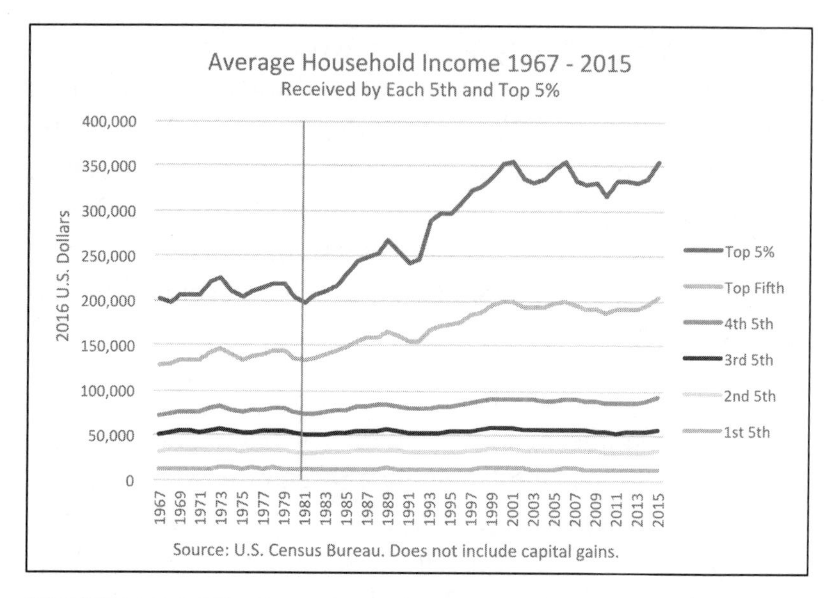

Mean Annual Household Income Received by Each Fifth and Top 5%						
(2016 Dollars)						
Year	1st 5th	2nd 5th	3rd 5th	4th 5th	Top fifth	Top 5%
1967	11,504	31,873	50,884	71,195	128,126	202,111
2015	12,582	32,957	57,400	92,951	204,390	354,379
% Change	9%	3%	13%	31%	60%	75%

And recall, this figure does not show the half of it, as it presents income without income from capital gains.

The Harsh Society

As these trends have played out in America, we are creating a harsh society, with ordinary Americans abandoned and betrayed by Wall Street, Washington, and the American consumer.

When I was starting out in Washington, I used to take my clothes to a laundry operated by a man from Korea. He told me that he had a rather high-ranking professional job in Korea. However, he had emigrated to the United States and was operating the laundry for the sake of his children. In Korea, jobs like the one he had were few and could be attained only by the small percentage who made the best grades on the national exams. He had brought his children to the U.S. at the expense of his career so they could have the broader opportunities afforded here.

But now we are becoming the Korea he left. In my school system, they show a film called "The Race to Nowhere," critical of the treadmill families get on to try to get their kids into the best schools. I used to agree with the criticism. But I have come to realize that we have become the "winner take all" society that Robert Frank described in his book of the same name.[77]

But it is even worse than that, because, even for those who "make it," having done all the right things and gone to school, and performed well on the job, there is no assurance of maintaining that status. Life in America has become a game of Chutes and Ladders[78] in which people climb their way up playing by the rules and working hard and them find themselves suddenly dropping down to the bottom of the board because someone decided that it was better to have their job performed in China or in India, or by someone imported from China or India.

There is no solid ground anymore. American families, blue collar and professional alike, are all standing on thin ice, worried that on any given day, they may fall through.[79] Or perhaps the better analogy is to have the rug pulled out from under them - because someone in a C-Suite or board room is going to actively make the decision to do so. In a poll of Americans in October of 2016, thirty percent were very fearful that they will lose their job in the next six months, up from 10 percent a year ago; 28 percent were afraid of not being able to pay their mortgages — up from 10 percent a year previous; and 39 percent said their personal financial situation caused them to lose sleep.[80]

Neal Gabler reports that in the Federal Reserve Board's annual survey of American consumers, when asked how they would pay for a $400 emergency, *47 percent* of respondents said either that they would cover the expense by borrowing or selling something, or that they would not be able to come up with the $400 at all.[81] Gabler reported that Edward Wolff, an economist at New York University, researched how long a family headed by someone of "prime working age," between 24 and 55 years old, could continue to self-fund its current consumption by liquidating all financial assets except home equity, if the family were to lose its income. He found that in 2013, such families in the bottom two fifths of income had no net worth at all. A family in the middle fifth, averaging about $50,000 a year, could last six days. So, three-fifths of American families with at least one prime-age wage earner, comprising two-thirds of the "middle class," are living week-to-week.[82]

Many working Americans are experiencing the outcomes the Fed survey respondents are anxious about. Across America, hard-working families are skipping meals and skipping days of heat during the winter. And, as captured by J.D. Vance in his recent book, it doesn't stop there, with some families enduring drug addiction and overdoses and even suicide.[83]

Key Finding: While the current situation is working for a few, millions of Americans are experiencing a hollow economy in which they are marking time at best, or slipping out of the "middle class," and fear for even worse for their children.

And so, we must consider, what does the future hold, if we stay on our present course? We will take up this question in Chapters 8 and 9.

Notes to Chapter 7

---

[1] The following discussion is based on material I have gathered in the online appendix titled Demystifying Unemployment. See "Demystifying Unemployment Statistics" at http://currentaffairspress.com/titles/what-if-things-were-made-in-america-again/.

[2] Includes those who did not actively look for work in the prior 4 weeks for reasons such as thinks no work available, could not find work, lacks schooling or training, employer thinks too young or old, and other discrimination. See Online Appendix, "Demystifying Employment."

[3] Includes those who were not currently looking for work for reasons other than discouragement, for such reasons as school or family responsibilities, ill health, and transportation problems.

[4] The BLS defines "employed" as follows: "Employed persons consist of: persons who did *any* work for pay or profit during the survey reference week; persons who did at least 15 hours of unpaid work in a family-operated enterprise; and persons who were temporarily absent from their regular jobs because of illness, vacation, bad weather, industrial dispute, or various personal reasons." [Emphasis supplied.] http://www.bls.gov/cps/lfcharacteristics.htm#laborforce.

[5] As defined by the BLS; see Online Appendix, "Demystifying Employment."

[6] Published online at http://currentaffairspress.com/titles/what-if-things-were-made-in-america-again/.

[7] Where not otherwise presented, the tables from which the figures in this chapter are derived are presented at http://currentaffairspress.com/titles/what-if-things-were-made-in-america-again/.

[8] The figure is derived from the following table:

Population and Potential Workforce			
	Civilian Pop'n over 16	Potential Workforce	Civilian Workforce
2007	232	157	152
2008	234	159	154
2009	236	160	155
2010	238	159	154
2011	240	159	153
2012	243	160	154
2013	246	161	155
2014	248	161	155
2015	251	162	156
2016	253	164	158
Source: Bureau of Labor Statistics; Author's Calculations http://www.bls.gov/cps/cpsatabs.htm			

[9] The figure is derived from the following table:

Workforce as % of Population (Civilian Non-Inst. over Age 16) (Millions)		
Year	Potential Workforce	Civilian Workforce
2007	67.5%	65.6%
2008	67.9%	65.9%
2009	67.8%	65.5%
2010	66.9%	64.6%
2011	66.4%	63.9%
2012	65.9%	63.4%
2013	65.3%	62.9%
2014	64.8%	62.5%
2015	64.4%	62.2%
2016	64.6%	62.3%
Source: Bureau of Labor Statistics http://www.bls.gov/cps/cpsatabs.htm		

[10] Christopher Erceg and Andrew T. Levin, "Labor Force Participation and Monetary Policy in the Wake of the Great Recession." Federal Reserve Bank of Boston, April 9, 2013.

[11] The figure is derived from the following table:

Employment as Percent of Population 1/					
1963	55.3%	1981	59.0%	1999	64.2%
1964	55.6%	1982	57.7%	2000	64.3%
1965	56.1%	1983	57.8%	2001	63.6%
1966	56.9%	1984	59.5%	2002	62.7%
1967	57.2%	1985	60.1%	2003	62.2%
1968	57.4%	1986	60.6%	2004	62.3%
1969	57.9%	1987	61.5%	2005	62.6%
1970	57.3%	1988	62.2%	2006	63.1%
1971	56.5%	1989	62.9%	2007	62.9%
1972	56.9%	1990	62.7%	2008	62.1%
1973	57.8%	1991	61.6%	2009	59.3%
1974	57.8%	1992	61.4%	2010	58.4%
1975	56.0%	1993	61.7%	2011	58.3%
1976	56.8%	1994	62.5%	2012	58.5%
1977	57.8%	1995	62.8%	2013	58.5%
1978	59.3%	1996	63.1%	2014	59.0%
1979	59.9%	1997	63.7%	2015	59.3%
1980	59.1%	1998	64.0%	2016	59.6%

1/ U.S. working age population over age 16.
Employed per BLS definition.
Source: Bureau of Labor Statistics

[12] The figure is derived from the following table:

Shortfall in Employment in Recovery from Great Recession (Millions of Jobs)				
Year	Potential	Projected	Actual	Jobs Gap
2006	154.8	139.3	139.3	-
2007	156.6	140.9	140.8	0.1
2008	158.8	142.8	139.4	3.5
2009	160.0	143.9	131.3	12.6
2010	159.3	143.3	130.0	13.3
2011	159.2	143.2	130.9	12.3
2012	160.3	144.2	133.6	10.6
2013	160.5	144.4	135.2	9.2
2014	160.9	144.7	138.2	6.5
2015	161.7	145.5	141.5	4.0
2016	163.5	147.1	143.7	3.4

Source: Bureau of Labor Statistics; author's calculations
Potential = Employed and Unemployed, Categories 1-6, 8
Projected = Employed full-time and voluntarily part-time at 2000 rate
Actual = Employed full-time and voluntarily part-time
Annual averages, except 2016 = Jan.-July 2016

[13] The potential workforce consists of Categories 1 through 6 and Category 8.

[14] The figure is derived from the following table:

Shortfall in Employment in Recovery from 2001 and 2008 Recessions (Millions of Jobs)				
Year	Potential	Projected	Actual	Jobs Gap
2000	145.5	132.7	132.7	-
2001	147.0	134.0	132.4	1.7
2002	148.4	135.3	131.5	3.7
2003	150.1	136.9	132.3	4.5
2004	151.1	137.7	133.9	3.8
2005	153.0	139.5	136.5	3.0
2006	154.8	141.1	139.3	1.8
2007	156.6	142.8	140.8	1.9
2008	158.8	144.7	139.4	5.4
2009	160.0	145.8	131.3	14.5
2010	159.3	145.2	130.0	15.2
2011	159.2	145.1	130.9	14.2
2012	160.3	146.1	133.6	12.5
2013	160.5	146.3	135.2	11.1
2014	160.9	146.6	138.2	8.4
2015	161.7	147.4	141.5	5.9
2016	163.5	149.1	143.7	5.3

Source: Bureau of Labor Statistics; author's calculations
Potential = Employed and Unemployed, Categories 1-6, 8
Projected = Employed full-time and voluntarily part-time at 2000 rate
Actual = Employed full-time and voluntarily part-time
Annual averages, except 2016 = Jan.-July 2016

[15] The figure is derived from the following table:

Shortfall in Employment in Recovery from 2001 and 2008 Recessions (Millions of Jobs)				
Year	Potential	Projected	Actual	Jobs Gap
2000	212.7	132.7	132.7	-
2001	215.3	134.2	132.4	1.9
2002	217.7	135.8	131.5	4.2
2003	221.3	138.0	132.3	5.7
2004	223.5	139.4	133.9	5.5
2005	226.2	141.1	136.5	4.6
2006	229.0	142.8	139.3	3.5
2007	232.0	144.7	140.8	3.8
2008	234.0	145.9	139.4	6.5
2009	236.0	147.1	131.3	15.8
2010	238.0	148.4	130.0	18.4
2011	239.8	149.5	130.9	18.6
2012	243.5	151.8	133.6	18.2
2013	245.8	153.3	135.2	18.1
2014	248.1	154.7	138.2	16.5
2015	251.0	156.5	141.5	15.0
2016	253.3	157.9	143.7	14.2

Source: Bureau of Labor Statistics; author's calculations
Potential = Civilian working age population
Projected = Employed full-time and voluntarily part-time at 2000 rate
Actual = Employed full-time and voluntarily part-time
Annual averages, except 2016 = Jan.-July 2016

[16] Note that this year, 2001, keeps popping up: the year that China obtained permanent normal trade relations with the U.S. and was admitted to the World Trade Organization.

[17] Jane M. Von Bergen, "Jobs Shortage," Philadelphia Inquirer, May 10, 2015. Citing: Paul Harrington, "Left Behind: Jobs Recovery Bypasses Philadelphia Teens." Drexel University (2015).

[18] Ronald D. White, "Near retirement, contending with unemployment, Los Angeles Times / Philadelphia Inquirer, May 10, 2015.

[19] "A Year of Unbalanced Growth: Industries, Wages and the First 12 Months of Job Growth after the Great Recession." National Employment Law Project Data Brief. February 2011. http://nelp.3cdn.net/35f827759654da7a74_0am6bt3s5.pdf

[20] "The Low Wage Recovery: Industry Employment and Wages Four Years into the Recovery.: National Employment Law Project Data Brief, April 2014. http://www.nelp.org/page/-/Reports/Low-Wage-Recovery-Industry-Employment-Wages-2014-Report.pdf?nocdn=1

[21] Tracking the Low-Wage Recovery: Industry Employment & Wages. National Employment Law Project.
http://www.nelp.org/page/content/lowwagerecovery2014/

[22] The N.E.L.P.'s report also documents severe job losses in manufacturing of durable and non-durable goods consistent with those we have reported. See Table 1 at p. 9 and following.

[23] Annie Lowrey, "Recovery Has Created Far More Low-Wage Jobs Than Better-Paid Ones." New York Times, April 27, 2014.
http://www.nytimes.com/2014/04/28/business/economy/recovery-has-created-far-more-low-wage-jobs-than-better-paid-ones.html

[24] *Id.* One of the big reasons for the movement towards lower-paying replacement jobs is that many of the new jobs are low-pay jobs in the warehouses and distribution centers that receive the foreign goods and distribute them to U.S. retailers and online buyers. See discussion below.

[25] Annie Lowrey, "Recovery Has Created Far More Low-Wage Jobs," *supra*.

[26] "Inside Amazon's Warehouse," *The Morning Call*, Allentown, Pennsylvania, www.mcall.com, September 18, 2011.
http://www.mcall.com/news/local/amazon/mc-allentown-amazon-complaints-20110917-story.html#page=1

[27] *Id.*

[28] Marc Lifsher, "Warehouse workers say Wal-Mart responsible for poor conditions," Los Angeles Times, November 30, 2012.
http://articles.latimes.com/2012/nov/30/business/la-fi-mo-warehouse-workers-say-walmart-responsible-for-poor-working-conditions-20121130

[29] "Bad Jobs in Goods Movement: Warehouse Work in Will County, IL." Warehouse Workers for Justice, with technical assistance from Center for Urban Economic Development at the University of Illinois at Chicago. 2010. http://www.warehouseworker.org/badjobs/.

In the "first large-scale study of workers in warehousing in the country" the worker advocacy organization Warehouse Workers for Justice, with technical assistance from the University of Illinois at Chicago, interviewed 319 workers from 156 warehouses, including both temp workers and direct hires.

[30] So, our warehouses are no better than the factories in China and Mexico, where these practices also are prevalent.

[31] Viscelli chronicled his experience and interviews with other truckers in *The Big Rig: Trucking and the Decline of the American Dream* (Oakland: University of California Press, 2016).

[32] "Eighteen Wheel Blues," *The Pennsylvania Gazette*, November-December, 2016, 18.

[33] The Bureau of Labor Statistics reported that among couples age 25-54, the average combined weekly hours worked increased from 56 hours a week in 1969 to 67 hours a week in 2000. "Working in the 21st Century," Bureau of Labor Statistics. Http://www.bls.gov/opub/home.htm.

[34] "Supply Chain News: Rise in China Wages Now Means Labor Costs about 20% Lower in Mexico, New Study Finds," Supply Chain Digest, Editorial Staff, April 8, 2013. http://www.scdigest.com/ontarget/13-04-08-1.php?cid=6913

[35] Joann Muller, "UAW's Loss and What It Means for Your Paycheck," Forbes.com, February 15, 2014. http://www.forbes.com/sites/joannmuller/2014/02/15/uaws-loss-and-what-it-means-for-your-paycheck/

[36] "The War on the American Worker – The Underemployed," http://www.payscale.com/data-packages/underemployment

[37] Josh Mitchell, "Students to Get Aid for Alternative Training," Wall Street Journal, August 17, 2016. The U.S. Department of Education has launched a program of loans and grants to provide training at non-college entities focused on such skills as software programming and computer-assisted manufacturing. *Id.*

[38] Emily Peck, "The Class of 2015 is in for a Rude Awakening on Pay," Huffington Post, May 12, 2015.

[39] Ronald D. White, "Near retirement, contending with unemployment, Los Angeles Times / Philadelphia Inquirer, May 10, 2015.

[40] Gordon M. Fisher, "The Development of the Orshansky Poverty Thresholds and Their Subsequent History as the Official U.S. Poverty Measure," U.S. Department of Health and Human Services (May 1992--partially revised September 1997). http://aspe.hhs.gov/poverty/papers/hptgssiv.htm

[41] For the 48 contiguous states. http://www.dhs.ri.gov/Portals/0/Uploads/Documents/Public/General%20DHS/FPL.pdf

[42] *See* Poverty Guidelines, Research, and Measurement - Further Resources on Poverty Measurement, Poverty Lines, and Their History; U.S. Department of Health & Human Services. http://aspe.hhs.gov/poverty/contacts.cfm

[43] How the Census Bureau Measures Poverty, U.S. Census Bureau. https://www.census.gov/hhes/www/poverty/about/overview/measure.html

[44] The figure is derived from the following table:

Federal Minimum Wage in Current-Year Dollars							
1961	1962	1963	1964	1965	1966	1967	1968
$ 1.15	$ 1.15	$ 1.25	$ 1.25	$ 1.25	$ 1.25	**$ 1.40**	**$ 1.60**
1969	1970	1971	1972	1973	1974	1975	1976
$ 1.60	$ 1.60	$ 1.60	$ 1.60	$ 1.60	**$ 2.00**	**$ 2.10**	**$ 2.30**
1977	1978	1979	1980	1981	1982	1983	1984
$ 2.30	**$ 2.65**	**$ 2.90**	**$ 3.10**	**$ 3.35**	$ 3.35	$ 3.35	$ 3.35
1985	1986	1987	1988	1989	1990	1991	1992
$ 3.35	$ 3.35	$ 3.35	$ 3.35	$ 3.35	**$ 3.80**	**$ 4.25**	$ 4.25
1993	1994	1995	1996	1997	1998	1999	2000
$ 4.25	$ 4.25	$ 4.25	$ 4.75	**$ 5.15**	$ 5.15	$ 5.15	$ 5.15
2001	2002	2003	2004	2005	2006	2007	2008
$ 5.15	$ 5.15	$ 5.15	$ 5.15	$ 5.15	$ 5.15	**$ 5.85**	**$ 6.55**
2009	2010	2011	2012	2013	2014	2015	2016
$ 7.25	$ 7.25	$ 7.25	$ 7.25	$ 7.25	$ 7.25	$ 7.25	$ 7.25
Source: Bureau of Labor Statistics Years when increased are indicated in bold.							

[45] The question must also be answered with reference to minimum wages that have been enacted by numerous states and localities that are higher than the federal minimum wage. In fact, a majority of states now have higher minimum wages than the federal level. The Economic Policy Institute has prepared an inventory of state minimum wages. At this writing, it is available online at http://www.epi.org/minimum-wage-tracker/. Governing magazine and institute have prepared an inventory of local minimum wages adjusted per the locality's cost of living. At this writing, it is available online at
http://www.governing.com/gov-data/economy-finance/city-minimum-wages-adjusted-for-cost-of-living-data-map.html.
Numerous jurisdictions have raised their minimum wage in recent

years, in response to the "Fight for $15" movement that began with a fast food worker walkout in New York City in November of 2012. The biggest beneficiaries, have been workers in jurisdictions that passed $15-an-hour ordinances: California, New York, Los Angeles, San Francisco, Washington, D.C., Seattle, and SeaTac, Washington. http://www.huffingtonpost.com/news/fight-for-15/ A number of companies also have raised their minimum pay scales independent of minimum wage requirements. Together with the minimum wage increases, these raises have added up to $62 billion in additional annual pay, according to a study by the National Employment Law Project. N.E.L.P., "Fight for $15: Four Years, $62 Billion," Data Brief, *National Employment Law Project* (December 2016).
http://www.nelp.org/content/uploads/Fight-for-15-Four-Years-62-Billion-in-Raises.pdf
More increases are on the way. In December of 2016, CNN Money reported that in 2017 the minimum wage was set to increase in 21 states, 22 cities, four counties, and one region. The increases ranged from small cost of living increases to jumps of one to two dollars. Jeanne Sahadi, "Minimum wage going up in 21 states, 22 cities," *CNN Money*, December 19, 2016.
http://money.cnn.com/2016/12/19/pf/minimum-wage-increases/index.html

[46] In creating this budget, I have relied largely upon the "allowable expenses" established by the Internal Revenue Service to determine a taxpayer's ability to pay a delinquent tax liability. They are those expenses "that are necessary to provide for a taxpayer's (and his or her family's) health and welfare and/or production of income." [Internal Revenue Service, Collection Financial Standards, effective Mar 31, 2014. http://www.irs.gov/Individuals/Collection-Financial-Standards.] In determining the allowable amounts, the IRS determines the amount actually spent for household expenses, using survey data from the Bureau of Labor Statistics. For some categories, a national standard is used; for others, amounts are determined for specific geographic areas. For the geographical region, we have used Summit County, Ohio, where the city of Akron is located. In selecting Akron, we have turned to the Census Bureau's "Cost of Living Index--Selected Urban Areas." The Index measures relative price levels for consumer goods and services in a geographic area for a "mid-management standard of living." The nationwide average equals 100 and each index is read as a percent of the national average. Akron is an area with an "average" cost of living: The Census Bureau gives it a composite score of 100.2, without substantial deviation by category.

[47] It should be noted that two children are not enough to sustain a population, as has been discovered in Japan (where the population is in

decline) and Germany (which must rely on immigrants). A more realistic budget for a sustainable future would be for a larger family, with perhaps an average of 2.5 children. However, for simplicity and ease of comparison with other studies, I have considered a four-person family.

[48] If one parent works twenty hours a week and child care is cut in half, then the hourly rate increases to $28.96. If one parent works twenty hours a week and child care is eliminated (i.e., after the children are in school full-time), then the hourly rate changes to $27.11.

[49] The Census Bureau described this variety in a report issued in June of 2012. "Monthly Child Support Payments Average $430 per Month in 2010, Census Bureau Reports," U.S. Census Bureau, Newsroom Archive. https://www.census.gov/newsroom/releases/archives/children/cb12-109.html

[50] U.S. Census Bureau, *op. cit.* http://www.census.gov/compendia/statab/cats/prices/consumer_price_indexes_cost_of_living_index.html

[51] Howard R. Gold, "Price tag for the American dream: $130K a year," Special to USA Today, July 4, 2014. http://www.usatoday.com/story/money/personalfinance/2014/07/04/american-dream/11122015/

[52] "Cash and Noncash Benefits for Persons with Limited Income: Eligibility Rules, Recipient and Expenditure Data, FY2002-FY2004," Congressional Research Service, Library of Congress, March 27, 2006. http://aspe.hhs.gov/poverty/contacts.cfm.

[53] U.S. Department of Health and Human Services. http://aspe.hhs.gov/poverty/faq.cfm. See also http://aspe.hhs.gov/poverty/contacts.cfm
See "Federal Assistance Programs" at Online Appendices, http://currentaffairspress.com/titles/what-if-things-were-made-in-america-again/.

[54]Autor, Dorn, and Hanson, "The China Syndrome."

[55] Alisha Coleman-Jensen, Matthew P. Rabbitt, Christian A. Gregory, and Anita Singh, "Household Food Security in the United States in 2015," U.S. Department of Agriculture, September 2016.

[56] Shawn Donnan, "A political trade-off," *Financial Times*, September 23, 2016, 9.

[57] They are the same researchers who found the connection between U.S. manufacturing job losses and China's gaining permanent

[58] Justin R. Pierce and Peter K. Schott, "Trade Liberalization and Mortality: Evidence from U.S. Counties." November, 2016. *See also* Max Ehrenfreund, "Researchers have found a troubling new cause of death for middle-aged white Americans," The Washington Post, November 23, 2016.
https://www.washingtonpost.com/news/wonk/wp/2016/11/23/trade-with-china-literally-kills-americans-economists-say/

[59] Christine Murray, "Mexico manufacturing surge hides low wage drag on economy," Reuters, June 2, 2014.
http://www.reuters.com/article/2014/06/02/us-mexico-economy-analysis-idUSKBN0ED20H20140602

[60] It has been pointed out that American consumer spending accounted for a rising percentage of GDP over the recent decades, rising from 61.8% of GDP in the 1960s to 70% of GDP in the 2000s, and that this may have resulted in "crowding out" of investment with possible ill effects on economic growth. William R. Emmons, "Don't Expect Consumer Spending to be the Engine of Economic Growth it once Was," *Federal Reserve Bank of St. Louis*, January 2012.
http://www.stlouisfed.org/publications/re/articles/?id=2201 I would agree that excessive consumer demand that is based on debt incurred on a base of inflated assets is not a sound foundation for the economy. However, Emmons notes the difficulty of replacing consumer spending with investment and increased exports, and does not contest the need for a robust consumer sector, at least at the levels of the 1960s and 1970s.

[61] Confidential online briefing attended by the author.

[62] Bureau of Economic Analysis, Table 1.1.1. Percent Change from Preceding Period in Real Gross Domestic Product, December 22, 2016. www.bea.gov/national/nipaweb/GetCSV.asp?GetWhat=SS_Data/Section1All_xls.
http://bea.gov/iTable/iTable.cfm?ReqID=9&step=1#reqid=9&step=3&isuri=1&903=1

[63] Bernadette D. Proctor, Jessica L. Semega, Melissa A. Kollar, Income and Poverty in the United States: 2015, U.S. Census Bureau, Report Number: P60-256 (September 13, 2016).
http://www.census.gov/library/publications/2016/demo/p60-256.html.

[64] See, generally, Martin Ford, *Rise of the Robots: Technology and the Threat of a Jobless Future* (New York: Basic Books, 2015).

[65] Timothy Noah, "The United States of Inequality," *Slate*, September 7, 2010. See also, Benjamin M. Friedmanmay, "Minding the

Gap," book review of *The Great Divergence* by Timothy Noah, New York Times Sunday Book Review (May 25, 2012). http://www.nytimes.com/2012/05/27/books/review/the-great-divergence-by-timothy-noah.html.]

[66] Greg Spotts, *American Jobs*, Documentary film. (2005) http://www.imdb.com/media/rm129073408/tt0461008?ref_=tt_ov_i.

[67] This is the category used for the IT workers at Bank of America, where Barlett and Steele reported the last worker fired committed suicide the day he was terminated from his computer programming job.

[68] For a summary of research on the effects of H-1B workers, see Ross Eisenbery, "H-1B Visas Do Not Create Jobs or Improve Conditions for U.S. Workers," Economic Policy Institute Blog, May 18, 2015. Http://epi.org.

[69] Bourree Lam, "America's Mixed Feelings About Immigrant Labor: Disney-Layoffs Edition, Atlantic.com, June 18, 2015 http://www.theatlantic.com/business/archive/2015/06/disney-h1b-visas-immigration-layoffs.

[70] Lynn Stout, "The Shareholder Value Myth," *Cornell Law Faculty Publications*, Paper 771, April 19, 2013. http://scholarship.law.cornell.edu/facpub/771. *See also*, Lynn Stout, *The Shareholder Value Myth* (San Francisco: Berrett-Khoeler Publishers, Inc., 2012).

[71] Macy, *Factory Man*, 349.

[72] Macy, *Factory Man*, 393.

[73] See http://nacdonline.org/sustainability.

[74] Broughton, *Boom, Bust & Exodus*.

[75] Emmanuel Saez, "Striking it Richer: The Evolution of Top Incomes in the United States (Updated with 2015 preliminary estimates)," UC Berkeley (June 30, 2016) http://eml.berkeley.edu/~saez/saez-UStopincomes-2015.pdf

[76] Income is pre-tax and does not include capital gains or government transfers.

[77] Robert H. Frank and Philip Cook, *The Winner-Take-All-Society* (New York: Free Press, 1995).

[78] Chutes and Ladders is a board game invented by Milton Bradley. A trademark registration for the game's name filed on behalf of Hasbro, Inc. is pending at the U.S. Patent & Trademark Office.

[79] MIT economist Thomas Kochan inventoried the stress under which American families were operating in 2005; the conditions he chronicled worsened during and following the next, Great Recession of

2008-2009. Thomas A. Kochan, *Restoring the American Dream: A Working Families' Agenda for America* (Cambridge, Massachusetts: The MIT Press, 2005).

[80] The telephone interviews were conducted from Oct. 1 to 8, 2016. Kai Ryssdal, "Poll finds Americans economic anxiety reaches new high," *Marketplace*, October 13, 2016.
https://www.marketplace.org/2016/10/13/economy/americans-economic-anxiety-has-reached-new-high.

[81] In an article in the May 2016 edition of The Atlantic magazine, Gabler, a successful author, admitted that he was one of them. Neal Gabler, "The Secret Shame of Middle-Class Americans," The Atlantic, May 2016.
https://www.theatlantic.com/magazine/archive/2016/05/my-secret-shame/476415/.

[82] Even in the second-highest fifth, a family could maintain its normal spending for just 5.3 months. Next thing you know, they are needing money from a charity to pay their electric bill.

[83] J.D. Vance, *Hillbilly Elegy: A Memoir of a Family and Culture in Crisis* (New York: HarperCollins, 2017). The title is misleading: Vance's focus is more on middle-American rust belt towns such as the Middletown, Ohio, where he grew up. Citing the Pew Economic Mobility Project, Vance notes that among working-class white Americans, only 44 percent expect their children to be economically better off, and fully 42 percent report that they are less well-off economically than were their parents.

Chapter 8

Looking to the Future – The Special Case of China

As I undertook the question of what the future holds, I kept noticing that so much depended on what happened with China. Like it or not, China is having an inordinate effect of world affairs, and is casting a long shadow on the future. As we consider what the future holds if we stay on our present course, China requires special consideration.

China's Project: The Great Restoration

In Chapter 1, we picked up the China narrative at the end of World War II in 1945. However, to understand where China is and where it may be headed we must take note of two aspects its past.

The "Century of Humiliation"

The first is this: during the hundred-year period beginning about 1840, China slid backwards economically as the West leapt forward during the industrial revolution, and suffered a string of humiliating military defeats at the hands of the West and Japan.

Following its defeat by Britain in the First Opium War in 1839-1842, China became a quasi-colony; five ports were opened to foreign traders, and the British colony at Hong Kong was founded, not to be returned until 1997. The impact on the Chinese psyche can be grasped by imagining the Chinese seizing control of New Orleans and plying the Mississippi with gun boats.

China suffered another defeat in the Sino-Japanese War of 1894-1895, losing control of Korea. From 1927 to 1937, China suffered through a civil war, which was interrupted by another war with Japan, subsumed into World War II, when China was invaded, defeated, and harshly occupied by Japan. The Chinese refer to the period 1840 - 1945 as the "Century of Humiliation."

Memories of Greatness

The century is all the more humiliating because it is set against a backdrop that I would call "memories of greatness" – the second aspect to be borne in mind.

The Chinese are fond of referring to China's "five thousand years of history." The Han ethnic group traces its origin to the "Yellow Emperor," Huang Di, who united his and neighboring tribes to form the Yanhuang: the Chinese people still refer to themselves as "Descendants of Yan and Huang." According to the founding myth, the first dynasty, the Xia, was founded by Emperor Yu, who tamed the flooding Yellow River, thus earning the "mandate of heaven" of governorship.[1] The first "imperial dynasty" was the Qin, founded by Qin Shi Huang after defeating the other six of the Seven Warring States to gain control of the whole of China, and, among other things, built the Great Wall. The second imperial dynasty, the Han, dating from 206 BC, spanned four centuries, and is considered a golden age in Chinese history. The Chinese refer to themselves today as the "Han" people. In the view of the ancient and pre-modern Chinese, Chinese culture was the most advanced civilization of the world, one that would influence surrounding "barbarians;" the Han ethnic group embodied the civilized values and norms of behavior, but they could be taught to others.[2]

Geopolitically, the Chinese had a concept of "all land under heaven," with China, the "Middle Kingdom," at its center. China ruled the land under heaven; surrounding countries were "vassal" states subordinate to China. The "kowtow," kneeling and touching one's head to the ground before the Emperor, was a symbol of deference, and the tribute given on such occasions was met with a return gift, often of more value. In 1820, China was a leading world power, perhaps accounting for as much as a third of global GDP.[3] When Britain and other western "barbarian" countries came knocking on China's door seeking trade in China's tea, silk, and porcelain, their emissaries were made to wait, ironically, in what is now the southern export-producing zone, while go-betweens carried communications to Beijing.[4]

Several concepts are important here. The first, is that the Chinese consider Han ethnicity and Chinese nationality to be pretty much one and the same thing. There are two edges to this sword. On the one hand, it is hard to lose one's Chinese nationality; even those who have relinquished it, or are Han offspring born in other countries, are expected to support China's interests and may become subject to the state's control. On the other hand, it is almost impossible to become a citizen of China if one is not ethnic Han; even spouses of Han rarely naturalize.[5]

The second concept is called to our attention by Henry Kissinger in his book, *World Order*: In the historical Chinese view, the world order was not an arrangement among equal sovereign states, but rather a "universal hierarchy," with all known societies being in a tributary relationship to China, the "Middle Kingdom" of "All Under Heaven." [6]

Third is that for the Chinese, history plays an important part in current affairs, more so than in the United States, and even Japan, at least with respect to World War II. Zhen Wang of Seton Hall University suggests that it is helpful to consider China and its people through the lens of "chosen-ness" (a people chosen for a special purpose), trauma, and myths. The Chinese have a proud sense of chosen-ness through their founding myths as citizens of the "Middle Kingdom," tempered by the trauma of their humiliation under Western and Japanese imperialism.[7]

Fourthly, while Western commentators refer to a "rising" China, the view of the Chinese leadership and populace is that China is involved not in a "rise," but in a return to greatness. Western geopolitical commentators refer to China as a "revisionist" state intent on upsetting the *status quo* of the global order. On the contrary, the Chinese view themselves and their nation as involved in restoring a *status quo ante*, with reference to the "golden age" of the Han and other dynasties, which existed prior to the injustices visited upon China by the Western powers and Japan during the Century of Humiliation. Indeed, in the view of Zhen Wang:

> China's memory of this period as a time when it was attacked, bullied, and torn asunder by imperialists serves as the foundation for its modern identity and purpose . . . After suffering a humiliating decline in national strength and status, the Chinese people are unwavering in their commitment to return China to its natural state of glory . . . .[8]

Shortly after assuming his position as China's leader, and on many occasions since, Xi Jinping has stated the objective of his government as pursuit of the "Chinese Dream" of the "great rejuvenation of the Chinese nation."[9]

If we are to understand where China may be headed in the future, we must understand this view of China, its people, and its past as held by the Chinese people and leadership. For in my view, the goal of populace and leadership alike is the restoration of China's rightful place as the economic, political and military leader, not just of the Asian region, but of the world.[10] Because the Chinese believe China once held this position, I refer to this vision of the future as the "Great Restoration."

The Mao Era

However, the Great Restoration got off to a bad start. As we saw in Chapter 1, following World War II, China suffered through a continuation of its civil war, resulting in a communist government in 1949, with the defeated Nationalists relegated to what is now Taiwan.

Under communism and the leadership of Mao Zedong, the country suffered under a series of economic and social calamities including The Great Leap Forward and the Cultural Revolution, resulting in hardship and death for tens of millions. These problems were compounded by the country's isolation, imposed both from within by its communist leaders, and from without, by the U.S. and its allies seeking to contain the spread of Chinese communism. Except for efforts to spread communism in Asia, the country remained largely insular, despite the opening created by the 1972 visit to the country by President Richard Nixon and Secretary of State Henry Kissinger. GDP remained low, at about five percent of world GDP.[11]

The Deng Era

Upon Mao's death in 1976, China went through leadership changes leading to the adoption under Deng Xiaoping in December, 1978 of the "Reform and Opening" strategy of limited capitalism and less central control, and opening to foreign investment and trade.[12] However, real take-off was delayed by the return of hardliners to the government and the repression of the nationwide demonstrations in support of the Tiananmen Square protesters in 1989. The new era in the Chinese economy can be marked from Deng Xiaoping's "Southern Tour" in 1992, in which he reaffirmed the Opening and Reform.

The Chinese Economy Takes Off

Methods and Means

At the outset, in early 1980, Deng Xiaoping had declared a goal of quadrupling the Chinese GDP by the end of 1999. How would China achieve these results? Economic takeoff would require four ingredients: natural resources, labor, capital, and technology.

Acquiring the Factors of Production

China had vast reservoirs of two of the factors: labor (and, in fact, very cheap labor consisting of impoverished peasants in a population of over one billion), and natural resources (in a land mass the size of the United States including monopolies on rare earth minerals). But how to acquire technology and capital?

As to technology, as Justin Lin points out, there are two possibilities: technological innovation in both product (computer over abacus) and process (mass production over handcrafting) can be sourced either from research and development in the home country, or by borrowing from abroad. Lin notes that for developed countries like the United States, Germany, and Japan, which already have the most advanced technologies, R&D is the only option available. However, for developing countries that lag in technology, the options include "borrowing," *i.e.*, "importing technology, copying, and purchasing patent licenses."[13]

Given the high costs and low percentage chance of commercial success of R&D, Lin notes that for developing countries like China, obtaining technologies from developed countries is preferable. He cites Japan and the four "Asian Tigers" as being adept at technology borrowing and industrial upgrading, resulting in high rates of GDP growth. Lin notes that after the Reform and Opening in 1978, China copied their model of importing technology and capital.

So, having two of the essential four factors of production, China set out to "borrow" the other two, technology and capital, from other Asian countries and the West. How did it do so? Through two incentives.

First Incentive: Cheap Labor and Subsidies

Under the Reform and Opening, the government permitted the establishment of private firms outside the existing State-Owned Enterprises, and permitted foreign investment. It also created the Special Enterprise Zones with additional subsidies and tax and customs incentives, with the purpose of attracting production of highly labor-intensive products for export. In this, China copied the methods of Taiwan and the other "Tigers." In fact, most of the companies coming to the Special Enterprise Zones have been from Taiwan, Hong Kong, and the other Tigers.

Between the basic reforms and the creation of the Special Enterprise Zones, the Chinese government created an environment to attract from abroad the two missing factors: capital and technology. The basic motivation of those investing the capital and technology was to benefit from cheap labor and government subsidies to lower the costs of production of their products.[14]

Second Incentive: Access to Selling in the Chinese Market

There has been another, in the long run perhaps more powerful, incentive for those investing the capital and technology: the lure of sales of their products into the already large and potentially immense Chinese market. Western companies, including multinational companies headquartered in the United States, have been falling over each other as they scramble to enter the Chinese market, by whatever means expedient. These companies range in sophistication from trinkets and toys to pharmaceuticals, automobiles and aerospace, and everything in between.[15]

"Borrowing" Technology and Attracting Investment

Did China successfully implement this strategy? As to technology, Justin Lin has concluded that the principal reason for China's rapid economic growth after the Reform and Opening has been China's "borrowing" of technology at low costs to achieve rapid technology change.[16] The "borrowing" has taken many forms, from joint venture agreements with companies requiring them to share their technology, to copying, to industrial and military espionage.

For example, in May of 2015, six Chinese citizens were indicted in a scheme to transfer cell phone filter technology they worked on at the University of Southern California and two U.S. tech companies to a new company in China that would "save 'a lot' of money by not having to conduct research and development."[17] In June of 2015, Chinese government hackers allegedly stole "all personnel data for every federal employee, every federal retiree, and up to one million former federal employees," as well as major health insurers, with the alleged aim of recruiting spies or compromising individuals for espionage purposes.[18]

As to investment of capital, China has become a leading recipient of "foreign direct investment" (FDI).[19] In the early years, the lion's share of this investment came from the "Chinese diaspora" of ethnic Chinese living in Taiwan, Hong Kong, Macau, and Southeast Asia. Later, western multinational companies joined in, investing in joint ventures as they set up operations in China. During the period 1990 – 2015, China amassed $2.8 trillion in FDI, measured in 2016.

The Chinese government reported that FDI in 2016 increased 4.1 percent over 2015,[20] and, indeed, foreign investment appears to continue unabated. For example, in December 2016, FoxConn announced that a joint venture with Sharp of Japan (of which FoxConn now is a 65% owner) would invest $8.8 billion in an LCD television screen plant in Guangzhou.[21] During Chinese leader Xi Jinping's visit to the U.S. in September of 2016, Boeing announced that it would build a "completion and delivery center" for 737 airliners with a Chinese joint venture partner,[22] and Apple announced that it would increase its investment in China, including the creation of Apple's first research center there.[23]

In addition to these investments, as China sold more and more of the export-oriented products produced under these arrangements, China amassed the world's largest foreign currency reserves, reaching as high as $4 trillion in 2014. In 2016, these reserves stood at just over $3 trillion, after the Chinese government used some of them in purchases to support the Chinese currency.[24]

And so, China was quite successful at applying its existing factors and attracting the ones it lacked. These arrangements are summarized in the following Figure:

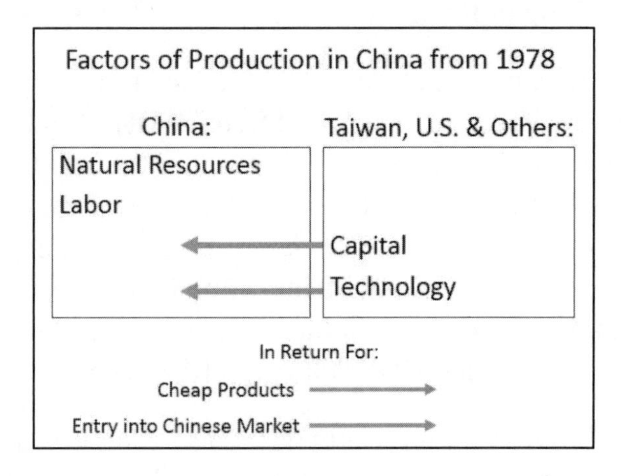

What other means did China employ in its pursuit of economic development?

Establishing & Subsidizing Industries: State Capitalism

China is operated by the Chinese Communist Party as a "socialist" country, to use their terminology. As such, it does not operate as a true market economy. The state remains heavily involved as an owner of business enterprises ("state-owned enterprises," or SOEs) and supports them, as well as most privately-owned enterprises, with heavy subsidies. A 2013 study found that most large Chinese companies receive substantial government subsidies. For example, Geely Automobile (owner of Volvo) got half of its net profits from government subsidies in 2011.[25]

Two economists, Usha C.V. Haley and George T. Haley, have concluded that China has pursued an "overarching policy of aggressively subsidizing targeted industries in order to dominate global markets."[26] In a series of studies, the Haleys added up the subsidies to major Chinese industries.[27] They determined that China provided energy subsidies totaling $27 billion from 2000 to 2007, as it moved from being a net importer of steel to the world's largest producer, creating an enormous overhang of excess supply in the process.

Similarly, they identified $33 billion in subsidies from 2002 to 2009 that enabled China to triple its paper production and overtake the U.S. to become the world's largest paper producer. In large part due to the subsidies, a country with one of the smallest amounts of forest in the world per capita, requiring it to import pulp and recycled paper, mostly from the United States, is able to undercut the price of U.S. and European paper.

China's industrial policy of targeting key industries, coupled with subsidies that are applied at the national, provincial and local level, result in entire sectors coming into being seemingly overnight, as in the case of solar panels.[28] Being a state-run economy, China could, and did, decide to get into the solar industry in a big way, increasing its capacity tenfold, building vast global excess capacity and driving down the price worldwide by 75 percent.[29]

One of the U.S. companies, SolarWorld, brought a trade complaint to the U.S. Commerce Department, which ruled that the Chinese were providing illegal subsidies and dumping the products into the U.S. market at below-cost prices, imposing stiff tariffs on the products. For its trouble, SolarWorld became the target of a Chinese military-operated espionage ring that was the subject of criminal indictments by the U.S. Justice Department earlier in 2014.[30] Even the Chinese companies have suffered from the overcapacity, with SunTech driven into bankruptcy requiring a bailout from Wuxi city.[31]

Much of the government assistance is local. This creates jobs and supports the local economy, helping politicians meet the GDP targets that are imposed on them by Beijing. Local officials see the support of new or expanded industries as a means for climbing the ladder of success within the Chinese Communist Party. However, this can work against the central government's efforts to eliminate overcapacity and inefficiency in the State-Owned Enterprises: as the Haleys note, "the central government's removal of subsidies has often resulted in the provincial governments increasing them." So, as The Economist has noted, "the unhappiest consequence of China's subsidy policy may be that it has created beasts too powerful to rein in."[32]

Indeed, a 2016 analysis of Chinese public companies conducted by the Wall Street Journal confirmed that the subsidies continue unabated. The Journal found continued Chinese government support including "billions of dollars in cash assistance, subsidized electricity and other benefits to companies" in sectors including steel, coal, solar, copper, and chemicals.[33] And a filing last year by U.S. Steel Corp., Nucor Corp. and the United Steelworkers union demanding countervailing duties on rolled steel, identified 44 separate subsidy programs, including seven that give Chinese steelmakers cheap or free land, iron ore, coal, and power;

eight that offer discount loans; 15 tax breaks; and 11 programs that give companies money directly.[34]

Of course, all of this is in violation of the rules of fair trade applied by the World Trade Organization and its constituent trading countries.

Legitimacy through World Institutions

Another tactic in China's economic development has been to obtain legitimacy and leverage through participation in international institutions.

We have noted the importance of China's 2001 admission to the World Trade Organization. In September of 2016, China achieved another milestone, with the Chinese currency, the yuan (aka Renminbi) being admitted to the "basket" of currencies used by the International Monetary Fund in its lending in emergency bailouts. The move gives the yuan a stamp of legitimacy, but is largely symbolic, questioned by many due to China's controls over exchange rates and capital movements. It is part of a broader strategy, in which China has "secured a foothold in nearly every major international financial institution, including installing senior executives at the IMF and the World Bank." For example, in September of 2016, China hosted the annual summit of the "G20" group of industrialized and emerging nations.

China also has pursued soft power and legitimacy through other organizations, such as winning rights to host the 2008 Olympic Games. Most recently, in January of 2017, Xi Jinping became the first Chinese president to attend the annual meeting of the World Economic Forum in Davos, Switzerland, where he was reported to receive a "fawning reception." [35]

China also has gone about setting up a number of alternative financial institutions of its own, including the $240 billion Chiang Mai Initiative, the $100 billion Contingency Reserve Arrangement, the $100 billion New Development Bank (with the BRICS countries of Russia, India, Brazil, and South Africa) and the $100 billion Asian Infrastructure Investment Bank, or AIIB. Washington had resisted the AIIB, but, outmaneuvered by China, has agreed to cooperate with it through the World Bank. (The AIIB is part of China's "One Belt, One Road" development and aid project, discussed below.)

At this writing, China hasn't yet achieved another milestone, designation as a "market economy" by the WTO. As a non-market economy, it is subject to anti-dumping actions with a lower burden of proof. This status has been elusive for the same reasons that China's currency is not considered safe :

> "because it doesn't have strong financial institutions like an independent central bank, trusted rule of law, and an open and transparent form of government with checks and balances. 'China has made abundantly clear it's not going to have any of these'" [36]

As 2016 ended, the United States had announced that it would not recognize market economy status for China and the European Union was rewriting its rules to the same effect, and China had launched a legal challenge with the World Trade Organization.[37]

Breaking Trade Rules

Which leads to another tactic China has employed in its pursuit of economic development: breaking trade rules.

With China's admission to the World Trade Organization in 2001, there were high hopes that it would move toward a market economy and abide by the WTO's fair trade rules. China has received enormous benefits from its WTO membership, in the form of elimination of tariffs on China's products and stability encouraging foreign investment. However, China but has not changed its behavior to conform to WTO rules:

- China heavily subsidizes both state-owned and private industry, as discussed above.

- China puts up a myriad of barriers to imports of products from other countries.

- When other countries contest these practices in the WTO dispute resolution mechanisms, China drags out the process before complying in the end, in the meantime doing much harm to the targeted industry in the U.S. or other country.

- China also has become adept at using unfounded claims of WTO violations by the U.S. and other countries to keep products out of China until the other country finally prevails after lengthy WTO proceedings.[38]

- China continues to fail to enforce intellectual property rights, resulting in high infringement levels in China, to the detriment of the patent and trademark holding companies whose products are being knocked off.

- China also keeps its economy opaque, failing to provide WTO-mandated information reports and translations.

Marking the tenth anniversary of China's admission, Long Yongtu, who helped China win admission to the WTO, said that China was "moving further away from the organization's principles. To modernize its economy, it has remained wedded to industrial policies, state-owned enterprises, and a 'techno-nationalism' that protects and promotes home-grown technologies." [39]

Nothing has changed in the ensuing five years. The Wall Street Journal has reported that WTO data show that China accounted for around 25 percent of all anti-dumping measures reported between 1995 and 2014, more than any other nation. The U.S. was the target in about 5% of measures.[40] And, as we will see, as of 2016, alleged illegal dumping of products by the Chinese was on the increase.

Economies of Scale and Industrial Clusters

Another aspect of China's economic development strategy is simply this: the country and its industrial enterprises are on a scale unmatched anywhere. Economic development professionals often speak of the advantages flowing from "economies of scale," and China, with its population and its methods of organizing industrial enterprises, can achieve these in spades. Reporting on the Chinese bid for the San Francisco – Oakland bridge project, Barlett and Steele noted a U.S. executive's reference to a Chinese steel fabricator with 32,000 employees, concluding: "It is not even a contest." [41] Or as Frank Yuan, a Taiwanese former middleman who did business with Wal-Mart, and who now heads an international apparel trade show, put it: "No one can compete with China. Such efficiency, such manpower." [42]

Furthermore, as export-oriented industrialization progressed, industry clusters sprang up, dedicated to manufacturing specific product lines, such as computers, household appliances, children's clothing, even specific products such as hosiery and neckties. These clusters included the entire supply chain associated with these end products, and they often account for a large percentage of the world's entire production of their specialty.[43]

Product Quality and Safety

It can also be argued that another of China's methods and means has been the reduction of costs via a widespread failure to apply standards adequate to assure the quality, and in some cases the safety, of products. This phenomenon has been reported periodically in the press, with respect to unsafe children's toys and tainted pharmaceutical products. Famous examples include Chinese drywall, which was found to be leaching hazardous chemicals into buildings in which it was installed, and, more recently, Chinese laminate flooring, which was found to be leaching formaldehyde.[44]

Imposing Social Costs

Perhaps most significantly, China has applied one more method in pursuit of its economic development: the failure to establish or enforce internal standards for health, safety, and living conditions in the workplace, and external protections against pollution and contamination of air, water, and soil by industrial operations. Avoiding these costs has played an important role in establishing the "China Price," but has resulted in social costs of a magnitude so large as to be difficult to grasp.

Harsh Working Conditions

We have seen that abundant low-wage labor has been a pillar of China's economic development strategy. However, in addition to paying low wages, Chinese companies have kept costs low by other means, at the expense of workers. These include the adoption of the "Factory Labor Camp" model, with harsh working and living conditions. Under this model, workers put in ten- and twelve-hour shifts six or seven days a week, often standing the entire time. They are housed in adjacent, Spartan dormitories with many workers sharing a room furnished only by bunk beds and shelves for a few belongings, with inadequate toilet and laundry facilities.

In Chapter 2, we saw how as early as 1979 the Chinese furniture industry also was reported to be following the model, and how even the Boeing factory in Xianjin was set up this way. Barlett and Steele compared the Vise-Grip employees who had "lived in neat, well-kept houses on quiet lanes nor far from the plant" in De Witt, Nebraska, to the plant making Vise-Grips for Newell in China, where workers were packed twelve to a room in dormitories next to the factory. [45]

Perhaps the most famous application of the model has been by the Taiwanese company Foxconn, in its "Foxconn City electronics production plant in Shenzhen, where it produces Apple iPads and iPhones.[46] In that enormous complex, eighteen employees committed suicide by jumping from the dormitory roofs, prompting Foxconn to install suicide-prevention nets, which at this writing are still in place.[47]

Perhaps an even more stark example of the Big Squeeze than Apple is provided by Dell computers. In February of 2013 the company's founder Michael Dell and a private equity firm "took the company private," that is, bought its stock and delisted it from the stock exchange, in a move to improve its sales and profitability. Dell promptly announced his intention to accomplish these goals by further squeezing costs out of Dell's supply chain, and wasted no time in doing so. In March of 2013, according to industry reports, Dell asked for price reductions from its two chassis suppliers, one of them a subsidiary of Apple computer maker FoxConn, and invited a third company to become a major supplier, putting pressure on the other two.[48]

How did Dell's cost cutting efforts play out on the ground? A few months later, in November of 2013, China Labour Watch and DanWatch, a Denmark-based independent watchdog, conducted a joint undercover investigation that provided a window into the working conditions Dell's suppliers imposed in their efforts to meet Dell's demands.[49]

Investigators found rural migrant workers, many of them under eighteen years of age, and many of them "student interns" paid even less than the standard wage, working seven day, seventy-four-hour weeks. Most of the work was done standing for ten to twelve hours a day, with the only rest during short meal breaks. Workers were expected to meet extremely high quotas set by supervisors on the factory floor, but with high quality, and were fined for their mistakes.

At one factory, three thousand workers lived in austere quarters adjacent to the factory, eight to ten to a room. They stood in line for one shower per ninety workers, running out of hot water, and in the women's dormitories, for one toilet for every fifty-five workers. They had to boil water to drink.

Rent, along with other fees, was subtracted from an already small pay check. The workers had to work excessive overtime to make ends meet, working up to 300 hours a month, in violation of Chinese law, International

Labor Organization rules, and Dell's policies. Even then, pay was $500 a month, half the average wage in Shenzhen.

One eighteen-year-old worker described the conditions on the factory floor saying, She said she found the work exhausting because of the repetitive movements and long hours. 'We have to stand up the entire twelve-hour shift; to sit down, you have to ask for permission."

Eva Hesse Lundström, editor of DanWatch, said: 'When companies compete on supplying computers in the cheapest way possible, and when our public buyers aim for the cheapest wares on the market, a high human cost is paid."[50]

Occupational Injury and Disease

But, in addition to long hours, low pay, and harsh working and living conditions, there are other practices, with far worse effects. Sometimes dangerous chemicals such as n-hexane and benzene are used because they dry quickly, permitting an operation such as cleaning a screen to be performed in less time. Sometimes ventilation, masks and protective clothing, and other standard measures are not implemented, to save costs. Sometimes machines are operated with safety features removed to increase production. Sometimes whole factories are operated without adequate precautions for flammable materials.[51]

The result: occupational disease, injury, and death: workers breathing and handling hazardous chemicals and metals resulting in neurological damage, leukemia, and other disorders; workers using unsafe machinery, resulting in loss of digits, limbs, and life; and workers dying when their factory explodes or catches fire.[52] In 2005, the United Nations reported that more than 200 million Chinese workers in 16 million companies were exposed to dangerous working conditions.[53]

The most immediately visible effects are workplace injuries. According to a 2007 report from China Labor Watch, workers in the Pearl River District lose 40,000 fingers to industrial accidents a year. One investigator who went to see firsthand reported thus:

> After witnessing the violence of China's manufacturing process over a couple of weeks in Shenzhen and Dongguan, I was reminded of the gun violence in certain American communities. It seemed like every Chinese migrant worker either had a hand injury, a repetitive stress injury or had lost a limb (or life). And if they themselves hadn't experienced this they knew someone who had.[54]

In addition to injuries, some hazards lead to occupational diseases. In some cases, there are immediate effects, as in the case of neurological damage. Long Li was a new member of the "global middle class." At age 18, in 2011, she left her parents' farm for Dongguan, where she cleaned cell phone screens, one every ten to twenty seconds, at Fangtai Huaei Electronic Technology. With overtime, she could make $485 per month, or $16 a day, putting her solidly in the "global middle class" according to the international economists. Except that the solution she used to clean the screens contained n-hexane, which caused her, and about thirty of her co-workers to lose the use of their fingers, then their arms, and then their legs, and to be hospitalized and endure painful injections in an effort to cure the neurological damage. Cases such as hers are widespread. In other cases, such as exposure to the carcinogen benzene, effects such as leukemia take longer to become evident.[55]

In other cases, occupational disease takes longer to have effect, as in exposure to industrial dust, resulting in silicosis. Silicosis is a debilitating lung disease; it and "black lung," common among coal miners, fall in the category of diseases known as pneumoconiosis. In 2005, China officially reported 665,043 cases of occupational disease, of which 606,891, about 90 percent, were pneumoconiosis patients.[56] By the end of 2013, China these numbers had risen to 833,700 cases of people with occupational diseases, of which 750,000 were pneumoconiosis cases.[57]

The computer and phone industry involves a high incidence of exposure not only to chemicals, but also to metallic dust. Another large Chinese industry, semiprecious stones, involves exposure to dust. Alexandra Harney followed the case of Deng Wenping, who died at age 36 after contracting silicosis while grinding semiprecious stones.[58]

In December of 2016, the central government announced its intention to step up its control of occupational diseases, calling for the transformation or phasing-out of hazardous workplaces and the expansion of health insurance coverage for affected people. Targeting major improvements in occupational health by 2020, the new guideline called on local authorities to support research, prevention, control, diagnosis and treatment of occupational diseases.[59]

The new guidelines were included in the Five-Year Plan issued in January of 2017, which included new requirements for companies, improved enforcement of standards, and improved compensation for victims. The plan acknowledged that "the level of occupational diseases can be classified as severe in China" and that more than 30,000 new cases are reported each year.[60]

However, because the plan is left largely to local implementation, and with economic pressure on local authorities to retain jobs, I would not expect any significant improvement in the foreseeable future. Meanwhile, those who are injured or contract occupational diseases face great challenges pursuing treatment and compensation.

Environmental Health

What of the failure to impose costs of environmental protection on Chinese companies? It has taken a heavy toll outside the factory, except in this case the harm is not limited to the workers, but rather is felt by the entire population.

Indeed, the consequences are not even limited to the Chinese. The U.S. tracks dust, sulfur, soot, and trace metals as they travel across the Pacific from China; on some days, the EPA estimates that twenty-five percent of air pollution from particulates in Los Angeles originates in China; rising deposits of mercury in American soil have been traced to Chinese power plants and cement factories; South Korea suffers from acid rain due to emissions from Chinese coal-fired power plants. China is the largest polluter of the Pacific Ocean; in 2007, more than 80 percent of the East China Sea, one of the world's largest fisheries, was rated unsuitable for fishing, up from 53 percent in 2000. Much of China's timber imports comes from illegal logging that is devastating environments in other countries. China has surpassed the U.S. as the largest greenhouse gas emitter; in 2007, it was projected to double the entire output of the industrialized west (the OECD countries) in 25 years. [61]

But, of course, the consequences are most severe within China. Alexandra Harney has reported that the Chinese landscape is dotted with "widow towns" and "cancer villages" where husbands have died of occupational disease and women give birth to babies with deformities and disabilities.[62]

China's energy consumption more than doubled from 2000 to 2010 alone, and about 70 percent of its energy comes from coal-fired power plants. Between power plants, industrial plants, and vehicle emissions, China's air is extremely polluted, largely with microscopic "particulates" from the coal-fired plants, that lodge in the lungs causing respiratory disease.

One expert says breathing Beijing's air is the equivalent of smoking almost forty cigarettes a day.[63] In January 2013, Beijing experienced a prolonged bout of smog so severe that citizens dubbed it "airpocalypse," prompting the establishment of an air quality alert system. Recurrent reports of severe smog appear regularly in the press, culminating in December 2015 with the first "red alert" in Beijing, requiring school closings and curtailment of vehicle use.[64] The problem is widespread: a 2012 Asian Development Bank report found that less than one percent of China's 500 largest cities meet the World Health Organization's air quality standards. A reported 83 percent of Chinese breath air that the U.S. Environmental Protection Agency would deem unhealthy or unhealthy for sensitive groups. Estimates of annual deaths due to air pollution run from 1.2 to 1.6 million, 13 to 17 percent of the total.[65]

Water is even worse. It is in severely short supply, especially in the northern, Yellow River basin, and pollution is at disastrous levels: almost 90 percent of underground water in cities and 70 percent of China's rivers and lakes are now polluted. A 2005 survey of 509 cities revealed that only 23 percent of factories properly treated sewage before disposing of it. According to another report, one-third of all industrial wastewater in China and two-thirds of household sewage were released untreated.[66] Combined with negligent farming practices, the water crisis has turned much of China's arable land into desert, which today claims around 27.5 percent of China's total land mass. Some 400 million Chinese lives are affected by desertification, according to the government.[67]

And then there is soil: A 2006 survey found that almost ten percent of farmland was contaminated with heavy metals, such as cadmium. The *Economist* reported that in 2013, the discovery of rice tainted with cadmium in Guangdong triggered panic buying of Thai rice.[68]

The effects on health have been serious: one study concluded that air pollution contributed to 1.2 million premature deaths in China in 2010; other studies have found that urban air in China causes respiratory, cardio-vascular, and cerebrovascular diseases. Studies have suggested that around eleven percent of digestive system cancers in China may stem from unsafe drinking water.[69]

The central government repeatedly has issued programs and plans to curtail the pollution. However, Deng Xiaoping's economic reforms diffused authority to the provinces, encouraging the creation of township and village enterprises (TVEs) to spread economic growth into the countryside. Today, adoption of effective environmental policies is hampered because local officials' incentives remain directed at economic, not environmental outcomes.

The central government also is keen to avoid public uprising over environmental issues, of the kind that led to the environmental movement in the U.S. For example, In March of 2015, *Under the Dome*, a TED Talk-style documentary on China's air pollution went viral, attracting hundreds of thousands of views before Internet censors blocked access to it.[70]

Since 1989, China has been operated under an implicit agreement: the regime promises improving material well-being of the people in exchange for their support of the party's monopoly on political power. With the advent of citizen unrest over environmental problems, solving the pollution issue is becoming very important to the Chinese party leadership; however, with the economy slowing, I would expect economic growth to take priority, and China to continue to pursue that growth by avoiding the costs of workplace safety and environmental health.[71]

The "Left Behind" Children

Another cost-saving device has had perhaps the most profound impact on workers and their families. Under the Chinese *Hukou* system of internal migration control, the government permits workers from remote regions to migrate to factory centers such as Shenzhen. However, to save the costs of schools and other infrastructure, the government does not permit these workers to bring their children with them. They must be left behind, to be cared for by grandparents or through other arrangements. Estimates of the number of these children range from 60 to 160 million.[72] Besides the emotional cost to them and their parents, their development is impaired by a second-rate, rural education and damage to their psychological and social development. The Chinese government has announced steps to ameliorate the problem, but they are limited in scope, and would require the workers to choose one place of residence: the rural workers often do not wish to give up their right to return to their rural home.[73]

A Joint Venture

It would be unfair to say that the use of these cost-saving tactics, at the expense of the occupational health of the Chinese workers and the environmental health of the Chinese populace, were all the doing of the Chinese government and companies. In many ways, they did take the initiative, to lure the foreign companies with low cost.

But perhaps the greater impetus has come from the foreign companies themselves. Wal-mart, Apple, Samsung, and the rest have applied ruthless pressure to their suppliers to cut costs, even while going through the motions of requiring workplace safety and protections against overwork and underpay. As Adam Matthews summed it up, "Apple leans on Foxconn, which leans on Wintek, which leans on its supplier, who skimps on safety to protect razor-thin margins." [74]

The "push" from the multinational companies and the "pull" from the Chinese government and companies becomes a "joint venture" that is a toxic mix for the Chinese people inside and outside the factories. And, of course, the final party to this arrangement is the American consumer, buying the product made under these conductions. As Alexandra Harney put it, "we all pay the China Price."[75]

Economic Results

China has acquired the factors of production, and has deployed them in a form of "state capitalism" using substantial state subsidies, access to international institutions while manipulating trade rules, taking advantage of huge economies of scale, and avoiding costs of workplace safety and environmental protection.

How has that turned out?

Gross Domestic Product

The first measure of China's economic development must be its annual Gross Domestic Product, the sum of its total economic activity. The following figure shows China's GDP, along with that of the U.S., from 1990, expressed in 2016 U.S. dollars, as reported by the World Bank.

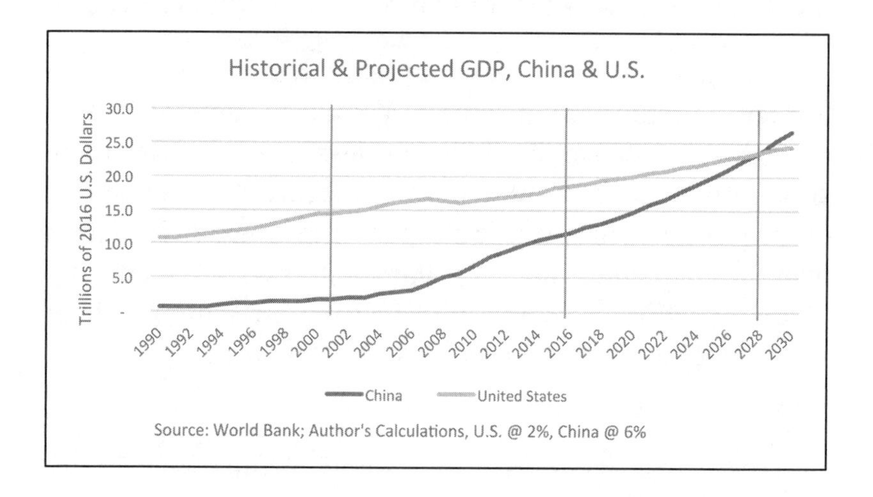

In 2015, China's GDP was $11 trillion, compared to $18 trillion for the U.S. Assuming a growth rate of two percent for the U.S., which is consistent with recent rates, and a growth rate of six percent for China, about a half percent lower than recent rates, China's GDP can be expected to surpass that of the U.S. in twelve years, in 2028.[76]

There is another way to measure GDP, known as "Purchase Power Parity," in which a country's GDP is adjusted to account for price differences in domestically produced goods and services. For example, if a meal or a haircut costs $20 in the United States, but only $12 in China, then the $12 of production in China is adjusted upward to equal $20, for an apples-to-apples comparison. The following figure shows China's GDP versus that of the U.S. as measured by purchase power parity, as reported by the World Bank:

Using this method of measurement, China's GDP passed that of the U.S. in 2013, when China's GDP was PPP$16.8 trillion, and U.S. GDP was $16.7 trillion. Looking forward, with growth rates of two and six percent for the U.S. and China, respectively, China could pull far out ahead of the U.S. However, whether China can sustain six percent annual growth is very much in question, and I have a prescription at the end of this book for how we can get the U.S. economy growing faster than two percent.

Manufacturing

Before you become too complacent about China's not yet having passed the U.S., at least in GDP measured in nominal dollars, I must point out that China already has outstripped the U.S. in manufacturing. As shown in the following figure, China passed the U.S. in 2010 and continued to grow, while the U.S. stagnated:

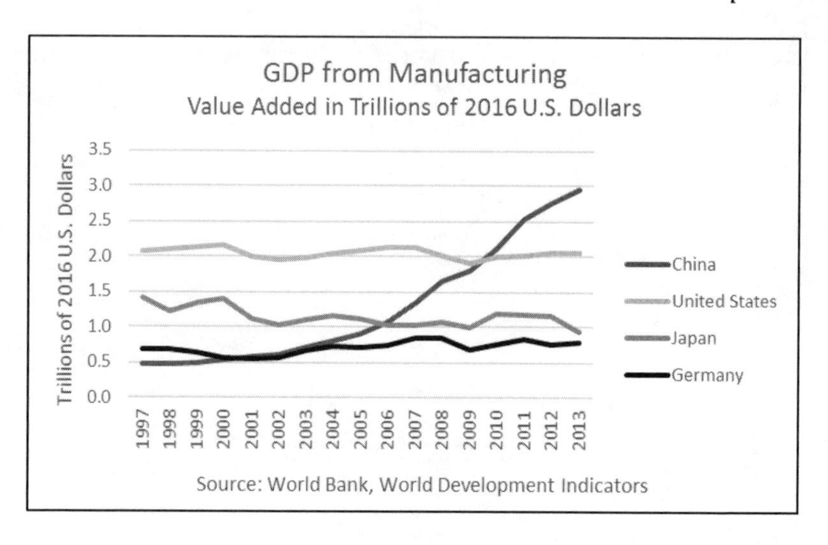

From 1990 to 2015, China's share of the world's manufacturing output rose from less than 3% to nearly 25%. China produces about 80% of the world's air-conditioners, 70% of its mobile phones and 60% of its shoes. Despite new competition from other low-wage producers like Vietnam, China has largely held onto its production of low-cost goods. For example, its share of global clothing exports has risen, from 42.6% in 2011 to 43.1% in 2013. One reason is China's clusters of efficient suppliers that are hard to replicate elsewhere. These clusters also have helped move China's domestic content in its exports from 40% to 65%.[77]

Vehicle Manufacturing

China is now by far the world's largest producer of automobiles (with the U.S. ranking a distant fourth), and the second largest producer of commercial vehicles, behind the U.S., as indicated in the following Table (The table also shows the percent change from the previous year):

Automobile & Commercial Vehicle Production in 2016				
Top Ten Countries, Millions of Units Produced				
Country	Cars	Comm Veh	Total	% Chge
China	24.4	3.7	28.1	14.50%
USA	3.9	8.3	12.2	0.80%
Japan	7.9	1.3	9.2	-0.80%
Germany	5.7	0.3	6.1	0.50%
India	3.7	0.8	4.5	7.90%
South Korea	3.9	0.4	4.2	-7.20%
Mexico	2.0	1.6	3.6	0.90%
Spain	2.4	0.5	2.9	5.60%
Canada	0.8	1.6	2.4	3.80%
Brazil	1.8	0.4	2.2	-11.20%

Prosperity, Unequally Shared

For many Chinese, these national statistics have translated into improved lifestyles. The Chinese state news agency reported that in 2014, the number of privately-owned passenger cars topped 100 million – an average of 25 for every 100 households. In a reflection of the uneven spread of China's economic prosperity, Beijing had the highest concentration, with 63 cars for every 100 households.[78] *The Economist* has concluded that "China is very unequal," noting that the fivefold spread between China's richest and poorest provinces exceeds even the four-fold spread of Brazil's.[79]

In China, with a few exceptions, the contrast is between the coastal manufacturing areas and the interior raw-materials producing areas. The interior made economic strides as the boom of the 1990s drove commodities prices up, and they used the new-found money in local building booms; when commodities prices dropped, the boom produced "ghost towns" they have been unable to fill. Some manufacturers have moved inland in search of cheaper labor, but the supplier "network effects" are mostly keeping them near the coast.

The New Chinese Imperialism

So, China has newfound wealth, that has come at a high social cost. What has it been doing with it? As I have said, in my view, the ultimate goal of the Chinese populace and leadership alike is the restoration of China's place as the economic, political and military leader, not just of the Asian region, but of the world, the vision I have referred to as the "Great Restoration." China's efforts toward this end constitute a new Chinese imperialism, that has economic, cultural, and military dimensions.

Economic Imperialism

Loans and Aid in Return for Business

One manifestation of China's economic materialism is the practice of providing development assistance in return for business for Chinese firms, access to raw materials, or both. Over the years, and especially since 2000, China has poured billions of dollars into Latin America, Africa, and worldwide, mostly in the form of long-term loans in support of infrastructure and other projects. One analyst counted $630 billion of Chinese overseas investments from 2005 to 2015, two-fifths of them in energy projects and sources;[80] China's state-owned development bank reportedly has surpassed the World Bank in international lending.[81]

China has been active in countries where western institutions have left openings, due to funding limitations, political considerations (e.g., Russia after the Crimean and Ukraine episodes), perceptions of risk levels, or preference of the receiving country. For example, developing countries may be reluctant to put on the "golden straight jacket" of the IMF, with respect to opening borders to capital flows and limitations on budget deficits.

In the case of Ecuador, the country defaulted on its previous IMF loans, which its president called "immoral and illegitimate;" the country since has borrowed some $11 billion from China, financing numerous infrastructure, mining, and energy projects across the country, and is looking for more.[82] In Nigeria, civil war, nationalizations, and broken contracts have led western companies to stay away or demand large profit margins. Chinese companies have stepped in, with construction companies, mostly state-owned, starting more than $24 billion in projects since 2005.[83]

But the Chinese financing comes with its own conditions. Interest rates can be high, and payment can be guaranteed in the form of rights to oil or minerals. For example, the New York Times has reported that China has tied up close to 90 percent of Ecuador's oil exports, most of it going to repay loans.[84]

In the case of projects financed by the Chinese Export-Import Bank, the very purpose of the financing is to support foreign countries' purchases of Chinese materials and services. But even projects financed with loans made through China's development bank often require, or wind up using, Chinese materials and construction services. China can impose these restrictions because it is still considered a developing country, not bound by the rules applicable to the U.S. and other industrialized countries.[85] In Nigeria, the local steel industry languishes, while Chinese construction companies bring in girders, beams, and other materials from China.[86]

The repayment terms may be beyond the borrowing countries' capabilities, especially when commodities prices fall, as they have in 2014 and 2015. A senior Chinese banker told the New York Times that China likely would restructure such loans, not by reducing the amount owed, but by extending the repayment period – locking up the borrowers' natural resources for a longer period. And, the banker told the Times, China could make the borrowers pay, by threatening to cut off the manufactured goods that the Chinese had come to dominate.[87]

A former U.S. State Department official characterized China as becoming "the new company store for developing oil-, gas- and mineral-producing countries . . . what we need to worry about is the way they are encouraging oil-producing countries to mortgage their long-term future through oil-backed loans." [88] As a former Ecuadorian official put it, "The problem is we are trying to replace American imperialism with Chinese imperialism." [89]

One Brazilian newspaper described Brazil's relationship with China as "semi-colonial," claiming that the country's economy "depends in excess on Chinese prosperity." At the time, Brazil's exports to China through July of 2015 were down nearly 24 percent from the same period the previous year. [90]

Ironically, it is the Chinese economy's slowdown that inhibits the borrowing countries' ability to pay. It is a vicious circle: China purchases oil and minerals and lends commodity-exporting developing countries the money with which to purchase Chinese materials and construction services on infrastructure projects. This props up both countries' economy for a while, but the Chinese economy slows down nonetheless. The Chinese slowdown reduces demand for commodities, and commodity prices drop. The borrowing countries have less capability to pay on their loans.

There also is concern that China is exporting its worst practices in terms of worker pay and safety and environmental impacts. A case in point is the $2.2 billion Coca Codo Sinclair hydroelectric project, which will divert water from the Coca river to eight giant Chinese-built turbines. with the goal of producing enough electricity to light more than a third of Ecuador. The hydroelectric project is led by Sinohydro, the Chinese engineering company, and financed by the Chinese Export-Import Bank.

On this project, workers were paid $600 a month, until, after work stoppages, pay was raised to $900 a month, more in line with Ecuadorean standards. Nevertheless, Ecuadorean workers have repeatedly protested about wages, health care, food and general working conditions.

The Chinese construction companies reportedly lord it over the local workers, whom they consider inferior. An Ecuadorean worker told the New York Times, "The Chinese are arrogant... They think they are superior to us." Another said, "You make a little mistake, and they say something like, 'Get out of here' ... They want to be the strongmen." [91] And conditions can be unsafe. After an underground river burst into a tunnel, killing a number of workers, a worker testified at a legislative hearing, "I am a welder, and on various occasions I have been obligated to work in extreme conditions of high risk, deep in water."[92] (And we thought using a hair dryer in a bathtub might be dangerous!)

The future calls for more of these kinds of deals; in January of 2015 China and the African Union signed a memorandum of understanding for development of Africa's rail, road, and air infrastructure, and industrialization.[93]

And in December of 2015, China pledged an additional $60 billion in financing to support sustainable development in African nations. The pledge came at a China-Africa summit China had been holding every three years since 2000, and tripled the $20 billion pledged at the previous meeting. China's leaders sought to dampen criticism that the relationship may have been in China's favor, promising a "win-win" arrangement, and casting China as a fellow developing country in league with the African nations. China positions itself as not imposing terms required by the West; critics contend that China is coddling authoritarian African governments. [94]

In another significant initiative, China launched the "One Belt, One Road" development and aid project, a kind of "Marshall Plan" involving financing and construction of infrastructure designed to export some of China's industrial overcapacity. Involving some 65 countries, with funding of $1 trillion planned in the first ten years and perhaps another $2 trillion afterwards, the initiative is designed to bring about a new economic order in Asia with China at the center.[95]

In all this activity, at the end of the day, the risk ultimately falls back on the Chinese government; a Chinese government agency, Sinosure, has guaranteed the loans. Sinosure insured a reported $427 billion worth of Chinese exports and overseas construction projects around the world in 2013 alone; by comparison, the U.S. Export-Import Bank issued a reported $5 billion worth of credit in 2013 and 2014.[96]

Buying Raw Materials and Selling Manufactured Goods.

But China is not content with this arrangement – it also is taking over the domestic markets of the developing nations. Simply put, China's manufacturing industry has destroyed its counterparts in countries in Africa, Latin America, and Asia.

The Nigerian textile and apparel industry serves as a case study. Over two decades, employment in the industry has fallen from 600,000 to 20,000.[97] "The Chinese basically copy every textile product in Nigeria," a town leader told the New York Times.[98] Chinese companies produce African designs using synthetic dyes, that are sold in the Nigerian markets at low prices. In Kano, employment in the local fabric-dying business has fallen from nearly 1,500 to 250 people over a decade. The city's tanneries also have laid off most of their staffs. Even with lower local wages, the Nigerian businesses cannot compete with the Chinese companies, which enjoy low-cost, subsidized energy and mass production. The loss of jobs has brought street protests blaming China.

The flood of Chinese products is not limited to apparel; low-cost Chinese goods are widespread. As in the United States, the benefits of low price are offset by the loss of jobs and depressing effect on wages. And many of the goods are shoddy and, in such cases as electrical products, dangerous. [99]

Nigeria and the other commodities-producing nations are desiring to develop their own manufacturing bases. But they cannot, when they are faced with the low-cost imports from China. So, at best, if they are lucky, they have some raw materials the Chinese want to buy, and they sell those to the Chinese in exchange for the manufactured goods. But, on average, the supplier of commodities always comes out on the shorter end of the stick than the manufacturer using those commodities; that is how colonialism works. That is what India rebelled against, when, at Ghandi's urging, they went back to their homespun garments in place of the clothing being made in English factories.

Buying Companies and Technology

Another aspect of China's economic imperialism is its practice of simply buying companies in other countries, gaining not only ownership of the business enterprise, but also of the company's technology, which can be put to other uses. Recent examples:

In June of 2016, China's Haier Group purchased General Electric's appliance division for a reported $5.6 billion. Haier, which previously had 1.1 percent of the U.S. market, would acquire GE's 14 percent market share. GE appliances employs some 12,000 workers, 4,000 of them at the "Appliance Park" in Louisville, Kentucky. (In November, the workers' union rejected a contract offer that included no pay raises and plans to bring in new hires at lower pay.)[100]

In 2016, the Chinese appliance company Midea purchased Kuka, a German maker of robots and one of Germany's most innovative companies. And a Chinese firm was seeking to buy a German lighting company that was second in size only to the Dutch company Philips.[101] In the first three quarters of 2016, Chinese companies spent nearly $11 billion purchasing German companies, far exceeding the previous record of $2.6 billion in 2014. The German government is seeking European regulations to strengthen its ability to stop sales "driven by industrial policy or to enable technology transfers." European Union officials have expressed sympathy for the idea that "Europe's high-tech industry should not just be 'sold off.'"[102] Similarly, Australia has resisted Chinese efforts to buy huge swaths of Australian farmland, and Chinese technology investments are receiving greater scrutiny in the United States.

China's total foreign direct investment abroad rose at a rate of 35 percent per year since 2003, and was expected to hit $170 billion in 2016. However, due to growing foreign resistance and Chinese government efforts to limit outbound capital flows, the Chinese are forecasting a slowdown to a level of $118 billion in 2017.[103]

Nevertheless, outbound FDI should remain strong. For example, China has a deal to invest $8 billion in a large, new nuclear power plant at Hinckley Point in southwest England, to be built by the French, with a second plant to follow, this one to be built by the Chinese.[104]

Cultural Imperialism

Some of China's efforts can best be categorized as "cultural imperialism," which I would divide into "hard" and "soft". The "hard" version is at work in the territories within China's national borders, such as Tibet, where local customs and languages are suppressed, and Han language and customs take over, partly through movement of ethnic Han into the territory. Monasteries and nunneries are destroyed, shut, or ordered to reduce their populations; schools teach entirely in Mandarin and people have been jailed for continuing to teach in the Tibetan language. The Tibetan leader in exile, the Dalai Lama, refers to these activities as "cultural genocide."[105]

The "soft" version is a form of "soft power," and is basically a public-relations or "propaganda" campaign spreading information supportive of the Chinese regime.

One example is the film industry. As of 2016, Dalian Wanda Group, the largest owner of movie theaters in China, had acquired or was acquiring several U.S. companies that would make it the largest movie exhibitor in North America. The company and its chairman, Wang Jianlin, reportedly have close ties to the Chinese government. Wang has told Hollywood that it needs to access the fast-growing Chinese market by "increas[ing] the Chinese element" of movies; "If you want to make a little money . . . You have to find ways to please the Chinese audience."[106]

However, one also must please the Chinese government and censors. Under the previous regime led by Hu Jintao, the Chinese Communist Party accused the West of waging "cultural warfare" against China, trying to "Westernize" and "divide" it. Feeling the urgency of "enhancing its soft power," the Party adopted guidelines designed to portray the Chinese regime in a good light and to prevent any mention of human rights violations, China's military adventurism, or conflicts in Tibet or other provinces. In the spring of 2014, under the current regime, several large deals were struck for Chinese-financed joint ventures with major U.S. film studios, whose projects must comply with these guidelines.[107] Films such as one opening at this writing are being made for display on both Chinese and U.S. screens; in such cases the U.S. film industry now effectively is operating under Chinese censorship.

Another example is the "Confucius Institutes" funded by the Chinese central government located within, and co-funded by, colleges and universities around the world.[108] As of 2012, there reportedly were more than 300 such institutes in more than 90 countries, with about 70 in the United States. The institutes are centers of Chinese language and culture education and research. However, they are intended to promote a positive and benign image of Chinese society and political systems, and China's propaganda chief is quoted as calling them "an important part of China's overseas propaganda setup."[109]

The Institutes are not unlike others such as the *Alliance Française*, British Council, and the *Goethe-Institut*, except that the Institutes are located within universities, which one commentator called "astonishing." Another, a professor at Columbia university, said it is fallacious to think that taking money from the Chinese government would not have any long-term consequences. A Stanford professor believes it inevitably will influence the way Chinese studies are taught.[110] Considering the social and environmental costs the Chinese government has been tolerating at home and imposing on developing nations abroad, and the human rights limitations and abuses I discuss below, I believe the universities hosting these Institutes are indeed engaged in a Faustian bargain.

Yet another example is Beijing's covert ownership and operation of some thirty-three radio stations worldwide, more than a dozen of them in the United States. The government's radio propaganda arm, Radio International China, refers to this as their "borrowed boat" strategy of using existing foreign media outlets. This, in turn, is part of a larger strategy, as expressed by Chinese President Xi Jinping in 2014: "We should increase China's soft power, give a good Chinese narrative and better communicate China's message to the world." Listeners to these stations and programs heard a quite different narrative of the 2014

Hong Kong democracy protests, for example, than was heard on mainstream news media.[111]

Military Imperialism

Another dimension of China's new imperialism involves imperialism conducted by flexing military muscle.

Military Buildup

To conduct this kind of imperialism, China has pursued an extraordinary, decades-long build-up in its armed forces, with annual budget increases in the double digits.[112] China's actual defense spending has been estimated to be as high as $200 billion. At those levels, the Chinese budget dwarfs those of neighboring countries, whose spending in 2012 the Pentagon estimated as: Russia, $61.3 billion; Japan, $58 billion; India, $45.5 billion; South Korea, $29.2 billion; and Taiwan, 10.8 billion.[113]

China's military is the largest in the world, with some estimates as high as 2.3 million total personnel, and is developing its own fleet of submarines and aircraft carriers, a new generation stealth fighter, and medium-range missiles capable of knocking out American aircraft carriers. China also is using state-sponsored industrial and economic espionage and technology transfer to acquire technology fueling its fast-paced military modernization program and cut its reliance on foreign arms makers.

In its introduction to a special series of reports in 2013 regarding China's "quest to counter U.S. military might", Thomson Reuters stated:

> China's military budget - second only to America's - has soared to almost $200 billion. Its top leader, Xi Jinping, is championing a renaissance aimed at

> China asserting its dominance in Asia and beyond. Its quest to modernize its military has been abetted by U.S. allies in Europe. And China's attempts to get American military technology it cannot legally acquire extends beyond cyber espionage to a broad smuggling effort that enlists local confederates whom U.S. authorities struggle to stop.[114]

Reuters also has reported on the "increasingly hawkish rhetoric coming from senior officers in the People's Liberation Army" gaining widespread coverage in the Chinese media, including one officer's call for a "short, decisive war, like China's border clash with India in 1962." Reuters also has reported that Japan's Defense Ministry has expressed concern over the possibility that the Chinese armed forces is acquiring a growing role in shaping foreign policy.[115]

In any event, with the buildup of funding and new weapons systems, according to Reuters, "For the first time in its modern history, China has the firepower to contest control of disputed territory far from its coastal waters." [116] In 2015, the Chinese State Council issued a policy document confirming these intentions, with the navy moving from an offshore to an open seas focus, and the air force moving from territorial defense to "both defense and offense." The government backed up the goals with an officially declared ten percent increase in defense spending.[117]

Territorial Claims

As China's military capabilities have grown, it has begun flexing its muscle in surrounding territory and waters.

East China Sea

One flash point has been the East China Sea, lying between China, Korea, and Japan. In November of 2013, China established an "air defense identification zone" in the East China Sea, which overlapped with Japanese and South Korean airspace.

China has claimed rights to uninhabited islands in the East China Sea, which Japan controls as the Senkakus and China calls Diaoyu. In the summer of 2016, a Chinese warship sailed into the islands' twelve-mile contiguous zone, and later in the summer, seven Chinese coast guard vessels accompanied an estimated 230 Chinese fishing boats, which entered the islands' waters. The incidents were among dozens reported by the Japanese during the year.[118] China and South Korea are in a dispute over rights to a submerged formation that China calls the Suyan Rock and South Korea knows as the Ieodo.[119]

South China Sea

Since 1947, China has been engaged in a program to assert control over the South China Sea, bordered by China, Vietnam, Malaysia, the Philippines, and Taiwan. The South China Sea possesses extensive fisheries and is crossed by important sea lanes, and since the early 1970s, has been thought to sit atop crude oil reserves.

In 1974, China defeated South Vietnam in a naval battle for control of the Paracel Islands in the northwest of the South China Sea. In 1988, after a deadly skirmish with the Vietnamese, China seized six reefs and atolls in the Spratly Islands in the south-central South China Sea. In 1994, China built structures on nearby Mischief Reef, which the Philippines claimed but were powerless to defend. In 2012, the Chinese forced the Philippines to relinquish control of Scarborough Shoal, in the eastern South China Sea.[120]

In response to the 2012 action, the Philippines filed a legal action with the Permanent Court of Arbitration in The Hague, asserting that Scarborough Shoal lay within the Philippines' 200-mile economic zone as established by the United Nations Convention on the Law of the Sea (UNCLOS). China did not make an appearance in the proceeding, but has stated that it has "historic claims" to nearly the entire area based in part on a "nine dash line" drawn on a map by Chinese officials of the Republic of China's Kuomintang government in 1947 and published in 1948, that runs close to the coasts of the surrounding nations.

Meanwhile, beginning in late 2013, China "embarked on a massive land reclamation project in the Spratlys, building up artificial islands that added thousands of acres of land. Some of the man-made islands feature military-grade runways, deep-draft piers to accommodate warships, facilities to host garrisons, and other support infra-structure."[121]

In July of 2016, the tribunal in The Hague unequivocally declared China's claims invalid.[122] The tribunal found that China had violated the Philippines' rights in its 200-mile economic zone by interfering with Philippine fishing and oil exploration, constructing artificial islands, failing to prevent Chinese fishermen from fishing in the zone, and physically obstructing Philippine vessels.[123]

Nine-Dash-Line as Submitted by China to U.N. in 2009

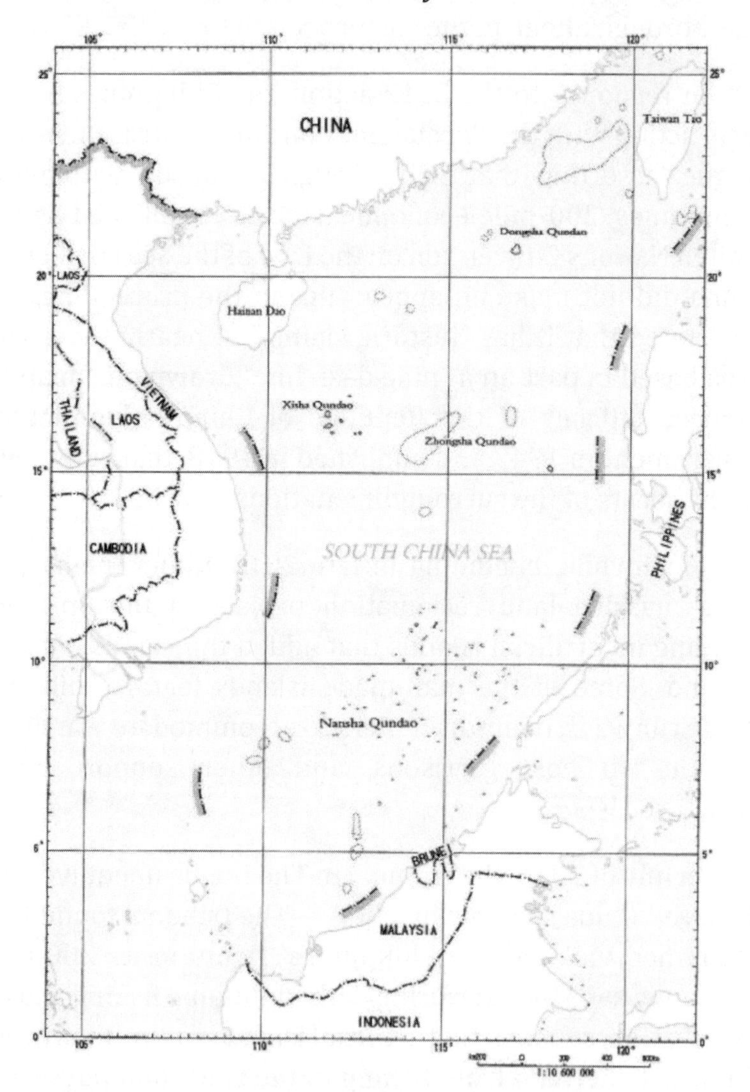

Figure 2: Map attached to China's 7 May 2009 Notes Verbales
Attachment to Note Verbale from the Permanent Mission of the People's Republic of China to the United Nations to the Secretary-General of the United Nations, No. CML/17/2009 (7 May 2009) (Annex 191); Note Verbale from the Permanent Mission of the People's Republic of China to the United Nations to the Secretary-General of the United Nations, No. CML/18/2009 (7 May 2009) (Annex 192).

Source: The South China Sea Arbitration Award of July 12, 2016, Permanent Court of Arbitration, 77.

The decision was a humiliation, and China's civilian government and military responded with harsh rhetoric, with the government warning its neighbors that it would "take all necessary measures" to protect its interests.[124] It is not clear, however, exactly what rights China is asserting within the area it has claimed, and how it will assert them.

For now, China has held off on developing Scarborough Shoal. However, the Chinese military appears determined to do so, emboldened by its experience in the Spratlys. As the head of the Chinese navy said: "We didn't expect President Xi would give us such robust support . . . and we didn't expect the Americans would be so slow to react."[125]

It is important to note, however, that the claims in the South China Sea are not only the Party's, Xi's, or the military's idea – they are deeply ingrained in the populace, and have been for a long time. Zheng Wang points out that geography textbooks teach Chinese students that "the southernmost point of our country's territory is Zengmu Ansha (James Shoal) in the Nansha (Spratly) Islands." James Shoal lies under 72 feet of water, fifty miles off the Malaysian coast and 1,100 miles south of the Chinese mainland. The claim dates at least to a 1936 map by a Chinese cartographer; generations of Chinese students have been led through an exercise measuring the distance from this southernmost point to the northernmost point in China.[126]

Zheng quotes the executive editor of China National Geography magazine from an article in 2013:

> The nine-dashed line has been painted in the hearts and minds of the Chinese for a long time. It has been 77 years since Bai Meichu put in his 1936 map. It is now deeply engraved in the hearts

> and minds of the Chinese people. I do not believe any Chinese leader would remove the nine-dashed line from the Chinese. I do not believe there will be any time when China will be without the nine-dashed line.[127]

According to Zhen Wang, the Chinese routinely have used a three-phrase narrative to describe these perceived violations in South China Sea: "water territories have been carved up," "islands and reefs have been occupied," and "resources have been plundered." Where other countries see China's actions as aggressive and bullying, "many Chinese genuinely believe that China is a peace-loving country and see themselves as the victims." Any sign of weakness on the subject on the part of Chinese leaders draws an angry response from the populace.[128]

The "Duterte Effect"

China has augmented the deployment of military might through use of the "soft power" of its economic weight as leverage to woo Southeast Asian countries into its orbit.

Despite the ruling on Scarborough Shoal, in October of 2016, the recently-elected Philippines president, Rodrigo Duterte, traveled to China and announced his country's economic and military "separation" from the United States, signing thirteen agreements for closer economic cooperation with China and $13.5 billion of deals and investments. The countries' leaders also announced plans for bilateral talks on conflicting claims in the South China Sea.

In what may be the first instance of what observers are calling the "Duterte effect," Malaysia's prime minister went to China in November of 2016 to negotiate the purchase of coastal patrol ships (over those made by the U.S. and Japan) and to explore closer defense and economic cooperation between the two countries. The Malaysian government thus far has sought to avoid confrontation over China's claims in the Spratly Islands and the South China Sea. However, Chinese fishing boats have been moving into Malaysia's fishing territory in the southern part of the Sea.[129]

Foreign Military Installations

China is not content to project its military power in its immediate surroundings. During 2016, China began construction of its first overseas military outpost, a naval installation in Djibouti on the horn of Africa. The installation, scheduled for completion in 2017, is to be next door to an existing American base. Djibouti's foreign minister said his country is "positioning itself in this big design China is putting in place." Chinese military officials have said that "[s]teadily advancing overseas base construction" is a top priority of the current regime, and the U.S. military is predicting that China will establish more overseas bases in the coming years.[130]

And China is taking its activity in the Western Hemisphere to a new level: The U.S.-China Economic and Security Review Commission has reported that in February of 2015, "China and Argentina announced prospective weapons sales and defense cooperation agreements extending beyond the scope of any made between China and a Latin American nation to date" including Argentina's purchase or coproduction of fourteen to twenty fourth-generation fighter aircraft, at least 100 armored personnel carriers, and five naval vessels; enhanced military-to-military exchanges; and China's construction in Argentina of a space tracking facility in connection with satellite imagery sharing. "If fulfilled, these agreements would vastly surpass China's previous regional arms exports in value and achieve several new benchmarks in the breadth, competitiveness, and technological sophistication of its regional arms sales." [131]

Summing Up

When I began this research, I thought the disputes over rocks and islands in the East China Sea and South China Sea were merely a matter of national pride. In fact, they are that and more – they are part of a Chinese intention to gain military and economic control of these areas.

The Chinese work a long plan. Thirty years ago, the Chinese established a plan to achieve naval power in stages, with goals for 2020 and 2030. In 1974, when they took control of the Paracel islands from Vietnam, they were content to let them sit for decades, knowing of their intended eventual use. The Chinese have been very clever in their use of a mixture of military and civilian assets, in the Paracels, on Scarborough Shoal, and now in the East China Sea.[132] And they have been clever in presenting a *fait accompli*, creating a new reality on the ground. Possession is nine-tenths of the law, in the South China Sea, as it has been in Crimea and Eastern Ukraine. They have been emboldened in this by the lack of a U.S. response.[133] And they have been emboldened by weakness in the U.S. economic position, as Southeast Asian countries like the Philippines increasingly have turned toward China, acquiescing in its aggression for perceived economic gain.

As China asserts its military and economic strength regionally and beyond, we have seen that it can be viewed as a "revisionist state" – seeking to change the current world order by becoming a regional hegemon and world superpower, or, as the Chinese leadership frame it, either as a "*status quo*" power, acting defensively, or, at most, restoring the "*status quo ante*" prior to injustices imposed by the West and the Japanese. Whichever way China's goals are framed, the Chinese strategy is to force the U.S. military presence out of Asia, in a strategy called "anti-access/area denial" (A2/AD). China wants to impose China's vision, with reference to its prior imperial glory.

It is dismaying to see so many in the U.S. intelligentsia oblivious to or in denial of these facts. For example, I was struck by two separate occasions when, in one case a professor at a prestigious liberal arts college and in the other a teacher at a prestigious preparatory school, independently brought up the subject of Chinese military inferiority, giving as an example their purchase of an aircraft carrier from the Ukraine.

As if they would stop there. The Chinese are inventive, imaginative, ingenious and excellent at copying. They don't need to spend billions on advanced designs for aircraft and submarines, when they can just steal the U.S. designs after we do so. And what do you do when they are four times larger? It calls to mind the German and Japanese soldiers in awe at the long lines of American soldiers and materiel during World War II. And the hordes of Chinese advancing toward the American lines in "suicide charges" during the Korean War, when the U.S. and China fought to a standstill.

In August of 2016, the Rand Corporation published the results of a study commissioned by the U.S. Army, in which Rand considered outcomes of a U.S.-China war, then and in 2025. The outcomes are grim, and become more so by 2025, when the balance will tip less in the United States' favor, as Chinese A2/AD capabilities improve. The study contained several recommendations for how to avoid a war. But with the hair trigger created by China's South China Sea assertiveness, the danger is that China will misjudge America's commitment to its Southeast Asia allies, as North Korea and the Soviet Union did in 1951. Rand reported "an increasing confidence among Chinese military strategists that they could conduct a short, sharp and victorious war."[134] There is no evidence that the growing economic ties between the U.S. and China are influencing China's military and civilian leaders' thinking in this realm.

Closing Thoughts on Chinese Imperialism

Looking back at China's emerging economic, cultural and military imperialism in pursuit of the "Great Restoration," we must consider, are we ready to have China take charge of Asia? Are we ready to pass to China the baton of world leadership?[135]

If those questions give us pause, then we must consider the future if we stay on our present course, a course that sends $370 billion unreturned dollars to the Chinese economy each year, and that removes one and a half times that much from the U.S. economy, with accompanying economic and social effects. Running decades of trade deficits with Japan and Germany, friendly, non-militarized democracies, stands in stark contrast to running much larger deficits with a fast militarizing, authoritarian government and military who consider themselves to be adversaries of the United States.

Problems in the Chinese Economy

Fortunately, it is not so clear that China can stay on its present course, regardless of the U.S. response.

Structural Problems in the Chinese Economy

In recent years, structural problems in the Chinese economy have become apparent. In the summer of 2015, the Chinese stock market suffered a severe crash, after the Chinese government had encouraged Chinese citizens to jump in, and then lost control of the process. In August of 2015, China widened the permitted spread of the price of its currency, resulting in a de facto devaluation and raising fears about the world market's confidence in the yuan.[136] 2015 and 2016 also were plagued with much labor unrest, as Chinese workers went without pay, were laid off and lost their pensions.[137] As the Chinese economy was slowing, the government continued to prop it up by priming the pump with more debt. Perceived structural weakness was leading to capital flight, via whatever means possible, including the purchase of companies in other countries, leading to government limits on capital outflows. Real estate prices were soaring, and in many markets there was an overhang of unsold properties.

Overcapacity Developed with Subsidies

But for our purposes, the most important structural problem is overcapacity in Chinese industry. In our discussion of state capitalism and China's use of subsidies, we saw that China's industrial policy of targeting key industries for development, coupled with subsidies, frequently resulted in overcapacity at levels far exceeding world demand. The problem was worsened by Beijing's use of a $850 million stimulus spending package to ride out the global recession with near double-digit growth in 2009 and 2010, in the process creating much of the excess capacity that plagues China, and the rest of the world, today.[138]

Once established, the new industries can come to dominate the world market due to the continued subsidies, which, in the view of some experts, are more important than low wages in China's comparative advantage. However, they typically develop overcapacity and begin competing based on low price, often operating at what would be a loss except for the continued subsidies.

Steel, Aluminum, and other Industrial Metals

China has been aggressively building up its capacity for producing industrial metals, including steel, aluminum, copper, and zinc, as part of a government-sponsored industrialization program. The capacity now far exceeds Chinese demand for the products, especially as the rate of growth of the Chinese economy has slowed during 2015 and 2016.

China has dealt with the resulting overcapacity by increasing exports of the products, "dumping" them on the world markets at cut-rate prices. As the dumped products captured market share, mills, smelters, and factories in the United States and Europe have lost money, laid off workers, and in some cases closed.

The Steel Industry

During 2015 the glut of Chinese steel pulled prices down and created havoc in the global steel industry.[139] In a report published in September of 2016, a unit of Duke University concluded that "the global steel sector is in crisis" due to overcapacity. The global steel market has grown to 2,300 million metric tons (MT) while only needing 1,500 MT to meet global demand. "[140]

The study concluded that since the year 2000, seventy-five percent of new steel production has come from China, and found that China's "state capitalism" model, heavily influenced and controlled by the central government in Beijing, "is at the core of the current overcapacity problem in the steel sector." The Duke researchers determined that China has pledged to cut its steel production, but leaders have been hesitant to act. As a result of the surge of underpriced steel from China, tens of thousands of Americans have faced layoffs and dozens of steel mills have shut down. The Duke researchers called for strong enforcement of America's trade laws to "address this growing crisis."

The U.S. steel industry has responded by bringing, and winning, trade cases imposing tariffs on the Chinese steel. In the Fall of 2016, U.S. steelmakers prepared to file further cases alleging that the Chinese steel producers have been circumventing the tariffs by shipping steel through Vietnam. (The U.S. Commerce Department also was investigating claims that one of China's largest aluminum producers was illegally shipping aluminum to the U.S. via Mexico to avoid U.S. tariffs.) [141]

To deal with the overcapacity problem, in addition to "dumping" production into the world markets, China is actively pursuing a restructuring of its steel industry through the closing, refinancing and combining of mills. However, closures and bankruptcies would depend upon the central government's ability to control provincial governments, which in many cases use subsidies to keep failing enterprises alive to maintain employment and tax revenues. Even with President Xi Jinping's centralization of power, such control has been lacking. Contrary to the government's goals, there are signs that Chinese steel capacity will be expanding, with reports of an additional fifty million tons of capacity to be added in coastal producers in the next two years.[142]

China also has made moves to get into production of high-end steel used in automotive and aerospace products; however, they allegedly didn't bother developing or even purchasing the technology, they just stole it. According to complaints in two cases filed in the Spring of 2016 by US Steel, in 2011 Chinese computer hackers stole secret information on methods for producing ultra-high strength steel used in the automobile industry. Within two years, the complaints allege, Baosteel of China was producing products using the stolen methods, which had taken US Steel more than a decade to develop. US Steel alleges that the cyberattacks were sponsored by the Chinese government and benefitted the entire Chinese steel industry. The complaints seek a ban on importation into the U.S. of steel products linked to the stolen intellectual property. At this writing, the case is pending before the U.S. International Trade Commission.[143]

The Aluminum Industry

As with steel, China has been expanding aluminum production for years, overtaking the United States in 2003; China now accounts for more than half of world aluminum production, over thirty million out of just under sixty million tons produced annually worldwide. And while most of the Chinese production is used domestically, overcapacity has led to soaring exports over the last decade - China's share increased from just over ten percent to just under forty percent of all aluminum exports.

China's excess capacity alone is now estimated at five times Europe's total production, which has declined by a third over the last decade and is under serious stress. In the United States, the aluminum industry has been in decline since the financial crisis of 2008, with production at a thirty-year low. From 2011 through 2015, world prices of aluminum fell by some forty percent, with producers blaming excess production by Chinese firms. U.S. and European producers accuse China of providing the Chinese aluminum producers with subsidized electricity, and the producers with dumping their products on the world market at artificially low prices.

Despite the overcapacity, in March of 2016, China Hongqiao, the world's largest aluminum producer, announced plans to *increase* its production capacity to some six million tons by year's end, one-third more than all U.S. production in 2015. And China now plans to push into the production of high-end aluminum for the automobile and aerospace markets, the province of American and European producers. In this case, rather than steal the technology, the Chinese plan to purchase it: a Chinese firm has agreed to purchase a U.S. maker of these products, raising further concerns in the industry.[144]

The Wall Street Journal reported that China's aluminum production rose to 32 million tons in 2015, double the level in 2005. Exports soared to 6.7 million tons from 2.6 million during the same period, helping push global prices down 40% in the past five years. The number of smelters in the U.S. has fallen to four from 23 in 2000, destroying thousands of jobs.[145] Europe has suffered a similar fate. In September of 2016 the Financial Times reported an industry analyst as asking:

> Does the west want an aluminum industry or not? They've got to make a decision if it's of strategic importance or not.[146]

The same question can be posed of the steel industry, where the Chinese deny the accusations of dumping and subsidies, claiming that the increased exports of steel are a sign of the Chinese industry's competitiveness.[147] An officer of the China Iron & Steel Association claims the U.S. is engaging in protectionism, and asks, why do so to help a "sunset industry?" [148]

And so, we must ask, does the U.S. want a steel industry or not? Is it of strategic importance, or not?[149] Meanwhile, without a change in course, the future holds more Chinese dumping of excess production, more Chinese movement into the higher-value products, by legal or illegal means, and more decline in the American steel, aluminum, and other industrial metal industries.

Growing Overcapacity in Other Industries

The European Chamber of Commerce in China also recognized the continued and growing problem of overcapacity in Chinese industry in a report issued in February of 2016. The report examined the causes and consequences of overcapacity in eight key industries including steel, aluminum, glass, paper and renewable energy products, and developments since the European Chamber published its original report on the issue in 2009. Concluding that "tackling overcapacity is now more urgent than ever," the Chamber made recommendations toward China's stated goal of "establishing the market as the decisive force in China's economy." The report noted that the Chinese Communist Party had listed addressing overcapacity as a priority every year from 2007 through 2015, but fundamental changes had not taken place.[150]

Reasons for this failure were described in a report in the Financial Times in June of 2013: Once industries are established, it is extremely difficult to close facilities down. For example, the Chinese government has found it nearly impossible to close steel mills because of the role they play in creating employment and paying taxes to local governments. The head of one of China's large steel companies told the Financial Times that "It is very difficult to find an effective remedy for China's production overcapacity problem. "Which company are you going to tell to shut down?" And at the same time, more capacity is added, in steel and other industries as well. At this writing, it appears the problem of overcapacity in China and several other countries will be going from bad to worse, and visited upon the United States and Europe unless adequate defenses are erected.[151]

More Subsidies

We have noted that one of the big causes of Chinese overcapacity has been government subsidies. It seems that we can expect more. Per a Wall Street Journal analysis of nearly 3,000 domestically listed Chinese companies in 2015, reported government aid rose to more than 119 billion yuan, or more than $18 billion in 2015 compared with about $14 billion in 2014. Reported subsidies rose roughly 50% since 2013.[152]

Some of this financial assistance went to assist companies to grow sales, including the American market; some went to keep ailing companies alive. For example, the Wall Street Journal reported that Yunnan Aluminum Co., obtained nearly $77 million in subsidies since late 2015. In securities filings, the company said that during first half of 2015, its production of alumina jumped 40 percent, even as revenue sank amid weakening prices. An official at the department that administered much of the cash assistance said it had acted to protect the company's 10,000 jobs, telling the Journal, "The government's aim is to help maintain social stability."[153]

More Protectionism

Meanwhile, China has delayed plans for reforms that would further open its markets, continuing to follow policies favoring domestic industries. A recent U.S. Chamber of Commerce survey reported three-fourths of American companies saying they felt less welcome in China than a year earlier. One U.K. company recently closed up shop after finding China's testing and other regulations more stringent than in the European Union.[154]

China's Economic Future

With all these structural problems, what does the future hold for China's economy?

Inherent Limits on How Far China Can Go?

A recurrent them is that there is some limit on the kinds of things the Chinese can do – that they can produce low-tech consumer goods but not more sophisticated products, or that they can manufacture, but cannot do design and engineering.

First, this assertion is contrary to our experience with the Japanese, who started out producing cheap toys when "made in Japan" was an epithet, and ended up selling us the Lexus and Infiniti. Or more recently, South Korea's Hyundai, which also began started out with a low-priced product of inferior quality, and now is producing name plates that compete with the Lexus.

Second, the Chinese have our great assistance, with U.S. companies avidly establishing R&D and design centers in

China within joint ventures, under arrangements that require the transfer of the U.S. companies' highest technologies. For example, in August of 2016, Apple announced plans to create that company's first research center in China.[155]

China in Space

A telling frame of reference in considering inherent limits on the Chinese is to consider the Chinese space program. On November 18, 2016, two Chinese astronauts returned to earth after spending thirty days in China's Tiangong-2 space lab. The lab was launched in September and the Shenzhou-11 spacecraft carrying the astronauts docked with it in October. The event marks the latest step in the modern Chinese space program, which dates from 1992.[156] On October 15 2003, China became the third nation to put a man into orbit, when Yang Liwei circled the earth for 21 hours.[157] Chinese astronauts later walked in space, and China sent a lunar probe to the moon; a second probe is planned.

The space lab visit is a precursor to China's planned launch of a space station, with a core module planned for as early as 2017, and a fully operational station by 2022.[158] China has been excluded from the International Space Station per a vote of the U.S. Congress in 2011. With the International Space Station set to be retired in 2024, a Chinese space station could become only country with an operational space station. China also has plans for a robotic probe to Mars, and for a potential manned mission to the moon.[159]

The space program is a source of intense national pride among China's populace. Yang Liwei, China's John Glenn, became a national hero. During a previous, fifteen-day mission, female astronaut Wang Yaping gained fame when she conducted a live space lecture for 60 million students across China.[160] The name of China's space lab, Tiangong-2, translates as "heavenly vessel," and China's launch rockets are named the "Long March." Joan Johnson-Freese, a professor at the U.S. Naval War College, told CNN, "China . . . wants a high-prestige achievement that allows the Chinese government to say to its people 'Look, this is what the Communist Party has done for you.'" [161]

China's ambitious space plans show no sign of abating, at a time when the Western democracies and Russia have cut back their space programs. India has a space program, and there is talk of an "Asian space race," but no one has a program nearly as ambitious as China's. China's space program may help Chinese industry, as the NASA program did in the United States. But the national security implications are likely more important. According to CNN, a recent, exhaustive review for the U.S.-China Economic and Security Review Commission reported that China's improving space capability "has negative sum consequences for U.S. military security."[162]

Shift to Higher-Value Products

In the commercial sphere, in 2015, China unveiled a plan called "Made in China 2025," designed to retain its manufacturing position through adoption of advanced manufacturing techniques.[163] The initiative reportedly "aims to expand the manufacturing sector's capacity to innovate, fully integrate IT into industrial processes, build quality brands and strengthen links with the international advanced manufacturing industry." Concentrating on ten priority industries including information technology, biotechnology, new materials and new-energy vehicles, the plan is the first step in a larger three-stage project that is set to run until 2049.[164]

Barlett and Steele reported that "[I]n 2008 the Chinese government created the Commercial Aircraft Corporation of China Ltd. (COMAC), a wholly-owned state enterprise, to 'build a large Chinese passenger aircraft that will soon be soaring through the blue skies.'"[165] In a visit to Boeing's headquarters in September of 2016, Chinese leader Xi Jinping confirmed that, notwithstanding its orders for Boeing planes, China would continue to develop its own larger commercial airliner, the C919.[166]

Venture Communism

The Chinese leadership also is pushing ground-up entrepreneurship as a means of moving beyond being the word's factory to creating ideas and technologies and the jobs that result from them.

At the national level, Premiere Li Keqiang has issued calls for "mass entrepreneurship." At the local level, governments are funding incubators, like the one in Hangzhou, called "Dream Town," that is providing startup companies with free rent, cash grants, and trading, funded by the city. The city of Suzhou, near Shanghai, has announced it plans to open 300 incubators by 2020, to house 30,000 startups. In Shenzhen, the government is offering rent subsidies of up to seventy percent for "creative" startups. In Chengdu, the government is creating a $28 million venture fund. Guangdong offers subsidies to cover startup losses. Hangzhou, home to Dream Town, is forming a public-private venture fund of some $650 million.

The government funding is in addition to a substantial private venture capital sector, which made $49 billion in investments in 2015, second only to the United States. Some worry that it will lead to a bubble and overcapacity of the kind that has plagued traditional industries that received government support.[167]

Which Way Forward?

China's economic future, then, is a function of a bundle of contradictions. As demonstrated in its space and military programs, China has the capacity to move into ever-higher value-added and technologically sophisticated manufacturing, especially with the help of western companies and a government ready to provide substantial financial sources. However, the Chinese economy suffers from a number of built-in limitations: Central and local governments alike misallocate resources toward building overcapacity in order to secure jobs and social stability. The focus on jobs and stability, a decentralized form of socialism, and the partial adoption of a harsh form of low price, low wage capitalism, creates in inability to pursue a consumer-based economy and to pursue non-economic goals such as worker safety and a healthy environment.

Several possibilities present themselves. One is a continuation of the past, which saw near-double digit growth for several decades. However, that pace likely is not sustainable, as evidenced by the slow-down of the last several years: in 2016, China reported GDP annual growth rates of 6.7 percent in the first three quarters and 6.6 percent in the fourth.

Another is that China's economy could collapse at any time. And it is true that it could; the Chinese economy is under tremendous strain. But I would not count on it, especially since so many American-based and other companies are contributing so massively to the continued buildup of technology and capital in China, and are continuing to take part in the drive to make products in China for sale into the U.S. and other foreign markets. This, and the Chinese government likely has the capacity to prop up the economy with further debt, at least in the medium term.

The most reasonable assumption is, in my view, for a more modest rate of GDP growth of approximately 6.5 percent, the floor below which Chinese policy makers likely would not let the economy fall. Meanwhile, China will continue to pursue the tactics I have described in terms of economic, cultural, and military imperialism, together with the creation of excess productive capacity and gaming the international trade system.

China's Political Future

So much for economics; what of China's political future? Since the Reform and Opening and especially since China's admission to the World Trade Organization, it is easy to become lulled into the impression that China is a normal country. By normal, I mean adhering to basic, widely accepted international norms of rights of people and their relationship to their government. It is not.

China is an authoritarian state in which the Chinese Communist Party is the paramount authority. CCP members, which number some 7.2 million, hold almost all top government and security apparatus positions. The first thing we must recognize in considering China is that the Communist Party is the be-all and end-all. Richard McGregor, formerly China bureau chief of the *Financial Times* and author of *The Party: The Secret World of China's Communist Rulers*, put it thus:

> In the words of Dai Bingguo, China's most senior foreign policy official, China's 'number one core interest is to maintain its fundamental system and state security.' State sovereignty, territorial integrity and economic development, the priorities of any state, all are subordinate to the need to keep the Party in power.[168]

The current leader of the Country, Xi Jinping, who took office in late 2012, reportedly was selected for just that purpose. The Economist has reported that a "broad spectrum of retired and serving leaders and their powerful families who felt that . . . the party might collapse . . . wanted someone who would keep the party in power and strengthen its grip on the military." [169]

Xi was a "princeling," i.e., the sons of one of Mao's lieutenants, who are generally regarded as having high loyalty to the party. He promptly began a series of actions aimed at tightening his control over the Party and the Party's control over the military. He launched an anti-corruption campaign that has resulted in the arrest of hundreds of thousands of officials nationwide, including generals in the armed forces previously thought untouchable. (It has been hard to distinguish cases of corruption and moves to purge individuals not in Xi's favor.)

Xi also has moved to consolidate personal power in a manner not seen since Deng, and perhaps Mao. His position makes him the head of the party, commander-in-chief, and head of state. However, he also has taken over responsibilities over the economy traditionally handled by the Premiere, and has appointed himself chairman of a multitude of existing and newly created committees, earning him the nickname "chairman of everything. " [170] He also has adopted the title of the "core" or *hexin*, a term used to describe strong leaders like Mao and Deng, and he is being referred to in the media, with his apparent approval, as "Uncle Xi." Five of the seven Standing Committee members are to retire after the 19th Party Congress in 2017, along with one-third of the remaining eighteen Politburo members. Xi is expected to use the occasion to further consolidate his power by arranging for the appointment of supporters. There also has been speculation that Xi will not step down after two five-year terms, as has become the tradition.[171]

Xi also has moved to strengthen and discipline the Party's propaganda machine. There are three main media organizations, all state-run: the People's Daily newspaper, the news agency Xinhua, and China Central Television. Xi told them in 2016 that they must "love the party, protect the party and serve the party." The Propaganda Department of the Central Committee of the Communist Party supervises some 3,300 television stations, nearly 2,000 newspapers, and almost 10,000 periodicals. It reportedly spends some $10 billion a year to get the Chinese government's party line into foreign countries' media. In June of 2016, the Central Commission for Discipline Inspection concluded an investigation of the Propaganda Department with a finding that the Department had failed "to implement the principle of the party managing the media."[172]

Xi also has presided over a wide-ranging program of stifling activism and dissent. In one aspect of the campaign, at the Party meeting in October of 2014, Xi and other leaders emphasized the "rule of law," ushering in a campaign of using new and existing laws to further restrict dissent. In 2015, the government launched the biggest crackdown on Internet speech in many years, using a law against "picking quarrels and provoking trouble". In July, police rounded up more than 200 civil rights lawyers.[173] During the first week of December, over fifty labor activists were rounded up in a coordinated police action in Guangdong province. Three of them, and later a fourth, were charged with "gathering a crowd to disturb public order". In fact, they had "provided assistance to workers engaged in collective bargaining in a number of cases including the Lide shoe factory dispute over compensation for relocation," according to the China Labour Bulletin.[174]

The lengths to which the Party has gone were conveyed in the U.S. State Department's report on human rights practices in China during 2015:[175]

> Repression and coercion markedly increased during the year against organizations and individuals involved in civil and political rights advocacy and public interest and ethnic minority issues. The crackdown on the legal community was particularly severe, as individual lawyers and law firms that handled cases the government deemed "sensitive" were targeted for harassment and detention, with hundreds of lawyers and law associates interrogated, investigated, and in many cases detained in secret locations for months without charges or access to attorneys or family members. Officials continued to harass, intimidate, and prosecute family members and associates to retaliate against rights advocates and defenders. Individuals and groups regarded as politically sensitive by authorities faced tight restrictions on their freedom to assemble, practice religion, and travel. Authorities resorted to extralegal measures, such as enforced disappearance and strict house arrest, including house arrest of family

> members, to prevent public expression of critical opinions. Five men working in Hong Kong's publishing industry disappeared between October and December from Thailand, Hong Kong, and Shenzhen; it was believed that PRC security officials were responsible for their disappearances. Authorities continued to censor and tightly control public discourse on the internet and in print and other media. There was severe official repression of the freedoms of speech, religion, association, and assembly of Uighurs in the Xinjiang Uighur Autonomous Region (XUAR) and of Tibetans in the Tibet Autonomous Region (TAR) and other Tibetan areas. . . .[176]

Writing in the December 2016 issue of *The Atlantic*," James Fallows, who spent the better part of the previous ten years living in China, took the measure of China's trends in an article titled "China's Great Leap Backward." [177] Fallows noted that daily life on Chinese streets appears "as free-form and commerce-minded as ever." However, the political climate was darkening. Comparing his previous and recent experiences in China, Fallows noted, among other things:

- During 2016, the Chinese government significantly strengthened the "Great Firewall" restrictions on Internet access, clamping down on the practice of accessing foreign Internet sites via private virtual private networks. Young journalists told him they were dropping out of their profession because it had become meaningless under increasing government restrictions. China has extended its repression of speech beyond its borders, for example in boycotting Norwegian salmon after the Nobel Prize committee awarded the peace prize to a jailed Chinese dissident. The government has been harassing the families of activists and dissidents who have left the country. During the past five years, organizations other than the Communist Party such as churches, labor unions, and non-governmental organizations, always repressed, have been more severely restricted. Even approved churches reportedly have been bulldozed, ostensibly in the name of urban renewal.

- The New York Times online version was banned in China after the Times' 2012 report that the family of the then-premier of China had billions of dollars in secret assets. (*The Economist* reports that in 2015 it joined the Times on the banned list.) LinkedIn reportedly has been removing posts critical of China even when they were intended for consumption outside China, as a condition of LinkedIn's operating in China. In the Spring of 2016, China blocked Apple's iTunes and iBooks apps in China.

- Three-fourths of businesses surveyed by the American Chamber of Commerce in Beijing reported that foreign businesses are less welcome in China, and nearly half reported a decline in revenues. Chinese companies report that they are being required to switch from foreign to Chinese suppliers.

Fallows noted that a Chinese law expert at Fordham University, Carl Minsner, wrote in 2016 that "China is experiencing the most sustained domestic political crackdown since Tiananmen Square."[178] Fallows himself concluded, "In my lifetime I did not imagine that I would see the day when China regressed back to its Maoist roots. I am fearing that now." [179]

Many of these trends pre-dated Xi Jinping's tenure; some experts believe they were a result of the financial meltdown in American and the West in 2008 -- China wanted to insulate itself from such risks, was emboldened by the West's weakness, and saw an opening to move.[180] But under Mr. Xi, China has made a turn from the Deng Xiaoping policies of putting the economy first, collective political leadership, and a cautious approach to foreign affairs, instead placing politics (protecting the Party) over economics, moving toward one-man rule, and a pursuing a muscular foreign policy.[181]

Ironically, despite all these moves to centralize power and increase party discipline, the decentralization of decision making instituted by Deng Xiaoping in the early 1970s has limited the capacity of the central government in Beijing to enforce national initiatives, such as environmental and food safety standards or the reduction of excess capacity in industry.[182]

This is a bad combination. Decentralization and the spread of "town and village enterprises" and privately-owned factories has left many businesses outside central control: They spring up causing overcapacity. They get in financial trouble or move with workers going unpaid. They don't enforce workplace health and safety rules, and workers are injured and get sick. They don't enforce environmental rules, and residents can't breathe the air, drink the water, or plant in the soil. All of this is adding up to significant social unrest. Environmental protests are common, as are worker strikes and demonstrations – The China Labour Bulletin reported 656 "events" in 2013, 4,154 in 2014, 5,437 in 2015, and 1,377 in 2016.[183] The reduction in 2016 likely was due to suppression by the government.[184]

In a November 2016 report, the International Labor Organization noted the contradiction between a statement from the Chinese government that "freedom of association is guaranteed through the explicit provisions of its Constitution", and provisions of China's Trade Union Law restricting freedom of association.[185] In fact, the Chinese people yearn for a government that is grounded in the constitution, not the Party.

The Economist has quoted Zhang Qianfan, a liberal legal scholar at Peking University, as concluding that "more than three-quarters [of the Chinese] would associate the Chinese dream with a dream of constitutionalism" -- the belief that the constitution should serve as the ultimate authority, overriding the whims of the party. Mr. Zhang told *The Economist* that more than 150 people, including many prominent scholars, had signed a petition he launched calling for full implementation of the constitution. And in January of 2013, a state-controlled newspaper, Southern Weekend, tried to publish a new-year message entitled "The Chinese dream: a dream of constitutionalism". [186]

However, the Party is having none of it -- the Southern Weekend article was replaced with a censored version. For Xi Jinping and the Party, the Party comes first. *The Economist* reported that in leaked unpublished remarks during his trip to southern China in December of 2013, Xi said: "The Chinese dream is an ideal. Communists should have a higher ideal, and that is communism."[187]

Nevertheless, the Party is confronting strong currents of public opinion. In March of 2013, a Party website ran an online survey to gauge support for Xi's "Chinese Dream," which the site said had "reignited hopes for the great revival of the Chinese nation". The page reportedly "was quickly deleted after around 80% of more than 3,000 respondents replied 'no' to questions such as whether they supported one-party rule and believed in socialism."[188]

This yearning for constitutional government and improved social and environmental conditions could at any time break out into widespread social unrest as occurred during the Tiananmen Square uprisings in 1989. In that event, only the People's Liberation Army would be able to restore order, as it did in 1989. If it did not side with the Party, as it did then, it would become the *de facto* ruling organization, at least for an interim period. It would have a shot at gaining legitimacy by tapping into the strong nationalist sentiments of the populace nurtured by the communist regime.

The Party leaders and the people alike are sensitive to these possibilities. Since the "mandate of heaven" settled upon Emperor Yu, for millennia China's leaders and populace have viewed coups, revolts, and natural disasters as signs from the heavens that a regime's right to govern had ended;[189] even today, they continue to harbor "a deep sensitivity to any phenomenon that smacks of end-of-dynasty symbolism."[190]

For the foreseeable future, it appears that the Chinese civilian and military leadership will continue to seek to avoid such signs, by increasing the repression of labor unrest and political dissent, by stoking nationalist sentiment through expansionist military activities, and by propping up the economy with exports and initiatives like the Silk Road. Economic and political "hard landings" are a possibility, but as Henry Kissinger once remarked, communists are remarkably adept at staying in power; in my view, we should prepare for a long haul of continued communist rule, economic mercantilism and military adventurism on China's part.

Notes to Chapter 8

[1] The idea is so important, that when scientists published evidence in 2016 of a great flood having occurred at about the right time and place, the state-run Xinhua news agency published reports of the "important support" for the existence of the Xia. "The return of the Xia," The Economist, August 20, 2016.

[2] Lizhong Xie, ed. *De-Politicization of Ethnic Questions in China* (Singapore: World Scientific, 2014),6. Even when China was occupied by the Mongols and the Manchus, the Chinese conventional wisdom is that the occupiers were "Sinicized," although recent research is reported to have cast this into doubt. "The upper Han," *The Economist*, November 19, 2016, 18.

[3] Lin, Demystifying, 1.

[4] James Bradley, *The China Mirage: The Hidden History of the American Disaster in Asia* (New York: Little, Brown and Company, 2015), 16.

[5] "The upper Han," *The Economist, supra.*,18.

[6] Henry Kissinger, *World Order* (New York: Penguin Press, 2014), 213.

[7] Zheng Wang, "Not Rising, But Rejuvenating: The 'Chinese Dream,'" The Diplomat, February 5, 2013.
http://thediplomat.com/2013/02/chinese-dream-draft/?allpages=yes

[8] *Id.*

[9] Following one such occasion, the head of the party's propaganda apparatus, Liu Yunshan, ordered the inclusion of the Chinese dream in school textbooks to assure that it "enters students' brains". "Chasing the Chinese dream." *The Economist*, May 4, 2013.
http://www.economist.com/news/briefing/21577063-chinas-new-leader-has-been-quick-consolidate-his-power-what-does-he-now-want-his

[10] Xi Jinping has been reluctant to explicitly state the goal of surpassing the United States. However, other officials have not been so circumspect, arguing that China must reassume its position as the world's most powerful nation, held for a millennium prior to the Great Humiliation. *Id.*

[11] Lin, *Demystifying*, 2.

[12] Building on the opening created in 1972, the United States established normal relations with China in 1979.

[13] Lin, *Demystifying*, 13.

[14] China offered other advantages as well: a stable political system (tested briefly during the Tiananmen Square incident), and, as time went on, good roads, communications, and ports. Harney, *China Price*, 9.

[15] For example, in 2016, Jörg Wuttke, President of the European Chamber of Commerce in China, reported, "Many European companies in the wind and solar energy industries . . . agreed to transfer technology to Chinese partners, and future competitors, as the price they had to pay to enter the market. However, few of them have ultimately prospered . . . Many have since vanished altogether." Jörg Wuttke, Does Made in China 2025 Mean Not Made by Europeans? Eurobiz.com, April 1, 2016. http://www.eurobiz.com.cn/does-made-in-china-2025-mean-not-made-by-europeans/

[16] Lin, *Demystifying*, 16.

[17] Ellen Nakashima, "Six indicted in plot to steal technology," *The Washington Post*, May 20, 2015.

[18] Ellen Nakashima, "China hacking into U.S. society," Washington Post, June 6, 2015. David Lerman, "After breach, calls to act," Bloomberg, June 8, 2015.

[19] FDI is the investment of capital from outside a country into an ownership stake of at least ten percent of a company inside the country. World Bank, World Development Indicators. http://data.worldbank.org/indicator/BX.KLT.DINV.CD.WD?page=1. Foreign direct investment are the net inflows of investment to acquire a lasting management interest (10 percent or more of voting stock) in an enterprise operating in an economy other than that of the investor. It is the sum of equity capital, reinvestment of earnings, other long-term capital, and short-term capital as shown in the balance of payments. This series shows net inflows (new investment inflows less disinvestment) in the reporting economy from foreign investors. Data are in current U.S. dollars.

[20] "Foreign direct investment to China rises 4.1 percent in 2016 on year," *Reuters*, January 13, 2017.

[21] "Foxconn joint venture to build $8.8 billion LCD plant in China," *Reuters*, December 30, 2016.

[22] Julie Johnsson, *Bloomberg News*, September _, 2015.

[23] Eva Dou, "Apple to Invest More in China," *Wall Street Journal*, August 17, 2016.

[24] Linglking Wei, "China Foreign-Exchange Reserves Keep Dropping," *Wall Street Journal*, January 8, 2017.

[25] "Most big Chinese companies get some kind of state subsidy". Quartz online, April 9, 2013.

http://qz.com/72354/most-big-chinese-companies-get-some-kind-of-state-subsidies/

[26] Usha C.V. Haley and George T. Haley, "How Chinese Subsidies Changed the World, Harvard Business Review, HBR Blog Network, April 25, 2013
http://blogs.hbr.org/2013/04/how-chinese-subsidies-changed/.

[27] Usha C.V. Haley and George T. Haley, Subsidies to Chinese Industry: State Capitalism, Business Strategy, and Trade Policy (Oxford: Oxford University Press, 2013).

[28] Jamil Anderlini, Chinese industry: Ambitions in excess, Financial Times, June 16, 2013.
http://www.ft.com/intl/cms/s/0/4d5528ec-d412-11e2-8639-00144feab7de.html#axzz36ARpURhy.

[29] Usha C.V. Haley and George T. Haley, "How Chinese Subsidies Changed the World," *supra*.

[30] U.S. Imposes Stiff Tariffs on Importers of Chinese Solar Panels. New York Times, June 3, 2014.
http://www.nytimes.com/2014/06/04/business/energy-environment/us-imposing-duties-on-some-chinese-solar-panels.html.

[31] "A new book lays out the scale of China's industrial subsidies," The Economist, April 27, 2013.
http://www.economist.com/news/finance-and-economics/21576680-new-book-lays-out-scale-chinas-industrial-subsidies-perverse-advantage.

[32] *Id.*

[33] Brian Spegele and John W. Miller, "China Continues to Prop Up Its Ailing Factories, Adding to Global Glut," *Wall Street Journal*, May 9, 2016.
http://www.wsj.com/articles/chinese-exports-surge-amid-overcapacity-at-home-1462746980

[34] *Id.*

[35] "The New Davos Man, *The Economist*, January 21, 2017, 33.

[36] Eswar Prasad, a Cornell University economist and former top China hand at the IMF, quoted in Ian Talley and Lingling Wei, "China Marks Milestone with Yuan's Entry Into IMF Reserve Basket," Wall Street Journal, September 30, 2016.
http://www.wsj.com/articles/china-marks-milestone-with-yuans-entry-into-imf-reserve-basket-1475260422

[37] Jeff Yoders, Lisa Reisman, Nick Heinzmann and Taras Berwzowsky, "China vs. the World: Why the Battle for New Trade Status is Such a Huge Deal," *MetalMiner*, December 30, 2016. Shawn Donnan, Lucy Hornby, and Arthur Beesley, "China challenges EU and US over market economy status," *Financial Times*, December 12, 2016.

[38] An example of this tactic is China's unfounded claim that the U.S. was selling automobiles into China at prices lower than their cost of production ("dumping"). Based on that claim, China had imposed "Anti-dumping duties" and "countervailing duties" on U.S. sport utility vehicles. On May 23, 2014, a WTO panel ruled in favor of the U.S., that the duties were violations of WTO rules and had to be removed. This was the third time the U.S. had won such a ruling against China. The two earlier disputes concerned U.S. specialty steel products and chicken broiler products.

[39] "China's Economy and the WTO," *The Economist*, December 10, 2011.
http://www.economist.com/node/21541461.

[40] Spegele and Miller, "China Continues," *supra*.

[41] Barlett and Steele, *Betrayal*, 226.

[42] Hornblower, "Joint Venture."

[43] Harney, *China Price*, 9-10.

[44] *See* Paul Midler, *Poorly Made in China: An Insider's Account of the China Production Game* (Hoboken: John Wiley & Sons, Inc., 2009, 2011).

[45] Barlett and Steele, *Betrayal*, 82.

[46] Foxconn is a unit of Taiwan's Hon Hai Precision Industry Company, which employs over a million people in factories across China.

[47] Rob Cooper, "Inside Apple's Chinese 'sweatshop' factory where workers are paid just £1.12 per hour to produce iPhones and iPads for the West," Daily Mail, January 25, 2013.
http://www.dailymail.co.uk/news/article-2103798/Revealed-Inside-Apples-Chinese-sweatshop-factory-workers-paid-just-1-12-hour.html

[48] Kevin Parrish, "Dell Demands Price Cuts from Component Suppliers," DigiTimes, March 17, 2013.
http://www.tomshardware.com/news/Chassis-supply-chain-lower-prices-Catcher-Technology-Fuyu-Precision,21527.html.

[49] Investigations were carried out at the MSI factory in Shenzhen city, the Mingshou factory in Suzhou city and the Hipro Electronics and Taida Electronics factories both in Dongguan city, Guangdong province.

[50] Daniel Miller, "Appalling conditions of factory workers who make Dell computers who are forced to work seven-day, 74-hour weeks and live in dorms with no hot water," Daily Mail, November 8, 2013. http://www.dailymail.co.uk/news/article-2492998/Revealed-Appalling-conditions-factory-workers-make-Dell-computers-forced-work-seven-day-74-hour-weeks-live-dorms-hot-water.html#ixzz36KOgSxPa.

[51] For example, in the recent Dell investigation, the eighteen-year-old worker described the conditions on the factory floor saying, "Because of the welding, the temperature is uncomfortably high and the smell is toxic. We don't get mouth protection and I get skin irritation if I touch my face at work." In factories in the Chinese provinces of Guangdong and Jiangsu, workers were also found to breathe chemical fumes all day long as they assembled components. Workers welding circuit boards also complained about skin rashes from direct and indirect contact with the electronics.

[52] Barbara Demick, "Explosion at factory in China kills 68," Los Angeles Times, August 3, 2014, reporting on 68 deaths in an explosion at a factory producing aluminum wheels for General Motors, likely from sparks igniting a highly flammable powder used in polishing the wheels, and referring to a June, 2013 fire at a poultry plant that killed at least 119 people, and a 1993 fire at a Shenzhen toy factory that killed 87, mostly young women.

[53] Harney, China Price, 57.

[54] Adam Matthews, "China's Bloody Factories: A Problem Bigger than Foxconn," Pulitzercenter.org, March 29, 2012. http://pulitzercenter.org/reporting/china-electronics-factories-injuries-labor-rights-foxconn-wintek-mike-daisey

[55] Michael Blanding & Heather White, "How China Is Screwing Over Its Poisoned Factory Workers," April 6, 2015.

[56] Harney, *China Price*, 57.

[57] Xu Wei, "Occupational diseases get new focus," China Daily, December 19, 2016. http://www.chinadaily.com.cn/china/2016-12/19/content_27704472.htm.]

[58] Harney, *China Price*, 56 *ff.*

[59] Xu Wei, "Occupational diseases get new focus," China Daily, December 19, 2016. http://www.chinadaily.com.cn/china/2016-12/19/content_27704472.htm.]

[60] Hu Yonggi, "Occupational disease patients to get additional benefits from new plan," China Daily, January 10, 2017. http://www.chinadaily.com.cn/china/2017-01/10/content_27907709.htm.

[61] Elizabeth C. Economy, "The Great Leap Backward?" *Foreign Affairs*, September/October 2007. http://www.foreignaffairs.com/articles/62827/elizabeth-c-economy/the-great-leap-backward.

[62] Harney, *China Price*, 57.

[63] "Mapping the invisible scourge," *The Economist*, August 15, 2015.

[64] Edward Wong, "Beijing Issues Red Alert Over Air Pollution for the First Time," New York Times, December 7, 2015.

[65] "Mapping", *supra*.

[66] Economy, "The Great Leap Backward?", supra.

[67] Bejna Xu, "China's Environmental Crisis," *Council on Foreign Relations*, updated February 5, 2014. http://www.cfr.org/china/chinas-environmental-crisis/p12608#p3

[68]"The East is grey," The Economist, August 10, 2013. http://www.economist.com/news/briefing/21583245-china-worlds-worst-polluter-largest-investor-green-energy-its-rise-will-have/.

[69] *Id.*

[70] Chai Jing's review: Under the Dome – Investigating China's Smog. At this writing, it is available at the following URL: https://www.youtube.com/watch?v=T6X2uwlQGQM#t=45is.

[71] For a discussion of the challenge of breaking out of this box, *See* Elizabeth C. Economy, *The River Runs Black: The Environmental Challenge to China's Future* (Ithaca: A CFR Book, Cornell University Press, 2004), and Yanzhong Huang, "Tackling Chinas Environmental Health Crisis," *Counsel on Foreign Relations*, May 14, 2015. http://www.cfr.org/china/tackling-chinas-environmental-health-crisis/p36538.

[72] Maura Elizabeth Cunningham, "The Vulnerability of China's Left-Behind Children," Wall Street Journal, March 21, 2014. http://blogs.wsj.com/chinarealtime/2014/03/21/the-vulnerability-of-chinas-left-behind-children/

[73] Richard Silk, "China's Hukou Reform Plan Starts to Take Shape," Wall Street Journal, August 4, 2015.

http://blogs.wsj.com/chinarealtime/2014/08/04/chinas-hukou-reform-plan-starts-to-take-shape/

[74] Adam Matthews, "China's Bloody Factories," *supra*.

[75] Harney, *China Price*, 289.

[76] Bloomberg has published a tool with which you can play with the percentages of growth for the U.S. and China. *See* "China's GDP will overtake the U.S. level in 2026 at these 2030 target growth rates: U.S. 2.0%; China 6.5%," *Bloomberg*. http://www.bloomberg.com/graphics/2016-us-vs-china-economy/.

[77] "Made in China?" *The Economist*, March 12, 2015. http://www.economist.com/news/leaders/21646204-asias-dominance-manufacturing-will-endure-will-make-development-harder-others-made.

[78] "Car ownership tops 154 million in China in 2014," Xinhua, January 28, 2015.

[79] "Rich province, poor province," *The Economist*, October 2, 2016, 41.

[80] Derek Scissors of the American Enterprise Institute, quoted in Clifford Krauss and Keith Bradsher, "China's Global Ambitions, Cash and Strings Attached," *New York Times*, July 24, 2015. https://www.nytimes.com/2015/07/26/business/international/chinas-global-ambitions-with-loans-and-strings-attached.html

[81] *Id.*

[82] *Id.*

[83] American Enterprise Institute, cited in Keith Bradsher and Adam Nossiter, "In Nigeria, Chinese Investment Comes with a Downside," *New York Times*, December 5, 2015. https://www.nytimes.com/2015/12/06/business/international/in-nigeria-chinese-investment-comes-with-a-downside.html

[84] Krauss and Bradsher, *supra*.

[85] *Id.*

[86] Bradhser and Nossiter, *supra*.

[87] Krauss and Bradsher, *supra*.

[88] David Goldwyn, the State Department's special envoy for international energy affairs during President Obama's first term, quoted in Krauss and Bradsher, *supra*.

[89] Alberto Acosta, who served as President Correa's energy minister during his first term, quoted in Krauss and Bradsher, *supra*.

---

[90] Editorial, August 25, 2015, O Estado de S. Paulo, cited in Keith Bradsher, "China Falters, and the Global Economy Is Forced to Adapt," *New York Times*, August 26, 2015.

http://cn.nytimes.com/business/20150828/c28chinaecon/print/en-us/

[91] Krauss and Bradsher, *supra*.

[92] *Id*.

[93] "Working together for development," *New African*, March 2015, 34.

[94] Norimitsu Onishi, "China Pledges $60 Billion to Aid Africa's Development," *New York Times*, December 4, 2015. https://www.nytimes.com/2015/12/05/world/africa/china-pledges-60-billion-to-aid-africas-development.html

[95] Brian Spegele, "GE Follows China into Developing Markets," *Wall Street Journal*, October 15, 2016. Jack Farchy, "The New Trade Routes: Silk Road Corridor," *Financial Times*, May 10, 2016. Amy Kasmin, Farhan Bokhari, and Christian Shepherd, "China and Pakistan pin hopes on Arabian Sea port," *Financial Times*, October 3, 2016.

[96] Bradsher and Nossiter, "In Nigeria, Chinese Investment Comes with a Downside," *New York Times*, December 5, 2015. https://www.nytimes.com/2015/12/06/business/international/in-nigeria-chinese-investment-comes-with-a-downside.html

[97] Bradsher and Nossiter, *supra*.

[98] Emir Muhammadu Sanusi II, the traditional ruler of Kano in northern Nigeria, quoted in Bradsher and Nossiter, *supra*.

[99] Bradsher and Nossiter, supra.

[100] Ted Mann, "Kentucky Workers Reject Chinese Firm's Offer," *Wall Street Journal*, November 23, 2016.

[101] William Wilkes, "Chinese Firm Circles Lighting Maker," Wall Street Journal, October 11, 2016.

[102] Guy Chazan and Sefan Wagstyl, "Berlin to harden stance on China investors," *Financial Times*, October 29, 2016.

[103] Lingling Wei, "China's Overseas Funding to Shrink," *Wall Street Journal*, January 14, 2017.

[104] "Hinckley Pointless," *The Economist*, August 6, 2016, 9.

[105] "The plateau, unpacified," *The Economist*, September 17, 2016.

[106] Erich Schwartzel, "Wanda's Chief Courts Hollywood," *Wall Street Journal*, October 19, 2016.

[107] Joshua Philipp, "Hollywood Trades Censorship for Chinese Market," Epoch Times, March 14, 2014. http://www.theepochtimes.com/n3/561356-hollywood-trades-censorship-for-chinese-market/

[108] Elizabeth Redden, "Confucius Says . . ." *Inside Higher Ed*, January 4, 2012.

[109] *Id.*

[110] *Id.*

[111] L. Gordon Crovits, "China's 'Soft' Power Exposed," *Wall Street Journal*, November 9, 2015.

[112] For example, in 2014, China announced a 12.2 percent increase in defense spending, to $132 billion, at a time when its GDP was growing at 7.5%, continuing years of double-digit increases. "China Announces 12.2% Increase in Military Budget," New York Times, March 5, 2014. http://www.nytimes.com/2014/03/06/world/asia/china-military-budget.html.

[113] "U.S. Official Warns About China's Military Buildup," New York Times, August 24, 2011. http://www.nytimes.com/2011/08/25/world/25military.html.

[114] Breakout: Inside China's military buildup; Reuters. http://www.reuters.com/investigates/china-military/
See also: Connected: China; Reuters, Special Reports. http://connectedchina.reuters.com/

[115] Breakout – Inside China's Military Buildup, Thomson Reuters, January 17, 2013. http://www.reuters.com/investigates/china-military/.

[116] *Ibid.*

[117] Simon Denyer, "China to extend military reach," *Washington Post*, May 27, 2015.

[118] Ankit Panda, "Japan: 7 Chinese Coast Guard Ships, 230 Fishing Boats in Disputed East China Sea Waters," *The Diplomat*, August 8, 2016.

[119] Source: News reports. See, *e.g.*, http://www.china-briefing.com/news/2011/05/31/chinas-territorial-disputes-in-the-south-china-sea-and-east-china-sea.html.

[120] Chinese officials have said that records show that China's sailors discovered Scarborough Shoal (Huangyan Island) 2,000 years ago, and "cite extensive records of visits, mapping expeditions and habitation of the shoal from the Song Dynasty (960-1279 AD) right through to the modern period." David Lague, "China's nine-dashed line in South China Sea." Reuters, May 25, 2012.

http://www.reuters.com/article/us-china-sea-boundary-idUSBRE84O07520120525

[121] Toshi Yoshihara, "The 1974 Paracels Sea Battle: A Campaign Appraisal," *Naval War College Review*, Spring 2016, Vol. 29, No. 2.

[122] The court first concluded that there was no legal basis for China to claim "historic rights" to resources within the sea areas falling within the 'nine-dash line' – any historical claims had been expunged with the ratification of convention, to which China was a party. The tribunal then determined that none of the Spratly Islands could generate a 200-mile exclusive economic zone for any party: therefore, the Philippines' 200-mile zone was exclusive.

[123] The tribunal also found that the Chinese had caused environmental damage in the construction of the islands and in permitting Chinese fishermen to use unlawful methods destructive of habitat. The South China Sea Arbitration. Tribunal Press Release, https://pca-cpa.org/wp-content/uploads/sites/175/2016/07/PH-CN-20160712-Press-Release-No-11-English.pdf

[124] "Courting trouble," *The Economist*, July 16, 2016, 35.

[125] Admiral Wu Shengli, quoted by Jin Canrong. in Jane Perlez, "Courting New President, China Slows Island-Building Off Philippine Coast," New York Times, September 25, 2016.

[126] Zheng Wang, "The Nine-Dashed Line: 'Engraved in Our Hearts,'" The Diplomat, August 25, 2014. http://thediplomat.com/2014/08/the-nine-dashed-line-engraved-in-our-hearts/

[127] *Id.*

[128] Zheng Wang, "The Perception Gap Between China and Its Neighbors," The Diplomat, August 6, 2014. http://thediplomat.com/2014/08/the-perception-gap-between-china-and-its-neighbors/

[129] Jeevan Vasagar and Charles Clover, "Malaysia ruffles feathers with closer China ties," Financial TImes, November 1, 2016.

[130] Jeremy Page, "China Builds First Overseas Military Outpost," *Wall Street Journal*, August 19 2016.

[131] Jordan Wilson, "China's Military Agreements with Argentina: A Potential New Phase in China-Latin America Defense Relations," *U.S.-China Economic and Security Review Commission*, Staff Research Report, November 5, 2015.
http://www.uscc.gov/research_security
http://origin.www.uscc.gov/sites/default/files/Research/China%27s%20Military%20Agreements%20with%20Argentina.pdf

[132] Yoshihara, *Paracels.*

[133] Perlez, "Courting New President," *supra*.

[134] Andrew Browne, "The Growing Risks of a China-U.S. War," *Wall Street Journal*, August 17, 2016.

[135]Henry Kissinger asserts that if America comes to be viewed as a declining power, then, "after an interlude of turmoil and upheaval," China and other countries will step in to exercise much of the leadership assumed by the U.S. since World War II. Kissinger, *World Order*, 232.

[136] See "Taking a tumble," *The Economist*, August 29, 2-15.

[137] Javier Hernandez, "Labor Protests Multiply in China as Economy Slows, Worrying Leaders," New York Times, March 14, 2016. http://www.nytimes.com/2016/03/15/world/asia/china-labor-strike-protest.html?_r=0
Hudson Lockett, "China labour unrest spreads to 'new economy'", *Financial Times*, February 1, 2017.

[138] Jamil Anderlini, "Chinese industry," *supra*.

[139] Christian Shepherd, "China adopts triple strategy to forge sleeker steel industry," *Financial Times*, September 28, 2016.

[140] Brun, Lukas. "Overcapacity in Steel: China's Role in a Global Problem." Duke University Center on Globalization, Governance & Competitiveness, September 1, 2016.
http://www.americanmanufacturing.org/research/entry/global-industrial-overcapacity-the-case-of-steel.
The report reviewed the results of a study of the global steel market commissioned by the Alliance for American Manufacturing.

[141] John W. Miller, "U.S. Steelmakers Ready China Complaints," *Wall Street Journal*, September 23, 2016.

[142] Shepherd, "China adopts," *supra*.

[143] Shawn Donnan and Lucy Hornby, "Blocking Moves," FT Big Read – Global Economy, *Financial Times*, October 13, 2016.

[144] Henry Sanderson and Michael Pooler, "Aluminum producers in west face fresh Chinese threat," Financial Times, September 19, 2016.

[145] Brian Spegele and John W. Miller, "China Continues to Prop Up Its Ailing Factories, Adding to Global Glut," Wall Street Journal, May 9, 2016, *supra*.

http://www.wsj.com/articles/chinese-exports-surge-amid-overcapacity-at-home-1462746980

[146] *Id.*

[147] Shepherd, "China adopts," *supra*.

[148] Donnan and Hornby, "Blocking Moves," *supra*.

[149] In a position paper published in the Spring of 2016, the Alliance for American Manufacturing pointed out that "If the current trend continues, in the long term the United States will end up reliant on Chinese steel producers—and by extension the Chinese government—for the steel needed to equip our armed forces or to quickly rebuild after a catastrophic event." "Steel Import Surge Threatens U.S. National Security," Alliance for American Manufacturing, Spring 2016, 4. http://www.americanmanufacturing.org/research/entry/global-industrial-overcapacity-the-case-of-steel.

[150] "Overcapacity in China: An Impediment to the Party's Reform Agenda," *European Chamber of Commerce in China*, February 22, 2016. http://www.europeanchamber.com.cn/en/press-releases/2423/european_chamber_releases_new_major_report_on_overcapacity_in_china.

[151] *See* Jamil Anderlini, Chinese industry: Ambitions in excess, Financial Times, June 16, 2013. http://www.ft.com/intl/cms/s/0/4d5528ec-d412-11e2-8639-00144feab7de.html#axzz36ARpURhy.

[152] Spegele and Miller, "China Continues," *supra*.

[153] *Id.*

[154] Ian Talley and William Mauldin, "Globalization on the Skids," Wall Street Journal, October 7, 2016.

[155] Eva Dou, "Apple to Invest More in China," *Wall Street Journal*, August 17, 2016.

[156] James Griffiths, "Shenzhou-11 astronauts return after China's longest-ever space mission," CNN, November 18, 2016 http://www.cnn.com/2016/11/18/asia/china-space-shenzhou-11/index.html.

[157] Katie Hunt and David McKenzie, "China: The next space superpower?" *Cable News Network*. Accessed February 9, 2017. http://www.cnn.com/interactive/2015/05/world/china-space/

[158] Xinhua, "China to begin building space station in 2017," China Daily Asia, September 16, 2016. http://www.chinadailyasia.com/nation/2016-09/16/content_15496444.html.

[159] Griffiths, "Shenzou-11," *supra*.

[160] Hunt and McKenzie, "China," *supra*.

[161] *Id.*

[162] *Id.*

[163] "Still Made in China," *The Economist*, September 10, 2015.

[164] Jörg Wuttke, Does Made in China 2025 Mean Not Made by Europeans? Eurobiz.com, April 1, 2016. http://www.eurobiz.com.cn/does-made-in-china-2025-mean-not-made-by-europeans/

[165]Barlett and Steele, *Betrayal,* 70.

[166] Julie Johnsson, "Boeing, China make deals as Xi visits U.S.," Bloomberg News, September _, 2015.

[167] Michael Schulman, "Venture Communism: How China is Building a Start-up Boom," New York Times, September 3, 2016. http://www.nytimes.com/2016/09/04/business/international/venture-communism-how-china-is-building-a-start-up-boom.html?_r=0.

[168] Richard McGregor, *The Party: The Secret World of China's Communist Rulers* (New York: Penguin Books, 2010), xii.

[169] "Chairman of Everything," *The Economist*, April 2, 2016, 43.

[170] *Id.*

[171] Tom Mitchell, "China speculation grows Xi will defy two-term tradition," *Financial Times*, October 12, 2016.

[172] "Who draws the party line?" *The Economist*, June 25, 2016, 36.

[173] Edward Wong, "In War on Internet 'Troublemakers,' China Turns to Law on Picking Quarrels," *New York Times*, July 27, 2015.

[174] "UN body urges China to allow labour activists to continue their job," China Labour Bulletin, November 14, 2016. http://www.clb.org.hk/content/un-body-urges-china-allow-labour-activists-continue-their-job. The All-China Federation of Trade Unions (ACFTU) is China's sole legally mandated trade union. However, like the Japanese trade unions after World War II, it is viewed as an instrumentality of management. Activities outside its structure result in arrests, charges, and imprisonment.

[175] The U.S. Department of State annually publishes its "Country Reports on Human Rights Practices." The Department advises: "Based on factual reporting from our embassies and posts abroad, these Congressionally mandated reports chronicle human rights conditions in almost 200 countries and territories."

[176] . . . Other human rights abuses during the year included alleged extrajudicial killings; executions without due process; prolonged illegal detentions at unofficial holding facilities known as "black jails"; torture and coerced confessions of prisoners . . . lack of due process in judicial proceedings; political control of courts and judges; closed trials . . .

extrajudicial disappearances of Chinese and foreign citizens; restrictions on nongovernmental organizations (NGOs); discrimination against women, minorities, and persons with disabilities; a coercive birth-limitation policy that, despite the lifting of one-child-per-family restrictions, in some cases resulted in forced abortion (sometimes at advanced stages of pregnancy); and trafficking in persons. Country Reports on Human Rights Practices 2015, China, U.S. Department of State.

[177] James Fallows, "China's Great Leap Backward," *The Atlantic*, December 2016, 58.

[178] The editors of *The Economist* reached the same conclusion. "Chairman of Everything," *supra*.

[179] Fallows, *supra*.

[180] Orville Schell, "China's Reckoning," *Wall Street Journal*, August 29, 2015.

[181] Gideon Rachman, "Xi has changed China's winning formula," Financial Times, May 31, 2016.

[182] "Master of Nothing," *The Economist*, October 22, 2016, 37.

[183] China Labour Bulletin, http://maps.clb.org.hk/strikes/en.

[184] Javier Hernandez, "Labor Protests Multiply," *supra*.

[185] "UN body urges," *supra*.

[186] "Chasing the Chinese dream," *The Economist*, May 4, 2013. http://www.economist.com/news/briefing/21577063-chinas-new-leader-has-been-quick-consolidate-his-power-what-does-he-now-want-his.

[187] *Id.*

[188] *Id.*

[189] "China's leadership risks a great leap backward," *Financial Times, October 12, 2016.*

[190] Schell, "China's Reckoning," *supra*.

Chapter 9

What does the future hold?

What, then, does the future hold? In Chapters 1, 2, and 3, we viewed the history of our trade and economic policy through a series of ten-year snapshots, ending in 2015. Now, we need to take one more snapshot, for 2025.

In the Introduction, I posed the question, what do we say to the high school and college Classes of 2020? In 2025, they will be one year out of college, and five years into their careers. What will their situation be? We can look to developments during 2016 for portents of things to come.

More Trouble with Trade

Mexico under NAFTA

What does the future hold for U.S. trade with Mexico under NAFTA? Several cases from 2016 tell the story.

Carrier Air Conditioning

Our first case begins on February 10, 2016.[1] Carrier, a heating, ventilating and air-conditioning manufacturer based on the west side of Indianapolis, announced that it was moving its main manufacturing facility, founded in the

1950s, to Monterrey, Mexico, eliminating 1,400 jobs. United Technologies Electronic Controls (UTEC), a nearby manufacturer of microprocessor controls for HVAC equipment that supplies Carrier, also announced it was moving its operation to Mexico, eliminating 700 jobs. Both companies are units of United Technologies Corp. based in Hartford, Connecticut.

The Carrier closing came as a surprise to employees, whose representatives said the company had made regular investments in the plant to keep it modern. And the company already had resorted to a two-tier wage system, with a quarter of the workers earning about $14 an hour, about $30,000 a year, and the rest about $26 an hour - about $55,000 a year, as much as $70,000 a year with overtime. No one is supporting a family on $14 an hour, even with two incomes. The Indianapolis Star reported that the Mexican workers replacing Carrier employees would be earning a base wage of $3 an hour. The Carrier executive announcing the move to the employees told them, "I want to be clear, this is strictly a business decision . . . in this extremely price-sensitive industry."

Under an agreement reached between the company and the union, Carrier's displaced employees would receive severance pay equal to one week for every year of service and six months of medical insurance; meanwhile the current contract would remain in effect until all the 1,400 jobs were eliminated, in three waves through 2019. A company spokeswoman said in a statement:

> Carrier recognizes the impact on employees, their families and the community. We appreciate their hard work and are pleased to have worked with the United Steelworkers to provide certainty

> through a comprehensive benefits package designed to help ease the transition.[2]

The employees and their union representatives were not "pleased" at all, and neither did they feel "appreciated." The union local president said:

> We feel like the people deserve a whole hell of a lot more for what they put into the facility. They are losing their jobs through no fault of their own due to pure and simple corporate greed.[3]

State and local officials were scrambling to help the displaced employees, with the city of Indianapolis amassing resources under a "Carrier Task Force" established by the mayor and funded with $1.2 million in repayments by Carrier of job retention incentives the city had given the company, and the state offering free job training services. However, as always, these efforts would fall short – from whence would anyone find jobs to replace those lost, even with retraining? Indirect job losses were projected at 1,358, with a statewide loss of income totaling $108 million a year. And this analysis did not include the job losses at UTEC. The local impacts would likely be catastrophic for families and the community, following a now all-too familiar pattern of home foreclosures, boarded-up shops, broken families, crime, and addiction.

However, note this: Carrier's residential HVAC headquarters and engineering organization will remain in Indianapolis. The United Technologies higher ups in Hartford and Indianapolis were happy to send their production to Mexico, but not to move there themselves.

I also was struck by this: "Experts" contacted initially in reaction to the announcement reassured a newspaper reporter that the move was an outlier, contrary to current trends. One "economic expert" from a local university said the decision was "out of sync" with other manufacturers, and that it is "highly unlikely that other manufacturers will uproot their factories and leave the country." Another "economic expert" at a Washington think tank echoed the sentiment, saying the days of companies leaving for cheap labor are mostly in the past.[4]

In my view, this is another example of our elites having their heads stuck in the sand, and of their utter failure to serve the interests of ordinary Americans. Their "opinions" could not be further from the truth.

The truth is that Carrier was aligning with powerful trends of profit-seeking and competition that are continuing to draw production out of the U.S. and into Mexico. Those trends were well captured in a company press release from Carrier:

> This move is intended to address the challenges *we continue to face in a rapidly changing HVAC industry, with the continued migration of the HVAC industry to Mexico,* including our suppliers and competitors, and ongoing cost and pricing pressures driven, in part, by new regulatory requirements.
>
> Relocating our operations to *a region where we have existing infrastructure and a strong supplier base* will allow us to operate more cost effectively so that we can continue to produce high-quality HVAC products that are competitively positioned while continuing to meet customer needs. [Emphasis supplied.] [5]

In late November, 2016, President-elect Donald Trump and Indiana Governor and Vice-President Elect Mike Pence announced an agreement with Carrier to keep 1,100 of the jobs in Indiana in return for an incentive package from the Indiana state government. However, it later was reported that the real number was 800 – more than 500 jobs were still going to Mexico, plus the 700 jobs at UTEC. The package reportedly included five million dollars in tax credits over the next decade in exchange for keeping the jobs at the Indianapolis plant, plus one million dollars in training grants and up to one million in additional tax credits based on Carrier's planned $16 million-dollar investment in the West Indianapolis factory.

So, there you have it: the continued migration of the HVAC industry to Mexico, ongoing cost and pricing pressures, and regulatory requirements, and Carrier air conditioning, a venerable American brand since the 1950s, is moving production to Mexico. That is the trend. That is the future.

And indeed, it did not take long for the "experts" to be proven wrong. On the afternoon of Friday, October 14, 2016, the employees of the Rexnord Corp. ball bearing plant in Indianapolis were told, without any advance notice, that the plant was closing and were ushered out the door. There, too, the company and union had agreed in 2012 to a two-tiered pay scale under which new hires were making five or six dollars an hour less. Average wages were reported at $25 an hour. The company recently had agreed to do away with the two-tier system, and now union representatives were thinking the company did so with the intent of moving and not having to pay the higher wages. As with Carrier, the city had given Rexnord job retention/creation incentives in the form of tax abatements on new equipment, and was investigating recovering them from the company.

So, the story is the same: the government gives up tax income and the employees give up pay, but, whether due to competitive pressures or a desire for larger profits, the lure of low wages in Mexico wins out in the end.[6] Meanwhile, the Rexnord workers fretted about where to find employment that would replace jobs paying about $25 an hour, and how they would make mortgage, car, and tuition payments.[7] Was Rexnord just another "outlier" as Carrier and UTEC were said to be? Hardly so, if you consider how the move to Mexico is playing out in another industry, in our next case.

Oreos®, Ritz® and Grahams

Our next case occurred a month after Carrier's, on March 23, 2016.[8] That was the last day on the job for 277 workers at the Chicago factory of Nabisco (National Biscuit Company, now called Mondelez International). Operating in Chicago since the 1950s and the company's largest, the factory had employed as many as 4,000 workers, but with modernization, that number was down to 1,200.

The company planned to replace nine of the plant's sixteen production lines with four new lines, spending $130 million on new equipment that would reduce employment on those lines from 600 to 300 jobs. But in the Spring of 2015, the company announced that it would not be installing the new lines in the Chicago facility after all, but rather in a $400 million plant the company had built the previous year in Salinas, Mexico.

The company said putting the new lines in the Chicago facility would cost $46 million more in annualized operating costs and capital expense than operating in

Mexico. The company met with representatives of the plant employees' unions; however, the company said the unions' "input did not provide a measurably impactful way to close the gap" between the costs in Chicago and Mexico.[9]

So, that's where we stand: an American company producing venerable brands such as Oreos®, Ritz®, and Grahams sold in the American market, calculates how much money it can save by making those products in Mexico, and tells its workers, "close the gap, or we're out of here." But notice, it is only the production that is out of here – the sales are still into the American market.

And note also, as in the case of Carrier and United Technologies, we don't see the top brass moving to Mexico; they want to retain all the privileges of living in the United States. Ron Baker, the strategic campaign coordinator for the Bakery, Confectionery, Tobacco Workers and Grain Millers union (BCTGM), told USA Today:

> The only reason they house their company in the United States is because they (the) CEOs can have security here and enjoy a civil society," he said. "You would never see them move themselves or their headquarters to places they are moving their production facilities." [10]

I would add that that is indeed a short-sighted strategy: as the effects of their ruthless business model spread, they eventually will find that they are unable to insulate themselves in their privileged enclaves from the depressed America they are creating.

Meanwhile, the effects are being felt by the laid-off Chicago workers. In an interview, one woman who had lost her hair from worry summed up the workers' plight:

> We're all . . . fighting for the same cause. . . and that's just to have a decent job, raise your kids, without having to, to worry.[11]

That is, to worry about your company sending your job to Mexico or some such place because it costs so much less to operate there. On March 23, 2016, that time had come for 277 of the workers at Nabisco's Chicago bakery.

One must wonder, what is next? According to reports, Mondelez's other facilities in the Chicago area include a Naperville plant focused on Triscuits, and a confectionary plant in the Rockford area that makes such products as chewing gum. A company spokesman said the company employs about 3,000 in Illinois. Applying the company's ruthless logic of operating costs, would the company not transfer those jobs to Mexico as well? That seems to be what the future holds.

Ford Sends More Production to Mexico

Our third case begins a couple of weeks later, on April 5, 2016. On that day, the Ford Motor Company announced that it was investing $1.6 billion in a new plant in Mexico's San Luis Potosi State to produce small cars. Later announcements made clear that Ford was referring to *all* its small car production. Ford said that construction was to begin in the summer, with new small cars expected to start rolling off the line in 2018, and that the plant would create *2,800 jobs* by 2020.[12]

As UAW President Dennis Williams pointed out in response to the announcement, there was nothing necessary about this move: "For every investment in Mexico it means jobs that could have and should have been available right here in the USA."[13]

Ford President of the Americas Joe Hinrichs made clear that the reason for the move was to maximize profits: "We're improving the profitability of our small cars," Hinrichs told the Detroit News.[14] The Wall Street Journal quoted industry experts as saying the move would yield cost savings of about $1,300 per vehicle, or about $300 million a year.[15]

The move was not new, to Ford or to the industry. A dozen motor vehicle manufacturing facilities were opened or announced for central Mexico's industrial belt between 2010 and 2015, part of a $20 billion investment by global automakers. U.S. auto makers, especially, have been active: The Wall Street Journal reports that after the 2008 financial crisis, the U.S. companies have placed a "disproportionate amount of new North American production capacity in Mexico in an attempt to keep up with record sales volumes."[16]

Some commentators have suggested that a reason for the increased auto production in Mexico is the country's entry into a large number of free trade agreements. Audi cited that reasoning for locating a $1.3 billion factory for the entire global production of its Q5 SUV in the south-central Mexico town of San Jose Chiapa.[17] In fact, the main difference from the United States is that Mexico has a free trade agreement with Europe, so a German company shipping to Europe from Mexico can avoid the ten percent duty that would apply to a car shipped from the U.S.

Nevertheless, while it is true that eighty percent of Mexico's production of cars and light trucks is for export, seventy percent is bound for the U.S. market.[18] Mexico's free trade agreements have little to do with it.

The fact is, U.S. and foreign auto companies have been placing production in Mexico for one simple reason: to produce products for the U.S. market at low wages. Audi executives have said the company will save 50 percent on labor costs at its Mexican Q5 plant as compared with Tennessee.[19] Mexican autoworkers reportedly make an average of twenty percent of what their U.S. counterparts earn.[20]

The Wall Street Journal reported that a contract for work at the announced Ford plant put factory wages at the facility at about $1.15 to $2.30 per hour, consistent with other auto-assembly plants in the region. (A Ford spokesman did not deny these amounts, but pointed to other worker benefits in the contract, such as life insurance, matching funds for worker-savings accounts and year-end bonuses equivalent to 20 days' pay.)[21]

And at other foreign company's plants? A worker at the Juarez plant of Lear Corp., a Michigan-based auto parts company, told a Journal reporter that the company recently increased wages at his plant, raising his pay by thirty-seven percent to about $46.00 a week, and by adding overtime bonuses and paid days off on birthdays. Assuming a forty-hour work week, he received a pay raise from $0.84 per hour to $1.15 per hour. A spokesman for the Korean auto maker Kia told the reporter that the company is paying an average of $7,200 a year, with engineers earning at least three times that, at the company's new factory outside Monterrey. At best, the Kia employees are averaging $3.50 per hour, with engineers making $21,600 a year.[22]

So, the going rate ranges from under $1 an hour at some parts factories to around $3 an hour at the large assembly facilities. The pay is higher than Mexico's minimum wage of is 73 pesos, or $4 a day. However, it still is so low that

Mexicans often can earn more in the "informal sector" that comprises half of the country's employment, such as working as street vendors.

And it is less than it costs to live, even in Mexico. For example, Monterrey, where many automobile and other factories are located, and where Carrier will be paying its workers $3.00 an hour, has a cost of living that is reported as only one-third lower than Indianapolis.[23] That is, trying to live on $3.00 an hour in Monterrey is like trying to live on $4.50 an hour in Indianapolis. It can't be done. And that's at the high end of the Mexican pay scale.

The Mexican workers are aware that they are being paid less than a living wage. During summer of 2016, in the border town of Ciudad Juarez across the border from El Paso, home to some 300 *Maquiladora* factories, workers staged demonstrations seeking pay increases and improved working conditions.[24]

Mexico's state and federal governments are trying to move workers up the value and pay scale, by turning out more engineers, expanding enrollment at technical schools, and creating special training programs tailored to factory needs. The Wall Street Journal reports that a $37 million state-funded facility was built on the grounds of Audi's plant near Puebla in 2014 as an incentive to win the company's business.[25]

However, the automobile, auto parts, and other manufacturing companies are caught up in a perverse effort to keep wages down. Employers are increasingly turning to perks such as athletic fields to attract and retain employees – anything to avoid increasing pay. One plant manager told a Journal reporter that it was important not to raise pay so much that industries would "move further south" looking for lower-cost labor markets.[26]

So, recruiters look for new hires to work in enormous automobile assembly and component factories built in the middle of nowhere in rural areas, for companies paying less than a living wage even by Mexican standards.

The future portends more of the same. Ford later announced that was canceling its plans for the new $1.6 billion small-car plant, but still planned to send all its small car production to other, existing plants in Mexico. And even without the new plant, Ford has been investing in Mexico, announcing plans to invest $2.5 billion in two new engine and transmission plants and an expansion of a diesel engine line that will create about 3,800 jobs. The new production is expected to double Ford's production in Mexico. General Motors also is investing $5 billion over the next several years, which will double its production in Mexico.[27] And Japanese and German auto companies have announced a long list of investments in new Mexican production capacity.[28]

Annual light-vehicle production in Mexico is forecast to climb to 5.1 million vehicles by 2020, a 50 percent increase from 2015's record 3.4 million units, with more than 70 percent of the cars and light trucks headed to the U.S. market.[29]

And the problem is not just with vehicles. Perhaps the greater problem is with vehicle parts and components. In 1990, total U.S. imports of car parts were $58 billion; by 2014, they had increased to $139 billion (both figures adjusted for inflation). Mexico was the largest source of imports that year, accounting for 34 percent of the total; China accounted for another 13 percent. Both countries' imports have grown dramatically, with Mexico up 86 percent since 2008, and China more than doubling during that period. The result is more U.S.-produced cars, with less U.S. content than ever: Government data show the Ford Escape having 55% U.S. and Canadian content in the 2015 model year, down from 90% for 2010 models.; the Honda Accord assembled in the U.S. went from 75% to 70% U.S. and Canadian content during the same period. [30]

The growth in parts imports has put tremendous pressure on wages in the American parts production jobs that have not yet been lost altogether. The average hourly wage for car-parts production workers was $19.91 in 2014, down 23 percent from ten years earlier; at automobile manufacturers, the wage was $27.83, down 22 percent over the same time.[31]

I was particularly touched by a Wall Street Journal report of a young couple in Three Rivers, Michigan, both working the night shift at a car parts manufacturer, he making $11.00 an hour stocking the line, she making $11.50 driving a forklift.[32] The story included a photograph of the couple and their five young children by previous marriages, standing on the stoop of the modest house they try to keep up on a combined income of $55,000 a year. All seven faces are bearing "grin and bear it" smiles, exuding good humor, energy, and a willing spirit – ordinary Americans wanting to make a go of it, trying to get by. But they are not.

The same article reported on a thirty-seven-year-old woman who was working in the Selma, Alabama plant of auto parts maker Lear Corp. -- the same company that recently had raised its workers' pay to $46 a week at its plant in Juarez, Mexico. In Selma, she was making $12.25 an hour. A company spokesman told the Journal that Lear was paying "competitive wages," the same refrain as heard from companies operating in Mexico. Referring to a turnover rate of less than two percent, he told the Journal reporter, "If our employees couldn't make ends meet, they would demonstrate their dissatisfaction with their feet by leaving and getting a job elsewhere."[33] As if they would stay there for one minute if there were any better-paying opportunities available.

And so ends our third case, a move by Ford to send its small car production to Mexico, a telling story that is part of a larger picture of offshoring parts and vehicle production, paying neither the Mexican nor the remaining U.S. workers enough to live on. And unfortunately, it is a continuing story that, if anything, is gaining momentum.

Sentry Safe goes to Mexico

Our final case winds up on Wednesday, June 29, 2016. That was the final day of work for 350 employees of Sentry Safe, "the world's leading maker of fire-resistant safes and security storage containers," operating from a factory near Rochester, New York. The company was founded in 1930 and operated by three generations of the same family until it was sold to Master Lock in July of 2014. In 2015, Master Lock announced it was moving production from the plant to Nogales, Mexico, a border city south of Tucson, Arizona to save on labor costs and keep the company competitive. In the corporate-speak of the official announcement, Master Lock said:

> This decision has been made to help us remain competitive in the marketplace as we optimize our operational footprint by consolidating locations and adding meaningful scale to our other existing facilities. Our decision is in no way a reflection of the successes, talents and skills of the Sentry Safe

team. We're incredibly impressed with their commitment to build a great company."

The third-generation owner of Sentry Safe told reporters he was "shocked and betrayed." He said he had an understanding with the former CEO of Master Lock that the operation would stay put, and that he and his brother would have never sold the company to Master Lock if they had known the company would move the jobs out of the area. Thinking of his father and grandfather, and the jobs, he said, "It makes me sick none of us saw this coming."

Locals pointed out that the closing would be hard on restaurants and other local businesses in the East Rochester area. One financial analyst estimated that the closing could remove some $30 million from the local economy. The economic activity has now been added to the economy of Nogales, where the Master Lock facility can be seen in an industrial park on the south side of the city, along with Otis Elevators, Kimberly Clark, and other companies.[34]

More of the Same

These snapshots from 2016 point to a continued movement to Mexico of manufacturing of goods for the U.S. market. Just as there are firms ready to help you outsource your white-collar functions to India, there are firms ready, willing, and able to provide you with "turn-key" services enabling you to outsource your manufacturing functions to Mexico.[35]

I visited the website of one recently, in response to an offer to "cut manufacturing costs and stating that their "Free Guide on Running Manufacturing in Mexico can save you money." The guide provides a "general outline of average monthly wages for typical manufacturing personnel," which

I have included in the following chart, along with projected hourly and yearly wages based on a 48-hour work week:

Maquiladora Labor Costs per IVEMSA				
	Pay/Mo.	Hrs./Mo.	Pay/Hr.	Pay/Yr.
Basic operator	$ 280.00	208	$ 1.35	$ 3,360
Semi-skilled operator	$ 408.00	208	$ 1.96	$ 4,896
Skilled operator	$ 456.00	208	$ 2.19	$ 5,472
Group leader	$ 560.00	208	$ 2.69	$ 6,720
Production supervisor	$ 1,440.00	208	$ 6.92	$ 17,280
Production engineer	$ 2,240.00	208	$ 10.77	$ 26,880
QA engineer	$ 2,240.00	208	$ 10.77	$ 26,880
Plant manager	$ 6,000.00	208	$ 28.85	$ 72,000
Source: IVEMSA promotional brochure, http://ivemsa.com				

The brochure goes on to state: "As well, productivity in Mexico is generally higher with typically a 48-hour work week (before overtime is required) vs the 40 U.S. hours per week. When compared to overall lower operational costs, the labor rate is an even better value. Thanks to the lower cost of living in Mexico, the labor rate is a win-win for all concerned." [36] Of course, we know this last sentence to be a lie, as these wages don't cover the cost of living in Mexico.

As of February 2017, President Trump has announced his intentions to renegotiate NAFTA and take other steps to stem the flow of American manufacturing to Mexico, a move with wide support among the American electorate. And dissatisfaction with NAFTA is not limited to the U.S. side. In August of 2016, tens of thousands of rural farmers protested in Mexico City against the flood of cheap American corn that had been coming to Mexico under NAFTA; in July, a polling company reported that, while 52 percent of Mexicans were opposed to exiting NAFTA, 33 percent were in favor.[37]

Meanwhile, however, news reports indicated Rexnord and other manufacturers such as Caterpillar are continuing with their plans to move manufacturing to Mexico.[38] While the future is uncertain, for now the trend is for more of the same.

More "Factory Asia"

So much for Mexico; what does the future hold for trade with Asia? In Chapter 8 we saw China's plans for continued expansion of its export-led manufacturing sector, while moving up the value chain and increasing the percentage of Chinese value-added. Meanwhile, pretty much every other Asian country is seeking to do the same thing.

Vietnam is pushing to become a regional manufacturing hub. Vietnam wants to capture the large companies that have been coming to Southeast Asia in response to investment incentives, seeking lower-cost alternatives to China, and in pursuit of the region's large markets. The Economist reported in September of 2016 that there were an estimated 2,000 Taiwanese companies operating in Vietnam, including one operating a $10.6 billion steel plant. Like China, Vietnam is focusing on new manufacturing techniques and increasing domestic share.[39]

Malaysia is seeking to replicate Shenzhen's growth into a 10-million-person urban manufacturing zone across from Hong Kong, with the development of Iskandar, across the Johor Strait from Singapore. Recognizing that "industries are the queen bee," Malaysian developers are recruiting foreign companies to locate production there to create jobs for local residents who will live in thousands of residential units being built by Chinese developers.[40]

In September of 2014, the newly appointed Prime Minister of India, Narendra Modi, launched his call to 'Make in India,' a campaign seen as one of the boldest international marketing initiatives from the Prime Minister's office. It was a call to nations focused on defense, aeronautics and other public sector enterprises to use India as a manufacturing hub. As of June 2015, numerous investments and commitments had been made, including $170 million in an R&D center for China's Huawei; an increase in French aerospace manufacturer Airbus' Indian outsourcing to $2 billion; and a commitment by Japan to pour $33.5 billion into Indian infrastructure projects over the next five years.[41]

But India is not only aiming at high-end manufacturing; it wants the low-end work too. A government program is recruiting rural women to work in the garment factories in cities like Bangalore. The government is trying to tap a pool of unused labor: in a 2012 survey, 205 million women aged 15 to 60 reported their occupation as attending to household duties; economists have projected that India's GDP could increase by as much as 27 percent if women were in the workforce on a par with men.

In 2016, a New York Times reporter visited a factory where girls recruited into the program make clothes for a leading western brand. Despite the presence of much machinery, she reported:

> And yet, incredibly, garments worn in the West are still made by humans - nearly all of them women, working exhausting hours with few legal protections and little chance of advancement, for some of the lowest wages in the global supply chain. . . . The girls' joints and back hurt, and their fingers have been punctured and sliced by needles

> and clippers. They live in a "hostel," and are locked in there except for alternate Sundays. . . . For two weeks' work, after deductions for room and board, health insurance and pension, they receive about twenty-eight dollars.[42]

The list goes on – we could include Indonesia, the Philippines, Thailand. Each of these countries is seeking to out-compete the others in export-oriented manufacturing, at ever-more sophisticated levels, using technology supplied by the multi-national companies. And if they are successful, it will be at the expense of both the developed and less-developed countries whose manufacturing they displace.

Meanwhile, Japan is working hard not to let China and Southeast Asia snatch away the American market. For example, in 2016, Japanese automakers were scaling up their efforts to capture market share in the American market for pickup trucks, where American companies have dominated. Nissan beefed up the warranty on its full-size pickup, and Honda and Toyota introduced new models.[43] And so, for Asia as well as Mexico, the future of trade looks to be "more of the same, except worse."

The Five Actors

In Chapter 1, I suggested that we bear in mind four "actors" in the drama of U.S. trade relations: (i) the U.S. public sector; (ii) the U.S. private sector; (iii) foreign countries' public sector; and (iv) foreign countries' private sector. It appears that we can expect more of the same from each of these, with the notable possible exception of the U.S. public sector, given the results of the 2016 presidential election. (For example, on his first full day in office,

President Trump signed a memorandum withdrawing the U.S. from the proposed Trans-Pacific Partnership.[44])

However, I also noted in Chapter 1 that there is another set of actors taking part in the situation: American consumers. As we consider what the future portends for trade, a case study should give us pause: in the Spring of 2016, General Motors started supplying U.S. dealers with the Buick Envision sport-utility vehicle entirely produced in GM facilities in China.

GM claimed that Buick had "holes in its lineup" as U.S. customers enjoying low gas prices moved toward S.U.V.s. The company had "ample Envision capacity" at a factory in Shandong province in China. The Envision is one of the first completely Chinese-made cars being sold in the U.S. Volvo, recently purchased by China's Geely, had begun shipping to the U.S. small numbers of its S60 model made at a plant in China. The Envision reportedly was designed and engineered at GM facilities near Detroit. It is built by Shanghai GM, a joint venture between GM and SAIC Motor Corp., and is enjoying strong sales in China. Sales of the Envision in American also have been brisk, as consumers have not been concerned with the cars' being made in China.[45]

China has a great deal of overcapacity in its automobile production market, with capacity to make 40 million light vehicles and sales expected to be 25 million in 2016. Much of this capacity is in joint ventures with U.S. automakers, so one can expect that the case of the Envision is only the beginning of things to come. And if American consumers are ready to buy Chinese-built Buicks and Mexican-built Fords without batting an eye, then the future does indeed hold "more trouble with trade."

More Job Losses

What do we see when we look to the future of employment? Every two years, the Bureau of Labor Statistics publishes its projections for employment for the coming ten years; in 2015, the BLS published its projections for the period 2014 through 2024.

More Job Losses in Manufacturing

For manufacturing employment, the BLS projected the loss of an additional 814,000 jobs, a seven percent decline, from 12.2 million to 11.4 million. Apparel, textiles, and leather goods, already decimated, were projected to shed an additional 135,000 jobs, a 34 percent decline. Computers and electronics were projected to lose an additional 130,700 jobs, a 12 percent decline. Of 21 manufacturing sectors, only one, fabricated metal products, projected an increase, of one percent; employment in all other sectors was projected to decline through 2024.

What will this look like on the ground? We can catch a glimpse in Granite City, Illinois, just north of St. Louis, where US Steel has operated a steelmaking plant since the end of the nineteenth century. An enormous, sprawling facility, US Steel describes it on its web site as "a leading supplier of high-quality hot-rolled, cold-rolled and coated sheet steel products to customers in the construction, container, piping and tubing, service center, and automotive industries." Only it is not -- it shut down at the beginning of 2016, laying off most of the 2,000 workers. The company said the shutdown was temporary, until sufficient demand returned; in November, the union web site was telling the still-idle workers about the union's food bank, and where they could pick up donated turkeys for Thanksgiving.

One worker told a New York Times reporter how he had taken a job there in 1999 at age 38, starting out shoveling slag and ending up operating the crane that carried the 350-ton ladle of molten steel. Making $24.62 an hour and overtime, he took home $86,000, enough to get a daughter through grad school and a son started in college. Now, his eyes were tearing up as he recounted telling his son he wouldn't be returning for his junior year. The head of the union local told the reporter of how his duties now amounted to that of a social worker, including dealing with the previous night's news that a worker, one of his high school classmates, had shot himself to death, leaving behind two children. [46] The American dream broken, because China had built too many steel mills and was dumping their product on the American market to stay operational, even as they built more mills.

If you go on Google Earth, you will see that the US Steel mill is about the only thing happening in Granite City. Surrounding it are residential neighborhoods largely populated by its workers. Neighborhoods that, if the mill doesn't reopen, will be like the neighborhoods around the Carrier plant in West Indianapolis, 240 miles up the road by I-70, where families will be riding it out until their homes are foreclosed.

Many of BLS' projected job losses in manufacturing will occur due to automation and the application of robots and artificial intelligence in the manufacturing process. [47] But this makes it all the more important that we do not send any of the remaining manufacturing jobs overseas.

More Job Losses in Services

Perhaps even more alarming than the trend in manufacturing jobs, is the future for service-sector jobs. It turns out that many industries and job functions that some thought were safely protected against offshoring, including the white-collar and high-skilled, are not.

In a 2007 study, Princeton economist Alan Blinder reviewed 800 occupations with respect to their potential to be offshored. His middle case conclusion was that 25 percent, representing some 33 million jobs in 2004, had the potential to be offshored.[48] A study by the U.S. Bureau of Labor Statistics reached similar conclusions. The BLS identified 160 service sector occupations that are susceptible to offshore outsourcing. (Blinder's study included all occupations.) The 160 occupations included a wide spectrum as to required skill and training and sophistication of services, from proofreaders to biophysicists. At the time of the study in 2008, there were 30 million people employed in these occupations.[49]

Since those studies were conducted, offshoring has continued, and has been moving up the value chain. Companies are increasingly moving sophisticated, mission-critical functions such as product design and research and development to China, India and other offshore locations, according to a study by Duke University and management consulting firm Booz Allen Hamilton (now Price Water-house Coopers).[50] Among the study's findings:

> The 'hot' sectors in offshoring these days are new product development and design, engineering services, R&D, and analytical knowledge services, including legal services. In fact, innovation services are now the second most prevalent set of services offered by providers (after IT) and among the fastest-growing service lines . . . .

The supply of outsourcing suppliers has grown dramatically: a Booz principal reported that the number of knowledge process outsourcing (KPO) providers grew 95 percent between 2000 and 2008, in areas such as engineering, design and research; 50 percent of providers offering innovation services were based in India, followed by China with 28 percent, and Russia at 15 percent.

Booz client companies that had outsourced functions offshore reported savings ranging from 29 percent for information technology and 41 percent for finance and accounting to 42 percent for research and development and 46 percent for engineering.

Global consulting services providers such as Booz (PriceWaterhouseCoopers), KPMG, and Accenture stand ready, willing, and able to assist U.S. firms in sending these jobs offshore.[51] But you don't need to engage them – the foreign firms will come to you. I recently received a personalized email solicitation from a company in India. It included a long list of administrative, technical, and research-oriented services that they stood ready to staff for me, beginning immediately.[52] I looked at the list, and the more extensive list provided on the company's website, and thought, "what do we tell our children?"

If we continue our current course, without a dramatic shift in direction, then we must tell our children and grandchildren to study the BLS list of 160 occupations, and *not* to aspire to any of those -- because there are several hundred million qualified individuals in India and elsewhere who stand ready to do those jobs for less than it costs to live in America, and U.S. employers are prepared to send the work to them to cut costs and maximize profits. Even if you do land one of those jobs, pay off your college loans, marry and have children, and spend fifteen years with your company, you may come to work some Friday and be told your Indian replacement is arriving on Monday, or will begin work in Bangalore.

And that leads to another conversation. Because then, we must say to our children, by the way, that means that there are going to be a lot more Americans vying for the remaining, non-tradeable jobs. So, there is going to be some very stiff competition, and unless you are the very best of the best, you are not going to make the cut. This is the harsh society we are creating, as discussed in Chapter 7.

More Hollowing Out

More problems with trade, and more job losses in manufacturing and services, will lead to more hollowing out: more stagnation in the economy due to lack of consumer demand, more underemployment and low pay, more dependency, and more social ills.

Progress, But Still Not Recovered

One cause for some hope was the report in September of 2016 from the Commerce Department that real median household income in the U.S. in 2015 was up 5.2 percent over the previous year, to $56,516. This was welcome news. However, as I discussed in Chapter 7, it is by no means a complete picture.[53] For example, the median income for both men and women was still lower than in 2007 before the onset of the Great Recession, and, for men, well below the peak of 1973.[54]

The Census Bureau reported that the official poverty rate in 2015 was 13.5 percent, down 1.2 percentage points from 14.8 percent in 2014; however, the 2015 poverty rate was still 1.0 percentage point higher than in 2007, the year before the most recent recession. And it was not just the poor: deeper losses in income were experienced in each layer of the distribution of income, with the most severe losses experienced in the bottom fifth.

I fear that Americans will hear the top-line news and think everything is just fine, and that we are on the road back. I am joined in this worry by Ian Rivkin, co-author of the Harvard Business School's annual survey, the 2016 edition of which is titled "Problems Unsolved and a Nation Divided":

> My fear is we could overreact and take it as a sign that we are just fine. . . . I don't see what has changed structurally that will sustain long-run improvements in real median household income.[55]

We are not just fine. Indeed, economists at the Economic Policy Institute have pointed out that:

> . . . despite the gains in 2015, household incomes have still not fully recovered from the deep losses suffered in the Great Recession—the bottom 95 percent of households still had incomes in 2015 below those of 2007 (while those in the top five percent are now three percent ahead).[56]

Problems in the Lowest Fifth and Upper Fifth

Two charities that operate in my area offer glimpses into the future from the perspective of the "lowest fifth" and the "upper fifth." One is an interfaith network of churches that take turns providing housing and meals for a week for families that have become homeless. The parents spend the days in job training and looking for a job; the goal is to get them back on their feet and off the street. There are children involved.

Mostly the family involves a single mother, often without much education, but always with a lot of drive and personality. There are not a lot of jobs for them -- often they are at call centers, but we've been offshoring those. These are young women who could and would wield scissors and a sewing machine if there were an apparel industry in Philadelphia. But the BLS says half of our remaining apparel jobs will be gone by 2024.

Another is a charity that helps economically struggling families in my school district. This is a district by and large composed of households in the upper twenty percent income range. And yet on any given day, many of these households have a secret: they are not making a go of it economically, because a spouse has lost his or her job, and it is taking a long time to find another one these days. So, things look fine on the outside, but they don't have the money to fill their heating oil tank, or pay their electric bill or make their car payment.

In response to a donation that filled one of these needs, a mother sent a message of thanks, then saying, "I am going to cut this off now because I am about to cry. I have tried so hard to keep everything in because I need to be so strong for my kids." This is an area that has been hit hard by the accelerating offshoring of white-collar jobs described in the previous section. This is what the future holds.

Social Ills Increasing

Meanwhile, the heroine/opioid epidemic in America increases unabated.[57] The annual meeting of a state chamber of commerce I attended in September of 2016 included, over the course of just two days, no less than three panel discussions devoted to how businesses could deal with the problem.

The drug epidemic has many causes, but one of them surely is the economic and social harm inflicted on communities when the jobs go offshore, as Pierce and Schott have shown. Recalling the head of the local union at the U.S. Steel plant in Granite City, Illinois that closed in 2016, dealing with news that a laid-off worker had committed suicide leaving behind two children, we can project that the measurable increases in suicides and overdoses that Deaton and Case and Pierce and Schott studied will continue.

Strategic Concerns

Economic Strategic Concerns

As we consider the future, we must take a big step back and engage in big-picture thinking that can only be described as "strategic."

Federal Deficits and Debt

When we do that, one of the first things we encounter is the fact that the federal government, every year, is spending a great deal more than it takes in, and in doing so, is piling up a mountain of debt. The Committee for a Responsible Federal Budget summarizes it this way:

> Arguably, the most important metric of a country's fiscal health is its ratio of debt to Gross Domestic Product (GDP). And unfortunately, even as deficits fell, debt continued to grow in nominal dollars and as a share of the economy. Since 2009, deficits have fallen by 60 percent, but nominal *debt held by the public has grown by about 90 percent – from $7.5 trillion to $14.2 trillion*. As a percentage of GDP, debt has also grown rapidly, *from 35 percent of GDP in 2007 to* 52 percent in 2009 and *nearly 77*

> *percent in 2016*. This puts debt at *twice the 50-year historical average* of 39 percent of GDP and leaves it near record-high levels not seen other than in the period around World War II. [Emphasis supplied.][58]

And, unfortunately, after a period of falling deficits since the 2008-2009 financial crisis, the Congressional Budget Office and the CRFB project increasing deficits in the coming years:

> The deficit remains over three and a half times as high as in 2007 (just over 2 percentage points higher as a percent of GDP) and is projected to grow over time. Under CBO's current law baseline, annual deficits will *return to trillion-dollar levels by 2024*. Under a more pessimistic Alternative Fiscal Scenario in which policymakers fail to pay for new spending and extended tax cuts, trillion-dollar deficits return by 2021 and *reach $1.5 trillion – a nominal-dollar record – by 2026*. *Id.* [Emphasis supplied.]

So, pull out your favorite picture of your kids, or of your grandchildren, and consider what we are leaving them on our current course: "unkeepable promises and unpayable debts," in the words of CRFB co-chairman Mitch Daniels, president of Purdue University.[59]

I agree with Mr. Daniels' prescription for the only way to avoid passing that legacy to our children and grandchildren: "a shift in national policy to the growth of the private, productive economy, as our all-out, primary priority" together with a moderation of those unkeepable promises.[60]

In short, we need to get the economy going again, so individual Americans and companies can afford to pitch in their fair share to pay for the things we do in common -- schools and parks at the local level, and Coast Guard cutters and interstate highways at the federal level. (And, of course, fix it so some of the most able to contribute are not avoiding their share through loopholes or offshore tax havens.) And, when people are self-sufficient and making a go of it on their own, they do not need support, reducing government spending. Moving people from receiving assistance to paying taxes has a double effect on deficit reduction.

As I discuss in this book, I am convinced that the essential first step to jump-starting the economy is to eliminate the trade deficit: to bring the jobs home, and pay people a decent wage for performing them.

Importance of Manufacturing

You probably have heard of the financial crisis in Greece unfolding in 2014 through 2016: the Greek government had been spending more than it took in, and had to borrow from the European Union (mostly Germany) to avoid bankruptcy. At this writing, in February of 2017, the crisis is not resolved.

When I first heard about the problem with Greece, the immediate thought that came to mind was, "do they make anything there?" I submit that a modern economy cannot thrive without a robust manufacturing sector. I am not alone in this assessment. In the introduction to his 2013 book, *Made in the USA: The Rise and Retreat of American Manufacturing*, Vaclav Smil tells us he wrote that book because he wanted to tell the story of manufacturing that built America, and that he believes preserving and reinvigorating manufacturing are essential to solving America's economic problems and it future as a nation.[61]

The breadth of the manufacturing sector in the economy is little understood, because it typically is narrowly defined. In a February, 2016 study,[62] the Manufacturers Alliance for Productivity and Innovation (MAPI) examined the total footprint of manufacturing at the center of a complex upstream and downstream supply chain. Accounting for manufacturing activities such as corporate R&D centers, the utility industry that produces the factories' electricity, logistics operations, corporate management, and providers of financial services and insurance, MAPI concluded that manufacturing and associated activities account for one-third (32%) of the U.S. economy.

The MAPI study also found that the domestic manufacturing value-added multiplier is 3.6, much higher than conventional calculations in the range of 1.4: for every dollar of domestic manufacturing value-added destined for manufactured goods for final demand, another $2.60 of value-added is generated elsewhere. So, too, for employment: MAPI found that for each full-time equivalent job in manufacturing dedicated to producing value for final demand, there are 3.4 full-time equivalent jobs created in nonmanufacturing industries.

Manufacturing is important; in fact, it is essential. At the end of the day, we must decide, who do we want to be: Germany, or Greece?

Global Political-Economic Concerns

Trade Deficits and Foreign Indebtedness

There is another result not pictured in the cascade but of great importance: the decline of the American position in the world order.

We previously have discussed the "Vicious Circle" of the low-price, low-wage economy. However, that is not the end of the story. The weak U.S. wage base does not generate enough taxes to fund the subsidies the U.S. government pays to the low wage earners, so the U.S. government borrows money from the Chinese government to fund its deficits. The Chinese government has money to lend, because it has been piling up dollars from all of the products the Chinese companies are selling to Wal-Mart and the like. Wal-Mart is selling to U.S. citizens whose wages are so low they can't afford to buy anywhere else, and who rely on government programs to subsidize their insufficient earnings. So, the "Pernicious Circle" is created:

The trade deficit is not merely a drain on the U.S. economy. The mercantilist nations piling up U.S. dollars through their trade surpluses, principally China, lend many of those dollars back to the United States, especially to the government. However, all this borrowing has converted the United States from the world's largest creditor nation to the largest debtor nation. America's position in the world order is weakened, as discussed below.

Australia provides a cautionary tale on the outcomes from such borrowing. Josh Bivens reports that the Australian *trade* deficit has been averaging around 2% of gross domestic product, however, Australia's *total* balance of payments deficit reached 6% of GDP. The 4% gap between the trade and total deficit was debt service — interest paid on the borrowing necessary to cover previously-accrued trade deficits. This large outflow of funds from Australia to pay interest on accumulated foreign debts "should be a red flag for the future of the U.S. economy." [63]

Economic Dependency

And then there is the question of whether it is wise to be dependent on China and/or other foreign suppliers for entire sectors and product lines. Is it well to have difficulty cobbling together enough steelmaking capacity to supply the Oakland-San Francisco Bay Bridge project? Are we to be co-opted in our foreign policy because we don't want to endanger our supply of things we can no longer produce ourselves?

National Security Concerns

These considerations quickly give way to national security concerns. In both *The Reckoning* and *Citizen*

Soldiers, David Halberstam and Stephen Ambrose, respectively, describe the surrendered Japanese and German soldiers standing in awe as they saw the interminable lines of American GIs in their jeeps, trucks, and tanks, and wondering how their leaders could have gone to war with such an industrial colossus. Then America's leaders decided that it was better to have the country's steel made in Japan and China, because it could be made less expensively there.

And it is not just steel - it's the "little" things, too. I once attended a conference at the National Bureau of Standards devoted to the topic of how to authenticate the origin of parts such as transistors and capacitors that were going into the avionics of sophisticated and very expensive fighter aircraft and other mission-critical situations. Having domestic sources for these components is important, and it gets very dicey when we must say, "no one is making those in the U.S. anymore."

It suffices to say, it is in our national interest to have a vibrant steel industry, and contrary to our national interest not to have one. If we don't have a steel industry capable of supplying the steel for the Bay Bridge, how would we have a steel industry capable of supplying our defense in the event of a major confrontation with another world power? And so, too, of many other industries that are strategically important from an economic and security standpoint.

World Order

Finally, these are matters of great consequence, not just to Americans, but to the rest of the world. We may have been involved in some misadventures of late, but whether China, Russia, Iran or any of a list of others holds sway can matter a great deal.

We do the world no favor by continuing to run these chronic trade-in-goods deficits and become reliant on China and others for key product sectors like steel and electronics. A weak America is not good for the United States or for the world.

Perceptions of weakness brought on by the failure of the American financial system in 2007 and 2008 and other events have emboldened America's adversaries and potential adversaries. Russian and Chinese warplanes are frequently buzzing, even colliding with, American ships and aircraft. China's muscle flexing was described in Chapter 8. Russia has seized territory using troops without insignia, engaged in war crimes in military operations on behalf of the Syrian regime, conducted cyber warfare, operated surreptitious false news operations, and interfered with elections. Iran tests American will with missile tests and military operations, as does North Korea.

Brazil has impeached its president and fallen prey to gang violence, Venezuela has food shortages, South Korea has impeached its president and is leaning away from the U.S. Militant Islamism controls a large swath of the Middle East through ISIS and is active worldwide through groups such as Boko Haram. Iran and Saudi Arabia are engaged in a proxy war in Somalia, and Libya is one of many "failed states." Europe suffers an unchecked migrant crisis, the potential for breakup of the European Union, and continued threat from Russia. The world order is in a precarious and in some places chaotic state, never more in need of a strong and steady American presence.[64] That strength is needed as a matter of American self-preservation, and as the world's only hope of a world order "affirming individual dignity and participatory governance, and cooperating internationally in accordance with agreed-upon rules," as Henry Kissinger has proposed.[65]

As Dr. Kissinger has suggested, one of the fundamental flaws in the current world order is that the international economic system has become global, while the political structure of the world has remained based on the nation-state." [66] Economic globalization has lurched from crisis to crisis, while political forces lead governments to seek national advantage through mercantilism. A sustainable world order will require moving beyond national advantage, and "the disciplining of globalization." [67]

Globalization Failing in the U.S. and Abroad

And what does the future hold for globalization? In Chapter 1, during the decade 1986-1995, we saw international trade morph into something called globalization – the free flow of capital, information, and technology across national borders, enabled by a new organization for regulating world trade, and by revolutions in shipping and communications and the organization of retailing and manufacturing.

The advent of globalization was accompanied by the beginning of the "Age of Oversupply" -- of people, as China, India, Russia and other countries brought three billion people into the world economy, of capacity, as they overbuilt their factories, and of capital, as they accumulated trade surpluses selling goods to the rest of the world.

How has this worked out, and what does the future hold? To answer these questions, we must recognize three key facts: (i) globalization is being conducted in a context of mercantilism, (ii) China's sheer size and the attractiveness of its market change everything, and (iii) in the end, globalization is simply about chasing the lowest wage around the world, without regard to health, environmental, and social effects.

Globalization in the Context of Mercantilism

You will recall that in Chapter 1 we were introduced to "mercantilism" – the practice of a nation deliberately selling more to other countries than it buys from them. Although globalization is implemented largely at a company level, it occurs in a context of nations, some of whom intentionally practice mercantilism through various means.

In Robert Isaak's view, globalization is guided by a kind of "corporate social Darwinism" in which "national teams" compete to capture maximum global market share through export-oriented growth.[68] However, one country can only succeed at this at the expense of one or more other countries. The following figure shows the balance of payments during 2015 for the top ten countries (greatest surplus) and lowest ten countries (greatest deficit):[69]

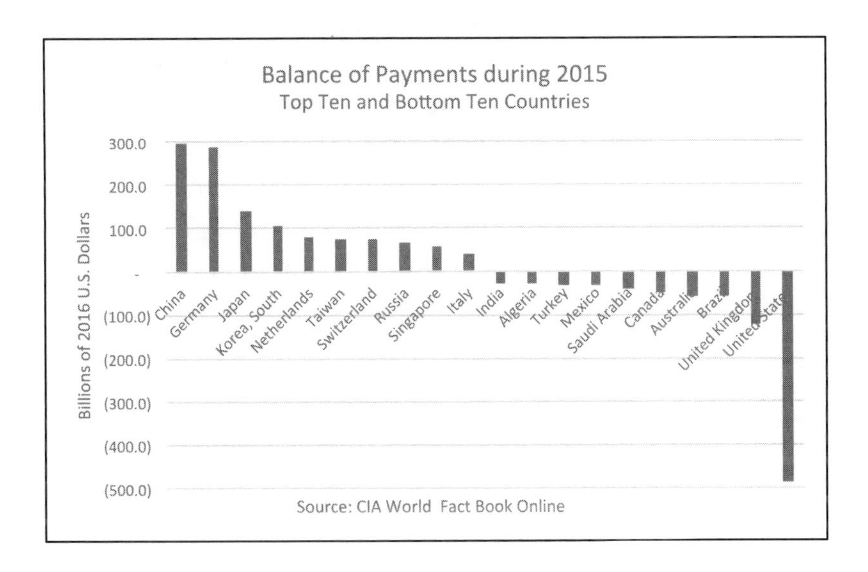

The figure puts into stark relief the "global imbalance" of payments. Perhaps the most striking aspect is the sheer size of America's balance of payments deficit, standing all alone out there, the worst of all nations, in 196th place. We saw in Chapter 1 that by 1995, in terms of its trade deficit, the United States had become the world's "biggest loser," an honor it has maintained in the ensuring twenty years. Todd Lipscomb spent many years as a U.S. executive operating in Asia. He reports in his book, *Re-Made in the USA*, that it was not unusual for him to see "amusement, or pride, or both" in the eyes of Asian businessmen regarding America's trade deficits in Asia.[70]

Running these deficits year after year adds up: the Treasury Department reported that in June of 2016, $6.3 trillion of the total U.S. government debt of about $17 trillion was in foreign hands. Of that, China held $1.24 trillion, and Japan held $1.15 trillion. Clearly this is not a sustainable path.

Another thing that struck me about it is that we are joined on the podium in second place by our free-trading partner, Great Britain. The size of Germany's surplus is striking – it shows the success with which Germany continues to pursue mercantilism, despite being a high-wage, developed country. Japan also has managed to continue to run a substantial surplus, even though its wages have been declining and it is in a perpetual state of near-zero economic growth. But the big story is China.

China's Effects on Globalization

Globalization would be proceeding without China. But it is important to note that China is having a profound effect on the way globalization is playing out, due to China's enormous size, with a population of some 1.3 billion.

India is of comparable size to China. What is the difference? First, China opened its markets to export processing and investment earlier and wider. Second, having done so, China benefited from entrepreneurs and companies with know-how and capital in nearby Taiwan who were ready to move in and seize the opportunity. Third, China benefited from the know-how and capital of U.S. and other western companies desiring not only to set up low-cost manufacturing for export, but also to gain access to the Chinese consumer market. Finally, China had an authoritarian form of government that was able, having decided on a path of export-led growth, to "make it so," and, at least to date, to repress complaints about how globalization has been working out for China's workers and their communities. So, India may soon be playing a larger role in globalization. But for now, there is nothing like China.

But China's crucial advantage has been its vast store of hundreds of millions of impoverished citizens practicing subsistence farming and ready to move into manufacturing, even for very low wages. Which leads us to the recognition of the essence and driver of globalization: wage arbitrage.

Globalization as Wage Arbitrage

For all the bookshelves full of discussion of globalization, it really is starkly simple when practiced as offshoring. Richard Baldwin sums it up succinctly when he tells us that offshoring is simply a method of arbitraging wage differences among nations.[71]

Arbitrage is the purchase of a commodity in one market for the purpose of immediately selling it at a higher price in another market.[72] So, Baldwin says, a firm wishing to combine its technology with low-cost labor can move production stages to Mexico. It effectively is purchasing low-price labor in Mexico for resale into the United States.[73]

Baldwin gives the example of Bombardier, the Canadian manufacturer of commercial aircraft, which moved production facilities to Santiago de Queteretado in North-Central Mexico. The company found ways to overcome the translation of technology from French to Spanish in order to make airplane tails using manufacturing engineers that cost $60 a *day* in Mexico rather than $35 an *hour* in Quebec.[74] This arguably has been good for Santiago de Queteretado, which went from two aviation companies with 700 workers in 2006 to thirty-three such companies with over 5,000 workers in 2015, but certainly not good for Quebec.[75]

But if globalization is essentially about wage arbitrage between low- and high-wage countries, we must ask, why does this big disparity exist?

The "Great Divergence:" "North" & "South"

Beginning around 1820, a handful of countries engaged in the industrial revolution and pulled away from the rest of the world in production and income, a phenomenon that has been referred to as the "Great Divergence." Mostly located in the Northern Hemisphere, these countries have come to be known as the "North," and consist of the western European countries, the U.S., Canada, Australia, Russia, and Japan. Among them, seven predominate — the United States, Germany, France, Italy, Britain, Canada, and Japan — and are referred to as the Group of Seven, or "G7." The G7 accounted for one-fifth of the world's income in 1820; by 1990 they accounted for two-thirds.[76] Their national incomes were high, and were broadly shared in the form of high wages, far higher than prevailed in the rest of the world. And so, the stage was set for the "wage arbitrage" of globalization.

The "Great Convergence"

With the onset of globalization, beginning around 1990, the G7 saw a rapid drop in its percentage share of world income, back to its level of 1914.[77] This drop of percentage of world income was accompanied by a drop in the G7's share of world manufacturing, which had been slipping since 1970, and then around 1990 began an accelerated decline. The drop in the G7's percentage of manufacturing was mirrored by a rise among six developing nations, which Baldwin refers to as the "Industrializing Six," or "I6:" China, India, Indonesia, and Thailand, Korea, and Poland.[78]

The share of the "I6" also grew at the expense of the rest of the world, which after modest increases from 1970-1990, saw its share of world manufacturing drift down and stagnate while the I6 advanced.[79]

Globalization's Effects

Global companies' dispersal of their supply chain in search of low wages has had profound effects. It is helpful to consider these effects in terms of three groups of countries: China and the other the newly industrializing export-oriented countries of the global South, the rest of the countries of the global South, and the countries of the global North.

Global South: China and the other Newly Industrializing Countries

One effect has been that growth in the world's economy is now concentrated in China and a handful of other newly industrializing, export-oriented countries of the global

South. At this writing, projections for 2016 are: China (6.6%), India (7.6%), Indonesia (5.0%), Malaysia (4.3%), Pakistan (5.7%), and the Philippines (6.4%).[80] As Robert Isaak has pointed out, the U.S. has subsidized this economic growth by running huge trade deficits, which have constituted huge trade surpluses on the part of China and other countries.[81]

The Promised "Global Middle Class"

What about the promised "global middle class?" In Chapter 4, we noted the second prevailing rationale for the pursuit of free trade: that the sacrifice of lost jobs, low pay, and social ills resulting from sending American production offshore is outweighed by lifting millions of foreign workers and their families out of poverty and "building a global middle class." How is globalization working out in terms of that goal, at least in these newly industrializing countries?

This issue is usually posed as "lifting hundreds of millions out of poverty" and "building a global middle class." But what is the reality? I would sum it up as follows:

> Many people have moved from abject poverty to extreme or middling poverty, and there has been a small increase in the middle and upper class, mostly concentrated in China. However, even these gains have come at a cost in both developed and developing nations.

How did I come to this conclusion?

We must begin by considering what we mean by "middle class." I think most people's thinking is well summed up in the definition offered by Homi Kharas, writing at the OECD:

> The middle class is an ambiguous social classification, broadly reflecting the ability to lead a comfortable life. The middle class usually enjoy stable housing, healthcare and educational opportunities (including college) for their children, reasonable retirement and job security, and discretionary income that can be spent on vacation and leisure pursuits.[82]

When it comes to counting up the members of the global middle class, however, such a definition can be difficult to apply.[83] Therefore, Kharas and others studying the matter tend to count people according to a range of daily income or expenditures, expressed in U.S. dollars. For example, Kharas uses a range of expenditures between $10 and $100 a day per person.

A note of caution here: The cost of equal goods and services can vary widely from country to country, so the unit of measurement is adjusted to achieve "purchase power parity," or "PPP." A PPP dollar theoretically will have the same purchasing power in India as in the United States. So, the income ranges typically are expressed in terms of PPP dollars. However, Kharas notes that, for a number of reasons, the PPP calculations may not be very accurate, and should be taken with a large grain of salt. We will see that to be true.

So, to my conclusions: One basis for these conclusions is a 2015 report from the Pew Research Center.[84] The categories used in the Pew study are as follows: [85]

Categories of Personal and Family Income					
		Per Person per Day		Family of Four per Year	
Category		Lower Limit	Upper Limit	Lower Limit	Upper Limit
1	Extremely Poor		$ 2.00		$ 2,920.00
2	Very Poor	$ 2.01	$ 10.00	$ 2,934.60	$ 14,600.00
3	Poor	$ 10.01	$ 20.00	$ 14,614.60	$ 29,200.00
4	"Middle"	$ 20.01	$ 50.00	$ 29,214.60	$ 73,000.00
5	Upper	$ 50.01		$ 73,014.60	
Source: Pew Research Center: Global Attitudes and Trends July 2015 Category labels are the author's.					

The percentage of the world population with income/consumption in these categories in 2001 and 2011 are as displayed in the following figure. It is important to note that these statistics already include adjustments for differences in prices between countries - when someone earns $2.00 a day in India, that is the same as earning $2.00 a day in the United States.[86]

Income per Person Per Day in 2011 Dollars (PPP) As Percentage of World Population					
	$0-$2	$2-$10	$10-$20	$20-$50	$50 >
2001	29%	50%	7%	7%	6%
2011	15%	56%	13%	9%	7%
Source: Pew Research Center analysis of World Bank Data					

Key Finding: So, with respect to poverty, the truth is this: there has been an historic shift as hundreds of millions of people have moved from abject poverty to extreme or middling poverty.

And even these gains have been unequally shared, concentrated in China, South America and Eastern Europe. The population earning more than ten dollars a day barely expanded in India and Southeast Asia, Africa, and Central America.

With respect to the middle class, Pew concluded: "the emergence of a truly *global* middle class is still more promise than reality." [Emphasis in original.] "In 2011, only 16% of the world's population was living on $20 or more daily, a little above the U.S. poverty line... And most of these people still lived in the economically advanced countries in North America, Europe and the Asia-Pacific region. . . In 2001, 91% of the [people earning more than $50 a day] lived in North America and Europe; in 2011, the share was 87%."

The true dimensions of the Asian "middle class" are illuminated in a 2010 report from the Asian Development Bank.[87] The report used an absolute definition of middle class as per capita consumption of $2–$20 per day in 2008. John West reports that "Many Chinese find this comical because no one could live on $2 or even $4 a day in a Chinese city today. Shanghai and Beijing are among the world's most expensive cities." [88]

However, unlike the Pew research, the ADB report included a category of two to four dollars a day. The report noted that "the majority of the Asian middle class still falls in the $2–$4 range, leaving them highly vulnerable to slipping back into poverty due to economic shocks."[89] One reason for this precariousness is that about two-thirds of these workers are employed in the "informal sector," for enterprises that are not registered or regulated; they have no contracts or rights, and wage and workplace standards simply are not applied.[90]

The ADB report concluded that China's improvement, though dramatic, had been concentrated below ten dollars a day, and that India had seen little improvement at all.

The report projected further improvement in the developing countries of Asia of population moving out of the extreme poverty range of less than two dollars a day; however, even these projections call for extremely modest income levels. Moreover, these income and consumption statistics fail to capture other dimensions of quality of life, such as lack of access to clean drinking water, hygienic toilets, basic healthcare, education, personal security, and individual liberty.

These are just gross statistics. What does this look like for an individual worker? There are some, such as the Indian IT workers in Bangalore and the urban Chinese professionals, who are living what we might refer to as a middle-class life. However, in the typical case, foreign workers are lifted above the two dollars a day that is the generally accepted standard for extreme poverty, but most definitely are not living a life that is anywhere near "middle class."

Typically, they are working long hours under strict circumstances for very little pay, living in what is closer to a cell block than a dormitory, very far from their home, where they may well have left their children behind. They may be contracting brown lung disease or other ailments from exposure to industrial chemicals, and are at high risk for injury on the job. If they are working in heavy industry, their factory is polluting the air and water around it. If they are working in an export-oriented business and succeed in bidding up their wages to something near a living wage, they will find that the entire operation will be moved on to another low-wage, low-regulation location, in their own country or in another. As Ellen Israel Rosen put it in *Making Sweatshops*, "It is essential to make clear that abuse is not economic opportunity." [91]

Why has globalization resulted in these conditions, and not had more widespread beneficial effects? In short, why has it not produced the promised "global middle class?"

Globalization and the "Smile Curve"

Here is why: In globalization, the treatment of production workers as commodities has effectively commoditized the fabrication process, permitting its performance anywhere using a firm's product and production technology.

This has resulted in a harsh competition based on price, and therefore, on production workers' wages. What were the "good jobs" when they were located in the developed countries have become the "bad jobs" when located in China and other developing countries.

This depression in manufacturing production wages has resulted in what has been dubbed the "smile curve," as represented in the following figure:

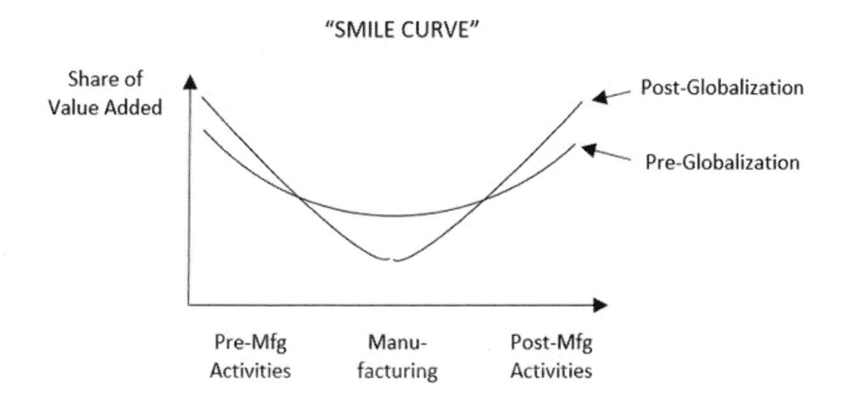

The "value added" before manufacturing in design, and after manufacturing in marketing, distribution, and service, is higher than the value added during the manufacturing process. This is so because the "value" is measured in terms of the cost of the inputs. Because of the global competition to provide low-price labor, the manufacturing part of a product's life has been devalued.[92]

South Racing South to the Bottom

This has not all been the doing of the global North. In an article in 2002,[93] Anita Chan and Robert Ross have recounted how the United States and other developed countries, at the infamous meeting of the WTO in Seattle in 1999, tried to secure the adoption of a "social clause" in WTO agreements that would link trade to environmental and labor standards.[94]

However, there was resistance from the governments and labor unions of many of the less developed nations, especially China and India, ostensibly on the ground that the social clause was a ploy to protect labor in the North from competition in the South.

Chan and Ross concluded that "[t]he absence of a mechanism establishing international labor standards is propelling the economies of the South in a race to the bottom in wages and labor conditions. . . . In rejecting a regulated international labor regime, countries of the South lower their own labor standards to remain competitive and provide a "good" investment climate."[95]

In China, they found that local governments offered companies the opportunity to pay less than the official minimum wage, and that the minimum wage was expressed as a monthly amount, ignoring actual work exceeding legal limits on hours. In footwear, they determined that workers averaged eleven hours a day, often with no days off. They also found widespread complaints of unpaid wages. It should be noted that the "race to the bottom" has not only been about pay and hours. Chan and Ross found occupational and safety hazards, including a "startlingly high incidence of severed limbs and fingers. . . . [D]espite China's dramatic export growth, the benefits have not trickled down to the assembly-line workers who make the exported goods." [96]

The Rest of the Global South

What happens when we look outside the fast-growing, export oriented countries? What has been the effect of globalization on "the rest of the South?"

The Formerly Fast-Growing Countries

First, we should note that the current growth is not coming from the "Asian Tigers" of Hong Kong, Singapore, South Korea, and Taiwan, all of whom are forecast to experience GDP growth of under two percent in 2016. Neither is the growth coming from the two "BRIC" countries of Brazil and Russia, which are forecast to experience *declines* of 3.2 percent and 0.7 percent, respectively.[97] These countries have seen their growth falter or decline as China and other countries have surged ahead.

What of "the rest of the rest?" Globalization is having ill effects on developing countries, especially as practiced by China. Several snapshots give us an idea of what is going on.

Mexico and China

Mexico is an example of a country in "the rest of the South," which, although it has greatly increased exports, mainly to the United States, has not achieved the strong growth enjoyed by China certain other Asian countries.

In their 2002 study of the lack of the "social clause" in trade arrangements, Chan and Ross found that pressures were increasing on Mexican factories to compete with China's long working hours and bargain-basement wages. Their conclusion: "[E]xport workers in China and Mexico have not benefited from the economic boom. . . . These assembly workers are caught in an internationally competitive race to the bottom." [98]

Latin America and China

Moving south from Mexico, the case of China in Latin America and the Caribbean is illustrative, as detailed in research by Kevin Gallagher and colleagues at Boston University and Tufts University.[99] From 2000 to 2009, during China's surge, Latin American-Caribbean exports to China increased dramatically. The great majority of these exports were commodities, primarily copper, iron and other metals, soybeans, and crude oil from a handful of countries. China also invested heavily in these industries in these countries. These exports to China benefited these countries' economies; however, there was the typical danger in trading in commodities -- as China's growth slows, these exports will decline, and the per unit price of these exports will fall.

More important is the other side of the coin: China's manufacturing exports have come to be a threat to manufacturing industries in Latin America and the Caribbean ("LAC"), in terms both of their exports outside of the region, and of their exports to other countries in the region. For example, China effectively prevented the Central American countries from benefiting from the

CAFTA free trade agreement., designed to make them a clothing manufacturing hub for exports to the U.S. Gallagher calculated that 94 percent of manufacturing exports from LAC were under threat from China, as well as high percentages of exports between LAC countries.

So, while Gallagher is likely correct in noting that "manufacturing and modern services are the key to long-term growth and prosperity," for the Latin American-Caribbean countries, globalization in a world occupied by China has meant a return to reliance on commodity exports, and a threat to what manufacturing they have developed.

Africa and China

Similar difficulties in the China relationship have been experienced in Africa, were there have been complaints across Africa that the Chinese are driving locals out of business. For example, poultry farmers in Zambia have complained that their markets were being invaded by Chinese poultry farmers; in Senegal, shopkeepers have claimed that Chinese traders have made the prices charged by local traders "uncompetitive."[100]

A 2008 case study by Sola Akinrinade and Olukoya Ogen is illustrative.[101] They examined "the impact of globalization, as exemplified in exterminatory Chinese export competitiveness, on the Nigerian textile industry." They noted "the phenomenal upsurge in Chinese textile trade in Nigeria" and the "debilitating nature" of the Chinese specialized goods market in Lagos on the Nigerian textile industry. In their opinion, with respect to the Nigerian textile industry, "China has been pursuing a policy of de-industrialization."

They concluded that, "while Chinese investments in the areas of infrastructural development could be crucial to Nigeria's socio-economic development, the skewed trading relationship that has turned Nigeria into a dumping ground for Chinese inferior and sub-standard textile products has wreaked havoc on the Nigerian textile industry and stifled the development of Nigeria's indigenous enterprise."[102]

In Ghana, the practice of illegal mining for gold in a way that destroys the country's rivers became a major problem when Chinese companies got into the game using Chinese equipment. The Chinese government has applied pressure against enforcement efforts, which the Ghana government has acceded to, coincidentally, at the same time as China "is facilitating the release of a $3 billion Master Agreement loan facility . . . to boost infrastructural networks."[103]

And it gets worse. Robert Isaak recounts how in the Congo, miners dig up coltan, the source of a vital ingredient for capacitors in electronic devices, by chopping down huge chunks of rain forest. The trade is so profitable that it spawns constant violence and civil war.[104] Without effective rule of law, the global free market can spell disaster - in this case, deforestation, disappearance of species, and constant violence. This should serve as a cautionary tale for those of us who think we are building a global middle class when we buy our smart phone.

Conclusions for the Rest of the South

Globalization's promotion of growth in China and a handful of other countries in "Factory Asia" has increased volumes and prices of commodities in countries producing raw materials for global industry. But prices fall when that growth slows; indeed, over the long term, a link has been observed between dependence on commodity exports and extreme poverty, especially in Africa.[105]

However, the big downside for "the rest of the South" is China's crowding out domestic industries, both in serving the domestic market, as in the case of Nigerian textiles, and in competing in the world market, as in Mexico. Globalization has produced a "South-South divide," in which China and Factory Asia are de-industrializing the other nations of the global South, forcing them into a reliance on provision of raw materials to the newly industrialized South, and left out in the cold when they have none to offer.

However, because of the "low price, low wage" dynamics of globalization, both the newly industrializing and "left behind" countries of the global South are engaged in a "race to the bottom," in a competition for low wages and low price.

The Global North

How has globalization been going for the countries of the "global North?"

Germany

First, I must note that Germany is an outlier. As we saw with respect to global imbalances, Germany's trade surplus is second only to China's, and higher as a percent of GDP. Germany focuses intently on exports as a source of economic growth and activity, and a high percentage of its GDP is attributable to exports. Germany also follows a "Germany first" mentality in its business dealings, for example, promoting German products as intermediate components in its manufacturing. We will look further at the German brand of capitalism in Chapter 11.

Under globalization, Germany has experienced some downward pressure on wages, competition from China, and efforts by China to buy German companies and assets. However, thus far, Germany has been weathering the storm of globalization relatively well.

Japan

When we looked at global imbalances, we also saw that Japan continues to run a surplus in trade. However, Japan has been locked in severe stagnation since the bursting of the Japanese "bubble economy" in 1990. Unlike Germany, Japan initially succeeded in international trade as a relatively low-wage country. It therefore was susceptible to being beaten at that game, first by the "Asian Tigers," and then by China — in a music store, you find that the musical instruments formerly made in the U.S. but taken over by Yamaha now are sold under the Yamaha brand, but are made in China.

Japan has responded by lowering wages dramatically, contributing to the country's general malaise. John West reports that in Japan, "the share of non-regular workers—part-time, temporary and dispatched workers—in the economy has more than doubled from 16 percent to 40 percent since 1990 . . . ."[106]

The United States

In the past, the United States created a vast American market of prosperous consumers, filling the demand side of the economic equation -- it was always consumers with a buck in their pocket ("demand" in economics lingo) that drove the economy. They had a buck in their pocket because the return on capital was shared with them through their wages – wages that were high enough to get them above subsistence and buy some of the things they were making, as envisioned by Henry Ford.

But that giant pool of demand in the U.S. domestic market became the envy of Japan, the Asian Tigers, and Germany. As we have seen, having little domestic demand of their own following World War II, they desired to build their industry by serving the demand the U.S. had built. And so, during the Japan/Asian Tigers era, *we began substituting foreign industry for U.S. industry in serving U.S. demand*. And, even as they grew their economies, these countries took steps to assure that U.S. industries did not serve their own growing domestic demand. This entire dynamic is being repeated, on a larger scale, during the China era since 2001.

However, it could not last. As U.S. industries declined, having been supplanted by the foreign industries, U.S. consumers lost their buying power, either directly through the loss of their jobs, or indirectly through downward pressure on their wages. We reviewed these effects in Chapters 6 and 7. The result:

The global low price, low wage economy has squeezed the vitality out of the American economy.

The Great Slowdown

And it is not just the United States. The countries using an export-led strategy of selling products into the developed countries' markets are effectively sapping the developed countries' growth. In September of 2016 the United Nations Conference on Trade and Development (UNCTAD) reported:

> Thirty quarters after the [2008 financial] crisis hit, developed countries are still struggling to return to a solid growth path, and policymakers were

> predicting tougher times ahead . . . . Growth forecasts have been regularly scaled back, and a new vocabulary has emerged to describe an underperforming economy . . . ." [107]
>
> UNCTAD contended that *economic slowdown in advanced economies is the biggest drag on global growth*, arguing that *the lack of global demand and stagnant real wages are the main problems behind the slowdown in international trade*. In many developed countries, a stringent fiscal stance and at times outright austerity have led to one of the weakest recoveries from an economic crisis on record. This has come on top of *a prolonged period of slow wage growth, leading to insufficient household demand* and weak spending on productive investment. The growth rate of the Eurozone is close to being matched by the slowing US growth rate, while Japan continues to stagnate." [108]

But it is not just the developed countries; the effects can be worldwide. Regarding the UNCTAD Trade and Development Report for 2016, the World Bank warned:

> [T]he slowdown in global growth – now in its sixth straight year –and the failure of advanced economies to boost demand, raise productivity and achieve fairer outcomes could intensify *as developing countries are now caught in the downdraft." Id.*

And so, we see effects that are worldwide, hitting China and the other "growing" developing economies, the rest of the global South, and the global "North" alike: In their annual updates for 2016, each of the international economic organizations has referred to stagnating growth and shrinking world trade. In September, UNCTAD reported:

> The world economy in 2016 is in a fragile state, with growth likely to dip below the 2.5 per cent registered in 2014 and 2015. . . .[109]

> The head of the Bank of England said:

> The global economy risks becoming trapped in a low growth, low inflation, low interest rate equilibrium. For the past seven years, growth has serially disappointed—sometimes spectacularly." [110]

The Global Big Squeeze

In my view, the cause of this worldwide economic slowdown is the global application of the "Big Squeeze," in which workers paid a pittance in developing countries have no money for discretionary spending, and workers in developed countries have lost their jobs or have taken low-paying jobs that leave them, too, shopping for necessities at a discount store.

Because the driver of globalization is the relentless pursuit of low wages, the life is being squeezed out of the global economy.

We have seen demand squeezed out of the U.S. and many other developed nations' economies, as low-cost imports have caused job losses and downward pressure on wages. This effect has been felt as well in many developing countries feeling competition from the export-oriented developing countries. Neither has consumer demand grown much in the export-oriented developing countries' economies, because the export industries have been under severe pressure from their global buyers to keep their wages low.

We have been engaging in a stark and ruthless global capitalism that applies the Big Squeeze throughout the global value chain, in a "race to the bottom" that benefits a few at the expense of the many. At the final stage of the chain, low-price, low wage continues to prevail. "The pressure to open new markets in lower and lower wage regions of the world has led to a Darwinian struggle, which is producing a race to the bottom."[111]

And we haven't seen the end of it. If current trends continue, Richard Baldwin's best guess is that, because there are still billions of low-wage workers who would love to move from agriculture into production, and because very large differences in wages persist around the world despite the "Great Convergence," manufacturing jobs will continue to move from the developed countries to a growing group of developing countries in search of lower wages.[112]

I would add that this "de-industrialization" will continue not just in the developed countries, but in the developing countries as well: the resulting job losses, and the accompanying downward pressure on wages, will be felt in *developing* countries who can least afford them.

And the Global Big Squeeze is not limited to manufacturing – globalization's "Darwinian race to the bottom" is felt, perhaps more so, in the mining and extraction industries, and in fishing, farming, and food processing. A vivid example is the Thai seafood industry, brought to light in a 2015 investigation by the Associated Press. The AP investigators discovered human trafficking in desperate Burmese workers, brought to Thailand under false promises. Once there, they were locked in shrimp processing sheds, where they stood from 3:00 a.m. to 7:00 p.m. with hands in ice water, removing the heads, tails, guts, and shells from shrimp, for $4.00 a day. The shrimp are supplied to major Thai seafood processing houses, which sell them to supermarkets, "big box" discount clubs, and restaurant chains in the United States and Europe. The workers are supplied by migrant brokers who lure them with promises of good jobs and then sell them into indentured servanthood for prices that are impossible to work off.[113]

An independent investigation by Nestle confirmed the AP's findings. Even worse are the conditions under which the shrimp and fish are caught: the slave ships. On them, migrants from Myanmar, Cambodia, and Bangladesh work for years, chained to the deck if they try to escape, and beaten, even murdered, for transgressions. Migrants are held in slave camps on both sides of the Thai-Malaysian border, and arrive by sea in Southeast Asia's "seaborne migrant crisis." Police and authorities are bribed, processing houses are lax in identifying the sources of their products, and the Thai national government stands by.[114]

The Thai seafood industry is not an outlier. Miners, foresters, factory workers, shipping crews, and their physical environment, all are exploited, because political and economic systems are too weak to stand up to the global competition in the "race to the bottom." An ethical cat-food maker can't operate a humane, but more costly, supply chain if its competitors are underpricing them with products made with slave labor, governments are on the take or looking the other way, and consumers are ready to buy the lower-priced product, no questions asked.

And so the race to the bottom continues.

Notes to Chapter 9

---

[1] Facts reported in this section are derived from the following sources:
Kris Turner, "Carrier, UTEC out of step with manufacturing industry, experts say," Indianapolis Star, February 12, 2016.
http://www.indystar.com/story/money/2016/02/11/carrier-utec-out-step-manufacturing-industry-moving-mexico-cutting-2100-jobs/80245446/.
IBJ Staff, "Update: Carrier plans to lay off 1,400 Indy workers in Mexico move," Indiana Business Journal, February 10, 2016.
http://www.ibj.com/articles/57162-carrier-plans-to-lay-off-1400-indy-workers-in-mexico-move.
Kris Turner, "Carrier closing to cost Indiana economy 108M a year," Indianapolis Star, June 17, 2016.
http://www.indystar.com/story/money/2016/06/17/carrier-closing-cost-indiana-economy-108m-year/85930170/?from=global&sessionKey=&autologin=.
Kris Turner, "Carrier reaches severance agreement with workers," Indianapolis Star, July 27, 2016.
http://www.indystar.com/story/money/2016/07/27/carrier-reaches-severance-agreement-workers/87621956/.
Network Indiana, "Only 800 Carrier jobs to stay in Indiana," WOWO Television, December 6, 2016.
https://www.wowo.com/800-carrier-jobs-stay-indiana/

[2] Kris Turner, "Carrier reaches severance agreement."

[3] *Id.*

[4] Kris Turner, "Carrier, UTEC out of step."

[5] IBJ Staff, "Update: Carrier plans."

[6] James Briggs, "Manufacturer Rexnord plans to move 300 high paying jobs to Mexico," Indianapolis Star, October 14, 2016.
http://www.indystar.com/story/money/2016/10/14/manufacturer-rexnord-plans-move-300-high-paying-jobs-mexico/92071104/.
Rob Williams, Rexnord Fires 350 Employees to Move High-Paying Jobs to Mexico, Newsmax, Monday, 17 Oct 2016.
http://www.newsmax.com/Finance/StreetTalk/Rexnord-Indianapolis-job-cuts-industrials/2016/10/17/id/753782/.
Susan Orr, "Mayor unsure how much of Rexnord incentives city could claw back," Indiana Business Journal, October 20, 2016
http://www.ibj.com/articles/60906-mayor-unsure-how-much-of-rexnord-incentives-city-could-claw-back.

[7] Andrew Tangel, "For Some Manufacturers, Mexico Still the Best Move," *Wall Street Journal*, February 9, 2016.

[8] Facts reported in this section are derived from the following sources:
Jessica Wohl, "Nabisco plant worker asks Emanuel, Obama to save Chicago jobs, Chicago Tribune, June 12, 2015.
http://www.chicagotribune.com/business/ct-nabisco-plant-unions-0613-biz-20150612-story.html.
Corilyn Shropshire, "Mondelez to cut Chicago jobs, send some work to Mexico," Chicago Tribune, July 29, 2015.
http://www.chicagotribune.com/business/ct-nabisco-mondelez-plant-0730-biz-20150729-story.html.
Aamer Madhani, "Oreo maker ignores Trump, Clinton criticism, begins layoffs in Chicago," USA Today, March 23, 2016.
http://www.usatoday.com/story/news/2016/03/23/nabisco-begins-layoffs-at-chicago-plant-despite-criticism-from-trump-clinton/82159194/.

[9] Corilyn Shropshire, "Mondelez to cut Chicago jobs."

[10] Aamer Madhani, "Oreo maker ignores."

[11] AFL-CIO Video, "Nabisco Outsourced Jobs."
http://aflcio.shpg.org/48/176224?link_id=0&can_id=d0809b5e64d3cce483dd852ff252f70b&source=email-layoffs-have-a-human-cost&email_referrer=layoffs-have-a-human-cost&email_subject=layoffs-have-a-human-cost.

[12] Company Press Release, "Boosting Small Car Profitability, Ford Invests in New Plant," Ford Motor Company, April 5, 2016.
https://media.ford.com/content/fordmedia/fna/us/en/news/2016/04/05/boosting-small-car-profitability-ford-invests-in-new-plant.html.

[13] Michael Strong, "Ford Plowing $1.6 Billion into Mexico Plant." The Detroit Bureau, April 5, 2016.
http://www.thedetroitbureau.com/2016/04/ford-plowing-1-6-billion-into-mexico-plant/.

[14] *Id.*

[15] Christina Rogers and Dudley Althaus, "It's Getting Harder and More Expensive to Make Cars in Mexico," The Wall Street Journal, August 14, 2016.
http://www.wsj.com/articles/mexicos-auto-production-boom-is-driving-up-labor-costs-1471201920

[16] *Id.*

---

[17] Dudley Althaus and William Boston, "Why Auto Makers Are Building New Factories in Mexico not the US," Wall Street Journal, March 17, 2015.
http://www.wsj.com/articles/why-auto-makers-are-building-new-factories-in-mexico-not-the-u-s-1426645802.

[18] Joanna Zuckerman Bernstein, "VW to spend $1 billion on Mexico assembly plant expansion for Tiguan," Chicago Tribune, Mar 9, 2015.
http://www.chicagotribune.com/business/ct-fiat-chrysler-ram-jeep-production-20160427-story.html.
Ben Bain, "Mexico auto exports forecast to hit record in 2015," Automotive News/Bloomberg, February 6, 2015.
http://www.autonews.com/article/20150206/OEM01/302069972/mexico-auto-exports-forecast-to-hit-record-in-2015.

[19] Dudley Althaus and William Boston, "Why Auto Makers Are Building."

[20] Ben Bain, "Mexico auto exports."

[21] Christina Rogers and Dudley Althaus, "It's Getting Harder."

[22] *Id.*

[23] Based on a cost of living index of 102 for Monterrey and 156 for Indianapolis. Source: Expatistan Cost of Living Index, http://www.expatistan.com.

[24]Christina Rogers and Dudley Althaus, "It's Getting Harder."

[25] *Id.*

[26] *Id.*

[27] Michael Strong, "Ford Plowing $1.6 Billion."

[28] Brendan Case, Mexico Surpassing Japan as No. 2 Auto Exporter to U.S., Bloomberg, January 31, 2014
fhttp://www.bloomberg.com/news/articles/2014-01-31/mexico-surpassing-japan-as-no-2-auto-exporter-to-u-s-.
Paul A. Eisenstein, "Ford Set to Double Mexican Production," The Detroit Bureau, February 8, 2016.
http://www.thedetroitbureau.com/2016/02/ford-set-to-double-mexican-production/.
Michael Strong, "Ford Plowing $1.6 Billion."
Christina Rogers and Dudley Althaus, "It's Getting Harder."

[29] *Id.*

[30] James R. Hagerty and Jeff Bennett, "U.S. Car-Making Boom? Not for Auto-Industry Workers," Wall Street Journal, March 23, 2015.
http://www.wsj.com/articles/u-s-car-making-boom-not-for-workers-1427154627

---

[31] *Id.*

[32] *Id.*

[33] *Id.*

[34] The foregoing discussion is derived from the following reports: Lynette Adams, "Final day for workers at Sentry Safe as company moves jobs to Mexico, WHEC Rochester, NY, June 29, 2016. http://www.whec.com/news/sentry-safe-plant-closes-jobs/4184858/. Rachel Spotts, "Former owner talks Sentry Safe's move to Mexico, Trump's comments," WHEC Rochester, NY, April 27, 2016. http://www.whec.com/news/former-owner-talks-sentry-safe-mexico-move/4119632/ Rick Moriarty, "New owner to close Rochester area safe maker, cut 350 jobs," Syracuse.com, June 24, 2015. http://www.syracuse.com/business-news/index.ssf/2015/06/new_owner_to_close_rochester_area_safe_maker_cut_350_jobs_1.html. Allison Norlian, "SentrySafe to move from Rochester – 350 jobs lost," RochesterFirst.com, June 23, 2015. http://www.rochesterfirst.com/news/news/sentrysafe-to-move-from-rochester-350-jobs-lost.

[35] There are such firms on the U.S. side of the border as well. In his 2015 book, *Boom, Bust, Exodus*, discussed in Chapter 3, Chad Broughton chronicled the history of the McAllen Economic Development Corporation, which stands ready to assist U.S. companies in locating manufacturing in Reynosa. Regarding the ill effects of these relocations on American workers, Keith Partridge, the president and CEO of MEDC, told Broughton, "there is no right to a living wage." Jose Skinner, "Book Review: How NAFTA Transformed a Mexican Border Town," Texas Observer, April 22, 2015. https://www.texasobserver.org/how-nafta-transformed-a-mexican-border-town/

[36] http://www.ivemsa.com/mexico-manufacturing.

[37] Ioan Grillo, "How Mexicans See Nafta," New York Times, September 25, 2016.

[38] Andrew Tangel, "For Some Manufacturers, Mexico Still the Best Move," *supra*.

[39] "The Other Asian Tiger," The Economist, August 6, 2016. As in China, the communist party's single-minded focus on economic growth is coming at a high environmental cost: smog covers Hanoi, two thirds of industrial wastewater is untreated, and Vietnam has its own "cancer villages" with high rates of the disease. "Red v Green," *The Economist*, February 18, 2017.

[40] Pooja Thakur Mahrotri and En Han Choong, "$100 Billion Chinese-Made City Near Singapore 'Scares the Hell Out of Everybody', Bloomberg (November 22, 2016), http://www.msn.com/en-us/money/realestate/dollar100-billion-chinese-made-city-near-singapore-scares-the-hell-out-of-everybody/ar-AAkB5nh?li=BBmkt5R&ocid=spartanntp#image=8.

[41] Bandana Tewari, "Making 'Made in India' Matter," Business of Fashion, June 17, 2015. http://www.businessoffashion.com/community/voices/discussions/does-made-in-matter/op-ed-making-made-in-india-matter.

[42] Ellen Barry, "Rural Reality Meets Bangalore Dreams," New York Times, September 25, 2016.

[43] Jonathan Bach, "Nissan Aims to Boost Sales of Pickups," Wall Street Journal, August 16, 2016.

[44] Carol E. Lee and Damian Paletta, "Trump Pulls U.S. Out of Trade Pact," *Wall Street Journal*, January 24, 2017.

[45] Mike Colias, "Americans Embrace a Chinese-Built Buick," Wall Street Journal, October 7, 2016.

[46] Peter S. Goodman, "More Jobs, But Not for Everyone," New York Times, September 29, 2016.

[47] Martin Ford has described how the regular doubling of computing power is driving the new automation trend. In manufacturing, it involves a transformation from machines as tools for workers, to machines as workers in themselves. But the trend also is extending to employment of skilled professionals, as machines take on more routine, predictable work at all levels. Martin Ford, *Rise of the Robots: Technology and the Threat of a Jobless Future* (New York: Basic Books, 2015). The trend toward automation is so pronounced that scholars and policy makers are considering how to structure a "post-work" society. See, e.g., Ford, *ibid*; Roberta Rehner Iversen, "What Do *You* Do? Ideas About Transforming "Work" in the United States." In *Social Policy and Social Justice*, ed. John L. Jackson, Jr., (Philadelphia: University of Pennsylvania Press, 2017), 87-96.

[48] Alan S. Blinder, "How Many U.S. Jobs Might Be Offshorable? Princeton University CEPS Working Paper No. 142, March 2007. https://www.princeton.edu/ceps/workingpapers/142blinder.pdf

[49] Roger J. Moncarz, Michael G. Wolf, and Benjamin Wright, "Service-providing occupations, offshoring, and the labor market," Bureau of Labor Statistics, Monthly Labor Review (December 2008). http://www.bls.gov/opub/mlr/2008/12/art4full.pdf.

---

[50] Vinay Couto, Arie Y. Lewin, Mahadeva Mani, and Vikas Sehgal, "Offshoring the Brains as Well as the Brawn – Companies Seek Intellectual Talent Beyond their Borders," The Duke Center for International Business Education and Research (2006). http://www.strategyand.pwc.com/media/uploads/OffshoringtheBrainsasWellastheBrawn.pdf. See also "Study Finds Companies Moving High-end Functions Offshore to Access Talent." *Duke Today*, https://today.duke.edu/2006/10/outsourcing.html.

[51] *See, e.g.*, Barlett and Steele, *Betrayal*, 112 *ff.* Of course, as we saw in Chapter 7, there is another way for companies to outsource these job functions to less expensive foreign workers, and that is to bring them to the U.S. under the H-1B and L-1B visa programs. These consulting firms will be all-too-happy to assist you with that, too.

[52] Although I had seen the offshoring offers of the big consulting firms like Accenture, I found this solicitation to be particularly chilling, because it was such a direct communication, and targeted small and medium size businesses that could not afford the big consulting firms. I have included a copy of it in the Online Appendix.

[53] In addition to the concerns discussed below, it is possible that this robust growth figure will be revised downward in later publications; many commentators, including Warren Buffett, have said their research does not indicate an economy growing at this rate.

[54] The Economic Policy Institute reports that "Since 1973, the median man working full-time, full-year has seen no sustained wage growth, with wages dropping from $53,364 in 1973 to $51,957 in 2002 and falling further over the 2002-07 recovery and the recession, before rising to $51,212 in 2015." Lawrence Mishel and Teresa Kroger, "Superb income growth in 2015 nearly single-handedly restored incomes lost in the Great Recession," Economic Policy Institute, September 13, 2016. http://www.epi.org/blog/superb-income-growth-in-2015-nearly-single-handedly-restored-incomes-lost-in-the-great-recession/.

[55] Ian Rivkin, quoted by Sam Fleming, "Still the economy, stupid?" Financial Times, September 18, 2016.

[56] Mishel and Kroger, "Superb income growth," *supra*.

[57] The Centers for Disease Control reported that in 2014, drug overdose deaths increased 14% from the previous year, and 137% since 2000. Deaths from opioids were up 200% since 2000. The 47,000 deaths from drug overdoses exceeded the 33,000 deaths from traffic accidents. Maggie Fox, "Drug Overdose Deaths Hit 'Alarming' New Levels, CDC Says," NBC News, December 18, 2015. http://www.nbcnews.com/health/health-news/drug-overdose-deaths-hit-new-record-u-s-cdc-says-n482746.

[58] Committee for a Responsible Federal Budget. http://crfb.org/blogs/wrapping-2016-fiscal-year. I must add that this report is only of debt held by the public. The federal government has borrowed money from itself to pay annual operating costs, for example, by borrowing from funds in the Social Security trust fund. As of January, 2017, the federal government owed itself $5.2 trillion dollars. These funds must be repaid in the future, by borrowing from the public. So, the federal government's real indebtedness as of January, 2017, was $19.9 trillion dollars, 106% of GDP.

[59] Mitch Daniels, "Washington's Wake-up Call," Wall Street Journal, September 14, 2016.

[60] *Id.*

[61] Vaclav Smil, Made in the USA: The Rise and Retreat of American Manufacturing (Cambridge, Massachusetts: The MIT Press, 2013), xi. I commend Smil's book to you for its rich portrayal of the history of American manufacturing, the fallacies of the arguments for the status quo, and the need for a resurgence of this vial sector of the economy. *See also*, Eamonn Fingleton, Unsustainable: How Economic Dogma is Destroying American Prosperity (New York: Thunder's Mouth Press/Nation Books, 1993, 2003). Previously published as In Praise of Hard Industries: Why Manufacturing, Not the Information Economy, is the Key to Future Prosperity (New York: Houghton Mifflin, 1989).

[62] Daniel J. Meckstroth, "The Manufacturing Value Chain is Much Bigger than You Think!" Manufacturers Alliance for Productivity and Innovation, PA-165, February 2016. https://www.mapi.net/system/files/attachments/files/PA-165_web_0.pdf

[63] Josh Bivens, "Trade, jobs, and wages: Are the public's worries about globalization justified?" Economic Policy Institute, Issue Brief #244, May 6, 2008. http://www.epi.org/publication/ib244/.

[64] To those of us who question American exceptionalism, I ask that you have another look at history. Despite our excesses and failures, America has twice saved the world, once from bludgeoning itself to death in the trenches of Europe and at countless other locations during World War I, and once from Imperial Japan and Nazi Germany during World War II. Thrice if you count the Soviets and the Cold War. South Korea could look like North Korea were it not for American sacrifice, and our misadventure in Vietnam was a failure of leadership, not of cause, as demonstrated by the current differences between Vietnam and South Korea. Our misadventure in Iraq involved a miscalculation of the prospects of democracy in a "nation" riven by deep divisions by sect and ethnicity, and created a power vacuum in which the "Islamic State" has arisen.

[65] Kissinger, *World Order*, 372.

[66] *Id.*, 368.

[67] *Id.*, 369.

[68]Robert A. Isaak, *The Globalization Gap: How the Rich Get Richer and the Poor Get Left Further Behind* (New York: Prentice Hall, 2005), 196.

[69] Balance of payments is measured as the "current account." The deficit or surplus is primarily the measure of a country's balance of trade in goods and services, but also includes net income, such as interest and dividends, and net cash transfers, such as foreign aid. The figure is derived from the following table:

Current Account Balance by Country during 2015 In 2016 U.S. Dollars					
1	China	296.1	187	India	(26.5)
2	Germany	288.1	188	Algeria	(27.3)
3	Japan	138.9	189	Turkey	(32.5)
4	Korea, South	107.0	190	Mexico	(32.7)
5	Netherlands	81.8	191	Saudi Arabia	(41.9)
6	Taiwan	76.9	192	Canada	(51.9)
7	Switzerland	76.6	193	Australia	(56.8)
8	Russia	66.5	194	Brazil	(59.5)
9	Singapore	58.1	195	United Kingdom	(124.7)
10	Italy	39.1	196	United States	(488.9)
Current account balance compares a country's net trade in goods and services, plus net earnings, and net transfer payments to and from the rest of the world during the period specified. These figures are calculated on an exchange rate basis. Source: CIA World Fact Book Online.					

[70] Todd Lipscomb, *Re-Made in the USA: How We Can Restore Jobs, Retool Manufacturing, and Compete with the World.* (Hoboken, New Jersey: John Wiley & Sons, Inc., 2011), 33.

[71] Richard Baldwin, *The Great Convergence* (Cambridge, Mass.: The Belknap Press of Harvard University Press, 2016), 296.

[72] Merriam-Webster Dictionary Online.

[73] Baldwin, *Convergence*, 296.

[74] Baldwin, *Convergence*, 79-80.

[75] Paul Gallant, "How Bombardier's Experiment Became Ground Zero for Mexico's Economic Revolution," Canadian Business, April 15, 2015, cited in Baldwin, *Convergence*, 79.

---

[76] Baldwin *Convergence*, 2.

[77] Richard Baldwin refers to this as the "shocking share shift," and the "Great Convergence" in his book of the same name.

[78] Baldwin, *Convergence*, 3. Three of Baldwin's I6, China (6.6%), India (7.6%), Indonesia (5.0%), are among the fastest-growing economies as projected by UNCTAD in 2016. The others are Malaysia (4.3%), Pakistan (5.7%), and the Philippines (6.4%).

[79] *Id.*

[80] "Economic and financial indicators," The Economist, October 22, 2016, 80.

[81] Isaak, *Globalization Gap*, 196.

[82] Homi Kharas, "The Emerging Middle Class in Developing Countries," OECD Development Centre Working Paper No. 285 (January 2010), 7.

[83] *See* discussion at Kharas, "Emerging," 12.

[84] Rakesh Kochhar, "A Global Middle Class Is More Promise than Reality," *Pew Research Center* (July 8, 2015). http://www.pewglobal.org/2015/07/08/a-global-middle-class-is-more-promise-than-reality/. The study analyzed World Bank data for 111 countries accounting for 88% of the global population and 85% of world output in 2011.

[85] I have provided my own labels for the categories. Pew's labels are as follows: Cat. 1: Poor; Cat. 2: Low Income; Cat. 3: Middle Income; Cat. 4: Upper-Middle Income; Cat. 5: High Income. However, I believe these labels are misleading, implying higher standards of living than the income ranges support. Even in my categories, the "middle" label is a bit of an exaggeration, as it includes a family of four with an annual income of $29,215; a true "middle class" income would be somewhere above that in any urban area of any country. So, too, a family of four in the United States with $73,000 in annual income is hardly "upper" income. As we saw in Chapter 5, at "The Real Cost of Living in America," in an average American town like Akron, Ohio, a family of four cannot make ends meet on $73,000 a year.

[86] The Pew income amounts are expressed in 2011 prices converted to 2011 purchasing power parity dollars. Purchasing power parities (PPPs) are exchange rates adjusted for differences in the prices of goods and services across countries. So, these are apples-to-apples comparisons.

[87] Asian Development Bank, "The Rise of Asia's Middle Class," special chapter in *Key Indicators for Asia and the Pacific 2010*, 3.

https://www.adb.org/sites/default/files/publication/27726/ki2010-special-chapter.pdf.

[88] John West, "Debunking the Myth of the Asian Middle Class," Brink News, September 20, 2016. http://www.brinknews.com/asia/debunking-the-myth-of-the-asian-middle-class/.

[89] Asian Development Bank, "Rise."

[90] West, "Debunking," *supra*.

[91] Rosen, *Sweatshops,* 251.

[92] *See* discussion in Baldwin, *Convergence,* 154 *ff.* Contrary to Baldwin, who thinks the two curves represent equal value, I would add that there is downward pressure on the outside edges of the smile curve as well: the design and some of the post-manufacturing jobs also have come under pressure from foreign competition, and the distribution jobs tend to be low-paying.

[93] Anita Chan and Robert S. Ross, "From North-South to South-South: The True Face of Global Competition," Foreign Affairs (September/October 2002). http://www.cfr.org/globalization/north-south-south-south-true-face-global-competition/p4960.

[94] The "social clause" would insert five core labor standards into trade agreements: freedom of association, freedom to organize and bargain collectively, and freedom from forced labor, child labor, and job discrimination. These rights are embodied in the conventions of the International Labor Organization (ILO); however, many less-developed countries lack laws protecting such rights or do not enforce such laws, at least for their export industries. *Id.*

[95] Chan and Ross, *supra*.

[96] *Id.*

[97] "Economic and financial indicators," *The Economist, supra.*

[98] Chan and Ross, "True Face."

[99] Kevin P. Gallagher, "China and the Future of Latin American Industrialization," Boston University Frederick S. Pardee Center for the Study of the Longer-Range Future, Issues in Brief No. 18 (October 2010), http://www.bu.edu/pardee/issues-in-brief-no-18/. Kevin P. Gallagher and Roberto Porzecanski, *The Dragon in the Room: China and the Future of Latin American Industrialization* (Stanford: Stanford University Press, 2010).

[100] "Chinese lessons: Past, present and future," *New African*, March 2015, 26.

[101] Sola Akinrinade and Olukoya Ogen, "Globalization and De-Industrialization: South-South Neo-Liberalism and the Collapse of the

Nigerian Textile Industry," *The Global South*, Indiana University Press, Vol. 2, No. 2 (Fall 2008), 159-170. https://muse.jhu.edu/ article/ 256188.

[102] *Id.*

[103] "Chinese lessons: Past, present and future," *New African*, March 2015, 26.

[104] Isaak, *Globalization Gap*, 188, 189. Tiffany Ma, "China and Congo's coltan connection," Project 2049. https://www.project2049.net/documents/china_and_congos_coltan_connection.pdf

[105] Isaak, *Globalization Gap*, 188.

[106] West, "Debunking," *supra*.

[107] UNCTAD, "TDR Overview, 2016," 2

[108] Maisei, Raman. "Trade and development requires an ambitious rethink." World Bank, September 22, 2016.

[109] UNCTAD, "TDR Overview, 2016," 2. The UNCTAD view was shared by the World Bank and the IMF. In June, the World Bank revised its 2016 global economic growth forecast down to 2.4 percent from the 2.9 percent pace projected in January, due in large part to sluggish growth in advanced economies, together with stubbornly low commodity prices, weak global trade, and diminishing capital flows. World Bank, Global Economic Perspective, June 2016. In October, the International Monetary Fund reduced its forecasts of global economic growth to 3.1 percent in 2016 and 3.4 percent in 2017, a downward revision of 0.1 percent for both years since its previous projection in April. International Monetary Fund, World Economic Outlook, 2016.

[110] Mark Carney, "Redeeming an unforgiving world," Speech given at 8th Annual Institute of International Finance G20 conference, Shanghai, February 26, 2016), 999. http://www.bankofengland.co.uk/publications/Pages/speeches/default.aspx.

[111] Rosen, *Sweatshops*, 250.

[112] Baldwin, *Convergence*, 290-292. Baldwin notes that computer integrated manufacturing could undermine this trend to some degree.

[113] Margie Mason and Robin McDowell, "Seafood from Slave Labor," Associated Press in Philadelphia Inquirer, December 15, 2015.

[114] Michael Peel, "Nestle admission underlines severity of labour abuses in $6bn Thai seafood industry," Financial Times, December __, 2015.

Chapter 10

A Call to Arms

I believe we are engaged in this global "Darwinian race to the bottom" because we have lost our ethical moorings.

You will recall that in Chapter 4, we reviewed the specific theories of free trade, which all started with "We should . . ." Sometimes the "should" is not so explicit. For example, in Chapter 4, we also considered the second prevailing rationale for the pursuit of free trade: that the sacrifice of lost jobs, low pay, and social ills in the U.S. resulting from sending production offshore is outweighed by lifting millions of foreign workers and their families out of poverty.

I noted that trading away American jobs in pursuit of alleviating poverty abroad has practical limits and raises ethical concerns about its impacts abroad. We reviewed those ethical concerns in Chapters 8 and 9, and in the foreign working conditions that came to light in Chapters 1 through 3. What of the ethical considerations raised by impacts in the United States?

These often go unspoken and implicit in assumptions of what is "socially optimal." In a recent interview, economist David Autor made them explicit. I would have expected differently of Mr. Autor, who has done much of the recent work on identifying the real costs of free trade in terms of lost jobs and lower wages.[1] However, Nathaniel Popper reports:

> When I spoke with David Autor, he told me that whatever the virtues or costs in the United States, *they pale in comparison* with the basic humanitarian benefits that people in places like China and Vietnam have experienced as a result of trade with the United States. "The gains to the people who benefitted are so enormous - they were destitute, and now they were brought into the global middle class," Autor says. "*The fact that there are adverse consequences in the United States should be taken seriously, but it doesn't tilt the balance.*" [Emphasis supplied.] [2]

For Autor, the math is simple: twenty million Americans thrown into poverty is worth a hundred million Chinese lifted out of poverty. He is just "doing the math." Popper goes on to suggest that we should consider trade "in moral and humanitarian terms, not just as political and economic matters" and should consider how to compare the value of a new job for someone in dire poverty and "a lost job for someone with at least some version of a safety net."[3]

So, it may be morally correct to transfer a job making products for the American market to a poor farmer in Vietnam from a factory worker in Reading, Pennsylvania, because at least the Reading worker can get food stamps. Yes, we should figure out ways to soothe the hardships, Popper says, "but trade inevitably involves some trade-offs."

You may be shocked, as I was, to hear an economist and a reporter blithely engaging in this moral calculus. However, Autor's and Popper's thinking is representative of many in our elites. *What are the ethical principles being applied here, and are they valid?*

It is pragmatically as well as morally essential that every American stop and think carefully about the ethics of destroying jobs, and with them, individuals, families and communities, in the name of low price or fighting global poverty. We need to stop and consider, what is the "should" that guides us? Let's do that now.

What is the "should?"

I have been surprised and dismayed at what little consideration the moral dimension receives in the social, political, and economic research and debate. In fact, there is an underpinning of ethics in all of this. As Ellen Israel Rosen has pointed out, "Economic systems embody moral and cultural norms . . . ." [4]

So, it is important that we stop and pay attention to the ethical dimensions of this subject. As Eli Ginzberg put it in the forward to his commentary on the works of Adam Smith:

> Economics can never answer the question of what men want from the economic activities in which they engage; economics cannot even tell us whether men should be encouraged to intensify their pursuit of material gain. Adam Smith was a moral philosopher before he became the founder of economics.
>
> It is important that we restudy his teachings, for *there is no future for an economics that sees itself as an end in itself.* [5]

The "should" is a moral should, or else nothing "matters," and we are left with nihilism. I am reminded of the motto on the seal of my alma mater, the University of

Pennsylvania: "Leges sine Moribus vanae" -- Laws without morals are in vain.[6]

The "Should" of Utilitarianism

I have mentioned that, in general, the efficient market hypothesis and market fundamentalism are based on the philosophical approach of utilitarianism, widely known for the maxim, "greatest good for the greatest number." For example, this thinking is embodied in the proposition that broad-based access to low-priced foreign-sourced products and services is worth the drastic losses that may be visited upon a minority.[7]

In the classical utilitarianism of Jeremy Bentham, right actions are defined as those that maximize pleasure and minimize pain, measured as "utility." John Stuart Mill expanded the concept to include happiness and fulfillment. Many modern philosophers (and economists) see utility, or intrinsic value, residing in the satisfaction of individuals' "preferences." [8] Preference utilitarianism unfolds like this:

Individuals have *desires*.[9] *Utility* is a measure of the satisfaction of the desires of an individual from the consumption of a good or service, or a set of goods and services. *Preference* is the ordering of alternatives based on their relative utility. Preference utilitarianism defines as the good those actions that maximize the fulfillment of individuals' preferences. The process is said to result in a "choice" that is "optimal."

Preference utilitarianism begs the question of what is "the good" or "the good life." The preferred outcome is the sum of individuals' preferences as expressed in the market. There is no consideration of how those individuals arrived at their preferences. But let us remember that there is an entire industry we refer to as "Madison Avenue," portrayed in the television series "Mad Men" but updated to a modern version, whose mission is to create preferences. I once attended an annual conference of a luxury marketing organization, and heard a featured speaker explain that the members' goal was to have someone walk into their store and point to a luxury handbag hanging on the wall and exclaim, "I *must* have that bag!" There also is no comparison of those preferences to any standard of morality or ethics. In fact, *preference utilitarianism is amoral; it has nothing to do with morals at all.*[10]

Preference utilitarianism also encounters the same problem as presented by classical utilitarianism — how "utility" is to be distributed across the population. In its simplest form, the theory calls for that distribution which maximizes the sum of satisfied preferences, with preferences weighted according to their intensity. Where outcomes are not known, expected utility is measured.[11] But how distributed? The maxim goes, "the greatest good for the greatest number." However, the theory begins and ends at "the greatest good," regardless of how many or how few individuals experience the good or in what measure.[12] So, even within the context of utilitarianism, we are confronted with the question of "distributive justice."

Distributive Justice

"Distributive justice" is a name for the moral principles guiding the choices a society makes, through its framework of laws and institutions, for the distribution of economic benefits and burdens across the members of the society. Those choices are being made every day, and cannot be avoided. The resulting distributions have a profound effect on people's lives.[13]

Those choices, and the principles that guide them, are commonly framed in terms of "equality" and "inequality." We have seen that utilitarianism is not very much concerned with the distribution of economic benefits, but rather focuses more on the total, as measured through gross domestic product or some such measure, in the belief that "a rising tide will float all boats."

There are two shortcomings to this approach: too much inequality may actually inhibit total growth; and too much inequality may violate our moral norms.

Inequality can slow growth.

Adam Smith believed too much wealth accumulation in too wealthy a society can cause problems. In *The Wealth of Nations*, Smith concluded that when a society becomes wealthy enough, opportunities to acquire extreme wealth can lead individuals to favor the benefits ("approbation") of wealth over those of moral behavior, with ruinous effects for individuals and society. At a certain point when an industrial society permits individuals to acquire large fortunes, Smith's general principle that pursuing one's own interest can better both the individual and the society gives way. As society becomes richer, the potential negative consequences of wealth accumulation grow larger.[14]

It makes intuitive sense that broadly shared prosperity will lead to more economic growth and that a failure to share prosperity ("inequality") will inhibit it. This intuition is confirmed in a recent study by economists at the International Monetary Fund. Looking at the experience of a large number of countries over time, they found a relationship between the degree of inequality and the pace and duration of growth: "[T]here is now strong evidence that inequality can significantly lower both the level and the durability of growth."[15] They also found that moderate use of progressive taxation to reduce inequality was associated with stronger growth, and that even large redistributions were growth-neutral.[16]

You be the judge: Do you think it makes sense that keeping the money in the hands of the wealthy will make for a stronger economy? Some argue yes, that the wealthy will then invest the money in business activities that will create jobs. But we know this is not happening: they are sitting on the money. The reason is there is little to invest in. And the reason for that is a lack of consumer demand: no one has the money to spend on the things they would produce if they invested. So there the money sits.

Now see if you think this makes sense: consumers with money in their pockets want to buy things. So, the wealthy (they are still wealthy by the way, just *not that wealthy*) invest their money in business activities that will produce products to *respond* to the demand. The job creators are middle class consumers who can afford to buy goods and services. This is what make sense to me, and to a goodly number of economists and others who study these things.[17] In my opinion, this is not rocket science, it is common sense.

Moral Concerns

The fact that utilitarianism, even while maximizing total utility, may result in extreme disparities in the distribution of economic benefits, also raises ethical concerns. For example, some individuals may not receive sufficient benefits to cover their basic needs of life. Other concerns may include notions of merit and fairness, where some individuals are not adequately compensated and some overcompensated, in relation to their effort or the value provided through their efforts.

These concerns give rise to a whole different approach from market fundamentalist utilitarianism, sometimes referred to as "family" or "stakeholder" capitalism. I will take up this approach in Chapter 11, "Is there a better vision?" There also is the question of "Who is us?" — Across what population are the economic benefits and burdens being distributed? There is some sentiment that these choices and distributions should be made on a worldwide basis. I will take up alternatives to that idea, too, in Chapter

11. For now, I will assume a worldwide perspective, since that is what is being imposed in the asserted project of eliminating poverty abroad.

But that leaves us with the major problem posed by utilitarianism: the treatment of the individual versus the whole.

Individual Sacrifice Compelled

A principal criticism of utilitarianism is this: It may be prudent for an *individual* to sacrifice and endure hardship at some points, to make his/her life better overall; however, utilitarianism applies this principle to a *whole population*, with some people suffering to achieve a net gain for others — the worth of the individual is lost in the process. "Utilitarianism, in even its most sophisticated and complicated versions, countenances the sacrifice of some persons to the happiness of others." [18]

Furthermore, the individual *chooses* to endure the hardship, whereas under utilitarianism there is no requirement of consent. Critics of utilitarianism argue that *it is immoral to make some people suffer for others to realize a net gain.*[19]

Adam Smith on What Can be Coerced

This distinction between conduct that can be coerced and conduct that is voluntary was well made by none other than Adam Smith, in his treatise *The Theory of Moral Sentiments.*[20]

Smith divided human actions into two categories: those that did harm to others, and those that provided benefit to others. Smith said the virtue of "justice" was the abstention from doing things in the first category, *i.e.*, that caused injury, "real and positive hurt to particular persons." We can think of it as a variation on the Hippocratic injunction to "first do no harm." This rule, Smith said, was of such importance that it could be enforced by the law and its violation could incur punishment.[21]

On the other hand, "beneficence," actions that provide benefit to others, cannot be elicited by force, and failure to perform them cannot be punished, because the failure "tends to do no positive evil." [22]

Here is an example of the category of beneficence: The commandant of the German concentration camp at Auschwitz, to discourage escapes, had a rule that if a man escaped, ten men would be killed in retaliation. In July of 1941 a man escaped from the bunker of a Polish priest named Maximilian Kolbe, prisoner 16770. The commandant, Karl Fritsch, announced that ten of the prisoners would be locked in the starvation bunker without food and water until they died. Ten were selected, including Franciszek Gajowniczek, who cried out in dismay, "my poor wife; my poor children! What will they do?" Hearing this, Kolbe stepped forward, saying he was a priest without a family, and asked the commandant to let him take Gajowniczek's place. For whatever reason, the commandant agreed. Kolbe died, and for the next fifty years Gajowniczek visited the prison in honor of his benefactor.[23]

What We've Been Doing

Compare that story to this one: the police in the surrounding towns round up men at random and inform them that they are going to Auschwitz, because the authorities have struck a deal with the camp commander: he will release ten men for every man they bring in. The townsmen are not asked to volunteer for this duty; they are just informed that they are going to be part of the exchange.

This story is hypothetical, but I tell it because that is exactly what we have been saying to the men and women working in the manufacturing plants that are being sent to

China and Mexico: we know you are losing your job, but we are raising ten people somewhere out there above two dollars a day into the "global middle class."

We are violating Smith's rule that beneficence will be applauded, but cannot be required -- Father Kolbe will be greatly admired for his action, but no one will be required to make such sacrifices. In fact, by requiring these sacrifices by American workers, we are violating Smith's other rule: to abstain from causing "real and positive hurt to particular persons" - to first, do no harm. I believe it is fair to say that preference utilitarianism is amoral in its formulation, but immoral in its consequences.

An episode of the television series on World War II, "The World at War" featured the British soldiers whose duty was to attempt to defuse unexploded German bombs in London. Workers would excavate a hole around the bomb, and the soldier would descend armed with information about how the fuse was thought to work, knowing a false move would prove fatal; the bombs not infrequently detonated. I remember a soldier, upon learning of his assignment to one of these units, telling his new commanding officer, "I thought people had to volunteer for that." That is how our factory workers feel when they learn they have been volunteered in the project of lowering American consumer prices and reducing poverty abroad.

That is how the entire textile industry felt on learning that they had been volunteered in the project of fighting communism by supporting the free Asian nations. The author of a 1957 study for the northern textile industry and the Textile Workers Union opposing further penetration of the Asian producers into the U.S. market argued that the problem of dollar shortages abroad was one of concern to the entire United States, which should not be solved by "excessive sacrifice by one segment of the economy, and a declining segment at that" -- the burden should be borne by taxpayers and strong industries, especially export businesses.[24] That is, if fighting communism was a national goal, then its costs should be spread across America, rather than singling out his industry to be sacrificed for the cause.

Destroying our Industrial Base

In my view, it is both a high moral crime and economic suicide to consciously, even intentionally, remove the factories, large and small, that are the productive engines driving the economies of communities across America.

During the Second World War, with some notable exceptions, bombing raids were directed at the industrial capacity of the enemy. I knew two men who during the war were children in the north and south ends of Manchester, England. The one who lived in the southern, industrial end, was bombed; the other who lived in the northern end was not. Now, our misguided trade and economic policies are having the same effect: it is as if we were intentionally bombing only the productive, industrial manufacturing centers of the United States. Except it is more like a neutron bomb, that leaves all the structures standing, but empty, with all the production, and even the formerly used machines, gone — to Mexico, or China, or Vietnam.

So it is with the Budd factory that used to make automobile bodies in Philadelphia. It is several city blocks on a side, six or seven stories high. It now stands empty, having closed in the 1990s. A sign outside announces the availability of one million square feet of space for purchase or lease.

And it is not just the factory that gets up boarded up. So, too, go the small businesses that supplied the factory and supported its workers. We hear of "food deserts," areas of our cities that are not served by a supermarket. The reason we have food deserts is that we have created "job deserts," neighborhoods and whole towns where there are no jobs to be had, because the factories stand empty, and there is nothing to replace them.

Hitting Hardest the Least Able to Bear It

What is worse, the effects are falling upon those least able to cope with them - Americans with a high school education and perhaps some junior college, or who perhaps earned a graduate equivalent diploma, or who perhaps never received their high school diploma.

Let us recognize that these are seventy percent of Americans, doing the seventy percent of jobs that do not require a college education. I think some of us tend to consider high-school educated, working Americans as some sort of minority, and one that may be worthy of disdain, even contempt.

As Beth Macy has pointed out, at the end of the day trade policies with fancy names implemented in Washington eventually make their way to small towns like Sumter, South Carolina, and Bassett, Virginia, where globalization's real-life burdens are shouldered by low-income workers.[25]

Not Just Low Price: Profits

We also must remember that moving all this production overseas has not been done solely, or even primarily, to offer lower prices to American consumers. At least for the first movers, the primary motive was profit.

Wal-Mart was in financial trouble after Sam Walton died in 1992, so they increased their sourcing in China. A store manager remembered "all of this stuff showing up," and being amazed that it had 60, 70, even 80 percent margins.[26] That is, Wal-mart was making that much gross profit on each sale. Apple's profit on a sale of an iPhone was 59 percent of the sale price; 30 percent for an iPad.[27]

Against Self-Interest

Ethical considerations aside, this is in almost no one's economic self-interest. So long as it was someone else whose ox was being gored, many of us thought this thinking was just fine. Oh, isn't that too bad, that all those shoe-making jobs went offshore. But it was inevitable, wasn't it? And aren't we better off with everyone being able to buy cheap shoes from abroad? And shouldn't those former shoemakers be doing something more befitting an American, requiring higher skills, while we give the low-skill work to those poor foreigners?

It is easy for us to think that way when we believe that what *we* do is immune from loss. Many people believed that about furniture, which was thought to be too bulky to be shipped long distances economically. They were wrong: the foreign producers figured out how to ship components to be assembled after arrival, and the container ships grew large and efficient enough to ship just about anything. And so has it been with many other industries and job functions that some thought were safely protected against offshoring, now including the white-collar and high-skilled, as discussed in Chapter 9. The offshoring is spreading to many previously thought immune.

And the effects are not limited to the occupations that are subject to offshoring: when those jobs are sent overseas, their former occupants, or people who were thinking of going into the field, are diverted into the non-tradable occupations, increasing competition and driving down wages. The downward effect on wages ultimately affects nearly everyone.[28] Even for those immune from these effects, when the economy has been sufficiently hollowed out by all this offshoring, there will be too few haves and too many have nots. In many ways, we are already there, but it will get worse, with suffering and social unrest.

Our elites have failed us

Our academic and political elites, while pursuing lofty policy objectives, have failed to serve the needs of ordinary Americans to be able to make a go of it in their lives. The elites who tell ordinary Americans that it is their duty to ruin their lives and give up everything they have worked for to lift someone in another country out of poverty — that each of them should enter a life of poverty to lift four or five people somewhere else out of poverty. And if they won't do that voluntarily, we will create a system that does that to them.

Except, of course, that those of us who are creating and perpetuating that system won't volunteer to do it ourselves. As one honest academic, Pietra Rivoli,[29] put it:

> [E]ven the most passionate defenders of free markets don't like to experience them up close and personal. Where do you find the most passionate defenders of free trade? You find them, you know, in the tenured members of economics departments all over the world. And so tenured members of economics departments have themselves created structures to protect themselves from markets, right? And their doing so has negative effects for people outside that particular group."[30]

She certainly is right on that last point: the universities are using "adjunct professors" who are being paid a pittance as the slack in the economy moves beyond blue-collar to every stratum of American society, and the "Big Squeeze" comes to bear on nearly all of us.

And I believe she is right in saying "the most passionate defenders of free markets don't like to experience them up close and personal." As I have discussed, MIT economist David Autor has said that the costs visited upon blue-collar Americans "pale in comparison" to the benefits to the hundreds of millions overseas who have been lifted from extreme poverty. But I don't see him volunteering to have his life destroyed in support of that cause. He probably has tenure, so he is one of the few people who are insulated from all of this, at least for the medium term.[31] I have a modest proposition: that no policymaker be permitted to promote policies requiring Americans to send their jobs to foreign countries unless and until the policymaker first matches the sacrifice, by giving thirty percent of his/her income to a foreign charity.

Shame on those of us who are members of the elite in secure positions at universities or think-tanks, imposing devastating harm on ordinary Americans and their families and communities in the name of low prices for the masses or eliminating global poverty. I am reminded of the passages in the Old Testament:

> "Son of man, prophesy against the shepherds . . . who have been feeding themselves! Should not the shepherds feed the flock? You eat the fat and clothe yourselves with the wool, you slaughter the fat sheep without feeding the flock . . . with force and with severity you have dominated them. . . ."
>
> Therefore, you shepherds, hear the word of the Lord: ". . . surely because . . . the shepherds fed themselves and did not feed My flock; therefore, . . I am against the shepherds, and I will demand My sheep from them . . . ."
>
> I will . . . raise up [new] shepherds over them and they will tend them; and they will not be afraid any

longer, nor be terrified, nor will any be missing," declares the Lord.[32]

Those of us who are policymakers, being in the position of a modern-day shepherd, have a high duty to look out for the interests of the ordinary American. If we don't, we need to be replaced.

Letter from Washington

But we have been failing in that duty. Here is what we have been doing instead:

LETTER FROM WASHINGTON to the residents of Anywhere, U.S.A.

Oh, your life has been ruined, and your community, too? Oh, I'm sorry, but you know, that's just the cost of the increase in welfare everyone is experiencing through the lower prices of the things made and done abroad. You know, this all is due to unstoppable forces beyond our control, and there are going to be winners and losers. And besides, you don't have to be a loser. You need to get out there and retrain yourself for a high-skill job. What's that, you say, you don't have money to live on while you go to school full-time? And what's that you say, there are no jobs to train for? And what's that you say, you have an IQ of 100 and aren't so good at school, but you're a hard worker? I'm sure you'll figure it out. In the end, though, it was worth it, because you and everyone else in America is better off, because we can buy our ten dollar shirts and get thirty percent off on our furniture, and, oh yeah, so are those foreign workers who got your jobs - we're raising them all up into a new global middle class. Isn't it wonderful? Thanks for doing your part to make it happen! You're the best! Say hello to everyone for me. I hope you guys are doing okay.

We are all complicit – Malign Neglect

But it is not just the policy makers. It is not just the companies who are operating the distribution centers through outsource contractors, claiming that they can wash their hands of the working conditions, that they have clean hands. It is not just the companies moving their factories to Mexico because their current workers can't match the Mexican wages. None of us has clean hands. Every time we go for the low price, we are complicit.

It is especially wrong if we are doing it in our perceived self-interest of being able to buy inexpensive foreign products and services.[33] The passage from Ezekiel directed at the shepherds also has something to say to the sheep:

> "As for you, My flock, thus says the Lord God, 'Behold, I will judge . . . between the fat sheep and the lean sheep. Because you push with side and with shoulder, and thrust at all the weak with your horns until you have scattered them abroad, therefore, I will deliver My flock, and they will no longer be a prey; and I will judge between one sheep and another.'" [34]

Not only this -- in my view, it also is morally wrong to stand by and watch others' lives being destroyed; we have a duty to intervene on their behalf. We are not unlike the cast of *Seinfeld* in part one of its *finale*, standing side-by-side facing the camera, watching someone behind the camera be carjacked at gunpoint. Instead of helping him, they crack jokes about his size while Kramer films it all on his camcorder, and then walk away. The victim notices this and tells the reporting officer, who arrests them under a duty-to-rescue law that requires bystanders to help out in such a situation.[35]

Instead of helping to rescue our fellow Americans, we are acting like Kramer did, saying, in effect, "Oh, isn't that too bad? They should have stayed in school and gotten a high-skill job that wouldn't be sent offshore." We have a duty to first, do no harm, and secondly, do what we can to repair the harm done.

Who will speak up?

Who will speak up for ordinary Americans? What has been happening calls to mind the famous quote of the German protestant theologian Martin Niemoller regarding the Nazis in the 1930s: [36]

> First, they came for the Socialists, and I did not speak out--
>
> Because I was not a Socialist.
>
> Then they came for the Trade Unionists, and I did not speak out--
>
> Because I was not a Trade Unionist.
>
> Then they came for the Jews, and I did not speak out-
>
> Because I was not a Jew.
>
> Then they came for me--and there was no one left to speak for me. [37]

Niemoller Paraphrased

Our situation is so dire, so many lives and communities have been destroyed, that, I believe, it is apt to paraphrase Niemoller:

> First, they came for the shoe industry, but I was not a shoemaker, so I did not speak out.
>
> Then they came for the furniture industry, but I was not a craftsman, so I did not speak out.

> Then they came for the steel industry, but I was not a steel worker, so I did not speak out.
>
> Then they came for the computer industry, but I was not an assembly worker, so I did not speak out.
>
> Then they came for the software industry, but I was not a programmer, so I did not speak out.
>
> Then they came for me – and there was no one left to speak for me.

It is interesting to note that Neimoller's construct is a combination of altruism and self-interest. As a matter of morality and ethics, we should be concerned with the plight of the worker whose job is being displaced. But as a matter of self-interest, we should be concerned that the next job to be lost may be ours, or that of a loved one, and even if not, we may feel downward pressure on our wages, and be left having to support the social needs of individuals and families who were forced into dependency, and to pay an ever-greater share of taxes for roads, education, and defense. Economic independence for every American household is a matter of altruism and self-interest alike.

Those of us who are doing well have both a moral obligation and a self-interest in promoting economic self-sufficiency for American families – so they can experience a decent life while making it on their own, and so we will not be required to subsidize their basic social needs. Ultimately, if we do not reverse current trends, those needs will become greater than the ability of the "haves" to subsidize. And ultimately, if we do not reverse current trends, the supposedly secure jobs of the "haves" will themselves be offshored, or lost in economic collapse.

For the Children

But the ultimate motivation is our concern for, and duty to, the next generations.

I have a favorite photograph of my children taken at the Memorial Day parade in Wayne, Pennsylvania in May of 2013. There they are, in their trappings of flags and red, white, and blue, full of happiness, energy and hope. Although I love that picture, it also haunts me. For while there are challenges in raising a child in America today, my real concern is the belief that there are things I haven't yet shared with them about their future. Yes, I am concerned that we are piling up federal debt every day on which they will be paying the interest; that college costs continue to outstrip inflation and earnings; and that health care is being priced beyond reach. But my major concern is that *we are busily trading away their opportunity for meaningful work.*

My question is this: When we have the conversation with our children as to what career direction they should consider, what do we tell them? For how many careers do we already say, "They don't do that here anymore; all that work went to (China or India, as may be the case), or will be gone by the time you enter the workforce"? Are we to say to them that they should aspire to be a designer somewhere like Apple, so they can have the one in 10,000 of the Apple jobs that are still located in the United States? Isn't that like telling them they should aspire to be in the NBA, with a similar percentage likelihood of success? And how many of such jobs that we now consider "non-tradable," or for which we currently think we have a comparative advantage, will be outsourced offshore before they enter the workforce?

Are we ready to offer up our children on the altar of global citizenry? Is our answer different if it is someone else's children whose future is at stake? *We are trading away our children's future.* We can't stay on our current course.

Breaking the Thrall of Free Trade

As we look at the sweep of history, decade after decade, one must ask, have we lost leave of our senses? For seventy years, our leaders have been in thrall to simplistic economic and trade ideologies that have been at odds with the facts and our real-world experience.

The continued propagation of the patently false propositions of "free trade," "win-win," and "socially optimal" results of the "rational market," and the patently unethical propositions of destroying lives of ordinary Americans and their communities in the name either of lower prices or of helping the teaming foreign multitudes out of poverty, make me wonder, are people being intentionally misleading? I am feeling like the character of Bid Daddy in Tennessee Williams' play, "Cat on a Hot Tin Roof," who strolls onto the stage and announces, "Mendacity; I'm surrounded by mendacity!"

I am sure some of that is going on. But I believe mostly we have been operating in good faith, but for some reason unable to see. It is as if we have been sleep walking in a trance, in the thrall of some wizard who has us under this spell called free trade.

A good example is Daniel Alpert, who gave us his extremely useful and insightful book, *The Age of Oversupply*, discussed in Chapter 2. Alpert is unusual in the clarity with which he describes the problem of global oversupply of cheap labor and productive capacity and the resulting global imbalances of trade and debt. If anyone understands the futility of engaging in free trade in the face of one and a half billion poor-but-able workers entering the global workforce and a glut of capital to set them up in business, it is he. Unfortunately, Alpert proves himself to be just as much in the thrall of the dogma of free trade as those whom he has criticized.

He points out that "[t]he developed world is facing nations that are acting in their own short- and medium-term (if not long-term) best interests by pursuing one version or another of state/oligarchic mercantilist capitalism." He says we cannot blame them for doing this, but "we do have the power to make it far less easy for them to do well as mercantilists," and calls on our governments to do so. He quotes former Intel CEO Andy Grove for the proposition that we are in the middle of an economic war for global supremacy, and shouldn't be carrying on as though it's business as usual.[38]

However, astonishingly, he immediately follows these warnings and call to action with this remarkable about-face:

> It would be nice to be able to coddle our private sector under the protective umbrella of tariffs and other trade restrictions as an incentive for them to spend, expand, and employ. *But after decades of advocating free trade*, acting as steward of the World Trade Organization, and enabling our emerging trading partners to achieve geopolitical and military strength and influence, *there is simply no going back*. I would hardly want to be the American president who calls the president of China and tells him, "Oh, you know that globalization stuff we've been advocating all these years? Well, it didn't work out so well for us, so . . ." [39]

As my kids would say, "OMG." It is as if the wizard stepped back into the room and swept him back into his thrall. Where to begin? Why does Alpert consider it "coddling" our private sector to use tariffs and other trade restrictions to level the playing field against the "state/oligarchic mercantilist capitalism" he recognizes is being deployed unfairly against them? Why, after decades of being the only free trader in a world of mercantilists whom we enabled to "achieve geopolitical and military strength and influence" is there "simply no going back"? Why would the American president not say that to China's leader? (And why hasn't any of them?)

Alpert has repeatedly said that the new "age of oversupply" requires the United States and other developed nations to "think outside the box." However, he has shown himself to be firmly trapped inside the box of free trade dogma, from which "there is no going back."

It seems that nearly everyone is in thrall to the dogma of free trade. We are free-trade zombies. We are like the workers marching in the trance of a "garden of pure ideology" in the famous Apple Macintosh® advertisement titled "1984" after George Orwell's book of the same name.[40]

The thrall of the dogma of free trade calls to mind the words of President Lincoln:

> The dogmas of the quiet past are inadequate to the stormy present. The occasion is piled high with difficulty, and we must rise with the occasion. As our case is new, so we must think anew and act anew. *We must disenthrall ourselves, and then we shall save our country.*[41]

Indeed, we must disenthrall ourselves of the dogmas of the past, of the notion –

- That free trade will be fair trade, or will result in balanced trade.

- That America is still the leading manufacturing country in the world.

- That manufacturing doesn't matter.
- That manufacturing in America is healthy, or at least recovering, through re-shoring and the application of new technologies.
- That our non-manufacturing, service jobs won't be offshored.
- That the remaining, non-tradable jobs are enough to support the economy.
- That a low-price, low-wage, "low road" economy is sustainable.
- That we can survive as communities and as a nation if current trends continue.

We must disenthrall ourselves, and the first thing we must do is imagine a better future.

Notes to Chapter 10

[1] *See* “The Great Employment Sag” and “The China Syndrome” discussed in Chapter 6.

[2] Nathaniel Popper, “How Much Do We Really Know About Global Trade’s Impacts?”, New York Times Magazine, September 6, 2016 http://www.nytimes.com/2016/09/11/magazine/how-much-do-we-really-know-about-global-trades-impacts.html?_r=0.

[3] *Id.*

[4] Rosen, *Sweatshops*, 19.

[5] Eli Ginzberg, *The House of Adam Smith* (New York: Columbia University Press, 1934; reprinted, New York: Octagon Books, Inc., 1964), xiii.

[6] The Penn motto is derived from the Roman poet Horace: “Quid leges sine moribus vanae proficiunt.” (Of what avail are laws without morals?)

[7] It is clear, moreover, as discussed in Chapter 4, that the losses are *not* only visited upon a minority, and that these low prices have a cost, in the form of lower wages and support for dependency, that are widespread.

[8] Under the influence of John Harsanyi, mainstream utilitarianism moved toward a preference-based version of utilitarianism that we see applied in much American economic thought. *See* John Broome, “Can There Be a Preference-Based Utilitarianism?” in *Justice, Political Liberalism, and Utilitarianism*, eds. Marc Fleurbaey, Maurice Sales and John A. Weymark, (New York: Cambridge University Press, 2008), 221. *See also* Julian Lamont and Christi Favor. "Distributive Justice," in *The Stanford Encyclopedia of Philosophy*, edited by Edward N. Zalta (Winter 2016 Edition), forthcoming URL = <https://plato.stanford.edu/archives/win2016/entries/justice-distributive/>.

[9] Desires may be categorized as wants and needs, needs being necessary for survival. However, it likely is more useful not to make this division, but instead to rank desires by importance. Food, clothing and shelter thus may begin as a need, but move toward wants as they improve in quality and expense.

[10] William Davies reaches the same conclusion. William Davies, *The Limits of Neoliberalism: Authority, Sovereignty and the Logic of Competition* (Los Angeles: Sage, 2014), 8. John Broome proposes that “preferences may partly determine good, but other things must enter

too," and questions whether satisfying preferences should be considered a moral aim at all. Broome, "Can There Be?", 221-222.

[11] *Id.*

[12] Lamont and Favor point out that many preference utilitarians nevertheless extend their theory to distributive results, with some prescribing strongly egalitarian structures with lots of state intervention and others a l*aissez faire* style of capitalism, as I discuss below. Lamont and Favor, "Distributive Justice."

[13] *Id.*

[14] According to Maria Pia Paganelli, Smith amends the sixth, 1790 edition of *Moral Sentiments* to account for this. Maria Pia Paganelli, "Theory of Moral Sentiments 1759 vs. Theory of Moral Sentiments 1790: A Change of Mind or a Change of Constraint," In *New Essays on Adam Smith's Moral Philosophy*, eds. Wade L. Robinson and David B. Suits, 35-44. (Rochester: RIT Press, 2012), 38, 40.

[15] Ostry et al, "Neoliberalism." "First, we continue to find that inequality is a robust and powerful determinant both of the pace of medium-term growth and of the duration of growth spells . . . . Thus, *it would still be a mistake to focus on growth and let inequality take care of itself*, if only because the resulting growth may be low and unsustainable. Inequality and unsustainable growth may be two sides of the same coin." *Id.* Emphasis supplied.

[16] *Id.* "Importantly, we established that growth is faster in more equal societies than in less equal ones, regardless of whether they have highly redistributive tax systems. The lower growth observed in highly unequal societies does not seem to be a side-effect of redistribution, as some people have claimed." Jonathan D. Ostry, "We Do Not Have to Live with the Scourge of Inequality," Financial Times, March 3, 2014.

[17] See, e.g., Homi Kharas, "The Emerging Middle Class in Developing Countries," *OECD Development Centre* Working Paper No. 285 (January 2010).

[18] Wolff, *Understanding Rawls*, 12. In this sense, utilitarianism can be thought of as a manifestation of the "tyranny of the majority," against which American founding fathers such as Alexander Hamilton tried to build institutional protections.

[19] Lamont and Favor, "Distributive Justice." This criticism was articulated by John Rawls, as failing to acknowledge the distinctness of persons. Rawls, *Theory*.

[20] Adam Smith, *The Theory of Moral Sentiments* (London: A, Millar, Second ed., 1761). The first edition was published in 1759, before *The*

Wealth of Nations. Smith's first, and continuing, field of interest was moral philosophy.

[21] Smith, *Theory*, 134.

[22] Smith, *Theory*, 132. Smith did think that there is a level of beneficence that is generally expected in society, above which a person's actions are "praiseworthy," and below which a person's actions may be "blamable," but not punishable. Smith, *Theory*, 135.

[23] Father Kolbe was canonized by Pope John Paul II on October 10, 1982 in the presence of Franciszek Gajowniczek. "St. Maximilian Kolbe," *Catholic Online*,
http://www.catholic.org/saints/saint.php?saint_id=370.
"Maximilian Kolbe," *Jewish Virtual Library*,
https://www.jewishvirtuallibrary.org/jsource/biography/Kolbe.html
"Kolbe, Saint of Auschwitz," *The Holocaust*, http://www.auschwitz.dk/.

[24] Seymour Harris in Rosen, *Sweatshops*, 86.

[25] Macy, *Factory Man*, 305, 336.

[26] Sam Hornblower, "Wal-Mart & China: A Joint Venture," *PBS Frontline*.
http://www.pbs.org/wgbh/pages/frontline/shows/walmart/secrets/wmchina.html

[27] Timothy Noah, *The Great Divergence* (New York: Bloomsbury Press, 2012), 101. Citations omitted.

[28] There is some evidence that the initial effect of trade with low-income countries is to drive up U.S. wages for skilled workers. See, e.g., Bivens, *Everybody Wins*. However, this effect is being countered by the advent of offshoring skilled work.

[29] Pietra Rivoli, *The Travels of a T-Shirt in the Global Economy: An Economist Examines the Markets, Power, and Politics of World Trade*. Dr. Rivoli is a professor of finance and international business at Georgetown University. In the preface to her book, *Travels of a T-Shirt in the Global Economy*, she says that when she set out to write her book, she thought that she would have a story that would help her students, who had been participating in anti-globalization protests, "appreciate the virtues of markets in improving the human condition." In the end, she believed that she had such a story, but that it is not the whole story - that progress results not only from competitive markets but also from "the forces of conscience that continue to rewrite the rules of global commerce." That is, that her students were right to be protesting how their T-shirts were made, and that moral boundaries had to be brought to the market.

[30] Pietra Rivoli, in Transcript of an IMF Book Forum--The Travels of a T-Shirt in the Global Economy: An Economist Examines the Markets, Power, and Politics of World Trade, International Monetary Fund, October 19, 2005.
https://www.imf.org/en/News/Articles/2015/09/28/04/54/tr051019.

[31] Let me say here that I admire and am grateful for the groundbreaking work Dr. Autor has done with his colleagues in taking the measure of the deep losses experienced by workers and their communities under pressure from imports. He is not alone in applying the "raising up millions" math and it is my hope that this book may raise some awareness and change some minds.

[32] Ezekiel 34:1-3, 10; Jeremiah 23:5.

[33] Or even with the intention of helping some foreign worker out of poverty, oblivious to the collateral damage.

[34] Jeremiah 23:17, 20-22.

[35] Wikipedia.
https://en.wikipedia.org/wiki/The_Finale_%28Seinfeld%29.

[36] Source: American Holocaust Museum;
http://www.ushmm.org/wlc/en/article.php?ModuleId=10007392.

[37] Niemoller eventually did return to Germany and did speak up, and paid for it with his life, being killed in a concentration camp shortly before war's end.

[38] Alpert, *Oversupply*, 254.

[39] *Id.* Emphasis mine.

[40] They march blank-faced in unison through a long tunnel, surrounded by television screens on which Big Brother celebrates the first anniversary of the "Information Purification Directives:" "We have created, for the first time in all history, a garden of pure ideology - where each worker may bloom, secure from the pests purveying contradictory truths.... We shall prevail!" At that moment, the female athlete featured in the ad hurls a sledge hammer at the screen, smashing it in a blast of light and smoke, breaking the trance of the marching people.

[41] Emphasis added. Abraham Lincoln, Second Annual Message to Congress, Washington, D.C., December 1, 1862. The American Presidency Project, University of California Santa Barbara. http://www.presidency.ucsb.edu/ws/?pid=29503.

Part Three

What can be done about it?

Chapter 11

Is there a better vision?

To imagine a vision of a better future, we must stop and ask, "What do we aspire to?" — What are our aspirations as individuals, families, communities, and a nation? But before we can answer that question, we must return to a question I raised in the introduction: who is "we" and "us?"

A Better Vision for Whom?

This question resurfaced in Chapters 4 and 10, as we considered the view that our economic and social goals should not be limited to the U.S. borders, and that we have a responsibility to do what we can to lift all peoples, even at the expense of those living in America. That is, eliminating poverty for the many in the world is worth imposing poverty on the few in the U.S. I came down in the camp that holds that even if we apply our ethics on a worldwide basis, it is morally wrong to impose this harm without the consent of those harmed.

But to imagine a better vision, we must ask again, a better vision for whom? For the purposes of this book, I have defined the "we" and the "us" as those who, by accident of birth or by choice through naturalization, have become parties to that social contract we call the U.S. Constitution.

The primary reason for this choice is that it is only within our national system that we really have any effective control.[1] We have very little to say about the social and economic conditions in Bolivia, or Madagascar, or any of the 190-some nations of the world. Pretending otherwise can lead to many unintended consequences, both here and abroad. As discussed in Chapter 9, I also believe a strong America is in the best position to be of help maintain stability and growth in the rest of the world.[2]

I therefore propose that our social, economic, and political goals and underlying ethics focus primarily on our system, and secondarily on the rest of the world. Let our focus be on "the American project" or "the American idea." I believe a good place to start is with what has been called "the American dream."[3]

A Better Vision for the American Dream

The historian James Truslow Adams named the collection of aspirations that Americans hold in common, "the American Dream." Many have pursued it, before and since he named it, including my father's parents, who emigrated to the United States from Czechoslovakia. But what is it, exactly? Adams' formulation was a dream of "a land in which life should be better and richer and fuller" for everyone, with opportunity to attain the fullest of their capabilities, and be recognized for what they are, regardless of circumstances of birth.[4]

Considering the American dream leads us to the larger question, "to what do we aspire?" What is the "richer, fuller life" Adams referred to? Adams' formulation, and mine, recognize that there are several dimensions of the "good life." As Adams said, obviously, "It is not a dream of motor cars and high wages merely . . ."

The British sociologist Sylvia Walby suggests that "progress," and therefore the vision of the good life, can be considered on four dimensions: economic development, aspects of equality, human rights, and human well-being." [5]

And what of "well-being?" For Walby, it includes education, health, and longevity. Well-being has been further teased apart by Martin Seligman as comprising those elements that permit a person to "flourish": happiness, engagement, relationships, meaning and purpose, and accomplishment.[6] Others have identified similar characteristics of well-being.[7]

The American Dream Today

Although many surely would offer different definitions, I would suggest that, in our day, there is common agreement on the following nine elements of our aspirations for the American Dream:

- **Opportunity:** to use one's abilities and to better one's lot, without regard to circumstances of birth.

- **Freedom:** to live and work where one wishes, to attend the house of worship of one's choosing, and to pursue the politics of one's preference, with the protection of due process of law.

- **Environment:** Enjoyment of a decent living environment: a modest home in a neighborhood with safe streets, good schools, drivable roads, dependable electricity, reliable fire and police protection, drinkable water, and breathable air.

- **Dignity:** the ability, independently and without resorting to a handout from government or a charity, to meet a family's basic needs for food, clothing, shelter and transportation, health care and education, and a little recreation.

- **Balance:** the ability to do so through a full week's work, with time to come home for the family dinner, little league practice, and helping with the homework; the freedom to choose whether and how much a second parent will work without giving up these things.

- **Stability:** freedom from fear of a capricious loss of one's livelihood, and confidence of finding new employment when changes do come.

- **A Safety Net:** that will catch those who, through no fault of their own, become ill or disabled or suffer some other personal calamity.

- **Dignity in Old Age:** Arrangements for a retirement without poverty.

- **A Better Future:** A well-founded belief that things will be better for the next generation.

To these elements of the American dream, I would add the following, to round out the American ethos, that is, the guiding beliefs that distinguish the character of Americans as a group:

- A well-founded belief that these aspirations are, and should be, available to each and every American; a sense that we are all in this together.

- A readiness to defend these aspirations when they are threatened, and to help others around the world to achieve and defend them, as our resources permit.

- A recognition that, at the end of the day, it is what passes between us that matters.

Again, as Adams, noted, "[i]t is not a dream of motor cars and high wages merely." Implicit in it is a life of dignity and of balance -- of dignity, in the ability to make ends meet on one's own, without government subsidies or charity, and of balance, in the ability to do so and still have time for relationships with our children, spouses, family and friends.

On a recent evening after dinner my wife and I took our recently-acquired puppy and one of our daughters on an outing to a community park. In the dusk one could hear whistles and the encouraging calls of coaching dads as ten-year-old boys practiced flag football, with other dads and a few moms talking in gaggles on the sidelines. Here was the American dream: families with parents who got home from work in time to have dinner and go to ball practice, to go home and read to their kids, who were making ends meet without working sixty hours or a second job. The dream was not about the big house or fancy car, it was about being able to afford the time to do those things, to have that time together, to have a life. And these are not "nice-to-haves." The importance of the family meal and of reading aloud to children are now well documented.[8]

Ethical Underpinnings of the American Dream

But why should this be the American dream, and why should we pursue it? We are back to the "should" -- we must recognize that there are ethical underpinnings to these expressions of the American "dream" of "the good life."

I suggest that a survey of Americans would find a strong majority, perhaps a consensus, around the following six ethical principles: [9]

1. A Decent Life. At bottom, I believe, is the notion of building a society that will assure that individuals' basic needs are met, as a matter of recognition of the dignity of each individual: that we don't just leave people to sleep in their cars or die of exposure. This notion has been promulgated through the work of John Rawls as the "Difference Principle" in his system of distributive justice. Rawls proposed that, once equal political liberties are established, social and economic inequalities are permissible if there is equality of opportunity to attain them, and if they provide the most benefit to the least advantaged.[10] That is, the rising tide must float all boats. An important aspect of this principle is that anyone doing work that needs doing, regardless of how menial, should have a decent life. But see also principle no. 3.

2. Opportunity. Next, is the idea of equality of opportunity, also embodied in Rawls' formulation. However imperfectly we have implemented it, there is widespread agreement among Americans that each individual should have some semblance of equal resources, for example, of education, should they choose to avail themselves of them, and of equal opportunity to compete for positions, for example in college admissions and in employment.[11]

3. Responsibility. Next, is the idea of responsibility — that an individual's outcomes will be in large part a result of one's effort and choices. Most people believe this principle limits somewhat the difference principle: basic needs are not a right of someone who is capable and has opportunities, but chooses not to work.

4. Sharing Risk. Next, on the other side of the coin from responsibility, there is the idea of sharing of the risk of misfortune — that when, despite industriousness, rectitude, and frugality, one has the bad "luck" to come down with multiple sclerosis or suffer some other misfortune, one will not lose everything one has worked for. We will find a way to share these risks.

5. Proportionality. Next, is the idea of recompense per the value one contributes: that someone who is doing brain surgery should be compensated more than someone emptying the trash, as important as emptying the trash may be. The larger idea is that more wealth will be generated when those who are more productive earn greater incomes.

6. Outer Limits. Finally, is the idea that there is some outer limit on what will be considered a fair distribution of income and wealth, on both an individual and a societal level. On the individual level is the notion that one should not be overcompensated for one's contribution, on some intrinsic scale of value.[12] On the societal level, there likely is a limit on what Americans would deem to be a fair distribution of the national income.[13] For example, what of the hypothetical case where one percent of the people were receiving 90 percent of the income? We don't have to move these percentages very far to reach our current state of affairs, one which hasn't pertained since the last "gilded age" in the 1920s.

More on A Decent Life

Let me expand upon the first and last points. As to the first, A Decent Life, this is an idea as old as the industrial revolution. For example, in 1906, John Augustin Ryan said, "Upon one principle of partial justice unprejudiced men are, however, in substantial agreement. They hold that wages should be sufficiently high to enable the laborer to live in a manner consistent with the dignity of a human being." [14]

A more modern statement of the idea was made by Warren Buffett in a 2016 interview: "We need to make sure that in a super-rich country everybody who's willing to work forty hours a week has a decent living." Indeed, in my view, if we have people getting up in the morning and working hard at a job that needs doing, and they are still poor, then our system is failing. We need to eliminate the term "working poor;" if you are working, you should not be poor. And, there is a practical aspect: enabling people to be self-supporting is also is the best way to shrink the government (less need for support, less crime) and balance the budget (fewer expenditures, more taxes coming in).

More on Outer Limits

As to the notion of Outer Limits, Americans have always looked down on those Central and South American countries, referred to as "banana republics," where most of the national income is captured by a small elite at the top and everyone else is struggling. We reject this arrangement because it doesn't work, and because it is unfair. It doesn't work, because when most people are poor, there isn't much spending going on, so the economy is smaller than it would be if most people were better off. It is unfair because it offends our sense of justice, what is referred to as "distributive justice."

On the other hand, Americans have always rejected the idea that the national income should be distributed equally among all persons. We reject this arrangement for the same two reasons: it doesn't work, and it is unfair. It doesn't work, because people produce more when they earn more for doing so. And it is unfair -- rewarding an able person who chooses to work less with the same income as one who works more offends our sense of justice.

My experience is that there is an American sense of distributive justice that lies between the two: that we are seeking a "golden mean" between the extremes of high income inequality and equal distribution of income. And we are wise to do so: as we saw in Chapter 10, there is research showing that this approach does, indeed, work best.[15]

Other questions abound. What of the tax structure? Warren Buffett has pointed out that his secretary pays a higher tax rate on her salary than he does on his hundreds of millions in income. What of the accumulation of unearned wealth? We Americans have never been big on aristocracy. In any event, I believe there is an American consensus around the idea that there is some outer limit on a fair distribution of income and wealth.

How to Achieve these Goals

The question, then, is how to achieve the American dream so stated, consistent with these ethics? It is now abundantly clear that blind faith in the market does not work, and the low price, low wage, free trade economy cannot deliver on the American Dream.

Family/Stakeholder Capitalism

So, what is our other choice? Some have proposed that the choice is between pure free market *laissez-faire* on the one hand, and socialism on the other. However, that is a false choice. There is another option.

We can be said to have practiced it, successfully, in the "mixed economy" described in Chapter 4.[16] However, it turns out that a more fulsome version is being practiced in places like Germany, in what George R. Tyler has dubbed "family" or "stakeholder" capitalism. In his 2013 book, *What Went Wrong*,[17] Tyler describes the northern European approach in which *capitalism is practiced in a way that includes the interests of workers and the communities where companies are located, pursues the national interest, and is focused on the long term.*

In Germany, a national "codetermination" law requires the presence of worker representatives on boards of directors: the German industrial giant Siemens reported in 2008 that its board of directors consisted of ten members elected by shareholders and ten members selected by employees. "Worker councils" provide input on operations. There is emphasis on lifelong "upskilling" of workers through apprenticeship and other programs and sharing productivity gains with employees. And, Tyler reports, German voters insist on both public and business policies that are supportive of families. The upshot? Germany is an industrial exporting powerhouse, consistently running a trade surplus second only to China, with an economy one-fifth China's size.[18] Importantly, Tyler points out that many American multinationals follow the stakeholder capitalism model in their operations in Europe.[19]

I have interviewed two Americans working in professional positions in the United States, one for a German publishing company and the other for a Scandinavian software company; their accounts bear out what Tyler has reported. For example, recently the German company, after having a profitable year, distributed a $5,000 year-end bonus to each and every employee, regardless of rank. The Scandinavian company flies every new employee to its home office for a week of intensive training, and has an annual retreat that is attended by every employee from the least to the highest. Both companies are highly competitive in the world market, despite, or one could say on account of, their investment in the training and compensation of their employees.[20]

Even in England, it is possible to practice enlightened capitalism. Richard Branson has often proclaimed that a key to the success of the Virgin companies has been their focus on the "well-being of our associates" as well as the customer experience. One thing they do is to strictly enforce a policy that employees must take 100 percent of their vacation, and are not allowed to take their company laptops with them. These company policies are complemented by public policies that support healthy families. There is another way of doing business that can deliver on the American dream.

In America, some companies are practicing something like this brand of capitalism; in her 2014 book, *The Good Jobs Strategy*, MIT economist Zeynep Ton describes how, even in the retail industry, they are making a high investment in their workers and yet achieving lower costs, greater customer satisfaction, and higher profits.[21] And, as I noted in Chapter 7, organizations like the National Association of Corporate Directors are recognizing "sustainability," broadly defined, as a principal goal to be pursued by companies.

A New Ethic of Dignity

A key to family/stakeholder capitalism is its emphasis on the dignity of the worker, who is valued and has a seat at the table. Dignity is our inherent value and worth as human beings; everyone is born with it. Donna Hicks has said:

> . . . [W]e all have a deep, human desire to be treated as something of value. I believe that is our highest common denominator. . . . This shared desire for dignity transcends all of our differences, putting our common human identity above all else.[22]

In formulating the American dream, it was this dignity of the individual that impressed James Truslow Adams. Adams tells of asking a young Frenchman what had struck him most on his first visit to the U.S., and the Frenchman's immediate reply, "The way that every one of every sort looks you right in the eye, without a thought of inequality." [23]

Thomas Kochan, a work and employment relations economist at MIT, laid out the virtues of a turn to family capitalism in his 2005 book, *Restoring the American Dream: A Working Families' Agenda for America*.[24] Kochan proposes replacing a view of workers as "costs to be traded and controlled like any other commodity" with a recognition that those who invest their human capital in a company should have an equal seat at the table with those who invest their financial capital (as in the German model), viewing their knowledge as an asset, and making full use of their skills.[25]

Kochan explains why this approach can be good for business, but most importantly, why it is necessary to realize our commonly held values of justice, fairness, families, and work -- values that are the foundation of the American dream of good jobs, fair pay, and opportunities for all.

The Virtuous Circle and the High-Road Economy

And so, there is another vision for life in America. It is a vision some commentators have referred to as the "high road economy." It is not new; it is the vision that gave us the Golden Age of 1947-1974, and created the American consumer-led economy in which economic gains were widely shared.

There is growing recognition of a need to return to this principle. For example, at Harvard Business School's "U.S. Competitiveness Project," [26] the authors of its most recent report propose that a nation is "competitive" only when business can compete successfully in domestic and international markets while also maintaining and improving the wages and living standards of the average citizen. "When these occur together, a nation prospers. When one occurs without the other, a nation is not truly competitive and prosperity is not sustainable." [27] "Competitiveness must lead to shared prosperity, in which all Americans have the opportunity to advance economically." [28]

With widely shared prosperity, the cascading effects of the low price, low wage economy and its vicious circle spiraling downward in a race to the bottom are replaced with a different cascade, creating a "virtuous circle."

The cascading effects now look like this:

- Robust labor market
  - Full empl. & skills use; living wage
    - Independence and social health
      - Robust consumer demand
        - Growing economy

Robust Labor Market

In a growing economy, there is strong demand by employers for employees to fill a wide range of roles in producing more goods and services.

Full Employment and Use of Skills, Living Wage

With strong demand for employees, the potential workforce is fully utilized, in both numbers, and in training, education, and skills sets. Efficient "job match" can be achieved, and the full potential of individuals realized. The "working poor" becomes a thing of the past, because in return for an honest day's hard work, an employee receives a living wage, a wage at which life "adds up." In this way, work is honored, and work has dignity. A living wage can be paid because economic gains, including gains achieved from increased productivity, are broadly shared, as they were in the past, as illustrated in the following Figure from the Economic Policy Institute, produced in Chapter 7 and reproduced here:

Figure 4U Cumulative change in total economy productivity and real hourly compensation of production/nonsupervisory workers, 1948–2011

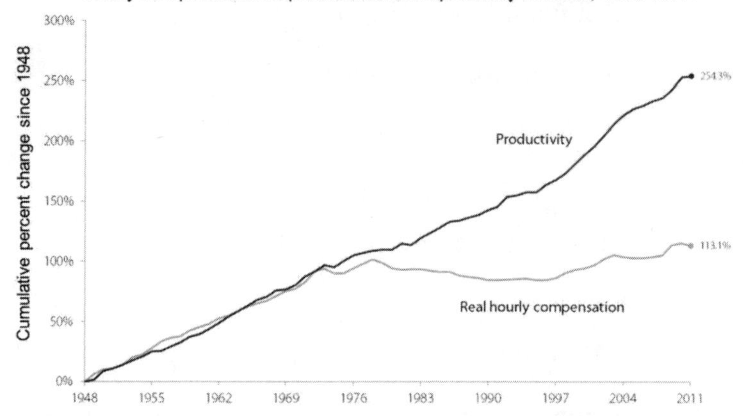

Note: Data are for production/nonsupervisory workers in the private sector and productivity of the total economy.
Source: Authors' analysis of unpublished total economy data from Bureau of Labor Statistics Labor Productivity and Costs program, wage data from BLS Current Employment Statistics program, and Bureau of Economic Analysis National Income and

EPI, *The State of Working America 12th Edition*, p. 236

These productivity-based wage gains can result in family income growth broadly shared across the population, as in the past, as illustrated in the following Figure from the Economic Policy Institute:[29]

Figure 2C Average family income growth, by income group, 1947–2007

Average annualized rate of growth

3.0%
2.5%
2.0%
1.5%
1.0%
0.5%
0.0%

1947–1979 1979–2007

2.5% 0.0% Bottom fifth
2.2% 0.4% Second fifth
2.4% 0.6% Middle fifth
2.4% 0.9% Fourth fifth
2.4% 1.2% 80–95th percentile
1.9% 2.0% Top 5 percent

*Data are for market based income of tax units.
Source: Authors' analysis of Current Population Survey Annual Social and Economic Supplement *Historical Income Tables* (Table F-2, F-3, F-5), and Piketty and Saez (2012)

EPI, *The State of Working America 12th Edition*, p. 67

Independence and Social Health

As more jobs provide family-sustaining pay and benefits, workers can make ends meet, and households can be independent -- not reliant on a benefit, subsidy or income transfer -- and in fact able to make their own contribution by paying taxes. Individuals, families, and communities all become healthier, as negatives become positives:

Potential Results for Communities

Reduced –	Increased –
• Unemployment	• Employment, self esteem
• Abuse	• Economic Independence
• Mental Illness	• Participation in tax burden
• Drug Use	• Tax collections for schools, etc.
• Crime /criminal justice spending	• Personal income and employment through multiplier effects
• Economic dependence, social welfare spending	
• Deficit, tax burden	

Robust Consumer Demand

Individuals and households who are "making a go of it" are out in the market, spending their earnings on goods and services comprising 60-70 percent of GDP.

Growing Economy

The robust demand for goods and services by consumers drives economic growth. A growing economy generates jobs, leading to a robust labor market, and the new cascade becomes a repeating, virtuous circle:

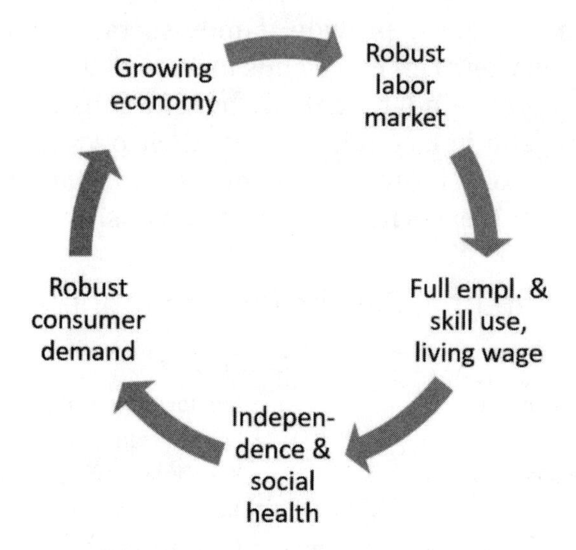

The virtuous circle leads to a building up, instead of a hollowing out, of the middle class.

Getting the Virtuous Circle Going

So, there is the vision, but how to get there? That is the subject of our next chapter.

Notes to Chapter 11

[1] For a detailed exposition of the arguments for a national focus in applying social and economic ethics, see Richard Arneson, "Egalitarianism," section 5, "Equality among Whom?" in *The Stanford Encyclopedia of Philosophy*, ed. Edward N. Zalta (Summer 2013 Edition). <https://plato.stanford.edu/archives/sum2013/entries/egalitarianism/>.

[2] There will be moral concerns regarding the fairness of four percent of the world's population having 25 percent of its income. But I submit that for the vast majority, perhaps 80 percent, of Americans, that is a very theoretical question, as they already are living at, or below, the level of basic needs, given the cost of living in America.

[3] This secondary focus would include, for example, assuring that America is not pursuing its goals by exploiting other peoples, and would include some "sharing of the wealth" in pursuit of the improvement of other peoples' lots.

[4] Adams wrote:

> If, as I have said, the things already listed were all we had to contribute, America would have made no distinctive and unique gift to mankind. But there has been also the American Dream, that dream of a land in which life should be better and richer and fuller for every man, with opportunity for each according to his ability or achievement. . . . It is not a dream of motor cars and high wages merely, but a dream of a social order in which each man and each woman shall be able to attain to the fullest stature of which they are innately capable, and be recognized by others for what they are, regardless of the fortuitous circumstances of birth or position.
>
> . . .
>
> "[T]he American dream . . . Has not been a dream of merely material plenty, though that has doubtless counted heavily. It has been much more than that. It has been a dream of being able to grow to fullest development as man and woman, unhampered by the barriers which had slowly been erected in older civilizations, unrepressed by social orders which had developed for the benefit of classes rather than for the simply human being of any and every class."

James Truslow Adams, *The Epic of America* (Boston: Little, Brown, and Company, 1931), 404, 405.

[5] Sylvia Walby, *Globalization & Inequalities: Complex and Contested Modernities* (Los Angeles: Sage, 2009), 5.

[6] Martin E.P. Seligman, *Flourish* (New York: Free Press, 2011).

[7] The Gallup organization has organized the Gallup-Healthways Global Well-Being Index into five elements:

- Purpose: liking what you do each day and being motivated to achieve your goals;
- Social: having supportive relationships and love in your life;
- Financial: managing your economic life to reduce stress and increase security;
- Community: liking where you live, feeling safe and having pride in your community;
- Physical: having good health and enough energy to get things done daily.

In analyzing the results of the index, Gallup and Healthways classify responses as "thriving" (well-being that is strong and consistent), "struggling" (well-being that is moderate or inconsistent), or "suffering" (well-being that is low and inconsistent). Interestingly for our present purposes, Gallup reports that the key, *sine qua non*, to all of this is "a good job" – a job in the formal economy working at least thirty hours a week. Jim Clifton, *The Coming Jobs War* (New York: Gallup Press, 2011), 2, 10. Melanie Standish and Dan Witters. "Americas Lead Highs, Sub-Saharan Africa Lows in Well-Being." *Gallup.com* (June 24, 2015), 999. http://www.gallup.com/poll/183710/americas-lead-highs-sub-saharan-africa lows.aspx?utm_source=World&utm_medium=newsfeed&utm_campaign=tiles

A French commission identified similar dimensions of well-being. In a 2010 report, the Commission on the Measurement of Economic Performance and Social Progress appointed by French president Nicolas Sarkozy identified the following:

- Material living standards (income, consumption and wealth);
- Health;
- Education;
- Personal activities, including work;
- Political voice and governance;
- Social connections and relationships;
- Environment (present and future conditions);
- Insecurity, of an economic as well as a physical nature.

Joseph Stiglitz, Amartya Sen and Jean-Paul Fitoussi, *Mis-Measuring our Lives: The Report by the Commission on the Measurement of Economic Performance and Social Progress* (London: The New Press, 2010), 61 *ff.* A research team led by Mark J. Stern at the University of Pennsylvania developed a Neighborhood-Based Measure of Social Well-Being with thirteen dimensions for measuring well-being in Philadelphia and New York City neighborhoods. Mark J. Stern, "From Poverty to Well-Being," in *Social Policy and Social Justice*, ed. John L. Jackson, Jr., (Philadelphia: University of Pennsylvania Press, 2017), 148-159.

[8] In recent years, the benefits of the family dinner have been well established. Anne Fishel, a professor at Harvard Medical School, author of "Home for Dinner," and co-founder of The Family Dinner Project, reports that researchers have found strong associations between family dinners and academic performance. Young adults who ate regular family meals as teens are less likely to be obese and more likely to eat healthily once they live on their own. Studies link regular family dinners with lowering a host of high risk teenage behaviors; there are also associations between regular family dinners and good behaviors: in a New Zealand study, a higher frequency of family meals was strongly associated with positive moods in adolescents, and other researchers have shown that teens who dine regularly with their families also have a more positive view of the future. Anne Fishel, "The most important thing you can do with your kids? Eat dinner with them," Washington Post, January 12, 2015.
https://www.washingtonpost.com/posteverything/wp/2015/01/12/the-most-important-thing-you-can-do-with-your-kids-eat-dinner-with-them/?utm_term=.6e560fcd0a12
See also, http://thefamilydinnerproject.org/resources/faq/.

The importance of reading aloud to children also is well documented. A joint position statement of the International Reading Association (IRA) and National Association for the Education of Young Children, states, "The single most important activity for building these understandings and skills essential for reading success appears to be reading aloud to children." "Learning to Read and Write: Developmentally Appropriate Practices for Young Children (1998)." The 1998 report of the Committee on the Prevention of Reading Difficulties in Young Children, "Preventing Reading Difficulties in Young Children," recommended three key practices to support language and literacy development. The first calls for adult/child shared book reading times that involve talking about the book and other topics. "Becoming a Nation of Readers," a 1985 report by the Commission on Reading, found that the single most important activity for building knowledge for their eventual success in reading is reading aloud to children,". Derry Koralek, Derry "Reading

Aloud with Children of All Ages," *National Association for the Education of Young Children*. http://www.naeyc.org/files/yc/file/200303/ReadingAloud.pdf www.rif.org.

[9] For a review and discussion of these ethical principles, see Lamont and Favor, "Distributive Justice;" and Richard Arneson, "Egalitarianism," in The Stanford Encyclopedia of Philosophy, ed. Edward N. Zalta (Summer 2013 Edition). <https://plato.stanford.edu/archives/sum2013/entries/egalitarianism/>.

[10] Rawls, John, *A Theory of Justice* (Cambridge, MA: Harvard University Press, 1971). Weisman, *Great Tradeoff*, 10.

[11] Equality of opportunity is applied to people in the "normal" range of cognitive and other abilities. We have developed policies under which we are devoting additional resources to individuals with disabilities to give them a shot at a decent life. This can also be thought of under the "basic needs" principle.

[12] James Truslow Adams put it this way: "For example, [Henry] Ford's fortune is often referred to as one of the 'honestly' obtained ones. He pretends to despise money, and boasts of the high wages he pays and the cheapness of his cars, yet, either because his wages are still too low or the cars too high, he has accumulated $1,000,000,000 for himself from his plant. This would seem to be a high price for society to pay even him for his services to it, while the economic lives of some hundreds of thousands of men and women are made dependent on his whim and word." Adams, *Epic*, 408.

[13] James Truslow Adams also recognized this principle: "In a modern industrial State, an economic base is essential for all. We point with pride to our 'national income,' but the nation is only an aggregate of individual men and women, and when we turn from the single figure of total income to the incomes of individuals, we find a very marked injustice in its distribution. There is no reason why wealth, which is a social product, should not be more equitably controlled and distributed in the interests of society." Adams, *Epic*, 410.

[14] Rev. John Augustin Ryan, S.T.L., *A Living Wage: Its Ethical and Economic Aspects (*New York: The MacMillan Company, 1906; Dissertation for the Doctorate in Theology at The Catholic University of America), vii. Ryan described the "right" to a personal living wage and a family living wage, and provided an estimate of a living wage for the time.

---

[15] Chapter 10, "Inequality can slow growth," citing the work of IMF economist Jonathan Ostry and colleagues showing that growth is faster in more equal societies.

[16] In my view, it was the oil embargo and quadrupling of oil prices in 1973 and 1974, and re-doubling of oil prices in 1979, that ushered in the period of "stagflation," ended the successful run of the "mixed economy," and set the stage for the beginnings of deregulation under President Jimmy Carter and the ushering in of the neoliberal agenda under President Ronald Reagan.

[17] George R. Tyler, *What Went Wrong: How the 1% Hijacked the American Middle Class . . . and What Other Countries Got Right* (Dallas: BenBella Books, 2013).

[18] Tyler, *What Went Wrong*, 51, 163, 442.

[19] Tyler, *What Went Wrong*, 246. One laughable exception was Wal-Mart, which tried to impose its low-wage, anti-worker model when it entered the German market through an acquisition. The Germans were particularly unhappy with Wal-Mart's attempt to impose its system of employees spying and reporting on each other – the Germans had had a bad experience with that when the Communists were in charge of East Germany. Wal-Mart ultimately failed, and left Germany after losing $5 billion. *Id.*

[20] I am not suggesting that we follow the German model exactly, only that, in broad strokes, there is a way of going about capitalism that does not result in the harsh society I described in Chapter 7.

[21] Zeynep Ton, *The Good Jobs Strategy: How the Smartest Companies Invest in Employees to Lower Costs and Boost Profits*. Boston: New Harvest/Houghton Mifflin Harcourt, 2014.

[22] Donnap Hicks, Ph.D., "What Is the Real Meaning of Dignity?" Psychology Today Online, April 10, 2013.
https://www.psychologytoday.com/blog/dignity/201304/what-is-the-real-meaning-dignity-0
Hicks is an Associate at the Weatherhead Center for International Affairs, Harvard University, author of the book, *Dignity: The Essential Role It Plays in Resolving Conflict*, published in 2011 by Yale University Press, and founder of Declare Dignity, http://www.declaredignity.com.

[23] Adams, *Epic*, 404.

[24] Kochan, *Restoring*. I referred to this book in Chapter 7, at The Harsh Society, with respect to Kochan's inventory of the stress under which American families are operating.

[25] *Id.*, xii.

---

[26] Operating since 2011, it states as its goal the identification of steps to restore "economic growth and prosperity shared across all Americans." http://hbs.edu/competitiveness.

[27] Michael E. Porter, Jan W. Rivkin, and Mihir A. Desai, with Manjari Daman. "Problems Unsolved and a Nation Divided: The State of U.S. Competitiveness 2016. Including findings from Harvard Business School's 2016 surveys of U.S. competitiveness," (September 2016), 7-8. Emphasis in original.
http://www.hbs.edu/competitiveness/research/Pages/research-details.aspx?rid=81.

[28] *Id.*, 2.

[29] These families' incomes were not equal, but they were growing at equal rates -- growth in the national income was being broadly shared, and that generated more growth.

Chapter 12

How can we make it happen?

How do we make the leap from the vicious circle to the virtuous circle?

The Individual Consumer Solution

Here is the good news: we, as consumers, can solve this problem ourselves. All we must do is choose to purchase quality products made in America, with money we are already spending, creating jobs in the communities where they are made. By bringing this spending home, we can be the "intervening cause" that breaks the downward cycle of the vicious circle, and ushers in the virtuous circle:

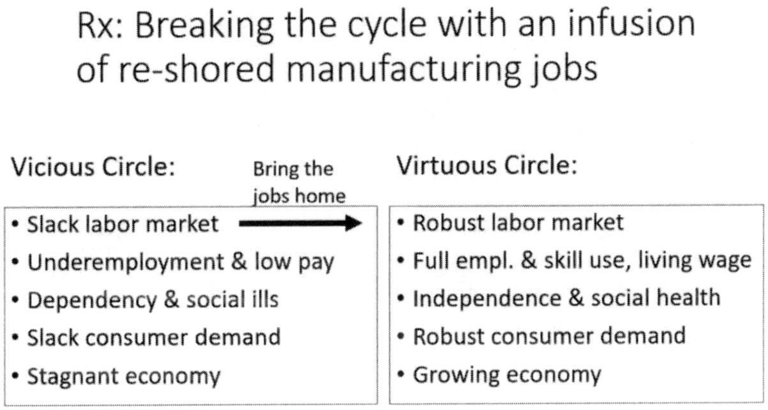

Rx: Breaking the cycle with an infusion of re-shored manufacturing jobs

Vicious Circle:	Bring the jobs home	Virtuous Circle:
• Slack labor market	→	• Robust labor market
• Underemployment & low pay		• Full empl. & skill use, living wage
• Dependency & social ills		• Independence & social health
• Slack consumer demand		• Robust consumer demand
• Stagnant economy		• Growing economy

We can say to the company that stayed the course and resisted the temptation to shut down its factory and send its production overseas, and say to the men and women who get up every day and go to work to make quality products, "we are going to reward you with our business."

I know you have questions about how this can work, so let me anticipate them:

Do consumers have enough spending power?

The fact is, consumer spending makes up nearly 70 percent of the $18 trillion U.S. economy. With this much spending power, American consumers are in a strong position to affect how things go, simply by redirecting spending to the purchase of products made in communities across America.

Is there enough spending to be redirected?

In Chapter 5, I described the $750 billion-plus annual trade in goods deficit -- imports into the American economy exceeding American exports to other countries' economies. Of that $750 billion, I have identified some $600 billion that is subject to consumer discretion -- choices we make every day, in the following categories:

U.S. Exports and Imports of Consumer Goods in 2015
in billions of 2016 Dollars

	Exports	Imports	Balance
Automotive Vehicles, Parts, and Engines	153	353	-199
Apparel, Household Textiles & Footwear	10	132	-122
Consumer Electronics & Other Goods N.E.C.	32	138	-106
Household Appliances, Furnishings & Equipment	15	76	-61
Pharmaceutical Preparations	56	109	-54
Recreational Equipment & Apparel	14	57	-42
Jewelry, Gems, Artwork & Collectibles	45	57	-13
Toiletries, Cosmetics & Other Nondurables	28	30	-3
Total	353	953	-600

Source: Bureau of Economic Analysis

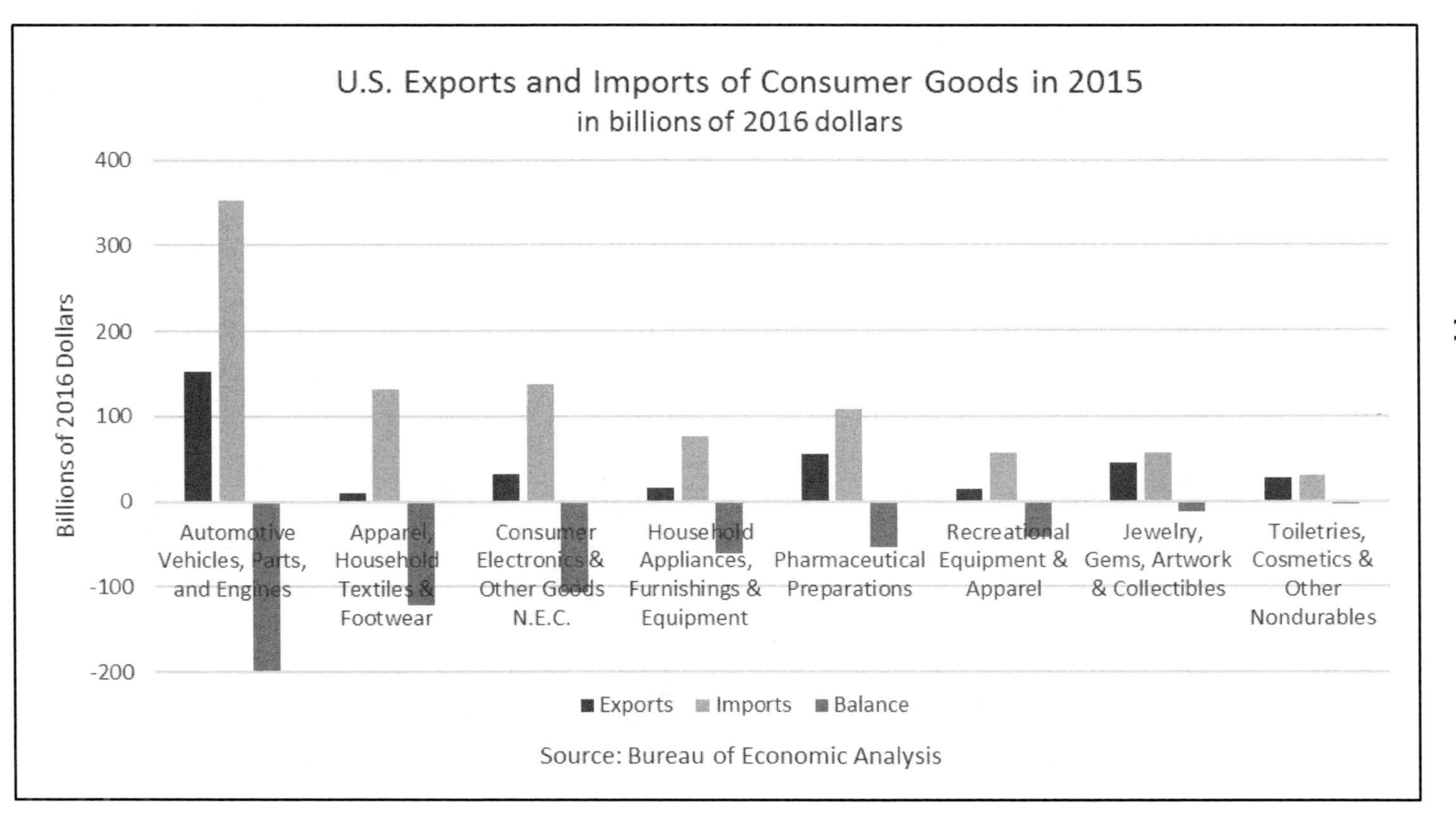
U.S. Exports and Imports of Consumer Goods in 2015
in billions of 2016 dollars
Billions of 2016 Dollars
400
300
200
100
0
-100
-200
Automotive Vehicles, Parts, and Engines
Apparel, Household Textiles & Footwear
Consumer Electronics & Other Goods N.E.C.
Household Appliances, Furnishings & Equipment
Pharmaceutical Preparations
Recreational Equipment & Apparel
Jewelry, Gems, Artwork & Collectibles
Toiletries, Cosmetics & Other Nondurables
Exports
Imports
Balance
Source: Bureau of Economic Analysis

Bringing home $500 billion of consumer spending would eliminate most of our consumer trade-in-goods deficit, and would restore our overall balance of trade.

If we did that, would it make a difference?

$500 billion would create a lot of jobs. How many? According to a study published in February 2014, 5.8 million, 2.3 million of them in manufacturing. Looking at the effects of a $500 billion shift in the balance of trade, the authors concluded that total economic production (GDP) would rise by $720 billion in the third year.[1]

Don't we need trade?

Let me emphasize, this prescription is not against trade. America needs to export, and needs vibrant trading relationships with other countries. But, those relationships need to be balanced.

The World Trade Organization and other organizations and academia refer to countries as "trade partners" vis-à-vis each other. In theory, the term is apt, as it implies a mutuality of benefits and obligations, in which each "partner" has a responsibility to manage the relationship for mutual benefit.

However, as we have seen, many trading nations act like anything but "partners." Instead, they adopt mercantilist, export-oriented policies designed to maximize their exploitation of the "partner" country's market (read United States), through subsidies and other forms of "state capitalism," and to minimize the "partner" country's penetration of their own market, through formal and informal barriers to entry, manipulation of currency relationships, and abuse of international trade rules.

At the end of the day, each trading partner has a duty to assure that the relationship does not become, or remain, out of balance. This is true even of trading partners such as Germany, who may not be engaging in the more egregious means of abusing the trade relationship, but who are running persistent large trade deficits with the U.S. nevertheless.

Ideally, we would have a trading environment where trade partners act like partners and keep their trade in balance, ensuring that trade is, as some theorists had hoped, a win-win for all involved. But, as we saw in Chapter 9, at More Trouble with Trade, there is no indication that our trading "partners" intend to give up their mercantilist ways. So, we will balance trade for them. Fair trade is balanced trade.

What about helping others?

As I discussed in Chapter 11, I believe there is a moral as well an economic imperative for America to lift poorer countries toward a higher standard of living. However, that cannot be done by the wholesale transfer to those countries of the production of products and services destined for the U.S. market. If we want to help other countries climb out of poverty, we need to do it in a more thoughtful way – in a way that is not causing poverty in the United States. A country that does not produce cannot be strong, and a strong America can best help the less fortunate.

Only consumers can do this

So, there is the answer, so elegant in its simplicity, that has been eluding us all these years:

> *Bring home $500 billion in spending, enough to balance trade, create six million jobs, take the slack out of the labor market, and start a "virtuous circle" of growth.*

But here is the thing – not only *can* consumers do this, consumers *must* do this, because *only* consumers have the capability to do this. Why is that? There are two reasons. First, consumer spending is where the problem lies: most of our trade-in-goods deficit is attributable to consumer spending, as indicated in the following table:

U.S. Exports & Imports of Goods by End-Use Category during 2015
in billions of 2016 dollars

	Exports	Imports	Balance
Consumer goods & automobiles & parts	353	953	-600
Industrial materials & capital goods	975	1099	-124
Foods, feeds, beverages & other goods	189	219	-30
Total	1518	2271	-753

Source: Bureau of Economic Analysis

And, the problem is getting worse. During the "recovery" from the Great Recession, the trade-in-goods deficit in consumer goods has progressively worsened – measured in 2016 dollars, it grew from $493 billion in 2011 to $600 billion in 2015, as indicated in the following figure and table:

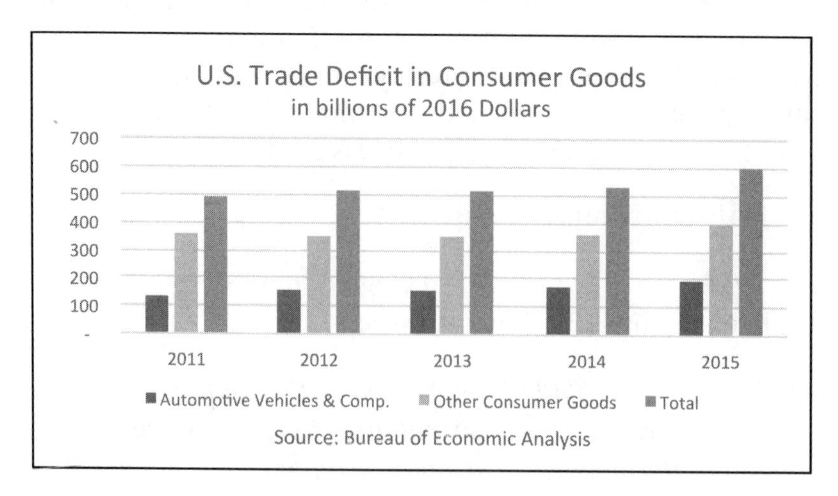

U.S. Trade Deficit in Consumer Goods in billions of 2016 Dollars					
	2011	2012	2013	2014	2015
Automotive Vehicles & Comp.	130	159	161	171	199
Other Consumer Goods	363	352	353	362	401
Total	493	511	514	533	600
Source: Bureau of Economic Analysis					

In particular, the deficit in automobiles and parts has grown, from $130 billion to $199 billion, as the industry has moved the production of more and more parts and components from U.S. to foreign producers.

Second, only consumer demand can solve the competition dilemma: A company facing thirty-percent lower-priced products from a competitor sourcing its goods in China will have trouble not following suit – that is why most of the case-goods furniture industry ended up going offshore, devastating communities in North Carolina and elsewhere. But if consumers are demanding products made in American communities, companies must respond.

We need to have retailers' purchasing agents telling their suppliers, "we can't move this Chinese stuff; can you please find me some of those made in America?" In short, in a play on the movie line,[2] one could say, "come, and they will build it." They will build new manufacturing capacity to make more of those products, employing U.S. workers in building the new plants, and in making the building materials for those plants, and in making the raw materials and components used in those plants, and in staffing those plants, and in staffing all the service industries connected to those plants and their workers. Next thing you know, you've created six million jobs.

What can one person do?

Well, you say, "$500 billion in spending and six million jobs is a lofty, worthy goal, but what can one person do?"

Let's look at what we each can do today, and what we can improve in the future.

Become a "Label Reader"

The first thing we each must do is to become an inveterate "label reader." The information can be hard to find (more on that later), but once you get going on this, I believe you will become quite adept at locating the country-of-origin label on packages and on products.

A Word about Labeling Laws

The labels are the result of a group of laws administered by the U.S. Customs Service and the Federal Trade Commission.[3] The Customs Service requires country-of-origin labeling on imported goods indicating the last country in which a "substantial transformation" of the product occurred.[4] Several other laws impose special country-of-origin labeling on categories of products, such as wool products and fur products. Automobiles have their own special law, discussed below.

Products that are *not* required to be labeled with statements of foreign origin *may* be labeled with respect to the U.S. and foreign origin of their content, per FTC rules to assure claims are not deceptive. In general, the FTC applies two standards: First, "Made in USA" and equivalent statements may be made for products that are "all or substantially all" made in the United States.[5]

Second, products that do not meet this test may make a "qualified claim" of U.S. origin so long as the claim is accurate and may be readily understood by the consumer. The FTC provides the following examples: "60% U.S. content." "Made in USA of U.S. and imported parts." "Couch assembled in USA from Italian Leather and Mexican

Frame."[6] "Assembled in USA" deserves special attention, as you may run across products labeled, *e.g.*, "Assembled in USA of global materials". The FTC staff guidance states:

> To avoid possible deception, "Assembled in USA" claims [made without further qualification] should be limited to those instances where the product has undergone its principal assembly in the United States and that assembly is substantial. In addition, a product should be last substantially transformed in the United States to properly use an "Assembled in USA" claim.[7]

The FTC staff has further noted in this regard:

> [A] "screwdriver" assembly in the U.S. of foreign components into a final product at the end of the manufacturing process doesn't usually qualify for the "Assembled in USA" claim.[8]

So, for our purposes, the takeaway is that "Made in USA" is the gold standard and always to be preferred, but in today's world of global supply chains, a qualified claim of substantial U.S. content is far better than "made in Korea," or some such place, and worth pursuing.

Also, please note: companies are *permitted* but not required to label the U.S. origin of products. I have noticed that some companies do not state U.S. origin, because they do not want to call attention to the fact that some of their products are not of U.S. origin – they just don't want consumers to be thinking about it. So, if after thorough examination, you can't find a country-of-origin claim, then you may be holding a made-in-USA product.

Sometimes it's easy

Although it does indeed seem like there are whole stores where we have trouble finding anything "made in America," I believe you will be pleasantly surprised at the hidden gems to be found out there. Often you will find an American-made product on the shelf next to the foreign one. For example, a personal planning notebook made in China sits next to one made in Maine. And one company sources one of its models of ball-point pens in both Japan and the U.S.; it is only a matter of checking to be sure you are getting the U.S.-made version. (So, too, of those Oreo® cookies we discussed earlier – some are still made in the U.S.) These small purchases made seem like they can't add up to much, but as we saw in the table and figure above, they can add up to billions of dollars of sales, and that is many thousands of jobs. And in most cases, there will be no difference in price.

Apparel and Electronics

Clothing and accessories are another matter. In Chapter 6, regarding "import penetration," I noted that 95 percent of our clothing is now coming from other countries. However, there still is plenty of clothing being made in the U.S. for us to get started. And as I have said, once the demand is there, companies will create new production capacity to meet it - "Come, and they will build it."

In the case of clothing, footwear, and accessories, there often will be a difference, sometimes a substantial difference, in price. The reason is simple: the U.S.-sourced products were not made with 16-cent-an-hour labor in Bangladesh. And likely were made better, with higher quality materials. Much apparel is so incredibly cheap these days because we have nearly completely devalued the labor that goes into producing it. And as I have pointed out, that is morally wrong. So, I invite you to go on your personal quest of identifying some reliable sources of U.S.-made apparel that suit your style, using some of the resources I refer to below.

Consumer electronics is another category that has substantially gone offshore: in Chapter 6, I reported that nearly 70 percent of computer and electronic component products purchased in the U.S. in 2015 came from other countries. It is going to take a while for us to turn this ship around. But we have seen recent announcements from Apple and Lenovo (the Chinese purchaser of IBM) that they intend to begin some production in the U.S., so we don't want to write this category off, and should do some detective work using the resources I describe below.

Buy an American Car

Here's the biggie: if you look back to my list of $600 billion of deficits in consumer products, you will notice that nearly $200 million, one-third of the entire deficit, is attributable to automobiles and components. This is the place where action is most effective, and most needed. But how to buy an "American" car? We have already noted the trend toward increasing the foreign content of cars that are assembled in the United States. With the global supply chain, it would be impossible to find a car that is 100 percent American-made. So, the simple answer is this:

> *Make sure the next car you buy has the maximum possible percentage of U.S. "content" (parts, labor, and manufacturing overhead).*

"And how do I do that," you ask. At this writing, there are two ready sources of information.

The American Automobile Labeling Act

The first is the American Automobile Labeling Act (AALA).[9] Since 1994, regulations under AALA have required that each automobile manufactured for initial sale in the U.S. bear a label disclosing where the car was assembled, the percentage of equipment that originated in the U.S. and Canada, and the country of origin of the engine and transmission.

The AALA is a vestige of the U.S.-Canadian Automobile Pact of 1965, described in Chapter 2. Due to its origins under the Pact, the label states the combined U.S. and Canadian content, without separating the two. The AALA has some other limitations, such as listing a percentage of parts content *not* including the content added in the final assembly – so, the percentage figure understates the U.S. content of a car assembled in the U.S., and overstates the U.S. content of a car assembled in Mexico or some other country.

However, it has the advantage of stating the location of the car's final assembly, where the car's engine and transmission are manufactured, and up to two countries responsible for fifteen percent or more of the equipment content of the car. In short, there is a lot of information to be derived from these labels. And, you don't have to go out to the dealer to see them; the National Highway Traffic Safety Administration publishes the information annually.[10]

The Kogod Made in America Auto Index

There is another listing that, in some ways, is more informative than the AALA list: American University's Kogod School of Business publishes a list developed by

Associate Professor Frank DuBois, the "Kogod Made in America Auto Index." Intended to provide a better read on the car's total effect on the U.S. economy, the Index is based on the AALA reports, but includes some additional criteria – for example, where the profits accrue.[11] The Index scores each car line, more than three hundred at this writing, with a possible maximum score of 100, on criteria including:

- where the manufacturer's headquarters is located;
- where most research and development (R&D) occurs;
- where assembly occurs;
- where the engine and transmission come from; and
- the AALA score.

Where does that leave us?

A couple of points jump out of both the AALA and the Kogod lists:

- For all the talk about how hard it is to tell where a car is made, there is a long list of cars that are made entirely, or almost entirely, in Japan, Korea, Germany, or some other country – you can be certain that when you buy one of these cars, you are helping the other country's economy and workers, and not the American economy and workers.
- There are many cars made by the "Detroit Three" that have very low U.S. content, and should be avoided for the same reasons.
- A number of cars are made in the U.S. by Japanese companies with rather high U.S. content scores, that may provide a second-best, but suitable option.

- There is a wide variety of high-quality cars with high scores, with profits accruing to U.S. companies, available to fund further R&D and other essential activities.

So, in order of preference, we should first choose a car with a high score that is made by one of the "Detroit Three," starting with Ford and GM, and then Chrysler, which, although at this writing a subsidiary of the Italian company Fiat, has substantial U.S. ownership. The companies' trade association, the American Automotive Policy Council (AAPC) states, without much exaggeration, I think, that "These three companies are the heart of the industrial base of the United States and an engine of the American industrial economy." [12] (Unfortunately, they are moving toward more foreign sourcing and production – but we will help them change that!) Next in preference is a car assembled in one of the U.S. plants operated by a foreign auto company, if its U.S. content rating is high enough. We should avoid buying cars, whether made by U.S.-headquartered or foreign companies, with low U.S. content – it won't take long for them to realize that, if they want to sell cars into the U.S. market, they will have to build them here.

Buy Yourself a Set of American Tires

What's that you say, you won't be in the market for a new car for a while? Well, then buy yourself a set of American tires. This is no small purchase, and an excellent way to get your feet wet in this product category. The tire industry is complicated, with numerous U.S. and foreign companies producing tires in many locations.[13]

So, the best way to go about this is to work with your tire dealer, explaining that you want to buy American-made tires, and providing some criteria and preferences. In the end, it is possible to know for certain where the tires are made from the sidewall imprint, which will state the country of origin or "Made in USA," and will indicate the tire's U.S. Department of Transportation identifier number. The prefix in this number (*E.g.*, DOT BE XX XXX XXX) indicates a particular factory.[14]

Find New Sources

A number of resources are available to help you identify companies still making things in the U.S. and locate and buy their products. Here are some examples:

Books

Roger Simmermaker has published a compendium of American manufacturers in his book titled *How Americans Can Buy American*.[15] For products directed towards babies and children, a special area of concern for product safety, Bruce H. Wolk has published a compendium of American manufacturers in his book titled *Made Here, Baby!*[16]

Both these books contain a surprising number of products and companies, as well as useful background information. Simmermaker is more comprehensive, but lists only companies, and so is more of a point of departure for further inquiry. (Simmermaker does go into greater detail regarding fifty American companies in his book, *My Company 'Tis of Thee*.[17]) Wolk's book provides useful company-level information, and often the companies offer products outside the baby and children's categories. Each of these books is worth getting to know, as they contain some pleasant surprises in categories we may have thought had gone entirely offshore.

Online Sites, Lists and Links

There are a number of online resources as well. In some cases, you can purchase the product right then and there. For example, this is the case for the online marketplace operated at http://www.madeinusaforever.com by Todd Lipscomb, author of the 2011 book *Re-Made in the USA*.[18]

Other web sites provide online, consumer-oriented compendia similar to those in Simmermaker's and Wolk's books. For example, Sarah Wagner founded and operates the USA Love List, http://www.usalovlist.com. The site offers a compendium of American-made brands, collections, blogs and tips. So, too, Michael Williams founded A Continuous Lean, http://www.acontinuouslean.com, offering a similar menu of content and services emphasizing durable products with the male shopper in mind. The blog at http://clothingmadeinusablog.wordpress.com offers advice directed at finding and purchasing clothing made in the USA.

Other sites are operated as organizations of American manufacturers of consumer products. American Made Matters®, http://www.americanmadematters.com, is an organization composed of companies manufacturing in a variety of industries, and service providers serving those companies. For consumers, the site offers a useful listing of products by categories with links through to the manufacturers' web sites.[19]

The Made in America Movement is a similar organization of American manufacturing companies, providing useful information to consumers seeking to connect with those companies and their products at a website located at http://www.themadeinamericamovement.com,

These examples are by no means a complete treatment; I have provided them to give you a taste of the resources available as of this writing.

Brick-and-Mortar Retailers

Another way to go at this project is working with existing brick-and-mortar retailers. That is, in addition to becoming a label-reader, you can get proactive with the store. Sarah Wagner of the USA Love List has pointed out that it is easy to ask for a store or department manager, explain that you've been trying to buy more American-made things, and ask if they can help you identify some in their store, for you and for recommendations to your friends. You may be surprised at what is on offer, and this will get store managers reporting back that people are looking for American-made products.

Other "Consumers"

You will recall that in Chapter 1 I noted that there are three categories of consumers: individual consumers, companies acting as consumers, and governments acting as consumers. For maximum success, we must assure that, when our local, state, and federal governments are procuring goods and services with our tax dollars, they are sourcing those goods and services in the U.S. So, too, our companies.

Clear Country-of-Origin Labeling

The beauty of this solution is that we do not need to ask the government for anything to carry it out. However, there is one thing that would be helpful.

The essence of the solution is to bring jobs home by exercising consumer choice. But it can be hard to choose an

American-made product when you can't tell where something was made. Online and hard-copy catalogs almost never mention a product's foreign origin, except occasionally to state "imported". And country-of-origin marking on packaging and products is indeed the "fine print," and hard to locate at that.

So, I propose changing the law to *require a clear statement of country-of-origin of foreign goods in all product descriptions and on the face of packa*ging. Enactment of such a law will enable consumers to make an informed choice.

Other Steps in Building the Virtuous Circle

Intervening in the vicious circle in the way I have described will jump-start the virtuous circle: bringing jobs home through the power of consumer spending will take the slack out of the labor market, the first step in the virtuous circle. That should get us moving toward full employment and wages rising toward a living wage. However, building the virtuous circle is not simple, or easy, especially in the face of the changes that are occurring in the very nature of work. Thomas Kochan has suggested that building an economy supportive of American working families will involve nothing less than creating what he calls the "next generation social contract" and has provided some ideas on how to get there.[20] There will be more work to do.

Stay Informed

The movement of American jobs offshore and its effects on American society and the world order are ongoing affairs, requiring our continued attention. I personally have committed to paying close attention to these matters in the news media, and encourage you to do so as well. There also are some special resources we can access regarding news, research, and public policy in this area.

The Alliance for American Manufacturing, is "a non-profit, non-partisan partnership formed in 2007 by some of America's leading manufacturers and the United Steelworkers . . . whose . . . mission is to strengthen American manufacturing and create new private-sector jobs through smart public policies." AAM operates a web site, http://www.americanmanufacturing.org, that offers a wealth of information as well as ways to help promote public policies in support of American manufacturing.

The U.S. Business and Industry Council Educational Foundation publishes research and information on its web site at http://www/AmericanEconomicAlert.org. The Foundation is the research arm of The U.S. Business and Industry Council, dedicated to the concerns of America's national manufacturing business community. USBIC reports that its "member companies are typically family-owned or privately held, and are often the major employers in their home communities and the mainstays of the local economy."

The Economic Policy Institute conducts research on these topics and broader economic topics from the perspective of the welfare of the American worker, and publishes reports at http://www.epi.org. Each of these web sites also carries news reports of current events. They also are a good means for each of us to enter the world of public policy. But back to the focus of this chapter, and this book: the consumer solution.

Spread the Word

Besides our personal and family commitments to buy things made in American communities, perhaps equally important is to spread the word. Each of us is an influencer, and I hope you will encourage those in your circles to read this book. Yes, my family went through a good bit of our savings while I was writing it and it would be helpful to sell some copies, but that certainly is not the point.

This is the book I wish someone else had written, and it contains information that I believe every American needs to know, and to act upon.

Just as important is for you to convey to those in your circles what you have learned and are committed to doing. And, of course, if you are a policy maker in an organization, you will have leverage giving your words and actions greater effect.

What else can we do? – "Made in America Again"

I believe we are going to have to figure out much of this as we go. I can foresee individuals and groups across the country coming up with ideas that haven't crossed any of our minds yet. For my part, I am committed to following this book with the following course of action:

- First, I am forming a non-profit educational organization that will continue this research, expanding and keeping it up to date, and disseminating it as broadly as possible.

- Second, I have formed a "public benefit company" dedicated to building healthy communities by helping people buy things made in those communities. I plan for this company to operate one or more online marketplaces where consumers can discover, purchase, and share a wide selection of American products of quality, safety, and durability.

- Third, I am forming a non-profit advocacy organization that will seek the enactment of clear country-of-origin labeling laws and the adoption of buy-American policies by governments and companies.

I am hoping that this coalition of organizations, operating under the umbrella of "Made in America Again," can provide a focus, a means, and a rallying point for those of us who want to bring our jobs home and get the virtuous circle going again. I will post updates on these efforts at www.miaa.us; I encourage you to visit it and register to receive email updates. You may think of even better things to do.[21]

A Different Final Chapter - An Actionable Plan

The story of the selling out of American workers and communities, as jobs have gone offshore, as we have taken part in the race to the bottom via low prices and low pay, and as we have broken faith with the idea that we should be sharing gains broadly across our society, is a sad tale. Other works have recounted much of this story, with different emphases. There didn't seem to be a comprehensive telling of the story of offshoring American industry and connecting those job losses with our larger economic malaise. Hopefully this book serves that purpose.

More importantly, in my view, the final chapters in other books often have fallen short, giving recommendations that miss the mark (e.g., a stronger social safety net and more income transfers) or won't get the job done (e.g., stronger enforcement of trade laws).

This final chapter, "How can we make it happen?" has the happy distinction of describing a plan of action that can immediately be acted upon by individual American consumers (and that is all of us) -- and that, when implemented, can "move the needle" on bringing jobs home, building healthy communities, eliminating dependency, and restoring the American middle class.

The beauty of this plan of action is that it is something we each can begin doing *right now*. No one can stop us from buying an American-made product, and no one can make us buy something that was made in Vietnam. Quite simply, we will be rebuilding the middle class through the power of consumer choice.

Endnotes to Chapter 12

[1] Robert E. Scott, "Stop Currency Manipulation and Create Millions of Jobs – With Gains across States and Congressional Districts," *EPI Briefing Paper #372*. (February 26, 2014) http://www.epi.org/publication/stop-currency-manipulation-and-create-millions-of-jobs/

[2] "If you build it, he will come." *Field of Dreams*, motion picture, 1989.

[3] I have prepared a summary of those laws in the Online Appendix.

[4] A substantial transformation is a manufacturing or other process that results in a new and different article of commerce, having a new name, character and use that is different from that which existed prior to the processing. Tariff Act of 1930; 19 C.F.R. § 102.

[5] Under this standard, parts and processing may contain only a *de minimis* amount of foreign content, and the last substantial transformation and final assembling and processing must occur in the U.S.

[6] Complying with the Made in USA Standard, FTC staff guidance document, 1998. https://www.ftc.gov/tips-advice/business-center/guidance/complying-made-usa-standard. Links to web pages containing the FTC's orders and letters, as well as policy statements and press releases, are collected on the FTC's web site at Tag: Made in USA https://www.ftc.gov/consumer-protection/made-usa.

[7] *Id.*

[8] Enforcement Policy Statement on U.S. Origin Claims, December 1997; https://www.ftc.gov/public-statements/1997/12/enforcement-policy-statement-us-origin-claims.

[9] 49 U.S.C. § 32304.
https://www.law.cornell.edu/uscode/text/49/32304
Regulations under the AALA are published at 49 CFR Part 583 – Automobile Parts Content Labeling,
https://www.law.cornell.edu/cfr/text/49/part-583

[10] At this writing, the information is published at Part 583 American Automobile Labeling Act Reports,
https://www.nhtsa.gov/part-583-american-automobile-labeling-act-reports.

[11] *See* About the Kogod Made in America Auto Index,
http://www.american.edu/kogod/autoindex/

[12] *See* http://www.americanautocouncil.org/about-aapc.

[13] See. E.g., Gene Petersen, "Where are Your Tires Made?" Consumer Reports, October 14, 2015.
http://www.consumerreports.org/cro/tires/where-are-tires-made.

[14] In 2014, the United Steel-workers posted the following list of codes for plants where their members were making tires:

BE: B.F. Goodrich, Tuscaloosa, Ala.
BF: B.F. Goodrich, Woodburn, Ind.
VE, YE, YU, 8B: Bridgestone/Firestone, Des Moines, Iowa
D2, E3, W1, Y7: Bridgestone/Firestone, La Vergne, Tenn.
2C, 4D, 5D: Bridgestone/Firestone, Morrison, Tenn.
UP: Cooper, Findlay, Ohio
UT: Cooper, Texarkana, Ark.
JU, PC, UK: Goodyear, Medicine Hat, Alberta
JJ, MD, PU: Goodyear, Gadsden, Ala.
DA: Dunlop, Buffalo, N.Y.
JN, MJ, PY: Goodyear, Topeka, Kan.
JE, MC, PT: Goodyear, Danville, Va.
JF, MM, PJ: Kelly-Springfield, Fayetteville, N.C.
CF: Titan Tire, Des Moines
JH, MN, PK: Titan Tire, Freeport, Ill.
B plus serial #: Titan Tire, Bryan, Ohio
CC: Yokohama Tire, Salem, Va.

"How to Find Union-Made Tires," USW.org, March 14, 2014, reposted from AFL-CIO,
http://www.usw.org/blog/2014/how-to-find-union-made-tires.

[15] Roger Simmermaker, *How Americans Can Buy American: The Power of Consumer Patriotism, Third Edition* (Consumer Patriotism Corporation, 2008).

[16] Bruce H. Wolk, *Made Here, Baby! The Essential Guide to Finding the Best American-Made Products for Your Kids* (New York: American Management Association, 2009).

[17] Roger Simmermaker, *My Company 'Tis of Thee: 50 Patriotic American Companies American Consumers Should Know About* (Consumer Patriotism Corporation, 2013).

[18] Lipscomb, *Re-Made, supra.*

[19] AMM applies a standard that at least 50% of the cost (labor, materials, and overhead) of a product is incurred in the United States and the final assembly or transformation takes place in the U.S.

[20] *See* Thomas A. Kochan, *Shaping the Future of Work: What Future Worker, Business, Government, and Education Leaders Need to Do for All to Prosper.* New York: Business Expert Press, 2016.

[21] I encourage you to share your ideas with me at jstuber@miaa.us.

Postscript

Looking to the Future

I drove out to Coatesville, site of the prison whose chaplain had been part of my "lightbulb moment." There I found an enormous steel mill, built on over 900 acres along the path of the Brandywine River. Across the street, a small portion of the mill, now owned by the global international steel conglomerate ArcelorMittal, is still operating, making steel plate. But most of the mill, covering many acres, stands empty and quiet. The building that formerly housed the executive and administrative offices is now largely occupied by the National Iron & Steel Heritage Museum, recounting the history of the mill, which produced the steel of which the twin towers of the World Trade Center were constructed. Between the building's parking lot, where I stood, and the high, blank wall of the mill ran a rail line, and on it came a single diesel locomotive. The engineer gave a long, loud blast of its air horn, and the sound reverberated off the walls of the mill.

I was carried back to a night when I was four or five years old. My family was paying a visit to my mother's parents in Braddock, Pennsylvania, just outside Pittsburgh, and they deposited me in a bedroom to sleep while the grownups visited. They lived in a group of buildings they called the "project", at the top of a hill overlooking the U.S. Steel corporation's Edgar Thomson steel works opened by Andrew Carnegie in 1875, where my grandfather worked. In the darkness, rolling up the hill, I could hear deep, booming sounds of large metal objects colliding, of things quite literally "going bump in the night." I had an abiding feeling that big things were happening down there. And they were.

That mill is still in operation. But the mill in Coatesville, like the mills in Bethlehem, and so many other places across America, now stands silent. Will the U.S. Steel mill in Granite City reopen? Or will it fall victim to the Chinese overcapacity in steel, and remain silent? I believe it is a metaphor for our future. As goes that mill, so will go our country.

As I was winding up my research on this book, we were celebrating Veterans Day on November 11, 2016. I thought back to 1945, to our "citizen soldiers" like Andy who came home and made the steel that went into the nation's power plants, bridges, automobiles, and appliances. And I flashed forward, through the time when we gave so much of our steel industry to Japan, to 2017, when we are giving the rest of it to China. Most of those citizen soldiers are gone now, but some of them, now in their nineties, are still with us.

And although I believe our primary duty is to our children and grandchildren, I can't help feeling a duty to these men and women, to assure that they will not have fought and sacrificed in vain, that we will not have squandered our patrimony and failed to pass it on to their grandchildren and great-grandchildren.

But time is running out. Fortunately, there is a way forward, if we will realize the urgency of the matter. But that window of opportunity will close. I just pray that we can disenthrall ourselves and pursue the American Project again, before it is too late.

It is a big project. But I believe the best, and necessary, first step is to decide that we are all in this together, and then do what we must for communities across America to say,

"We make things here again."

U.S. TRADE AGREEMENTS

AGREEMENT	COUNTRY	ENTRY INTO EFFECT	TPP TTIP*
NAFTA	Canada	1994	TPP
NAFTA	Mexico	1994	TPP
Bilateral FTA	Israel	1/1/1995	
Bilateral TA	Vietnam	12/10/2001	TPP
Bilateral FTA	Chile	1/12004	TPP
Bilateral FTA	Singapore	1/1/2004	TTP
Bilateral FTA	Morocco	6/15/2004	
Bilateral FTA	Australia	1/1/2005	
Bilateral FTA	Bahrain	1/11/2006	
CAFTA/DR	Costa Rica	2009	
CAFTA/DR	Dom. Repub.	2007	
CAFTA/DR	El Salvador	2006	
CAFTA/DR	Guatemala	2006	
CAFTA/DR	Honduras	2006	
CAFTA/DR	Nicaragua	2006	TPP
Bilateral FTA	Oman	1/1/2009	
Bilateral FTA	Peru	2/1/2009	TTP
Bilateral FTA	Jordan *	1/1/2010	
Bilateral FTA	South Korea	3/15/2012	
Bilateral FTA	Colombia	5/15/2012	
Bilateral FTA	Panama	10/31/2012	
	Brunei		TTP
	Japan		TTP
	Malaysia		TTP
	New Zealand		TTP
Bilateral FTA	UAE	In negotiation	
	European Union		T-TIP

TPP: Proposed Trans-Pacific Partnership. TTIP: Proposed Transatlantic Trade and Investment Partnership.

Recommended Further Reading

Of the works to which I have made reference in this volume, I especially recommend the following titles for your further reading, for their in-depth treatment of key aspects of this story.

Barlett, Donald L. and James B. Steele. *America: What Went Wrong.* Kansas City: Andrews and McMeel 1992.

Barlett, Donald L. and James B. Steele. *America: Who Stole the Dream?* Kansas City: Andrews and McMeel 1996.

Barlett, Donald L. and James B. Steele. *The Betrayal of the American Dream.* New York: Public Affairs 2012. In this series of books, investigative reports Donald Barlett and James Steele provide clear analysis and in-person reporting on the forces undermining the American Dream, including trade. Read together, they present a trend, and leave us wondering, "how could we continue doing this, decade after decade?

Harney, Alexandra. *The China Price: The True Cost of Chinese Competitive Advantage.* New York: Penguin Press 2007. Harney takes us on a personal tour of the human and environmental costs of China's economic development, in which we are all complicit, and in which we all pay the "China Price."

Macy, Beth. *Factory Man: How One Furniture Maker Battled Offshoring, Stayed Local - and Helped Save an American Town.* New York: Little, Brown & Company, 2014. Macy provides a compelling, readable, and informative narrative of an industry's capitulation to the forces of globalization, with the exception of one man and a band of like-minded manufacturers who thought they had a responsibility to their communities.

McGregor, Richard. *The Party: The Secret World of China's Communist Rulers*. New York: Penguin Books, 2010. McGregor provides an inside look at the machinations and motivations of the Chinese Communist Party. He provides insights into the CCP as the "be-all and end-all" of Chinese society, helping us understand why China's current leader, Xi Jinping, would say, "The Chinese dream is an ideal. Communists should have a higher ideal, and that is communism."

Smil, Vaclav. *Made in the USA: The Rise and Retreat of American Manufacturing*. Cambridge, Massachusetts: The MIT Press, 2013. Smil provides a rich portrayal of the history of American manufacturing, the fallacies of the arguments for the status quo, and the need for a resurgence of this vital sector of the economy.

Bibliography

Books

Adams, James Truslow. *The Epic of America.* Boston: Little, Brown, and Company, 1931.

Alpert, Daniel. *The Age of Oversupply.* New York: Portfolio/Penguin, 2013.

Ambrose, Stephen E. *Citizen Soldiers: The U S Army from the Normandy Beaches to the Bulge to the Surrender of Germany.* New York: Simon & Schuster, 1998.

Appelbaum, Richard B. and Gary Gereffi. "Power and Profits in the Apparel Commodity Chain." In Global Production: The Apparel Industry in the Pacific Rim, ed. Edna Bonacich et al. Philadelphia: Temple University Press, 1994.

Arndt, Sven W. "Free Trade and Its Alternatives." In The Oxford Handbook of International Commercial Policy, edited by Mordechai E. Kreinin and Michael G. Plummer, 3-31. New York: Oxford University Press, 2012.

Arneson, Richard. "Egalitarianism." In *The Stanford Encyclopedia of Philosophy*, edited by Edward N. Zalta (Summer 2013 Edition). URL <https://plato.stanford.edu/archives/sum2013/entries/egalitarianism/>.

Baldwin, Richard. *The Great Convergence.* Cambridge, Massachusetts: The Belknap Press of Harvard University Press, 2016.

Baldwin, Robert E. "U.S. Trade Policy Since 1934." In The Oxford Handbook of International Commercial Policy, edited by Mordechai E. Kreinin and Michael G. Plummer, 177-197. New York: Oxford University Press, 2012.

Barlett, Donald L. and James B. Steele. *The Betrayal of the American Dream.* New York: Public Affairs 2012.

Barlett, Donald L. and James B. Steele. *America: What Went Wrong.* Kansas City: Andrews and McMeel 1992.

Barlett, Donald L. and James B. Steele. *America: Who Stole the Dream?* Kansas City: Andrews and McMeel 1996.

Batra, Ravi. The Myth of Free Trade. New York: Charles Scribner's Sons, 1993.

Bernstein, Jared. *All Together Now: Common Sense for a Fair Economy.* San Francisco: Berrett-Koehler, 2006.

Bivens, Josh. *Everybody Wins, Except Most of Us*. Washington, D.C.: Economic Policy Institute, 2008.

Block, Fred and Margaret R. Somers. *The Power of Market Fundamentalism: Karl Polanyi's Critique*. Cambridge: Harvard University Press, 2014.

Broome, John. "Can There Be a Preference-Based Utilitarianism?" In *Justice, Political Liberalism, and Utilitarianism*, edited by Marc Fleurbaey, Maurice Sales and John A. Weymark, 221-238. New York: Cambridge University Press, 2008.

Broughton, Chad. *Boom, Bust, Exodus: The Rust Belt, the Maquilas, and a Tale of Two Cities*. Oxford: Oxford University Press, 2015.

Brown, Phillip, Hugh Lauder and David Ashton. *The Global Auction*. New York, 2011.

Clifton, Jim. *The Coming Jobs War*. New York: Gallup Press, 2011.

Collins, Larry and Dominique Lapierre. *Is Paris Burning?* New York: Simon and Shuster, 1965.

Davies, William. *The Limits of Neoliberalism: Authority, Sovereignty and the Logic of Competition*. Los Angeles: Sage, 2014.

Eckes, Alfred E., Jr. "Administration of Trade Policy." In The Oxford Handbook of International Commercial Policy, edited by Mordechai E. Kreinin and Michael G. Plummer, 50-74. New York: Oxford University Press, 2012.

Eckes, Alfred E., Jr. Opening America's Market: U.S. Foreign Trade Policy Since 1776. Chapel Hill: The University of North Carolina Press, 1995.

Economy, Elizabeth C. *The River Runs Black: The Environmental Challenge to China's Future*. Ithaca: A CFR Book, Cornell University Press, 2004.

Fingleton, Eamonn. *Unsustainable: How Economic Dogma is Destroying American Prosperity*. New York: Thunder's Mouth Press/Nation Books, 1993, 2003. Previously published as *In Praise of Hard Industries: Why Manufacturing, Not the Information Economy, is the Key to Future Prosperity*. New York: Houghton Mifflin, 1989.

Fleurbaey, Marc, Maurice Sales and John A. Weymark, eds. *Justice, Political Liberalism, and Utilitarianism*. New York: Cambridge University Press, 2008.

Frank, Robert H. and Philip Cook. *The Winner-Take-All-Society*. New York: Free Press, 1995.

Frank, Robert H. *Falling Behind: How Rising Inequality Harms the Middle Class*. Berkeley: University of California Press, 2007.

Kevin P. Gallagher and Roberto Porzecanski, *The Dragon in the Room: China and the Future of Latin American Industrialization* (Stanford: Stanford University Press, 2010).

George, Rose. Ninety Percent of Everything. New York: Picador, 2013.

Ginzberg, Eli. *The House of Adam Smith*. New York: Columbia University Press, 1934; reprinted, New York: Octagon Books, Inc., 1964.

Gocmen, Dogan. "The 'Adam Smith Problem' and Adam Smith's Utopia." In *New Essays on Adam Smith's Moral Philosophy*, edited by Wade L. Robinson and David B. Suits, 45-70. Rochester: RIT Press, 2012.

Goodwin, Doris Kearns. *The Bully Pulpit: Theodore Roosevelt, William Howard Taft, and the Golden Age of Journalism*. New York: Simon & Schuster, 2013.

Hacker, Joseph S. and Paul Pierson, *American Amnesia: How the War on Government Led Us to Forget What Made America Prosper*. New York: Simon & Schuster, 2016).

Halberstam, David. *The Reckoning*. New York: William Morrow and Company, Inc., 1986.

Haley, Usha C.V., and George T. Haley. *Subsidies to Chinese Industry: State Capitalism, Business Strategy, and Trade Policy*. Oxford: Oxford University Press, 2013.

Harney, Alexandra. *The China Price: The True Cost of Chinese Competitive Advantage*. New York: Penguin Press 2007.

Irwin, Douglas. *Peddling Protectionism: Smoot-Hawley and the Great Depression*. Princeton: Princeton University Press, 2011.

Isaak, Robert A. *The Globalization Gap: How the Rich Get Richer and the Poor Get Left Further Behind*. New York: Prentice Hall, 2005.

Iversen, Roberta Rehner. "What Do *You* Do? Ideas About Transforming "Work" in the United States." In *Social Policy and Social Justice*, edited by John L. Jackson, Jr., 87-96. Philadelphia, University of Pennsylvania Press, 2017.

Keynes, John Maynard. *The General Theory of Employment Interest and Money*. New York: Harcourt, Brace and Company, 1936.

Kissinger, Henry. *World Order*. New York: Penguin Press, 2014.

Kochan, Thomas A. *Restoring the American Dream: A Working Families' Agenda for America*. Cambridge, Massachussets: The MIT Press, 2005.

Kochan, Thomas A. *Shaping the Future of Work: What Future Worker, Business, Government, and Education Leaders Need to Do for All to Prosper*. New York: Business Expert Press, 2016.

Lamont, Julian and Christi Favor. "Distributive Justice." In The Stanford Encyclopedia of Philosophy, edited by Edward N. Zalta (Winter 2016 Edition), forthcoming URL = <https://plato.stanford.edu/archives/win2016/entries/justice-distributive/>.

Lichtenstein, Nelson. "Walmart's Long March to China." In *Walmart in China*, edited by Anita Chan, 13-33 (ILR Press an imprint of Cornell University Press: Ithaca, 2011.

Lin, Justin Yifu. *Demystifying the Chinese Economy.* Cambridge: Cambridge University Press, 2012.

Lipscomb, Todd. *Re-Made in the USA: How We Can Restore Jobs, Retool Manufacturing, and Compete with the World*. Hoboken, New Jersey: John Wiley & Sons, Inc., 2011.

Macy, Beth. *Factory Man: How One Furniture Maker Battled Offshoring, Stayed Local - and Helped Save an American Town*. New York: Little, Brown & Company, 2014.

McGregor, Richard. *The Party: The Secret World of China's Communist Rulers*. New York: Penguin Books, 2010.

Noah, Timothy. *The Great Divergence*. New York: Bloomsbury Press, 2012.

Okun, Arthur M. *Equality and Efficiency: The Big Tradeoff*. Washington, D.C.: Brookings Institution Press, 1975.

Paganelli, Maria Pia. "Theory of Moral Sentiments 1759 vs. Theory of Moral Sentiments 1790: A Change of Mind or a Change of Constraint." In *New Essays on Adam Smith's Moral Philosophy*, edited by Wade L. Robinson and David B. Suits, 35-44. Rochester: RIT Press, 2012.

Prestowtiz, Clyde. *The Betrayal of American Prosperity: Free Market Delusions, America's Decline, and How We Must Compete in the Post-Dollar Era. New York*: Free Press, 2010.

Rawls, John. *A Theory of Justice*. Cambridge: Harvard University Press, rev. ed. 1999 (first published 1971).

Ricardo, David. *The Principles of Political Economy and Taxation*. London: J.M. Dent & Sons Ltd., 1911.
Available online at Library of Economics and Liberty: http://www.econlib.org/library/Ricardo/ricPCover.html.

Rivoli, Pietra. *The Travels of a T-Shirt in the Global Economy: An Economist Examines the Markets, Power, and Politics of World Trade.* Hoboken: John Wiley & Sons, Inc., 2009 and 2015.

Robinson, Wade L. and David B. Suits, eds. *New Essays on Adam Smith's Moral Philosophy.* Rochester: RIT Press, 2012.

Rosen, Ellen Israel. Making Sweatshops: The Globalization of the U.S. Apparel Industry. Berkeley: University of California Press, 2002.

Ryan, Rev. John Augustin, S.T.L. *A Living Wage: Its Ethical and Economic Aspects.* New York: The MacMillan Company, 1906. (Dissertation for the Doctorate in Theology at The Catholic University of America.)

Seligman, Martin E.P. *Flourish.* New York: Free Press, 2011.

Simmermaker, Roger. *How Americans Can Buy American: The Power of Consumer Patriotism, Third Edition.* Consumer Patriotism Corporation, 2008.

Simmermaker, Roger. *My Company 'Tis of Thee: 50 Patriotic American Companies American Consumers Should Know About.* Consumer Patriotism Corporation, 2013.

Smil, Vaclav. *Made in the USA: The Rise and Retreat of American Manufacturing.* Cambridge, Massachusetts: The MIT Press, 2013.

Smith, Adam. *An Inquiry into the Nature and Causes of the Wealth of Nations.* London: W. Strand and T. Cadell, 1776. Available online at Library of Economics and Liberty: http://www.econlib.org/library/Smith/smWNCover.html

Smith, Adam. *The Theory of Moral Sentiments.* London: A, Millar, Second ed., 1761. Available online at Library of Economics and Liberty: http://www.econlib.org/library/Smith/smMSCover.html

Stern, Mark J. "From Poverty to Well-Being." In *Social Policy and Social Justice,* edited by John L. Jackson, Jr., 148-159. Philadelphia, University of Pennsylvania Press, 2017.

Stiglitz, Joseph, Amartya Sen and Jean-Paul Fitoussi. *Mis-Measuring our Lives: The Report by the Commission on the Measurement of Economic Performance and Social Progress.* London: The New Press, 2010.

Stiglitz, Joseph E. *Globalization and Its Discontents.* New York: W.W. Norton, 2002.

Stiglitz, Joseph E. *The Price of Inequality: How Today's Divided Society Endangers Our Future.* New York: W.W. Norton & Co., 2012.

Stout, Lynn. *The Shareholder Value Myth: How Putting Shareholders First Harms Investors, Corporations, and the Public*. San Francisco: Berrett-Khoeler Publishers, Inc., 2012.

Ton, Zeynep. *The Good Jobs Strategy: How the Smartest Companies Invest in Employees to Lower Costs and Boost Profits*. Boston: New Harvest/ Houghton Mifflin Harcourt, 2014.

Tyler, George R. *What Went Wrong: How the 1% Hijacked the American Middle Class... and What Other Countries Got Right*. Dallas: BenBella Books, 2013.

Vance, J.D. *Hillbilly Elegy: A Memoir of a Family and Culture in Crisis*. New York: HarperCollins, 2017.

Viscelli, Steve. *The Big Rig: Trucking and the Decline of the American Dream*. Oakland: University of California Press, 2016.

Walby, Sylvia. *Globalization & Inequalities: Complex and Contested Modernities*. Los Angeles: Sage, 2009.

Weisman, Steven R. *The Great Tradeoff*. Peterson Institute for International Economics: Washington, D.C., 2016.

Wolk, Bruce H. *Made Here, Baby! The Essential Guide to Finding the Best American-Made Products for Your Kids*. New York: American Management Association, 2009.

Xie, Lizhong, ed. *De-Politicization of Ethnic Questions in China*. Singapore: World Scientific, 2014.

Papers

Akinrinade, Sola, and Olukoya Ogen, "Globalization and De-Industrialization: South-South Neo-Liberalism and the Collapse of the Nigerian Textile Industry," *The Global South, Indiana University Press*, Vol. 2, No. 2 (Fall 2008), 159-170. https://muse.jhu.edu/article/256188.

Asian Development Bank. "Key Indicators for Asia and the Pacific 2010; Special Chapter: The Rise of Asia's Middle Class." https://www.adb.org/sites/default/files/publication/27726/ki2010-special-chapter.pdf

Atkinson, Robert D., Luke A. Stewart, Scott M. Andes, and Steven J. Ezell. "Worse Than the Great Depression: What Experts Are Missing About American Manufacturing Decline," Information and Technology Innovation Foundation (March 2012). http://www2.itif.org/2012-american-manufacturing-decline.pdf

Autor, David H., David Dorn, and Gordon H. Hanson. "The China Shock: Learning from Labor Market Adjustment to Large Changes in

Trade." NBER Working Paper No. 21906, Issued in January 2016. doi: 10.3386/w21906. http://www.nber.org/papers/w21906 Published: David H. Autor & David Dorn & Gordon H. Hanson, 2016. "The China Shock: Learning from Labor Market Adjustment to Large Changes in Trade," Annual Review of Economics, vol. 8(1).

Autor, David, David Dorn, and Gordon H. Hanson, "The China Syndrome: Local Labor Market Effects of Import Competition in the United States." Massachusetts Institute of Technology Department of Economics Working Paper Series, Working Paper 12-2. May 2, 2012. http://ssrn.com/abstract=2050144. *American Economic Review* 103:6 (2013): 2121-2168. http://doi.org/10.1257/aer103.6.2121.

Autor, David H., David Dorn, Gordon H. Hanson, and Jae Song. "Trade Adjustment: Worker Level Evidence." Massachusetts Institute of Technology Department of Economics Working Paper Series, Working Paper 13-21, June 30, 2013. http://ssrn.com/abstract=2323054. NBER Working Paper No. 19226, Released on July 23, 2013. http://www.nber.org/papers/w19226. The Quarterly Journal of Economics, Oxford University Press, vol. 129(4)(____), 1799-1860. See also http://www.nber.org/digest/nov13/w19226.html.

Baldwin, Richard. "The World Trade Organization and the Future of Multilateralism." Journal of Economic Perspectives, Volume 30, Number 1—Winter 2016—Pages 95–116. http://dx.doi.org/10.1257/jep.30.1.95.

Bivens, Josh. "Trade, jobs, and wages: Are the public's worries about globalization justified?" *Economic Policy Institute*, Issue Brief #244, May 6, 2008, http://www.epi.org/publication/ib244/.

Bivens, Josh. "Using standard models to benchmark the costs of globalization for American workers without a college degree." Economic Policy Institute, Briefing Paper #354 (March 22, 2013). http://www.epi.org/publication/standard-models-benchmark-costs-globalization/.

Blinder, Alan S. "How Many U.S. Jobs Might Be Offshorable? Princeton University CEPS Working Paper No. 142, March 2007. https://www.princeton.edu/ceps/workingpapers/142blinder.pdf.

Carney, Mark, "Redeeming an unforgiving world." Speech given at 8th Annual Institute of International Finance G20 conference, Shanghai (February 26, 2016). www.bankofengland.co.uk/publications/Pages/speeches/default.aspx.

Chan, Anita, and Robert S. Ross, "From North-South to South-South: The True Face of Global Competition," *Foreign Affairs* (September/ October 2002).
http://www.cfr.org/globalization/north-south-south-south-true-face-global-competition/p4960

Clinton, Bill. "Expanding Trade, Protecting Values: Why I'll Fight to Make China's Trade Status Permanent." New Democrat, vol. 12, no. 1, 9–11 (2000).

Couto, Vinay, Arie Y. Lewin, Mahadeva Mani, and Vikas Sehgal. "Offshoring the Brains as Well as the Brawn – Companies Seek Intellectual Talent Beyond their Borders." The Duke Center for International Business Education and Research (2006). http://strategyand.pwc.com.
http://www.strategyand.pwc.com/media/uploads/OffshoringtheBrainsasWellastheBrawn.pdf

Dorman, Peter. "The Free Trade Magic Act: In dubious study, first you see the benefits of globalization, then you don't." *Economic Policy Institute*. Briefing Paper #111 (September 1, 2001).
http://www.epi.org/publication/briefingpapers_dorman-bp2/.

DuBois, Frank. "Evaluating 'Made in America': A Critique of the American Automotive Labeling Act and a Proposed Alternative," accepted by the Academy of International Business Annual Meeting (July 2013).
https://aib.msu.edu/events/2013/pdfs/AIB2013_Proceedings.pdf

Ebenstein, Avraham, Ann Harrison, and Margaret McMillan. "Why are American Workers getting Poorer? China, Trade and Offshoring." NBER Working Paper No. 21027 issued in March 2015, doi: 10.3386/w21027 http://www.nber.org/papers/w21027.

Eggertsson, Gauti B., Neil R. Mehrotra and Lawrence H. Summers. "Secular Stagnation in the Open Economy." American Economic Review, 106(5): 503-07 (2016).DOI: 10.1257/aer.p20161106.

Eichengreen, Barry. "The Political Economy of the Smoot-Hawley Tariff." NBER Working Paper No. 2001, issued in August 1986.
http://www.nber.org/papers/w2001,doi:10.3386/w2001.

Fisher, Gordon M. "The Development of the Orshansky Poverty Thresholds and Their Subsequent History as the Official U.S. Poverty Measure." U.S. Department of Health and Human Services (May 1992-- partially revised September 1997).
http://aspe.hhs.gov/poverty/papers/hptgssiv.htm.

Gallagher, Kevin P. "China and the Future of Latin American Industrialization." *Boston University Frederick S. Pardee Center for*

the Study of the Longer-Range Future, Issues in Brief No. 18 (October 2010).
http://www.bu.edu/pardee/issues-in-brief-no-18/.

International Monetary Fund. "World Economic Outlook – Subdued Demand: Symptoms and Remedies. (October 2016).
http://www.imf.org/external/pubs/ft/weo/2016/02/.

Kharas, Homi. "The Emerging Middle Class in Developing Countries." *OECD Development Centre* Working Paper No. 285 (January 2010).

Kimball, Will and Robert E. Scott. "China Trade, Outsourcing and Jobs." *Economic Policy Institute* Briefing Paper No. 385 (December 11, 2014).

Kochhar, Rakesh. "A Global Middle Class Is More Promise than Reality." *Pew Research Center* (July 8, 2015).
http://www.pewglobal.org/2015/07/08/a-global-middle-class-is-more-promise-than-reality/.

Ma, Tiffany. "China and Congo's coltan connection." *Project 2049*.
https://www.project2049.net/documents/china_and_congos_coltan_connection.pdf.

Meckstroth, Daniel J. "The Manufacturing Value Chain is Much Bigger than You Think!" Manufacturers Alliance for Productivity and Innovation, PA-165, February 2016.
https://www.mapi.net/system/files/attachments/files/PA-165_web_0.pdf.

Moncarz, Robert J., Michael G. Wolf, and Benjamin Wright, "Service-providing occupations, offshoring, and the labor market," Bureau of Labor Statistics, *Monthly Labor Review* (December 2008).
http://www.bls.gov/opub/mlr/2008/12/art4full.pdf.

N.E.L.P., "Fight for $15: Four Years, $62 Billion." Data Brief, *National Employment Law Project* (December 2016).

OECD. "Education Indicators in Focus. - 2012/5 (May)." *Organization for European Cooperation and Development* (2012).

Oreopolous, Philip, Marianne Page, and Ann Huff Stevens. "The Intergenerational Effect of Worker Displacement," *National Bureau of Economic Research*, Working Paper No. 11587 (2005).

Ostry, Jonathan D., Andrew Berg, and Charalambos G. Tsangarides. "Redistribution, Inequality, and Growth." IMF Staff Discussion Note 14/02 (2014).
http://www.imf.org/external/pubs/ft/sdn/2014/sdn1402.pdf

Ostry, Jonathan D., Prakash Loungani, and Davide Furceri. "Neoliberalism: Oversold?" *Finance & Development*, International Monetary Fund, Vol. 53, No. 2 (June 2016). http://www.imf.org/external/pubs/ft/fandd/2016/06/ostry.htm.

Pierce, Justin R. and Peter K. Schott. "The Surprisingly Swift Decline of U.S. Manufacturing Employment." NBER Working Paper Series, Working Paper 18655. National Bureau of Economic Research. Cambridge, MA December 2012. http://www.nber.org/papers/w18655.

Pierce, Justin R. and Peter K. Schott, "Trade Liberalization and Mortality: Evidence from U.S. Counties." November, 2016. http://www.nber.org/papers/w22849

Porter, Michael E., Jan W. Rivkin, and Mihir A. Desai, with Manjari Daman. "Problems Unsolved and a Nation Divided: The State of U.S. Competitiveness 2016. Including findings from Harvard Business School's 2016 surveys of U.S. competitiveness." (September 2016). http://www.hbs.edu/competitiveness/research/Pages/research-details.aspx?rid=81

Proctor, Bernadette D., Jessica L. Semega, Melissa A. Kollar, Income and Poverty in the United States: 2015, U.S. Census Bureau, Report Number: P60-256 (September 13, 2016).

Rocha, Cynthia and Felicia McCant, "Closing Time: Workers' Last Call," Forum for Applied Research and Public Policy 14, no. 1 (1999), http://www.questia.com/read/1G1-54370218/closing-time-workers-last-call.

Saez, Emmanuel. "Striking it Richer: The Evolution of Top Incomes in the United States (Updated with 2015 preliminary estimates)," UC Berkeley (June 30, 2016). http://eml.berkeley.edu/~saez/saez-UStopincomes-2015.pdf

Samuelson, Paul A. "Where Ricardo and Mill Rebut and Confirm Arguments of Mainstream Economists Supporting Globalization." *Journal of Economic Perspectives*, 18(3) (2004): 135-146. DOI: 10.1257/0895330042162403.

Schlefer, Jonathan. "There is No Invisible Hand." *Harvard Business Review* (April 10, 2012). https://hbr.org/2012/04/there-is-no-invisible-hand.

Scott, Robert E. "The effects of NAFTA on US trade, jobs, and investment, 1993–2013." *Review of Keynesian Economics* Vol. 4, Issue 4 (2014): 429-411. doi: 10.4337/roke.2014.04.02.

Standish, Melanie and Dan Witters. "Americas Lead Highs, Sub-Saharan Africa Lows in Well-Being." *Gallup.com*, June 24, 2015. http://www.gallup.com/poll/183710/americas-lead-highs-sub-saharanafrica-lows.aspx?utm_source=World&utm_medium=newsfeed&utm_campaign=tiles

Stiglitz, Joseph. "Moving Beyond Market Fundamentalism to a More Balanced Economy." *Annals of Public and Cooperative Economics*, 80:3 (2009): 345-360. http://www8.gsb.columbia.edu.

Stout, Lynn. "The Shareholder Value Myth." *Cornell Law Faculty Publications*. Paper 771. April 19, 2013. http://scholarship.law.cornell.edu/facpub/771.

United Nations. "Trade and Development Report, 2016." *United Nations Conference on Trade and Development* (September 2016). http://unctad.org/en/PublicationsLibrary/tdr2016_en.pdf.

United Nations. "Trade and Development Report, 2016 - Overview." *United Nations Conference on Trade and Development* (September 2016). http://unctad.org/en/PublicationsLibrary/tdr2016overview_en.pdf.

U.S. International Trade Commission. "Economic Impact of Trade Agreements Implemented Under Trade Authorities Procedures, 2016 Report." USITC Publication No. 4614, June 2016.

U.S. International Trade Commission. "U.S. Trade Policy Since 1934" in "The Economic Effects of Significant U.S. Import Restraints: Sixth Update 2009," Chapter 3. USITC Publication 4094 (August 2009), 59-123. https://www.usitc.gov/publications/industry_econ_analysis_332/2009/economic_effects_significant_us_import_restraints.htm.

Weisbrot, Mark and Dean Baker. "The Relative Impact of Trade Liberalization on Developing Countries." *Center for Economic and Policy Research* (June 12, 2002). http://cepr.net/publications/reports/the-relative-impact-of-trade-liberalization-on-developing-countries.

Williams, Brock R., *et al.*, "The U.S.-Korea Free Trade Agreement (KORUS FTA): Provisions and Implementation." *Congressional Research Service*, September 16, 2014.

Wilson, Jordan. "China's Military Agreements with Argentina: A Potential New Phase in China-Latin America Defense Relations."

U.S.-China Economic and Security Review Commission, Staff Research Report, November 5, 2015.
http://www.uscc.gov/research_security
http://origin.www.uscc.gov/sites/default/files/Research/China%27s%20Military%20Agreements%20with%20Argentina.pdf

World Bank. "Global Economic Prospects: Divergences and Risks." (June 2016).
http://www.worldbank.org/en/publication/global-economic-prospects

Yoshihara, Toshi. "The 1974 Paracels Sea Battle: A Campaign Appraisal." *Naval War College Review*, Spring 2016, Vol. 29, No. 2.

Documentary Films

Hornblower, Sam. "Wal-Mart & China: A Joint Venture." *PBS Frontline*.
http://www.pbs.org/wgbh/pages/frontline/shows/walmart/secrets/wmchina.html

Koppel, Ted. "The People's Republic of Capitalism." Documentary Film, 2008.
https://archive.org/details/ThePeoplesRepublicOfCapitalism

LeDuff, Charlie. "Happy Twentieth Anniversary, NAFTA!" *The Americans with Charlie LeDuff.*
https://www.youtube.com/watch?v=Tg605ALJStY

Spotts, Greg. *American Jobs.* Documentary film. (2005)
http://www.imdb.com/media/rm129073408/tt0461008?ref_=tt_ov_i

* * *

Name Index

Subject Index